Playing Underground

THEATER: THEORY / TEXT / PERFORMANCE
Enoch Brater, Series Editor

Recent Titles:

Trevor Griffiths: Politics, Drama, History by Stanton B. Garner Jr.

Memory-Theater and Postmodern Drama by Jeanette R. Malkin

Performing America: Cultural Nationalism in American Theater
  edited by Jeffrey D. Mason and J. Ellen Gainor

Space in Performance: Making Meaning in the Theatre by Gay McAuley

Mirrors of Our Playing: Paradigms and Presences in Modern Drama
  by Thomas R. Whitaker

Brian Friel in Conversation edited by Paul Delaney

Sails of the Herring Fleet: Essays on Beckett by Herbert Blau

On Drama: Boundaries of Genre, Borders of Self by Michael Goldman

Contours of the Theatrical Avant-Garde: Performance and Textuality
  edited by James M. Harding

The Painted Word: Samuel Beckett's Dialogue with Art
  by Lois Oppenheim

*Performing Democracy: International Perspectives on Urban
  Community-Based Performance*
  edited by Susan C. Haedicke and Tobin Nellhaus

A Beckett Canon by Ruby Cohn

David Mamet in Conversation edited by Leslie Kane

The Haunted Stage: The Theatre as Memory Machine
  by Marvin Carlson

Staging Consciousness: Theater and the Materialization of Mind
  by William W. Demastes

Agitated States: Performance in the American Theater of Cruelty
  by Anthony Kubiak

Land/Scape/Theater edited by Elinor Fuchs and Una Chaudhuri

The Stage Life of Props by Andrew Sofer

*Playing Underground: A Critical History of the 1960s Off-Off-Broadway
  Movement* by Stephen J. Bottoms

Playing Underground

A Critical History of the 1960s
Off-Off-Broadway Movement

Stephen J. Bottoms

The University of Michigan Press
Ann Arbor

to Michael Smith,
for "keen inspiration"

and to Paula,
for everything

Copyright © by the University of Michigan 2004
All rights reserved
Published in the United States of America by
The University of Michigan Press
Manufactured in the United States of America
♾ Printed on acid-free paper

2007   2006   2005   2004   4   3   2   1

A CIP catalog record for this book is available from the British Library.

Library of Congress Cataloging-in-Publication Data

Bottoms, Stephen J. (Stephen James), 1968–
    Playing underground : a critical history of the 1960s off-off-
  broadway movement / Stephen J. Bottoms.
      p. cm. — (Theater: theory/text/performance)
    Includes bibliographical references and index.
    ISBN 0-472-11400-X (cloth : alk. paper)
    1. Off Off-Broadway theater—History—20th century.   2. American
  drama—20th century—History and criticism.   I. Title.   II. Series.
  PN2277.N5B47   2004
  792'.09747'1—dc22   2004001248

He came to the altar with flowers
He came to the altar with flowers
But the preacher did not hear
No the preacher did not hear
For the preacher was singing a folksong
Not knowing the folks had all but gone.

Each man chooses the stations
That he waits at while choosing his cross
Each man chooses the stations
As each man chooses his death.

Everyone took his life for granted
Refused to grant logic to his joy—

Now that joy's gone
Now that joy's gone
Now that joy's gone
Now that joy's gone

No one need be bothered by his joy.

—H. M. Koutoukas, Elegy for Joe Cino

Preface

I'm not interested in the sixties. I'm not interested in any of these nostalgic eras
they're reviving. . . . That's just people trying, so desperately, to find some—
(*Laughs lightly.*) "meaning for their own time."
> —"Carla," in Robert Patrick's *Kennedy's Children*

For as long as I can recall having an opinion on the subject, the theaters that
have seemed most alive to me—the most exciting to be at or a part of—have
been those generally regarded as "illegitimate" by the established apparatus of
press, funding bodies, and professional theatrical institutions. Basement theaters. Café theaters. Hole-in-the-wall theaters. Theaters thriving on rough
edges, raw passion, and a fierce sense of the immediacy and "liveness" of both
the stage event itself and of the audience. A church gymnasium; a disused
warehouse; the underground arches beneath a railway station: these are the
performance spaces where I have been thrilled and moved far more often than
I have been in the relatively comfortable, controlled spaces of the professional
theater. My own first experiences as a director—in a tiny black-box space converted from a reading room in the University of Bristol's students' union,
where the crammed-in audience seemed almost to sit on top of the stage, and
the ceiling was so low that the barn-doors on the lights could scrape the tops
of actors' heads—made most of the "real" theaters I have worked in since
seem lacking in atmosphere by comparison.

For some years, I harbored these thoughts rather guiltily, believing that I
must, at heart, be some kind of rank amateur to feel this way. During my doc-
toral research on the work of Sam Shepard, however (cf. Bottoms 1998a), I
became fascinated by his background in the off-off-Broadway movement of
the 1960s—a movement that seemed to have been largely airbrushed out of
the history books, but which had thrived in precisely the kinds of spaces that
interested me, and which, far from being merely some amateur or student
affair, had produced an explosion of genuinely innovative theater. My
research for this book has thus been an attempt to explore and document a
movement that offered real alternatives to institutionalized professionalism. In

today's theater scene, often intent on recycling familiar formulas—whether big-money commercialism, subsidized classicism, or purportedly avant-garde gimmickry—a new injection of anarchic, underground energy is devoutly to be wished for.

Excavating the movement's history proved no simple task, since so little of critical or historical substance has previously been published on the subject. Albert Poland and Bruce Mailman's *The Off-Off-Broadway Book* (1972) remains the most useful source, but is mostly comprised of play-texts, and its "factual" details are often inaccurate. My work has involved dredging used bookstores for long-out-of-print play collections, wading through avalanches of archived newspaper clippings, and tracking down playwrights, directors, and actors to request interviews and, where possible, beg for copies of unpublished scripts. The surviving documentation, moreover, covers only a fraction of what occurred on off-off-Broadway's ad hoc stages, some of which mounted new plays every week or two, for years. Much of what was instantly forgotten probably deserved no better fate, but much that was of value has also, undoubtedly, been lost forever: the creators of off-off-Broadway were always more concerned with what was happening *now*, in the present moment (one of the central imperatives of the 1960s counterculture), than with documenting events for posterity. Playwright H. M. Koutoukas claims he went as far as shredding all copies of some of his plays after opening night, partly to prevent script piracy, but also partly to ensure the ephemerality of performances that had been designed to "hit the air" and then vanish forever. The venues themselves were only slightly more concerned with recording their achievements: the archives of the period held by La Mama and Judson Church consist of clipped-out *Village Voice* reviews, typed or hand-printed programs and posters, scratchy photographs, and letters recording the day-to-day business of trying to keep the venues afloat. The most vivid accounts of the performances themselves are to be found in the memories of those who were there, but, as many of them are quick to point out, time can play tricks on the memory.

In short, all that is really left of Off-Off-Broadway is fragments—fragments that require a good deal of creative interpretation if one is to assemble them into a coherent narrative. The notion of writing anything "objective," let alone "definitive" on the subject seems nonsensical: there was and is no one set of truths about off-off-Broadway to uncover, since the entire scene was always more a matter of competing perceptions than of a singular, concrete reality. For this reason, my ironic working title for this book was *What Happened*, and although my publishers—for sound marketing reasons—suggested that I go with something snappier, the impishness of my original choice still appeals. Gertrude Stein's short play *What Happened* (1913), which became the basis for a landmark production by the Judson Poets' Theater (1963), uses rhythmically repetitive, self-referential language to capture a subjective impression of endlessly circling chatter, rather than attempting in any way to record the representational "truth" of the dinner party Stein was apparently inspired by. Conversely, though, *What Happened* also appealed as a title because it can be taken as a direct statement, perhaps even a challenge: for the off-off-Broadway movement *did* happen, and *can* be narrativized, and it is long past time that its significance was acknowledged.

Unfortunately, even in a book of this scale, it is possible only to sketch out an initial mapping of "what happened." For example, in seeking to set out an intertwined history of the venues and companies involved in the movement, I have often had to rein in my own impulse to reflect at length on individual works. Few of the plays and performances discussed in this book are covered in anything like the detail they deserve, and—while I have attempted to cover most of the major "landmarks" of the movement's development—the materials I focus on often say as much about my own critical preoccupations as they do about their renown at the time. Much more research could, and I hope will, be done, by other scholars with different concerns. But what follows is, at least, a start.

Off-off-Broadway was a theater movement founded on collaborative creation, and this book too is very much a group effort. I owe an enormous debt to the many people who have shared their time and expertise with me. I am grateful to my interviewees, in particular, for providing insights that none of the existing documentation could have offered: a full list of their names, and of when and where we met, is provided in appendix B. (Please note that quotations in the text from these artists that are otherwise unattributed to bibliographic sources come from these interviews.). Further thanks are due to the following "OOBniks" for consenting to read and comment on chapters in progress: Tony Barsha, Hal Borske, Jerry Cunliffe, Paul Foster, Walter Hadler, Robert Heide, Lawrence Kornfeld, H. M. Koutoukas, Murray Mednick, Tom O'Horgan, Robert Patrick, John Vaccaro, and Doric Wilson. Further invaluable advice has also been provided by friends and colleagues including Greg Giesekam, Francis Hagan, Katherine Morley, and, especially, Sarah Kornfeld.

My most important collaboration of all has been with Michael Smith, the chief theater critic for the *Village Voice* throughout the period discussed in this book, whose reviews—clear-sighted, provocative, personal—I have come to appreciate as my own set of eyes on what actually happened, in performance, off-off-Broadway. Latterly, via e-mail, Michael has also stepped in as an indispensable critic and editor of my writing. Long before this personal contact was established, however, I had been struck by the frequency with which his *Voice* reports resonated with, and indeed helped crystallize, my own accumulated impressions of the plays and players involved. If I quote him frequently, it is because I trust him and because, still more importantly, he was trusted by the artists themselves. "He loved the theatre as much as we did," notes playwright Megan Terry: "he let people know where to come and what was happening. When there was a breakthrough, he would be the first to proclaim it" (Savran 1988, 244). Smith's unapologetically subjective reviewing style consciously eschewed the conventional notion that the critic's function is to provide a "service" to an anonymous public, by setting oneself up in judgment over what is or is not worth seeing. Instead, always acknowledging his own preferences and interests, he sought to speak to and for the creative community of which he was a part—as a playwright, as a director, and as "key grip" for his longtime lover, lighting designer Johnny Dodd. He sought to generate debate rather than to close it down, and proved willing to open himself up to criticism in the process: "I got mocked sometimes for writing about myself," he notes, "but it was a deliberate choice. I love the theater and wanted to be a friend of the theater and an advocate of the theater and keep the theater alive and healthy and wonderful. That was my aim—not to be right all the time." If there is a better goal for a theater critic to aspire to, I don't know what it is.

During my research, I have also become aware that many librarians and archivists see their function in very similar terms: to keep the future of theater bright by keeping its memory alive. My thanks go especially to Chris Karatnytsky and her colleagues at the Billy Rose Theatre Collection of the New York Public Library, to Ozzie Rodriguez at the La Mama archive, to Amy Wilson and Judson Memorial Church, and to Martha Coigney of the International Theatre Institute. Finally, I am profoundly grateful to my own immediate community here in Glasgow—to the actors and directors who collaborated with me in bringing so many of the plays discussed in this book back to life in three dimensions, and to the students who sat my courses on this subject, and who fed back to me, I am sure, many more insights than I imparted to them. And then of course there is Paula, who has put up with everything, and fed me with joy.

Contents

1. Digging (Up) the Scene: An Introduction   1
2. Setting the Scene: A Look at the Fifties   16

Part One: Emerging Venues, Emerging Playwrights, 1960–66

3. Caffe Cino: The Birth of a Movement   39
4. Judson Poets' Theater: Verse Plays and Vaudeville Skits   61
5. La Mama ETC: Hurrah for the Playwright   83
6. Theatre Genesis: Urban Prophecy   105
7. In One Act: On the Aesthetics of Off-Off-Broadway Playwriting   124

Part Two: Present Collaborations, 1963–68

8. The Judson "Musical": Sublimely Ridiculous?   147
9. The Open Theatre: Transformations   169
10. La Mama Troupe: The Kernel of Craziness   192
11. The Play-House of the Ridiculous: Beyond Absurdity   215
12. Other Kinds of Cruelty: Ritual, Participation, and the Plague   237

Part Three: Changing Times, 1966–73

13. Going Overground: Changing Profiles in the
    Later 1960s   259
14. Death and Disaster: Leaving the Caffe Cino   279
15. The Absence of Peace: Changing Politics, Changing Communities   301
16. Going Solo: Auteurs, Poseurs, and La Mama   322
17. Signals through the Flames: The Afterlife of a Movement   344

Appendix A: Chronology of Notable Events and Productions   367
Appendix B: Interviewees, Correspondents, and Discussants   375
Bibliography   377
Index   389

1 Digging (Up) the Scene: An Introduction

> I have chosen to focus primarily on the experimental ensembles in the United States rather than on the more complex Off-Off-Broadway movement as a whole. . . . Someone else would have written a different book on this period, and it is hoped that there will be reports from other points of view. One might concentrate on individual artists, or on the development of the important houses like the Caffe Cino, Judson Poets' Theatre, La Mama, and Theatre Genesis.
> —Arthur Sainer, *The Radical Theatre Notebook*

Today, almost thirty years after Sainer's *Radical Theatre Notebook* was published, the standard conception is that the American experimental theater of the 1960s consisted of performer-centered ensembles—most notably the Living Theatre, the Open Theatre, and the Performance Group—and little else. Politically oriented companies best known for their open-air protest theater, such as the San Francisco Mime Troupe or the Bread and Puppet Theatre, are also often recognized, usually in a secondary role. Yet the "off-off-Broadway movement" and its four "important houses," which—as Sainer implies— were just as worthy of critical attention as the ensembles, barely rate a footnote in most histories of postwar American theater. In Christopher Bigsby's third volume of his *Critical Introduction to Twentieth Century American Drama*, to take but one obvious example, off-off-Broadway is dispensed with on a single page of the book's introduction, prior to an extensive first section dealing with the three ensemble companies cited above. Usually in such histories, individual playwrights and companies whose work first emerged "off-off" are discussed in some detail (Bigsby features Sam Shepard and the Open Theatre), but precious little is said, or apparently known, about the broader scene of which they were a part.

This book is an attempt, at long last, to write the account of the Caffe Cino, the Judson Poets' Theater, La Mama, and Theatre Genesis that Sainer envisaged. Though there were also many more theaters designated "off-off-Broadway" during the 1960s, there was a general consensus that these four venues— along with a few itinerant companies, such as the Open Theatre and the

Play-House of the Ridiculous, which also feature prominently in this book—made up the core of an identifiable, alternative theater movement. Today, of course, the term *off-off-Broadway* (coined by the *Village Voice* in 1960) is used in a catchall manner to designate any enterprise on the bottom rung of the New York theater world's notional ladder of cultural and economic significance, below the professional off-Broadway houses, and "above" them, Broadway itself. Most such productions are simply "showcases," by which actors, paid a profit share if at all, are hoping to attract attention from press or agents, and thus gain a leg up toward a professional career. This conception of the scene, however, did not become common until the early 1970s, more or less concurrently with the demise of the 1960s movement.

This is not to suggest that the dream of a professional career was absent from the equation in that first decade: off-off-Broadway owed its genesis in part to the fact that New York's established theaters were no longer offering parts so readily to young actors as they once had. The increasing commercialization of off-Broadway theaters during the 1950s had effectively wiped out their traditional role as a training ground for the next generation, and the next generation, consequently, began to resort to performing in tiny, nontheater spaces such as cafes, churches, basements, and lofts, mostly in Greenwich Village and the East Village. Yet the emergence of these venues, coinciding with the increasingly countercultural trajectory of the downtown arts world in the 1960s, also allowed for the emergence of a whole new generation of young practitioners who, for the most part, cared very little about whether or not their work would translate into the milieu of the mainstream, commercial theater. Indeed, the term *off-off-Broadway* is itself somewhat misleading in this respect ("let's call the calling *off-off* off," Astaire and Rogers might suggest), since it implies an integral, vertical relationship with the establishment. During the 1960s, this was in fact far less pronounced than the scene's *horizontal* relationship with the poets, dancers, painters, musicians, and filmmakers who were, simultaneously, experimenting in directly comparable ways. Today, the achievements of many other downtown artists of the period—from Allen Ginsberg to Andy Warhol, and from the Judson Dance Theater to the Velvet Underground—are regarded as being of pivotal importance in the histories of their respective art-forms, a fact that makes the collective "forgetting" of the alternative theater movement all the more extraordinary. Was the experimental theater simply insignificant or unimaginative by comparison with what was happening in the other arts? Certainly nobody thought so at the time: if anything, theater was regarded as a medium in which artists from different backgrounds could cross disciplinary borders and experiment together, collaboratively.

If the term *off-off-Broadway* needs to be considered skeptically, it is also necessary to establish in what sense the four venues and two companies cited above can be seen as constituting the core of a "movement." This was a loose constellation of enterprises, whose aesthetic concerns often seemed wildly divergent: there was never a single leader or a manifesto for this movement, or even a coherent set of objectives. There was, however, a very clear sense of shared community, and a shared resistance to the economic imperatives of mainstream American culture. Allowing theater artists the freedom truly to speak with their own voices meant creating a context that sidestepped any question of commercial viability. Not one of the key off-off theaters of the period charged money for tickets, and each subsidized itself by other means: this was, as Elenore Lester titled the first major *New York Times* article on the scene in 1965, "the pass-the-hat circuit."

That original, radically anticonsumerist vision of off-off-Broadway—as "free theater" in every possible sense—ultimately proved unsustainable, not least because practitioners eventually had to face up to the need to make a living. In the later 1960s, some off-off theaters sought to resolve their ongoing financial and legal difficulties by pursuing grant funding and institutional legitimacy. The end of the movement is perhaps marked most clearly by the voluntary dissolution of the Open Theatre in 1973, precisely in order to avoid becoming a grant-dependent administrative entity that perpetuated itself simply for the sake of perpetuating itself. While it lasted, though, that defiant resistance to economic convention was one of the key features that distinguished off-off-Broadway from other new theater ventures of the time. For example, subscription-subsidized bodies such as the American Place Theatre—founded in 1964, at St. Clement's Church on West Forty-sixth Street—were less in thrall to the market than were New York's commercial theaters, but nevertheless had to produce, consistently, a certain type and standard of play, in order to persuade their subscribers to resubscribe.

A second unifying aspect for the movement was the simple fact of geographic proximity: artists and audiences were able to move quickly and freely between the different theaters, located as they all were in the adjoining bohemian neighborhoods of Greenwich Village and the East Village. While each space had its own distinct character and core staff, there was a constant, freely circulating traffic of personalities and ideas around this downtown scene. In this regard, the off-off-Broadway movement was distinct from other countercultural phenomena, such as the black theater movement of the later 1960s, which was at once more unified in its thematic and political concerns, and more diversified geographically. Ed Bullins's New Lafayette Theatre in Harlem; Amiri Baraka's Spirit House Movers in Newark, New Jersey; Douglas Turner Ward's Negro Ensemble Company in the East Village; Vinnette Carroll's Urban Arts Corps in Chelsea: these and other enterprises sought to speak to and for the area's African American communities (albeit with varying degrees of radicalism), and they too deserve detailed examination on their own terms. They remained fundamentally separate, however, from off-off-Broadway's racially mixed but predominantly white community of downtown bohemians: any attempt to wedge them under the same umbrella—as Poland and Mailman do in the *The Off-Off-Broadway Book*—would be both tokenistic and misleading.

Text and Performance

A third cohering factor for the movement, and arguably the most significant in understanding its subsequent historical eclipse, was the centrality of the playwright to the creative process. This factor distinguished it from the director-led performance work that became the new "big idea" among many theater scholars during the 1960s: "We were carving out a domain for ourselves, overthrowing the writers," Richard Schechner, both a critic and a director, has famously claimed of this period (1981, 55). Responding to such newfound inspirations as the manifestos of Antonin Artaud (first published in English in 1958) and the largely nonverbal "happenings" of Allan Kaprow et al. (first seen in New York in 1959), Schechner and others began to champion a new, body-oriented anti-textualism, which perceived playwriting as an unwelcome incursion of literature into the realm of the performative. The notion that a neat, binary separation developed between a text-based theater world—old-fashioned, bourgeois, mainstream—and a radical, director-led avant-garde is still taken for granted in all too many critical discussions of this period. Yet this opposition of writer versus director, text versus performance, while attractively clear-cut in theory, rarely fit in with reality. Joseph Chaikin's Open Theatre, one of the most celebrated director-led collectives of the period, always worked closely with living playwrights like Megan Terry, Jean-Claude van Itallie, and Susan Yankowitz. Drawing on material from the company's workshop processes, these writers created texts for its public performances, contributing both linguistic precision and dramaturgical structure. This is one of many reasons why the Open Theatre was identifiably a part of the off-off-Broadway movement, which was in large part defined by the collaborative, interactive relationships that developed among playwrights, directors, and performers. "There was an ambivalence about words which we all had," van Itallie acknowledges, "because we had been lied to. We were discovering in the sixties that we had been lied to by the establishment in every way. Yet the very words we were being lied to with, still we had to use them to speak." Text was distrusted, certainly, and particularly if it seemed categorical and closed in its "truth" statements: yet text was also recognized as a powerful creative tool, to be explored rather than dispensed with. "You *are* trapped by language," notes Maria Irene Fornes, a playwright associated with both the Open Theatre and Judson Poets': "you're trapped by language in the way that in the city you're trapped by streets. You cannot walk across a building. But you wouldn't say, 'Oh, it's not fair, I wanted to walk this way but there's a building in the way. You'd just walk around the building!" As a Cuban immigrant whose English was self-taught, Fornes knew well the power of language both to limit and liberate.

In retrospect, one can see a great deal of off-off-Broadway playmaking as attempting to "walk around the building," by fusing text and performance in ways that complement and assist each other. The new playwrights championed by venues like the Cino and Judson—far from simply writing their plays as self-contained literary entities that had to be interpreted "correctly" by directors and actors—were often *wrights* in a literal sense, outlining plans for three-dimensional events that sought to respond directly to the peculiar physical circumstances of these unorthodox theater spaces, and that created particular types of experiential dynamic for spectators, rather than treating them as passive observers. Freed by circumstance from the commercial expectation that they write so-called full-length works prioritizing linear narrative or psychological characterization, off-off-Broadway playwrights specialized in creating one-act pieces cohering around distilled, emblematic images or confrontations, which often had as much in common with performance poetry or visual art as with conventional drama. They wrote for particular spaces, particular actors, even particular props, adopting intuitive or improvisatory writing methods that often resembled the practices of other downtown artists of the time. "I'm opposed to whole idea of conception-execution—of getting an idea for a picture and then carrying it out," Robert Rauschenberg once commented, in what could easily have been adapted as a statement of intent for off-off playwrights as diverse as Irene Fornes and Sam Shepard: "I've always felt as though, whatever I've used and whatever I've done, the method was always closer to a *collaboration* with materials than to any kind of conscious manipulation and control" (Tomkins 1968, 204).

In the context of theater, of course, an open-ended, collaborative approach to developing new work could also be applied to the rehearsal process. The familiar, hierarchical power structures of the professional theater simply did not apply off-off-Broadway, and the onus, instead, was on a kind of reciprocal, freewheeling creativity. A playwright, for example, might form a friendly alliance with a director, and then supply him or her with a deliberately provocative or ambiguous script that not only invited but *required* that director to find innovative creative solutions to the problems posed. The radically nonspecific play-texts of Gertrude Stein—the one dead playwright to become a kind of honorary, posthumous member of the movement—were regarded as exemplary in this respect (they tend not even to assign particular lines to particular characters). Conversely, directors might come up with staging suggestions that, in pursuing their underlying vision for the play, might seem utterly counter to the playwright's intentions—as for example when Jacques Levy proposed chopping up the three scenes of Michael Smith's *The Next Thing* (1966) into eleven shorter scenes, and then reshuffling them to create a radically disorientating sense of narrative discontinuity. Smith, however, accepted the idea, saw its relevance to what he had written, and eventually had the text published in Levy's amended format.

Levy and other leading off-off-Broadway directors such as Chaikin, Lawrence Kornfeld, Tom O'Horgan, and John Vaccaro were rightly celebrated for their strikingly distinctive creative talents. Yet they rarely functioned as "auteur" directors in the now-familiar sense of channeling every aspect of production through a personal, stylistic vision. Rather than appropriating "authorship" in this way, these directors worked with living writers, who were often close colleagues, seeking to create something greater than the sum of the individual parts. They also tended to use unorthodox performers who had more than a few ideas of their own about how to take possession of their roles, and who would be encouraged to make those ideas felt during the rehearsal process. Indeed, many of the plays of this period might now, with the benefit of after-the-fact terminology, be considered "performance pieces," in the sense of providing opportunities for performers to shine as individual personalities, rather than simply as actors of character roles. Penny Arcade, who first appeared onstage with the Vaccaro's Play-House of the Ridiculous in 1969, and later became one of the most distinctive solo talents to emerge from New York's performance art scene of the 1980s, points to the 1960s movement as the unacknowledged precursor to much of that later work: "everybody knows where performance comes from when it's the visual, gallery-based stuff," she notes, "but nobody knows where performance comes from when it's the text-based theater stuff. And it comes from John Vaccaro, and Jack Smith, [and] what I call the 'criminal psychedelic homosexual avant-garde.'" That label covers the likes of H. M. Koutoukas, Ondine, Jeff Weiss, and Charles Ludlam, all major players on the off-off-Broadway scene, as writers or actors or both. For his part, Vaccaro points back to the Caffe Cino as the inspirational starting point for such queer performance work, and for much else besides: "This is the beginning! This is *it!* The major things done in New York were done *there*, and nowhere else. I don't give a shit what anybody else says. They're lying."

What Happened?

For Penny Arcade, the lack of recognition of such work by historians and critics amounts to nothing short of "cultural amnesia"—a condition that she blames squarely on "sloppy scholarship and lack of primary research." It is difficult to dispute her perspective, especially when one examines the reasoning behind the customary sweeping dismissals of off-off-Broadway in historical surveys. In his recent book *American Avant-Garde Theatre*, for example, Arnold Aronson claims that "in retrospect, much [off-off playwriting] reads as rather conventional and even sentimental" (2000, 79). In literal terms, that is probably true: given that, as Aronson notes, off-off-Broadway venues presented "hundreds [of plays] a year," a sizable proportion of them were always going to be mediocre, or even downright bad (as indeed is a sizable proportion of all theater, everywhere). Yet to offer this by way of curtailing discussion of the whole topic is simply irresponsible. Looking at *Eight Plays from Off-Off-Broadway*, for example (the first such anthology, published in 1966), it is difficult to see how Aronson's description could be applied to any of texts presented. Moreover, given Aronson's own insistence that "in the avant-garde . . . meaning is inherent in the [performance] and cannot be separated from it without destroying both sense and art" (7), his dismissal of off-off-Broadway in terms of plays to be *read*, without the slightest attempt to investigate their performance conditions, is plainly inconsistent.

Equally plainly, though, the lack of serious critical attention received by the movement since its demise is a logical product of the lack of attention paid during its life span. The only consistent and reliable commentary on the scene came from the *Village Voice*, which had been founded in 1955, and which continued through much of the 1960s to be a small-scale, local paper that performed the function indicated by its name, and paid devoted attention to experimental theater. The mainstream press, however, had little interest in the Village's makeshift, underfunded venues. Presented by unpaid actors and directors, and with little or no obvious publicity, off-off-Broadway productions usually paid little attention to the standards expected of professional theater (indeed they were often of questionable legality), and it is thus hardly surprising that the scene was largely ignored even by the *New York Times* until 1966, when the first successful transfers of off-off-originated work began appearing in commercial off-Broadway venues.

Perhaps more surprising is that it took until that year for the *Tulane Drama Review* (later just the *The Drama Review*) to acknowledge the movement's existence. By far the most widely circulated, most pugnaciously controversial theater journal of the period, *TDR* was the first to report the emergence of many leading experimental theatermakers: from 1965, for example, it championed the work of Jerzy Grotowski and his Polish Laboratory Theatre, which might never have become so famous in the West without this coverage. The vanguard artists that editor Richard Schechner and his colleagues chose to devote attention to during the 1960s are, not coincidentally, still the ones recognized in subsequent histories. And yet *TDR* almost completely ignored the off-off-Broadway movement: the journal's self-declared "absolute commitment to professional standards" (Schechner 1963b, 10) meant that anything as "illegitimate" as off-off-Broadway simply failed to register on its scanners. Time and again, its editorials of the early to mid-1960s frothed with rhetorical condemnations of the state of New York's "commodity theater," but continued to insist and assume that the alternative would have to be found in the resident professional theaters that were then beginning to emerge in regional centers outside New York. (This despite the caustic observation of *TDR*'s own former editor, Robert Corrigan [1964, 14], that these theaters were developing repertories of classics rather than new voices.)

When *TDR*, belatedly and tokenistically, acknowledged off-off-Broadway by commissioning the *Voice*'s Michael Smith to write a summary survey article, Smith made a point of emphasizing that "the very unprofessionality" of the movement was perhaps its greatest contribution to the American theater: "it implies a particular point of view: that the procedures of the professional theatre are inadequate; that integrity and the freedom to explore, experiment and grow count more than respectable or impressive surroundings" (1966,

159–60). Such observations failed to alter *TDR*'s priorities, however. Throughout the decade, serious-minded outsiders tended to dismiss the movement, usually on the basis of only the sketchiest knowledge, as a mere countercultural "fad." That tendency was exacerbated, moreover, by the Broadway success of the musical *Hair* in 1968, as directed by La Mama's Tom O'Horgan. Though it was an unashamedly commercial popularization of off-off ideas and techniques, and featured a simplistically idealistic hippie ideology that had little in common with the more sophisticated, skeptical tone of most off-off productions, *Hair* was assumed by many to be an accurate representation of the scene. Hence the condescending tone of commentaries like Robert Brustein's, in his *New Republic* review of Rochelle Owens' *Futz* (another O'Horgan production that opened off-Broadway later in 1968): "next season, the commercial theatre may confidently expect a siege of hippie rock musicals and avant-garde theatricals, complete with pansexual love-ins, nude tableaux, mixed media, Oriental dances, Yoga exercises, raga music, cunnilingus and fellatio—in brief, the whole mixed bag of the Off Off Broadway movement" (1970, 68). As a caricature of *Hair,* and perhaps even of *Futz,* the description may be fair, but beyond that it says far more about Brustein's ignorance of his subject than it does about the irreducible diversity of the underground movement he purports to describe.

Brustein's use of the term "avant-garde" also points to another factor in the movement's neglect. That label, then as now, was often casually thrown around as a term of dismissive abuse for anything that seemed stylistically unusual or difficult to understand by conventional standards: off-off-Broadway productions caught a lot of this kind of flak. At the same time, however, those critics actively championing the notion of a new avant-garde largely ignored off-off-Broadway, because of their emphasis on this notion of a quasi-Artaudian, antitextual revolt against the mainstream theater. This new take on the avant-garde's time-honored role as the champion of both political and aesthetic progressivism meant that the rejection of playwrights came to be viewed by some as a radical gesture, in and of itself: "as the object against which the avant-garde was able to define itself . . . text-based theater served not only as a foil for the avant-garde's anti-textualism, but more generally for its opposition to the institutions of bourgeois culture" (Harding 2000, 9).

Looking back, we may find it difficult to understand why this opposition to text was considered revolutionary. The link is comprehensible, certainly, in the work of the Living Theatre, whose commitment to "the beautiful anarchist-pacifist revolution" was clearly genuine: during the 1960s, the company evolved into a traveling commune, whose work was collectively created as a manifestation of group beliefs. Less apparent, however, is the social-political relevance of Jerzy Grotowski's experiments with "poor theater," which were often held up by academic avant-gardists as a shining example to follow. (Grotowski's free adaptations of texts by dead writers rendered much of the language as guttural sounds, rather than comprehensible speech.) Whatever resonance Grotowski's works may have had in the context of his native Poland, it was difficult to perceive productions such as *The Constant Prince* and *Akropolis* as anything other than hermetic, aestheticized experiences when they finally reached the United States in 1969. Yet Grotowski's troupe had by then been so extensively heralded that they were greeted with the kind of fawning awe accorded to royalty. Undoubtedly their work deserved many of the plaudits it received, but it is notable that one of the few dissenting voices was that of *Village Voice* critic Ross Wetzsteon, who—steeped in the free-for-all experimentalism of New York's underground theater community—was repelled by the air of trendy exclusivity surrounding Grotowski's visit. (Since the environmental performances seated very few spectators, the entire run had been sold out weeks in advance.) "A Grotowski production is a mass in worship of its own devotion," Wetzsteon wrote: "[Its] air of self-celebrating piety . . . combines with the fashionable, even superciliously elitist ambience of the company's New York performances to produce that most noxious of attitudes: chic spirituality" (1969d).

This confluence of the "avant-garde" with the fashionably sophisticated—which provided anything *but* an "opposition to the institutions of bourgeois culture"—became far more pronounced in the 1970s. The coolly formalistic creations of directors such as Robert Wilson and Richard Foreman were heralded as the next phase of avant-garde antitextualism—thanks to their use of strange, abstract stage imagery (where language was used at all, it tended to be in the form of collaged, seemingly nonreferential fragments). Again, though, the *Village Voice* provided dissenting voices. Michael Feingold scathingly pointed out the degree of "cultural capital" to be accrued from attending events such as Wilson's mammoth minimalist opera, *Einstein on the Beach* (1976), by drawing an explicit comparison with underground work of the previous decade:

> The theatre that was made in the days of the Caffe Cino, the Open Theatre, and the Bread and Puppet Theatre was a theatre for people who wanted to have an experience. The theatre of, say, Robert Wilson, in contrast, seems to me a the-

atre for people who want to purchase a painting. In contrast to the over-touted innovations of the last decade (e.g. Richard Schechner's asinine claim that in the sixties an "anti-literary revolution" took place and "the writer was out"), these alterations are significant and will probably have the effect of sealing the current experimental theatre movement off from the public for good. (Marranca 1977, 23–24)

After a further quarter-century of niche-marketed, avant-garde-flavored performance work, Feingold's comments seem peculiarly prescient. Moreover, his attempts to direct attention back to other experimental approaches proved largely futile. As several of my interviewees for this book noted, it was during that same, late-1970s moment that academic historians began appearing in the Village, digging for material on New York's newly *historical* avant-garde, while applying a freeze-dried set of criteria for what they were looking for: "Avant-garde theatre was primarily formal, schematic, intellectually derived, and dependent upon aesthetic rather than visceral emotion" (Aronson 2000, 5). Thus, for example, the primarily formalistic work of the Judson Dance Theater became retrospectively celebrated, even as the closely allied Judson Poets' Theater, with its unabashedly joyous sense of vaudevillian showmanship, was studiously ignored. It simply did not fit the agenda.

Underground versus Avant-Garde?

A distinction needs to be drawn, it seems, between the "avant-garde" (at least as familiarly constituted) and the "underground"—and this book deals primarily with the latter. Although undergrounds may of course contain elements of avant-gardism, the crucial distinction is their relative disregard of "agendas," whether political or aesthetic. This very disregard, novelist Ronald Sukenick argues in his book *Down and In,* may paradoxically lend the underground a more genuinely antiestablishment dynamic: "In 1939, [Clement] Greenberg claimed that the avant-garde, rather than revolutionary, has traditionally been attached to the ruling elite because it needs the ruling elite's money. . . . An avant-garde leads the pack, [but] it does not necessarily oppose it" (1987, 248). By contrast, Sukenick argues, "the underground can provide an adversarial alternative," because of its absolute disinterest in following any dictates but those of creative freedom:

Cultural undergrounds are notoriously unreliable in terms of ideologies and politics, but the other side of the coin is that they can free themselves of politi-

cal cant and ideological rectitudes to make their judgments as they will. [The]
underground, independent, exploratory, and inventive, remains as the critical
and even prophetic component of the culture. (241, 249)

Sukenick's description can be applied directly to off-off-Broadway. The
movement's emphasis on new playwriting may have cast it on the wrong side
of the bourgeois textuality versus radical antitextuality dichotomy, but it was
nevertheless—in practice rather than in theory—fundamentally nonbour-
geois, simply because the underground scene comprised artists of all social
backgrounds and classes. Joe Cino, for example, came from a working-class,
Italian-American family in Buffalo, and set up his Caffe as a place for his
social circle to hang out. He was, in William Hoffman's words, "the least
avant-garde person I ever met." The intuitive, rough-edged playmaking that
Cino began sponsoring on his premises had everything to do with personal
experimentation—his motto was "do what you have to do"—but nothing
whatever to do with academic debates about art.

In retrospect, the "adversarial" significance of the Caffe Cino's casual disregard for conventional mores is most clearly apparent in the platform that it
provided for young, gay artists to reflect theatrically on their sexuality. They did
what they had to do—at a time when homosexuals were still widely assumed
to be both degenerate and mentally ill. Indeed, the off-off-Broadway movement that developed in the Cino's wake was so openly gay-influenced, across
the board, that the director of Theatre Genesis, Ralph Cook, once made a
point of stressing that his group was notable, "within the Off-Off Broadway circuit" for its "almost conspicuous heterosexuality" (Orzel and Smith 1966, 94).
The queer spirit of the theatrical underground was surely another reason for
the manly arm's length at which it was held by the leading theater critics of the
time, many of whom frequently expressed virulently homophobic sentiments
in print (cf. Bottoms 2003). Significantly, the avant-garde-oriented *TDR* was
among the most vocal exponents of this particular prejudice. In 1963, for example, Schechner wrote an editorial condemning Edward Albee's *Who's Afraid
of Virginia Woolf?* as "decadent": "I am tired of morbidity and sexual perversity
which are there only to titillate an impotent and homosexual theatre and audience" (1963a, 9). In 1965, he published an extended, quasi-psychoanalytic article by Donald Kaplan that concluded that the American theater was rife with
the corrosive influence of "homosexual ideology" (1965, 55). Never mind
Albee and Tennessee Williams; even Arthur Miller was "a latent homosexual,"

Kaplan insisted: "the distinction between heterosexuality and homosexuality in the world of current theatre is a thin line of illusion" (53–54). It was not until the end of the decade that gay artists were treated favorably in *TDR*, as Stefan Brecht and others began covering the Ridiculous. Even Brecht's commentaries, however, later collected in his book *Queer Theatre*, betrayed a certain homophobic distaste for the artists' sexualities.

In a telling juxtaposition, *TDR*'s first articles on Jerzy Grotowski appeared in the same, 1965 edition as Donald Kaplan's jeremiad: his starkly ascetic brand of "poor theater" must have seemed like the perfect antidote to the American theater's swishy decadence. There is, however, one more dimension to the journal's advocacy of Grotowski that is worth drawing attention to here: his work was seized on as the long-sought-for theatrical equivalent to the kind of high modernism that had dominated debate elsewhere in American culture in recent decades. Grotowski's stated desire to purify his theater of all nonessential elements, to create an unmediated physical confrontation between actor and audience by stripping away costumes, makeup, lighting and sound effects, as well as any reverence to the literary text, fit in well with the dictates of modernist art critics like Clement Greenberg, who had argued that the goal of each artistic medium was to emphasize and distill its own essential properties. "All the arts have purified themselves, eliminating the intrusions of other arts," Eugenio Barba wrote in that first *TDR* article on Grotowski's Polish Lab: "Only the theatre has not done this," he adds—until now (1965, 153).

One might caricature subsequent critical assumptions as follows: in the 1960s, experimental theater was modernist, and then, in the 1970s, via Wilson and Foreman, it became postmodernist. I should stress that I am in no way attempting to diminish the cultural and artistic significance of Grotowski, Wilson, Foreman, or anyone else. But the often obsessive attention of scholars to questions of modernism and postmodernism has resulted in a small handful of experimental artists being accorded an enormous amount of critical attention, while many others have been all but forgotten. One of the particular ironies of this erasure is that academia—in its general lack of awareness of New York's underground theater scene in the 1960s—has been deprived of a potentially rich source of grist for its postmodernist mill. "If nothing else is clear about Postmodernism," writes Ronald Sukenick, "it is glaringly obvious that it is impelled by a passion for reengagement with common experience." The key to the concept, he suggests, lies in this "need for a new realism, more available and more inclusive," which in the 1960s "was being expressed by the art originating in the Lower East Side and elsewhere" (1987, 150).

Sukenick's assessment is clearly consistent with the "postmodern turn" that the visual arts took in Lower Manhattan during the early to middle 1960s: pop art, assemblage, minimalism, and happenings all abandoned the modernist notion of the transcendent, self-contained artwork in favor of a more contingent sense of responding to the immediate time and place in which the work was made and displayed. What is less widely recognized is that a similarly contingent attitude was adopted by off-off-Broadway theatermakers, many of whom shared the pop artists' fascination with contemporary pop-culture iconography, and demonstrated a fondness for junk and "found objects" akin to that of happenings-makers. On a textual level, too, many underground plays bore resemblances to the material being produced in this period by "postmodernist" literary figures like Sukenick, John Barth, and Donald Barthelme, whose 1967 cut-up novel *Snow White* was described by the *New Republic*'s Richard Gilman (also a theater critic) as "open-ended, provisional, characterized by suspended judgments, by disbelief in hierarchies, by mistrust of solutions, denouements and completions, by self-consciousness issuing in tremendous earnestness but also in far-ranging mockery." As I hope will become clear, this could also stand as a description for any number of off-off-Broadway plays of the same period: frequently drawing inspiration from high and low culture alike, the scene's writers created playfully distorted, provocative reflections on the contemporary American landscape. The Warhol "superstar" Ondine might not have thought he was being postmodern when, in Soren Agenoux's Caffe Cino play *Chas. Dickens' Christmas Carol* (1966), he played Donald Duck playing Ebenezer Scrooge parachuting into Vietnam while screaming speed-driven psychobabble, but if the label cannot be applied here, it is hard to know where it can.

My purpose here, though, is not to seek to reclaim off-off-Broadway, retrospectively, as a postmodernist theater movement. Any such categorical pigeonholing would simply run the risk of turning the movement into another theoretical abstraction—one that has precious little to do with the irreverent, often ecstatic creativity of the artists whose work this book seeks to document. Instead, I would argue that the real importance of the off-off-Broadway movement lay in its blithe, "underground" disregard for conventional wisdoms and categories, and thus in its playful blurring of the borders between artistic "isms." The theater scene that evolved around the Caffe Cino, Judson Poets' Theater, La Mama, and Theatre Genesis drew freely for inspiration on everything from the most esoteric poetry to the most conventional "soap opera" realism, from Greek tragedy to Hollywood movies, from absurdism to burlesque, Artaud to opera. Radically pluralistic, radically promiscuous in its creativity, this theater was not "postmodernist" in the sense of reacting to and against modernist agendas, but—if anything—"*post*-modernist" in the sense of rendering such agendas largely irrelevant. "One of the most American things about the off-off-Broadway movement," observes playwright Robert Patrick, "was that there was no movement—no manifesto, no credo, no criteria. It just happened."

2   Setting the Scene: A Look at the Fifties

You can't understand the sixties if you don't understand the fifties. People nowadays think *Grease* and *Happy Days* were what it was like in the fifties, but those are just reflections of the movies we saw. The only works from the time that really express what it was like are a play called *Tea and Sympathy* and a movie called *Invasion of the Body Snatchers*. . . . Very few people had any real education in the fifties in America. In fact it was a lot harder being bright than it was being gay, because very few people knew there *were* any gay people, but it was horrifying being bright: it was like there was a law against intelligence. The McCarthy thing was only the tip of the iceberg of a horrifying anti-intellectualism, antiprogressivism. It was a great, big, gorgeous, turquoise-plastic and gleaming-chrome toaster, that was the goal in life, that was what everyone wanted. . . . It was *so* oppressive, but you just can't push people down that far without them springing back up.

—Robert Patrick

Mr. Patrick, as should be becoming clear, has a quotable quip for every occasion, and his description of growing up in the 1950s vividly captures the sense of mindwash conditioning experienced by a whole generation of American children born during or just after World War II. The return to peacetime brought with it a concerted program of reactionary social propaganda: women, for example, having been obliged to surrender their jobs in offices and factories to men returning from the war, were reminded insistently that their proper place was in the home, baking apple pie. Meanwhile, as the nation's antipathies were rapidly refocused away from Germany and Japan toward Soviet Russia, sufficient paranoia had to be manufactured to justify the continuing expansion of America's nuclear arsenal. The McCarthyite anti-Communist witch hunts enforced an almost fascistic level of conformity by redefining the activities deemed "un-American," and effectively silencing most forms of political dissent. It is hardly surprising, then, that the 1950s also became the age of juvenile delinquency, James Dean's causeless rebel, and the emergence of the Beat movement.

The publication in 1956 by San Francisco's City Lights bookstore of Allen

Ginsberg's era-defining poem "Howl" brought to a generation of lonely, voiceless young Americans the relief of knowing that they were not, after all, alone. Though San Francisco was the city initially associated with the Beat movement, its center of gravity had begun to shift to New York by the late 1950s. With that shift, a new wave of what Patrick calls "rabid, freedom-seeking, art-loving outcasts" came washing into the city from all parts of the nation, as if in the wake of Ginsberg and Kerouac. Most sought to settle in Greenwich Village, which, since the early days of the century, had been seen as a haven for artists and freethinkers. Its chaotic, zigzagging street layout, an oasis of the illogical set within the otherwise rigid uniformity of the Manhattan grid-plan, was only the most obvious, outward sign of the Village's dissenting spirit. The area's landlords, however, had entirely conventional profit motives, and responded to the new rise in demand for apartments by pushing their rents up. Many newcomers thus began searching for living space in the less desirable but noticeably cheaper area to the east, roughly between Cooper Square and Tompkins Square Park. This new "boarding house for the Village" quickly became known simply as the East Village: it was in this run-down region of deserted lofts and cold-water tenements where Ginsberg himself lived, in a top-floor apartment on East Fifth Street furnished mostly by mattresses.

These demographic shifts also brought about significant changes in Village lifestyles. In the 1950s, the Village still retained a good deal of its traditional, bohemian atmosphere, manifested especially in its lively bar culture. The San Remo, on MacDougal at Bleecker Street, a traditional New York tavern of old wood walls and pressed-tin ceilings, was a locus for artists and hedonists of all descriptions, and seemed to carry an infectious spirit of wild, emotional theatricality in its smoky air. By contrast, the Cedar Tavern, on University Place, was known for its more coolly laid-back atmosphere, and as the favored hangout for New York School painters such as Willem de Kooning, Franz Kline, and, until his death in 1956, Jackson Pollock. As the new vogue for "beat" or "hipster" lifestyles began to take hold, though, newer establishments began to appear. Jazz clubs became a vital part of the new scene: rooted in improvisation and thus constant innovation, jazz was a key inspiration for action painters and Beat writers alike, and became the soundtrack for the Village's incoming generation. The Five Spot club in Cooper Square, for example, became the home venue for the new brand of "free jazz" being pioneered by the likes of Charles Mingus and Ornette Coleman.

Playwright and poet Amiri Baraka (then LeRoi Jones) identifies the opening of the Five Spot as a turning point of sorts: "I still went to the Cedar and bellied up to the bar, but now . . . the Five Spot was the center for us. [This] was right in tune with the whole movement of people East, away from the West Village with its high rents and older bohemians. Cooper Square was sort of the border line; when you crossed it, you were really on the Lower East Side, no shit" (Sukenick 1987, 58).

Another major new development was the sudden explosion of the coffeehouse scene. Cheaper and easier to establish than bars (not least because, since liquor licenses were not involved, there was less harassment from police and Mafia protection rackets), small cafés began opening all over the East and West Villages during the latter half of the decade. Often, they were run by enterprising young artists who saw an opportunity to create meeting places for their social circles, and to provide walls on which paintings or photographs could be hung. In the East Village, the Tenth Street Coffeehouse initiated another trend by establishing a regular program of poetry readings, by familiar and emerging voices. Presenting their work in such contexts, many poets quickly realized that writing pieces to be read aloud was a very different discipline from writing for the page, requiring more attention to vocal rhythms and to keeping an audience's attention. Despite the protests of purists, the new poetry began to evolve toward a more marked theatricality—just one example of how traditional disciplinary boundaries between the arts began to be blurred or traversed in the changing downtown culture of this transitional period. Another was the way that Beat-style performance poetry got further mixed up with the older tradition of protest music, to generate the Village folk revival that spawned, among many others, the young Bob Dylan. Such developments were, of course, quite logical. As long as the social life of Village was based around bars (and thus inebriation), the actual creative work of the artists frequenting them remained separate, confined to studios and garrets. Caffeine, though, is a stimulant, and customers at the new coffeehouses proved to be amenable and focused audiences for those experimenting with newly performative fusions of music, poetry and art. The cafés thus played an important role in the gradual blurring of disciplinary boundaries that characterized the Village arts scene in the late 1950s and early 1960s. They also provided the seedbed for off-off-Broadway, as young theatermakers too began to experiment with fusing text, image, and sound into tightly focused events designed specifically for the tiny, platform stages provided by cafés.

The Qualified Failure of Off-Broadway

Greenwich Village was, of course, no stranger to theatrical experiment. It had long been favored as home base for those playwrights, actors, and directors who saw themselves as standing at an uneasy arm's length from the full-on commercialism that characterized midtown's Broadway theater district. Independent attempts to foster serious theater enterprises "off-Broadway" had traditionally been based in this area, initially as a modest, amateur alternative to the professional glitz of the Great White Way. In the 1910s, amid a nationwide trend toward the establishment of "little theaters," companies such as the Washington Square Players and the Provincetown Players were established by members of Greenwich Village's bohemian intelligentsia. The latter group, which created its theater at 139 MacDougal Street by converting the house's dining room into a stage and two parlor rooms into an auditorium, was explicitly committed to encouraging the emergence of new American playwrights, and first staged the early, experimental works of Eugene O'Neill and Susan Glaspell. The 1920s saw the formation of a number of other Village-based theater groups, among them the Cherry Lane Players, whose Cherry Lane Theatre—like the Provincetown Playhouse—outlived the company itself to become a key venue for the next major wave of off-Broadway activity.

In years following World War II, the need for an alternative to Broadway once again became keenly felt, as the economic imperatives of commercial theater became more cutthroat than ever. Producers and investors were caught in a two-way economic pinch: a consumer-driven inflationary boom was driving the costs of production to unprecedented heights, while theater audiences were being seduced away by the ever-more-spectacular offerings of cinema and by that newest home-comfort appliance, the television. The significant new voices of Tennessee Williams and Arthur Miller managed to establish themselves on Broadway in the late 1940s, but by the 1950s, the incidence of unknown playwrights being launched with full-scale productions fell almost to zero. Producers simply would not risk capital on new voices or untried material, and relied instead on familiar names, formulaic entertainments, and the wholesale pilfering of successful product from London's West End.

The potential of the Village theaters to provide a real alternative to all this seemed greatly enhanced when, in 1949, Actors' Equity ruled that their members could work in these smaller houses for a lesser pay-rate than on Broadway—a move that opened the door to the professionalization of off-Broadway theater. Two new pay scales were introduced, for theaters of up to 199 seats, and those up to 299 seats, and this prompted a new wave of building conversions—with several old movie houses, for example, adding stages and subtracting sufficient seats to bring them in line with the new regulations. Its newly professional status meant that, in the 1950s, off-Broadway acquired a new legitimacy. With running costs substantially lower than those on Broadway, the Village venues began to be seen as providing new hope for a theater premised on art rather than commerce.

In 1952, off-Broadway scored its first critical and commercial hit, in the form of Tennessee Williams's *Summer and Smoke*, as directed by Jose Quintero at the new Circle in the Square Theatre. A former nightclub on Sheridan Square, the venue's name derived from the circular, low-ceilinged dance floor that had become an arena-style auditorium, with seats facing a thrust, platform stage from three sides. This arrangement was indicative of the growing postwar movement to create alternatives to the overfamiliar, end-on dynamics of proscenium-arch staging, and it created a sense of intimacy that proved ideal for Williams's play. Having flopped on Broadway just four years previously, *Summer and Smoke* seemed suddenly transformed: the production made a star of Geraldine Page and ran for 357 performances—an achievement that prompted other producers to sit up and look at off-Broadway's new possibilities.

However, the Circle's association with established Broadway names like those of Williams and O'Neill (Quintero staged an acclaimed revival of *The Iceman Cometh* in 1956) was indicative of the fact that the new off-Broadway scene was not particularly daring in its choice of material. In effect, the serious drama being squeezed off Broadway by economic forces found an alternative home in these smaller theaters: revivals of plays by established American and European dramatists were far more likely to be mounted than new, untested work. "Off-Broadway was really the residue of the things that students learned in their college university courses in theater, and in Eric Bentley and John Gassner anthologies," Leon Katz comments dryly: "They would simply do those plays in very interesting and respectable productions." For the most part, though, unknown American dramatists were no more likely to find exposure off-Broadway than on, and that situation worsened over the course of the 1950s as the commercial pressures on the new theaters grew steadily tighter.

Simultaneously, across the Atlantic, the "pocket theaters" of Paris, very much the French equivalent of off-Broadway, were mounting the work of a new wave of playwrights—including Samuel Beckett, Eugène Ionesco, and Jean Genet—whose plays were revolutionizing the possibilities for dramatic writing (cf. Cohn 1998). As a result of their European acclaim, these writers began attracting attention in New York too, but a misconceived Broadway production of *Waiting for Godot* in 1956 quickly proved they had little commercial potential. There were off-Broadway successes such as Alan Schneider's highly praised version of *Endgame*, which played at the Cherry Lane in 1958, but Beckett was still considered such a risk with audiences that early discussions for Schneider's premiere of *Krapp's Last Tape* centered around the concept of playing it several times nightly in the back room of the Five Spot jazz club (an off-off-Broadway idea predating the fact). Those plans changed, however, after *Krapp* was successfully mounted in Germany, in double bill with the world premiere of *The Zoo Story*, by the previously unknown Edward Albee, who had found it impossible to get his work produced in the United States. Producer Richard Barr now stepped in to mount the same bill as the pilot project for his new off-Broadway company. It opened at the Cherry Lane Theatre in January 1960, and Albee became, by proxy, part of the European new wave.

One of the New York theater establishment's few genuine risk-takers, Barr had abandoned a lucrative Broadway producing partnership in order to champion the work of new American playwrights. His faith in Albee proved fully justified: *The Zoo Story* was so popular with audiences that it was remounted eight times over the next six years, becoming the defining off-Broadway play of the era. The play revived, almost single-handedly, the American little theater tradition of the self-contained one-act drama, and did it by fusing a distinctly American urban realism with new ideas derived from the European "theater of the absurd" (as Martin Esslin would label the works of Beckett, Ionesco, et al.). Albee acknowledges Beckett as a key influence, and *Zoo Story* clearly owes an enormous debt to *Waiting for Godot*—in its use of a single, crystallized stage image (two figures on an almost bare stage fill time with stories and games), in its emphasis on the rhythmic textures of its dialogue, and in its focus on apparently banal, inconsequential events. All of this can be read as generating a sense of ennui, of the meaninglessness or "absurdity" of existence. Yet Albee, unlike Beckett, locates his play in an identifiable, "real world" location, beside two park benches on the west side of Central Park. The play stages a confrontation of specific social types—Jerry is the lonely, desperate, but fiercely articulate dropout; Peter the comfortably numbed bourgeois family man—and thus brings a specifically urban, contemporary twist to its themes of alienation and helplessness. Indeed, Albee's depiction of Jerry as a "beat" character, in the original sense of being "beaten down" by society, of living on its margins, helped to legitimize such alternative voices as a subject for dramatic treatment. By casually breaking down the theatrical taboos surrounding topics such as homosexuality (Jerry mentions, in passing, his repression of his own homosexual urges as a teenager, his living next door to "a colored queen," his familiarity with the cruising areas in Central Park), *The Zoo Story* articulated on the off-Broadway stage the kind of frank, anti-bourgeois, New York–centric sensibility that would subsequently become a hallmark of the underground theater scene. Albee himself subsequently adopted a very different trajectory, graduating to Broadway and to the more privileged social milieus depicted in plays like *Who's Afraid of Virginia Woolf?* and *A Delicate Balance.* Yet he and Barr remained very supportive of young writers whose stance remained more explicitly oppositional to mainstream mores.

In requiring only a small performance space and almost no set (two benches and a painted backdrop), *The Zoo Story* was a powerful reminder that large budgets, large casts, and lengthy plots can be as much a hindrance as a help in creating memorable drama. The intimacy and immediacy of the play, its emphasis on verbal and physical confrontation (and thus on the performance skills of actors, rather than on theatrical effects), provided a blueprint of sorts for much of the low-to-no-budget off-off-Broadway theater of the 1960s—"a theatre that was bone-clean, depending on the very vigor of the production to make it work" (Poland and Mailman 1972, xiv). As playwright Robert Heide notes, "No one other than Albee was doing one-act plays off-Broadway. . . . He helped open up the way for off-off-Broadway, because there were all these young writers, including probably myself, who said, 'Oh, I can do that too!' And we wound up at places like the Cino."

In the immediate aftermath of *Zoo Story*'s success, Albee's sudden fame and notoriety also persuaded a number of off-Broadway producers that there might be money to be made promoting other new playwrights. A handful of young writers including Jack Richardson, Arthur Kopit, and Murray Schisgal thus succeeded in having plays produced professionally. This trend was short-lived, however, and other new playwrights like Heide were thus "driven underground." By the early 1960s, the off-Broadway scene was already sagging under the weight of inflated and unsustainable speculative activity. The 1959–60 season in which Albee emerged was the first year in which over one million dollars had been invested in off-Broadway productions (the number of which was by then already double that of productions on Broadway itself), and by 1966, Michael Smith was looking back on an era that already seemed long gone:

> Off-Broadway's happy days were over quicker than anyone expected; ironically nearly a dozen new Off-Broadway theatres were built or reconstructed just too late, and Off-Broadway today is glutted with empty theatres. As the movement became established, rents went up, unions moved in, ticket prices climbed, audiences were reduced in number and ever more subject to "hit psychology." A play could be produced for a few hundred dollars in the middle fifties; in the sixties Off-Broadway productions have required initial investments ranging from a minimum of $10,000 to upwards of $40,000. (Orzel and Smith 1966, 4–5)

Thus, for the most part, the supposed alternative had become simply a smaller-scale version of Broadway itself. By the early 1960s, many people's hopes for a revival in serious professional drama in America had shifted toward the new resident theaters being established with foundation grants in cities elsewhere in the country. (Changes in the tax laws in 1954 had resulted in corporations such as Ford and Rockefeller establishing foundations to provide grants to artistic causes, as a philanthropic tax dodge.) The regional theaters, however, needed reliable product to attract regular audiences and thus prove themselves worthy of support: they tended to offer much the same kind of "library" repertory as off-Broadway, and did little to pioneer new directions. Faced with these dead ends, many young theatermakers began to take matters into their own hands. Smith dates the beginnings of off-off-Broadway as a conscious theatrical movement to a September 1960 revival of Alfred Jarry's grotesque classic *Ubu Roi*, at the Take 3 coffeehouse on Bleecker Street: the program note called for "a return to the original idea of Off-Broadway theatre, in which imagination is substituted for money, and plays can be presented in ways that would be impossible in the commercial theatre" (Orzel and Smith 1966, 6).

Alternatives to the Alternative?

If *Ubu* marked a beginning, of sorts, for the 1960s scene, it was not without precedent. The new generation of underground theaters owed a significant debt to the pioneering work of a few, consciously experimental companies that had struggled to lay the foundations for a genuine alternative to commercialism. Chief among these was the Living Theatre, which had itself produced a version of *Ubu* at the Cherry Lane in 1952, and which—led by Judith Malina and her husband, Julian Beck—fought its way past seemingly insuperable obstacles to become the single most influential American company of its era. From the outset, the company was driven by a consciously avant-gardist commitment to the fusion of both aesthetic and political radicalism. Malina, who had studied with the great German director Erwin Piscator, in his Dramatic Workshop at the New School for Social Research, notes that she and Beck wanted to create a theater of "pure art, pure poetry, [with] the highest level of artistic adventure, the highest level of experiment, the highest level of political advance." However, as Malina herself is the first to acknowledge, such lofty aspirations were absurdly at odds with the practicalities imposed by their humble resources. The story of the Living Theatre in the 1950s, like that of many underground artists of the 1960s, is that of a company constantly trying to find a viable context in which to perform.

Always more concerned with the *nature* of their contact with audiences than with totting up the numbers of spectators present, the Becks first attempted to establish a performance space, in 1948, by converting an intimate basement room on Wooster Street into a theater that would accommodate no more than thirty seats. These plans had to be abandoned, however, when the city concluded from their license application that this was to be a cover for a brothel (Ellen Stewart was to encounter the same prejudice fourteen years later). The Becks subsequently began to plan performances for the living room of their own Upper West Side apartment, and as many "private guests" as they could squeeze in. The Living Theatre thus premiered with "theater-in-the-room" in 1951, before presenting its first public productions later that year in the more professional surroundings of the Cherry Lane Theatre, which they rented using money recently inherited by Beck. During the 1951–52 season, the company staged its first repertory season, presenting poetic dramas such as Gertrude Stein's *Doctor Faustus Lights the Lights* and Kenneth Rexroth's *Beyond the Mountains*, but the residency was brought to an abrupt end when, three nights into *Ubu Roi*, the fire department closed the show for using flammable set materials. The Cherry Lane's new owner took this as an excuse to terminate their contract. After another period of hiatus, the company relocated to another nontheater space—a large loft, way uptown at One Hundredth Street and Broadway—where, during 1954 and 1955, they produced plays including Pirandello's *Tonight We Improvise* and Jean Cocteau's *Orphee*, before being closed again for building code violations.

The Living's insistence at this time on presenting plays by poets and aesthetes sprang in part from an interest in the plays themselves—so radically distinct from the formulaic naturalistic dramas of the mainstream. The Becks also, however, had a shrewd awareness that plays using abstract language and imagery tended to dictate little about their actual staging, and were thus wide open to creative innovation. Their objective, which again set important precedents for off-off-Broadway, was to mount collaborative, multidimensional events, with the playwright's text functioning as a starting point in the creation of productions that belonged, uniquely, to their participants. They sought, as Malina puts it, "to bring theater, which was a little retarded, up to the level of experiment in dance, in music, in painting, in poetry." To this end, musicians and choreographers were brought on board alongside actors, and Julian Beck—who was also an abstract expressionist painter of considerable repute—applied a trained visual eye to the creation of sets and costumes. The company's example seems also to have inspired similar experiments by the shorter-lived Artists' Theatre, which director Herbert Machiz battled to keep afloat between 1953 and 1956, and which prioritized work by New York–based poets such as Frank O'Hara and John Ashbery, while commissioning set designs from painters like Larry Rivers.

Predictably, though, the primary difficulty faced by both the Living Theatre and the Artists' Theatre during this period (aside from financial problems) was that their insistence on staging complex, "high-brow" texts made the task of attracting regular audiences very difficult. The Living had a small coterie of devoted admirers: the poet William Carlos Williams, for example, hailed Stein's *Doctor Faustus* as "the first really serious, really cleanly written, produced and acted play" that he had seen in a long time (Tytell 1995, 77). Yet much of their early work was regarded, even by those sympathetic to their cause, as simply too esoteric to connect meaningfully with audiences. Often the company's intentions seemed unclear even to their performers. One telling incident occurred during their 1952 staging of Paul Goodman's *Faustina*—a production derided by observers and later described by Beck as a "humiliating agony" (Tytell 1995, 83). The young actress cast in the lead role, Julie Bovasso, was required by the script to address the audience directly at the play's conclusion, dropping Goodman's language and expressing her own feelings as they occurred to her, spontaneously, in that moment. A precursor to the company's later experiments with improvisatory immediacy, this moment nevertheless seemed pretentious and redundant to Bovasso, who stepped forward on the first night to tell the audience how irritated she was at being expected to do this. According to Lawrence Kornfeld (who later became general manager of the company), Goodman himself thought her reaction perfect in its authenticity. Yet Bovasso, who had clashed with the Becks throughout rehearsals, walked out on the show after just a few performances.

The Tempo Theatre

In 1955, Bovasso set up her own small company, in an enterprise that owed an obvious debt to the do-it-yourself spirit of the Living. The Tempo Theatre, however, was in many respects a more representative precursor of the down-to-earth practicality of the off-off-Broadway movement than was the more self-consciously avant-gardist work of the Living Theatre. "The Becks were like the godparents," Michael Smith explains, "but they were kind of a little above everything else." By contrast, Julie Bovasso's approach was unassumingly direct. An Italian-American from Brooklyn, she came—as did many leading figures of the 1960s underground—from a blue-collar background, and had little patience with anything that struck her as "arty." She wanted to experiment, but she was also not shy about wanting to entertain.

The Tempo Theatre was established with an initial investment of just $250, from the sale of a painting by Bovasso's husband, George Ortman. She rented and overhauled the larger-than-average parlor of a ground floor apartment at 4 St. Mark's Place, in what was then just beginning to be called the East Village, and built a small proscenium stage and a birdcage box office. The auditorium consisted of just sixty or seventy folding chairs. This semilegal enterprise was plagued, and in 1957 forced to close, by precisely the kind of pressures to which the 1960s café venues were later subjected: Jerry Tallmer recalls that the odds stacked against her "included the cops, who on any given evening might come in with a jovial: 'Okay, Julie, whattaya got in the register?' and clean her out—all $30 or $40 of it, if she didn't want to be closed down for one violation or another" (1991b, 31). Yet in this tiny theater, during its short life, Bovasso presented the first productions on American soil of plays by Jean Genet, Eugene Ionesco, and Michel de Ghelderode—writers whose work was then considered too "way out" for any kind of commercial production. In 1954, Grove Press had published a reading edition of Genet's *The Maids* and *Deathwatch*, but there seemed no danger of anyone wanting to stage them until, as Tallmer recounts, "Ortman [came] back from Paris talking about the new playwrights he'd seen. . . . Julie sat down and wrote a bunch of airmail letters. 'Dear Mr. Genet (Ionesco, etc.), my name is Julie Bovasso, I am starting a theatre in New York and I would very much like to . . .' They wrote back: Yes" (1991a).

According to playwright H. M. Koutoukas, Genet himself attended the 1955 premiere of *The Maids*, the Tempo's inaugural production, only to be arrested in the lobby as an undesirable alien: "Immigration would just send homosexuals right back. And of course he was an ex-con." The production, however, which Bovasso both directed and starred in, went on to become a cult success, and in 1956 her performance as Solange won her one of the first ever Obie Awards for distinguished acting. The *Village Voice*, published for the first time in October 1955, had quickly established an annual ceremony to honor the work of Greenwich Village's "O.B." theaters, which it was one of the paper's key missions to document. (Michael Smith recalls that, when he joined the *Voice* in 1958, "the theater reviews were like, half the paper.") It was Jerry Tallmer's initiative as the paper's chief theater critic that ensured that hole-in-the-wall shows such as *The Maids* were treated with the same respect and seriousness as the more seemingly professional work of, say, the Circle in the Square (whose *Iceman Cometh* that year won Obies for Quintero's directing and Jason Robards's acting).

Bovasso's productions were driven by a brand of low-budget dynamism that displayed the same, refreshingly direct approach she had used in writing to the authors. "As I sit here, 36 years later," Tallmer wrote in Bovasso's obituary, "I can still see . . . writhing up from behind the chaise longue onstage . . . two menacing, red serpents—the arms of a venom-spitting Julie Bovasso in rubber scullery gloves" (1991b, 30). The rubber gloves are a feature of Genet's script, but the degree of theatrical emphasis that Bovasso gave them directly anticipated off-off-Broadway's penchant for colorfully makeshift theatricality. In the absence of sufficient resources to realize the elaborately decorated boudoir imagined by Genet ("Louis-Quinze furniture. Lace" [Genet 1954, 35]), Bovasso compensated by drawing special attention to isolated elements like the rubber gloves—make them bright red!—so as to give them a focus and resonance akin, perhaps, to that with which Robert Rauschenberg invested the "found objects" in his combines, or to the consumer iconography that would later be associated with pop art. The choice is indicative of Bovasso's ability to blend experimentalism with a self-consciously populist touch that made her productions both challenging and accessible: "I know that it wasn't arty," she herself said of *The Maids*, "because my father came to see it and liked it, and he's a truck driver" (Benevy 1955). For precisely such reasons as this, the Tempo is remembered by some observers, such as Maria Irene Fornes, as "in a sense the first off-off-Broadway theater." Many off-off playwrights, including Fornes herself, went on to domesticate the inspiration of Genet, Ionesco, and

Beckett in very similar ways to those employed by Bovasso as a director. By the late 1960s, after several years as a jobbing actress, Bovasso herself returned to make some major contributions to the alternative theater scene she had inadvertently helped inspire (see chapter 16).

The Living Theatre at Fourteenth Street

In the meantime, the Living Theatre had successfully regrouped. Having been forced into silence since 1955, the company relaunched itself in January 1959, in a new theater that they themselves had created within the structure of an old department store at Fourteenth Street and Sixth Avenue, on the northernmost edge of Greenwich Village. The building took a year to renovate and remodel, at a crippling cost of twenty thousand dollars (which Beck sought to cover through relentless fund-raising), but by the time it opened it had been transformed into a shining jewel box of the arts. The walls and ceiling, for example, had been painted in black alternating matt and gloss stripes, which became progressively narrower toward the stage, thereby creating the impression for spectators of sitting inside an old-fashioned concertina camera. In this lovingly created space, the Living presented a new repertory of work that, while reflecting the same aesthetic and political concerns as before, also embraced a grittier, more distinctly American spirit—just as the traditional bohemianism of the Village was giving way to the raw energy of jazz musicians and Beat poets.

These changes were epitomized by the company's groundbreaking production of Jack Gelber's new, "hipster drama," *The Connection*, which premiered in 1959 and remained in the repertory—thanks to popular demand—over the next two years. Despite being dismissed as "a farrago of dirt" by the *New York Times* for its frank exploration of the lives of a group of New York heroin addicts (and indeed for Gelber's unprecedentedly liberal use of the word *shit* in its many and various vernacular contexts), the play became something of a cause célèbre among enlightened Villagers, and attracted critical acclaim from figures as diverse as Jerry Tallmer, Robert Brustein, and Kenneth Tynan. Like *The Zoo Story*, which appeared almost simultaneously, Gelber's play effectively adapted the influence of *Waiting for Godot* to the realities of New York low-life: a racially mixed group of junkies (the integrated casting was itself a bold political statement at the time) hang around in Leach's run-down apartment, passing time with idle talk and activities while waiting for their "connection" to arrive. Unlike Godot, the connection—a dealer named Cowboy—does in fact show up, and administers heroin to all and sundry in the offstage toilet. His arrival, however, simply results in further listlessness as the effects of the drug set in. Eventually, and anticlimactically, Leach collapses from a self-administered overdose.

In Gelber's play, the characters' dialogue is markedly less textured and seductive than in Albee's: it really does suggest the kind of conversational banality of the hyperrealistic situation that it depicts. The intrigue of *The Connection* lies not in its language but in its conceptual structure, which suggests a debt to Pirandello or Genet: the junkies' behavior is metatheatrically framed, from the start, by the use of two other characters identified as the playwright and the producer, who speak to the audience from the stage, explaining that they have assembled a cast of authentic heroin addicts, rather than mere actors, and that they will not simply be speaking pre-scripted lines, but improvising in the manner of jazz musicians around a loose scenario. In short, the audience is told that they are not watching a fictional situation set in a fictional location, but actual people, actually in front of them, on a set that is merely masquerading as Leach's apartment for the sake of added authenticity. The natural tendency of most spectators, of course, would be to doubt such claims and regard this all as theatrical pretence, but Gelber sows seeds of doubt by a kind of double bluff: his producer character, Jim, insists (in direct contradiction of other statements) that, "I and this entire evening on stage are merely a fiction. And don't be fooled by anything anyone else tells you. . . . What I mean to say is that we are not actually using real heroin. You don't think we'd use the real stuff? After all, narcotics are illegal" (Gelber 1960, 19). Such provocations may well have prompted spectators to wonder whether something illegal *was* in fact be going on under the guise of a fictional drama. Indeed, production anecdotes suggest that some members of Freddie Redd's quartet—the jazz ensemble who played live onstage during the performance—were indeed drug users, and that, on occasion, one or other of them would pass out, for real, during the performance.

In retrospect, the hall of mirrors surrounding the question of the play's "reality" is perhaps less interesting in itself than for what it effected; namely, a heightened awareness on the part of audience and actors alike of the play's existence in the *now* of performance. The traditional separation between the representational (the fictional elsewhere of the play) and the real (here, now, in the theater) had been blurred, thrown into question—not least because the almost constant coexistence onstage of a fifteen-strong cast meant that the actors were obliged to find simple, everyday activities of their own with which to occupy themselves—from making tea to rolling a hula hoop to simply sitting. This was particularly the case during the lengthy periods (ten minutes or more at a time) when the musicians would improvise jazz while the other characters simply listened. The actors thus had to learn to follow the example of the musicians, and become comfortable simply "being" on stage, rather than constantly feeling the need to act or emote. For this reason, argues Arthur Sainer, *The Connection* signaled a "radical loosening of the fabric of drama," in that what was being staged "had to do not with character being made but with performers ceasing to make performances" (1975, 11–12).

"We began to understand in the 60s," Sainer continues, "that the events in plays were too often evasions. . . . At best they were *about* something rather than *some* thing; they were ideas describing experiences rather than the experiences" (1975, 15). Following on from *The Connection*, the Living Theatre continued to explore, in different ways, the complex relationship between dramatic fiction and real-time, onstage behavior. In their 1963 production of Kenneth Brown's *The Brig*, for example, the actors played inmates in a U.S. Navy brig. Again rooted in a kind of extreme, documentary realism, the production was also partially inspired by Artaud's manifestos for a "theater of cruelty": the play depicts soldiers being pushed through a series of ritualized humiliations, as guards order them up and down the stage space in a numbingly repetitive cycle of movement drills. In executing these instructions, the actors' bodies were subjected to a visibly real process of physical exhaustion. Both *The Brig* and *The Connection* demonstrated clearly that—despite the antitextual rhetoric of some 1960s theorists—dramatic text and "live," physical performance were in no way incompatible. Several leading off-off-Broadway playwrights subsequently experimented further with the creation of dramatic fictions that, paradoxically, highlight the immediate presence of the actor in front of the audience. Such strategies, of course, made a virtue of necessity: the very fact of performing in cafés and church halls, rather than in dedicated theater spaces, meant that the maintenance of conventional theatrical illusion was a virtual impossibility.

In 1963, with *The Brig* still running, the Living Theatre building was seized by the Internal Revenue Service for nonpayment of taxes: without external financial support, the company had been unable to make financial ends meet as a professional, off-Broadway venture. The Becks and a committed, core group of company members subsequently went into self-imposed exile in Europe, where, as a traveling community, they went on to create their most famous works. They left behind them, however, a number of associated artists—including Joseph Chaikin, Lawrence Kornfeld, Warren Finnerty, and Rochelle Owens—who subsequently became leading participants in the off-off-Broadway movement.

Several of these figures had cut their creative teeth by creating performances for the Living's Monday Night Series. These informal, one-night-only events, which took advantage of the acting company's night off, featured mixed programs of short plays or dance pieces, and music or poetry recitals. The series provided further evidence of the company's attempts to generate a creative dialogue between the arts—also apparent in their decision to lease the top floor of the Fourteenth Street building as studio space for modern dance pioneer Merce Cunningham (who had previously worked with the company as both actor and choreographer) and his close colleague, composer John Cage. These revered "tenants" also occasionally offered work at the Monday night events, which—like the café performances of the period—contributed substantially to the gradual blurring of disciplinary boundaries between the arts at this time. According to Michael Smith, the Monday Night Series was an important inspiration for the subsequent development of off-off-Broadway theater, thanks to the relaxed, casually creative atmosphere of these events, and the free exchange of ideas across art forms.

Happenings

One other vital, formative factor in the theater scene's "radical loosening" was the emergence—also from 1959—of the loose genre of non-text-based performance events known as "happenings." The first such event, from which the name was derived, was Allan Kaprow's 18 *Happenings in 6 Parts*, mounted at the Reuben Gallery in the East Village that October. Kaprow himself, originally a painter, did not conceive of the event as "theater" at all, simply because no playscript or dramatic fiction was involved: what happened was simply what happened. For many, though, the three-dimensional, time-based events created over the next few years by Kaprow and artist colleagues including Red Grooms, Claes Oldenburg, Jim Dine, and Robert Whitman, were indeed a new brand of theater—insofar that they employed sight, sound, and live performers, who would enact simple tasks "scripted" for them by the artist-author. Indeed, for composer John Cage, who did more than any other individual to kickstart this trend during the 1950s, there was no question that happenings—

and indeed the related "Fluxus" events then being created by another group of New York artists—were symptomatic of the gradual evolution of other art forms toward the condition of theater.

In 1952, Cage had organized a one-off "Theatre Piece" that became, for many, the touchstone for subsequent cross-disciplinary experiments. He and Merce Cunningham, then working as instructors at Black Mountain College in North Carolina, collaborated with painter Robert Rauschenberg and others to create a mixed media event in which an audience, seated in an unusual, in-the-round formation, witnessed several distinct activities taking place simultaneously. Cage's pianist David Tudor performed a composition while Cage himself stood on a step ladder and read a fragmentary lecture; Cunningham and some of his dancers improvised movement around and between the triangular blocks of audience; Rauschenberg, whose series of all-white canvas paintings were suspended at different angles above the audience, played records on an old phonograph. The performance was an experiment with structured randomness, juxtaposing disparate elements so as to explore chance interrelationships between them. Owing a clear debt to the dada and futurist performances conducted in Europe during the 1910s and 1920s, the Black Mountain event helped inspire many other similar experiments. Cage himself continued to play extensively with the inherent theatricality of musical performance. In his most famous composition, 4'33" (also 1952), a pianist lifts the piano lid, sits without playing a note for four minutes and thirty-three seconds, and then closes the lid again: this is at least as much a theater event as it is an exploration of the unsilence of silence, and could perhaps be retitled *Waiting for Music*. Cage also went on to teach a highly unorthodox composition course at the New School, attended by Kaprow and others, which directly inspired experiments such as 18 *Happenings in 6 Parts*. For that event, the Reuben Gallery's long, narrow loft space was subdivided into three smaller rooms by erecting semitransparent screens of plastic sheeting: each of these spaces was used, simultaneously, for the enactment of six compartmentalized sequences of events, involving both living bodies and moving objects ($6 \times 3 = 18$).

Many of the New York happenings that followed, over the next few years, have been well documented elsewhere, and it would serve no purpose to re-rehearse details here (cf. Kirby 1965; Sandford 1995). The focus of this book, as has been noted, is on theatrical experiments that continued to prioritize the playwright's text, and that, in doing so, have been comparatively neglected by subsequent scholarship. Nevertheless, happenings proved to be a vital influence on the off-off-Broadway movement—not least because many of its leading playwrights and directors had themselves been directly involved in the making of happenings. "They were really fundamental, in my experience, for seeing theater," says Maria Irene Fornes, who participated as a performer in one of Claes Oldenburg's "Ray Gun Theatre" events, "because it was *all* theater, but it had nothing to do with traditional dramatic structure. Not even the language: language was used almost as if it were objects. Words were spoken as if it were a cashier saying $3.75 [she taps the table]; $3.75 [tap]; $3.75 [tap]." This refocusing of attention away from "meaning" and toward the basic, phenomenological properties of language, objects, and action—toward their shapes, textures, and rhythms—opened up all kinds of possibilities for theatrical experimentation. For example, the multiple-focus abundance of simultaneous actions in many happenings seemed to invite further explorations in "total theater." This was the trajectory pursued by director Tom O'Horgan, who created several happenings of his own before turning to work with La Mama's playwrights, and who notes that—in his text-based and non-text-based work alike—"essentially my concern was trying to find that kind of form which would utilize all the arts, painting and sculpture and music."

Conversely, though, since happenings seemed to legitimize dispensing with the traditionally assumed components of theater, a new minimalism was also possible. If plot, character, and the rest are optional, then what *are* the minimum requirements for an effective and engaging piece of theater? That question seemed to be asked, equally, by a composition like 4'33" and by a play like Paul Foster's *Balls*, in which the only onstage action is a pair of Ping-Pong balls swaying mesmerically in pin-spot light, to the sound of disembodied voices. Even playwright Jean-Claude van Itallie, who found happenings "completely uninteresting as theater," precisely because they often seemed so devoid of content ("the audience has got to attach its feelings to something that has denotative value!") points to their importance as "a leveling of the ground. It was like, OK, this is ground zero, and you've rejected the usual forms, which for us were Broadway, psychological realism. And then you think, *now* what's possible?"

One final point to stress is that off-off-Broadway theatermakers also seem to have responded enthusiastically to the fundamentally democratic, antiauthoritarian nature of happenings. From the outset, Cage had conceived of events such as his Black Mountain theater piece in these terms, believing that—by allowing spectators to focus in whichever direction they chose, and by allowing chance juxtapositions to dominate the performance itself—artists and audience alike became equally important to the creation of the event as it occurred. (Cage in fact strongly objected to Kaprow's 18 *Happenings* on the grounds that the instructions issued to the audience, telling them when and where to move within the gallery's three rooms, felt like a form of policing.) Subsequent happenings followed similar principles: by reframing everyday objects and actions in a different light, and by leaving spectators to choose for themselves how to respond to those objects and actions, the artists did away with any notion that the artwork could or should be a fixed, unchanging entity that expressed to the viewer a particular point of view or emotional dynamic. Spectators at happenings were invited, instead, to come up with their own interpretations and conclusions with regard to the events that they witnessed and participated in. Much the same was true of the developing off-off-Broadway scene.

Perhaps the most obviously "democratic" feature of the happenings was their embracing of the detritus of American popular culture as source material that could be valued as much as the most elevated of classical or modernist art. "The theatre of Happenings," Allan Kaprow wrote, "if [it] is theatre . . . is close in spirit not to Racine or even Beckett, but to the theatre of . . . drag races, one day supersales, march-ins, rocket launchings, Pentagon meetings, brain operations, and the subway rush-hour" (Benedikt 1968, 358). The implications of this declaration, which would have been unthinkable to artists just a few years beforehand, were perhaps most fully realized in the happenings of Claes Oldenburg, who took to mounting performances as a regular weekend event in a disused store on East Second Street, changing the entire decor and dynamic of the space from week to week. One of the artists who also became integrally associated with pop art during the early 1960s, Oldenburg filled this store space with his iconic representations of contemporary consumer products, and had his performers perform nostalgic re-creations of silent movie slapstick, or vaudeville and burlesque routines.

As Oldenburg wrote in the program notes for *Store Days* in 1961: "I am for Kool-art, 7 Up Art, Pepsi Art, Sunshine Art, 39 cents art, 15 cents art, Vatronol art, Dro-bomb art, Vam art, Menthol art, L&M art, Ex Lax art, Venida art, Heaven Hill art, Pamryl Art, San-o-med art, Rx art, 9.99 art, Now art, New art, How art, Fire Sale art, Last Chance art, Meat-o-Rama art" (Lahr and Price 1974, 297–98). The playful exuberance of such sentiments could also be taken as a manifesto for much of the work that appeared off-off-Broadway in the 1960s. This was theater created largely by young, disaffected refugees from the American heartlands, who found their way to downtown Manhattan in the late 1950s and early 1960s, and who—for the most part—had little or no formal education in the arts. These "new bohemians" were as likely to be inspired, creatively, by B-movies and comic books as by Baudelaire or Cocteau. By the early 1960s, moreover, the need to throw off traditional conceptions of high and low art, respectable and despised, was being felt even by those with more self-conscious artistic agendas. "We needed to get out," observes Lawrence Kornfeld of the new underground's unashamedly populist brand of experimentalism: "To get out from inside. To get out from Eisenhower time. To get out from those constraints. To create a very, very American form."

part 1 Emerging Venues, Emerging Playwrights, 1960–66

3   Caffe Cino: The Birth of a Movement

You see, we weren't there to develop new theater. We didn't have an anti-Broadway philosophy. It's just that we stumbled into a place where we could develop our craft, and we loved it, it was a lot of fun to do it. . . . We were experimental, sure, but *truly* experimental, in the sense that we were trying things out: "Let's see if it works." I wrote my first play, *Goodnight I Love You* [1965], about a gay man talking to a straight friend, a girlfriend, on the telephone, and explaining that he's been impregnated by his boyfriend. The audience was disgusted by this. Gay audience. I mean, where did I get the nerve to write this?

          —William M. Hoffman

The Caffe Cino was the first off-off-Broadway venue of importance to emerge in the early 1960s, but as Hoffman's comments indicate, the development of its theater program was more accidental and incremental than self-consciously experimental. At the turn of the decade, nobody would have thought seriously that an alternative theater movement could have its beginnings in a setting as cramped, inappropriate, and underfunded as this tiny backstreet café. The Cino initially developed as a venue in which young writers, directors, and actors, deprived of opportunities in the commercial theater, whether on or off-Broadway, could exercise their skills. Many of these artists fully intended to seek careers in the mainstream whenever the chance arose, but in the meantime they discovered that the Cino was a space so free of commercial concerns that they could try out anything, even if this meant casually breaking rules of form and content that were sacrosanct in the professional theater. Moreover, the fact that the Cino's regular staff and customers were largely (though certainly not exclusively) gay, made them outsiders of another sort in relation to mainstream culture: though sexuality was by no means a defining theme in the Cino's hugely diverse range of work, there was an underlying awareness of difference—of being, on some basic level, *excluded* from the mainstream—that facilitated the celebratory abandon with which Cino writers embraced the bizarre, the ridiculous, and the taboo. Paradoxically, though, as the Cino's first resident playwright, Doric Wilson, also stresses, the essential spirit of the venue lay in a fundamentally innocent sense of playfulness: "It was Mickey Rooney and Judy Garland getting together and saying, 'Let's put on a play in the barn!'"

Transcending the Context

Contrary to popular belief, the Caffe Cino was not, strictly speaking, the first off-off-Broadway venue. The emerging coffeehouse culture in Greenwich Village in the late 1950s provided new platforms for painters, poets, and musicians, and it was natural enough that plays, too, began to be mounted in a number of cafés, more or less simultaneously. "It began as a few very isolated productions here and there," *Voice* critic Michael Smith remembers: "There were two or three cafés in the Village that occasionally did a play. It wasn't any movement. But then a couple of places started doing them all the time, so I could write something." Smith initiated a review column headed "Café Theatre," and by September 1960, there were sufficient performances being mounted in coffeehouses such as the Take 3, the Phase 2 and the Cafe Manzini that the *Voice* began listing "Café Dramas" in a separate classified section. Then, in the November 24, 1960, edition of the *Voice*, that section was retitled "Off Off-Broadway," in recognition of the fact that this new wave of small-scale theater was no longer confined merely to cafés.

The new label, which neither Smith nor the *Voice*'s chief drama critic at the time, Jerry Tallmer, will now confess to coining, was in all likelihood intended more as a joke than as serious recognition of a new substratum of New York theater. Many of the early café offerings were simply fly-by-night attempts by MacDougal Street establishments to cash in on the boho-tourist trend that peaked in the summer of 1960. "The Beat movement," noted poet Howard Ant, had by then "clambered—or been ferried—up to its latest stage, the Strident Commercial. Up and down MacDougal, all that summer, beat poets played to the tourist hordes of habitats from Dubuque to the Bronx" (Sukenick 1987, 137). Simultaneously, cabaret-style comedies and musical spoofs became the most familiar forms of café theater, playing alongside the musical entertainments that quickly became such a noise nuisance in the area that the city authorities began cracking down. That summer, the fire department issued temporary closure orders against the Gaslight, the Café Bizarre, and the Take 3 for breaches in fire regulations, and by the fall, the police were targeting café owners for staging entertainments without cabaret licenses. Technically, such licenses were only needed by venues selling liquor, but café theater per se had no legal status at all, and existed only at the indulgence of the authorities. Coffeehouses continued to be subjected to harassment for the most minor infringements: by 1964, the operator of the Gaslight estimated that he had made seventy-four court appearances in four years. Few cafés could stay open for long under that kind of pressure, much less attempt to maintain theater programs.

That the Caffe Cino became the single noteworthy exception to this rule was thanks primarily to two factors. First, founder Joe Cino learned early on that pressure from city officials was often best handled "out of court": "Never have so many payoffs been made for so many ripoffs to so many jerkoffs," playwright Paul Foster notes of Cino's under-the-counter dealings with New York's civic servants (1979, 7). Second, as financial constraints forced other cafés of the period to close when they could not pay basic wages, Joe Cino found that a close, inner circle of friends were willing to work for him without pay. Such volunteerism might have smacked of exploitation were not Cino himself the most exhaustively self-sacrificial of them all: far from profiting from the enterprise, he frequently pursued other work during daylight hours or on late-night shifts, going without sleep in order to subsidize his own and the Caffe's survival with this extra income. Inspired by his example, the Cino's "temple slaves," as Robert Patrick labeled them (including himself), volunteered to make and serve food and drinks, wait tables, wash dishes, and mind the door. If they sought anything in return, it was only the opportunity to participate in the new plays that were constantly being scheduled for production.

Thus, unlike its early counterparts, which mostly discontinued theater production within a year or so, the Cino survived long enough to develop sufficient reputation to attract a stream of hopeful playwrights, directors, and actors to its tiny stage. Throughout the decade, plays continued to appear intermittently at other Village coffeehouses, but none of these projects acquired any regularity or consistency. Only Ellen Stewart's Café La Mama achieved anything like the longevity of the Cino, and even La Mama only survived its infancy by turning itself into a semiprivate club. By 1966, Michael Smith could plausibly write that the Cino was "the only true cafe-theatre now functioning in New York City" (Orzel and Smith 1966, 9).

Beginnings

Joseph Cino was born in 1931 and raised in Buffalo by his first-generation Sicilian-immigrant parents. He moved to New York City aged sixteen, and studied performing arts for two years at the Henry Street Playhouse. Cino dreamed of becoming a dancer—a career he pursued through much of the 1950s, with modest success—but his constant struggle with weight eventually led him to surrender that hope. His world instead began to revolve around a group of other young, gay men, including Charles Loubier—an artist friend who waited tables at the Playhouse Café, and who got him a job there in 1958. The café, so-named because it was located next door to the Provincetown Playhouse on MacDougal Street, was one of the very first to schedule play-readings as entertainments, and according to Joe Davies—one of the young actors who frequented the café—Cino planned to direct a version of *Lysistrata* there, in which Davies would perform. That plan never came to fruition, but by December 1958, Cino had teamed up with his then-lover, painter Ed Franzen, to rent a storefront of his own, a few blocks west at 31 Cornelia Street. For Joe Cino, as for many of his contemporaries, setting up a café was primarily about having a place of his own that could provide a focal point for friends and local artists: from the outset, he was supported in this vision by a tight community of core staff, including Davies, Loubier, and painter-dishwasher Kenny Burgess (later renowned for his lovingly hand-painted posters for Cino plays). Their group bond was symbolized by the evolution of their own patois, known as "simulata"—a campy, idiosyncratic fusion of Italian and English. With affectionate cruelty, the overweight Cino was nicknamed "porcino," little pig.

The new Caffe (Italian spelling) was established with personal savings of just four hundred dollars, with which Cino rented and modestly refurbished the derelict ground floor store space—a long rectangle about forty feet deep and just fourteen feet wide. At the front, on either side of the door, were window cases featuring a decorative coffee-machine and an easel-mounted poster advertising current attractions. Immediately inside, the main body of the room was filled with a motley collection of tables and chairs salvaged from a variety of sources, amid which a space could be cleared to create a temporary "stage" area. The counter area, complete with working coffee machine and sink, was located toward the back of the room. A partition wall then masked off the toilet and a small private room, which came to double as a dressing room. Eventually, on either side of the entrance to the narrow passageway leading to these rooms were placed a lighting control board and a record player for music and sound effects. Staging theater in such a tiny venue was not, however, part of Cino's initial plan. He sought only to provide walls on which his painter friends could display their work, and to lay on simple entertainments: "Tuesday was poetry night," recalls Joe Davies, "and then there was a music night and a dance night, and finally somebody said, well, let's have a play reading!" The spirit of these enterprises was at first gloriously amateur. Dance night, for example, might consist of little more than Davies himself doing "an impromptu, almost modest male-less-strip-than-tease" to the accompaniment of records: this was the spectacle that Doric Wilson remembers witnessing on his first visit to the Cino late in 1960 (1979, 7). Nevertheless, the play readings were, from the start, of a decent standard precisely because the participants were often professional actors. "Slowly, through networking, [the Cino] became a kind of green room," Davies points out:

> The first place people would come after summer stock would be the Cino. Or people from a Broadway show, when they'd finished the run. I was working at the off-Broadway houses at that time—the Actors' Playhouse and the Sheridan Square. We were Equity actors, and they wouldn't allow us to work for nothing, but as long as we had the scripts in our hands, we were just doing a "reading" and we could say we weren't acting.

Clearly there was a thin line between reading and full-blown performing even at this early stage: actors did not, for example, restrict themselves to sitting in chairs and avoiding eye contact. The introduction of off-script performances was perhaps inevitable, and seems to have begun when Phoebe Mooney, a theater student from Uta Hagen and Herbert Berghof's nearby HB Studio, asked for permission to perform one of her "acting exercise" scenes in the Caffe. Since they were not yet Equity members, the students had nothing to fear from the union, and benefited from the chance to perform more publicly than they could at school. The first such scenes were performed at some point in 1959, and the practice continued over the next year. The first mention of the Caffe Cino in the *Village Voice* was in February 1960: "Scenes from Giraudoux's *Madwoman of Chaillot* and Williams' *This Property is Condemned*" were advertised in the paper's "What's On" section. Since the Tennessee Williams play is only fifteen or twenty minutes long in its entirety, the suggestion that only certain scenes were performed is probably disingenuous—an attempt to avoid possible legal infringements, given that performing rights had not been applied for. Concerns over issues such as licenses and Equity regulations gradually seem to have been forgotten, however, as the Cino's habitués began to enjoy and further exploit the possibilities for performing there. According to Joe Davies, another Rubicon was crossed in the summer of 1960, when the Cino mounted its first fully staged play, "with a set and everything": *The Lady of Larkspur Lotion*, another Williams one-act, was performed by Davies, Larry Johnson, and Regina Oliver, all regulars at the Caffe. A few weeks later, the Cino's first new playwriting premiere took place: James Howard, a student at Lee Strasberg's Actors' Studio, persuaded Davies and Johnson to appear with him in a forty-five-minute modern morality play he had written, titled *Flyspray*. The Flyspray, a kind of Everyman character, was played by Howard himself, and his innocent companion, the Mate, by Johnson. "And I was this romantic fool who had the big white shirt, big boots, and huge hat with a plume on," Davies recounts, "and I was asleep up this tree, which was actually a ladder. That was the set."

Flyspray is long lost as a text, apparently at little cost to the annals of dramatic literature: Davies remembers it as a long-winded exercise in moral posturing. The more important innovation at the Cino that fall was its gradual move toward a regular, weekly programming schedule, which was quite distinct from the more sporadic offerings of the other early café theaters. This development was largely thanks to director Robert Dahdah, who brought to the Cino his amateur repertory company and their entire back catalog of work. "I had what I called the Only Permanent Floating Repertory in New York City," Dahdah explains: "I had about fifteen actors, and we did a lot of one-act plays, just about every one-act play ever written, and we would tour in the veterans' hospitals, at the Seamen's Institute, at the Federation of the Handicapped. Anywhere that couldn't afford to pay for a show, we would go there." Dahdah had been introduced to Joe Cino by a mutual friend and employee of the American Laundry Company, where Cino was working as a typist during the Caffe's first year to help cover the bills. Since a director had just walked out on the Caffe's advertised production of Jean-Paul Sartre's *No Exit*, Dahdah agreed to take over the reins. The resulting show's popularity with audiences convinced Cino to give Dahdah a free hand to bring in his own company, which thus ceased "floating" for a while: "I brought down *Hyacinth Halvey, The Stephen Foster Show*, and then I did a show almost every week there, for months. I did all of William Inge's one-act plays, all Tennessee Williams' one-act plays, I did some Noël Coward plays, you name it." Chestnuts like Lady Gregory's *Hyacinth Halvey*—the Cino show advertised in the *Voice*'s first ever "Off Off-Broadway" listings, in November 1960, and originally a curtain-raiser for Dublin's Abbey Theatre—seem an unlikely foundation for an underground theater movement. Yet Dahdah's period at the Cino was crucial in providing a consistency of production standards and a reliable supply of new material. With the Caffe producing regularly, Joe Cino also began to be approached more frequently with proposals for other productions, proposals that he did his best to accommodate. "After a while they started booking other people," Dahdah remembers, "and I started petering out. But I think that happened a lot—that someone would have a regime for a while, and then make way for someone else."

One notable feature of the Cino's early programming, which Dahdah's "regime" certainly reinforced, was that the established writers whose back catalogs were most extensively plundered were gay men. Inge, Williams, Coward, Truman Capote, Oscar Wilde, André Gide, and Jean Cocteau all popped up repeatedly. Although very few of the plays featured anything that could even be construed as gay content, the Cino regulars seem nevertheless to have shared a sense of common identity with these writers. Moreover, the context in which the plays were presented made it more than usually likely that any homosexual undertones in the work would be apparent to audiences. Despite the strong social taboos at this time against any display of same-sex affection, the Cino was identifiable from its earliest days as a gay-friendly venue, as is clear from the first-ever review of a Cino production to appear in the *Village Voice*, in December 1960. Critic Seymour Krim seemed less concerned with examining the merits of Dahdah's "responsible" revival of *No Exit* than with drawing public attention to the "incense burning and faggots camping (a big boy in glasses offered his hand to be kissed by a smaller guy wearing a single earring and chewing on a toothpick)." If this innocuous gesture could inspire such fascinated revulsion, one can only guess what Krim's response might have been had he seen Joe Davies' frankly homoerotic production of Gide's *Philoctetes* in August 1961. The chorus was played by a group of hustlers, who used to hang out regularly at the Cino: "I had dressed them all in little fur loincloths," Davies recalls, "and at a certain moment of truth, they came off." Doric Wilson recalls that moment gleefully: "Here were our straight boys doing the first gay exploitation theater in New York."

Improvising a Theater

The staging conditions that evolved in this early period at the Cino were, to say the least, basic. When readings and scenes were first mounted in the space, the "stage" was simply an open area of floor. With the advent of fully staged plays at the Cino, this space became defined as a square of about eight by eight feet, backing onto one of the Caffe's side walls, and surrounded on three sides by tables. The sight-line problem was addressed with the introduction of a platform stage constructed from wooden milk crates, and covered by pieces of old carpet. (Lanford Wilson, coming into the Cino to mount his first play in 1963, was the first person to think to nail the crates together to stop them from wobbling underfoot.) Later on, sturdier platforms were constructed, but this up-against-the-wall staging layout remained standard. Occasionally, alternative arrangements were adopted: the stage might be thrust right out to the opposite wall, for example, creating two separated blocks of audience on either side. On rare occasions, a small booth stage was constructed with strips of wood and curtains at the far end of the room, to create a kind of parodic evocation of more conventional theater spaces. Whatever the configuration, however, the basic experience remained one of intimacy bordering on claustrophobia: the most successful Cino plays were invariably those that took full account of that dynamic, and found a theatrical premise that capitalized on it.

Settings on this tiny stage remained necessarily minimal, usually consisting of single items of furniture, like a bed, a sofa, or a table. Sometimes, painted flats were propped against the wall behind the stage, although less obviously two-dimensional solutions, such as draped fabrics, tended to work better. Given these limitations, Cino shows relied heavily on their lighting for the creation of visual effects and atmosphere: the lights were hung from three scaffolding ceiling bars, which ran parallel down the length of the room. The Caffe's resident lighting magician was John P. Dodd—known to everyone as Johnny—a startlingly handsome young man who was also one of Cino's most indispensable waiters, adept at moving mercurially between tables to ensure everyone was served before showtime. Essentially self-taught as a lighting designer, Dodd had also apprenticed himself for a season to the Living Theatre's lighting man, Nikola Cernovich. He regarded lighting as an art form in itself, and his great skill lay in conjuring dramatic atmospheres using the limited resources available to him: one show might use a single, naked bulb; another might involve Dodd "playing" the simple control desk as if it were an organ, in order to create colorful, shifting moods for more abstract pieces. Dodd's "vision of the light 'breathing,' never still, interactive with the living performance on stage" (Smith 1991), eventually made him the single most in-demand member of the off-off-Broadway community. He regularly designed for other venues, and in the 1970s went on to work for everyone from director Robert Wilson to the New York Dolls rock group.

Many of the lights used at the Cino, and indeed the electricity itself, were stolen. Joe Cino's lover, electrician Jon Torrey, succeeded in the risky, highly illegal task of wiring the lighting rig up to the city grid, thereby securing a free power supply: "at dusk, the Cino lights would go on with the City street lamps," remembers Robert Heide (1985, 30). Joe Davies confesses to stealing lights—"follow spot, roof cables, and all"—from the Actors' Playhouse, when working there as a janitor. Most of the Cino's more impressive wares, he notes, were "borrowed" in this manner:

> The play would close, the theater would close, and I'd help them break apart the set. In payment for that I'd sort of claim whatever I wanted and take it over to the Caffe. [The Actors' Playhouse] did a big production called *Here Come the Clowns* with a huge damask maroon-and-gold front curtain, so I brought it over, and we'd use different sizes. All the fabric we used in different shows for wall hangings was from that main curtain. And they had a gold curtain and a cyclorama and a scrim, so we'd "borrow" those. . . . We got a new floor when they tore down a bunch of old houses across from my house on Houston Street, and they brought all the hardwood flooring out, stacked up. So a bunch of us carried it off to the Cino over a whole weekend, while the guard was off duty, and we put in a new floor.

Such activities may sound ethically dubious, but the Cino had no money for production budgets, and most of its devotees regarded such theft as a justifiable, Robin Hood–style enterprise, especially since many of these materials would otherwise have been trashed. On many occasions, moreover, sets would literally be built from garbage and abandoned objects picked up from the street. Robert Rauschenberg had used this method to construct his famous "combine" sculptures in the 1950s, but by all accounts Joe Cino himself was also a master of creative assemblage. Paul Foster recalls meeting him in the street once, while wondering how to find a set for his play *The Recluse* (to be performed at La Mama), and finding a willing, highly adept collaborator in his quest:

> As we walked, Cino picked up a red box from the top of somebody's garbage. At the corner he found ten yards of perfectly good, cheap, green nylon. . . . We found a store window mannequin, minus arms and one leg, and just before we got to Sam Tepper's Used Clothes on the Bowery (I was getting into it now), he found the *pièce de pièce*, a stuffed cat! (True!) . . . And I had an A&P shopping cart full of the most beautiful set I ever built. . . . Later, NET filmed the play for television and spent [thousands] on the same set which Cino found for me. (1979, 7)

Foster's anecdote says a lot about Joe Cino's own creativity and generosity, and also about the alchemical spirit of his whole enterprise—the conviction that gold could be spun from trash. There was never the vaguest possibility that his makeshift café theater would make a good home for conventional, naturalistic theater of the sort still dominant at the time, with its detailed box sets and studied observance of the "fourth wall." Yet this unlikely space lent itself to the creation of a different kind of magic—a kind that openly flaunted its homespun artifice, and in doing so acknowledged the immediate coexistence of spectators and actors, mere inches away from each other. Playwrights and directors coming into the Cino had to find ways to work with this basic dynamic. "You felt," Michael Smith notes succinctly, that "a certain level of theatricality was called for" (1985, 13).

Among the Cino's early productions, those of director Andy Milligan were probably the most charged in their theatrical immediacy. Owner of a dress shop on West Fourth Street, Milligan had also worked professionally as an actor and costume designer. He created lushly decadent spectacles for the Cino's tiny stage through the use of simple but striking props such as blood-red roses—a signature feature of his productions of both Genet's *The Maids* (July 1961) and Arrabal's *The Two Executioners* (September 1962). "Every night a hundred fresh roses," recalls actor Jack Delucia of the latter: "The Cino was reeking of these flowers" (McDonough 2001, 39). Still more striking was the way in which Milligan directed his actors to literalize the lurking, ritualistic violence in his chosen scripts—which also included Genet's *Deathwatch* (October 1961) and his own adaptation of Tennessee Williams's homoerotic short story, *One Arm* (July 1962). Often establishing a deceptively controlled, relaxed pace to begin with, his productions would then explode into orchestrated hysteria, in which the line between the acted and the actual seems to have been extremely fragile: "they were really beating each other up, like for real," Johnny Dodd noted of Milligan's female leads in *The Maids*: "It scared me, made me sick to my stomach" (McDonough 2001, 39). Similarly, Bob Dahdah remembers that, in the final scene of *The Two Executioners*, one actor was dragged offstage into the bathroom at the back of the Cino, where his screams "were so loud, so terrifying, so horrifying that police cars came to almost all the performances. . . . Andy wanted more, more. I always thought he was doing something to this guy to make him scream like that. Screams that could be heard in hell" (McDonough 2001, 35). Milligan's productions were either unforgivably sick, or chillingly beautiful, depending on one's point of view, but it was he that first gave the Cino a reputation for genuinely risky, deviant theatrical experimentation.

A Tale of Two Wilsons

Milligan, however, moved into underground filmmaking after 1962, and the Cino's programming subsequently became dominated not by directors, but by writers. This shift of emphasis was in large part thanks to the impact of the plays of Doric Wilson, the first new dramatist to be repeatedly produced at the Caffe, with four one-act plays appearing there during 1961. A twenty-two-year-old from the state of Washington, Wilson was first invited to the Cino by actress Regina Oliver. His witty, satirical plays proved well suited to the Caffe's minimal staging conditions because of their incongruously down-to-earth depiction of mythic or historic figures: placing these characters on a small coffeehouse stage furthered this sense of demystification. Wilson's first play *And He Made a Her*, for example, is ostensibly set in the Garden of Eden immediately after the creation of Eve, but was staged using only a stepladder and a chair. Its humor lies largely in the very human bickering of a group of conservative angels who are vehemently opposed to this latest innovation of the Almighty's, which they believe will disrupt the neat order of heaven and earth, by causing "a marked rearrangement in the basic respect which keeps the subversive element under control" (Wilson 1961, n.p.). The angels make common cause with the rather dim Adam, who is angry over the theft of his spare rib. When Eve arrives, however, and attempts to persuade Adam to help her propagate the human race, her wily use of reverse psychology overcomes his objections, and he agrees to try out her new "game." The angels (who are told they cannot watch), believe that this development will push them from center stage into creation's sidelines, and bemoan the fact that nothing will ever again be as simple as it was—predicting that "some lowly creeping thing" (a snake, perhaps) will be scapegoated for this loss of innocence, when it is clearly Eve's doing.

Wilson now sees the play as wryly protofeminist: the audience is invited to view the serpent myth as reactionary disinformation—designed to dissuade humans from further experimentation, and to deny Eve her achievement in bringing about a more democratically human world. The main appeal of *And He Made a Her*, however, lies in its sure sense of verbal wit and irony (accompanied by a healthy dose of sexual innuendo), which allows for a deceptively lighthearted treatment of its mythic material. The play can be seen, in retrospect, as establishing a precedent taken up by many subsequent Cino playwrights: "We were really the heirs to Italian opera," Bill Hoffman notes, in reference to Joe Cino's own love of the form; "we were lighter in spirit [than many theaters]; not lighter in meaning, but lighter in surface." *And He Made a Her* proved so popular during its initial, three-night engagement that it became the first Cino play to be invited back for a second, consecutive week.

Although *And He Made a Her* was written before Wilson had even discovered the Cino, his next piece, *Babel Babel Little Tower* (June 1961), was the first new play to be tailor-written for the venue, and set another important precedent by exploring the highly theatrical uses that could be made of the coffeehouse environment. Rather than work again within the small stage area, Wilson opted here to use the entire room, by setting the piece *in* a café, and using the street door for the entrances and exits made by his mythic-historic characters—St. Augustine, Hector, and Helen of Troy—who come in to sit down, drink coffee and read their papers. Jane Lowry, the young actress who had starred as Eve in *And He Made a Her*, here played a waitress, Eppie: since she also served the Cino's actual customers throughout the evening, it was never clear exactly when the "play," as such, had begun. Wilson even notes that, at one point, the backstage toilet was flushed on cue, further blurring the line between drama and actuality.

Ralph, a young man bent on impressing Eppie, begins at one point to pile café tables one on top of another, to create a tower—an illustration of the dynamic, world-moving personality he is trying to project. The tower, however, is promptly appropriated by the mythic-historic characters as, variously, a religious icon, a military memorial, and a phallic symbol. Their inability to agree on its meaning prompts vehement arguments—thus turning it into the proverbial Tower of Babel. Meanwhile Eppie, appealing for a more grounded, levelheaded approach to the world (and courting), begs Ralph to take the tables down before she gets into trouble. In the midst of all this, another actor dressed as a policeman would enter the Caffe and begin ad-libbing an argument with the Cino's actual doorman, threatening to close the show for license violations in exactly the manner that real cops had. He would then take the tables down himself, citing public safety reasons. On one night, Wilson recalls, this performance was so "real" that the policeman was physically attacked by a group of strippers from a club around the corner on West Third Street, who had been enjoying the show and were angered by the interruption.

Wilson's seamless fusion of his dramatic themes with the specifics of the location made this an example of "environmental theater" predating the term itself. The play also anticipated many subsequent off-off-Broadway pieces in creating a strong, central visual metaphor (the tower of tables) that functioned sculpturally as well as dramatically, its possible meanings proliferating on reflection, rather than pointing toward some neatly resolved "message" or thematic statement. *Babel Babel*'s most immediate impact, however, lay in the fact that it was the first play at the Cino to be scheduled for a full week of performances, with only Monday "dark"—a pattern that subsequently became standard. It was also during this period that Cino and his colleagues, responding to expanding custom, sawed down the size of the café's table-tops, so as to be able to wedge more people and chairs into the space. A comfortable capacity of about thirty people was thus expanded to accommodate a crush of up to ninety—although Robert Patrick, who worked as the Cino's doorman from 1961, claims he could sometimes squeeze in many more for popular shows, by asking people to sit on tables and stand against the wall.

Wilson mounted two more one-acts—*Now She Dances!* and *Pretty People*—at the Caffe that year, but in December, with plans being made to mount yet another showing of *And He Made a Her* (it had already had two runs), Cino proposed levying a one-dollar door charge for spectators. This seems to have been motivated less by financial opportunism than by a desire to control the flow of people trying to see the show, but the proposal caused an angry argument with Wilson, who withdrew his play. Wilson was concerned, particularly, for his actors, since he feared a door charge would be a step too far for Equity: the union had tended to turn a blind eye to its members performing in coffeehouses so long as no money was involved, but was showing signs of cracking down. Following the fracas with Wilson, Cino abandoned door charges forever, opting instead to control numbers by instituting a one-dollar minimum purchase from the menu for those who came to see plays—much as other cafés levy a minimum during the lunch hour rush. All moneys made from selling food and drink in this way went toward the Caffe's rent and maintenance, while the actors—as they had always done—took a share of whatever could be made by passing round a hat after performances. The arrangement was loved by customers, but Cino himself continually struggled to balance his accounts.

Wilson never again wrote for the Cino, instead moving on to form an association with producer Richard Barr, whom he hoped would further his professional career. Subsequently, however, the programming of work by new playwrights became increasingly frequent: Joe Cino could see that there was real audience interest in work by new writers. It took time for the trickle to become a stream, and the regular plundering of one-act anthologies continued for a couple of years yet, thanks to the venue's unending demand for new shows, to feed the weekly or biweekly turnaround. Yet several new playwrights began to develop profiles in 1962 and 1963. The most prolific, Jerry Caruana (four plays), seems to have been favored less for the quality of his work than because he was an inspector for the city's license department (a form of bribery via flattery?). More significant, however, were Claris Nelson and David Starkweather. Nelson, like Jane Lowry, was a graduate of Alvina Krauss's theater program at Northwestern University, and came to the Cino as a result of that connection. She had three highly regarded plays produced at the Cino during 1962, including *The Rue Garden*, a tragic-comic fable that marked the directorial debut at the Cino of yet another Northwestern alumnus, Marshall W. Mason. David Starkweather's first plays, *You May Go Home Again* and *So Who's Afraid of Edward Albee?* appeared within two weeks of each other in February 1963, and also proved very popular with audiences. The former, a bittersweet family drama presented as a kind of ghoulishly satirical cartoon, is, like *The Rue Garden*, discussed in some detail in chapter 7.

These successes notwithstanding, the most significant and prolific new playwright to emerge at the Cino around this time was another Wilson, Lanford (no relation), who eventually presented a total of nine plays at the venue between 1963 and 1966. A native of Lebanon, Missouri, Lanford Wilson had made his way to New York with the explicit intention of becoming a playwright. He had, however, become immediately disillusioned: "I saw every play on Broadway and hated everything!" (1978, 40). His discovery of the Cino came as a kind of revelation: he was astonished by the quality and immediacy of the January 1963 production of Ionesco's *The Lesson*, and by the following month's Starkweather plays, which struck him as vastly more interesting than anything he had seen uptown. Wilson persuaded his friend Michael Warren Powell (with whom he had come to New York from Chicago) to check out the Caffe too, and Joe Cino—on discovering that the pair aspired, respectively, to be playwright and actor—suggested that Wilson should write a play for Powell to star in. The result was *So Long at the Fair*, written in a matter of hours, and premiered in August 1963. Lost to posterity, it was, Powell recalls, "a play about an artist who has arrived in New York and thinks he's destined to be the greatest." It is now remembered chiefly, however, for its extraordinary ending, in which Powell's character killed a woman who was trying to seduce him, and hid the actress's inert body inside a foldaway sofa bed (the single set item). "What were we thinking of?" Wilson exclaims in retrospect: "We could have killed her!" (Absher 1990, 85).

In his subsequent Cino work, Wilson's integration of character and theatricality became far more accomplished. *Home Free!* for example (January
1964), which again featured Powell, was tailor-made for the tiny Cino stage: it
movingly explores a strange, incestuous relationship between an adult, but
emotionally childlike brother-sister couple, who live together in a tiny, claustrophobic apartment. In here, the seemingly agoraphobic Lawrence, who
dares not leave the room, is steadily losing all touch with reality, despite
Joanna's best efforts. The pressure-cooker intensity of the piece is so dependent on being played in a tightly confined space that, as Powell notes, the
stage area had to be artificially restricted whenever *Home Free!* was subsequently presented at larger theaters (as when La Mama toured it in 1965). By
contrast, with *This Is the Rill Speaking* (July 1965), Wilson used the Cino stage
to suggest a much broader canvas, creating a "play for voices" reminiscent of
Under Milk Wood. A small Missouri town community was evoked by six
actors, playing seventeen parts, who created a series of shifting groupings and
tableaux against the simple, representative backdrop of a white porch. The
constant onstage presence of all six, in immediate proximity to each other
even during ostensibly private duologues, created a powerful image of the
smothering closeness and interdependence of small-town life. Wilson himself
directed, ensuring that the actors voiced the regional, Ozark accent as accurately as possible.

Wilson's most acclaimed and controversial Cino play was *The Madness of
Lady Bright* (May 1964), which finally traversed the huge psychological barrier between making gay-friendly theater, and making theater about gay characters—a move that shocked even the Caffe's clientele, considerably more
than had Wilson's affectionate treatment of incestuous siblings. *Lady Bright*'s
portrait of an aging drag queen, tortured by loneliness and memories of his
former lovers, slowly going mad in his own apartment, succeeds in deftly evoking sympathy and understanding for a figure taught by society to loathe himself. Based loosely on a hilariously queeny desk clerk with whom Wilson then
worked at the Americana Hotel, the play is a roller-coaster monologue of emotional highs and lows, punctuated by self-conscious comic patter. Leslie
Bright constantly theatricalizes himself, conducting conversations with imaginary companions and talking to himself in his mirror: "Mirror, you are—I am
sorry to report—cracking up. . . . I am losing my mind. I am. I am losing my
faggot mind" (Wilson 1993, 28). It is as if Wilson has taken the self-dramatiz-
ing tendencies of Tennessee Williams's Blanche DuBois to their logical
extreme: indeed the ending of the play, in which Leslie imagines doctors

coming to take him away, seems to be a wry reference to the climax of *A Street-car Named Desire*. In this piece, though, the inner mind itself is also theatricalized, through Wilson's creation of two other roles. The Boy and the Girl function to literalize the voices in Leslie's head, echoing, mocking, and judging him with a dismissive, caustic humor that reflects his own self-hatred: "He wants to die, I believe. . . . I mean you couldn't expect him to live like that." / "He's effeminate." / "No-one can want to live if they're like that." / "It's all right on girls" (34–35). The additional actors also function as figures from Leslie's memories, recalled in fragmentary "flashback" scenes, as his past and present blur together in a sped-up, unhinged variant on the structure of *Death of a Salesman*. In one particularly poignant moment, Leslie remembers his first attempt to pick up another man, when he was just twenty: this creates a sudden inversion of the age dynamic between Leslie and the Boy, as the forty-year-old plays out the role of an inexperienced youth, seen by the twenty-one-year-old hustler as appealingly naive. There is a cruel, almost heartbreaking irony to the image of Leslie's older face speaking with his younger voice, looking bravely forward to a future that will bring only loneliness.

Neil Flanagan, the Cino stalwart who had directed *Home Free!* loved the script of *Lady Bright* so much that he insisted on playing the lead role himself (Denis Deegan instead took the directing reins, as he had for *So Long at the Fair*). Flanagan's sympathetic portrayal was described by Michael Smith as "expert and delightful, with a clear sense of modulations between joy and manic desperation" (1964c), and the production proved so popular with audiences that Joe Cino immediately extended the standard two-week engagement and, in Wilson's words, "ran it forever." With repeated revivals over the next three years, *Lady Bright* eventually clocked up over two hundred performances, and became the first Cino production to be reviewed anywhere other than the *Village Voice*, when Jerry Tallmer—by then writing for the *New York Post*—paid a visit. However, while grudgingly conceding its "brutal honesty," Tallmer condemned the play as "repulsive" in every respect (1964b). At a time when gay characters, if they figured in plays at all, were almost invariably off-stage or already dead, this was, perhaps, a predictable response—but it neatly articulated the Cino's increasingly countercultural status. "There were some outsiders who came and were shocked," Wilson remembers, "but I decided they shouldn't have come in the first place. . . . Besides, I didn't think I was being a bad boy or anything. I was just writing what I saw" (Wilson 1984, 31). *Lady Bright*'s success encouraged other Cino playwrights to follow suit, and experiment with similarly "out" gay material.

Programming and Environment

Wilson's play was so significant to the Cino that its history can effectively be divided into periods "before" and "after" *Lady Bright*. Prior to its appearance, a sizable proportion of the Caffe's program was still made up of revivals; subsequently, it became devoted almost exclusively to new writing, as more and more young playwrights began to present their work for consideration. Increasingly, a kind of friendly rivalry developed, with new and established Cino faces competing to see who could be next to produce a piece exciting and innovative enough to pack out the Caffe through word-of-mouth "buzz." Playful experiments in theatrical form and content became commonplace, yet the quantity and the diversity of the new plays produced at the Cino make it impossible to say that any particular house style or aesthetic developed. Indeed, the underlying ethos of the venue was simply that anything was permitted. "Neil, what exactly can we get away with at the Cino?" Wilson had apparently asked Neil Flanagan after conceiving the idea for *Lady Bright*: "I mean . . . can we just do anything we want *at all?*" (Wilson 1984, 31). Joe Cino's only stipulation to his writers and directors was "do what you have to do": they were to follow their instincts rather than adhering to preconceived notions of what might be acceptable or conventionally entertaining.

Similarly, in selecting productions, Cino himself relied largely on gut instincts. Doric Wilson's account of his first "programming meeting" with Cino is fairly typical: "[I went to] the Caffe Cino to meet Joe and ask him to read my play, *And He Made a Her*, for possible production. Joe was busy behind the counter. He smiled, asked my birth sign . . . gave me a cup of cappuccino (my first) and a performance date, and politely refused to read my offered script" (1979, 7). Cino rarely, if ever, read a play, preferring instead to rely on intuitive judgments about whether or not the artists themselves had anything original to say. Inevitably, perhaps, his judgments were often flawed, and the theatrical results embarrassing: many observers stress that a sizable proportion of the Cino's shows, throughout the 1960s, were poor in both conception and realization. Yet the question of whether work at the Cino was, by conventional standards, either "amateurish" or "professional" is somewhat beside the point. Joe Cino's deliberately anticuratorial programming policy, his refusal to make advance judgments as to the artistic worth (or otherwise) of the plays proposed to him, meant that the Caffe set the tone for the open-ended, experimental dynamic of the off-off-Broadway movement as a whole. If Cino had subjected prospective shows to assessment according to any accepted standards of dramaturgy (standards in which, in any case, he had no training), the Caffe might never have programmed many of its more memorable productions. His advocacy of the new and untested was never self-consciously programmatic, but true experimentalism demands the right to fail, and that—as former Caffe regulars always stress—is the great gift he gave them.

Cino also fostered a sense of warmth and creative community at the Caffe that appealed equally to trained, professionally oriented theatermakers, such as Marshall Mason and Lanford Wilson, and to those without a career thought in their heads. "Many of us had never dreamed of being playwrights," Robert Patrick points out, "but because Joe gave us a floor, we became playwrights. If Joe had had a bowling alley, there were those of us who would have become champion bowlers. To be with Joe." It should be noted, perhaps, that Patrick's own first play, *The Haunted Host*, was initially, uncharacteristically, rejected by Cino. Apparently he feared that if Patrick too began writing, he might lose his valuable services as doorman. He was brought to account, however, by the combined appeals of playwrights Lanford Wilson, David Starkweather, and Tom Eyen, acting in solidarity with Patrick. *The Haunted Host*—another take on the insane queen theme, this time with less self-pity and a more forthright, comic defiance of the straight world's disdain—was duly programmed for December 1964. Marshall Mason stepped in to direct, generously applying himself to the task of drawing effective performances out of Bill Hoffman and Patrick himself, neither of whom had ever acted before. As such cases clearly illustrate, the Cino's work was characterized by a deeply egalitarian approach, which meant that the have-a-go amateurs were never looked down on by the would-be professionals. Rather, both camps were able to learn from each other, as traditional theatrical skills were fused with a more rough-edged, impulsive creativity.

In effect, the only restrictions placed on the creative freedoms of the Cino were the practical constraints: "You couldn't get more than two or three people on the Cino stage," Lanford Wilson notes, explaining the preponderance of Cino plays featuring only one, two, or three actors, "and people couldn't sit in those seats for more than forty minutes. It was physically impossible. So we had our time span" (Dace 1981, 10). The one-act play remained standard at the Cino even after some other off-off-Broadway venues began to present longer shows, simply because of this physical restriction. Intermissions might have been introduced to combat the sore bottom issue, but the Cino's constantly embattled financial circumstances meant that keeping one audience around for more than an hour or so was impractical. "The idea, of course, was to sell as much coffee as possible," Claris Nelson points out, "so after the show you'd have to collect the checks, clear the tables, get the audience out, and get the next batch in." The scheduling format typically required repeat performances of the same play at 9:00 P.M. and 11:00 P.M. every night, with a 1:00 A.M. late show on weekends.

The other, unavoidable contextual factor for any play at the Caffe was the environment itself, into which Joe Cino poured most of his own creative energies. On a few, rare occasions, he participated directly in the mounting of plays: in July 1963, for example, he directed a version of Strindberg's *Miss Julie*. Yet it was the Caffe itself that preoccupied him: "Joe Cino," Michael Smith wrote, "is mainly concerned with the ambience of the room, in which the play is only one ingredient" (1966, 161). Cino's objective was always to create a warm, relaxing atmosphere in which spectators felt invited to engage personally with the performance, rather than feeling intimidated or "talked down to," as in so many arts venues. It took time for his vision to be fully conceived (Doric Wilson recalls a quite sober tone and decor in the early days), but the Cino gradually evolved into a kind of magical grotto. First came the twinkling fairy lights, strung liberally across the ceiling, and then the sprinkling of glitter dust on the floor for show nights. Festoons of hanging decorations followed— cutouts, mobiles, baubles, glitter angels, miniature Chinese lanterns, and ever more fairy lights: eventually, one reporter noted, there were enough "to decorate a forest of psychedelic Christmas trees" (Sullivan 1967). For Claris Nelson, these features were crucial to the relaxed, nonthreatening atmosphere of the Cino: "It all had that gentle sort of twinkly feeling. You were totally safe in this environment."

The Cino's walls also gradually became bedecked with crunched-up silver foil, old posters, photographs of movie stars and opera singers, portfolio shots of actors who frequented the Caffe, and whatever other memorabilia Cino had seen fit to fasten up. "Say you left your jacket there," suggests Joe Davies; "that'd get nailed to the wall, and it became part of the Caffe. It was sacred. And if somebody tried to move it to get a set up, Joe was furious. He wouldn't let anything be taken down." The wall decorations sometimes accumulated several layers, and thus invited infestations of cockroaches: periodically everything would be taken down and deloused, then put back up again. Adjustments in the decor were also made, week by week, to enhance whatever show was coming in: "We try to change the feeling of the room as much as possible to go with the current production," Cino once explained: "It's never really planned, but somehow we make it happen within that 24-hour changeover between productions" (Orzel and Smith 1966, 53). Maria Irene Fornes recalls visiting the Cino for a Valentine's Day play and finding the walls bedecked with painted hearts, which promptly disappeared again the next week: "Every day it was like throwing a party!"

Cino's creative interventions inevitably had an impact on the reception of the plays themselves: "You'd work so hard to set up a mood," Lanford Wilson recalls, "then the lights would fade and Joe would come onstage and give this utterly ludicrous introduction to your play, embarrassing you totally, completely *destroying* the mood, then ring his bell and say 'It's magic time!' and go back behind the bar." He stresses, however, that nobody resented these contributions, because "the mood turned out to be far better that way than anything it was you wanted. Joe Cino *was* the mood" (Wetzsteon 1982, 44). Indeed, for the Caffe's regulars, the room itself acquired near-mystical significance, thanks to the love and energy that Cino had invested in it. Sometimes productions would be performed simply for the sake of being in the space itself, since it was not uncommon, especially during the early years, for attendance at some shows to be very small. The late-night, 1:00 A.M. slots at weekends were especially prone to this fate, but Cino would never cancel a performance: he simply asked the actors to "do it for the room." Wilson had just such an experience on the opening night of *So Long at the Fair:* when no spectators had arrived at ten after nine, Cino ordered the door closed and the show to begin. "It happened to me more than once," Wilson notes: "We'd just play to the room. But the thing you have to remember is that *it was some room*" (Wetzsteon 1982, 40).

Even those off-off writers who primarily worked elsewhere, such as La Mama's Paul Foster, regarded the Cino as a uniquely special environment in which to mount a play: "That room," Foster has written, "motivated you to want to possess it, to conquer it, to make it identify with you" (1979, 7). The challenge for the playwright was to write something that might simultaneously complement the surroundings and draw the viewer's focus away from other distractions toward the play. *The Madness of Lady Bright* was apparently conceived with this in mind: "The stage within a stage is set as Leslie Bright's one-room apartment," read the opening directions (1993, 23), as if to acknowledge that the Cino's interior, and all its inhabitants, were in some sense a part of the performance, and Leslie's drag-queen boudoir merely an intensified reflection of that environment. Yet if Wilson, among others, found ways to adapt psychological realism into innovative forms appropriate to this space,

the writer whose work seemed to belong most organically to the Cino environment was H. M. Koutoukas (nicknamed "Harry," although his real fore-
names remain a closely guarded secret: he has variously offered "Hieronymus
Monroe," "Haralumbus Medea," and "His Majesty" as options). The only
playwright to match Wilson's record of mounting nine different plays at the
venue, Koutoukas seemed almost to mirror the Cino space itself, in person:
known for his elaborately colorful sense of costume, his glittered fingernails,
cobra-jewel rings, and, at one point, his habit of wearing a stuffed parrot on his
shoulder, he was "the archetypal Cino playwright; his combination of
whimsy, speed, camp and insanity was precisely right for Joe's sensibilities"
(Poland and Mailman 1972, xvii).

Koutoukas was no mere joker. Like Judith Malina, he had trained as a
director with Erwin Piscator at the New School, and although he did not
share their political earnestness, his embrace of the Cino was based on a self-
conscious rejection of the commercial theater establishment. Koutoukas was
so repulsed by the mercenary attitudes he had encountered among producers
and agents that he instead sought out an alternative environment more con-
ducive to his blend of heightened aestheticism and anarchic wit. For him, as
for many others, the Cino's nonjudgmental, laissez-faire attitude toward programming was liberatory, and the theatrical immediacy that could be
achieved by capitalizing on the Caffe's limited size and finances proved ideal
to his needs. Many of his plays were (like *Lady Bright*) monologue-based, consisting of a kind of fantastic solo portraiture projected straight out to the surrounding audience, and they thus made far more sense in this tiny, intimate
space than they could have in a conventional theater. His concern was with
exploring what he calls the "internal journeys" of the deviant and the marginal: "I really wanted to write about people that nobody was interested in
writing about," he explains, "the ones over there that were a bit crazed by life
and the cosmic encounter. The mad, the people who thought differently." In
All Day for a Dollar, for example, "a divine Christmas ecstasy" commissioned
by Cino for December 1965, the central figure is an eccentric theater director
named Sascha Stavropoulos (played by director Robert Dahdah), who is
damned to a heaven of broken toys and broken dreams, peopled by the faded
stars of theater ages past. His eternal torment is to see all his plays rehearsed,
without ever opening. As with *Babel Babel Little Tower*, the action was scattered all over the Caffe, which was filled with glittering Christmas trees,
painted stars, and actors on stepladders, and given ravishing colors and textures by Johnny Dodd's lighting. It was, Michael Smith reported in the *Voice*,

"a perfect meeting of event and place, and within its confines was a source of special pleasure" (1965h).

If Stavropoulos the Greek was based loosely on Koutoukas himself, his one-man piece *With Creatures Make My Way* (May 1965) was a kind of deranged homage to Joe Cino. The "Creature," initially performed by Warren Finnerty (the original Leach in *The Connection*), is an androgynous, semihuman figure who lives in an irridescent underworld of sewers beneath the city, accompanied only by mice, rats, "little tweekies," and "the baby alligators that are flushed down toilets every day" (Koutoukas 1965, 1). The setting is both a metaphorical invocation of the Cino, that peculiar refuge for artists and outsiders, and a "mouldy" subterranean inversion of the "the churches of the White Anglo-Saxon Protestants, known as WASPS, that exist everywhere" (stage directions, 1): in practice, it was again created through a combination of atmospheric lighting and knowingly "tacky" theatrical artifice (cutout paper spiders, for example, dangled above Finnerty's head). Here the Creature, exiled from the WASPs' ostensibly normal world, passes his time making music, playing Mozart on the giant pipe organ in which the mice and rats live. He dreams longingly of the day in which he will be reunited with the one creature he can share eternity with—a lobster onto which he dripped water from the fountain of youth, all those centuries ago. At the end of the play, he discovers that his newest companion in the sewers, a pearl-encrusted lump of ectoplasm, is in fact that very lobster, and the two join in an ecstatic union of song and dance. For, as the creature notes, "music Scotch-tapes the whole world together, doesn't it?" (6). The entire scenario is knowingly preposterous, and yet behind the surface absurdity lies a genuine sense of poetry: "Float, float, to where all water ends and sky begins," the creature tells a broken, wayward moth whom he has set on a leaf in the sewer stream: "there's light there, indeed, indeed" (6). *With Creatures Make My Way* is infused with a peculiar sense of tenderness, made all the more poignant by the fact that its nonsensical premise cancels out any danger of mere sentimentality. Koutoukas invited his audience to empathize with this seemingly freakish figure—and in doing so, to share and celebrate the underground, queerly alternative existence of the Caffe Cino itself.

4 Judson Poets' Theater: Verse Plays and Vaudeville Skits

> What is really happening in these verse plays? . . . What is the failure, and where? Instant answer: we don't know how to do them right. The actors don't know how to speak the verse, make it come alive, nor the directors, nor do we know how to make glow the formal structures and theatrical devices of the theatre of verse, that is, a formal theatre, a theatre not of the realist style.
>
> —Julian Beck, "Storming the Barricades"

Café theater had been a feature of *Village Voice* listings for over a year before the next significant feature of the nascent off-off-Broadway scene made its initial appearance. In the fall of 1961, both the New York Poets' Theatre and the Judson Poets' Theater launched themselves with mixed bills of one-act plays. In the spring of 1962, the Hardware Poets' Playhouse added itself to the short list of companies whose titles indicated a self-conscious attempt to create a serious theatrical environment in which poets could be given voice. With the "poet playwright" implicitly being distinguished from the mere journeyman dramatists of the commercial theater, these new ventures marked themselves out as more consciously avant-garde than other early off-off concerns, such as the Caffe Cino. Yet there was also an earthy, do-it-yourself spirit about these ventures that connected them directly to the café theaters: the mini-renaissance in poetry-based playwriting at the turn of the decade was, after all, integrally linked to the burgeoning Village coffeehouse scene, and the popularity of its performance-poetry events.

Ironically, this revival of interest in poets' plays was developing at precisely the time when the Living Theatre—which had championed verse-based theater during the 1950s—was beginning to shift the focus of its explorations away from the poet's word toward the immediate physical presence of the performer (with plays like *The Connection* and *The Brig*). As Julian Beck acknowledged (Brown 1965), the Living's productions of poetic dramas had often baffled audiences, and the company itself had never felt happy with much of the work. Loathe as Beck might have been to admit it, even the best poets did not necessarily make good writers for a visual and physical medium like the stage, and indeed many of those who did experiment with dramatic form were really writing "closet dramas"—literary exercises not seriously intended for staging. As some of the Living's would-be successors quickly discovered, theaters dedicated to mounting verse plays ran the risk of seeming esoteric, overly wordy, or simply impenetrable to audiences. The question was how best to find a balance between poetic aspiration and theatrical viability.

Striking the Balance

The New York Poets' Theatre found particular difficulties in striking this balance. This collective group included some of the leading young artists on the downtown scene, several of whom had been associates of the Living Theatre. Nik Cernovich, the Living's lighting designer, and also an aspiring director, had collaborated with composer John Herbert McDowell and director-choreographer James Waring on a number of presentations for the Monday Night Series. Their stage manager had been the poet Diane di Prima, who—together with her sometime lover LeRoi Jones—was editor of *The Floating Bear*, an informal, mimeographed arts journal reviewing the avant-garde scene. These artists, and other friends including dancer Fred Herko and his lover, director Alan Marlowe, decided in 1961 to form an ad hoc production company.

Marlowe found the venue for their first production—the "Off-Bowery Theatre" on East Tenth Street. This turned out to be the large, cold, gloomy back room of a newly appointed storefront art gallery, which had, di Prima recalls, "nothing going for it except the location . . . and the price—it was *very* cheap" (2001, 276). The company performed two triple bills there, opening in October and December 1961, but subsequently abandoned this obscure, unappealing space. In 1962, they took out a two-month lease at the Maidman Theatre on Forty-fourth Street, and mounted a series of happenings, film screenings, and music and poetry recitals, but no plays. It was not until February 1964 that the group—whose members were constantly engaged in a variety of individual projects—organized themselves sufficiently to coordinate their next production. Now performing under a new name, the American Theater for Poets, the group presented a new triple bill at the "New Bowery Theatre" at 4 St. Mark's Place (the same small space that had housed Julie Bovasso's Tempo Theatre). After just two months, however, the company was evicted by the police, for reasons that remained unclear even to them. Subsequently, they produced a few new plays in various locations, but their output was sporadic at best. The company's story was a too-familiar one: a promising lineup of artists proved unable to find the venue, the finances, or the administrative coherence necessary to establish themselves as an ongoing concern.

Part of the problem, however, was the company's choice of material, which—like the Living Theatre's work in the 1950s—tended to be too abrasive, or esoteric, or both, to attract more than a coterie audience of avant-garde aficionados. The most accomplished piece on its inaugural bill was LeRoi Jones's *The Eighth Ditch* (from a larger work titled *The System of Dante's Hell*): "Where the other two plays [by di Prima and Michael McClure] were exercises," wrote the *Voice*'s Sandra Schmidt, "this is drama." Yet it was also "lurid" and "unquestionably obscene" (1961). Presenting a military camp as the eighth circle of hell, the play consists of a series of violent confrontations between characters whose only names are numbers (46, 64, 62), and concludes with one of them being subjected to anal gang rape. *The Floating Bear*, which had published the play in a previous edition, was being prosecuted for doing so under obscenity laws, so the Poets' Theatre spent the entire run of the show fearing closure, and trying to guess which spectators might be plainclothes detectives. Yet the production proved obscure enough to escape such attention: emboldened, the company mounted a second bill of plays by Waring, John Wieners, and Robert Duncan, which confirmed to the *Voice* that "this poets theatre goes in for scary sensationalism" (Herschberger 1961).

When not setting out to shock, the group's emphasis was often on a kind of neodadaist formalism. The February 1964 bill, for example, included di Prima's *Murder Cake*, a text composed by chance techniques using the I-Ching, and *Love's Labor* by Frank O'Hara—one of New York's most prolific and celebrated poets of the period. Both pieces were composed almost entirely of lengthy, seemingly unrelated speeches, from seemingly unrelated characters. *Love's Labor*, for instance, features Venus, Paris, Metternich, Irish Film Star, Alsatian Guide, and others. One of a series of eclogues by O'Hara, it is a wry pastiche of the pastoral form, complete with baa-ing sheep. The non sequiturs pile up, often to hilarious effect, but the piece makes little sense as theater. Indeed Joseph LeSueur, introducing O'Hara's *Selected Plays*, suggests that his eclogues were not even written with performance in mind (O'Hara 1978, xiii).

The potential with such texts was that—in the absence of coherent narrative or characterization—a kind of pure theater could be constructed by juxtaposing the words with a similarly alogical use of movement and imagery.

Indeed, di Prima describes *Murder Cake* as a "word score" rather than a play, "for a director to do with as s/he wills" (2001, 376). James Waring, who directed it, seems to have been particularly adept at this approach. As a chore-ographer, he was celebrated for his creation of "exquisitely lyric" visual forms through the collagelike assembly of abstract movement and everyday materi-als: dance critic Jill Johnston once described his work as "a 'happening' with dance as the protagonist . . . any token from life as we see it or know it is acceptable at any time in this illogical scheme of things" (1961, 9). With *Mur-der Cake*, Waring simply treated di Prima's language as a kind of found object, as abstract sounds forming another layer of the collage.

John Vaccaro, who acted with the company at this time, found Waring's work inspirational because it helped him realize that a director is free to take all kinds of creative license with such open-ended textual material. This prin-ciple became crucial to his own directing work on Ronald Tavel's knowingly ill-made plays for the Play-House of the Ridiculous, which they cofounded the following year. Vaccaro seems also to have taken direct inspiration, though, from Alan Marlowe's production of *Love's Labor*, which turned the piece into a kind of outrageous, transvestite farce (much to the disgust of Waring, who had staged an earlier version of the piece for the Monday Night Series in 1960). With a wild, campy cast including Vaccaro, Fred Herko, and the drag queen and freak-show artist Frankie Francine, the production was, di Prima remembers, "a great demonstration of harmony in chaos . . . there were moments when twenty or more people were cavorting separately on that little stage" (2001, 376). With the forgetful Francine constantly looking for his lines, written onto various parts of his costume, this was a flagrantly tacky display of queer excess: staged several months before the Cino premiere of *Lady Bright*, it proved a direct precursor to Vaccaro's work with the Ridiculous. Neverthe-less, Vaccaro remained extremely skeptical about the value of the texts chosen by this poets' theater, which seemed to pretend to artistic sophistication while making no viable contribution to their own staging. "I never forgot the open-ing line [of *Murder Cake*]," he notes: "'Uninjured I have evolved from burnt velvet toast!' What the hell do you do with *that*?" Vaccaro slightly misquotes di Prima's text, but he accurately conveys its densely nonsensical quality. "I began to see that they weren't really *good*," he notes mischievously of the group's writers: "They wrote these poetic things, which were kind of nice, but they couldn't write for the theater. They were poets!"

The Hardware Poets' Playhouse sought to avoid such potential pitfalls by adopting a more hard-nosed approach to its programming. According to director Peter Levin, Hardware's preference was for poets who were interested in writing "pretty solid theatre, direct and straightforward," rather than "precious verse plays" (1965). Located in a midtown loft, above a hardware store on West Fifty-fourth Street, with running costs subsidized out of the pockets of its four founders (Levin, Audrey Davis, Jerry and Elaine Bloedow), this venture survived for four seasons before folding quietly in 1966. This company's problem, observers agree, was that it always lacked directors or performers who could make its selected plays "come alive" (to use Beck's words). Robert Pasolli's *Voice* review of Ilya Bolotowsky's *Visitation*, for example, noted that "a quite good and imaginative play" had been ruined by the Hardware's thrown-together, "botched job" of a production (1965). "I kept imagining that the bland, unfinished, even amateurish surface of their work concealed an aesthetic of some kind," Michael Smith later commented, looking back over several years of Hardware productions (in a review of two "only mildly dull" plays by poet Susan Sherman): "But the persistence of their style and its resistance to all my attempts to get interested leads me to believe that they have nothing special in mind [besides] over-acting" (1966a). With hindsight, Hardware Poets' Playhouse seems to have been more notable for its guest events than its plays: these included avant-garde music and dance concerts, such as LaMonte Young's "Theatre of Eternal Music" (playing the same, mesmerizing chord for hours on end), and Meredith Monk's early solo choreography.

Of the three poets' theaters founded in the 1961–62 season, the one based at Judson Memorial Church became by far the most accomplished in balancing textual and theatrical innovation. Afforded stability and longevity by its sponsor—the church itself—it sought to program a wide range of material, from the "direct and straightforward" to the wildly abstract. (Indeed, di Prima's *Murder Cake* in fact received its premiere at Judson in 1963, under Waring's direction, prior to the reformation of their own company.) The Judson Poets' Theater's reputation, however, came to rest primarily upon the productions mounted by the resident creative team of director Lawrence Kornfeld and composer Al Carmines. Their ability to excavate a play for its underlying meanings, and then vividly theatricalize them through movement, imagery, and music, meant that Judson productions were usually more accessible and appealing than those of the other poets' theaters, achieving a clear, synergistic relationship between text and performance.

With the Poets' Theater developing alongside the church's equally significant programs in the visual arts, happenings, and dance, it was appropriate that Judson became widely regarded as "the heir apparent and real to the gone but not forgotten Living Theatre" (Tallmer 1966), once the latter had decamped to Europe after 1963. Yet while emulating the the Living's sponsorship of a cross-disciplinary community of artists within its walls, Judson's theater work proved considerably more playful and irreverent than that of its predecessor. Drawing inspiration and energy not only from poetry and art but from popular entertainment forms like vaudeville and movies, this poets' theater thrived on an unabashed sense of showmanship: just as at the Cino, the "high" and "low," the serious and the frivolous, were fused together in productions that could be as entertaining as they were innovative.

Beginnings

Judson Memorial Church is an elegant, Italianate building designed by renowned architect Stanford White, which stands on the southern lip of Washington Square in the heart of Greenwich Village. Founded in 1892 by Baptist minister Edward Judson, its initial mission was to be a church that would "cross the tracks," by serving both the wealthier families to the north of the Square and the Italian immigrant ghetto to the south. Judson also sought to provide direct, practical help to the Italian community, establishing a health clinic and a clean water fountain. Thus, from the start, the church's history was bound up with social activism, which was considered integral to its identity and mission, rather than a mere sideline to religious observance. This was a heritage taken very seriously by Dr. Howard Moody, who in 1956 began a pastorate that was to last almost four decades: Moody involved himself and the church directly in social and political campaigns, and also commissioned a young pastoral assistant named Bud Scott to go out into the local creative community and find out what its particular needs were. Scott reported that the greatest need was for an open space for artists to come together to share ideas *as* a community, and Judson responded by opening its doors to artists' forums, poetry readings, and exhibitions. The Judson Gallery was established in 1958, in the church's basement Ping-Pong room, and in 1959–60, its program was curated by Allan Kaprow—fresh from his success with *18 Happenings in 6 Parts* at the Reuben Gallery. Consequently, Judson became an early center for happenings such as Kaprow's *The Shrine* and Claes Oldenburg's "Ray Gun Specs" events—which incorporated work by Jim Dine, Al Hansen, Dick Higgins, and Robert Whitman. Over the next few years, the church was also to initiate dance and poetry programs.

   Also around the turn of the decade, Moody instituted a two-year-long review of Judson's liturgical practices, inviting local artists onto the review committee (regardless of their religious beliefs, or lack thereof) in order to help develop an approach to Sunday worship meetings that would seem relevant and accessible to the community. As a result of this review, the church's pews were torn out and replaced with movable chairs, and the liturgical sessions acquired a distinctly unorthodox tone. At one Sunday meeting, for example, witnessed by an *Esquire* journalist,

> a young woman and a young man [stand] at one side of the raised altar, beneath the thirty foot cross . . . singing a blues by Bessie Smith. In the center of the altar a male dancer, naked to the waist, moves jerkily in place. . . . Bending slowly, he picks up a tin can from the floor, raises it over his head, and turns it upside down. A stream of blue paint pours over his head and shoulders. (Kempton 1966, 106)

The relationship of such events to the cross-disciplinary art work being sponsored by Judson was obvious. Indeed, on one Easter Sunday, a dawn service was held in Washington Square Park in which celebrants enacted a series of everyday "transformations" (haircuts, shaving, changing clothes) very similar to the kind of simple actions that had been part of the earliest happenings. Here they were contextualized in relation to the Easter message of new life, but Michael Smith reviewed the service in the *Voice* as a theater event.

In accordance with the radical thinking of contemporary theologians such as Paul Tillich, Judson Church was seeking to blur and even erase the traditional divide between the sacred and the secular. For some, this approach was interpreted as an attempt to sanctify the activities of everyday life; for others, it represented a secularizing of the church itself: "They were trying to take the veil off," notes Lawrence Kornfeld. Under Howard Moody, Judson eventually removed even its altar and the large wooden cross that hung over it, turning the church sanctuary into a "meeting room" in which a variety of activities could take place, including theater and dance performances. This was a logical development given that, for Moody and associate minister Al Carmines, the creative activities at the church were as much a form of worship as anything that took place in a Sunday service: "The two great doctrines of Christianity are salvation and creation," Carmines once noted: "There's been too much concern with the first. Judson wants to do more about the second" (Poland and Mailman 1972, xxv).

Judson's first, less than successful attempt at initiating a theater program came in May 1959, when actor-director Charles Gordon coordinated a large scale production of Goethe's *Faust*, by the "Judson Studio Players." According to the program notes, this was indicative of the church's desire to "recover a vital relationship with the imaginative and artistic life going on about it." Yet the production, complete with elaborate lighting rig, electric sound system (projecting the voice of God), and massed chorus, was universally judged by reviewers to be a *folie de grandeur*, "slow moving and occasionally just plain dull" *(Show Business)*. Gordon's staging scheme within the church sanctuary proved particularly unpopular: by using not only the raised altar area as a stage but also two additional platforms running down either side of the still-extant pews, the production forced spectators to crane their necks around in order to follow much of the action. "The director," one critic felt, "should be wrapped up in strudel and rolled out of town" (Swan 1959). (Adding an "e" to his name, Charles Gordone later became an award-winning playwright.)

The mistake with *Faust* was to attempt initiating a full-scale, off-Broadway-style production company, using ostensibly professional actors, just at the point when off-Broadway was proving increasingly unviable financially. Something much less grandiose in scale was needed to forge a truly "vital relationship" with the local community, and in 1961, another theatrical experiment at Judson suggested that this lesson had been learned. On March 23, on the same night that Doric Wilson's *And He Made a Her* opened at the Caffe Cino, the "Judson Gallery Players" premiered another new play, William Packard's *In the First Place*. No doubt partly inspired by the recent emergence of the low-budget café theater scene—a clear and viable alternative to the "off-Broadway" approach—this production took place in the more intimate surroundings of the church's choir loft, a gallery area overlooking the main sanctuary. This rectangular space, measuring approximately twenty-two feet by forty-two feet (comparable in scale to the Cino, though somewhat wider), provided an open, flexible space that could comfortably seat audiences of ninety to a hundred in a variety of configurations, and proved an ideal space for mounting small-scale theater.

Unfortunately, *In the First Place* was, like *Faust*, poorly received. Michael Smith, in one of his earliest *Voice* reviews, noted the potential of the space, but dismissed the play as an "overly pretentious . . . jungle of quasi-beat religiosity" (1961). Director Robert Nichols, however, refused to be deterred by such responses. A busy professional architect, he was in no position to mount a sustained theater program at the church, but he lobbied Howard Moody to find a way of using the choir loft for theater on a more regular basis. Moody decided to seek out an assistant pastor who could take on regular ministerial duties while also coordinating the church's arts programs, and he found his man in Alvin Carmines, who had graduated that year from Union Theological Seminary. Carmines had demonstrated an enthusiasm for theater during his time as a student, and had been particularly impressed by the Living Theatre's work, and by a "thrilling and bizarre" Claes Oldenburg happening at Judson itself, in which the artist had walked through the basement and gymnasium reading *The Scarlet Letter* aloud in Swedish. With such experiences in mind, he responded excitedly to Moody's offer of what was initially a part-time position: "I was given a very skimpy salary and coffee money and beer money to go hang out in the bars and meet playwrights, which I did."

With Robert Nichols's assistance, Carmines relaunched the church's theater program under the name Judson Poets' Theater, with the specific intention of presenting new, experimental writing. As he later explained, "one need in our community was for a space where new playwrights could be produced free from certain commercial pressures and popular taste. Another concern was for the church itself, that it might be exposed to the work of these playwrights and thus hear the secular prophets in our city" (Orzel and Smith 1966, 123). With these points in mind, Carmines and Nichols agreed on two founding principles with regard to the selection of scripts: "One, not to do religious drama. Two, no censorship after acceptance" (Kauffmann 1966c). The first principle was in line with the general policy of the church to serve rather than preach to its community, but perhaps also reflected an awareness that *Faust* and *In the First Place* had both been perceived as having suspiciously religious overtones. Carmines's determination that the Poets' Theater should send out very different signals was reflected in his choice of Joel Oppenheimer's play *The Great American Desert* for its first production, in November 1961. Since that play included a coarseness of dialogue that would then have been unthinkable on the commercial stage (the first word spoken, "Goddamn," crops up three more times in as many sentences, with "fuckin' desert" appearing shortly afterward), it also occasioned an immediate test of the second founding principle. A vote was taken among the congregation as to whether it was acceptable to present such work in the church premises, and a large majority agreed that plays should never be censored for language or content. From then on, the church's great gift to its theater artists—much like Joe Cino's to his playwrights—was to avoid interfering in any aspect of their work, however controversial it sometimes became.

The Poets' Theater's first program also included an adaptation of Guillaume Apollinaire's *The Breasts of Tiresias* (1917), a choice suggesting that Judson was seeking to locate itself in relation to a lineage of avant-garde poetry plays that stretched back to the Parisian salons of the 1910s and 1920s. Indeed, it became common practice at Judson to mount new plays by Village poets alongside older pieces by more famous writers—from Gertrude Stein to Michel de Ghelderode to Georg Buchner. This first bill, however, seemed unevenly balanced: Apollinaire's piece, now chiefly notable for its subtitle, "a surrealist drama" (the earliest documented use of that particular "ism"), is something of a curiosity and very difficult to translate effectively into English. Nichols's directing apparently did little to elucidate it, and Jerry Tallmer felt that his production was notable primarily for the "grave, sad, ludicrous" performance of Al Carmines himself as the pregnant protagonist (the first of many memorable roles for the Poets' Theater). This potential false start, however, was more than compensated for by the strength of Oppenheimer's play.

Written entirely in vernacular prose rather than verse, and taking the distinctly un-avant-garde theme of the Wild West as its starting point, *The Great American Desert* was a highly original new work suggesting the combined inspiration of the theater of the absurd and the Hollywood western. It is, in fact, a kind of antiwestern, which focuses attention on aspects of the frontier experience that Hollywood traditionally avoids; most notably, boredom and genocide. Three itinerant cowboys, each a different age and personality type, wander about the eponymous desert, making camp, going to sleep, waking up, and talking incessantly in their foul-mouthed, self-regarding manner about little of any substance. The play thus evokes a kind of existential tedium reminiscent of Beckett, while also suggesting that the reality of the West was always far less romantic than the myths would suggest. Oppenheimer wittily underlines this point with an extended dream sequence, in which four "heavenly heroes" appear to the cowboys to impart wisdom. One of them, Billy the Kid, is relabeled as "the first juvenile delinquent," and Doc Holliday as "the original hipster" (a reference to his drug habit as much as to his sense of style). "I sure hope all you fellows are doin' your best to do your part," says the first of the heroes, Wyatt Earp, in a sermonizing mode that satirizes church custom as well as the character's mythic status:

> That's what I wanted to talk to you about today. *Doin' your part.* I know there are some around today who'll try and tell you boys I was a psychopath, because, they'll say, I liked to lop my buntline special, all that big long barrel, across some baddie's face, but, boys, I was just doin' my part as I saw fit. The West had to be made fit to live in, and by providence I was the man picked to do my part. There's no denyin' that all the shootin' and killin' and hootin' and hollerin'

wasn't fun too, but most of all it was plain and simple, doin' my part. Boys, what I got to say to you is, like it says in the Good Book: go thou and do likewise. (Orzel and Smith 1966, 151–52)

The ironic tone of Oppenheimer's dialogue belies his serious concerns, which are made most apparent by the documentary-style speeches that are cut in between the cowboys' dialogue scenes, and played "out of character" by the heavenly heroes, as if they are newscasters. Without ever stating a case overtly, these inserts repeatedly allude to the destruction of Native American tribes by white settlers in the West, and position the play in direct opposition to the racist, chauvinist stereotypes propagated by so many movies and television serials of the 1950s. Although these points might now seem familiar ones, Oppenheimer's subtly nondidactic approach to his material, and his subversive use of irony, mean that the piece still rewards close examination. "It seems a very simple little play," Jerry Tallmer commented in the *Village Voice*, "but there are layers within it, and layers within those layers. Perhaps that's why it's poetry after all" (1961).

The Great American Desert was also significant in launching the full directorial career of Lawrence Kornfeld. A native New Yorker, Kornfeld had worked for the Living Theatre since the mid-1950s, after getting out of the army (it was he who first read and recommended *The Connection* for production—a play whose combination of structural ingenuity and gutter vernacular may well have helped inspire Oppenheimer's). During his apprenticeship with the Becks he had gained directing experience through the Monday Night Series, but had eventually realized that he would never be given the opportunity to direct a mainstage Living Theatre production. He thus seized on Oppenheimer's invitation to direct his play at Judson as an opportunity to launch an independent career.

Many of Kornfeld's directorial ideas for *The Great American Desert* are still apparent in the published script, in which details of his staging are reproduced as stage directions. His approach to the piece, which made highly inventive use of space and movement while simultaneously serving the thematic concerns of the text, served as a model for much of his subsequent work at Judson. By arranging the choir-loft audience on three sides of the cowboys' acting area, Kornfeld ensured a three-dimensional, sculptural feel to the piece—in counterpoint to the two-dimensionality of the movies that Oppenheimer's text satirizes. He seated the heavenly heroes above and behind the blocks of audience, and whenever one of their speeches interrupted the cowboys' scenes, the lights would dim on the central area. This allowed the cowboys to relocate their campfire scene to a different part of the space, and in doing so, to rotate the configuration of their seating arrangement, thereby creating a sense that the audience was viewing the same scene from different camera angles, at varying distances. One observer suggested that this strategy enabled "a small area of the choir loft to successfully convey a vast sense of the desert" (Marlowe 1963). Furthermore, by contextualizing the play's ostensibly naturalistic campfire episodes within this highly formalized use of spatial framing, Kornfeld created a striking visual complement to Oppenheimer's concerns with highlighting and "making strange" the constructedness of Hollywood's conventional representations of the West. As Kornfeld himself notes of this and subsequent productions he directed at Judson, "I would try to find out what the author really, really wanted, and then to find an original way to realize it, that would satisfy the author." Rather than seeking to establish a distinctive, individual style as an "auteur" director, Kornfeld sought to respond with fresh eyes to each new text he staged, so as to create a complementary relationship between writerly intention and directorial invention.

Emerging Collaborative Dynamics

Kornfeld's success with *The Great American Desert* meant that he quickly became a fixture at Judson. He struck up a close working relationship with Carmines, aiding substantially, for example, with programming decisions for the new theater. Scripts submitted to the church were read and assessed on a number of criteria, including their appropriateness to the venue's profile, and the degree of interest that Kornfeld, or other regular directors like Nichols, had in staging them. Thus, from the outset, Judson displayed a greater degree of selectivity in its production choices than did café venues like the Cino or La Mama, which needed to stage new pieces every week or two in order to keep regular customers coming back. By constrast, Judson Poets' Theater typically presented just six to eight new programs per year, usually in the form of double or even triple bills (though longer, single plays also appeared occasionally), giving four performances over a weekend, for three or four weekends. There might then be a month or more before the next program was presented. This greater selectivity meant that the standard of work at Judson was generally more reliable than at the café venues. Yet the "right to fail" was also held as sacrosanct, and as a result, as Michael Smith observed in 1966, "Judson's work, like the rest of Off-Off-Broadway, has been inconsistent and uneven"

(Orzel and Smith 1966, 10). The church's desire to serve and encourage the local artistic community meant that, just as at the Cino, "simple artistic quality is not an absolute value" (Smith 1966, 171).

Because the Poets' Theater was conceived as a part of the church's ministry (and also partly for legal reasons), all performances were free of charge to audiences, and everything had do be done at low cost: the church's annual grant to the theater was $200. The budget for that first double bill—including costs for sets, lights, costume, publicity, and all—was $37.50, a figure that remained standard for the next five years. As at the café venues, financial shortfall was covered by passing a hat around after each performance, but the actors at Judson did not take a share of these donations: casts were frequently a good deal larger than the two or three typical at the Cino, and distributing the money evenly would have been fairly pointless. Kornfeld himself, however, did receive a small wage as resident director: "They gave me about twenty dollars a month, and I ate there. It wasn't poverty, I was just always short of money." This retainer was indicative of the particular importance of directors within the Poets' Theater's operations, since, with so little cash available for use on design elements like sets, costume, or lighting, it was crucial that a coherent production approach be created using only the actors' bodies and voices, and the available resources of the raw space itself. It was not uncommon for a production's only "set" to consist of strategically hung paintings by Judson-associated artists such as Jon Hendricks, who ran the Judson Gallery after Allan Kaprow stepped down, and who regularly stage-managed and designed for the Poets' Theater.

Working with such limited resources, but in such close proximity to a cross-disciplinary community of artists, a particular emphasis on the collaborative dynamics of performance quickly emerged at the Poets' Theater: dancers and musicians, for example, could bring extra dimensions to a theater piece without adding to its material requirements. The Poets' Theater's fifth production, in August 1962, of a double bill headed by George Dennison's *Vaudeville Skit*, proved particularly important in this regard. This was another beautifully written one-act play suggesting the twin influences of Beckett and popular culture, in which three homeless hobos attempt to build a habitable structure from cardboard boxes, on the outskirts of a city dump site near Wichita, Kansas. (Again and again in poets' plays of this period, the expanses of the American heartlands seem to encompass both the nation's myths and the figures who live on its margins.) The circularity of their language and activities is clearly indebted to *Waiting for Godot*, but also—as the play's title suggests—to the comic patter of traditional American vaudeville, of which Dennison was a devotee.

The skit form was ideal for Judson because it prioritized performance values (speech rhythms, sight gags) while minimizing set requirements (cardboard boxes only). Moreover, Dennison's use of the genre prompted Kornfeld, in an early rehearsal for the play, to request that Carmines try punctuating the text with music, using the church's piano to improvise a barrel organ–style vaudeville accompaniment. This was initially intended simply as a rehearsal exercise, to help the cast develop a sense of vaudevillian rhythms in their line delivery, but the results proved so perfect for the material that Carmines's piano became an integral part of the production: "And [so] I was a composer. That was the first thing I had ever composed" (Wallach 1968, 56). Michael Smith provided a rave review for Carmines's "jangly, jouncy piano accompaniment," which complemented Dennison's text by "commenting, counterpointing, answering." The result was "stunning theatre. . . . It is not to be imagined, it is only to be seen" (1962a).

Two months later, Carmines was also acclaimed for the "infectious music" he wrote to accompany Kornfeld's "joyous" bare-stage production of *Malcochon*, a lyrical West Indian folk drama by the Trinidad-based poet Derek Walcott (Smith 1962b). Then in June 1963, he took another step by composing a collection of songs for inclusion in Robert Nichols's play *The Wax Engine*— again directed by Kornfeld. Echoing some of the more serious concerns of *The Great American Desert*, this bizarre variation on William Inge's *Bus Stop* (or perhaps John Ford's movie *Stagecoach*) depicts a collection of mythic Americans—from Jean Harlow to Andrew Carnegie to John Dillinger— stranded in a hellish highway diner, where they inexplicably become co-opted into a telethon-style variety show in aid of cancer research. On the page, there is a macabre, eerily unsettling tone to the whole play, and although the text does not call explicitly for songs or music, some of the metered language certainly lends itself to such a treatment. *The Wax Engine* paints a grotesque portrait of the United States as a cliché-ridden wasteland of the soul, and that vision was further enhanced by rendering certain sequences in the form of gruesomely upbeat songs and jingles, of the type used in telethons.

Carmines subsequently collaborated with Kornfeld, and indeed with other Judson directors, on a regular basis. He became renowned for a bright, playful style of music that drew, pastiche-like, on a very broad range of musical idioms, often using radically different styles within the same piece to create unexpected juxtapositions. "I like everything from Beethoven to Purcell to

Schoenberg to John Cage to Richard Rodgers to gospel songs," Carmines once explained: "A line from the text will suddenly suggest something operatic, or Spanish, or ragtime, and I do it in that style" (Burke 1969, 7). This eclecticism inevitably attracted critics who accused Carmines of having no original musical voice of his own, but it seems, with hindsight, that it was precisely this stylistic promiscuity that made his music so "original." Carmines's blurring of musical boundaries, his ability to place the high modern and pop-cultural on the same playful plane of consideration, made him one of the first "postmodern" composers. More importantly, he had a strong sense of how music could complement the emotional complexity of a play: as productions like *The Wax Engine* demonstrated, Carmines's music tended to foreground upbeat whimsy, while also suggesting darker undertones or elements of disharmony (he cites Kurt Weill as a key inspiration in this respect). His evolution as a composer became a central factor in the development of the Judson's richly theatrical approach to its chosen play-texts.

As the Poets' Theater's collaborative profile began to develop, it was also logical that certain writers began to participate in the process themselves. Kornfeld and Carmines found that new texts were beginning to be provided in response to their work, as well as vice versa. George Dennison, for example, wrote two more pieces for Judson that played further on his love of vaudeville while capitalizing directly on the theater's strengths. *Patter for a Soft Shoe Dance*, as its title indicates, was a short, rhythmic text written to be spoken by two men performing a soft-shoe routine—their patter lightly satirizing the recent arts scene, from Ginsberg and Kerouac, through Cage, to *The Connection*: "'Act one they scratched their faces / act two they fell asleep' / 'It doesn't *sound* so very deep' / . . . / 'In fact it was the rage / putting jazz right on the stage'" (Dennison 1964, 3). Carmines composed a suitable piano accompaniment, and the piece was directed and choreographed by Remy Charlip, another former Living Theatre associate who became a regular Judson contributor.

More significantly, Dennison also wrote *The Service for Joseph Axminster* (1963), as a more complex sequel to *Vaudeville Skit*. "Ladies and gentlemen, welcome back to the choir loft," announces the Master of Ceremonies in the play's first line, directly locating the theatrical space as Judson itself—and thereby minimizing the need for stage illusion—before going on to announce that the dramatic scene is, once again, a wasteland near Wichita (Dennison 1963, 1). Subsequently, the piece plays cleverly on this doubling of space and time. The MC tells the Judson audience that they will witness the restaging of an impromptu funeral service held, beside railroad tracks, for an old hobo named Joseph Axminster. This restaging is ostensibly for the benefit of two "actual" New York Bowery bums, friends of the deceased, who are seated to the side of the stage as audience members. The show is mounted, however, not by the three derelicts who "actually" found the body of "Little Joe," but by three actors who have been hired to re-create their parts—and who repeatedly remind us that they are "just acting." As the play progresses, it becomes increasingly unclear when they are speaking "in character" and when "as themselves." The fact that one of them, the pompously hammy W. C., is instantly recognizable as a W. C. Fields type, adds a further layer of artifice to the proceedings: even the "actual" actors are theatrical types. (Perhaps in wry homage to the father of such "estrangement" tactics, Bertolt Brecht, the second derelict is named B. B.) Meanwhile, the presence of passing trains is signified by a patently two-dimensional, shoulder-height cardboard cutout of a train, carried back and forth across the space by stagehands.

Joseph Axminster, however, is no mere theatrical game: Dennison uses these devices to create genuine humor, but also to develop a complex meditation on the limitations of theatrical representation itself when considering the value of an "actual" human life: "In such moments as these," the MC tells us grandly at one point, "the resources of naturalism are powerless" (18). The play thus makes a virtue of Judson's limited resources: the yawning gulf between the supposedly real events being depicted and the company's limited ability to re-create them functions as a mirror of the tramps' inability, during their "service," to account meaningfully for the life of the deceased man. Feeling it their duty to give Axminster a memorial, they stumble their way through misremembered fragments of the ritual lines they have heard at other funerals, and do their best to eulogize a man they barely knew and did not particularly like. The effect is both hilarious and poignant, as snippets of Axminster's life story—none of them particularly reliable—are recalled in the futile hope that some narrative coherence might emerge. Even the watching Bowery bums chip in to try and help: Joe was investigated by the House Un-American Activities Committee, they recall, but "the Committee was unable to prove that any activity had taken place" (14).

With no coherent picture emerging, the service disintegrates into cross-talk and is interrupted by the arrival of a woman, Lisa, who is expecting the imminent escape of her husband from the nearby Wichita jail. In a beautifully judged comic sequence, the characters all look offstage in the direction she indicates, watching and applauding the daring jailbreak—invisible though it is in the theater—and sharing her disappointment when her husband is recaptured. Subsequently, W. C. and B. B. compete with each other to comfort the lonely Lisa, but in doing so, they return once again to wistful, even nostalgic reflections on the nature of time and memory (and the loss thereof)—just as they had during the "service." Even those alive in the present, it becomes clear, are haunted by indeterminate pasts.

The third, most curmudgeonly derelict—the aptly named Rage-in-Age—provides the play's most direct expressions of this disorientating sense of the present's being somehow absent, even as the past is spectrally present. Riffing bitterly on the ritual phrase "Man, thou are dust," for example, he barks:

> As if I didn't know it. Sometimes I get up in the morning and stand at the window and look out at the world . . . and I think *(shakes his fist)* You lie! You lie! . . . I fall asleep at night and hear all those bloody voices from approximately fifty years ago. What is time? Time is nothing. Time does not exist. That's what those voices have been telling me. . . . And then I wake up. And that proves that time *does* exist. And so I sit there in the dark and I say to each one of those voices, *You lie! You lie!* And then I get up and turn on the light . . . and what do I see? A thirty-watt light bulb swinging at the end of a dusty cord. Is that *serious?* Can you find some *meaning* in this? Axminster—you're lucky to be out of it! (9)

A further twist is added by the fact that, in addressing Axminster's "corpse," what Rage-in-Age "sees" is the Master of Ceremonies, who (ostensibly owing to an actor shortage) doubles as the body, and has to keep popping up to give narration before lying down again to play dead. Such comic disruptions, and the incongruous fact that the MC is played by "a young girl," mean that there is never any chance that the dead man will become illusionistically "present" to the audience: the absence of an adequate onstage corpse further highlights the fundamental absence, in death, of Joseph Axminster himself. He remains a mystery, an unaccountable loss, a hole in the very fabric of the play.

Thus, in *The Service for Joseph Axminster*, as in *The Great American Desert*, innovative theatrical form complements and indeed extends the play's thematic (and traumatic?) content. "Under Lawrence Kornfeld's direction," Michael Smith noted in the *Voice*, "the devices fuse with the material inseparably" (1963a). (As if acknowledging the play's incompleteness without this staging, Dennison later simplified the text for a reading version published in his 1979 short story collection, *Oilers and Sweepers*—silencing the MC and eliminating the Bowery bums.) Yet although *Joseph Axminster* was written with Judson in mind, it was nevertheless a fully conceived play before it went into rehearsal. The next logical step was for the Poets' Theater to experiment with workshopping textual material that seemed less "finished" conceptually—dictating less from the page about how it should be staged, and leaving more of those decisions to the collaborative rehearsal process.

To facilitate such an experiment, Kornfeld and Carmines turned that fall to Gertrude Stein's *What Happened*, a seemingly abstract poetic text that claimed to be "a play in five acts," but that offered nothing in the way of stage directions, characters, or even dialogue (the lines are printed without ascription to particular speakers). It was precisely the kind of text likely to be dismissed in some quarters as an unstageable closet drama. Yet by workshopping the play with a team of three singers and five dancers, Kornfeld and Carmines built a theatrical, musical structure around Stein's language that seemed to complement it organically. (This as opposed to devising a staging—as James Waring might have—that placed the text in formal juxtaposition with other, unrelated elements.) As Alan Marlowe remarked in his review for the *Floating Bear*, the piece exuded "all the child-likeness and queerly logical sensibility of Saint Gertrude Stein. [As] bouncing and lively as a new born baby," it was "all that Miss Stein could have wished for—and more" (1963). Audiences agreed: the ecstatic, celebratory performance had to be revived repeatedly over the next few years to satisfy demand, proving conclusively that Julian Beck's dream of a theater that could "make glow the formal structures and theatrical devices of a theatre of verse" was indeed possible.

The significance of *What Happened* and its ensemble-based devising process is such that it is discussed at length in chapter 8, alongside other, subsequent Judson pieces created by similar means, such as Rosalyn Drexler's *Home Movies* (1964) and Maria Irene Fornes's *Promenade* (1965). Unlike the Stein piece, these were both by living playwrights, yet the initial texts were similar to *What Happened* in that their primary emphases on language and wordplay dictated little in advance about staging. In these instances, the writers worked collaboratively with director, composer, and performers, developing their texts throughout the rehearsal process.

Expanding the Possibilities

The expansive theatricality of *What Happened*, and particularly its use of dancers, was facilitated in part by the Poets' Theater's move "downstairs" into the main sanctuary of the church. The removal of the pews meant that, from 1963, this airy, high-vaulted room—roughly seventy feet by ninety—could also be used for theater and dance performances. Poets' Theater productions could now opt for either the upstairs or downstairs space: the former was more commonly used for pieces requiring greater intimacy and closer attention to dialogue, the latter for productions oriented toward choreographic spectacle and music (although this was by no means a clear-cut distinction). Judson's reputation as the off-off-Broadway venue in which directors played a particularly vital role was thus cemented further by the move downstairs, since commanding this larger space with the same tiny production budget required still greater directorial ingenuity than the choir loft. Particularly intriguing was the way that the sanctuary offered further options for varying the audience-performer relationship. Some productions were staged, proscenium-style, on temporary platforms extending apronlike from the shallow altar dais. More commonly, however, theater and dance performances were staged at floor level: different productions were staged across the length or width of the room, or at angles across its various corners. There were also experiments with placing audiences on two, three, or all four sides of the performing area. As Kornfeld notes, "We had plays in every possible configuration of space." In every instance, the basic architectural properties of the church itself (bright, spacious, elegant) remained the primary scenic elements.

One striking example of spatial experimentation was provided by the Poets' Theater's production of *Asphodel, in Hell's Despite*, which appeared in double bill with *What Happened* in September 1963. John Wieners's darkly intense variation on the Adam and Eve myth was furnished with an experimental, rock-based score by John Herbert MacDowell and a design layout by Andy Warhol—then enjoying his first flush of fame as New York's leading pop artist. (Warhol's connections with the downtown poetry community are well documented in Reva Wolf's recent book, *Andy Warhol, Poetry, and Gossip in the 1960s.*) With these collaborators, director Jerry Benjamin created a staging approach that followed certain happenings in dismantling the conventional stage/auditorium divide altogether: spectators entered the room to dance hall music and were invited by the performers to dance and drink wine, before seating themselves on chairs arranged throughout the room, facing in different directions. Apples were placed and hung around the space within easy grasp of the spectators, so that the spatial/visual concept tied in with the thematics of the play: the spectator, seated within a church, is implicated directly in the act of eating—or at least being tempted to eat—Eden's forbidden fruit. Similarly, at the end of the play, in which two Adam and Eve couples—the younger naive and energetic, the older experienced and world-weary—fail to learn from each other, everyone is consigned to hell: the Judson audience was subjected to a bombardment of noise, lighting, and other effects (tactics that Warhol was later to develop further in his assaultive multimedia spectacle, the Exploding Plastic Inevitable). According to Jerry Tallmer, this climax suc-ceeded in "[bringing] an onlooker quite close to the edge of felt terror . . . he comes out of the dark with confetti and streamers in his hair, hysteria in his ears, whispers in his brain" (1963).

The *Asphodel* experience, however, "was unfortunately blotted out by the sheer exuberance of the Stein work," which followed it on the bill (Smith 1963b). Such unhelpful juxtapositions were, unfortunately, a familiar result of Judson's somewhat haphazard programming of double bills. In May 1965, for example, Kornfeld's production of *Devices*—a subtly understated three-han-der by Kenneth Brown, author of the Living Theatre's *The Brig*—was treated by many observers as little more than a curtain-raiser for the boisterous musi-cal piece *Promenade*, despite being, at least in Smith's opinion, "the more intricate and provocative of the events" (1965c). In the same review, Smith pointed out that this pairing of plays neatly summarized the two, broadly dis-tinct strands of work that had developed at Judson: "Kenneth Brown's play deals with ideas about life, love and politics," as had, for example, *The Great American Desert*, *The Service for Joseph Axminster*, and *The Wax Engine*, whereas *Promenade* "is compounded of bouncy, paradoxically cheerful non-sequiturs," as were other musical pieces such as *What Happened* and *Home Movies*. It is unfortunate, perhaps, that the more immediate audience appeal of the latter category meant that they subsequently overshadowed the former in the recollections of observers and critics. Certainly the musical pieces stood among Judson's most theatrically innovative work and (as chapter 8 demon-strates) were far from lacking in dramatic complexity. Yet it is also important to stress that Judson's more ostensibly serious plays—which often communi-cated their "ideas about love, life and politics" through deadpan humor or vaudevillian showmanship—remained an important part of the theater's pro-gramming even after its reputation for alternative musicals was firmly estab-lished. Following the Living Theatre's example, Judson was a director-led the-ater even before such approaches became fashionable, but it was also, consistently, a theater for writers.

Indeed, the theater work at Judson seems to have helped inspire a number of poets to forsake the safety of closet dramas and seek instead to respond directly to the physicality of the stage. It is, perhaps, no coincidence that it was in the wake of Judson's early successes that Frank O'Hara (a regular audience member at the church) wrote his most accessible and stageable play, *The*

General Returns from One Place to Another (1964). Written in prose, in a series of short, pithy scenes separated by blackouts, it was clearly composed with production in mind, employing as it does some striking visual imagery and a deftly economical use of spoken language (some scenes consist of only a single line, with the subsequent blackout acting as a kind of deadpan exclamation point). The piece was not staged at Judson, but at a makeshift East Village venue called the Writers' Stage Theatre, as the first production by "Present Stages"—a new venture by *Asphodel* director Jerry Benjamin. Nevertheless, *The General*'s use of bone-dry humor and skitlike scenes, to playfully subvert American myths and heroes, is strongly reminiscent of several key Judson plays.

O'Hara's piece satirizes the postwar years of General MacArthur (who died the month after the March premiere), presenting a comic, seminaked General who constantly tours around Southeast Asia posing for cameras and making speeches. At root, the play is an attack on America's imperialist attempts to maintain influence in that region: "To be independent! How ironic and how lovely," laughs the General at one point: "As if anyone could be! And if one were, immediately the others would arrive and tear you down, exploit you, rape you and murder you. 'Self-determination!' What an odd slogan" (O'Hara 1978, 198–99). There, in a nutshell, is the reasoning behind the placement of U.S. forces in Vietnam—initially as protective "peacekeepers." Yet the play avoids any explicit address of "issues," opting instead for an insistent tone of gently ironic whimsy: thus the main action concerns the budding romance between the General and Mrs. Forbes, a wealthy tourist (another kind of neo-colonialist?), who falls in love with him when she sees him in a field of flowers. Paradoxically, by "avoiding the issues" in this way, and by dropping them in as little more than asides, O'Hara creates an oddly unsettling sense that the generals, and perhaps the rest of the distracted world, are merely fiddling and diddling as Rome burns. "Honestly," declares Chiang Kai-shek to General Franco, mid-sentence, as if irritated by a fly: "If they don't stop that bombing, I'm going to . . ." (208).

The General Returns was first performed in double bill with LeRoi Jones's *The Baptism*, another new play demonstrating a disarmingly playful wit, as well as its author's characteristically abrasive assault on establishment values. In this case, Christianity was the chief target, with Jesus being portrayed as a "thin Jewish cowboy." "I was delighted to discover," Michael Smith noted, "that Jones has, in addition to his strength as a playwright, a wildly satirical sense of humor" (1964a, 15). Unfortunately, like many other small companies of the period, Present Stages had trouble finding the resources with which to follow up on this promising first bill. Judson Poets' Theater, however, secure in its church sanctuary, continued throughout the decade to provide a home for the endeavors of many of those exploring the fertile border territory between theater and poetry, satire and myth.

5   La Mama ETC: Hurrah for the Playwright

> Off-Broadway . . . is more and more beset by commercial problems—greedy
> landlords, union demands, costs. . . . The Village coffeehouses have taken over
> the job of putting on the furthest-out, most risky plays of young writers restless
> with even the standard experimental forms. If you had gone to the Caffe Cino,
> on Cornelia Street, for example, in the past few months . . . you might have
> stopped wondering where all the vital new theater is these days. Now that the
> bars are opening in the theaters uptown, you can get scotch with your dross.
> Cappucino with gold is better.
>
> —Edward Albee (1964), "Where the Action Is"

Though neither the Caffe Cino nor the Judson Poets' Theater had set out with
any programmatic intention to promote new playwriting, the localized success of their early ventures quickly sparked a variety of attempts to build on the
foundations they had established. Ellen Stewart's Café La Mama opened in
1962, and initially appeared to be a kind of East Village twin for the Cino, but
soon established itself as an enterprise that sought, more single-mindedly and
forcefully than its counterpart, to expand its horizons and raise the profile of
its resident writers in the wider world. The following year, another new venture, the Playwrights' Unit, was established by the off-Broadway production
partnership of Richard Barr, Clinton Wilder, and Edward Albee at a small theater in the West Village, with the explicit intention of helping the new generation of downtown playwrights to develop their work toward full commercial
production. The contrasting achievements of these organizations, however,
spoke volumes about the increasing size of the gulf—in both operational and
attitudinal terms—between the commercial sector of which the Barr partnership was a part, and the emerging off-off-Broadway movement.

The Playwrights' Unit

Albee and Barr were often in the audience at the Caffe Cino during its early
years, and were among its most prominent supporters: indeed, Albee went on
record several times in the press with comments like those cited above. When

his first multiact drama, *Who's Afraid of Virginia Woolf?* became the controversial, must-see hit of the 1962–63 season, he and Barr resolved to direct some
of the profits toward supporting this new wave of playwrights: "We were making an awful lot of money," Albee has acknowledged, "and it was going to go
to taxes if we didn't figure out something else" (Kolin 1988, 200). An initial
requisition of around twenty-five thousand dollars was put toward founding
the Playwrights' Unit, and in the fall of 1963, the Village South Theatre on
Vandam Street was rented as a space dedicated exclusively to the new venture.
In this 199-seat, proscenium arch venue, new plays would be staged each
weekend, in workshop-style productions, to invited audiences.

The "free show" setup was clearly indebted to the café theaters' example,
and the Playwrights' Unit too worked to tight budgets — with each production
being staged for about one hundred dollars (almost three times the Judson
allocation, this was still a mere pittance by professional standards). Yet the
Unit was less an off-off-Broadway venture than an instance, as Doric Wilson
puts it, of "noncommercial off-Broadway." The intention was to provide a
kind of halfway house between the café scene and the commercial theater, by
using a roster of recognized professional actors and directors, who volunteered
their services free of charge. Once a play had been accepted for production, it
was the writer's responsibility to assemble his or her own chosen production
team from this list of volunteers, and to decide which prospective agents or
producers they might want to invite to the performances. This opportunity to
see their work produced "professionally," in a proper theater, was one that
many aspiring playwrights saw as a godsend. The Playwrights' Unit, recalls
John Guare — whose early one-act, *To Wally Pantoni We Leave a Credenza*,
was produced there — was "a profoundly important place for a number of people" (Savran 1988, 87). Ironically, however, those writers who had already had
work produced at the café venues tended to find the setup (to quote Doric
Wilson again) "somehow bloodless."

For "underground" playwrights like Wilson, Paul Foster, and Robert
Heide — all of whom were initially affiliated with the Unit, but failed to produce a single play for production there — the drawbacks were several. The
scheme of presenting each new play just two or three times in a single weekend, for example, was clearly less attractive than, say, the Cino's practice of
mounting a dozen or so showings a week, sometimes for two weeks or more —
thereby allowing the play time to find its feet in front of an audience. Moreover, audiences were often difficult to gather at the Village South: without the
coffee, the company, and the atmosphere of the café theaters, there was little

incentive to risk an evening on an unknown playwright (with new plays every week, the quality of the writing could be every bit as haphazard as at the Cino), and it was common for the auditorium to be sparsely filled.

The Unit's imposition of professional standards and structures, for all its obvious advantages, also seemed awkwardly offputting by comparison with the anarchic creativity that characterized the emerging off-off scene. As the Unit's manager, Charles Gnys, once commented to a reporter, the playwright "is not allowed to bring his roommate in to direct. We try to get him the best professional help . . . none of this, you know, 'I have a friend who directs,' or 'I want my cleaning woman to design the sets'" (1968). These remarks, alluding dismissively to practices common at the Cino or Judson, are a telling indicator of the somewhat superior attitude adopted by the Playwrights' Unit toward its "less professional" cousins. And yet a play like *And He Made a Her* had been directed far more successfully at the Cino by Doric Wilson's *roommate*, actor Paxton Whitehead, than it was by Richard Barr himself when he showcased it at the Cherry Lane in 1962 (effectively a "Playwrights' Unit" production before the fact).

Working with inexperienced but enthusiastic peers was, for many writers, preferable to scouring the Unit's roster of volunteer professionals, since there was always a danger that those donating their services in the spirit of charity would treat untested material with a degree of condescension. "It was kind of patronizing," Jean-Claude van Itallie remarks of the Unit's whole approach: "I mean it's great, when there's nothing, to be thrown something, [but] this was a place for the *little* playwrights. That was the aesthetic: 'These are baby plays by baby playwrights, and we're going to offer a kind of nursery school.' Which is not the most pleasant situation." Van Itallie's first play, *War*—ingeniously depicting an ongoing, improvised war-game between two male actors, older and younger (they also seem, on some level, to be father and son)—was staged at the Unit in December 1963, but he subsequently pursued production opportunities in the café venues instead. This was the reverse of the progression that Albee and Barr had envisaged.

Perhaps the biggest problem with the Playwrights' Unit, however, was the very promise of upward mobility that was also its biggest draw. The Unit's raison d'être was to find and try out material that might potentially be moved "up the ladder" to a commercial off-Broadway production. Yet since plays submitted to the Unit were selected with this factor firmly in mind, programming was dictated by the opinions and preconceptions of the readers (usually Barr and Gnys) as to what might potentially be commercially viable. Barr, for example, would habitually mark submitted scripts with jotted notes such as "highly promising" or "N.G." ("no good"). As a result, a large majority of the plays produced at the Unit adhered to established theatrical forms. That tendency was already apparent in the 1965 anthology *New Theatre in America*, edited by Edward Parone (Unit manager in its first year of operation), which is mostly composed of plays presented by Albee-Barr-Wilder over the previous couple of seasons, at either the Playwrights' Unit or the Cherry Lane. Five of the seven plays included are essentially slices of domestic realism, and the other two—Lawrence Osgood's *The Rook* and LeRoi Jones's *Dutchman* (both premiered at the Unit)—bear striking resemblances to Albee's *The Zoo Story*. In both these plays, casual encounters in public spaces in New York (Washington Square Park and a subway car, respectively) gradually mutate from the realistic to the ritualistic, as the protagonists' exchanges grow more menacing and confrontational: *Dutchman* even ends, just as does *Zoo Story*, with a knife killing. As Susan Sontag remarked, when Jones's play opened at the Cherry Lane as the Unit's first off-Broadway transfer, in 1964, "There is a smell of a new, rather verbose style of emotional savagery in *Dutchman* that, for want of a better name, I should have to call Albee-esque" (1967, 156).

Dutchman is, it should be stressed, a striking play in its own right, which broke important new ground in its forthright treatment of racial tensions. Clay, a young black man who has assimilated himself into middle-class white society, is goaded for his apparent passivity by a sexually provocative white woman, Lula. (Also referring to herself as "Lena the Hyena . . . the famous woman poet" [Parone 1965, 199], Lula seems modeled in part on Jones's former lover, Diane di Prima.) Finally pushed to cracking point, Clay begins to articulate a suppressed rage that threatens to erupt into revolutionary militancy—at which point, Lula and the other subway passengers respond by killing him. The play is a powerful and still controversial metaphor for the Catch-22 situation faced by blacks in a white-dominated society, and anticipated Jones's own transformation into Amiri Baraka, and his adoption of a black nationalist stance that separated him entirely from the commercial theater. Yet it remains questionable whether *Dutchman* would ever have achieved the exposure it did had it not fit so readily into an already recognizable "genre" of new playwriting. When it opened off-Broadway, it was billed alongside Samuel Beckett's *Play* and Fernando Arrabal's *The Two Executioners*, apparently in an attempt to contextualize it not as a drama about race, but as "theater of the absurd"—a category that, thanks to Martin Esslin's book of that title, could now be sold to discerning theatergoers.

Thus, while the Playwrights' Unit clearly sought to encourage new play-wrights, its approach to their work—like that of the commercial theater itself—was dictated ultimately by marketing concerns rather than by the creative needs of the dramatist, and by the need to accommodate new talent within existing institutional structures. By contrast, the first concern of Ellen Stewart, the maverick impresario and self-appointed earth mother who founded Café La Mama in 1962, was to provide young playwrights with a theater space in which they could develop work on their own terms, without fear of creative interference. The Cino's open-ended programming approach provided her with a model of sorts, but Stewart was far more concerned than was Joe Cino with gaining wider recognition for the playwrights she championed. To do that, she eventually sidestepped New York's commercial theater system altogether, and began promoting them overseas. Having grown up in the cultural melting pot of Louisiana, and having traveled extensively overseas, Stewart's perspective was somewhat more multicultural and internationalist than that of counterparts like Joe Cino and Al Carmines. In hindsight, La Mama seems always to have had its sights set well beyond downtown Manhattan, even if, for much of the decade, those living in the same neighborhood had difficulty in finding the place.

Beginnings

Nobody seems sure exactly how old Ellen Stewart is, although since she gave birth to a son in 1943 (the same year in which, for example, Sam Shepard was born), she was of an age to act as "mama" to many of the young playwrights she took under her wing in the 1960s. Stewart moved to New York from Chicago in 1950, and secured a menial job at Saks Fifth Avenue, where she—like other African Americans employed there in the days before the civil rights movement—was obliged to wear an unflattering blue smock. Underneath it, however, she wore her own, home-designed clothes, and when customers at Saks began to ask where they could buy the clothes worn by the exotic model they had seen in the elevator (Stewart, on her way to or from lunch), she was promoted to a position as designer. In 1953, two of her creations were worn to the coronation of Queen Elizabeth II. Despite her success in this role, however, Stewart never felt entirely fulfilled by the work. After illness forced her to take a leave of absence from Saks, she decided to take a chance and launch herself as a freelance designer. Renting a basement at 321 East Ninth Street, she made plans to open her own boutique.

At around this time, Stewart's friend Jim Moore (who was to become La Mama's long-term business manager) introduced her to Paul Foster, a young law graduate and would-be playwright who had already dipped his toe, unsuccessfully, in do-it-yourself theater. He and three friends—including director Andy Milligan—had poured their available resources into converting a disused Russian restaurant near Union Square into a performance space. For their first production, Milligan directed John Ford's bloody tragedy 'Tis Pity She's a Whore, but it bombed so badly that it put paid to the entire enterprise. "He really botched it," recalls Foster: "I remember one critic said, 'They should cordon off Second Avenue to make sure nobody goes in this theater.' And the whole thing collapsed." Penniless but still hopeful, Foster offered to help Stewart start up her boutique, if she would consent to let him use the basement room as a theater after hours. Stewart says that she initially pursued this idea in the hopes that her foster brother, playwright Fred Lights—a graduate of the Yale drama program, who had been badly burned by the commercial theater system—would also be persuaded to write for the new space. Nothing came of this (Foster says he never met Lights), but Stewart's enthusiasm for the theater project quickly eclipsed her own, initial idea for the boutique. Her inspiration, she claims, was "Papa" Abe Diamond, the owner of a portable merchandise stand—or pushcart—who had donated fabrics from among his dry goods to help her start making her own clothes. This small theater could be a "pushcart" of her own, which might, in turn, help others fulfil their dreams.

Stewart, Foster, and a volunteer crew including another aspiring playwright, Ross Alexander, set about converting the small, dingy basement—just twenty feet by thirty—into a usable space. They boarded the floor with wood from orange crates, installed plumbing, built a coffee bar next to the fireplace, and stripped the walls to bare red brick—an earthy visual feature that became standard at all La Mama's subsequent venues, and that marked it out from the layered impedimenta of the decor at Caffe Cino. Five hundred bricks were stolen from a nearby construction site to help repair these walls, on which the main hanging decoration—in homage to Papa Abe—was a single pushcart wheel. It took Andy Milligan, however, to make the room workable as a theater space. "I went back to Andy because he was the only person I knew," Foster explains:

> So we called him over, and he said, "Are you sure you want to put a play on?" Because this room was as big as a postage stamp. He said, "Do you have any

gels?" Ellen and I just looked at each other, because we didn't know what a gel was, and Ellen said, "Honey, I'll look in my pocketbook." And at that point Andy realized we didn't know what the hell we were talking about.

Milligan took matters into his own hands, rigging up stage lighting, and then bringing in his own adaptation of *One Arm*, the Tennessee Williams short story, as the inaugural La Mama production. It opened on July 27, 1962, as a direct carryover from the Caffe Cino, where it had played two weeks earlier. The next week, Milligan's staging of Eugene O'Neill's melodramatic monologue *Before Breakfast* was presented—also revived from an earlier Cino engagement. Over the next few months, La Mama came to rely quite heavily on such "transfers," in order to build a regular program schedule. Other early productions were supplied by Cino regulars like Neil Flanagan and Joe Davies, and in March 1963 Joe Cino himself brought in his praised production of Tennessee Williams's *Auto da Fe*, as previously seen at Café Bizarre. The Cino connection also helped flesh out La Mama's early audiences, although as Robert Patrick recalls, the attraction was as much Stewart herself as the plays she sponsored: "Someone said why don't you come on over to La Mama, but they didn't say, come and see the play, they said you won't believe this woman, she's a black Marlene Dietrich. Ellen got up to introduce the show with a big Afro hairdo, huge hoop earrings, a car coat, skintight red-and-white checkered stretch pants, high heels, and rang a bell, and we all just fell in love with her."

Perhaps unsurprisingly, La Mama's early operations closely resembled those of the Cino in many respects. The small, square stage area was initially just a clear space between tables, in front of the wall opposite the coffee bar. A one-dollar minimum purchase from the menu was required in order to watch a play, and a basket would be passed around after the show, for donations to the actors. Scheduling policy also echoed the Cino: at first, plays typically ran for just one week, Wednesday through Saturday, and Stewart chose her presentations not by reading scripts but by trusting intuitive hunches (or "beeps," as she called them) about prospective writers and directors. A crucial difference between the two venues, however, is pointed out by Cino stalwart Joe Davies. "Ellen did a different thing" in opening La Mama, he notes: "She made it for the playwrights," rather than creating a "room" characterized by a particular ambience or clientele. The stripped-down, functional look at La Mama meant that the space did not predetermine an atmosphere for the pieces appearing there. Jean-Claude van Itallie is among those playwrights who saw La Mama as the most inviting off-off space because it "imposed no aesthetic, made no artistic suggestions. Ellen presented us with a benevolent context within which to work" (1981, 8). By contrast, van Itallie found the Cino (where his play *War* was revived in March 1965) to be "too full of sequins, fishnets, a generally swishy loudness" (1979, 6).

In 1962, however, when the La Mama basement first opened for business, van Itallie and other writers later associated with La Mama had yet to appear on the scene, and even Foster and Alexander had yet to write any plays. The first signs of La Mama's distinctive identity, however, were already becoming visible in this early, foundational period. Its third production, and also its first premiere of an original play, was *A Corner of the Morning*, written by a young Mexican playwright, Michael Loscasio, who was then visiting New York. La Mama's eighth production was *Head Hunting*, a new play by Korean writer Pagoon Kang Wook, again directed by Andy Milligan. Stewart professes not to remember how these pieces arrived on her doorstep—"I don't know. It was God!"—but they signaled La Mama's nascent internationalism at a time when very few people even knew the place existed. Stewart's early presentations were ignored even by the *Village Voice*, partly because her venue was well beyond Greenwich Village itself: *Voice* critic Arthur Sainer recalls receiving a letter from "some lady way over east," begging someone to come and review her shows. With many people even in the immediate vicinity unaware of La Mama's activities, Paul Foster took to operating as a sidewalk barker, often hauling passers-by in off the street to generate an audience. It was by this means that playwright Leonard Melfi first discovered the venue's existence: his first produced play, *Lazy Baby Susan*, was La Mama's tenth, opening in October 1962.

These beginnings were inauspicious, and little of lasting note was produced at La Mama during its first year of operation. The most noteworthy production was the American premiere of Harold Pinter's one-act play *The Room*, which succeeded *Lazy Baby Susan*, opening on Halloween night. Set in a lowly bed-sitting room, which is essentially the play's central character and subject, Pinter's play must have benefited atmospherically from being presented within the claustrophobic La Mama basement. There must also have been a nice irony in the characters' repeated insistence that "the room keeps warm. It's better than the basement" (Pinter 1976, 101). The play, however, was presented without licensing permission: Stewart assumed the production was so low-profile that nobody would care, but her transgression prompted a surprise visit from Pinter himself. In New York for the off-Broadway premiere of

The Dumbwaiter and *The Collection*, he had been interviewed for the *Village Voice* by Michael Smith, who mentioned the La Mama production to him. Pinter promptly went to the Ninth Street basement with his American agent to demand that performances of *The Room* be halted forthwith. Yet when the agent angrily informed Stewart that nobody, not even the author, could mount a Pinter play in New York without her permission, the indignant playwright decided to prove her wrong, granting La Mama performance rights on the spot.

82 Second Avenue

Stewart was less fortunate in her encounters with other authority figures. Throughout 1963 and 1964 she was plagued by harrassment from a rotating cast of civic authorities, who were again clamping down on the semilegal entertainment activities of the downtown cafés. The first La Mama basement operated for just nine months before being closed down, in April 1963, by New York's buildings department. Prompted by continued complaints from Stewart's neighbors (whom she believes were prejudiced against her color as much as her activities), they informed her that East Ninth Street lay in an area zoned against cafés. It later emerged that this edict was in error, and that the café was perfectly legal, but by then Stewart had moved operations to another, larger location at 82 Second Avenue, in a second floor loft space (about twenty feet by fifty feet) where she could legally seat seventy-four customers. Having been given clearance here, she was told less than a month later that this too was an error and that she *was* now in an area zoned against cafés. Stewart protested that a "Zen teahouse" had previously existed on the same premises, and produced sworn affidavits to that effect, but the buildings department refused to budge. At this point, though, Stewart discovered that she could continue to operate legally if she simply ceased to claim café status, stopped charging for coffee, and ran a "permanent private party" instead. Since La Mama could not pay its way as a café anyway, this was no great loss in the short term. (Stewart was subsidizing the whole venture by continuing to work freelance as a designer and seamstress.) La Mama operated "in private" from the late summer of 1963, eventually formalizing its club status by issuing membership cards and retitling itself La Mama ETC—for "Experimental Theatre Club," but also for "etc." (as in "mama and friends").

The year and a half that La Mama spent at 82 Second Avenue was a pivotal period that saw the theater's homegrown playwrights begin to establish themselves: Stewart relied heavily for her programming on regular contributions from a small group of writers including James Eliason, Bruce Kessler, Robert Sealy, and particularly Ross Alexander, who had five new plays produced at La Mama between August 1963 and August 1964. The most significant new voice, though, was Paul Foster's: he finally debuted with *Hurrah for the Bridge* in September 1963, and followed up with *The Recluse* (June 1964) and *Balls* (November 1964). All three were accomplished, theatrically ingenious works, which greatly enhanced La Mama's claim to be an experimental theater worthy of attention. All three, moreover, were deftly directed by Sydney Schubert Walter (an early associate of the Open Theatre). Although Walter left New York in 1965 to run the Firehouse Theatre in Minneapolis, thus ending La Mama's first significant writer-director partnership, Stewart learned from him the vital importance of finding directors capable of breathing life into such unorthodox new plays.

Each of Foster's three earliest works is distinctly different in tone and style, but each creates a dreamlike, sometimes nightmarish otherworld; an alternative reality that resists rational explanation, while setting up peculiar resonances for the spectator. Indeed, it seems to have been Foster's work that first inspired Stewart's conviction that La Mama should prioritize the creation of theater that appealed to the instincts more than to the intellect. "Criticism as to the incomprehensibility of the works offered comes invariably from the audience person who has yet to recognize the subconscious stimuli," she commented in a note for *Eight Plays from Off-Off-Broadway*: "This is the way I feel, and I feel very strongly about this" (Orzel and Smith 1966, 164). Foster's *Balls*, which represented La Mama's work in that collection, was often mocked by witless observers for being no more than its title suggested, or else for being (as Arthur Sainer suggested in his initial *Voice* review) simply a rip-off of Samuel Beckett's recent radio play *Embers*. Like that piece, *Balls* is ostensibly set on a deserted seashore, and its characters are heard only as voices, mixed in with the sounds of waves and gulls. Yet as Michael Smith observes, while the "beautifully written [text] sounds surprisingly Irish, reminiscent of Beckett and Synge," this is just one layer of a complex theatrical event (Orzel and Smith 1966, 13). While listening to the voices of characters—whom, it emerges, are dead, buried in graves in muddy coastland that is slowly eroding into the sea—the audience is confronted with a stage image that seems representative of nothing other than itself, in the theatrical here and now: two swinging Ping-Pong balls oscillate in and out of pin-spot light beams, while moving gradually toward each other, then apart again. The unexplained juxtaposition of soundtrack and image sets up an eerily hypnotic effect for the spectator. "Seeing the play, I was held in tension between the calm of detachment and the disquiet of mysteriousness," Smith wrote: "the play's strengths lie in [the strange] disjunctions between realism and abstraction, between rational and arbitrary levels of action" (Orzel and Smith 1966, 13). There is also a delightfully oblique humor at work in the play, as the title and visual perhaps indicate: the dialogue between the dead Wilkinson and Beau-Beau is marked as much by grumpiness as by lyricism, particularly when they find their graves being urinated on by a group of children taking a rest-stop from a bus journey. Foster also sets up a few bleakly comic moments in which the play's two distinct worlds abruptly and inexplicably collide: "Us and a pair of balls," Beau-Beau remarks glumly at one point, "*I AM* so tired of them" (Foster 1967b, 1.13).

Hurrah for the Bridge is more identifiably a stage play than *Balls*, but is no less intriguing. Perhaps owing again to Beckett, it is set in an abstracted, postapocalyptic landscape, but Foster creates here a fable without a moral, a puzzling but disturbing tale of violence and helplessness. Offstage somewhere, a bridge is being built to an undefined other shore, but it seems that the stanchions will only hold if human bodies are embedded in them. Consequently, a gang of thugs (reminiscent of the Droogs in Anthony Burgess's 1962 novel *A Clockwork Orange*) are in search of living victims, and pick each other off when nobody else is available. Into this alarming situation comes the Rover, an old man pushing a handcart piled with fabrics, who talks incessantly to an unseen companion within the cart, whom he seems to love without compromise or question: "I'll push ye over every street and stone with me raw nubs, an if they wear out . . . why I'll tie a rope on me neck, and by God, I'll pull ye! I will thet, Ruby. Pull ye by me neck" (1967b, 2.34). Ruby, however, seems to be as much succubus as lover, constantly issuing impossible demands by sending written messages up a string pulley from inside the cart. When she finally descends from the cart, after the Rover has been attacked and stabbed by the thugs, she appears as an apparition "in a long, white, gauzy peignoir, overhung with a tattered, ragged net. Her light hair hangs loose and unbrushed on her shoulders, and on her head a wreath of dry, brittle flowers. Her face is impassive and chalk-white" (2.51). She stands over the dying Rover, utters a brief, detached laugh, and then exits as the lights fade. No explanation for any of this is offered, but Foster's text—with its detailed orchestration of sound, lighting, costume, and dialogue—suggests a poetic vision that resonates with possible political, and sexual meanings, while generating a kind of gut-level disturbance.

One subtextual level to *Hurrah for the Bridge*, for those in the know, was its homage to Stewart herself: the play's central prop is the Rover's pushcart, "piled enormously, precariously high with rags; rich colors, black, purple silks, gold tassels, velvet remnants" (2.29). That pushcart, moreover, was equipped with a bell that Stewart subsequently appropriated: she would ring it to attract audience attention at the start of each performance, before welcoming them "to La Mama, dedicated to the playwright and all aspects of the theater."

122 Second Avenue

Foster's *Balls* was the last production at 82 Second Avenue. The venue had been under a suspended stay of execution since July, when it had been closed yet again as a result of concerted action by the police, fire, health, and license departments. Under the terms of a temporary reprieve, La Mama was instructed to make fifteen thousand dollars' worth of repairs on the building to make it safe for occupancy. By the fall, however, the necessary finances had not been raised, and La Mama was scheduled for permanent closure. Secretly, Stewart and friends hunted out a new location and refurbished it. Following the opening night of *Balls* on November 4, the members-only audience was asked to pick up their tables and chairs and carry them up the street to the new premises—another second-floor loft at 122 Second Avenue. La Mama resumed production there just one week later. Meanwhile, *Balls* had moved directly to the Cino on November 5.

Ironically, the new space was La Mama's largest and best yet, measuring twenty-three feet by seventy-five, and with a twelve-foot ceiling. The legal limit for occupancy was again seventy-four, due to the second-floor location. Many more spectators could be and often were admitted, but much of the expanded floor space was devoted to creating a larger and more flexible stage area than had previously been possible. Using an arrangement of platforms, two main spatial configurations were established: a raised stage, about ten feet deep, could be set up across one end of the rectangular room, or alternatively, a larger, floor-level space about twenty feet deep could be cleared across the middle of the room, with the platforms being used to help create two seating areas raking back on either side (still holding the café tables). Along one of the side walls, a wooden construction was built to house the bathroom, dressing room, and a serving counter (an old A&P counter fixed to the top of a cut-down shoeshine stand). The opposite wall showcased La Mama's characteristic naked brickwork, and was decorated with framed pictures and a large banner carrying the venue's logo.

La Mama remained in residence at 122 Second Avenue for three and a half years, a relatively stable period that enabled the theater, finally, to establish itself firmly as a leading alternative venue. Throughout that time, however, it continued having to hide behind the "private club" premise: no shows were advertised externally to passers-by, and the street-level door was only ever labeled "122 Delivery Entrance." (Stewart herself would sit on the stairs leading up to the café during performances, to intercept possible visits from minions of the city.) The only outward sign of La Mama's activities was its weekly listing in the *Village Voice*, but no address or telephone number was ever given in the ads: only members could attend shows, and members knew how to get there. To become a member, however, one had to know to go in person to 122 Second Avenue. In short, the whole operation worked via word of mouth, but the clandestine methods proved no obstacle to attracting members: by 1967 there were an estimated three thousand card-carrying La Mama members, including such luminaries as Leonard Bernstein and Peter Brook.

Unlike most clubs, La Mama's membership dues operated on a weekly rather than an annual basis: for one dollar you could renew your membership for the week, and see the featured performance as many times as you liked. Since most people went to see each show only once, they were, in effect, paying a one-dollar entry charge. Every penny of these takings, however, went straight into paying the building's rent and overheads: nobody was paid anything, except from pass-the-hat takings, and Stewart continued to subsidize the theater's activities from her own pocket. "There's this fiction that off-off-Broadway was done 'without money,'" Stewart told me in 1995: "Well, dear, I paid the rent, I paid the electric, I bought the material, I made all the costumes. I worked five jobs and I paid all the bills." To help cut overheads, Stewart cut the café menu items at the new venue to a functional minimum of coffee, tea, and hot chocolate. Nobody went to La Mama for the refreshments anyway (the coffee was notoriously bad), but as Michael Smith observed, "The café gesture is important, since part of Ellen's basic idea is to release the audience from the rigidity of numbers and rows, and to make them comfortable" (1966, 164).

La Mama thus retained its casually informal spirit, but the new, larger space also gave it a more distinctive profile than previously. The size of the stage proved very attractive to writers and directors who had cut their teeth in tiny spaces like the Cino, but who needed room to expand their ideas: Lanford Wilson's *Balm in Gilead*, for example, which opened in January 1965, was the first full-length play written for off-off-Broadway, and required a stage area large enough to contain a cast of over twenty-five. Set in a seedy all-night coffee shop on the Upper West Side—a hangout for pimps, prostitutes, hustlers, and petty criminals, as well as the city's waifs and strays—the play was designed to capitalize on being performed in an actual café environment. Yet by his own account, Wilson had, in part, written it "to break out of the physical limitations inherent in writing a play for the Cino. The original version of the play had 55 characters. After I brought it down to 33, I gave the script to Marshall to read" (Wilson 1984, 31). According to director Marshall Mason, it simply never occurred to him to mount *Balm in Gilead* anywhere other than La Mama.

Mason and Wilson, though both firmly established at the Cino, had never previously worked together. They were introduced following an August 1964 revival of *Home Free!* and quickly struck up a rapport that became the foundation for a lifelong creative partnership. Sharing a similar aesthetic preference for a theatrical lyricism grounded in realism, each found he could rely on the other to help hone his work through questioning and cajoling. *Balm in Gilead* became their first collaboration and was soon followed by a second, *The Sandcastle* (September 1965), a drama based on Wilson's experiences at San Diego State College. Wilson's third La Mama piece, *The Rimers of Eldritch* (July 1966) was another kaleidoscopic, large-cast play, this time based on his youth in small-town Missouri: as with the earlier *This Is the Rill Speaking* at the Cino, however, Wilson directed *Rimers* himself to ensure that it had an authentic Ozark feel.

All these plays were highly regarded, but it was *Balm in Gilead* that really broke new ground for Wilson, Mason, and La Mama. A three-ring circus of overlapping dialogues and multiple-focus staging, the play creates a vibrant, sweaty sense of being right there in the café with these "low-life" characters. Although Wilson gestures toward a narrative through-line, in the tale of a young couple freshly arrived in the city, this was, Michael Smith observed in the *Voice*, one of the "not quite successful" elements of an often "brilliant" piece of theater (1965a). The play's impact, as Wilson himself stresses, lies in its overall design rather than any individual plotlines: "Everything seems to move in a circle," he says, a "general large pattern" within which the separate characters "constitute a whole, moving around some common center" (1988, 3). That group dynamic is reinforced by the fact that most of the dialogue is intended to be played "breakneck fast," so as to bombard the audience with an overload of information: this is in sharp contrast to a more traditional play like O'Neill's *Iceman Cometh*, which evokes a similar milieu but works out its dialogues with ploddingly methodical deliberation. "Wilson's kaleidoscopic technique frees him from the obligation to show these characters only in formed dramatic confrontations," Smith noted; "[he] describe[s] a wider reality by reproducing its texture" (1965a).

In creating a kind of hypernaturalistic drama, Wilson had also—paradoxically—created one that was highly theatrical. As if in recognition of this, the play repeatedly breaks its own frame by punctuating the dramatic illusion with moments in which the here and now of the theater event is underscored. Certain characters make frequent use of asides delivered directly to the audience, and Wilson also sets up an exterior, street area to one side of the stage that is necessarily less convincing, illusionistially, than the café setting (this would have been especially the case at La Mama). The actors are also used choreographically, as a wall of bodies, grouping and ungrouping to delineate new spaces, a strategy that also facilitates the play's one, extraordinary coup de théâtre: while one group of characters sings a song, as a round, the rest of the cast "silently lift every stick of furniture, the 'set,' about three feet off the ground and turn the set—as a turntable would—walk the set in a slow circle until it is facing the opposite direction" (Wilson 1988, 42). This moment was, by Wilson's admission, directly inspired by Lawrence Kornfeld's choreographic directorial work at Judson (he had been particularly struck by *What Happened*, in which a piano is moved around the stage by the cast, while still being played). The roundabout sequence could never have been performed in the Cino, but, equally, would have made little sense in a conventional, end-on theater. It worked perfectly at La Mama, though, with the two, facing blocks of audience being shown the other's perspective on the scene.

Balm in Gilead, in short, represented a striking fusion of some of the different strands of experimental work that had been developing off-off-Broadway. The production proved so successful with audiences that they lined up around the block to get in. Stewart held the show over for a second week, but on closing night, Wilson remembers, "There was practically a riot in the street" when the door closed with people still outside: "Finally Ellen just let everyone in, so there were about 180 people in there, though God knows how" (Wilson 1984, 32). The production brought La Mama a much higher profile on the downtown scene than it had previously enjoyed, and—just as *Lady Bright* had done for the Cino the previous year—seemed to attract many more playwrights to submit work to the venue. The first half of 1965 saw the La Mama debuts of several other writers whose work had already appeared elsewhere off-off-Broadway, and who took advantage of the larger La Mama stage to experiment with visual spectacle. For example, H. M. Koutoukas's *Tidy Passions (or Kill, Kaleidoscope, Kill)*, which premiered in June, required an eight-strong ensemble cast, who engage in a bizarre, dancelike ritual of worship to the mythic Cobra God.

June also saw the premiere of Jean-Claude van Itallie's *America Hurrah*, which needed an end-on stage to accommodate its motel room setting: this patently two-dimensional mock-up of the conventional box set was then systematically trashed each night by performers dressed as giant paper dolls. Never speaking a word, the visiting couple would enter the room, strip down to their giant paper underwear, daub obscene graffiti on the walls, smash the TV, and wreck the furniture, all to the accompaniment of a droning, monotonous voice-over describing in detail the banal appeal of this "cozy, comfy, nice" motel room on "route Six-Sixty-Six" (van Itallie 1978, 139). This unsettling juxtaposition of image and sound perhaps owed something to *Balls*, but *America Hurrah* (later retitled *Motel*) has a very different impact onstage, presenting a no-holds-barred expression of cultural self-loathing that fuses consumer-icon pop art and Artaudian cruelty. The play subjects its audiences to an ever-intensifying sensory assault, as rock music and sirens are added to the aural melee, and blinding headlights are turned on spectators. The La Mama production, directed by Michael Kahn, also benefited from the creative input of Robert Wilson, who would become famous in the 1970s as a visionary director-designer, but whom van Itallie had plucked from obscurity to help with this show. Initially, Wilson had been lined up to design the set, but his plans to render it as a giant yellow submarine had, as far as van Itallie could see, nothing to do with the play he had written. Wilson was persuaded to create the doll costumes instead, which he did using glistening, obese chunks of crumpled, painted paper. The dolls, described by Michael Smith as "truly grotesque and marvelously theatrical," contributed greatly to this "savage and unrelenting satirical outcry at the vulgarity of the highway civilization" (1965d).

If writers like van Itallie and Foster helped La Mama establish a reputation for serious-minded experimentalism, Stewart's most prolific resident playwright during this period—and indeed throughout the decade—was Tom Eyen, whose unashamed instinct for "showbiz pizzazz" represented another important strand of La Mama's work. A former sketch-writer for the revue club Upstairs at the Downstairs, Eyen made his La Mama debut at 82 Second

Avenue with *Little Miss Frustrata; or, The Dirty Little Girl with the Paper Rose in Her Head Is Demented* (May 1964), and quickly followed up with *The White Whore and the Bit Player* and *My Next Husband Will Be a Beauty* (both August). He then became a fixture at 122 Second Avenue with shows such as *Why Hanna's Skirt Won't Stay Down* (June 1965), *The Demented World of Tom Eyen* (September), and *Miss Nefertiti Regrets* (December). The last, a trash-Egyptian musical about a Cleopatraesque queen, is now chiefly notable for marking the acting debut of Bette Midler. Eyen's less distinguished efforts, characterized by the kind of slapdash wit also apparent in his titles, could be as throwaway as a comic strip, and not to be taken any more seriously. He could also, however, be an acute observer of human pain as well as a purveyor of pleasure: works such as *The White Whore* and *Hanna's Skirt* were notable as much for their underlying pathos as for their wild, satirical humor. Both became much-revived favorites of the off-off-Broadway scene, proving ideal not only for La Mama, but also for the cabaret-sized intimacy of the Cino.

Why Hanna's Skirt Won't Stay Down is clearly indebted to Eyen's revue-writing experience: set in an abstracted carnival funhouse, it cuts quickly between stand-up-style monologues, delivered direct to the audience, and short, skitlike flashback scenes in which the two characters—Hanna and Arizona—recall moments from their past, using each other to play a variety of remembered characters. Playing Hanna, both in the premiere and in frequent revivals, Helen Hanft became something of an underground star in the smart-talking "sassy dame" role that Eyen had tailor-made for her (Bette Midler admits that she freely plagiarized from Hanft to create her own stage persona). Beneath the showbiz shtick, however, as Hanft herself points out, the play is about loneliness, and particularly the sense of isolated inadequacy induced by the popular culture industry's obsession with image and glamor. Hanna stands over a blowhole, à la Marilyn Monroe in *The Seven Year Itch*, eternally exhibiting her sequined crotch, while Arizona, a self-confessed narcissist, poses in his stars-and-stripes jockstrap in a hall of fun-house mirrors. "I come and go," Arizona states repeatedly, neatly summing up the hollowness of his too-active sex life.

"I think the exploitation of sex in this country is just disgusting," Eyen (a bisexual Catholic) once explained of his overtly eroticized plays (Klemesrud 1970, 5). That conviction is given still more extreme realization in *The White Whore and the Bit Player*, which is set—we are informed—in the mind of a famous blonde, during the ten seconds between her act of suicide and her actual death. Invoking both the death from uremia of Jean Harlow and the barbiturate overdose of Marilyn Monroe, as well as the Hollywood myth of fading stars being killed off to boost their box office value, *The White Whore* is a savagely satirical indictment of a culture in which the only self-images available to many women are defined by the black-and-white dichotomy of virgin and whore. The play's two characters present two sides of the same troubled psyche, enacting the stereotypes of blonde movie temptress and penitent nun, but also frequently switching and doubling these roles to suggest a kind of schizophrenic confusion. This is matched by an abrasive and—for the earlier 1960s—shocking use of sexual self-display: the nun, for instance, masturbates by rubbing herself against the life-size crucifix that is the only set item. Directed ineptly, the play could easily disintegrate into a kind of gross, misogynist parody, but the intent is clearly to capture a visceral sense of psychic breakdown, of the feelings of self-hatred and worthlessness that could drive someone to suicide. *The White Whore and the Bit Player* still reads as a startling and disturbing piece of small-scale theater, a kind of demented, self-abusing cousin to *The Madness of Lady Bright.*

Promoting the New Wave

By the end of 1965, La Mama was no longer out on a limb in the East Village, but recognizable as off-off-Broadway's most feverishly active venue, in terms of the diversity of the work, and the sheer number of writers, that it sought to support. At the Obie Awards that year, La Mama and the Cino were rewarded with a joint citation for creating new opportunities for playwrights. The close relationship between the two cafés was further demonstrated by Stewart's hosting of benefit nights for the Cino, after it was severely damaged by fire that March. These "Caffe Cino at La Mama" evenings kept the Cino program alive while the Cornelia Street venue was being restored (it reopened on Good Friday). In November, the favor was reciprocated when the Cino's Robert Patrick helped Paul Foster to organize a benefit revue for La Mama called "BbAaNnGg!" to help raise funds for urgently needed electrical repairs (as demanded by the city's buildings department). Twenty-nine writers, including both Cino and La Mama regulars, contributed three-minute sketches to make up the evening.

Such collegiality, however, did not disguise the fact that Stewart's vision for the future of her theater was profoundly different from Joe Cino's. Where he was content simply to provide a space and create an inviting atmosphere for his playwrights to work in, she had her sights firmly set on having her "biddies" (as she called the playwrights she adopted) recognized by the world at large. The question, of course, was how best to achieve this without them having to compromise their ideas or sacrifice their creative independence. Stewart's solution, very much that of a fashion designer, was to "brand" her writers as a new wave, rather than as individuals seeking admission to the established commercial theater world. The earliest instance of this approach was the so-called Coffee House Theatre Festival, which Stewart presented in June 1964 at the Playwrights' Unit's theater on Vandam Street. Despite a concerted blitz of press releases, however, this one-off event—a double bill of Foster's *The Recluse* and David Starkweather's *So Who's Afraid of Edward Albee?*—failed to attract any more attention from the mainstream press than had La Mama's previous productions.

That same year, though, La Mama plays began to attract some genuine interest in Europe. Mari-Claire Charba and Jacque Lynn Colton, the two actresses for whom Eyen had written *The White Whore and the Bit Player*, took a trip to Paris, and wound up performing the piece at the Shakespeare & Co. bookstore, and then at the city's American Center, where there was considerable interest. Meanwhile, Paul Foster was making connections in Denmark, where a production of *The Recluse* was mounted by a local producer, Jens Okking. These links prompted Stewart to reason that, if La Mama could establish a reputation in Europe, and return home with positive press from abroad, then New York might be obliged to pay more attention. Thus, in the fall of 1965, a troupe of actors and directors embarked on La Mama's first European tour. They crossed the Atlantic by the cheapest means available—ship—with each person having purchased a one-way ticket at his or her own expense, trusting Stewart's promise that they would be provided for in Europe, and that their tour schedule would generate the finances to bring them home. The tour destinations, thanks to the previous year's exploits, were Paris and Copenhagen.

The story of this first European tour is recounted in more detail in chapter 10, as it resulted directly in the genesis of the "La Mama Troupe" ensemble company. It is relevant here, though, to highlight the mix of material that the touring party performed. Some of the pieces were homegrown plays from La Mama, including *Hurrah for the Bridge*, *America Hurrah*, and works by other, largely forgotten La Mama playwrights such as Bruce Kessler, Robert Sealy, and Mary Mitchell. Yet the program also included a judicious selection of plays first presented at other off-off-Broadway venues, such as *Home Free!*, *The Madness of Lady Bright*, and William Hoffman's telephone monologue

Thank You, Miss Victoria, from the Cino, and Leonard Melfi's *Birdbath* and Sam Shepard's *Chicago* from Theatre Genesis. In choosing this range of material, Stewart and her colleagues were positioning themselves as international ambassadors not just for La Mama, but for new Village playwriting generally. The tour publicity announced pointedly that "La Mama Experimental Theatre Club presents: Off-Off-Broadway Theater."

Stewart was thus promoting the La Mama brand name by associating it, almost metonymically, with the broader movement. That strategy became even more apparent in March 1966, when, following the touring company's return from Europe, Stewart teamed up with off-Broadway producer Theodore Mann (cofounder of the Circle in the Square), to present *Six from La Mama* at the Martinique Theatre. Two alternating triple bills of one-act plays were put together to showcase the troupe's work, which had been precision-polished by their time on the road. Foster's *The Recluse,* however, was the only one of the selected plays to have originated at La Mama. This was again a program more representative of the movement as a whole than of any individual theater—and that was the line fed to the New York press corps. Predictably, however, their responses were largely those of a disgruntled establishment, singularly unimpressed by these underground upstarts. The reviews were negative, and frequently patronizing, with the first bill, in particular, meeting a uniformly hostile response. Only Melfi's *Birdbath* met with qualified approval: as a two-hander with a basically realistic premise and a strong, central dramatic confrontation, it sat more easily on a conventional stage than either *Thank You, Miss Victoria* (dismissed as a weak exercise in monologue) or Wilson's "play for voices," *This Is the Rill Speaking,* which was thought overly indebted to *Our Town, Under Milk Wood,* or both. (*Rill,* another Cino original, was a recent addition to the group's repertoire, since Wilson's *Home Free!* and *Lady Bright* had been optioned for a more conventional off-Broadway production: opening the following month at Theater East, this too received a volley of critical abuse and closed quickly.)

The second Martinique bill fared slightly better, winning some praise from the *New York Times*' Stanley Kauffmann. Though he dismissed *The Recluse* as "a tedious attempt at Gothic grotesque," Kauffmann saw real innovative value in van Itallie's *War* and Shepard's *Chicago,* both of which, he felt, "share[d] certain characteristics" in their plotless playfulness and flights of imagination (1966b). Kauffmann deemed *Chicago* "the best play on both bills," and its lead actor Kevin O'Connor went on to win a Vernon Rice Drama Desk Award for his performance. This was small compensation, however, for the fact that, following the critical slating, *Six from La Mama* ran for just two weeks.

The Martinique shows were a well-intentioned attempt to showcase off-off-Broadway writers to a wider public, and *as* off-off-Broadway writers rather than as individuals picked up by commercial producers. In retrospect, however, the plays seem to have been poorly served by being grouped together under this banner heading. The individual values of each piece were somewhat obscured by the externally imposed publicity agenda: responding to the plays on the plays' own terms was difficult when the context was a "bill" that was being "sold" as something noteworthy. An identical problem had in fact arisen a year earlier, when the Playwrights' Unit had made a single, comparable attempt at collectively promoting off-off-Broadway voices to commercial audiences, with a "New Playwrights" bill presented at the Cherry Lane Theatre in February 1965. This triple bill also featured just one piece original to the presenting organization—Shepard's still-unpublished *Up to Thursday*, which Charles Gnys had directed at the Playwrights' Unit the previous November— alongside Foster's *Balls* and Wilson's *Home Free!* Richard Barr went to some lengths to publicize the bill as a significant conjunction of new talents, and succeeded in having Shepard, Foster, and Wilson photographed together for a feature article in the *New York Times*. Critics' reactions, however, ranged from boredom to bemusement, and one of the most negative was from Michael Smith, in the *Voice*. These were all plays that he had admired on their own terms, in their original settings, Smith stressed,

> yet the triple bill is not a good theatre experience. The plays represent radically different visions and methods, and each of them seems diminished in context of the others. . . . The program as a whole lacks direction and clarity of intention, and as a result seems to be nothing but a showcase . . . a collection of works lumped together in a vaguely educational manner, as if the only reason for attending is self-improvement, and the experience is necessarily a chore. The impression I get is of laziness, and nothing new seems to have been accomplished beyond a photograph on the front page of the *Times*' Sunday drama section. (1965b)

As Smith's comments indicate, the problems with the New Playwrights bill, and indeed with *Six from La Mama*, were primarily to do with context. In the café venues, a one-act play could stand alone as a piece sufficient in itself, and not require to be paired with something else simply to fill up an evening. More important still, the intimacy of the off-off venues generated a particular kind of intense, two-way relationship between viewer and viewed, militating against the voyeuristic distance permitted by a darkened auditorium. Previously in this book, several plays—including *Babel Babel Little Tower, The Service for Joseph Axminster,* and *Balm in Gilead*—have been described as being to some degree "site-specific," designed for the spaces in which they first appeared. In a broader sense, however, many more off-off-Broadway plays—including most of those on the Martinique and Cherry Lane bills—were specific to their sites insofar that they were created for performance in small, atmospheric café spaces. "When I now go to see something on a proscenium stage it's like something else," Joe Cino remarked in 1966, "with no comparisons to what is done here" (Orzel and Smith 1966, 54). Attempts to relocate such plays to larger, more conventional theaters, without regard for the change in theatrical dynamics (the Martinique had a three-quarter-round stage, but was quite sizable, with a high roof), rendered many of them small and odd-looking—just as conventional theater itself appears small and odd when filmed "as is" for television.

Sam Shepard, for one, seems to have learned important lessons from these early "commercial" experiences. "I have to work Off-Off-Broadway," he explained in a 1966 interview: "It's an environmental choice. . . . The plays can't be done anywhere else, economically or any other kind of way. Anywhere else the value systems are completely different. . . . You have to conform in a certain way" (Lerman 1966, 146–47). Ellen Stewart, however, seems to have drawn somewhat different conclusions from *Six from La Mama.* Clearly, small-scale playwriting did not translate easily to more public contexts, but one artist whose reputation was substantially enhanced by the Martinique engagement was Tom O'Horgan, director of all six plays, for whom the critics were united in their praise. According to Stanley Kauffmann, O'Horgan's was "the major contribution" in making the event worth seeing: despite the variable standard of writing, he possessed "the ability to see in a script the physical unfolding which will articulate its essences and rhythms" (1966a). Realizing O'Horgan's achievement, Stewart resolved to place him, and subsequently other directors, at the heart of her operation. La Mama thus began to follow the Judson example, pursuing a more self-consciously collaborative synthesis of text and performance. In the longer run, Stewart's commitment to the new playwright was to become secondary to her interest in directors whose visual and musical flair made their work directly accessible across borders of language and culture. More so than any other off-off-Broadway programmer, Stewart sought to forge new trends rather than be led by them, and to reach out beyond the Village context.

6   Theatre Genesis: Urban Prophecy

> Here, now, in lower Manhattan, the phenomenon is taking place: the begin-
> ning, the Genesis, of a cultural revolution. It is taking place out of utter neces-
> sity. Out of the necessity to survive. . . . Personally I have little hope for the sur-
> vival of our civilization. But whatever hope we have lies with our artists. For they
> alone have the ability (if we do not continue to corrupt them) to withstand the
> onslaught of the mass media and the multitude of false gods. They alone have
> the ability to show us ourselves.
> —Ralph Cook, in Orzel and Smith, *Eight Plays from Off-Off-Broadway*

Theatre Genesis, the fourth and last of the four key off-off-Broadway venues to
be founded, was also the most self-consciously programmatic in its approach
to presenting new playwrights. Based at St. Mark's in the Bowery, a church on
the corner of Second Avenue and East Tenth Street, it was the brainchild of
Ralph Cook, whose approach—as the somewhat portentous statement above
indicates—was more overtly politically oriented than that of Joe Cino, Al
Carmines, or Ellen Stewart. Cook also made a more specific commitment to
professionalism in presentation, as his adoption of the title "artistic director"
clearly indicated (this was an industry term never embraced by his counterparts, with their comparatively ad hoc programming practices). Cook's
earnestness made him a figure of fun among some other members of the off-
off scene, but his devotion to the nurturing and development of all his Theatre
Genesis artists, and particularly the playwrights, made him a deeply loved
figure at St. Mark's.

A native of California born in 1928, and a former Hollywood bit-part actor,
Cook was a good deal older than the playwrights he nurtured, becoming a
mentor or father figure, just as Ellen Stewart was "la mama." Yet where she
was very much the internationalist entrepreneur, he was more the local
activist. For Cook, Theatre Genesis existed, first and foremost, to speak to
and for its immediate locality—the deprived, run-down area of the Lower
East Side in which St. Mark's was located: "the actors, directors and writers
are members of a geographical community and we are presenting plays for

members of that community," he stressed, "not as a special gala event but as an integral part of the life of the community" (Orzel & Smith 1966, 94). Consequently, Genesis never showed much interest in publicizing its work more broadly, and this relative insularity helps explain why Genesis remains the most underdocumented and underrecognized of the key off-off-Broadway venues. That comparative obscurity seems particularly surprising when one considers that Genesis was the artistic home of Sam Shepard—now off-off-Broadway's most famous son. Yet Shepard's growing renown in the 1960s hinged largely on the fact that, being well aware of Cook's lack of interest in promoting his playwrights in the outside world, Shepard took it upon himself to pursue productions at Cino, Judson, La Mama, and the Playwrights' Unit. That Shepard nevertheless remained rooted at St. Mark's throughout this period, and more often than not ensured that members of the Genesis acting fraternity played key roles even in these "outside" productions, speaks volumes about the sense of community and belonging that Cook succeeded in fostering.

Beginnings

St. Mark's in the Bowery is an elegant yet modest Episcopal church, which stands on the oldest continuously consecrated religious site in Manhattan. Peter Stuyvesant, governor of New Amsterdam, first erected a chapel there in the 1650s, on land purchased from the Dutch West India Company. The present church, with its distinctive tall, narrow spire, was erected in the 1790s, in the very earliest years of the United States itself. By the 1950s, however, St. Mark's had fallen on hard times: its traditionally white, middle-class congregation had declined sharply in numbers as the surrounding neighborhood evolved into a multiethnic mix of blue-collar whites, African Americans, Puerto Ricans, and Ukrainians. Yet the appointment of a dynamic young pastor helped to revivify the church and redirect its sense of mission. Reverend Michael Allen made it his priority to minister to the entire neighborhood rather than just to those parishioners attending services. He established various social programs for the local community, and in 1963 was appointed chairman of the Lower East Side Civil Rights Committee. Allen sought to have the church address the needs of everyone from the street people and drug addicts living in the Bowery area to the artists and intellectuals who were increasingly moving to the East Village as rents rose in Greenwich Village proper.

All of this was, of course, similar to the approach being adopted by Howard

Moody at Judson Memorial Church, but Allen stresses that he did not share Moody's secularizing vision of the church, and placed more stock in traditional Christian values: "We were perceived, and perceived ourselves, as a parish church, the church for the parish, doing what we did as ministry." His particular emphasis on ministering to the needy and disenfranchised—a core Christian principle—was one of the features that attracted Ralph Cook when he first visited St. Mark's. At that time he was himself recovering from a nervous breakdown and a period in a mental hospital, and he greatly appreciated Allen's support and friendship, which was offered regardless of Cook's professed atheism. When Cook asked if he could contribute to the church's ministry by running an acting workshop for local youths, and possibly establish a theater program, Allen enthusiastically agreed, and Cook was appointed "lay minister to the arts."

Theatre Genesis was established in a second-floor meeting room of the parish hall, a building attached to the back of St. Mark's itself. This separation of church and theater, in contrast to the arrangement at Judson, was in part a reflection of Allen's more traditional theological perspective, but also of Cook's desire to have a dedicated theater space. Converting the room into a small, black box–style studio, he presented the first Theatre Genesis production in July 1964. The show, however, was a prepackaged, touring production of *Study in Color*, a play by Malcolm Boyd designed for presentation in churches. Cook did not like it, and quickly resolved in future to present only those plays that he thought both artistically valid and socially relevant in some way. For some months, nothing interested him enough to want to present it, but he eventually found what he was looking for when the twenty-year-old Sam Shepard handed him his first two plays, *Cowboys* and *The Rock Garden*. Shepard, who had recently arrived in New York from California (with, ironically enough, a touring religious theater group, the Bishop's Repertory Company), was working as a busboy at the Village Gate nightclub, where Cook was headwaiter. He produced the scripts on learning of plans for the new theater, and these two very different one-act pieces were presented in October 1964. They provided a clear indication of Cook's priorities: here was a young writer, relatively uneducated in theater or literature, who was finding his way intuitively toward his own theatrical style. For Cook, Shepard's was the voice of a kid off the local streets, and as such *Cowboys* and *The Rock Garden* seemed ideal to launch a theater program whose purpose was, in part, "to help reopen communications between church and community" (Orzel and Smith 1966, 11).

"I know it sounds pretentious and unprepossessing," Michael Smith noted in his *Village Voice* review of the double bill: "'Theatre Genesis . . . dedicated to the new playwright.' But they have actually found a new playwright, [and] he has written a pair of provocative and genuinely original plays" (1964d). Smith's belated response drew a curious audience to the new venue for the final weekend of performances, and helped counteract the negative impact of an earlier, more dismissive review from Jerry Tallmer in the *Post*, who saw *Cowboys* as a pointless Beckett imitation. Though obviously indebted to *Waiting for Godot* in its presentation of two men who fill in time on an all-but-bare stage with games and rhythmic language, *Cowboys* was also a fairly direct translation to the stage of the playful street antics of Shepard and his friend Charles Mingus III, who used to wander lower Manhattan as a kind of anarchic double act, adopting comic voices and dodging traffic. To its admirers, it seemed to capture both the energy and disaffection of the Lower East Side's large, and largely rootless, youth population, brought up on 1950s platitudes and television serials: "Their basic mood is exhaustion bordering on despair," Smith wrote of the play's two young male characters, "but from it they rouse themselves into bursts of wild energy, alternately joyous and desperate, in which they impersonate Wild West heroes surrounded by marauding Indians and relish in memory the sensate details of breakfast" (1964d). Although he did not say so in the review, Smith also felt that the play's minute attention to such details, together with its free-form linguistic playfulness, brought it closer than anything he had yet known to creating a theatrical equivalent for the subjective experience of being high on pot. Shepard's writing seemed to him to suggest a kind of alternative, liberated state of mind, an intuitive rejection of traditional dramatic logic. (The text of *Cowboys* is unpublished, but is described in detail in the 1992 book *Sam Shepard*, by David DeRose, who acquired the only extant manuscript from Ralph Cook.)

If *Cowboys* seemed to celebrate the attempts of two young men to create new roles and even headstates for themselves, *The Rock Garden* summarized what they were fleeing from. In a triptych of simple domestic scenes, Shepard depicted the banality and tedium of life in an archetypal, middle-American family home (complete with white picket fence). "The writing is beautifully controlled," Smith noted, "and conveys the overpowering boredom of the situation without being boring for a moment" (1964d). Moreover, Shepard's precise attention to visual, theatrical detail is as accomplished here as his language: indeed the first scene contains no words, simply a telling sequence of looks between family members, which are never met with a returned gaze. The resulting tense, seized-up atmosphere is then shattered with the Girl's deliberate knocking over of a glass of milk; in this context it is a simple but shocking gesture, and white liquid drips onto the floor in silence. Later, in the play's crucial, climactic moment, the Boy effects his own, more pronounced revolt against the family's repressive mediocrity by launching into a vividly detailed monologue on the joys of sex and the advantages of small vaginas. This prompts his father—in a wonderfully understated final image—to fall off his chair. It was this speech that brought immediate notoriety to the production and the new theater, which was condemned for promoting obscenity in a church building. Yet Pastor Allen himself, in a move indicative of his ministry's priorities, publicly spoke back in support of the play, arguing that it was more Christian to use offensive language in pursuit of truth than to use decent language in defense of conventionalized lies. *The Rock Garden*, Allen argues in retrospect, "was really an attack on the pornography of American life," and for him represented exactly the kind of social and spiritual conscience that St. Mark's stood for. "One day Sam and I were talking," Allen adds: "I said to him, 'One day you will be recognized as America's greatest Christian playwright.' He responded that he hoped that would be true."

Programming, Personnel and Environment

This first homegrown production at Theatre Genesis was staffed almost entirely by a core group that Cook had gathered from among his associates at the Village Gate. The cast included fellow waiters Lee Kissman and Kevin O'Connor, as well as Stephanie Gordon, daughter of the club's hostess. The stage manager was Mimi Davies, who also worked at the Gate. Right from its inception, then, there was a sense of "gang" or "family" to the setup at Genesis, with others being drawn into the group through their friendships with individual members: Barbara Eda Young, for example, who like Kissman went on to act regularly at St. Mark's for the rest of the decade, was first invited along by her friend Mimi Davies, to see a rehearsal of *Rock Garden*. Young was so shocked by the play's final speech—"I was so completely provincial!"—that she almost did not come back. Conversely, however, the notoriety of the Shepard plays meant that the theater quickly began to attract the interest of other would-be playwrights, who began submitting scripts for consideration.

Ralph Cook's selection policy for new plays was, however, more rigorous

than that adopted at other off-off-Broadway venues. He would typically program shows to run for about twelve performances over three weekends, as did
Al Carmines. Like Judson, Genesis also tended to present double bills. However, Cook's pairing of one-act plays was less arbitrary than Carmines's, usually focusing on work by a single writer (as with the opening Shepard bill) or
on plays that were deemed to be related in some way. Indeed, Cook's insistence on presenting new work only when he had a bill of plays with something
worthwhile to say meant that Theatre Genesis had a more erratic production
schedule than any of its counterparts, sometimes going two or even three
months without a new production. This prizing of quality over quantity meant
that the standard of the work produced at Theatre Genesis was more consistently reliable than at other off-off venues: "Some of the plays were bad," Barbara Young acknowledges, "but I'd say 70 percent of them were good, and the
ones that were good—that was how you learned to act." Meanwhile, the regularly pumping heart of the Genesis operation was the weekly Monday night
play-reading workshop, in which participating actors read submitted scripts.
Cook himself read all the submissions, and chose for the play-reading sessions
those that he felt showed evidence of "talent and ability" (the anticuratorial,
open-door policies of Joe Cino and Ellen Stewart meant little to him). He
then looked to see what the actors and directors at the readings would make of
the material: "The decision for production is made," he explained, "when a
director connects with a play and both meet with the approval of the artistic
director" (Orzel and Smith 1966, 93).

In practice, of course, since Cook himself was both artistic director and,
initially at least, the director of most of the actual productions, a meeting of
minds between Cook and any prospective writer was a primary requirement.
From the outset, it was his sense of taste and judgment that determined the
theater's trajectory. Nevertheless, Cook was, in his own way, a remarkably
nonprescriptive leader. He was particularly appreciated by playwrights
because of his clear concern to present their material in as unmediated a manner as possible, to find out how *they* wanted their plays to appear, and to pursue that. Though he was noted for his clean, cool, no-nonsense directorial
style, this was largely a result of his determination not to bring any extraneous
vision of his own to bear on a play. Colleagues remember him as a director
whose approach to new material was so "hands off" as to sometimes give the
impression that the playwrights were directing their work *through* him.
"That's what they liked about him," notes Tony Barsha, a writer-director who
joined the Genesis setup in 1966:

It was almost like he didn't know what he was doing, except that he knew exactly what he was doing. It was like watching John Huston direct; he worked like that too. He'd come on set hungover and acted as if he had not a clue as to where he was or why he was doing it and people would start filling in. He had the right people around him, and they'd start giving him all these ideas, and he'd say, "Oh, we'll take that, we'll take that . . ." Ralph was like that, and he was very good at it.

Cook's approach succeeded not only in forcing playwrights to think through and articulate their intentions for their work, but also in drawing strongly personal performances from his actors. He avoided the familiar directorial habit of simply telling actors what to do, and instead required that they find an understanding of the material for themselves, however opaque it might sometimes seem. Barbara Young asserts that, working with him, she gained a greater sense of each role's possibilities than she has ever subsequently been allowed to find by directors in the professional theater:

> Ralph did something really wonderful, which also made it very difficult later for all of us, because he absolutely gave you space. [He] was the only director I've known who told you that you had to figure it out for yourself. He said: "You can do it! That's why you're playing this part!" And sometimes that could be so infuriating, and I would be in tears, because I wanted him to give me the solution. But he forced me to find the solution. . . . You're motivated to move onstage because of what's going on, not because someone tells you to go from A to B. I never found that experience again, after Theatre Genesis. You were a *part* of it, not just a robot who's hired and learns lines.

The sense of intimacy and belonging that Cook's approach helped to generate was further enhanced by the particularities of the performance space itself. The "black box" had at that time only recently emerged as a favored concept for flexible, multipurpose theaters, and Cook's conversion of the church meeting room into such a space was another clear indication of the differences between Genesis and the other off-off-Broadway venues, with their more makeshift performance environments. Few previous black boxes, however, could have been quite this small: Michael Smith estimates that the entire room was around thirty by thirty-five feet, which made it somewhat wider than, but not as deep as, the Caffe Cino. (The space has since been remodeled and expanded for its present occupiers, Richard Foreman's Ontological Theatre.) The intimacy of the room, combined with the blacked-out neutrality of its walls, made Theatre Genesis into a kind of womblike sweatbox. Various audience configurations were possible, but no spectator was ever more than a few feet from the action, and in the absence of distractions like coffee machines and exterior windows, the intensity of the atmosphere was unrivaled. Performing at Genesis was thus akin to movie acting insofar that, within this "black cube," the subtlest vocal or facial inflection could be picked up by audience members.

Similarly, the focus that the space afforded to onstage *objects* was unusually sharp. Pared-down settings consisting of only a few key items were of course a common feature of the plays presented in other spatially and financially constrained off-off-Broadway theaters, but at Genesis—where set or prop items stood out sharply against the uniform black background—a particular emphasis on the sculptural or iconic quality of those objects was possible. In this respect, lessons seem to have been learned from that opening Shepard bill: *Cowboys* had cleverly used a couple of sawhorses on an otherwise bare stage, whereas *The Rock Garden* had been criticized for the production's somewhat unconvincing attempt, in such a tiny space, to construct a realistic domestic environment using theatrical flats. Although there were other, subsequent uses of such flats, Genesis plays tended increasingly to focus around single objects—such as the freestanding bathtub in Shepard's *Chicago* (1965)—which could act as visual anchors for plays that were otherwise chiefly dominated by language (necessarily, given the size of the space). Playwright Murray Mednick confirms that this minimalist approach to sets and props became a conscious element of the Genesis aesthetic: "[We found that] you could use a certain kind of visual symbology . . . to great effect in a small space. We were really interested in discovering iconographic usages: what would have the resonance of an icon, a newly discovered icon, so that you can communicate directly to the audience's subconscious?" Again, this concern related to the idea of evoking alternative headstates: Mednick suggests that this visual emphasis on found objects and cultural icons—from Coke bottles to cowboy hats—was partly inspired by an awareness of the way that everyday objects can become strangely fascinating, or be viewed with an uncanny clarity of focus, when under the influence of certain drugs.

One further advantage of the tiny black space was that the walls themselves (unlike those at other off-off venues) could be repainted for particular productions. The most extreme example of this came in 1968 when, for Walter Hadler's first play *Solarium*, the entire room—walls, floor, and ceiling—was temporarily repainted bright yellow, so as to completely engulf the audience within this vivid color. "Johnny Dodd lit the place," Hadler recalls, "and it went from the crack of dawn through high noon and into late night, in a sort of twenty-four-hour cycle. Around 'noon,' the place became so brilliant in this yellow that it felt like you were levitating. A couple of truck drivers were sitting there—they're like, 'What the fuck's going on?!'"

Dodd was the most relied-upon lighting designer at Genesis throughout the 1960s, just as he was at the Cino. As this anecdote illustrates, however, the simple uniformity of the Genesis space meant that he customarily used subtler, more subliminally atmospheric lighting states than he did at the Cino, where the glitter and baubles encouraged a wilder, more self-demonstrative approach. Indeed, though Genesis and the Cino, thanks to their size, shared a particular emphasis on small casts and the spoken word, the distinctions between the two were quite marked. The point is neatly demonstrated by contrasting the ways in which H. M. Koutoukas's version of *Medea* was produced at each venue, almost simultaneously, in November 1965. (Koutoukas, it emerged, had submitted the piece to Genesis partly as a subversive prank, and Cook was outraged when he discovered that *Medea* was being presented elsewhere at the same time.) The piece is set in a laundromat (see next chapter for an explanation as to why), and at the Cino this was suggested simply by lining up some large cardboard boxes with circular holes cut out of their fronts to indicate washing machines. This consciously "tacky" choice was complemented by the twinkling walls of the Cino space itself, and by the use of actor Charles Stanley as a six-foot-plus drag Medea. The failings of the available resources, as ever, became the production's virtues. Conversely, at Genesis, with the black space lending no built-in atmosphere, the laundromat setting was created by commissioning iconic washing machine sculptures from a local pop artist. In the play's final moments, when, according to the stage directions, Medea "ascends to the constellation Virgo," planetarium-style projections of the cosmos were cast onto the black walls and ceiling to create a climactic coup de théâtre.

The Evolving Profile

The very presence of Koutoukas's *Medea* on the Genesis program in 1965— with its campy, faux Greek extravagance standing in such stark contrast to, say, Shepard's coolly abstracted realism—is indicative of the genuine diversity apparent in Cook's programming during Genesis's first couple of seasons. Other plays produced during this early, embryonic period ranged from two experimental one-acts by historian-playwright Charles L. Mee, to a piece by the soon-to-be cult novelist and screenwriter Rudolph Wurlitzer, to the more-

or-less conventional realism of Leonard Melfi—who had five plays mounted on three different bills during the latter half of 1965, making him at that point Cook's most produced playwright. Melfi is a good example of a writer who benefited considerably from Cook's play-reading-into-production scheme. An aspiring commercial playwright whose various attempts at full-length plays had been repeatedly turned down by agents and producers, he had had one previous one-act piece produced off-off-Broadway: *Lazy Baby Susan* had appeared at La Mama in October 1962, but while Melfi had appreciated the chance to see his work staged, he had subsequently gone back to peddling his longer scripts (unsuccessfully). Early in 1965, an actor friend, David Miller, started taking him along to Cook's Monday play readings. Melfi submitted *Lazy Baby Susan* and another one-act to be read in this forum, where they failed to impress. Yet Melfi was sufficiently galvanized by this rejection, and sufficiently inspired by actor Kevin O'Connor's performances in the readings, that he sat down and wrote *Birdbath* explicitly for Genesis, with O'Connor in mind for the male role. Cook loved the results, and directed the show himself that June, in double bill with a shorter Melfi piece, *Sunglasses*. Opposite O'Connor's Frankie, he cast Barbara Young, in her first role: her "polished, beautifully detailed portrayal of Velma" (Lester 1965a), distinguished by a disturbingly tiny, high, birdlike voice, added greatly to the play's impact. This combination of script and performers proved to be Genesis's most popular show yet with audiences, and both performers were invited to tour with the piece on the first La Mama excursion to Europe (although Young could not afford to go).

Birdbath is, in many respects, a straightforward slice of stage realism, presenting a late-night encounter between a would-be-poet bartender and a psychologically damaged waitress. There is a clear narrative trajectory to the piece, and a melodramatic secret in the waitress's past to be climactically uncovered (she killed her mother first thing this morning). Yet Melfi's restraint in his handling of this material, and his carefully judged use of ironic subtext (perceptible to the audience but not the characters), draws audiences in despite the stretches in narrative plausibility. Moreover, something about the controlled intensity of the encounter, and the way in which Melfi manipulates audience sympathy so that it swings back and forth from one character to the other, as each gets steadily more drunk and more unstable, lifts the piece above run-of-the-mill realism toward the level of archetype. As Melfi explained, *Birdbath* was written at a time when, as a bartender himself, "I was almost always dealing with people who were practically strangers to me, but

whose lives and beings suddenly seemed more meaningful than my own existence" (1967, viii). The play transforms these experiences into an encounter
that evokes a whole world of late-night collisions and broken individuals. Still
regularly revived, the piece is relished by actors, and let down only by its final
moments, in which Frankie writes and then reads out a rather weak poem
dedicated to the sleeping Velma.

Birdbath was tailor-made to take full advantage of the claustrophobic intimacy of the Genesis space, but it also translated adequately to the stage of the
Martinique Theatre, where (as previously noted) it fared relatively well with
the New York press as part of the 1966 *Six from La Mama*. Such opportunities
for exposure seem to have drawn Melfi away from Theatre Genesis and back
to La Mama: he never worked with Cook again after 1965. This parting of
ways, however, seems to have been felt mutually: none of Melfi's other plays
at Genesis that year had proved nearly as powerful as *Birdbath*, and his subsequent work swung back toward a sweeter, rather more sentimental tone,
which would have made him particularly out of place at Theatre Genesis,
where Cook and his colleagues were developing a more distinct, harder-edged
aesthetic.

That aesthetic was defined by Cook in a 1966 statement as being characterized by "a deeply subjective kind of realism," and his emphasis here was
clearly more on the subjective than on any conventional understanding of
realism (Orzel and Smith 1966, 94). He encouraged playwrights to empower
themselves by valuing and exploring their own perspectives on the world—to
ask basic, existential questions about being and consciousness, about what
seemed fundamentally "real" to them, and to articulate those questions poetically and theatrically. Cook's notion of subjective realism was initially most
clearly embodied, and probably partly inspired, by the work of Sam Shepard.
By grounding his early plays in recognizable, everyday realities (a bathroom, a
motel room, etc.) but refracting and abstracting these images through the
application of a very personal, subjective vision, Shepard had begun to
develop a kind of raw, neoexpressionist theater that had recognizable
antecedents in the work of Beckett, Albee, and Pinter, but that was also unmistakably individual in tone and execution. Particularly important here was
Shepard's freely spontaneous, rhythmic use of theatrical language, which was
immediately recognized by critics as his most distinctive gift, and which
allowed his characters to give voice to vividly imagistic monologues that
seemed to spring, uncensored, from the wilder regions of the mind. Shepard's
acknowledged influences in this regard were the beat writings of Ginsberg and

Kerouac, the action painting of Pollock, and the improvisational jazz of Charlie Parker, Ornette Coleman, and Charles Mingus (father of his roommate)—all of which were enthusiasms shared by Cook. Indeed, the notion of "subjective realism" was at root an attempt to map out a theatrical equivalent for the expressive spontaneity apparent in those other art forms.

Theatre Genesis's association with this type of material was strongly reinforced in 1965 by the foundation of the St. Mark's Poetry Project, which met elsewhere on the church premises. By this time, many of the leading figures in the East Village poetry movement had grown weary of the limitations and interruptions attendant on the coffeehouse readings that had been standard since the turn of the decade, and the establishment of more organized meetings at St. Mark's was widely welcomed: indeed, they regularly attracted such prominent figures as Beat pioneers Allen Ginsberg and Gregory Corso. As lay minister to the arts at the church, Cook was notionally the project's sponsor, but the real impetus for its foundation came from Joel Oppenheimer, its first director, who became an inspirational figure to many at St. Mark's. (His play *The Great American Desert* now reads as a kind of precursor to a whole strand of western-obsessed Genesis playwriting.) The project was run with the assistance of another poet, Ann Waldman, who later took over as director herself, and also occasionally acted with Theatre Genesis.

Although there was no formal collaboration or crossover between the theater and the Poetry Project, the presence of both organizations within the same building helped to define the trajectory of both. Just as the coexistence of theater, dance, gallery, and happenings at Judson Memorial Church led to that venue being associated with a richly visual, choreographic mode of theatrical presentation, so St. Mark's became identifiable as the proponent of a more directly emotive, densely verbal theatricality: Beat-style performance poetry translated to the stage. "The reading of the poems became a kind of performance art," explains Murray Mednick:

> There was a kind of presentational quality to the language which I think we [in Theatre Genesis] were very influenced by. We had a similar attitude toward language, which has to do with a feeling about the spoken word as an almost shamanistic act, incantatory, ritualistic, as opposed to the theatrical [dialogue] tradition. . . . We had a very high estimation of the idea of the word itself coming through the medium of the actor.

Tony Barsha wryly notes that such "incantation" eventually became such an integral part of the Genesis approach that "it became a necessity" even in the most dialogue-based plays: "There came a moment when the monologue had to come in. It had to be a revelatory monologue, a scatalogical monologue, a monologue of entropy, whatever." Such verbal flights became as central to the Genesis aesthetic as the solo breaks were to jazz performance.

An early Genesis production that clearly demonstrated this language-based, "subjective realist" approach was the April 1965 double bill of Shepard's *Chicago* and Lawrence Ferlinghetti's *The Customs Collector in Baggy Pants*. Ferlinghetti, as one of San Francisco's leading Beat poets, had already published *The Customs Collector* in his short-play collection *Unfair Arguments with Existence* (1963), and it seems to have been selected by Cook specifically to stand alongside *Chicago*. Both pieces are essentially rhythmically driven monologues (although *Chicago* also has a number of subsidiary characters), and in both, the trajectory is one of gradual intensification in the monologuist's mood, from playfully ludicrous beginnings toward an eruption of near-hysterical anxiety by the end. In Ferlinghetti's piece, this is achieved partly by the sheer breathlessness of the actor after an increasingly frantic, seven-page monologue that includes not one single period or pause. *Chicago* is more rhythmically complex, ebbing and flowing like the sea into which the inhabitants of Stu's story finally walk, but the effect is all the more disquieting for that: Shepard's use of humor is deft (where Ferlinghetti's plays relentlessly around the same sexual innuendo), and it is in the steadily darkening accumulation of telling details and comic-grotesque observations that the play's impact lies. In Stu's narrative, a smelly, overpopulated train journey gives way to a beach scene, a wild orgy of sand and sperm, a frantic attempt to make smothering rugs, and finally a ritual drowning by suicide. *Chicago*, like much of Shepard's early work, is difficult to make rational sense of, but through rhythm and image it conjures a vivid sense of a "subjectively real" trip into a nightmare world that Stu appears, finally, to crave escape from, as he leaps from the bathtub he has been confined in throughout the play and exhorts the audience to embrace life: "Breathing, ladies and gentlemen . . . it's fantastic!" (Shepard 1986, 59). The ominous knocking of a policeman's nightstick from the behind the audience as the lights fade clearly implies that, whatever Stu fears, they are not so easily escaped.

Juxtaposition with Ferlinghetti's play seems to clarify the nature of Stu's anxiety. The customs collector characterizes his location as the ladies' restroom on the "lifeboat full of flush toilets we call civilization" (Ferlinghetti 1963, 79), and his listeners as "all the women I have ever loved and known" (85). He asks—at first threateningly and finally desperately—for them to return to him the jewels they have stolen, "the twin gems" and "the great King of Diamonds" (81). The castration terror so obviously underlying this piece, and so beloved of the Beat movement in general, throws into relief Stu's obvious anxiety over the plans of his girlfriend, Joy, to go out and leave him alone. (Joy was played by Shepard's girlfriend, Joyce Aaron, who had recently spent time away, acting in a play in Chicago.) Her departure seems to leave Stu impotently stranded in his (womblike?) bathtub. "The movement of the play," Ralph Cook comments, "is from Stu's minute particular subjective problem . . . to the universal problem of Man's being civilized to the suffocating point of losing his balls" (Shepard 1967, 10). The double bill, taken together, thus indicated a developing concern at Theatre Genesis with exploring the underside of a specifically masculine subjectivity—a concern that could at times, all too easily, spill over into a misogynistic depiction of women as the threatening "other," but that could also, in the best instances, be deeply revealing and even cathartic in the honesty of its confrontation with repressed male fears.

This bill was also distinguished, once again, by some highly accomplished performances, in which actor and role seemed seamlessly fused. As Stu, Kevin O'Connor's "ecstatic plunges into the rich language are breathtaking," Michael Smith noted in the *Voice*: "he is unfalteringly attuned to the play's impulsive, fragmented rhythms" (1965d). In *The Customs Collector*, former Living Theatre actor Warren Finnerty (who also played the silent, threatening cop in *Chicago*) gave another virtuoso performance—definitive, according to Ferlinghetti. Murray Mednick, a poet before he was a playwright, was attracted to Theatre Genesis for the first time by Ferlinghetti's name, but was "so intrigued" by Finnerty's pulsating delivery of the text that he too began to experiment with writing for speaking voices. He met Cook through Finnerty, and shortly after gave him his first one-act play for consideration at the Monday night play readings: *The Box* interested Lee Kissman sufficiently that he volunteered to direct it, in a December 1965 production. Thereafter, Mednick became an almost ever-present figure at both Theatre Genesis and the Poetry Project: "I felt really, really helped by Ralph, and by the church," he recalls, "and I was also influenced by that approach that Ralph called subjective realism. He was interested in the inner life of people—in a Christian sense—an inner quest for meaning. I think of him as a mentor, because he really saved my ass. . . . I don't know what I would've done if I didn't have that support."

Mednick's story is just one of several indicating the development of a core group of like-minded artists at Theatre Genesis. As Leonard Melfi and indeed Kevin O'Connor began to detach themselves from St. Mark's, others began to be attracted by the theater's increasingly distinctive profile. Tony Barsha, for example, arrived at St. Mark's early in 1966: a former beatnik who had dabbled in poetry and playwriting, he found himself "staying across the street on Eleventh Street, and somebody said go check them out because they do play readings there." That April, Genesis premiered Barsha's one-act plays *The Pattern* and *The Trunk*. He too subsequently became a familiar face at St. Mark's, and acknowledges a profound personal debt to Cook. (Prior to discovering Genesis, he confesses, "I didn't know what the fuck I was doing. I was totally lost.") At around the same time, Walter Hadler, who with Mednick, Barsha, and Shepard was to become one of the four key, resident playwrights at Genesis for the remainder of the decade, was also finding his place there. A trained actor, he was first cast in David Scott Milton's play *The Interrogation Room* (January 1966), in which he played the sinister inquisitor of Barbara Young and Murray Paskin (another regular Genesis actor). Hadler's acting experiences at St. Mark's led directly to a desire to articulate his own vocal rhythms and "subjective reality" through playwriting.

Developing Attitude

The emergence of a distinct community of writers and actors at Theatre Genesis was also strongly related to a factor identified by Ralph Cook in his statement for the *Eight Plays from Off-Off-Broadway* anthology: "Theatre Genesis has defined itself in terms of a deeply subjective kind of realism and, within the Off-Off Broadway circuit, an almost conspicuous heterosexuality" (Orzel and Smith 1966, 94). Tony Barsha, who admits that the predominantly heterosexual character of the theater made it the only off-off venue he would have felt comfortable working at, describes the situation even more bluntly when he quips, at least half-seriously, that Genesis consisted of "a bunch of guys, and their babes, and their drugs." It would be worryingly easy to conclude that Cook and his colleagues extended their admiration for the Beats and abstract expressionists to the point of self-consciously recreating the kind of male-dominated environment typical of those scenes in the 1950s, rather than embracing the (notionally) more gender-liberated mood of the 1960s.

Women in fact played a more important part at Theatre Genesis than first meets the eye. From its inception, many of the vital roles both onstage and off were played by such women as Stephanie Gordon, Mimi Davies, Barbara Young, actress O-Lan Johnson (who married Shepard in 1969), and stage manager Georgia Lee Phillips (who married Hadler in the same ceremony).

Asked whether Genesis was essentially a "boys' club," Young acknowledges that "Ralph liked to present that as an idea," but she never saw this as the theater's reality and never felt excluded or belittled: "I think there were some men who maybe thought it was a boys' club, but they were disabused of that notion!" The fact remains, however, that the real creative power at Genesis rested almost solely with a core group of men, while women played subsidiary, supportive roles. Only two plays by female writers (one-acts by Sally Ordway and Shirley Guy) were produced there during the whole of the 1960s, both in the theater's first, most embryonic year of operations.

In terms of "balance" between male and female playwrights, of course, other off-off theaters were not much more equitable: in this prefeminist era, the vast majority of plays being submitted for consideration were by men. Only Judson Poets' Theater made any visible effort to prioritize the work of female playwrights—part of a consciously progressive approach that also saw them explicitly advertising for the services of both white and black actors (this mixed-race casting was another direct legacy of the Living Theatre). Nevertheless, Theatre Genesis was regarded with some suspicion elsewhere on the off-off-Broadway scene precisely because its gender profile was so overt. "I always felt everyone was trying to be butch," Al Carmines notes of his own tendency to avoid St. Mark's, "and I didn't want to be butch. I didn't want anyone to tell me how to be butch." Robert Patrick argues that the macho posturing, such as it was, stemmed from Ralph Cook's unease with the rest of the downtown theater scene, in which "of course almost everybody was gay, and he was a little afraid of that. That was OK, it wasn't like a big thing (except maybe with him), but Theatre Genesis was, you know, what the straight boys were thinking."

Maria Irene Fornes offers what is perhaps the most insightful external analysis of Theatre Genesis in observing that, while much of the work was certainly male-oriented, "it was not macho in the usual way, but something very kind of *defeated*." Here echoing the original sense of the term *beat*—as in beaten down; dropped out—Fornes implicitly connects the attitude of the Genesis writers to the specific environment within which St. Mark's was located. The general attitude projected by their work was, she says, "not *macho* macho, but macho drug, which is different. These were straight men but from the street drug world. Macho drug has this kind of undercurrent of anger, disappointment, possible violence." As has been noted, part of St. Mark's mission was to speak to and for the disaffected people of its immediate neighborhood, and it was thus logical that such "urban alienation" found a voice at Theatre Genesis, especially given that its key writers mostly came from less-than-affluent, blue-collar backgrounds. If Caffe Cino was responding in part to the tastes of the West Village gay community that made up a large proportion of its staff and clientele, and Judson Poets' Theater to the cross-disciplinary interests of Village bohemians, Genesis was, in turn, responding to the genuinely local audience that its free-ticket policy had generated. As Murray Mednick stresses,

> Our audiences were quite mixed. More than most. There were a lot of blacks. We had a lot of street people come to our plays. [St. Mark's is] right next to the Bowery, Second Avenue, First Avenue, and then you get over into Alphabet City. So we were aware of the street element. Guys who didn't understand shit but would really hold you to account for your attitude.

Mednick, himself a heroin user during the later 1960s, is the first to admit that the Genesis writers sometimes tried a little too hard to appear tough or "with it." Yet their attitude was in large part a logical response to these factors, an attempt to reflect—through "subjective realistic" means—on the environment surrounding them. "The reality of St. Mark's community is turbulent, explosive, changing too fast for fixed values or identities, and forbiddingly hard to find a theatrical language for," Michael Smith wrote in 1966, "but Cook [and his playwrights] are hot for adventure," and their plays reflect "reality at a more abstract level: contemporary, urban rhythms of speech, deflected and diffuse communication between characters, disquieting patterns of self-awareness" (1966, 174–75).

Tony Barsha's small but perfectly formed play *The Trunk* (1966) exemplifies several of Smith's points, and goes beyond simple attitude or "vibe," to offer a sophisticated reflection on the lives of the disenfranchised figures it represents. Two wandering men are depicted in the transient nowhere of a bare stage, engaged in the Sisyphean task of dragging a large trunk (the single, focal prop-icon) to some undefined destination. Unable to move it without each other's help, they are bound together in this task, but uncertain of its purpose. To fill in time in their otherwise vacant lives, Jerry repeatedly asks Al, "What's in the trunk?" Al responds with a series of stories that contradict each other. The play is obviously indebted, as were so many others of the period, to the example of Samuel Beckett, and the quickfire dialogue and comic twists make this every bit as much a "vaudeville skit" as George Dennison's play of that title. Nevertheless, Barsha's treatment of his material is distinctive and original. Al and Jerry are unmistakably working class and unmistakably American, with a more-than-passing resemblance to John Steinbeck's Lenny and George, in *Of Mice and Men*—the one is slow and vulnerable, the other sharp and wary. Dragging the trunk along is a labor-related task, and their conversation is more proletarian than those of Beckett's tramps: Al distracts Jerry for some time, for example, with the exciting suggestion that the trunk contains a woman, a stripper, "with blue eyes, pink titties and the little . . . furry thing she keeps between her legs" (Barsha 1966, 6–7). This woman, Al assures Jerry—who has no memory of his past—was in love with him, but felt unworthy of him. Jerry overcame this objection, Al says, by assuring her that "our love is stronger than time" and marrying her, only to leave later, saying, "*(deep male voice)* I have to go. It is something I must do" (9). This is, of course, a ludicrous conflation of pop stereotypes of masculinity (the romantic hero; the troubled loner). Barsha thus playfully manipulates exactly the kind of mass-cultural clichés that, Marxist critics might argue, keep workers blinded to their exploitation.

Having persuaded Jerry to go to sleep, Al confides to the audience (not necessarily any more reliably) that big, dumb Jerry was once a highly articulate union organizer who stood up manfully for the rights of his fellow workers, and who then lost his mind in a suspicious-looking industrial accident. This implausible tale appears to be corroborated when—after Al kicks Jerry in the butt so that he falls and hits his head on a rock (slapstick of the purest kind)—Jerry miraculously rediscovers his lost articulacy. He begins a lengthy address to the audience, a manic monologue in typical Genesis style, on the necessity of not being bought off by deceptive pay rises offered by management:

> Any raise in pay is instantly offset by a raise in prices, which is then rippled across the country in every industry into management's "god of gods"— inflation. That means, my friends and fellow workers, we must say, "Shove your fucking raise. Let's talk about real working class gains." Can you say that? Can you? Well, you'd better. You've got to learn to pass on the buck. The buck means you get fucked. Fucked by the buck. What do we really want? I'll tell you . . . (19)

Jerry continues in this vein, his rhetoric becoming steadily wilder, until he climaxes with an exhortation to the audience that recalls not *Waiting for Godot* but Clifford Odets' quasi-revolutionary drama *Waiting for Lefty*: "Strike until we have won everything. Strike for humanity, for dignity, for power. Strike. Strike. Strike" (19). He then collapses on the floor, holding his head, and reverts to big, dumb Jerry:

Jerry: Boy, that was some kick, Al.
Al: How's your head?
Jerry: My head? Fine. My butt sure hurts. (20)

By returning again to knockabout comedy, Barsha cunningly avoids any suggestion that Jerry's oratory be taken seriously, as agitprop: the whole tone of the play is comic-ironic rather than socially didactic. And yet something about Jerry's socialist analysis, parodic as it is, resonates nonetheless with the basic stage situation of two working men locked into the performance of a task they cannot control, comprehend, or complete. Much the same is true of Al's subsequent stories, which include a fairy-tale rendering of the history of poor Europeans emigrating to the promised American Oz of liberty and abundance; and a meditation on the wonders of consumer goods, which can distract one from the traumatic violence of everyday life. When the trunk is finally revealed to be empty, the sense that there is no adequate explanation or solution to their dilemma is underlined. As they set off again with their burden, Jerry instantly forgets what he has just seen, and asks, with the play's final line, "Hey Al, what's in the trunk?" (30).

The Trunk epitomized the tendency of Theatre Genesis playwrights to create distilled stage metaphors that fuse an implicitly politicized depiction of socially marginal figures with an underlying sense of existential or metaphysical malaise. "The thing that made Genesis," Walter Hadler suggests, tying all this back to the role of the church itself in the theater's foundation, "was that there was a question about the mystery of life, a holy question that was always at work, and that always transcended the politics." As we shall see in subsequent chapters, however, the group's ever-skeptical engagement with the increasingly controversial politics of countercultural dissent was also one of its most significant contributions, as the decade heated up.

❡ In One Act: On the Aesthetics of Off-Off-Broadway Playwriting

A lot of us were working on things we'd call performance pieces now. . . . I wasn't interested in writing "play" plays. I like it when there's a pileup and everyone dies at the end because it makes for such a nice curtain, but I was more interested in the inner life of the character. A lot of the things I did were monologues, and you can do that with one act. For a three- or four-act you wouldn't have enough material—much better to bop them with a couple of metaphors, slip them a simile or two, and let the audience get to a nice late dinner.

—H. M. Koutoukas

By mid-decade, it was clear to many observers not only that a new playwriting "movement" had emerged off-off-Broadway, but that the plays staged by the Cino, Judson, La Mama, and Genesis had become an identifiable alternative to the mainstream, rather than a tryout for it. Other new theaters continued to pop up (many of them short-lived), but these ventures tended simply to reinforce the importance of the leading four. Early in 1966, for example, Ntoni Bastiano established his Playwrights' Workshop Club in a Chelsea loft, on Seventh Avenue at Twenty-third Street, adopting the same operating approach as La Mama, with private club status and a one-dollar weekly membership fee. An actor and writer who had worked around the downtown scene, Bastiano believed his venue would fill a need that the other off-off-Broadway houses were not addressing. There had to be a place, he suggested, dedicated to the writers of realist dramas and musical comedies, rather than to the "avant-garde and abstract." Within a year, however, as Robert Pasolli noted in the *Voice*, Bastiano was forced to close the loft because of "the mounting debt problem produced by his absent audience. . . . Part of the club's problem has been its commitment to the naturalistic playwright, [which has] cut off his theatre from the animating spirit of off-off-Broadway. If the traditional play has its place, it is the new forms and the experiments that provide the milieu with its juice" (1967a).

As Pasolli's comments indicate, off-off-Broadway productions had developed an audience that expected the alternative and challenging, rather than the more conventional. And yet, as has been indicated in previous chapters, this experimental profile had come about as much by accident as by design, as writers began to respond not only to the opportunities offered by these new spaces, but also to the peculiar physical challenges they presented, and particularly to their emphasis on presenting one-act plays. Initially the necessary result of practical considerations, this prioritization of short plays had liberated writers from the conventional expectation that they stretch their material over two or three acts to create a "full evening's entertainment"—an expectation that tends necessarily to place emphasis on a play's *linear* trajectory, in terms of cause-and-effect narrative and developing "themes." By contrast, the one-act form relies less on linear dramatic development than on the presentation of an immediate, theatrical "moment"—staging not so much a story but a *single act*. Rather than "covering ground" narratively, off-off-Broadway writers tended to stay in one place—literally, the small space of the stage—and to view that place prismatically, creating a variety of perspectives on the central dramatic circumstance by "riffing" improvisationally around it. They keenly felt the need for a central, theatrical image around which a play could cohere. Jean-Claude van Itallie, for example, notes that he learned from Ellen Stewart the importance of finding such a focus point: "The creative question is, 'What do you want to see up there on stage? What is visually exciting?'" (Bryer 1995, 248).

This emphasis on the one-act form is, of course, one of the major reasons for the comparative critical neglect of off-off-Broadway playwriting. One-act plays have always tended to be underrecognized and underanalyzed, simply because they are rarely produced professionally (for obvious commercial reasons). The length of a dramatic text, moreover, can be all too easily confused with "depth": a widespread, largely unexamined assumption is that if it's shorter, it must "say less." However, a painting or sculpture may be taken in by the viewer in a few moments, but linger in the imagination for a lifetime—longer than many a full-length "moving picture." Anyone who has seen the ten- to fifteen-minute plays of Samuel Beckett staged well—*Rockaby*, for example, or *Not I*—knows that less can indeed be very much more. As has often been noted, Beckett's short pieces are akin to paintings for the stage, and his work demonstrates incontrovertibly that the one-act form is distinctive in being able to focus with greater clarity on a particular moment, a distilled image, a character in crisis. These pieces for single actors are also, of course, far more striking in an intimate theater space than in a large one (just as it is difficult to appreciate most paintings from the far end of the gallery).

Koutoukas's suggestion that many off-off-Broadway plays might best be described as "performance pieces" is significant in a number of respects. For one thing, the term indicates that these works tended to acknowledge their own status *as* performances. With limited resources for sets, and with the proximity of actors and audiences creating an inescapable sense of face-to-face intimacy, it made little sense to pretend that these plays were simply fictions taking place in another time and place. Creating a self-contained "play" world, through conventional, fourth-wall illusionism, was an impractical response to these spaces. A better option was to acknowledge the audience's presence, by addressing them directly or by emphasizing the theatrical artifice of the play itself—by setting up a double exposure of competing realities, balancing the provisional creation of a dramatic elsewhere with a self-conscious acknowledgement of the "real time" theatrical present. Such strategies are apparent in most of the pieces discussed in the preceding chapters.

Second, the term *performance piece* also stresses the fundamental importance of the performer to these plays. Off-off-Broadway playwrights rarely wrote texts for themselves to perform onstage, in the way that the "performance artists" of more recent decades have (although chapter 16 deals with some notable exceptions). Yet they were well aware that, with limited staging resources and limited playing time with which to draw in an audience, the performers' presence, wit, and charisma were central to a play's impact. Whether they were writing monodramas, as Koutoukas often did, or multi-character pieces, off-off writers, knowing their community, frequently wrote with particular actors in mind. In the best cases—as we saw in the last chapter, for example, with Kevin O'Connor and Warren Finnerty—the virtues of performer and text became inseparable, symbiotic.

Third, the designation *performance piece* might also be taken to imply a connection with those forms of performance art that spring more directly from visual art practice (the happenings of Kaprow and others were, of course, an early form of such work), and which thus emphasize the immediate physical, sculptural, and visual dimensions of the staged event, rather than more "dramatic" concerns like character and narrative. Similarly, off-off-Broadway plays frequently stressed the immediate, "phenomenological" presence of onstage bodies and objects, at least as much as their signifying functions. For example, a particular prop or costume might be seen not only to symbolize something within the world of the play, but to "be" onstage, in the more immediate, three-dimensional sense so often neglected in the mainstream theater (the sculpted doll outfits for *America Hurrah* are a prime example). In Foster's

Balls, the use of swinging Ping-Pong balls in sharp points of light replaced the physical presence of actors altogether: semiotically speaking, the balls "mean" little or nothing in relation to the play's spoken text, but their simple, rhythmic presence functioned as a mesmerizing counterpoint to the offstage voices.

I do not want to overstate the connection to visual art (one that probably never occurred to many of the writers themselves), but it is worth noting that visual art was itself, during this period, being described in some quarters as "theatrical." For example, in his famously intemperate essay "Art and Object-hood" (1967), the modernist critic Michael Fried accused the new wave of minimalist sculptors like Donald Judd, Robert Morris, and Carl Andre of abandoning the traditionally self-contained nature of fine artworks, by creating pieces that depended for their meaning and impact on their contextual location as objects within the gallery space, and on their contingent, physical relationship with the viewer. Tony Smith's *Die*, for example, was a six-foot cube that, standing on the gallery floor at fractionally above average head height, was neither tall enough to be monumental nor small enough to be looked down on as an object: instead, it invited one's direct, physical engagement by, say, getting up on tip-toe to look at the top surface. For Fried, this active, three-way dynamic of object, viewer, and space constituted "a kind of *stage* presence," and therefore disqualified such works from being considered as "art," on the grounds that "art degenerates as it approaches the condition of theatre" (Battcock 1995, 127, 141). Fried's attack is ironically amusing, given that conventional drama, and indeed conventional dramatic criticism, was at the time so *little* concerned with the physical context in which a play appeared, and tended to assume passive reception as the standard audience response. Conversely, though, off-off-Broadway plays were often highly "theatrical" in exactly the way Fried outlines: although the spectator might not be able to move physically around the stage, he or she was nonetheless brought into an active engagement with the event by a variety of playwriting strategies that responded directly to the specifics of site and scale.

In order to start unpacking this and the other broad points sketched in so far, I want to turn to a more detailed analysis of three contrasting plays. Each was mounted on the same, small platform stage of the Caffe Cino, but made very different uses of the conditions that that context imposed. The plays are strong pieces of work individually, but I have selected them not for their "exceptional" qualities but as exemplars of certain approaches and strategies common in off-off-Broadway playwriting. In each case, audiences were presented with immediate *experiences* rather than just dramatic narratives, and the spectator—rather than passively absorbing neatly worked-through themes or ideas—was directly implicated in, or interpolated into, the event itself.

The Bed

"I think it's time you wrote that 'existentialist' play," Joe Cino reportedly told Robert Heide early in 1965: "But make it a play for blond men" (Gordy 1998, 317). The resulting play, *The Bed* (1965), runs only a few pages and presents a banal, desultory conversation between Jack and Jim, two figures who seem almost incapable of getting themselves out of bed. Despite its brevity, however, *The Bed* usually ran for thirty to forty minutes in performance, simply because of the extended pauses that Heide calls for in his stage directions, during which nothing of any consequence happens. The play, in short, is set in real time, which *drags*. Unlike most Cino plays, the script is almost entirely lacking in humor, or in other entertaining elements that might distract from Heide's primary emphasis on the passing of time. It sounds terminally tedious, but Robert Dahdah's production of *The Bed* proved so popular with audiences that it became the third most frequently presented play in the Cino's history, eventually clocking up over 150 performances.

What prevents the piece from becoming merely boring is its almost microscopic attention to detail—which capitalizes on the constricted stage space and the immediate proximity of the spectator. At the Cino, the eponymous, large white double bed, tilted slightly toward the audience for visibility—filled almost the entire platform stage. Effectively framed by the white rectangle of the bed itself, the lethargic behavior of Jack and Jim becomes a strangely compelling spectacle: at such close range, every little twist of the neck, stretch of an arm, or flicker of an eye can be a source of voyeuristic intrigue. At the Cino, part of the appeal for the audience was this frank objectification of two attractive, underwear-clad male bodies—actors Larry Burns (blond) and Jim Jennings (not). Indeed, simply placing two men in bed together onstage was, at this time, a near-revolutionary gesture. And yet the men's sexuality, perhaps even their gender, is also, on some basic level, incidental: the play refers, beyond these specifics, to the universal experience of waking up to a sour, bored, nothing-to-do kind of day.

In a sense, *The Bed* provides the missing link between Beckettian absurdism (two men filling in empty time) and the New York avant-garde's fascination with the detailed observation of banality. Andy Warhol's films *Eat* and

Sleep, for example, each show a young man performing just those activities for extended periods of time. Warhol, in fact, loved *The Bed*, and shot a film version in a loft setting, using the original Cino actors: he then spliced sections of it into his 1966 split-screen movie *The Chelsea Girls* (a film about people sitting in rooms at the Chelsea Hotel). What the film experience could not reproduce, however, was the raw physical proximity of performers and spectators in the tiny space of the Cino. While it is often said that Warhol's movies highlight the fact of the spectator's voyeurism, the viewer is still "protected" by the fact that the thing being stared at is not actually there. Onstage, *The Bed* is, in effect, all about the act of watching real bodies just a few feet away, and as such induces a self-consciousness in the audience that is at once pleasurable and discomforting. At such close quarters, moreover, it is difficult for the spectator to watch *The Bed* without falling into a similarly torpid mood, and thus becoming strangely complicit in the proceedings.

The spectator's self-consciousness is further heightened by the fact that *The Bed* does not render itself up easily to "interpretation" of its "dramatic content." The play's broken, stilted dialogue communicates a few basic facts about the character's lives, but it is essentially little more than a skeleton on which to hang the nonact of nothing happening. While Heide's subject matter may be said to include "existential ennui, boredom, drugs, booze, alienation" (as he himself indicates in a note preceding the text), none of these things is actually discussed, "thematically," by the characters, except in a kind of jaded, heard-it-all-before tone of self-emptying parody:

Jim: On and on and on. You. Me. Sex is dead. No, it's God. God is dead. No,
        it's Nietzsche, Nietzsche is dead. No, I am alive, here, and yet . . .
Jack: Why don't you just drop dead? (Heide 1965, n.p.)

To hear these lines delivered in an appropriately lethargic, slowed-down manner, is to hear Martin Esslin's meaningful explanation of "the theater of the absurd" being reduced, itself, to an absurdity. Similarly, when Jack at one point picks up his bedside clock—which has stopped—and subjects it to extended scrutiny, the play seems both to invite "interpretation" and to sardonically reject it: "Shakes clock. Indicates throwing of object (clock) out of window. Image: shortstop hurling a baseball. Looks at object clock. Studies it for a moment. Laughs. Puts clock back in its place." The tight focus of the play has shrunk even tighter, to the examination of an ordinary household object, but is this stopped clock symbolic of something—a sense of being frozen in time, perhaps, or even the fact of mortality itself—or is it simply, physically, a stopped clock?

The play's tendency to present its audience with blank, unspoken questions becomes inescapable when Jim turns on a phonograph to play a pop song (the Dave Clarke Five's "Anyway You Want It") at full volume. The song is played from start to finish, and during these few minutes neither actor moves or speaks: "They wear blank expressions on their faces and appear not to be listening to the sound." Subsequently, Jim gets up and leaves the space—"maybe. . . . for a cup of coffee . . . To . . . uh . . . get some cigarettes." After another silence, Jack restarts the turntable and plays the song all the way through, all over again, sitting almost motionlessly. "Record end: reject," reads Heide's final stage direction. This repeated playing of an entire song bears similarities, perhaps, to Jack Gelber's *The Connection*, with its long jazz interludes between dialogue. In that play, however, one can watch the music itself being played, and the junkies nodding along to it. The musical sequences in *The Bed*, by contrast, are theater as deadly still life. An unsettling incongruity is created through this juxtaposition of bright, upbeat, canned music with the rigid, empty stares of the "live" actors. A space has been opened up, a yawning gap between sound and image, and again, spectators have little choice but to insert themselves into that gap and choose a response—be it irritation at the inaction, enjoyment of the music, heightened awareness of one's voyeuristic scrutiny, or whatever. The play, Elenore Lester noted tellingly in the *Voice*, "achieves its most alive moments in complete stasis" (1965b).

Medea

The use of such disjunctive juxtapositions was a recurrent feature of off-off-Broadway plays—and indeed of other creative experiments of the period, in dance, music, films, and visual arts. In few cases, however, was incongruity pursued to quite such a bewildering degree as in H. M. Koutoukas's version of *Medea*, subtitled *The Stars May Understand* (1965), which converts Euripides' scenario into a "single act" by eschewing most of the narrative, and focusing all its attention on the crucial, climactic scene in which Medea carries out the murder of her children, in vengeance on their father Jason. This version of the tale, however, is set in a self-service laundromat, and Medea kills her baby son by placing him in a washing machine. "She closes the door," reads the pivotal stage direction: "Slowly she puts a coin in. Chaotic music up."

> *Medea* (SCREAMING): Oh wretched fate—damned destiny
> That such love should turn to THIS.
> (Koutoukas 1965, 11–12)

Jason arrives in high dudgeon and attempts to turn off the machine, only to have Medea hurl Clorox in his face.

This collision of classical tragedy and contemporary "pop" banality might appear to render the piece a mere "put-on" (to use a phrase much beloved of 1960s critics). Indeed, Koutoukas himself described the piece, as he did all his work, as a "camp" rather than a "play." Appearing the year after Susan Sontag's landmark essay "Notes on Camp" (1964), which had for the first time made "the camp sensibility" a topic for intellectual discussion, *Medea* appeared at first glance to fulfil Sontag's description of camp as essentially lacking in depth or seriousness, as a prizing of style and artifice over substance. Certainly, the piece is intended to be delivered in an exaggeratedly theatrical manner, as the description of the heroine's first entrance makes clear: "Her arm covers her whole face excepting her eyes," the stage direction reads; "the drape of her sleeve veils her whole body and facial features" (3). Accompanied by ominous music and an "intense violet light upon MEDEA," this high-melo-dramatic entrance was played with aplomb in the Cino production by Charles Stanley's tall, gangling drag Medea. Each of these elements added further to the play's jarringly incongruous mix of elements, its foregrounding of theatrical artifice.

Perhaps most jarring of all is the play's highly formalized language, an accomplished pastiche of the declamatory verse style of the Greek original, which would be suitable for broadcasting the voice to a giant amphitheater, but must have seemed absurdly excessive within the intimate spaces Koutoukas was writing for. And yet, crucially, that language seems to demand to be delivered with the utmost seriousness, rather than in any knowingly "campy" way. By Koutoukas's own account, the play was initially inspired by a newspaper report of a woman in Harlem who killed her child by placing it in a washing machine. That story instantly connected, in his mind, with the Medea myth, and in many respects the play suggests a sincere attempt on its author's part to come to terms with the horrific reality of such an act. Accordingly, Medea's extended central monologue articulates her passion and anger with real force:

> I am the rage
> I am the scourge
> The heart and tenderness and hurt
> Of all things that have been left to die—
> Wasted on the shores of useless love.
> Features lost and confused in another image—
> Medea draws her portrait anew.
> Medea draws her features strong, alone,
> In fire, madness and with bloody soil.
>> No one, no thing, no God
>> Dare deny Medea the rightness
>> Of her insanity.
>
> (6)

This forceful, rhetorical tone is pursued throughout most of the play's text, which contains few overtly humorous lines. "The language is high-flown as befits tragedy, the tragic impulse is pursued without deviation, and Koutoukas has injected a philosophical content of evident seriousness," Michael Smith noted in the *Voice:* "But the comic effect of the setting is certainly not unintended. And what," he concludes, "are we to make of that?" (1965e).

The spectator is thus left uncertain, even bewildered, by the juxtapositional incongruities inherent in Koutoukas's basic premise. This loss of bearings is exacerbated because the piece—playing on the immediate proximity of audience to stage—interpolates its viewers into the action from the outset, rather than allowing them to observe passively. The piece opens as the child's nurse (the only character besides Medea and Jason) appears onstage and directs her monologue toward the audience:

> WOMEN OF CORINTH LAY DOWN YOUR LAUNDRY!
> The grandson of the SUN sleeps—
> The son of a demi-goddess dreams
> Of glories he will never see
> Honors he will never be paid
>
> (*Rocks the baby in her arms, then lays it in a clothes basket. Viper-like, hissing:*)
>
> Must you always gather like maggots
> At tragedy's door
> Or do you free yourself of guilt
> By coming here to bleach your clothes?
>
> (1)

The lines are calculatedly ridiculous, yet it is not easy simply to laugh at the speech, if it is delivered with the required passion and urgency. Cast in the role of the "women of Corinth"—who in Euripides' original make up the play's chorus—the spectators are immediately confronted, challenged: they become party to events in the present, rather than simply observing a distant Greek past. Moreover, this blurring of dramatic past and theatrical present adds further to the play's disorienting impact, since the nurse, like the audience, appears already to know the outline of the narrative that is about to unfold: "Medea comes to this place this night," she tells us, "Preceded by her myth!" Medea enters on cue, veiled up to her eyes, groaning: "Oh wretched, wrecking myth!" (3). She seems haunted not only by her anger at Jason, and her murder of Creon, but by centuries of being mythologized as a murderous child-killer. And this before she has killed him.

To return to Smith: what *are* we to make of all this? As scholarly analyses have noted, the use of radical incongruity is often central to what has been called high-camp comedy. In Oscar Wilde's *The Importance of Being Earnest*, for example, the humor of the dialogue depends on its being performed absolutely deadpan by the actors, as if they are discussing matters of the deepest importance: it is the rift between form and content—between the ridiculousness of the subject matter and the formal seriousness of the language patterns and delivery—that drives the play's hilarity. In *Medea*, however, Koutoukas takes this principle to another level. In this case, the content is both serious and ridiculous, and the incongruities seem to create not only high-camp comedy, but a kind of high-camp *tragedy*. Camp, Koutoukas maintains, is "deadly serious," and the sense of viewing an insane, out-of-joint world is communicated powerfully to the audience through his bewildering, multilayered use of dramatic disjuncture. The familiar, comfortable devices of dramatic logic are dispensed with, to create— perhaps—a deranged modern equivalent of ancient Greek myth, in which rationality and order collapse under the inexorable onslaught of fate.

Tellingly, this approach to the material is complemented by the play's depiction of Jason's Corinth as a culture in which the rule of rationality has numbed human passion. Medea the barbarian foreigner, guided by unfettered passion, thus becomes its avenging antithesis:

> Medea and Medea alone revenges all nature and will send
> Greece screaming from its vile logic, its agoras,
> its chattering imitations of its cheap clever Gods.
> (*Softly*) MEDEA WILL REMIND THE GODS OF WHAT FURY MEANS.
> She will shake the foundations of their laws, rape open
> the fears of the young, quake up a thousand fears and
> force them down Corinth's throat.
> (5)

Koutoukas here raises the murder of Medea's son beyond the simple, personal level of revenging Jason's treachery to a kind of cultural terrorism (or even radical feminism?). The sheer rhetorical force of her language and rage invites the spectator toward an unexpected empathy with her "insane" actions. As the speech continues, moreover, the titanic tone gradually gives way to quieter reflection, on Medea's lost innocence, on the loss of her homeland, on her shattered dreams of love, all of which are delivered with similarly affective language: "I have wept till my eyes could no longer see the reason. I have screamed out with pain that made music seem inconsequential" (8). When she finally places the child in the washing machine, her claim that this is an act of saving love, delivering him from the world's cruelties, seems almost plausible. Paul Foster recalls this climactic moment as one of off-off-Broadway's defining moments, stressing both the immediate proximity and the disturbing incongruity of the events: "Medea was there for you to reach out and touch, forming the unspeakable crime of infanticide in her mind. Then she threw her baby into a laundromat and washed it to death with Oxydol. She slammed the lid down and set the dial on HEAVY LOAD. How can you forget things like that?" (1979, 7). Smith's *Voice* review put it slightly differently: "*Medea* is so eccentric as to be nearly unthinkable, [but] I can't swear that the quality is wrong for the subject" (1965e).

You May Go Home Again

Koutoukas's *Medea* was one of a number of off-off-Broadway plays demonstrating that explicit theatricality—almost demanded by the particulars of the spaces themselves—could be used not just to entertain but to facilitate the development of the event's emotional complexity and poignancy. Rather than being guided in its emotional responses and identifications by the pretense of conventional storytelling and characterization, the audience is made to grapple with its own conflicting responses, as it attempts to make sense of the often contradictory information it is asked to assimilate. This is also true of David Starkweather's *You May Go Home Again*, which, though less abrasively disorienting than *Medea*, is still more sophisticated in its use of theatricality. First produced at the Cino in 1963 and then reworked under the author's direction in 1965, this is a "total theater" event, combining dancelike movement sequences, physical comedy, and tableaux vivants, and a detailed musical score that provides line-by-line rhythmic commentary on the spoken dialogue. *You May Go Home Again* is thus the functional antithesis of *The Bed's* hypernaturalistic minimalism, yet this play too depends for impact on its staging in a constricted space, into which a family of four—mother, father, sister, brother—are permanently crowded. Even during private moments of individual reflection, these characters perform their lines and movements in immediate proximity to one another, as if to emphasize the smothering closeness of the family bond.

Compression is in fact the key structural principle here: where time seems elongated by Heide's play, Starkweather squeezes it like a concertina, using a quasi-filmic "editing" approach to cut rapidly from scene to scene, moment to moment. Yet this fluidity functions not to open out the dramatic space, as film would, but to reinforce the sense of confinement. The family is introduced, for example, using a "dining room scene" in which the actors bend their knees and perform a stylized mime to indicate sitting and eating. In a matter of seconds, the play cuts from breakfast ("Good morning, dear"; "Good morning, Mom") to lunch ("A nice lunch, Mom") to supper ("Oh, look at the sun"; "Time for bed for you"), the shifts punctuated only by lethargic movements suggesting the passage of the day (Poland and Mailman 1972, 15). The play thus sketches in a sense of the family's life as somnolent, static, and dull, while never boring the audience. As the action progresses, we are presented instead with neatly compressed "takes" on the family's circumstances—as when Mom performs her Sisyphean labors of scrubbing and cleaning, while her family assembles first into an audience, "in positions suggesting a bleacher," cheering her on, and then as cheerleaders themselves: "U rah rah, Perfect Ma" (16). Abandoning her cleaning, Mom imagines an idealized picture of the family, as Dad, Peter, and Linda form freeze-frames suggesting happy snapshot poses. Yet her daydream morphs into a nightmare vision of being "SWALLOWED BY HER CHILDREN" (17), as her menfolk pick her up bodily, turn her upside down, and hold her as if feeding her into Linda's gaping mouth. Hopes and fears are thus deftly juxtaposed, with the overt theatricality evoking an immediate sense of the family's underlying emotional turmoil.

Again and again in this play, complex feelings and relationships are sketched in quickly and powerfully, without the need for extended exposition. The piece thus provides excellent examples of another key off-off-Broadway playwriting strategy. "It seems to me that you can speak to people in a new kind of shorthand, by the use of dramatic clues," the Open Theatre's Megan Terry has noted, pointing to the influence of popular media on this approach: "People are very well educated, from films, radio, television—we know all the stories now. [We can] connect the dots, the incomplete completes itself"

(Savran 1988, 245). The spectator, in other words, is required actively to "fill in the gaps" between the quickly changing images and scenes. This imaginative involvement becomes such an integral part of viewing *You May Go Home Again* that the spectator creates a whole other layer of images, "in the mind's eye," as it were, to complete the incomplete. In describing his sister's fiancé, whom the family considers beneath her, Peter declares that "he just doesn't measure up. Well look at him!" Pointing down at floor of the stage in front of him, he adds, "At the very most he's only fourteen inches high!" (20). The play's blurring of fantasy and physical fact are by this point so well established that, in that moment, the spectator "sees" a fourteen-inch-high man in front of Peter, staring back up at him. The effect is both comic and oddly unnerving, particularly in the way it seems to bring the spectator "onside" with Peter, in his patronizing treatment of Linda. Yet in other moments, the temptation is to side with Linda against Peter, or with the children against the parents: the play leaps so quickly from point to point that it creates a kaleidoscopic swirl of conflicting sympathies and identifications.

The audience thus becomes implicated in an emotional tug-of-war, a fact emphasized, in particular, by the presence of a fifth character, "the Executioner." This dark, embittered figure, with black hooded gown and ax, turns out to be the externalized self-image of "David," the family's long-lost elder son, whose bleak outlook on the world is clearly bound up with his own conflicted feelings toward his family and their views. "Where is that boy that all the world loves?!" Mom asks, receiving the distant reply, "In the basement, Mama, chopping up God" (19). Yet David is ostensibly many miles away, presumably in the big city to which David Starkweather himself had fled, and so is represented—via another neat compression of space—standing on a second small platform, placed in the audience area. The Executioner, who opens the play with a gloriously bizarre, misanthropic monologue, views the family scathingly from a distance, and thus becomes a framing device for the rest of the action: the audience, physically aligned with this figure as external observers of the family, seems to view them *through* the distorting lens of his loathing (whether they like it or not).

It also becomes clear, however, that this loathing is helplessly entangled with an intense love and pity for the family: try as he does, David cannot separate himself from them emotionally. In a strange, dreamlike sequence, they attempt a nighttime boat journey toward him (without moving off their stage), which he rebuffs. Yet in the play's climactic moments, he himself crosses the gulf between them, shedding his executioner's robes along the way. Stepping onto the main stage, he is welcomed by his family as if in an airport arrivals hall. The play's fluency and theatricality are also shed at this point: in a devastatingly simple, naturalistic scene, the characters haltingly search for appropriate words of greeting, in inadequate but heartfelt attempts to bridge the emotional divisions between them. *You May Go Home Again*, Lanford Wilson recalls, "just ripped me apart. [It] was filled with hate but was all about love. It was filled with horrible, horrible portraits that were all done so beautifully" (Bryer 1995, 290).

String Games and Card Tricks

As should be clear from these brief analyses, the three plays discussed thus far, though widely variant in style and tone, are best regarded not as self-contained works of dramatic literature, but as blueprints for performance events. All three reinvent theatrical convention for their own ends, setting up complex confrontations in time and space between actors and audiences. Moreover, while each one implies an outsider's perspective on social mores and institutions—as one might expect from playwrights who, as gay men, were very conscious of their own position on the social margin—these pieces never impose a particular viewpoint or "message" on their audiences, engaging them instead in an open-ended process of negotiated response. "I purposely made it so that anybody could project whatever they wanted," Koutoukas notes of his work: "I left all public statements wide enough so that [he flicks his hand], 'As you desire!'"

   This sense of performative interaction divides off-off-Broadway playwriting from the self-consciously earnest work of mainstream dramatists like Arthur Miller: "No playwright can be praised for his high seriousness," Miller wrote seriously, "and at the same time be praised for not trying to teach" (1958, 12). If the playwright's task was to teach, it followed that the audience's task was to decode the lesson, to correctly interpret the play's content and learn from its conclusions. Even the younger, "off-Broadway" generation led by Edward Albee tended to adhere to similar assumptions. As Albee himself proposed in notes to *Box-Mao-Box* (1968), playwrights had an "obligation" to "make some statement about the condition of 'man' (as it is put)" (Albee 1971, 124). The underground generation, however, tended to adopt the attitude outlined by Susan Sontag in her landmark 1964 essay "Against Interpretation." "Real art has the capacity to make us nervous," she stressed: "By reducing the work of art to its content and then interpreting that, one tames the work of art" (1967, 8). For Sontag, artists were not teachers or philosophers, but the creators of aesthetic experiences. Sam Shepard made a similar point, more bluntly: the notion that "playwrights are some special brand of intellectual fruitcake with special answers to special problems that confront the world at large" was, he insisted, "a crock of shit. When you write a play you work out like a musician on a piece of music. You find all the rhythms and the melody and the harmonies and take them as they come" (1971, 1).

None of this is intended to suggest that off-off-Broadway plays were empty of potential meaning or substance, simply that—as Shepard has pithily put it—"ideas emerge from plays, not the other way around" (Marranca 1981, 215). The emphasis, in other words, was not so much on the writer's "intentions" for the play as on the audience's reception of it: the traditional hierarchy of playwright as author(itarian) and audience as passive receiver was rejected in favor of a cocreation of meaning. For Ellen Stewart, the determination of her leading playwrights to pursue an intuitive, spontaneous creativity, by tapping into subconscious impulses rather than strictly rational ones, helped to create a "subliminal rapport" within the theater space that "eliminates the separation of artist and audience that one is so aware of in 'contemporary' theatre" (Orzel and Smith 1966, 163).

The titular activity of Rochelle Owens's *The String Game*, produced at Judson in 1965, provides an appropriate metaphor for this kind of playful exchange. A group of Eskimos sit throwing a piece of knotted string into the air and arguing about what picture it makes when it falls: "This is a seal or maybe a vulva" (Owens 1968, 35). The missionary priest to this imagined polar community, Father Bontempo, thinks it must be "an angel or the Lord," but the Eskimos find this unlikely: "this is the vulva of a seal." Truth, like beauty, Owens seems to imply, lies in the eye of the beholder rather than in any absolute reality, and those who force their beliefs on others are not to be trusted. In *The String Game*, the attempts of traders and churchmen to impose a foreign worldview on the Eskimos—by colonizing their culture with capitalism and Catholicism—are particularly suspect. And yet this is no neat, anti-imperialist tract of a play: Owens avoids imposing political interpretations of her own on the situation, presenting instead a series of ironically ambiguous twists. It seems, for example, that Bontempo suffers more from his own absolutism than do the Eskimos: driven by doctrine to live in an alien culture, he feels deprived of the comforts of home, and when he is finally supplied with a good Italian meal, he gorges himself and chokes to death. Meanwhile the Eskimos, rather than coming across as innocent victims of exploitation, seem drily resigned to the loss of the old ways, and quite content to sit idly around playing games while collecting "government checks." They also enjoy ridiculing Cecil the half-breed, although it remains unclear whether Cecil is ridiculed because he is racially impure, or because he is an idiot. (Or is he an idiot because he has been ridiculed?) Desperately trying to prove himself, he buys into the capitalist myth of the self-made man and—responding to an implausibly long advertisement on the back of a matchbook—sets himself up in business as a shoe salesman. He then attempts to enlist the Father's help in his sales campaign, by bribing him with Italian food.

The String Game is a beautifully judged little play: bizarre, funny, and sad by turns, it seems inherently political, and yet completely nondidactic. As in many other plays of the period, it uses irony to subvert and question both received assumptions and its own implied concerns. It thus stands as a neat illustration of Owens's suggestion that, in the 1960s, she was part of a generation of experimental dramatists whose work implied a resistance, "in both form and content, [to] the absolute power of organized doctrine, principles, and procedures" (1989, 20).

In some cases, this ingrained suspicion of authority led writers to distrust even their own received assumptions about the world. Maria Irene Fornes, for example, notes that her musical play *Promenade*—also first produced at Judson in 1965—started out as an entirely open-ended writing exercise, an attempt to evade conscious manipulation of her material. She sought, instead, to take her own subconscious "by surprise." Adopting a method of chance juxtaposition, Fornes began by writing words on three different packs of cards: the first was a series of generic scene locations, the second, a series of character types, and the third, a series of possible opening lines. Shuffling the decks and picking a card from each, she began her first scene in response to the words "Jail" and "Aristocrats," by depicting two prisoners—105 and 106—digging their way out of jail and surfacing at a dinner party for the decadent rich. Instantly, certain possible narrative threads appeared, but Fornes continued to draw new cards whenever she needed fresh inspiration for a new scene, rather than allowing herself to impose too many conscious "ideas" about where the play should go, or what it was "about." The result of this improvisatory approach is that—considered as "a single act"—*Promenade* coheres around the image of a crazy, freewheeling journey, moving from one short, skitlike scene to the next. At Judson this was literalized by Malcolm Spooner's set design—a huge, illustrated storybook backdrop, whose pages were turned to depict different locales for each scene, even as the performers themselves stayed, physically speaking, in the same place.

Ever since *Promenade*, Fornes has regarded her task, as a playwright, as akin to that of a permissive parent, allowing her "children" to run and play rather than forcing behavioral patterns on them. Indeed, she now draws a clear distinction between her first play, *Tango Palace* (1963), and her work from *Promenade* onward, regarding the first as an "off-Broadway play" and the others as "off-off-Broadway." The fact that *Tango Palace* was not originally produced off-Broadway, but rather by Herbert Blau's San Francisco Actors' Workshop, indicates that her distinction is qualitative rather than geographic. *Tango Palace*, Fornes explains, is the only piece she ever wrote by starting out with a clear, conscious idea—a preconceived intention—for what the piece was to become. Appearing to owe something to Ionesco or Genet, and based—by Fornes's admission—on personal experiences, it depicts two characters locked in a nightmarish closed circle: everything that Leopold says and does seems preempted and determined by a deck of cards that Isidore holds in his hands. The metaphorical implications are clear (Isidore "holds all the cards"), and the play provides a powerful and disturbing image of a kind of sadomasochistic interdependence. *Promenade*, by striking contrast, breaks away from this closed system by envisaging a world in which the characters' identities and relationships—far from being fixed into predetermined patterns—are constantly being reimagined through performative role-play. The prisoners, for example, are portrayed less as criminals than as childlike innocents, abroad in a strange world like latter-day Candides. Lacking clear identities of their own (they have only numbers, not names), 105 and 106 observe the behavior of those around them in order to decide what roles they should adopt for themselves: "I've just discovered what life is all about," declares 105 at one point, before bursting into song by way of demonstration:

> To walk down the street
> With a mean look in my face
> A cigarette in my right hand
> And a toothpick in the left
> To alternate between the cigarette
> And the toothpick
> Ah! That's life."
>   —(Schroeder 1968, 17–18)

Promenade often seems reminiscent of Brecht, in its use of such pithily aphoristic observations, set to music. Where Fornes differs from Brecht, however, is that her aphorisms cannot be pinned to an authorial statement on the social conditions that 105 and 106 observe. As with Owens, a social conscience supports the writing but never dictates a response: rather, the text is dominated by a sense of contradiction and paradox, which always throws the onus back on the spectator to respond to the material. "Riches made them dumb. Yes, riches made them dumb," the aristocrats' Servant (who has taken on the role of guide and mentor to the prisoners) notes of her masters: "It's not worth it, then?" ask 105 and 106, to which she replies, simply, "It's worth it" (15). Performing the role of the idle rich might render one mentally vacuous, but who would not choose wealth over poverty? Such perverse (a)logic recurs throughout the play almost as a formal principle, alongside the equally persistent concern with the transformability inherent in role-play. To avoid capture by the jailer, for example, the prisoners switch their costumes with a reckless driver and the man he has just run down. The latter duo are promptly arrested, the numbers on their jackets being taken as proof of their identity. "Neither probe nor ignore / That the clothes make the man," notes the Servant: "Isn't it true that costumes / Change the course of life?" (Schroeder 1968, 20).

Promenade epitomizes the off-off-Broadway movement's widespread rejection of the psychological determinism that dominated American theater at the time, thanks particularly to Method-school acting and naturalistic dramaturgy. "The biggest thing that actors have to get over," Lawrence Kornfeld notes of directing work like Fornes's, "is what they're taught about motivation. 'The character can't do this,' they'll say: 'It's not in their psychology.' Nonsense! People can do anything, and people *do* almost anything." Even in those off-off plays where characters seem trapped by fate or family or circumstance, the potential for sudden revelations or turnabouts is always there—as in *You May Go Home Again*, when Starkweather's David does indeed return home, despite the past. Circumstances and identities can shift at will because, for playwrights embracing the kind of creative freedoms encouraged by Joe Cino and others, the familiar dynamics of cause-and-effect narrative logic were far less important than the physically limited, but imaginatively limitless potential of the stage event itself. As Michael Smith indicates in his play *The Next Thing* (La Mama, 1966), *anything* can happen next. Arthur murders his mother after dinner, but whether this is the result of Oedipal compulsion or a random impulse is impossible to say. "And what happens next will be the next thing," he tells his date, Sue:

Whatever it is. If the police pound down the door and rush me to jail or an asylum, it will be the next thing. If your hair is a wig and you take it off and are a man, it will be the next thing. If that sheet moves and Mother speaks again or a bomb drops here and now or we go on talking and marry and have children and lead ordinary lives and die peacefully in each other's arms at 80, it will be the next thing. Absolutely whatever happens. And there *will be* a next thing. We can choose, or we can just go on without choosing. We need not fear that nothing will happen. (Smith 1969, 116–17)

Proto-feminism?

Therein, of course, lies the rub: "We can choose, or we can just go on without choosing." The question of agency in one's choices *is* often socially determined, and while one can seek to imagine new, liberating possibilities, it would be foolish to pretend that no obstacles exist. Considering *Promenade* from this perspective, it is striking that—with the notable exception of the ever-mischievous Servant—the play's female characters seem hemmed in by restrictive gender roles that it does not occur to them to challenge. In particular, the three aristocratic ladies—Miss I, Miss O, and Miss U—appear helplessly dependent for self-esteem on attracting the amorous attentions of their male companions. For example, in the song "Four Naked Ladies," the women take turns tearing off their clothes—"I want to be naked too"—in a desperate attempt to draw the men's attention back from the provocative Miss Cake (who has just stepped, scantily clad, from a cake). Nakedness, of course, is another kind of costume; one that tends to objectify the wearer. The men respond to this group striptease with feigned disinterest—"Only one naked lady . . . All right, two naked ladies" (10)—prompting the women to thank them profusely for permission to disrobe. Without their to-be-looked-at-ness, it seems, they would have no sense of identity at all.

Characteristically, Fornes never pushes any of this as an "issue": the spectator is again left to make her own connections. Yet the heavily gendered assumptions underlying questions of individual agency were underlined in several other female-authored plays of this period. Claris Nelson's *The Rue Garden*, for example (Caffe Cino, 1962), reads at first as a lighthearted pastiche of Victorian society comedy, in which Agatha Apfeather and Prudence Humper-Bentcroft comically bemoan the loss of Henery Chiggins, who deserted them without explanation many years ago. The tone of the piece, however, gradually mutates from blithe wit toward something more poignant and bleakly poetic: locked in behind their gate, nursing painful memories of the past, the women have cultivated a garden that grows only rue. The bitter shrub has obvious symbolic overtones—even if one is unaware that, according to middle European tradition, a maiden is expected to keep a rue garden as an outward sign of her continuing virginity, and of her wifely potential. Tightly hemmed in by the small dimensions of the Cino stage, the garden setting provided a resonant stage metaphor: these women, in Smith's terms, have "gone on without choosing." Henery Chiggins, when he eventually returns, is by contrast someone who has chosen his future and chosen again—to the extent that he appears incapable of remembering anything of the past. He lives only for the joys of the present: "The birds and the grass and the ocean don't remember pain," he tells the women, in bewildered noncomprehension of their resentment toward him (Nelson 1962, 36). Henery then liberates a young flower-girl, Jennifer, from the potentially stifling company of the older women, taking her away with him on a new adventure: "Goodbye rue!" she declares, in the play's final line (41). This conclusion, however, seems crafted to beg questions rather than provide resolution. Will Jennifer be any better off with Henery than the other women were? They may be locked in the past, but isn't his inability to remember it indicative of a pathological failure to feel sympathy for anyone but himself? Aren't all these characters locked into prescribed, self-destructive gender roles? Can Jennifer, perhaps, break that pattern? Nelson's deftly written play contains all these questions within its deceptively simple, fable-like narrative.

At this point, it is relevant to note that Rochelle Owens' previously cited comments on resisting "organized doctrine, principles, and procedures" relate to her conviction that several experimental playwrights of her generation might now be viewed, with hindsight, as "proto-feminist." Owens is careful to specify that this claim relates to their attempts to create work that sought "a redefinition of aesthetic possibilities, [going] beyond static notions of consciousness," rather than making any kind of propagandist statements on the condition of women. Too much purportedly political playwriting, she argues, expresses its opinions "in culturally approved and conservative modes [having] little to do with re-definitions and experimentation. . . . One ought to question the assumptions of the culture which created the social role of women" (1989, 20). This entails challenging familiar perceptions, rather than simply making points about what we can already see. In this sense, perhaps,

Fornes's desire to "take the subconscious by surprise" can be seen as implicitly progressive—an attempt to discover what she did not realize she knew, rather than assuming that what she already "knows" defines the limits of the possible.

It is notable that several of the artists who might, with hindsight, fall into Owens's "proto-feminist" bracket—including herself, Fornes, Rosalyn Drexler, Ruth Krauss—were championed by Judson Poets' Theater. As we shall see in the next chapter, that group's particular aptitude for staging poetically oriented, language-driven plays full of playful paradox seems to have made it well suited to exploring the performative possibilities of work that, in some cases, can be seen as a precursor to what Hélène Cixous would later label *l'écriture feminine*—writing freed from the traditionally masculine demands of logic, order, rationality. It would be a mistake, however, to propose any crude separation of off-off-Broadway's female and male playwrights: the latter, as should by now be clear, were also frequently concerned with playfully undermining conventional logic. Men or women, gay or straight, these were bohemian, underground artists whose unorthodox plays were rooted in and informed by their socially marginal position, and Owens's comments count, in a sense, for all of them. If there was a progressive dimension to their work, it lay not in overt sociopolitical statements but in their ongoing determination to keep imagining new possibilities, to challenge or subvert received conventions and assumptions, and—crucially—to invite audiences to share in the experience.

Part 2 Present Collaborations, 1963–68

8   The Judson "Musical": Sublimely Ridiculous?

> What happened in these productions was what happened to the people who did them; the words and music were not what happened: what happened was that the people who acted and sang and danced *were* the action the music and the dancing. . . . Many of them didn't know this or don't believe this, but it's true and they are mistaken: they were only doing what they were doing at that moment on that stage, even though they repeated the same thing night after night and were not improvising.
>
> —Lawrence Kornfeld, "How the Curtain Did Come"

If off-off-Broadway developed initially as a theater scene dedicated to presenting the work of new playwrights, the increasingly self-conscious emphasis of many of those writers on emphasizing the experiential dimensions of the theater event—as something taking place onstage, "in the moment"—also helped to focus creative attention on the act of staging itself. Innovative directors and performers gradually began to be recognized more and more for their own, distinctive contributions, and by the mid-1960s, many, varying collaborative experiments were being conducted in the direction of creating a more fluid, reciprocal relationship between text and performance. The next few chapters examine a number of groups notable for such work—groups whose impulses to innovation came from a range of sources, from experiments in actor training to the "nonacting" of underground film. This chapter, however, returns to the Judson Poets' Theater, where a particular confluence of theater, visual arts, music, and dance created what were arguably the purest examples of a theater emphasizing the immediate present of performance.

Ironically, the artist whose work provided the single biggest influence on this evolving aesthetic was not, in fact, physically present. The plays of Gertrude Stein (whose witty, paradoxical writing style Kornfeld pays homage to in the article cited above) were often ridiculed in her own day, and are still rarely produced, simply because these largely abstract poetic texts tend to feature little in the way of comprehensible dramatic narrative or characterization, and rarely even ascribe lines to particular characters. To the artists at Judson, however, this was precisely their attraction: her work required a high degree of creative innovation, rather than simply "interpretation," on the part of the production team. Stein herself had intended as much, delineating her play-texts from her other work by stressing that the former required someone else's "vision" in order to be completed: "When I see a thing it is not a play for me, but when I write something that somebody else can see then it is a play for me" (Stein 1975, viii). More important still was her emphasis on the notion of plays as "landscapes," as things that are simply there, for the viewer to behold in the present: "I felt that if a play was exactly like a landscape then there would be no difficulty about the emotion of the person looking on at the play being behind or ahead of the play, because the landscape does not have to make an acquaintance. [It] is there [but] it is of no importance unless you look at it" (1985, 122). Freed from the need to pay attention to a linear, narrative progression, Stein reasoned, the spectator—no longer having to cross-reference present with past, or project possible futures—might be able to respond more personally and spontaneously to the stage events presented. Hence the meditative circularity of her playwriting.

Stein was concerned, in short, with the possibility of creating a theater of phenomena, rather than representation—with emphasizing the perceptual processes of the spectator, rather than imposing some particular scheme of authorial meanings. As such, her work seemed consistent with many of the other experiments being carried out off-off-Broadway in the 1960s. Moreover, her desire to focus attention on a kind of heightened awareness of the moment helps explain the appeal of her work at Judson, in particular. Al Carmines, apparently influenced as much by Heideggerian philosophy as by his theological training, believed that the theater, like religion itself, could be a source of spiritual enlightenment, by helping audiences look toward a simple, numinous experience of being alive, here and now. "All of us constantly have these little revelations in our lives, little epiphanies," he once remarked in an interview: "People who don't believe in God have them all the time, you know. I don't think it matters whether they *say* they believe in God or not. I do think that . . . all these things have their roots in some kind of creative love. A reality. And I call that God" (Burke 1969, 7). It might be tempting, given these words, to see Judson's group-devised work as a latter-day attempt to evoke the sublime, were it not for the fact that, as we shall see, much of their work—wild, raunchy, irreverent—also anticipated the theater of the ridiculous.

It is worth noting, in passing, that Stein's ideas—which she herself regarded as "theological" in a certain sense—also provided primary inspiration for the work of Richard Foreman, the avant-garde writer-director who came to prominence in the 1970s, and who also sees himself as an artist whose "erotic, playful and schizoid" work nevertheless displays "essentially religious concerns" (1992, 5). Foreman's phenomenological emphasis on the present moment of performance has been well documented, not least in his own theoretical writings:

> A critic once told me that his problem with my plays was that when he was watching them he thought they were fantastic, but once he'd left the theater they seemed to vanish from his memory. As if that were bad! [An] art that affects you in the moment, but which you find hard to remember, is straining to bring you to another level. If offers images or ideas from that other level, that other way of being, which is why you find them hard to remember. (Foreman 1992, 23–24)

What is less well documented is that very similar points were being made about the work of the Judson Poets' Theater, almost a decade before Foreman began to be critically recognized. As Michael Smith wrote of their 1964 production of Rosalyn Drexler's *Home Movies*, "Kornfeld has again contrived an experience that functions in direct theatrical terms; the emotional content is conveyed by the shape of the event rather than in its particular 'meaning.' The memory finds nothing verbal to attach itself to, but the sense lingers of an hour joyfully spent" (1964a). Smith's emphasis on "joy," however, is perhaps what distinguishes the Judson work from Foreman's, which, as even his admirers acknowledge, can easily seem "abstruse, elusive, or not worth the trouble" to the untrained eye (Peter Sellars, in Foreman 1992, vii). Judson's collaboratively developed pieces, built around Stein texts like *What Happened* (1963) and *In Circles* (1967), as well as new plays like *Home Movies* and Irene Fornes's *Promenade* (1965), were defined not only by aesthetic innovation but by their immediate accessibility as entertainment. Looking back on *What Happened*, for example, Kornfeld acknowledges that, while it may indeed have been historically significant as an experimental fusion of theater, music, and dance, "what was very important for us as a Judson Poets' Theater was that it was an enormous hit! Audiences loved it and came back again and again and again. It was thirty-two minutes long, and it still amazes me how people responded to it."

What Happened

Gertrude Stein's first attempt at a play, written in 1913, *What Happened* had to wait fully fifty years, until September 1963, for its first complete staging. Also Judson's first attempt at Stein, this was—Al Carmines noted later—a "turning point" in the Poets' Theater's practice, since it was their first production fully to succeed in drawing "a certain attention . . . to what you're doing as what you're doing at that moment, and not as it refers to something else" (Smith 1966, 172). Besides Stein herself, the key influence on the piece in this regard was the Judson Dance Theater, which had been formed in the summer of 1962 by a group of young choreographers (many of them graduates of the Merce Cunningham company) who had approached Carmines to ask whether the church would be willing to sponsor a concert of new dance pieces. The series of workshops and performances that the group went on to mount in both the Judson gymnasium and the main sanctuary—thoroughly documented in Sally Banes's book *Democracy's Body: Judson Dance Theater, 1962–64*—proved highly influential in moving dance practice beyond both the expressive modernism of Martha Graham and the purist formalism of Merce Cunningham. This new generation, like their contemporaries in visual art and theater, sought a less exclusive, more "democratic" style of dance experiment. Often dancing in casual clothes and sneakers rather than leotards and point shoes, they explored the possibilities inherent in reframing the simplest forms of everyday movement—such as walking, sitting, even vacuum-cleaning—as "dance."

The importance of the Judson Dance Theater for the development of the Poets' Theater's work lay in this disciplined exploration of simply moving and "being" on stage. As a theater director whose primary interests lay in the highly choreographic staging of written texts, Kornfeld was fascinated with the possibility of using dancers as actors because they felt no need, as most actors did, to start artificially "emoting" the moment they stepped onstage. Having used two of the Dance Theater's members (Rudy Perez and Judith Dunn) in his production of Paul Goodman's *Hagar and Ishmael* (July 1963), Kornfeld wanted to extend this collaboration. For *What Happened*, he persuaded five of the Judson dancers—Yvonne Rainer, Lucinda Childs, Aileen Passloff, Arlene Rothlein, and Joan Baker—to commit to a four-week period of workshops and rehearsals directed toward a staging of Stein's text. Also involved were Carmines, as composer-pianist, and three male actor-singers.

From the outset of the project, Kornfeld was concerned to facilitate a process whereby each of the participants would be able to contribute creatively. The objective was to follow an intuitive process of group exploration—to find what the play might mean for this particular group of people, rather than to impose a preconceived directorial reading. "Only Gertrude Stein knew what the words were about," Kornfeld wrote later: "I only care what they will mean after we all fight over them" (1990, 136). To help facilitate this kind of creative tussle in rehearsal, he also suggested that, rather than dividing the performers' tasks according to their own disciplinary proficiencies, all nine would speak and sing and move: they were thus challenged to step out from their familiar "comfort zones," and find new ways of working and interacting with each other. At times, this approach led to a degree of tension and uncertainty among the participants. Stein's text, however, provided a point of common contact for all involved: as an exploration of language and verbal rhythms rather than dramatic content, it proved intriguing, on a formal level, to the dancers, actors and musicians alike, and it was here that the project found its starting point. Stein's division of her short, seemingly abstract text into five "acts," for example, appears entirely arbitrary at first glance, but on closer examination each act turns out to have its own structural logic. Act 3, for example, plays over and over on the relationship between the words *cut* and *slice*: "A cut. A cut is not a slice, what is the occasion for representing a cut and a slice. What is the occasion for all that. / A cut is a slice, a cut is the same slice. The reason that a cut is a slice . . ." (Benedikt 1968, 312). By contrast, act 4 has a more consistent rhythm and less contradictory approach, but lists many more objects: "A birthday, what is a birthday, a birthday is a speech. . . . A blanket, what is a blanket. . . . A blame, what is a blame. . . A clever saucer, what is a clever saucer . . ." (312–13). Stein's use of such repetition and variation inspired similarly playful experiments in echoing and layering her words in performance. Some were spoken, some sung, some spoken *and* sung; some were delivered solo, some chorally, some as call and response. Carmines even coordinated the reworking of some sequences into densely layered four-part harmonies for himself and the three male singers. "Kornfeld and his cohorts have taken [Stein's] phrases and repeated them, staggered them, contrapuntalized them one against the other," Jerry Tallmer wrote of the opening performance, "in infinite combinations and permutations until the whole emerges as an exquisite semi-comic harmony" (1963).

The company also worked to create a visual equivalent for these verbal games, by developing a pageant of vignette-like images and movement sequences that could be repeated and varied in different combinations.

Attempting to mirror the playfulness of the text, these sequences were linked by a sense of adults playing in a disarmingly childlike manner—with the dancers adapting and framing simple activities as dance, just as they would in their individual work. Lucinda Childs, for example, would play at rolling jacks on two imaginary jack boards, set at a ninety-degree angle from each other, so that as the game progressed, she had to stretch farther and farther in opposite directions. Aileen Passloff would perform a hilariously awkward dance wearing a man's oversized boots, while sniffing the audience suspiciously. At one point, Joan Baker would lie down inside Carmines's grand piano, as if it were a bath: basking in the vibrations from a rolling, swirling Rachmaninov pastiche, she would then perform an extravagant pantomime of "bathing in music." This sequence, like many, was initially suggested by Kornfeld, but Baker made it her own: since he was not a choreographer in the conventional sense of specifying every movement, but rather a director suggesting images for the performers to inhabit, there was plenty of room for creative interplay. Each of the dancers became, in effect, the choreographer of her own movements, while being placed within a "landscape" masterminded by Kornfeld.

Stein's landscape concept was treated quite literally in this production: the performance space chosen stretched across the entire width of Judson's "downstairs," and this horizontality was emphasized by placing it just in front of the overhanging choir-loft—whose bottom edge, from which curtains were hung as a backdrop, thus formed a low frame for the action. Adopting Cezanne's principle of treating every part of the canvas equally, Kornfeld sought to populate the whole expanse of the wide, shallow stage area with activity: "his actor/dancers snap smartly across the length of it like banners," Alan Marlowe wrote in his *Floating Bear* review, "they are everywhere, filling the stage with life and movement" (1963). The horizontality of the space was most dramatically emphasized, however, during a sequence in which the entire cast gathered behind the piano and pushed it, as if pushing a boat out, clear across the stage from upstage left to downstage right. With Carmines continuing to play as he walked, the cast would all keep singing, and Aileen Passloff danced along behind them with the piano stool. On opening night, Kornfeld remembers with amazement, the audience "started to applaud and yell, stamping their feet," as this sequence unfolded. The response was often similar at subsequent performances. "I mean even today, something like that is just breathtaking," Maria Irene Fornes notes of her own sense of awe at the moving tableau: "Larry was like a sculptor who would see these things, that you had never seen before, and mold the whole piece around them."

If *What Happened* is remembered most vividly for its unorthodox choreography, it was, nevertheless, as much a text-based theater piece as a dance piece. Kornfeld was never interested in exploring movement as a purely formal concern: "The source of movement is the feeling of people in a circumstance," he insists: "I am interested in form and rhythm, but not to the exclusion of idea, relationship, and feeling." Along with the fun and spectacle, the collaborators also worked to bring a poignancy to the performance. This was, again, in response to Stein's text, which though relentlessly non-specific, contains many intimations of emotion, from great joy to great sadness: "Four and nobody wounded, five and nobody flourishing, six and nobody talkative, eight and nobody sensible" (311). The climax of the piece was particularly moving in its execution. "A regret a single regret makes a doorway," Stein's text reads for the short fifth act: "What is a doorway, a doorway is a photograph . . . a photograph is a sight and a sight is always a sight of something" (313). These lines, delivered by Yvonne Rainer in a tone that "made it sound like Mohammed!" (Kornfeld), were accompanied by the "sight" of the performance itself beginning to melt away ("a single regret"?). As the lights gradually faded, the performers began, again, to move the piano, this time directly upstage, away from the audience (again: repetition with variation), as if they were leaving this dimension, via some unseen "doorway," and moving on into another.

"The correspondences between the words and the actions are on some other level than sense or reason can determine," Michael Smith wrote in his *Voice* review, "but unquestionably they exist. Everything that happens has the casual inevitability of great art . . . it is a divine slight moment of joy, it is a theatrical fountain of youth, and you should go drink" (1963b). Other commentators were equally ecstatic: "Not only was there a conversation between music, singing and dancing throughout the piece," Michael Benedikt noted,

> but these roles were constantly interchanged. Dancers called out the text, the chorus began to dance, the pianist sang and spoke and sometimes danced, [and] even the piano was converted from one medium (musical instrument) to another (portable sculpture). The whole was converted into a theatrical conversation in which, appropriately enough, not individuals but whole arts took part. (1968, 308)

The production played to packed audiences in the main hall of Judson Church, and, by popular demand, was revived five times over the next few years. It also received three Obie Awards for the 1963–64 season—for best production (musical), distinguished direction, and best music. The Living Theatre's *The Brig* received the other key awards, for best production (play) and design (Julian Beck), while Judson Church itself was awarded a special citation "for its sponsorship of experiment in the performing arts."

Theater as Collage Composition

The creators of *What Happened* did not attempt to repeat their achievement or work together again as an ensemble, and the Dance Theater and Poets' Theater resumed their own separate programs of work. Subsequently, however, the latter's program was often defined by the attempt to find afresh that elusive collaborative magic, by putting together new teams of artists for new production experiments—artists who might push and pull at each other's ingrained habits and assumptions. The objective was not to form a single, clear ensemble group with an identifiable performance style, but to draw on different combinations of contributors for each new project, in an attempt to respond to the particular needs of each new text. Christmas 1964, for example, saw another Kornfeld-directed workshop group performing *Sing Ho for a Bear!*—a musical adaptation of A. A. Milne's Winnie the Pooh stories. Carmines himself was Pooh, dressed in furry tunic and two furry ears: "it's an outlandish idea," Smith wrote, "but forget the idea. The experience is authentic [and] the production is a treat" (1964e).

Still more noteworthy were the first stagings of *Home Movies* and *Promenade*, two highly unorthodox new plays that probably could not have been mounted anywhere but Judson. "I didn't even know it was a play," Rosalyn Drexler recalls of the former: "I wrote it at home to amuse myself." Her initial draft of *Home Movies* was simply a collection of whimsical jottings that she showed to a friend, the critic Richard Gilman. Having rave-reviewed *What Happened* for *Commonweal*, however, Gilman suggested that the Poets' Theater might be able to perform similar alchemy for her. "*Home Movies* was all over the place when it came in," Kornfeld remembers, "but Al, Rosalyn, and I got together and said, 'What's in this that needs to come out?'" He stresses that the objective was never to "fix" scripts like this: "I hated that Broadway thing of, after one reading, rewrite it! My motto was 'Make it work': if the play has value, it has to have its own way of working." Responding to the energy and bizarre wit of the raw text, he and Carmines worked with Drexler to develop a coherent production approach, bringing structure to it by adding complementary layers of visual, musical, and performative material. The published version of *Home Movies* is, in effect, a transcription of the Judson production, containing numerous stage directions and exchanges that were developed collaboratively through rehearsal. Irene Fornes's *Promenade*, conversely, was more finished as a script when Carmines first received it, and was first published in its original form. Yet this too was an open-ended piece that positively invited creative intervention during the rehearsal process. "My script was not delightful," Fornes remarks simply: "it was just a possible *setup* for something delightful." Like Drexler, she had initially written the piece for fun, "and I thought for sure that no one was going to do this, because it doesn't sound like any musical ever written." After seeing *Home Movies*, however, Fornes realized that "it *would* be done" if she took it to Carmines.

The suitability of both *Home Movies* and *Promenade* to the evolving Judson approach is clear from the texts themselves. As with Stein, the primary virtues of both lie in their rhythmic, playful, enigmatic use of language: they are full of strange rhymes, grotesque puns, silly songs, mock dialects and foreign phrases, rat-a-tat word association exchanges, and vaudevillian "bits." Although both pieces gesture toward a narrative through-line, their emphasis is always on the immediate experience of the theatrical moment, rather than on being "about" some external subject. "There aren't any truths about human life that can be extrapolated like lecture titles from Rosalyn Drexler's work," Gilman noted in the introduction to her first collection of plays, *The Line of Least Existence* (whose title piece was also produced at Judson in 1967): "Imagination equals style equals play; until we learn that this is so, we are going to go on hunting like demented ferrets for the truth underneath the surfaces of plays we see, snuffling, rooting around, and never experiencing what is there to be experienced" (Drexler 1967, ix). Similarly, *Voice* critic Robert Pasolli noted in 1969 that Fornes's work presented a world of pure spontaneity: "everything is random and everything seems arbitrary. This is a phenomenological approach to character, the most advanced that I know of" (1969b, 58).

Both Fornes and Drexler acknowledge European antecedents like Beckett, Ionesco, and Jarry as major inspirations for their playwriting, particularly in the license they seemed to provide to break with dramatic convention. "As an untutored young person, reading *Ubu*, I fell on the floor I couldn't stop laughing," Drexler notes: "It was so wonderful, the plumping up of the main character, what he thought about himself. . . . I said aha! That's right, I can do that! There's a place for my kind of mind too!" Crucially, though, both women also had the "kind of mind" that had initially been drawn to the visual arts—a factor that helps explain their disinterest in linearity, their attraction to collagelike assembly. Fornes had trained with the leading abstract painter Hans Hoff-mann, and Drexler was already well known in the art world in the early 1960s, particularly for the large, colorful paintings she had made using images drawn from newspapers and pulp fiction magazines. Not trusting her own ability with figurative drawing, she had adopted the strategy of pasting blown-up reproductions of these images onto canvas, and then painting over them. This compositional method, which she was initially ashamed to admit to, meant that she came to be seen as an early member of the pop art movement. It was by a similar method of intuitive fumbling in the dark that *Home Movies* came to be written. "I see words as found objects too," she later commented: "I col-lage things in my writing as well" (1986).

The text for *Home Movies* is largely composed of recycled language. Stock phrases are twisted against themselves or crunched together into bizarre rhymes: "Let no man now diminish / What takes two falls to a finish" (Drexler 1967, 118). Quotations are corrupted and recontextualized: "Ask not what the Lord has done for you / Ask what you can do for the Lord" (108). Language from different arenas of discourse collides in jarring non sequiturs: "Charles dear, I know you think of me as an old cow, but time is running out and I must know. Is a woman's brain smaller than a man's?" (95). This "fast and witty script," Susan Sontag noted, created a verbal leveling of ground, "in which the oldest cliché and the fanciest fancy are meant to be uttered with the same solemnity" (1967, 159). A connection can be drawn here with New York's hap-penings artists, and their "witty appreciation of the derelict, inane, *démodé* objects of modern civilization" (Sontag 1967, 271). Fornes and Drexler had both participated as performers in happenings by Claes Oldenburg and Robert Whitman, respectively, and shared their playfully nostalgic affection for the dated escapism of 1930s popular culture. *Home Movies* features a slapstick punch-up described in the stage directions as "a Mack Sennet fight" (105), while the jailer's inept pursuit of the prisoners in *Promenade* feels like a Key-stone Cops chase. "It's like a lot of movies from the 1930s, like Fred Astaire and Ginger Rogers," Fornes herself suggests: "Everybody is lightweight, you know, you run, you cry, there's a meeting and then something happens and you go somewhere else." *Home Movies*, by contrast, remains rooted in one location, but transforms a banal, bourgeois domestic situation into a three-ring circus of zany absurdity, reminiscent of a Marx Brothers routine.

The Judson team responded to these texts by applying a similarly playful approach to the production process, appropriating and juxtaposing ideas from numerous sources, and particularly from old pop-cultural forms. The musical accompaniment that Carmines developed for *Home Movies*, for example, drew on a perverse variety of "found" styles, to create "an extraordinary and on every occasion on-target disbursement of torch songs, Latin motets, 1890s mother melodies, Minsky motifs, ragtime penances, barbershop chorales, spirituals" (Tallmer 1964a). Meanwhile, Kornfeld conceived the staging of *Home Movies* as a kind of homage to burlesque. He proposed constructing a booth stage, complete with show curtain, at one end of Judson's narrow choir loft, thereby mimicking the layout of a small burlesque house. The little stage contained a simple set suggesting a bourgeois lady's boudoir: here, Mrs. Verdun and her sexually budding daughter Vivienne would entertain a variety of gentleman callers. Their costumes, too, implied a burlesquing of burlesque conventions, with the female characters being dressed in a variety of bizarre, overtly sexualized outfits: "one-piece knickers with a zipper running full-length, [and beneath,] a white brassiere with crisp, huge daisies pinned to the cups"; "a sweeping lace peignoir over a silk or satin sheath, so that her gestures flow around her" (77). Far from being rendered simply as sex objects, however, the female characters were far sharper and wittier than the men: controlling the stage action, Gretel Cummings (Mrs. Verdun), Sudie Bond (Vivienne), and Barbara Ann Teer (Violet, the maid) threw the spectators' gaze right back at them.

The actors were directed to develop broad, outlandish performances in the burlesque style. Kornfeld had consciously extended the objets trouvés principle to his casting, selecting performers not for their skills or training as actors but for their dynamism as stage personalities, and the relevance of their personae to the roles in question. Carmines's position as Judson's minister, for example, was exploited by casting him as the randy priest, Father Shenanagan, while the most flamboyantly gay member of the Judson Dance Theater, Freddie Herko, became the raging queen, Peter Peterouter. This was, as Michael Smith noted in the *Voice*, an outrageous extension of the approach adopted with *What Happened*, in which the dancers had simply performed versions of themselves on stage: "Kornfeld's method as a director is to release and use the personalities of his performers; the play is not 'acted' in a normal sense, [but] when he finds performers with [this kind of] energy and presence . . . the results are marvelous and make ordinary theatre look contrived and unconvincing" (1964b). The roles in the play thus became inextricable from the people playing them, and Drexler made various textual adjustments in response to material the performers developed in rehearsal. "Watch me metamorph into a mannered and pompous queen," Peter Peterouter declares at one point in the script, and the following stage directions describe him "pranc[ing] around making grotesque faces at the audience" (91–92), while stripping off his outer clothes to reveal a rhinestone necklace and knee-length red dress. This was Drexler's attempt to annotate Herko's burlesque take on the idea of queeniness—a camping up of camp itself, played directly toward the astonished spectators. For Michael Smith, Herko's "vivid confrontation with the audience" was one of the most extraordinary moments in an extraordinary show.

Sadly, Herko did not appear again at Judson: he committed suicide later that year by dancing out of the second floor window of Johnny Dodd's Cornelia Street apartment. Yet the casting of personalities as actors became a staple approach of the Poets' Theater. *Promenade*, for example, made a minor celebrity of Florence Tarlow, a librarian by day, and a Judson church member. Untrained as an actor, she stole the show as Miss Cake, leaping semiclad and singing from a large cake during the play's banquet scene. Tarlow became a recurrent favorite in subsequent Judson productions, one of a number of "divas" whose audience appeal owed everything to their personal stage charisma. A similar approach, of course, was being adopted at the same time by Andy Warhol, whose underground movies featured his own band of self-proclaimed "superstars." From 1965, the idea was pushed still further by the Play-House of the Ridiculous.

To Camp or Not to Camp?

This stress on the exaggerated enactment of one's individuality, rather than on creating a theatrical illusion of natural, "authentic" behavior, was widely regarded at the time as a manifestation of "the camp sensibility." "Camp sees everything in quotation marks," Susan Sontag explained in her 1964 essay "Notes on Camp": "to perceive Camp in objects and persons is to understand Being-as-Playing-a-Role. It is the farthest extension, in sensibility, of the metaphor of life as theater" (1967, 280). Given this definition, "camp" does indeed seem an appropriate descriptor for the Drexler and Fornes plays, with their emphasis on spontaneous, self-inventing behavior rather than psychological determinism. Similarly, if one accepts Jack Babuscio's later summary of the camp sensibility as foregrounding "irony, aestheticism, theatricality and humor," then a number of Poets' Theater productions could be so described (Cleto 1999, 119). What could be more campy, in these terms, than pushing a piano across the stage while still singing and playing? Irene Fornes (who was Sontag's partner for several years during the 1960s) sees the archly sophisticated wit exhibited by several Judson productions as epitomizing a kind of "high camp" aesthetic, akin to that of Noël Coward or Oscar Wilde, and as distinct from the more overtly swishy "gay camp" characteristic of certain performances at the Caffe Cino. Michael Smith made the same distinction in his review of *Promenade*, a play treated by Kornfeld not as burlesque, but as a decadent comedy of manners, complete with Beardsley-esque backdrop designs.

Significantly, though, both Kornfeld and Carmines remain resistant to the Judson work being labeled camp—particularly, it seems, because the word became widely used at this time as a shorthand means of dismissing such highly stylized work, by implying that it celebrated mere surface style, at the expense of emotional substance. "Our style was more grotesque than camp," Carmines maintains: "we took the grotesque very seriously." That term implies a discomforting clash of emotional opposites that is anything but superficial—an incongruous coexistence of, for example, both the comic and the disturbing or horrific—and relates closely to the kind of jarring juxtapositions being used by numerous off-off playwrights during this same period. For evidence of Carmines's claim, moreover, one need look no further than his superb score for *Promenade* (which, unlike *Home Movies*, is still available in recorded formats). Drawing on his usual range of eclectic influences, from torch songs to operatic arias, the music is mostly brisk, exuberant, and thoroughly enjoyable. Yet there is also a darker, more abrasive edge lurking beneath the high spirits—perhaps suggestive of some sleazy Berlin cabaret. The recording features elements of dissonance, minor keys, and the use of deep, rasping male vocals set jarringly against soaring, high-pitched females. The music perfectly complements Fornes's deceptively simple lyrics, which in songs such as "The Moment Has Passed" mix blithe joviality with a bleak subtext of emotional isolation and violence:

You have perhaps made me feel something
But the moment has passed (the moment has passed)
And what is done cannot be undone
Once a moment passes, it never comes again. . . .

He said he would kill for me.
And I said, "like, for instance, whom?"
And he said, "like, for instance, you,
Like for instance you."

Sometimes it hurts more than others
Sometimes it hurts less. . . .
But never mind that, no never mind that
God gave us understanding just to confuse us.
And it's always the same anyway.
                    (Schroeder 1968, 17–18)

As Smith remarked in his review of *Promenade*, "The dominant emotion is romantic melancholy but the tone is vapid frivolity, and the delicate tension this creates gives the event its distinction. . . . The ideas that are used for comic effect are by no means trivial, and the glassy glibness of their expression is devastating" (1965c). Not all the Judson musicals made this clash of emotional textures quite so discomfortingly apparent: the boisterous irreverence of *Home Movies*, for example, admitted little in the way of melancholy. Kornfeld maintains, however, that the Poets' Theater's complex use of theatrical and musical form was always directed toward the exploration of feeling, rather than just aesthetic exhibitionism. Even when they adopted arbitrary, gamelike rules as a compositional tactic, the challenge was to see if something fresh or surprising could be created from the available components:

> For instance, every show had what we called a compulsory tango. Sometimes the tango was funny, sometimes it was scary: it was just a formalism. But what a lot of people forget is that formalisms like that can contain many subjects and ideas, and that's what we tried to do: say serious things in a comic way, and comic things in a serious way. Al's music had a deep sense of irony, but it was not irony for irony's sake.

The irony here, perhaps, is that Kornfeld's comments can from certain angles be seen as a kind of manifesto for camp. According to Christopher Isherwood, "true High Camp always has an underlying seriousness. You can't camp about something you don't take seriously. You're not making fun of it, you're making fun out of it. You're expressing what's basically serious to you in terms of fun and artifice and elegance" (Cleto 1999, 51). Isherwood's comments are rooted in gay experience—in the impulse to mock and ironize the dictates of a culture that declares one's deepest emotional needs to be "unnatural." Similarly, although not identified with any particular sexual orientation, the Poets' Theater's work adopted a consistently subversive attitude toward mainstream morality—as one might expect from a radical church. Thus *Home Movies* made farcical burlesque out of bourgeois attitudes toward domestic decorum and pious religiosity, presenting a rampant polysexuality underlying the Verdun family's thin veneer of respectability. The text revels in a gleeful excess of innuendo and double entendre: "Oh yes, I adore fruit in the summer / So refreshing / Succulent" / Ripe / Juicy! / Dripping / Ever so wet / Would you care for a fruit? / But your bowl is so delightful to look at, I wouldn't dream of disturbing the arrangement" (87). The company also created visual imagery to match, as for example when Sister Thalia—in "whorish" blonde fright wig under her nun's wimple—knelt in front of Father Shenanagan, thereby suggesting fellatio as much as prayer. A few years later, none of this would have seemed particularly shocking, but in 1964, with the sexual revolution in its infancy, *Home Movies* would have seemed in scurrilously bad taste had its sense of warmth and delirious silliness not largely disarmed criticism. "Camp is a solvent of morality," Sontag suggests: "it neutralizes moral indignation, sponsors playfulness" (1967, 290).

In effect, *Home Movies* was all about the tearing down of facades and appearances, and another important element in this respect was its playful subversion of social stereotypes. Most notably, the production used two black actors—Barbara Ann Teer and Jim Anderson—as the two servants, Violet the maid and John the delivery man. Both parts were played as the very embodiment of white prejudices regarding their sexuality: Violet evoked the black exoticism of Josephine Baker, "a gorgeous supple beauty [wearing] practically nothing: a top of feathery petals and a bottom of the same" (77–78), while John produced a "huge, phallic pencil" from his pants pockets in order for Mrs. Verdun to sign for the closet he has delivered (an old vaudeville trick, recontextualized). The patently excessive manner in which these stereotyped attributes were paraded and played with also functioned to mock and query them. "You wouldn't take li'l ol' me fresh fum de sharecroppers shack where I was born," pleads Violet at one point, in mock "colored folks" accent. "Don't pull that ol' darky act on me," Mrs. Verdun retorts: "I didn't hire you for your sense of humor. I'm completely aware of the race hatred you bear me" (84–85). The recurrence of such quips through the play—"Sometimes I feel like a chocolate turkey," Violet sings later, "Gazing out of cellophane windows" (108)—indicates a seriousness of intention underlying the wit, a "spoof[ing of] white liberal values in the most transgressive terms" (Banes 1993b, 156). A similarly progressive subtext also seems to underlie the play's absurd exaggeration of homosexual stereotyping. Mr. Verdun, presumed dead, turns out not to be dead at all, but instead—in a literalization of the familiar metaphor — is locked inside the closet that John delivers to the house. He and Peter, the prancing queen, have been having a relationship ever since they met at — where else? — the gymnasium.

The company carried this playful treatment of stereotype on into the production of *Promenade*, opting to play Fornes's archetypal mother figure, for example, as the "Alabammy mammy" type used in so many old Hollywood movies. They even inserted a silent, Mr. Moto-style "mysterious Oriental gentleman" into proceedings, although the script mentions no such figure. Yet the drawback with such ironic representational games is, of course, that they rely on the audience to demonstrate a degree of ironic sophistication in response. The camp sensibility, Sontag argued, is located principally in the eye of the beholder: one needs to be "in on it" to "get it." The point was demonstrated all too clearly by the transfer of *Home Movies* to a commercial, off-Broadway run. Opening in May 1964, two months after its Judson premiere, and just around the corner from the church at the Provincetown Playhouse, this was the first off-off-Broadway production to move intact to a "proper" theater (nine months before the "New Playwrights" triple bill of Foster, Shepard, and Wilson plays at the Cherry Lane). The comedian Orson Bean, a collector of Drexler's paintings, loved her play so much that he sponsored its relocation. However, the show's playful irony and breezy transgression of taboo proved too far ahead of the times for more conventional theatergoers. *New York Times* critic Louis Calta spoke for many in dismissing it as "a dismal melange [of] questionable worth and taste," and failed to comprehend its satirical edge: "It is difficult to identify the objects that Miss Drexler is jabbing at" (1964).

The Provincetown production survived for a few weeks on the strength of its alternative cachet, but closed during the summer when, with New Yorkers going out of town, it failed to attract a tourist audience. Many of the show's admirers, however, felt that something fundamental had been lost as soon as it moved: "the nice thing about the production is that it is not slickly professional," Jerry Tallmer had noted of the Judson premiere, "it has all the loose edges of high vitality and low budget" (1964a). At the Provincetown, Michael Smith observed, "the performances are more evenly professional, [but] *Home Movies* has lost its direct contact with the audience and become less fun. . . . The open directness of the production faded when it stepped into the show-business arena; audience and actors are friendly peers in the hominess of Judson Church, but in the 'professional' theatre they are employers and employees" (1964b).

A Playmaking Circle, a Circle for Plays

Smith's comments are telling, given that the Poets' Theater's creative process depended for its success, in part, on the necessary avoidance of an employer/employee relationship with its performers. Since the church could not pay actors a wage, there was no "contract" involved: participants volunteered their time for love, and on the understanding that—rather than simply being hired for a prescribed job—they would be able to contribute directly to the creative process. The loose ensemble of regular performers that Carmines and Kornfeld built up during the mid-1960s included not only "inspired amateurs" like Florence Tarlow, but also a number of established professionals who were attracted by this playful approach. Both George Bartenieff (Mr. Verdun in *Home Movies*; 106 in *Promenade*) and Theo Barnes (who first worked at Judson directing his own, Kabuki-inflected adaptation of *Antigone* in 1966), had extensive professional credentials, and had featured in the original cast of the Living Theatre's *The Brig*. Bartenieff's partner, Crystal Field, played Miss O in *Promenade*, fresh from her stint in the Lincoln Center premiere of Arthur Miller's *After the Fall*. Dancers like Arlene Rothlein, Aileen Passloff, and David Vaughan also continued to act regularly in Judson plays, and the theater came to thrive on the complementary virtues brought by its various performers—as craft and discipline combined with wild individuality and risk taking.

It is worth stressing, also, the number of strong female presences in the Judson camp, including Field, Tarlow, Gretel Cummings (Mrs. Verdun and Miss I), Passloff, Rothlein, and in time Lee Guilliatt, Julie Kurnitz, and Margaret Wright. At a time when most roles for women in the mainstream theater were still those of wives, mothers, and other male appendages, Judson became noted for its championing of female performers as well as its unusual proportion of scripts by female playwrights. In Rochelle Owens's *Istanboul*, for example, Tarlow and Field were considered by Jerry Tallmer to have stolen the show in their respective roles as "the horrifyingly self-elected earth-mother lady saint" and "a pampered, drawling, colonialistic adulteress." These "champion muses" were "actresses with a wide command of the absurd in its purest sense," heading up "the beautiful, not-too-silly-just-crazy-enough deadpan clowning by the entire cast" (Tallmer 1965).

Kornfeld again masterminded this production, but he was not the only director to use the evolving Judson group to advantage. Indeed, one of the Poets' Theater's most celebrated pieces was Remy Charlip's December 1965 production of Ruth Krauss's *A Beautiful Day*. Another former associate of both Merce Cunningham and the Living Theatre, the multitalented Charlip was drawn to Judson by its growing reputation for innovative, interdisciplinary performances, and worked there regularly from 1964, as a director, choreographer, performer, and costume designer. *A Beautiful Day* was a project designed to capitalize directly on Judson's interactive working process, by taking a dozen of Krauss's short poem-plays and creating a revue-style piece using different performers in different sections. Irene Fornes designed the costumes, Johnny Dodd the lights, and Carmines, as ever, provided music.

Among the open-ended texts that Judson had by now made its signature, Krauss's pieces represented a near-vanishing-point extreme. The titular poem-play *A Beautiful Day*, for example, consists in its entirety of the following:

> *Girl:*   What a beautiful day!
> *the sun falls down onto the stage*
> *end*
>   (Poland and Mailman 1972, 26)

Using this tiny fragment as his starting point, Charlip created a suite of five different variations on the same simple action—which are annotated as stage directions in the published version. The sun, for example, appeared variously as a gold-covered ashcan lid crashing to the floor, and a large orange balloon that was exploded with a pin. Each new version was a new creation, but their serial juxtaposition also created an oblique narrative relationship between the ever-more-wary girl (Florence Tarlow) and a boy (Charles Adams) who manipulated the balloon's appearance and destruction. By the fourth variation, for example, the girl appeared "grimly and cautiously" through a trapdoor, to find herself bathed in bright, warm sunlight. Overcoming her caution, "the Girl smiles and says, 'What a beautiful day!'"—only to be hit on the head by a large orange ball dropped from the ceiling. Once again, then, the formal properties of repetition, variation, and counterpoint were used to create both poignancy and humor. Charlip extrapolated a rich variety of emotional textures from Krauss's simple texts, so much so that Michael Smith was moved to declare him "a genius. The word is dangerous in a critic's vocabulary but I kept thinking it. . . . *A Beautiful Day* is insistently human, grounded in the reality of human feeling and experience (tenderness, surprise, amusement, comfort, nostalgia). . . . Its distinct and incisive bite produces the nourishment of astonishment and delight" (1965f).

Given the Poets' Theater's recurrent emphasis on "the reality of human feeling," it was perhaps logical that these musical theater experiments would eventually circle back to an investigation of character, and the dramatic interplay between individuals. With *In Circles* (1967), Judson's second musicalization of a Gertrude Stein text (*A Circular Play, a Play in Circles*, written in 1920), the company elected to focus on these more traditional theatrical concerns, rather than on interdisciplinary experiment. Yet the emphasis on the present moment of performance remained central. Kornfeld sought to stress not the dramatic illusion of actors playing characters, but "the reality of pretence," in the theatrical here and now: "pretending is very real," he wrote, "and only unwelcome when it is not recognized as a real event" (1990, 140).

From the outset, work on *In Circles* focused on the basic "reality" of the interplay between the cast members in the rehearsal room. If *A Beautiful Day* had been created by having different participants collaborate on different segments, this piece was created through an almost organic group process by participants who, by now, knew each other very well. Kornfeld and the ten-strong cast (five women and five men—Carmines and his piano included) developed the performance by working their way through Stein's text, literally page by page, responding to whatever ideas were sparked among the people in the room. Thus David Vaughan, who was a few days late coming into rehearsals owing to other commitments, also "arrived late" in the performance itself, entering at the point in the text where he had entered the process. This organic approach was also applied to the distribution of Stein's lines among the cast. Each of the performers selected the lines that particularly appealed to them, and then sought to extrapolate a "pretend" character by imagining a figure whose personal story might provide an emotional "through-line" linking these seemingly abstract statements. During rehearsals, the actors would then argue for the right to "own" their chosen lines: "We'd be in rehearsal," Theo Barnes recalls, "and I'd say, 'Can I say that?' I chose lines, and I fought for them." Barnes secured a selection of lines that he imagined belonged to a character he dubbed "Cousin Frederick," who was "an outsider, a First World War veteran—I thought of the English war poets." The other performers imagined characters of their own, and discussed their stories with Kornfeld, but he instructed them not to reveal these "subtexts" to each other, but rather to react—in character—to whatever seemed to be happening onstage, in the moment. "I was very, very interested in what went on inside characters," he explains: "I wanted to have real characters, alive and reacting, but not to have to tell a story that dragged them around by the nose."

Meanwhile, Carmines treated the development of his score as another "character" in this interactive process, writing music day by day, in response to whatever was happening in rehearsal. He would teach new material to the cast each morning, and then Kornfeld would listen to the new sequences and consider how best to stage them, sometimes calling for adjustments to pace, mood, and so forth. A responsive feedback loop—a circle—thus developed between staging and score (which featured strings and percussion, as well as piano). The result was a performance in which the majority of the text's lines were sung, and without clear-cut distinction between songs and spoken scenes: instead music, song, and speech blended, as Steinian phrases and musical themes circled around each other. Somehow the deliriously eclectic score developed into a "rounded" whole by constantly switching musical moods, circling from rabble-rousing group choruses to gentle, poignant solos and back again; from raunchy barrelhouse numbers to solemn plainsong. Typical of the formal, textural contrasts that emerged was the recurrent juxtaposition between "round as a round as my apple" (Stein 1975, 139), gorgeously sung as a sweet, whimsical round, and "Cut wood cut wood" (140), spoken slowly in a hard-edged staccato while backed by sharp, atonal notes on the piano. The music also responded directly to the personal qualities of the performers: dancer Elaine Summers, for example, who was not a confident singer, had a sequence written for her based on the phrase "I hear a sore" (140), in which she was encouraged to elongate the words "hear" and "sore," so that she could take her time sliding up and down the scale to find the right notes. "It had that Dietrich kind of thing," Kornfeld remembers, "her fighting for the notes and sliding around was beautiful."

As director, Kornfeld chose to foreground this seamless fusion of performers and score by using a comparatively restrained staging approach. There were a few, signature moments of dancelike movement and vaudevillian comic business, but the piece was largely staged using a series of tableaux that emphasized the performers' relationships with the music, and with each other. At the very start of the performance, for example, as the audience were still entering the auditorium, all the performers (except the absent Vaughan) would gather "in a circle" around Carmines's piano while he taught them, bit by bit, a new song composed that day: from the start, the piece was thus rooted in a sense of genuine, in-the-moment spontaneity. Subsequently, as the play proper got going, this united group would fragment and disperse across a wide platform stage—again stretched landscape-like across the entire width of the Judson sanctuary—to form smaller "circles," which then recurrently regrouped into larger or smaller groups. Often, in the process, certain individuals—most notably Barnes's Cousin Frederick—would be left isolated, alone, sometimes having to move a long way to rejoin their peers. "Larry likes people to walk long distances onstage," Barnes observes, "because you see them. You see who they are."

The performance, in short, seemed to hinge around the Stein line, "A circle is a necessity. Otherwise you would see no-one" (141). The unsettling implications of that observation—do we gather together simply to avoid being alone? do we always trust or even like our companions?—were developed visually through the piece by suggesting that some kind of garden-party gaiety is going on, in which not everyone is having an equally good time. (The abstracted garden setting included a huge painted backdrop with colorful paper flowers collaged onto it, and looked, one observer suggested, "like something from the children's version of *Last Year at Marienbad* [Sullivan 1968b].) "It had what I call the generic Chekhovian story," Kornfeld notes wryly: "people in a garden, coming in and out. It's as if you turned a Chekhov play inside out, so what you heard in the show was the melodies, the songs, the fragments of ideas that were the subtext underneath the Chekhovian drama." The success of this playful strategy is clear from the show's reviews, which stressed a sense that—lurking behind the joyous frivolity—were all kinds of unspoken pain. "Charming, charming, charming—and sad," wrote the *Times*' Clive Barnes of the October premiere at Judson:

> The terrible sadness of the not-quite-seen, the not-quite-comprehended. . . . The words fall easy off the tongue like tart raspberries in sweet cream, and Mr. Carmines' music sprays evocative sugar over all, [but] occasionally ominous Stein-lines (such as "no-one, no-one is certain") cut like sniper-fire across the genial fabric of verbiage. In fact such assaults, to the sensitive, may become distressingly frequent. A question like; "Do little children have hernia?" brooks no answer. (1967)

Dan Sullivan concurred that the production succeeded "by imposing an ever-moving and ever-interesting pattern of feeling on Miss Stein's apparent nonsense," and picked out Theo Barnes's performance for special mention: "[He] keeps being reminded of some intolerable personal anguish that he would never complain about in these circles" (1968b). Intriguingly, though, Kornfeld himself retained certain reservations about the performances of *In Circles*, which—for him—sometimes lost that vital sense of occurring in the present moment, and instead slid back into the conventional theatrical safety of rehearsed illusion: "The actors [were] so good at what they could do, that they

. . . would often be compelled to think of pretence outside the realm of reality" (1990, 140).

The challenge for the Judson Poets' Theater was always to keep its work fresh, to keep seeking new ways to take audiences by surprise, and so bring about those momentary perceptual epiphanies that might bring the observer to a renewed awareness of Being. The company's musical theater pieces (and there were many more besides those addressed in this chapter) constantly experimented with new angles, new conjunctions of people and ideas, but were marked nonetheless by an underlying consistency of quality and approach. "Mr. Kornfeld and his Judson Players have established a completely distinctive style of acting," Clive Barnes noted in reviewing *Peace*, Judson's 1968 musical adaptation of Aristophanes' satire: "It is like the choreography of James Waring, or perhaps even the collages of Robert Rauschenberg. It has within it the elements of self-mockery, a certain quizzical detachment, and yet it takes itself totally seriously, and properly so" (1968a).

9 The Open Theatre: Transformations

In order to "make it," we need to make images of ourselves. We compose ourselves from the cultural models around us. We are programmed into a status hunger. Once we have masked ourselves with the social image suitable to a type, we enter the masquerade of the setup. . . . An actor who approaches character without having considered the setup falls into it.

—Joseph Chaikin, *The Presence of the Actor*

Of all the leading off-off-Broadway groupings, the Open Theatre was the most intent on fusing an exploration into theatrical forms—specifically new acting techniques—with a challenge to the everyday "norms" of American society. The group's inspirational leader, Joseph Chaikin, had inherited a concern for political activism from his mentors at the Living Theatre, but also brought a quieter, more reflective approach to theatermaking. The evident seriousness with which his company operated—unsullied by "camp" frivolity or other modish distractions—helps explain why their work, in contrast to that of their underground colleagues, was given sustained coverage in the scholarly press almost from the outset (notably in the *Tulane Drama Review*—to which critic Gordon Rogoff, an active associate of the company, was a regular contributor). In time, Chaikin came to be regarded by critics as one of a select band of international "guru" directors—along with the likes of Peter Brook and Jerzy Grotowski, with whom he built important working relationships. Yet although the Open Theatre eventually transcended the New York context, touring nationally and internationally by the later 1960s, they remained very much an off-off-Broadway company in many key respects, not least in their insistence on maintaining dynamic collaborative relationships not just between actors and directors but also with living playwrights. While stressing Chaikin's catalytic role in the group, this chapter also seeks to emphasize some other, comparatively neglected contributions, which were crucial in the company's evolution toward a balance of the technically accomplished and the socially relevant.

Workshop Beginnings

Born in Brooklyn in 1935 and raised in Iowa, Joseph Chaikin returned to New York as a young man with the express intention of becoming a Broadway star. This career plan, however, was abandoned as a result of his work with the Living Theatre, which first hired him in 1959. He played a number of roles for the company, including taking over as Leach in *The Connection*, after Warren Finnerty left the cast. It was not until he featured as Galy Gay in Judith Malina's 1962 production of Brecht's *Man Is Man*, however, that the company's artistic and political stance began to sink in personally. "There I was, night after night," he wrote later, "giving all my attention to pleasing, seducing and getting applause from the audience, which is the very process wherein Galy Gay allows himself to be transformed from an innocent and good man into a machine—all because of flattery, one flattery after another" (Pasolli 1970, xiv). Chaikin began to reflect on his own ingrained assumptions, concluding that the pursuit of conventionally defined success would entail succumbing to what he came to call "the setup"—a prescribed role dictated for him by the existing sociopolitical system, rather than one he had defined for himself. And in succumbing, would he, like Galy Gay, eventually internalize the mask and become the thing demanded by the setup? Chaikin became fascinated by the question of the actor's social function. In effect, *Man Is Man* had brought about a kind of Brechtian estrangement from his own chosen profession, and provoked him to analyze its processes more carefully.

Chaikin found, however, that the Living Theatre had little interest in his new enquiries. The specific requirements of each production often demanded that actors adopt experimental approaches to performance, but exploration of the actor's craft, in and for itself, ranked low on the Becks' agenda. Chaikin twice initiated acting workshops for company members, and twice had to shelve them due to lack of interest. Knowing of his concerns, however, some students of acting teacher Nola Chilton, who had recently emigrated to Israel, approached him about working with them instead. The resulting, first meeting of the Open Theatre took place on February 1, 1963, "in the borrowed auditorium of the Living Theatre. Seventeen actors and four writers declared themselves to be a new theatre group, did some warm-up exercises and two improvisations, and then went across the street for coffee" (Pasolli 1970, 2). This group met regularly through the spring and reconvened in the fall in a borrowed space on Third Avenue. When the Living Theatre's Fourteenth Street theater was closed by the IRS, pushing the company into voluntary European exile, Chaikin stayed behind with his new colleagues.

Initially, the Open Theatre had no designated leader: its membership operated as a collective, and continued to do so throughout its history, taking practical decisions about company policy, finances, and so forth on the basis of group consensus. Nevertheless, Chaikin's inventiveness and sense of purpose quickly made him the de facto leader of their creative activities: "He tried not to be," observes Michael Smith (one of the four writers affiliated with the group from the outset), "but it was inevitable. His kind of leadership was indirect, a matter not of asserted authority but of the force and perseverance of his presence" (1973c). Workshop enquiries were driven by his attempts to find a viable alternative to the kind of emotional exhibitionism taught by the Method school, which he saw as designed to manipulate audience responses. He was drawn, instead, to the Brechtian notion that the performer should be visibly "estranged" from her or his role, and thus critically engaged with it. Yet even Brecht's alienation techniques, he felt, could too easily become merely ingrained habits, convenient artifice. Chaikin sought to find ways for actors to explore and harness their own spontaneous creativity, rather than resorting to intellectual rationalization for every gesture. How could the actor learn to be fully "present" onstage, rather than simply an agent for the dry reproduction of a prerehearsed illusion?

As we have seen, that same quest for disciplined spontaneity was also at the heart of much off-off-Broadway playwriting of the period, and lay behind some of the performance experiments at Judson Church. Larry Kornfeld's interest in working with charismatic nonactors sprang from his conviction that even a performer playing a character role should acknowledge the present "reality" of this "pretense"—something that was perhaps easier for those who had acquired less proficiency in the illusionistic tricks of the trade. For Chaikin, however, such approaches were in danger of throwing the baby (of actorly craft) out with the bathwater (of theatrical "fakery"). Methods had to be found for harnessing and directing the spontaneous impulse, rather than relying on "inspired amateurism."

In this respect, Nola Chilton had left a promising legacy. Like most acting teachers in New York, her work was based on a version of the Stanislavski method, but she had devoted serious attention to developing exercises intended to help actors performing in the new wave of absurdist dramas, in which psychological explanations for characters' behavior were often in short supply (to take an example from Ionesco: what is one's motivation to turn into a rhinoceros?). In Chilton's "weapons" game, for example, actors were asked to imagine the emotional states they associated with guns or swords, and then to externalize those feelings physically, so as to create not a crudely literal image of person being weaponlike, but a bodily expression of the essence of that idea.

Chaikin picked up on such ideas and developed them with new workshop exercises, such as the "Inside/Outside" game, which experimented with finding direct, outward expressions—however abstract or nonnaturalistic—for internal emotional states. Part of the purpose of such games was to help actors overcome acquired inhibitions about what was "appropriate" onstage, and thus liberate them to play freely with bodies and voices. This was still more apparent with the so-called transformation exercise, in which actors improvising a scene together could respond to the established situation not just by coming up with a new line, but by following an intuitive process of lateral connection, transforming themselves physically from one character or animal or object into another, sometimes altering the inferred context of the scene in the process. This exercise could result in responsive jamming sessions akin to jazz improvisation, or in rolling, confrontational status games, with actors seeking constantly to gain an upper hand by trumping each other's leaps of imagination. "Whatever realities are established at the beginning are destroyed after a few minutes and replaced by others. Then these are in turn destroyed and replaced," wrote director Peter Feldman (another Living Theatre veteran, and an important contributor to the Open Theatre's early experiments):

> The transformation, besides questioning our notion of "reality" in a very graphic way, also raises certain questions about the nature of identity and the finitude of character. At the Open Theatre, we tend to define character by what a person does that we can see, not by what society or his childhood experiences have produced in him. (Feldman 1966, 201–3)

Thus, like many off-off playwrights, Open Theatre began to reject the deterministic mechanics of naturalism in favor of a liberatory sense of free play, of the potential for transforming a situation rather than being confined by it. Chaikin's interest in Brecht was a contributory factor here, but so too was Erving Goffman's *The Presentation of Self in Everyday Life* (1959), which became something of a handbook for the company. This landmark sociological study examined the ways in which "character," in life as much as onstage, is determined by costume, setting, and linguistic patterns, rather than being a fixed, essential entity. Yet it is also, according to Goffman, something that is more often imposed on a person than consciously chosen (a "setup"). Various Open Theatre exercises sought to explore these impositions: "Perfect People," for instance, involved playing out the imagined lifestyles of the picture-perfect figures found in movies and magazines: "Perfect People are sanitized, regularized and glamorized types which the image-makers have us all secretly believing we ought to be" (Pasolli 1970, 37). Much fun was had improvising satirical scenarios for these impossible people with plastic smiles. Where the transformation exercise liberated participants to play, the Perfect People were trapped grotesquely in their assigned image.

Early Presentations

The Open Theatre initially had no plans to perform publicly. The workshop was dedicated to open-ended exploration rather than to production, and was, as the name further implied, open to anyone interested in the process. Since Chaikin's methods often seemed haphazard and unstructured, the group lost as many members as it attracted during this early, formative period. Nonetheless, his rigorous commitment to exploring the actor's craft was enthusiastically embraced by many of the young actors who were simultaneously cutting their performative teeth in front of off-off-Broadway audiences. Open Theatre actors appeared regularly in productions at the Cino, La Mama, Judson, and Genesis, often taking with them the ideas and techniques they had been working with, which thus became influential in other rehearsal contexts. The Open Theatre became a kind of research and development arm for the off-off-Broadway movement, since the busy producing venues tended to have little time for such reflective self-examination.

There was also, however, an increasing desire among some company members to present some of the results of their workshop explorations publicly, *as* the Open Theatre. Chaikin himself was highly ambivalent about such suggestions, but the eventual group consensus was that the value of their experiments, as theater, could only be properly judged if they were presented to an audience. During the 1963–64 season, two one-off evenings of improvisations and sketches were presented on dark Monday nights at the Sheridan Square Playhouse (December) and the Martinique Theatre (April). The following year, the company committed itself to presenting a further eight programs of improvisations and short plays at the Sheridan Square, on alternating Mondays between February and May 1965. Though presented in an off-Broadway house, the spirit of these programs was unmistakably "off-off." Admission was free (although donations toward costs were welcomed), and a virtue was made of the rough-edged quality of the presentations: designated as "open rehearsals" rather than as finished performances, they used a bare stage and a minimum of props. The actors presented themselves simply as themselves, as actors stepping in and out of a series of roles. The primary reality of the performer's presence onstage took clear precedence over dramatic illusion.

These public presentations necessarily brought a new focus to the role of playwrights within the group. Until this point, they had played a largely observational role, and some, like Sam Shepard, preferred to maintain that status. Shepard never wrote a play for the Open Theatre as such (although when *Icarus's Mother* premiered at Caffe Cino in 1965, it was in a production directed by Michael Smith, with a cast of Open Theatre regulars). He drew inspiration, however, from witnessing Chaikin's group in rehearsal, as they examined ideas of self-performance and role transformation—ideas that had been present in his own writing from the outset, on a more intuitive level. Irene Fornes, too, saw herself as observer more than participant, although her short play *The Successful Life of 3* was presented, in different versions, on two of the Sheridan Square bills in 1965. This piece applies the rapidfire shifts of the transformation exercise to a breakneck narrative about a curious ménage à trois. He, She, and 3 keep their names and basic characteristics throughout, but race with breezily deadpan detachment through an entire lifetime of changing circumstances—courting, marriage, childbirth, separations, global adventuring, and criminal racketeering—within the space of an act. Significantly, though, the characters' transformability does not appear to offer positive or liberatory potential: indeed they remain determinedly, sometimes outrageously amoral throughout. These are, Michael Smith observed, "brightly cold-blooded, ingratiating monsters, and in performance the play is chilling because it is so very charming" (Orzel and Smith 1966, 15). With its grotesquely clashing tones, *The Successful Life of 3*, subtitled "a skit for vaudeville," proved to be more at home at Judson Poets', where it was eventually given a full production in 1967.

The Open Theatre's inclination toward social critique was more clearly expressed in the short plays that Jean-Claude van Itallie wrote for the Sheridan Square season. From the outset, van Itallie was more directly involved with the Open Theatre's work than either Shepard or Fornes, often writing sketches and scenarios for them to work with in rehearsal. In 1965, he wrote two one-act plays based on the Perfect People exercise—fast-moving parodies of Hollywood's face-achingly wholesome Doris Day–Rock Hudson movies of the 1950s. The "Doris plays," *I'm Really Here* and *Almost Like Being*, were written to be presented as staged movies, in the sense that the actors were always to know which imaginary camera they were playing to, at what angle. "On camera," they were bouncy, smiling and impossibly happy; "off-camera" they appeared bored and drained of life. Under Chaikin's direction, *Almost Like Being* was presented with a precision of caricature and a tone of brittle jollity not dissimilar to *The Successful Life of 3*. In marked contrast to Fornes's play, however—or indeed many other off-off-Broadway plays drawing on popular culture sources—there was no sense here of a layered or ambivalent response to the material. The play's "statement" was made crystal clear by a final "freeze frame," which cut off the last two words of its sung finale. "Doris Day had a song called 'It's Almost Like Being in Love,'" Irene Fornes explains dryly: "so the profound thought of that piece was, 'It's Almost Like *Being*.' They were saying that being like that is not really being. Now [who], even at that time, would need to be told that Doris Day was not 'real?'" Her remarks point up the fact that, initially at least, the technical expertise demonstrated by the Open Theatre's actors was not always matched by a comparable subtlety or complexity in their approach to dramatic content. As van Itallie himself acknowledges in retrospect, "That caricature stuff is pretty facile," useful only for "making fun of things that are obviously facades and lies." The Doris plays typified the Open Theatre's early tendency toward a rather clumsy didacticism in its presentations: "Many of its initial statements were glib and self-congratulatory," Arthur Sainer recalls: "Here were performers and writers making an effort to see something of the inherent falsehood in the way our culture stated things. . . . When it failed, I suspect it was because the audience felt it was being gratuitously attacked for behavior which it hardly needed to be reminded of" (1984).

Megan Terry's contributions to the Sheridan Square season were somewhat more successful in balancing the Open Theatre's technical experimentation with a similarly open-ended approach to social enquiry. Her two plays based directly on the transformation exercise, *Calm Down Mother* and *Keep Tightly Closed in a Cool Dark Place*, were first showcased in March 1965. The latter takes the imprisonment of three men for murder as its basic premise, but runs through a dazzling series of variations on their basic circumstance, pastiching different dramatic genres and character types, so as to emphasize in different ways the characters' shared sense of claustrophobic entrapment and mutual distrust. The play implicitly addresses the psychologically damaging consequences of imprisonment, without ever turning it into an "issue."

Directed by Peter Feldman, and featuring three of the ensemble's leading actors—James Barbosa, Ron Faber, and Chaikin himself—*Keep Tightly Closed* was a tour de force in performance.

With hindsight, however, *Calm Down Mother* is the more historically significant of the two plays, in being one of most distinctively "proto-feminist" pieces of the period. This "transformation for three women," initially performed by Sharon Gans, Isabelle Blau, and Cynthia Harris, even ends with a mantralike sequence—"Our bellies / Our bodies / Our eggies" (Orzel and Smith 1966, 280)—which playfully but unequivocally advocates a woman's right to exercise birth control. The bulk of the play, however, avoids such neat statements, instead playing a series of subtly textured variations on the central thread of relationships among women—some of which are seen as positive and supportive, others destructive or problematic. In the process, Terry again utilizes a wide range of theatrical styles: thus, a divorcee and a friend whose mother is dying of cancer confront their fears in a moving, naturalistic scene, only to transform immediately into two old ladies rocking on a porch, whose comic banter is straight out of vaudeville. They then turn into a pair of prostitutes discussing clients with their madam, in a scene that seems at once to parody Hollywood's depiction of hard-boiled whores and to raise serious points about the dangers they face daily. Within a taut, compact structure, *Calm Down Mother* presses all sorts of emotional and intellectual buttons for its audience: exploding reductive stereotypes and using transformation to suggest a sense of the potentially limitless variety of women's lives and hopes, the play epitomized the Open Theatre's desire to speak to issues of consequence, while also allowing the complexity of their workshop investigations to be reflected on the level of content.

Directorial Innovation

In the fall of 1965, with many of her regular performers away on La Mama's first European tour, Ellen Stewart persuaded the Open Theatre to commit to performing a new program of work for a week or two each month, between October and May. As a progression from the Sheridan Square one-night stands, this residency provided production opportunities for all of the actors, directors, and writers involved with the company. Chaikin opposed the move, feeling that too much vital energy would be siphoned away from the continuing workshop explorations, and certainly, during that season, the company became somewhat fragmented, as different subgroups worked on different plays. Yet the La Mama residency also created the opportunity to focus further on the question of how the group's workshop explorations might be developed into a distinctive performance aesthetic.

A significant figure in this endeavor was director Jacques Levy, a friend of Sharon Gans's who became actively involved with the Open Theatre during the 1965–66 season. Levy was fascinated by Chaikin's workshop process, and his effort to entwine artistic investigation with social-political awareness. As a director, though, Levy was more interested than Chaikin in using the insights of the workshop to create finished performances. Levy's orientation, like Larry Kornfeld's, was toward finding radical directorial solutions for "difficult" texts: "I mean, unless there was something really, really strange going on with the intention of the playwright, why would I do the play?" He also felt, though, that he needed the playwright's consent to theatricalize those intentions in ways of his own devising. He formed just such an alliance with Sam Shepard, whom he met through the Open Theatre, and whose *Red Cross* he directed at Judson in January 1966. The venue was significant, as Judson liked to support such reciprocal, writer-director partnerships, but whereas the Kornfeld-Carmines works tended to leap out at the audience with an obvious desire to engage, Levy adopted a studiedly "cool" approach to Shepard's play: "We were edgier in the sense that there was a lack of concern about whether the audience is 'getting it' or not. It's not reaching out to the audience. It's giving them the credit for being intelligent: '*You* figure it out.'" With hindsight, Levy sees this attitude as relating closely to the post-Brechtian orientation of the Open Theatre. He directed his cast of three (Judson's Florence Tarlow, Genesis's Lee Kissman, and the Open Theatre's Joyce Aaron) to acknowledge the spectators but treat them with a kind of distanced disregard, as if they were behind translucent glass. That coolness was also reflected in the look of the piece: *Red Cross* is ostensibly set in a hotel room, in a wooded ski resort, but Levy chose to present it on an entirely white set with white costumes, as if this were a hospital or asylum—or, more abstractly, a white colorfield uniting figures and ground—and to light it with an almost oppressive glare. Shepard liked the effect so much that he wrote this design into the permanent text of the play—one of his very best from this period.

Levy's reconception of Michael Smith's *The Next Thing*, presented as part of the Open Theatre's La Mama residency that March, was still more radical. Originally written in three scenes, Smith's play is set before, during, and after a dinner at the home of Arthur and his mother, and owes something to Chaikin's "inside/outside" experiments, in that the characters seem

unashamed to enunciate and calmly act out the most taboo of inner urges—
even to the point of Arthur killing his mother. Smith aspired to an impact akin
to that of Strauss's opera *Salomé*, steadily building up to a sustained pitch of
ecstasy or hysteria, but his text perhaps had more in common with Oscar
Wilde's original *Salomé*, in being somewhat overwritten. Levy, however,
solved the potential pitfalls by chopping the text into eleven smaller scenes
and staging them out of chronological order. Apparently a response to the
obliquely distanced quality in much of Smith's dialogue, this approach rendered the play less "ecstatic" than coolly unnerving, creating an insoluble
puzzle-box of a play, with eerie blank spaces between the discontinuous
scenes. One moment, for example, mother is dead and covered with a sheet;
the next she is sitting up to the table. How did she die? Is she really dead? Is
there some metaphor to be unraveled? Or is her death simply what happens
in Arthur's mind, over and over again? Needless to say, the cutting back and
forth required total focus, "in the moment," from the actors, who could not
rely on conventional emotive through-lines.

Thanks to the resequencing, the murder itself, instead of occurring,
unseen, between the during- and after-dinner scenes, became the final, climactic event. Directly after scene 11, Levy staged a dumb show in which the
killing was repeatedly reenacted in agonizing slow motion, while a recording
of the last scene's dialogue was replayed behind it. Between all the other
scenes, he had Robert Cosmos Savage play manic harpsichord music, coming
in full tilt as the lights went out and cutting dead as they came back up. This
demented, vaudevillian twist ratcheted up the audience's disorientation: "If
Brecht was doing Marx," Levy quips, "we were doing the Marx Brothers."
Smith himself, having initially been skeptical about Levy's approach, came to
appreciate his interventions, and even had the play published in its rese-
quenced format (see Smith 1969, 87–118). "It probably hadn't occurred to me
to play with form so boldly," he notes, "and it opened me up to all kinds of possibilities I explored in later plays—making the form itself active, not just a con-
tainer of the action."

The organic relationships between form and content, text and process,
were explored still more fully in the Open Theatre's last La Mama offering, in
May 1966. *Viet Rock*, scripted and directed by Megan Terry, represented a real
step forward for the company, as the first piece to be entirely created through
the ensemble workshop process. It was also notable as one of the first theatrical responses to U.S. involvement in the Vietnam War, which had escalated
markedly in 1965 with the beginning of Lyndon Johnson's second term as

president. Running a weekly Saturday workshop over the course of the season, Terry led sixteen actors in applying some of the exercises developed by Chaikin to an exploration of the participants' responses to the war. She then selected images, scenes, and dialogue that emerged from these workshops, shaping them into a performing text that, though it bears her name as author, was also very much the work of the actors. In Europe, the Living Theatre was using "collective creation" in freely adapting existing narratives like *Antigone* and *Frankenstein*, but this was something else again—a new drama created from scratch by its performers. *Viet Rock* fully embodied the Open Theatre's conviction that actors were creative artists rather than mere interpreters of a playwright's words, but that a playwright was also needed to give form and voice to their experiments. As Peter Feldman memorably remarked, "When I read words which have been spoken by actors in an improvisation, I realize again what banal and clichéd writers actors usually are" (Terry 1966, 197).

Technically and visually, *Viet Rock* was a triumph, providing a virtuoso display of the Open Theatre's increasingly physicalized performance style. Without ever resorting to blackouts, the actors rapidly morphed from character to character, image to image, to create a kaleidoscopic array of war-related scenes. Group tableaux and gestural shorthands created everything from pulsating flower images (or were they wounds?) to parachute descents. Critic Michael Feingold, still a student when he first saw the piece, later recalled its extraordinary impact:

> On stage the men of the troupe are enacting a scene of battle in Vietnam. They create the jungle terrain with their bodies, the battle sounds with their voices, and the lines they speak are the random thoughts of people under stress. They advance. One mimes being hit, the others catch him, then, abruptly, the sounds change, the body is held high, and the group, rotating weirdly, has become a helicopter, transporting the wounded to Saigon. . . . I am enthralled. (1973)

Impressive as the piece was technically, however, it also brought into sharp focus the unresolved tension within the company over how best to balance its exploratory creative approach with its desire to be politically relevant. Feldman and Chaikin, who were drafted into the process shortly before the La Mama premiere to help tighten it directorially, came to the conclusion that— given its subject—the play needed an angrier tone and a more overt antiwar message than Terry's leadership had given it. During the following month, they attempted to rework the piece for a projected return engagement at La Mama, but Terry, feeling that her work had been violated, rejected their changes. Thanks in large part to the play's topicality, the troupe went on to play invited dates at the Yale School of Drama in September (the first guest production under Robert Brustein's deanship). *Viet Rock* then opened off-Broadway in November, at the Martinique Theatre (scene of *Six from La Mama* earlier that year), but the serious divisions that had by then opened up within the company were illustrated by Chaikin's request (reluctantly adhered to) that *Viet Rock* should not be advertised as an Open Theatre production.

With hindsight, it is easy to see why Terry felt that her coolly ironic approach to the material was the more appropriate. Because the piece was initially designed for presentation at La Mama, whose bohemian audiences were largely opposed to the war already, she was less interested in preaching to the converted than in adopting—like Levy, and indeed like many of her fellow off-off playwrights—a more oblique approach that would empower the audience to respond on their own terms. The piece clearly seeks to raise questions, and to present resonant theatrical metaphors for the sense of confusion and anxiety felt by so many over the escalating war. Terry's objectives, it seems, were for the presentation to mirror the enquiring nature of the process: "We tried to work on personal drives toward aggressive and warlike behavior. We worked on grief and regret. We played war games similar to those which American children play and we found the line between play and real was not too wide" (Terry 1966a).

This questioning approach informed many of the play's key features, including its title and its accompaniment by folk-rock songs (composed by Marianne de Pury, who worked with Terry on the project from its inception). As Terry noted, "A song seemed necessary to develop the strange feelings of today when we are fighting in Viet Nam with a discotheque soundtrack at home" (1966a). That sense of disjuncture is captured with savage irony by the show's opening "title track": "When the bombs fall / The Viets rock and rock / When the napalm bursts / Then the Viets roll. . . . Rock and roll / Rock and roll / How the sweet Viets / Love to rock and roll" (Terry 1966, 198–99). A similarly unsettling collision of war narrative and pop culture occurs when a platoon of new recruits parachutes into Vietnam, only to find themselves in a "Shangri-La" of exotic beauties—straight out of Hollywood's Oriental fantasies—who invite them to participate in a "slow motion orgy," until their sergeant reminds them bluntly that they are here to make war, not love. What exactly are the "realities" of this conflict, the piece seems to ask, when news and movies are jostling for space on television? A further twist is added by the sequence, at the end of act 1, when the actors—following the cry "Let freedom ring! Kill for freedom!"—exit singing "America the Beautiful" with, the stage directions say, "all the genuine fervor and gusto they can muster. Big, big, big" (211). Sung rousingly, without irony, the sequence confronts its audience with the fact that, even for sworn dissenters, that song has a kind of mythic emotional pull, which implicates its listeners in its patriotic fervor, and hence, whether they like it or not, in the violence justified by its invocation.

In his *Voice* review of the Martinique opening, however, Joseph LeSueur suggested that, in moments like this, "blind patriotism is held up as a virtue" (1966b). LeSueur and other critics balked at *Viet Rock*'s refusal to adopt a more overt antiwar position: "Being on the side of the angels isn't the same thing as having a point of view." Such objections seem, in some respects, to miss the point, yet LeSueur is correct insofar that the play, for all the provocative ingenuity of its individual moments, lacks coherence. Read now, as a text, *Viet Rock* seems too long and sprawling to sustain itself as a collage of devised sequences: "[Miss Terry] has simply hurled a style at the wall and let it splatter," Walter Kerr remarked in the *Times* (1966b, 1). Terry seems to have succumbed to the now-familiar hazard of collectively created theater, in being too fond of the actors and their "favorite bits" to be as ruthless as she needed to be in editing out redundant material. There are, for example, far too many weak comic sequences, featuring "an exceedingly unsophisticated form of irony" (LeSueur 1966b), cluttering up an otherwise promising script. More problematic still is the fact that, rather than focusing its attention on the conflicted, bewildered feelings of Americans at home, as initially intended, the bulk of the final piece is composed of on-the-ground combat experiences. These are rather crudely and naively imagined by young artists with no first-hand knowledge of war conditions.

Commercial Breakthrough

Following the uniformly negative press response, *Viet Rock* ran for six weeks at the Martinique before closing quietly. The most demoralizing thing for Terry's cast, however, was that another troupe of Open Theatre actors had premiered another, far more successful off-Broadway production four days prior to the Martinique opening. Jean-Claude van Itallie's *America Hurrah*, presented at the Pocket Theatre, had Chaikin's cooperation and achieved substantial critical acclaim (indeed, several reviews directly compared the two shows, using the virtues of van Itallie's as a means of highlighting *Viet Rock*'s failings). *America Hurrah* ran for over a year, becoming something of a "must-see" event, and played a short engagement in London in the summer of 1967—quite an achievement for a trilogy of one-act plays that, as van Itallie now readily admits, was initially mounted as a kind of "vanity" production. Largely financed using money from his wealthy family, the venture was his attempt to launch a professional playwriting career: "I thought my God, I'm nearly thirty, I haven't had any public exposure, I've been writing for little lofts and dark corners, and in terms of my parents' ethic I'm a total failure. Let me at least try once." In terms of Chaikin's ethic, however, such an ego-driven venture was questionable, and threatened the cohesion of the workshop process. Van Itallie, Chaikin's lover at the time, had to drag him aboard, "kicking and screaming," to direct *Interview* as the first piece in the trilogy.

First presented under Feldman's direction, in a draft version titled *Pavane*, at one of the Sheridan Square evenings the previous year, *Interview* had been written for the Open Theatre company, and made full use of their technical virtuosity and transformational abilities. It was, van Itallie notes, written in direct response to one of Chaikin's workshop exercises, "where they were being sensitive to everybody speaking at the same time, and knowing how to stop at the same time, without giving a prearranged signal. I began to think what it would be like to write something for many voices at once." *Interview* makes superb use of rhythmic, choral language patterns that are structured almost musically, as "an oratorio with an opening chorus, eight arias . . . and a closing chorale recapitulating the aria motifs" (Pasolli 1970, 89). As taut and punchy as *Viet Rock* is loose, the piece uses a cast of eight (four interrogators, four victims) to evoke a powerful sense of the ritualistic humiliation of job interviews, through a cacophonous layering of questions and responses. It then opens out to create a similarly noisy, impersonal urban landscape of offices, streets, and subways, as the actors enact a series of rapidfire scenic shifts and group tableaux. Chaikin's work on the production allowed him to consolidate and clarify his technical achievements with the company, and van Itallie further developed the text in response to these rehearsals, to create a piece finely tuned to the voices and abilities of the performers.

A similarly collaborative dynamic developed in relation to the other plays in the trilogy, *TV* and *Motel*, which were directed by Jacques Levy, using the same cast. *TV*, a new piece, was initially intended by van Itallie as the centerpiece for the evening. A satirical, McLuhanesque attack on the vapidity of the new televisual culture, it was a development on the techniques of the "Doris plays": the dull, "real" people working in a television studio are juxtaposed, on the other side of the stage, with the impossibly perky stars of the shows they program. The text pastiches numerous generic styles, from sitcom to soap to documentary, colliding violent war news with "human interest" stories. But though Levy pulled out all the showbiz shtick he could in rehearsing these scenes, he found that the satire somehow "wound up just being ponderous." He proposed the radical solution of intercutting the two "worlds" much more forcibly, by playing scenes simultaneously with each other to create a bewildering double-focus effect. "It's like with music," Levy notes of the aural layering created by the overlapping dialogues, "you can hear the brass and the reeds and the strings: you can hear it all, if you just let it happen to you." The "real" and "virtual" characters also gradually moved toward each other physically, so that the spatial separation between them was eventually erased completely. At that point, the two halves of the cast could only be distinguished by the thin black lines painted across the whitened faces of the TV people (a makeup suggestion of Remy Charlip's). These effects, written into van Itallie's published version of the play, are difficult to appreciate on the page, but were so tightly orchestrated in performance that audiences were again amazed by the company's virtuosity.

The final piece of the evening, *Motel*, had been premiered at La Mama in 1965, as *America Hurrah*. Arguably the most striking and forceful of the three plays (as well as the shortest), it was played exactly as written. Critics who had seen Michael Kahn's version at La Mama, however, felt that Levy brought a more incisive directorial edge. The difference between the productions was, in Levy's own view, epitomized by the doll-people's appearance: "The Robert Wilson masks were big and monstrous, and I didn't want that. We finally decided to use these clear plastic masks, which weren't outlandishly sized, but made the actors seem *totally* dehumanized." Similarly, rather than building the pitch of the performance up to a level of hysterical excess, Levy instructed his actors to carry on tearing the motel room apart at a consistently cool, robotically deliberate pace, thereby emphasizing an unsettling formal contrast with the blaring rock music, sirens, and blinding lighting effects. Levy had the noise and intensity build, inexorably, over an extended period, "higher and higher and higher until you could hardly stand it, until *boom*. It just stops dead." Deafening noise was followed by a deafening silence, which dared the audience to have the temerity to applaud.

In all three of its parts, then, *America Hurrah* assaulted its audience with layered sound and spectacle. It was an unlikely candidate for commercial success, but it benefited considerably from fortunate timing. Earlier in the year, Peter Brook's Artaud-inspired production of Peter Weiss's *Marat/Sade* had played to great acclaim in New York, acclimatizing critics and public to the arrival of "new theater techniques" (a label increasingly applied by the press to anything nonnaturalistic). Van Itallie suggests, moreover, that 1966 was "the right historical moment" for countercultural voices to break through to mainstream recognition: "If they couldn't suppress us, they would applaud us, [so] society co-opted us at that time." That analysis seems to be confirmed by the reviews: in the *Times*, Walter Kerr celebrated *America Hurrah* as "a whisper in the wind." Noting the lack of clear narrative lines in the three pieces, and their emphasis on theatrical effect, Kerr spoke of van Itallie as if he were heralding a theatrical revolution: "One of the things the theater is trying to discover at the moment is a means of approaching poetic effect on stage without reverting to echoing forms. And these deliberate 'primitives' come to seem a valid, perhaps necessary, first try—almost as though we were Greeks again, searching out a right sound for the stage" (Kerr 1966a).

America Hurrah was not, of course, a "first try" by any standards but those of the mainstream critics previously unaware of the underground theater scene. Significantly, the *Village Voice*'s Ross Wetzsteon stood out as a dissenting voice amid all the critical praise, arguing that these plays were, in fact, rather simplistic. Referencing the show's subtitle, "Three Views of the U.S.A.," Wetzsteon suggested that these could be summarized as follows: "Modern life is mechanical and unfeeling; television is banal and irrelevant; motels are slick and lifeless. . . . All this applies, by and large, to the scripts as well." The contribution of actors and directors could not be faulted, he stressed, but "all that talent and ingenuity" had been wasted on material that, in the case of *TV*, "would make a just passable college revue" (Wetzsteon 1966a). This analysis is reductive in its emphasis on content at the expense of form, and pays too little attention to the specific, experiential qualities of each piece. (The notable exception is the "perfectly balanced" *Motel*, praised by Wetzsteon for provoking uneasily conflicting responses: "We delight in seeing that obscenely slick motel turned into rubble, while at the same time we're painfully aware that this contradicts our aversion to violence.") And yet Wetzsteon's broader point is telling, for the framing of these three plays, in a commercial production under this title and subtitle, inevitably tended to flatten out their individual qualities. The audience was, in effect, told what to think in advance: here were three theatrical metaphors for the dehumanized state of America—or what Robert Brustein chose to call "the national malaise we have been suffering in Johnsonland" (van Itallie 1978, 6). This reduction of the plays to the level of political sound-bite permitted their comfortable absorption into a mainstream theater culture that, then as now, prized neatly packaged explanations over stylistic innovation or artistic ambiguity. *America Hurrah* thus succeeded in "crossing over" where previous commercial transfers from off-off-Broadway—from Judson's *Home Movies* to *Six from La Mama*—had largely failed. Appearing at a pivotal moment in the mid-1960s, it blazed a trail for future marketing of "countercultural" material.

The "Second" Open Theatre

Joe Chaikin, however, remained far from comfortable with this commercial breakthrough. With *America Hurrah* playing throughout the 1966–67 season, its performers' energies were again diverted away from the Open Theatre's week-to-week workshop programs. The company also continued to be riven by internal tensions—not least because eight of their number were being paid regularly as actors in van Itallie's show, while the others were not. Various new workshop projects were initiated that season—the most coherent of which was Jacques Levy's attempt to coordinate an ensemble investigation into the Kennedy assassination—but nothing solid came of them. After a year of tension and indecision, Chaikin concluded that firm action was needed to save the company and reassert its original objectives. Thus, when the Open Theatre reconvened in the fall of 1967, he announced that, for the first time, he would handpick the membership for his own workshop, and that the chosen group would meet four times a week—a more intensive commitment than had ever previously been demanded. Subsequently, although less exclusive workshops continued to be run by other company members, the focus of attention and energy moved decisively back to Chaikin's explorations. The excluded rump of the company began to drift away and look for other projects, while Chaikin's select group became closer than ever, forming what he came to refer to as "the second Open Theatre"—a company now dedicated to the careful pursuit of just one project at a time. At this juncture, Chaikin later noted, "I committed myself to never doing anything Off-Broadway or on Broadway ever again, and it's a commitment I hold to. That performing arena is not one I want to have anything to do with, because I think that the commercial interests, and the real estate, and the critics, and the unions contain it in a particular way" (Feingold 1973).

In subsequent years, the Open Theatre resisted commercial pressures by performing only occasionally in public, either by invitation, at colleges and theater festivals, or within the confines of its own loft workshop space. Here, performances remained free of charge—although audience members who could afford it were asked for a "donation" of two dollars toward overheads. The company thus reaffirmed its commitment to the raw simplicity of off-off-Broadway theater: "This whole setting makes La Mama look very commercial by comparison," one observer noted wryly after his first visit to the company's space at 60 West Fourteenth Street (which they inhabited from 1968 to 1973). In this "austere loft furnished in old office furniture and hanging natural-color burlap, with a highly polished linoleum floor," the audience seated themselves on cushions, pillows, old mattresses, and a few folding chairs. The stage area, "on the same floor level as is the audience, [is] lighted and set with the utmost simplicity. . . . Here the performance really *is* all" (Buck 1970).

The Open Theatre thus embraced the ideal of "poor theater," a term that was just coming into vogue as the ideas of Jerzy Grotowski began to be publicized in theater circles. Grotowski advocated the rejection of all extraneous staging apparatus, and even of conventional stage/auditorium divisions, in favor of creating a direct communion between actor and spectator in one shared space. Chaikin was clearly inspired by his Polish counterpart, whom he first met when Peter Brook invited them both to London in the summer of 1966, to participate in workshops toward his own group-devised production on the Vietnam War, *US*. When Grotowski subsequently visited New York in November 1967, with his leading actor Ryszard Cieslak, they demonstrated various of their techniques to the Open Theatre workshop. That same fall, the newly handpicked company began to apply a still greater physical rigor to their work than previously, regularly using Grotowskian exercises in their warm-up sessions.

These connections notwithstanding, Chaikin always maintained that the Open Theatre was on a "journey" different from that of Grotowski's ensemble. Certainly, the new piece that the company premiered in 1968, *The Serpent*, was a long way from the self-sacrificial anguish of Grotowski's *Akropolis* or *The Constant Prince*. Thoughtful, articulate, and downbeat, *The Serpent* finally pulled the previously disparate strengths of the company's work together into an extraordinary whole—dependent not only on the careful deliberation of Chaikin's workshop process, but also on group devising methods pioneered by Terry, on the coolly distanced performance aesthetic developed by Levy, and on a beautifully measured text provided by van Itallie. Subtitled "a ceremony," the piece was a meditation on biblical creation myths, and as such was superficially connected to other ritual-theater pieces of the time, such as the Living Theatre's *Paradise Now* or the Performance Group's *Dionysus in 69* (both also premiered in 1968—see chapter 12). Yet *The Serpent* belonged not so much to an Artaudian "theater of cruelty" as to the lineage of Brecht's "epic theater," in being composed of a carefully arranged sequence of self-contained episodes, each with a central "action" that the audience is asked to consider critically.

The Serpent was also firmly grounded in certain key principles of off-off-Broadway playmaking. Provocative structural juxtapositions and familiar imagery drawn from contemporary culture are used to spark questions and associations in the spectator's mind, without dictating a response. The piece contains, for example, staged reconstructions both of John F. Kennedy's assassination and of the very first murder, Cain's killing of his brother Abel. With the assassination having acquired at least as much mythic weight in the modern American mind as the biblical narrative, it was used—in effect—as a way *into* thinking about that more "primal" scene. Both killings are on some level inexplicable, products of some basic human urge to violence—a concern that, in 1968, was unmistakably immediate and relevant as a dramatic subject. Indeed, Martin Luther King and Robert Kennedy were both assassinated during the making of *The Serpent*, and these killings were interpolated into the scene depicting Jack Kennedy's death using imagistic shorthand references. By avoiding the temptation to draw explicit or didactic links between these disparate events, the company instead created a meditative experience for spectators, allowing them the time and space to bring their own associations and thoughts into play. If the piece was indeed "a ceremony," it was in the sense of providing not teaching or enlightenment to audiences, but the opportunity to participate in a process of community reflection; "in a kind of eucharist," as van Itallie put it, "where the actors are in some sense priests or celebrants" (1978, 2.6).

It should be noted that van Itallie's relationship with the rest of the company during this project was not always an easy one. Chaikin's workshop had remained closed to anyone but the actors themselves for most of the play's devising period, and van Itallie was brought in, late in the process, to start shaping the rich but rather amorphous mass of material they had developed into a workable presentational form. His imposition of words and structure on the material inevitably caused tensions in the group, especially when some individuals' favorite sequences were cut out. Yet van Itallie's relative distance seems also to have been very important, allowing him the objectivity and ruthlessness that Megan Terry had been unable to impose on *Viet Rock*. Taking the major scenes developed by the actors, he devised a structural sequence designed to maximize the reflective possibilities. Thus, after an opening scene in which a corpse, dead of a gunshot wound, is ritualistically autopsied, we are presented with the Kennedy assassination sequence: the corpse, initially symbolic of universal mortality, thus acquires a more specific and immediate identity. From here the piece backtracks to the Bible, presenting a "gardenscape" in Eden, in which the serpent tempts Eve to eat the apple, Adam follows suit, and God arrives to curse and evict the offenders. In following on from the assassination sequence, this familiar tale prompts new questions: is the world's current violence, for example, reflective of some deeper, innate "fallenness" in humanity? Next comes the Cain and Abel sequence, in which the murder is carried out with a kind of experimental brutality that seems both horrific and strangely innocent: "And it occurred to Cain to kill his brother," states the chorus, "but it did not occur to Cain that killing his brother would cause his brother's death" (2.42). As Cain tries desperately to revive the corpse, further questions arise: does any of us really know what the consequences of our actions will be? What is "innocence" anyway?

This process of open-ended questioning, partly engendered by the sequencing of the scenes, is greatly enhanced by the series of layered, echoing "chorus" speeches that van Itallie wrote for female voices, after interviewing several of the women in the company about their lives and hopes. Providing oblique links between the major scenes, these speeches consist of pithy comments on the life experiences of ordinary people, which rub provocatively against the "mythic" events being enacted. Their effect is to ask spectators to acknowledge their own state of bewilderment and uncertainty: "In the beginning anything is possible / I've lost the beginning / I'm in the middle / Knowing neither the end nor the beginning" (2.35). Such lines echo in the mind, begging further questions and suggesting connections, during the often largely nonverbal scenes that follow them. "The word is one element," van Itallie comments pointedly, "but . . . it's the top of the iceberg; it's what clicks everything else into place" (Venza 1970).

Van Itallie's contribution would not have been possible, however, without the weight and subtlety of the performance sequences developed by the company, which also tend to rely on structural ingenuity for their meditative effects—as is particularly apparent from viewing the surviving television recording. The Kennedy sequence, for example, which was lifted almost wholesale from work done in Jacques Levy's 1966–67 workshop, breaks the Dallas assassination down into twelve frozen images, based on a sequence of twelve stills from the notorious Zapruder film, as printed in *Life* magazine (the film itself was not seen by the public until the 1970s). In performance, the twelve tableaux are played in sequence, forward and backward, sped up and slowed down, like a videotape being played back again and again. (The gunman himself "calls the shots" by counting out the number sequences.) Rather than numbing the viewer to the horror of the real events, however, as tends to happen with television replays, the onstage repetitions become more agonizing as they go on. At first the scene even seems slightly comic, with a waving crowd making "ooh aah" noises in the background (the crowd shuffles sideways while the "car" stays center stage, to suggest its movement). Gradually, though, the extraneous details are cut out, as the repetitions focus on the victims themselves, rocked again and again by the impact of bullets, yet returned again and again to the happy smiling and waving at the beginning of the sequence. The pop-art ironies of the Open Theatre's early work are thus themselves recycled into a sequence of eerie poignancy. Brief, iconic representations of the King and RFK killings are also layered into the scene as the sequence continues to repeat, and as a chorus of onlookers begins to chant a mantra of helpless denial: "I was not involved / I am a small person / I hold no opinions / I stay alive . . . I keep out of big affairs / I am not a violent man / I am very sorry, still / I stay alive" (van Itallie 1978, 2.21).

Here again, the content of van Itallie's words is perfectly judged: they succinctly encapsulate themes of guilt, responsibility, and innocence that recur in similar verbal motifs throughout the piece, triggering thoughts like small pebbles being dropped into water to create ripples. Yet, as the recording makes clear, the performers' delivery of these words is also crucial in lodging them, echoingly, in the viewer's mind: a kind of hollow, guttural pulse, emphasizing different syllables during different repetitions of the phrases, gives the words the pull of a shuffle drumbeat (or a heartbeat?). In such moments, the company's collaborative dynamic reaps rich rewards, as the writer's words, inspired by the company's enquiries, are given life by the actors' technical skills. The same is still more powerfully true of the Cain and Abel scene. Here, the chorus of women chants the story of the killing in a cyclical, plainsong recitation, *before* the scene itself has got under way. The singsong narrative, with its pointed commentary on the events, then seems to hang in the air during the almost total silence that accompanies the enactment of Abel's death. Cain twists and mauls his brother's body casually, experimentally, his actions punctuated only by a plaintive bleating sound representing the presence of his sheep, and the occasional thudding of Abel's limp limbs onto the stage floor. For Ross Wetzsteon, this superbly constructed sequence was "the most profound and terrifying image of murder I've ever seen in the theatre. [In] their desperate unity, murderer and murdered become a kind of black and violent pieta" (1969b).

The heart of *The Serpent*, though, the center from which all the rest seems to flow, is the scene in the Garden of Eden, which is also established using an extended period of near silence. Here, the company's technical achievements in using their bodies to suggest plants and animals is deftly complemented by the way these images seem to comment further on the themes of the piece. Paul Zimet, for example, makes a wonderful movement solo out of his choice of creature, the heron, who stands tall and aloof, gently flexing his "wings." He seems graceful, beautiful, but is also notably detached from the rest of the action: when Zimet re-creates the same image in later scenes, one begins to wonder if the heron represents a narcissistic self-involvement, a refusal to see and engage with the world ("I stay alive"). Related questions arise when God curses Adam and Eve after they have eaten the apple: "He" speaks to them, weirdly, through their own bodies and voices, as if they are possessed by his spirit in those moments. Could this also suggest that God is in some sense their creation, not they his? "So man created God," the chorus announces later on, in one of a series of "Statements" designed to be questioned: "What for? To set limits on himself" (49).

The need for such limits and laws is apparent in the violent deaths of Abel and Kennedy, but the piece also clearly implies that remaining pure and innocent is never an option. In the garden, the serpent is also the tree of the knowledge of good and evil: six men form a tight grouping of writhing, serpentine arms and legs, which simultaneously suggests a tree waving in wind, dangling apples from its "branches." Temptation comes inextricably entwined with knowledge. And if the loss of innocence means that humanity is capable of violence, of murder, does not greater self-knowledge also bring with it the potential to aspire to greatness, to goodness—to paradise, even? "There is no measure / To what degree / The mind imagines, receives or dreams," the doctor announces in the opening autopsy scene (18). "Imagine. Imagine," the serpent hisses at Eve, tempting her with what she might be able to see and know if she takes the apple:

Eve:	But, is what you can imagine
	What will be?
Serpent 1 & 2:	How can you know
	Until you eat?

(26–27)

These lines could stand as a loaded motto for the entire countercultural experiment of the 1960s. For the Open Theatre, there was no pretense to the prelapsarian innocence that so many hippies claimed for themselves in this period. Rather, *The Serpent* suggests an acute awareness of the potential of each individual—not just of governments and armies—to do terrible harm. And yet the necessity to eat of the apple, to experiment with experience even though the consequences may, on occasion, be horrific, also seems strongly apparent. We may fall, we may die, the piece implies, but in the process, maybe we will imagine and create something new, something outside the present cycle—the present "setup"—of fixed roles, fixed enmities, fixed laws and hierarchies and conventions (both social and theatrical). In this sense, *The Serpent* encapsulated and articulated the dreams not only of the Open Theatre, but of the off-off-Broadway community at large.

10   La Mama Troupe: The Kernel of Craziness

O'Horgan is getting all the blame for the gimmicky excesses of "the new theatre" but little of the credit for its fluent physicality and disciplined spontaneity.
Those who use the word "O'Horganism" as a pejorative seem to me to mistake
fluidity for sloppiness, imagistic intelligence for mindlessness, and evocative
artifices for stage trickery. . . . Acting "with the body," or the "physicalization of
language" are not rejections of mind and language, as commonly argued, but
rather the method of seeking [a] fusion of body and mind, of the physical and
the spiritual.

—Ross Wetzsteon, *Village Voice*, March 6, 1969

The success of the Open Theatre in developing an ensemble-driven performance approach, allowing for a reciprocal relationship between the creative
work of actors, directors, and writers, inspired many other groups to attempt
similar collaborations. Primary among these was La Mama Troupe, under the
direction of Tom O'Horgan, which single-handedly revived the exuberant
spirit of the traveling minstrel show and became internationally renowned for
the no-holds-barred theatricality that they applied to a series of unusual plays
pushed in their direction by the ever-watchful Ellen Stewart. In line with
Stewart's policy of forcefully promoting her artists in the wider world, La
Mama Troupe capitalized much more than did the Open Theatre on the critical and commercial breakthrough of van Itallie's *America Hurrah*, and by
mid-1968, two of their productions—Rochelle Owens's *Futz* and Paul Foster's
Tom Paine—were running simultaneously off-Broadway. In the same year,
O'Horgan also had his first freelance directorial success, pouring many of the
theatrical ideas he had developed at La Mama into the hit Broadway production of the hippie musical *Hair*.

O'Horgan's commercial successes made him a controversial figure at the
time, particularly among those purists who accused him of "selling out." The
extraordinary, Dionysian physicality of La Mama Troupe's work was often
unfavorably compared with the meditative precision of the Open Theatre, or
the harsh asceticism of Grotowski's Polish Lab—as if the unbridled expression
of bodily joy were somehow tasteless or exploitative. To his admirers, though,

O'Horgan's work was more than worthy of comparison with that of other lead-ing experimental directors. He shared with Chaikin, Kornfeld, and Grotowski a fundamental concern with emphasizing the immediacy of the theatrical event as "an appointment in time" (as he puts it) between actors and audi-ence. The difference was simply that the energies invoked by La Mama Troupe were earthy, bodily energies—effervescent and erotically charged, sweaty and excessive—which seemed to hostile observers to smack of indisci-pline, or even anti-intellectualism.

Similarly, they were accused by some of riding roughshod over the texts of the plays their productions were based on, of treating them simply as pretexts for theatrical showmanship. Certainly, the troupe treated the script as only one element among many, and their layered use of visual, verbal, and musical registers meant that individual components had to compete for attention. Yet as O'Horgan himself stresses, "The *sense* of a play, the textures of a play, the language of a play" provided the vital raw material and starting point for each new production. Whereas the Open Theatre evolved toward creating its own collective texts, which were then structured and given words by playwrights, La Mama Troupe began with the text's structures and language, and built around them. "Ninety-nine percent of the stuff I've done," O'Horgan points out, "has been new pieces, sitting right with the writer." For playwright Paul Foster, who collaborated directly with O'Horgan on a string of plays for La Mama, he was, "quite simply, the greatest living director for the insane and lively art of the theatre" (1970, 6).

Early O'Horgan

The originality of Tom O'Horgan's work as a director stemmed largely from his unorthodox background. An autodidact with no conventional theater training, he was first and foremost a musician. During the 1950s, he wrote music for a number of theater groups in Chicago, and also worked as an off-beat variety entertainer, playing twelve-tone songs and early English ballads on a harp, while cracking jokes (he once appeared on Ed Sullivan's television talent show). He then became musical director for the New York branch of the Chicago-based improvisational comedy club Second City, an experience that further developed his sense of the immediate, "in the moment" relation-ship between performer and audience. The New York club, however, closed in 1963: "There was a period just about the time Kennedy was shot," he recalls, "when satire suddenly just dried up." Finding himself without a career, O'Horgan began creating small-scale, mixed-media happenings in his loft, two of which—*A Masque* and *Love and Vexations*—were performed at Caffe Cino in August and September of that year. His breakthrough production, however, came in 1964 with his first attempt to apply his evolving, cross-disciplinary approach to a prewritten play-text. Genet's avowedly metatheatrical play *The Maids* proved an ideal starting point for his experiments with staging character-based, representational plays in ways that emphasized their theatrical immediacy.

The third significant downtown staging of *The Maids*, following Julie Bovasso's in 1955 and Andy Milligan's in 1961, O'Horgan's was also the first American production to use male actors in the roles of Claire and Solange, as Genet had allegedly intended. In an America recovering from the repressions of the 1950s, transvestite casting was still taboo, and as O'Horgan recalls of the rehearsal process, "even with my crazy background, it was hard for me to concentrate on the play with these guys dressed as ladies." Realizing that audiences were likely to spend the first ten minutes of the show simply trying to absorb the implications of the gender switch, rather than paying attention to the dialogue, O'Horgan decided to shoot a filmic prologue to help them adjust. Thus, the actors were seen gaily running around Abingdon Square in their frocks, until lights came up behind the gauze projection scrim, and the actors were revealed, in the flesh, on set. The device was typical of O'Horgan's emerging aesthetic—to take a problem presented by the desire to serve the text itself, and solve it with a highly theatrical twist of convention that drew attention to the actors' physical presence.

The Maids was first presented in the small dance studio that was part of O'Horgan's Third Street loft apartment, and quickly became a talking point in the local arts community. Never one to miss an opportunity, Ellen Stewart invited him to re-present it at La Mama's venue at 82 Second Avenue, which he did in October 1964, a month before that space was closed. He remounted it again at 122 Second Avenue that December, and again the following August—an indication both of the show's popularity with La Mama audiences and of Stewart's determination to woo O'Horgan, by establishing him as a leading presence at her theater. "Her original intention was to evolve new playwrights," O'Horgan recalls, "but these writers of hers were from outer space; they just wrote whatever they wanted. She needed a couple of good directors so that she could take all this very weird stuff and somehow make it function, on no budget whatsoever." From 1965, he began directing regularly at La Mama, accepting whatever new scripts Stewart thrust in his direction. Some of them were, he admits, distinctly unpromising on the page, but he developed a tactic of searching out "the kernel of craziness" in each one and building a theatrical experience around these key ideas or motifs: "Frequently what I wanted was just to do the stage directions."

O'Horgan's importance to La Mama was demonstrated incontrovertibly by the events of La Mama's first European tour, in the fall of 1965. He and Stewart's other favored director at the time, Ross Alexander, led a company of sixteen actors to Europe by ship, which then split into two troupes. Alexander took one to Paris, to perform their repertoire of off-off one-acts at the new American Center, while O'Horgan took the other to the Aaso Skole Theatre in Copenhagen, believing they had drawn the short straw. They were greeted, however, with open arms: "Within a week at this theater there were lines around the block," he recalls with amazement: "You couldn't get into the damn place. We were like stars in this little country!" By stark contrast, Alexander's troupe bombed in Paris, and when the two troupes switched cities, as planned, it did neither any favors: Alexander's work proved a relative disappointment to the Danes, while O'Horgan's group faced an uphill struggle to interest the turned-off French. "We got no reviews, nothing," recalls actor Michael Warren Powell, "and we were starving!" After the scheduled programs had played out, both troupes found themselves penniless and stranded, without the funds to return home to the United States. Left to their own devices, Alexander's actors dispersed quietly: devastated by the whole experience, he never directed a play for La Mama again. O'Horgan's group, however, traveled back to Glumso, Denmark, where they had been offered an unofficial "residency" at an old schoolhouse, which functioned as the local arts center.

Reduced by circumstance to a core of just five actors—Powell, Mari-Claire Charba, Jacque Lynn Colton, Victor LiPari, and Kevin O'Connor—the troupe stayed in Denmark throughout the winter, rehearsing a stack of new plays and traveling with their host, Elsa Gress. A lecturer on Denmark's circuit of small, community-based arts colleges, Gress arranged for them to perform in "these little dinky places" (Powell), to help pay their way. During this time, the group began to develop a real sense of cohesion as an ensemble, and the first signs of their distinctive identity began to emerge. Even at this early stage, for example, there was a strong sense of physicality about their work. Mari-Claire Charba recalls O'Horgan's version of Foster's *Hurrah for the Bridge* as being built around the image of the Rover's weighty cart being wheeled up and down ramps, in and out of the stage space: "the whole production was this cart-carrying."

Eventually the funds were found for the troupe to return to the United States, where they showcased six plays at the Firehouse Theatre in Minneapolis, before remounting them off-Broadway as *Six from La Mama* in March 1966. Observers were struck by how tight and cohesive the group had already become: "I had heavy misgivings about the company's work," Firehouse director Sydney Schubert Walter wrote to former Open Theatre colleague Michael Smith (perhaps with some of La Mama's more ramshackle café productions in mind), but "I was all wrong and am delightfully surprised. [There is] no slapdash feeling, no sense of a touring company in makeshift relation to the place. . . . The look, the feel, the overall tone of the plays is just right" (Smith 1966b). O'Horgan's central role in the troupe's evolution was not lost on Stewart, who became convinced that it was the dynamic, theatrical manner in which the plays had been presented, rather than the specifics of the texts themselves, that had made them appealing and accessible—particularly to foreign audiences. "I learned in 1965," she remarks bluntly, that "English is not the beginning and end of anything. Generally it's the ending; it messes you up." It might be countered that La Mama's relative success in Copenhagen, as against Paris, was related to the fact that Danes generally speak English with greater fluency and willingness. For Stewart, though, the lesson was clear: "I found that the plays that were the most visual were the ones that people liked." From this point on she began to shift the emphasis of her operations toward the development of director-led projects in which the visual and musical aspects were at least as significant as the verbal. That shift of emphasis also allowed Stewart herself to make greater use of her own gifts for team building: "Her great talent was in seeing how this person fit with that person," O'Horgan recalls, "in creating the kind of chemistry that you can make something from. She was an absolute genius at this."

Workshop Developments

Following the closure of *Six from La Mama*, O'Horgan and his actors resolved to consolidate their almost accidental status as an ensemble group by establishing an ongoing workshop. Having just witnessed the obvious benefits of the Open Theatre's workshop process during their 1965–66 performance residency at La Mama, Stewart willingly assented to their request for a permanent rehearsal space, renting a large basement on East Ninth Street. The newly titled La Mama Troupe went back to work almost immediately, experimenting with a variety of staging methods. This was not, however, a long period of isolated workshopping of the kind favored by Chaikin. The company had been forged through the challenges presented by staging unorthodox, one-act plays to tight production deadlines, and they continued to operate this way, being stretched constantly by new material.

The troupe premiered a string of plays at La Mama through 1966, and, during the summer, also worked on filming *Three from La Mama* for National Educational Television. Commissioned to shoot three plays of their own choosing, they recorded van Itallie's *Pavane* (later *Interview*) in a studio, and Foster's *The Recluse* and Shepard's *Fourteen Hundred Thousand* on location in "found" buildings on Welfare Island and Park Avenue. Broadcast in the fall of 1966, in the wake of the off-Broadway premiere of van Itallie's *America Hurrah* (which of course included *Interview*), *Three from La Mama* added further to the company's growing renown. Then in October, the now nine-strong troupe embarked on a second European tour, playing in Sweden, Yugoslavia, and England, with a number of plays from their back catalog, as well as new pieces including Tom La Bar's *Tattoo Parlor* and Rochelle Owens's *Homo*. By Christmas they were back home at La Mama premiering a new Paul Foster piece, *The Hessian Corporal*.

At this point, O'Horgan decided to shake things up. During the winter of 1966–67, he expanded the workshop group to a roster of thirteen. This included all of the original troupe (except Jacque Lynn Colton), as well as influential new members like Peter Craig, Claris Erickson (aka playwright Claris Nelson), Jerry Cunliffe (who had worked with O'Horgan in Chicago in the 1950s, and had played the lead in Judson's ill-fated 1959 production of *Faust*), and Seth Allen. Rated by O'Horgan as "one of the greatest actors this country has ever had," Allen joined the troupe from the Open Theatre, where he had been a key member of the *Viet Rock* ensemble. He thus brought new insights and exercises to their work, as indeed did Marilyn Roberts and Victor LiPari, who had participated in workshops with Jerzy Grotowski in Europe. It is notable that the kind of physical discipline demanded by Grotowski began to feature more prominently at this time in the La Mama Troupe's work, as well as in the Open Theatre's. "We'd do exercises from 8:00 A.M. until noon," Powell recalls: "headstands and calisthenics and acrobatics and dance, and then work on the plays." O'Horgan, however, sought to apply this new physicality in directions very different from Grotowski's stark asceticism.

One of the original physical exercises developed by O'Horgan, known as "the Row," gives a good indication of his troupe's objectives. This involved dividing the actors into two groups and placing them at opposite ends of the rehearsal space. They would then walk toward each other, pass, and keep going to the opposite wall—the twist being that they must take forty-five minutes to an hour to accomplish the task. During this slow-motion cross-over, which necessarily concentrated attention on the basic physical process of placing one foot in front of the other, the actors might also be asked to perform additional activities, from standing on one's head to exchanging a piece of clothing with an oncoming person: "And this is quite complex when you slow it way down," O'Horgan notes, "because the gravity aspect works upon you."

According to troupe members, such exercises worked to develop their abilities in a number of directions. First, Jerry Cunliffe suggests, "It's about connecting body and mind—a very eastern kind of thing—keeping the body active and expressing things through the body." As O'Horgan explains, "If you really get your body to move in slow motion, some other part of the brain takes care of it, and then your mind is free to free-associate in different ways." As the actors tuned themselves into this "wavelength," they found that the possibilities for improvisation in rehearsal extended greatly, as they responded to the words and ideas in a play-text not just on a rational level, but on an intuitive, physical level. Michael Warren Powell recalls "the Row," in particular, as an exercise that helped develop the troupe's aptitude for making fluid transitions from one role or mind-set to another, thanks to the game of using found objects as imaginative triggers: "You'd pick up a hat, and then meld that into a character. Then you'd come across a shoe, and that would sort of modify the character. And someone else would pick up another shoe, so you'd become a pair with this person."

A second key function of O'Horgan's rehearsal exercises was to develop the troupe's awareness of time and rhythm: "Working at different speeds," he notes, "in slow motion and fast motion, in staccatos," was fundamental to the troupe's aesthetic:

> It's sort of like applying music to movement. We did an awful lot of work in that direction, because improv is great, but you have to have guidelines, you have to have structure, so that it goes someplace. So we had the chordal structure of a play, and how to divide that up into moments and beats was what our rehearsals were all about. Trying to figure out where the beats were, and who's in charge of this beat and how far you can go with it.

Thus, although the troupe's work often appeared wild and loose, it was timed to the second. Actors might be given leeway to improvise in performance, but within a specific period of "beats," measured against lines in the text: "He'd give us a frame," Peter Craig recalls, "and he'd say, you can do anything you want, but don't go out of the frame."

Another key musical concept adapted by O'Horgan was that of counterpoint. Imagine a room full of people performing the Row together, and one begins to have a sense of the kind of multiple-focus "chaos" that was a hallmark of the La Mama Troupe's work. What all involved stress, however, was that there was nothing haphazard about the simultaneous juxtaposition of images and activities in their work. Exercises like the Row taught the performers to be attuned to the actions of everyone in the room, so that their own moves complemented or competed with them at just the right moment: "It was all about trust," Peter Craig emphasizes. Paul Foster, who worked closely with the troupe at this time, became fascinated by the theatrical potential of such layered activity, and applied it directly in writing *Tom Paine*—a historical drama that he developed collaboratively with the troupe, by bringing in a few pages at a time for them to rehearse and develop. Numerous passages in the play feature simultaneous action and dialogue on two or more parts of the stage. Foster also specified that the actors should play musical instruments, including O'Horgan's own collection of often freakish antiquities—"harpsichord . . . crumhorn, oboes, recorders, cymbals, serpent, triangle" (Foster 1967a, 9)—so as to create a cacophonous soundtrack of anachronistic noise.

O'Horgan's "total theater" of multilayered sound and image—sometimes jarringly abrasive, sometimes deliriously appealing—was thus the polar opposite of Grotowski's "poor theater," which emphasized the stripping away of all theatrical components "extraneous" to the essential confrontation of actor and spectator. O'Horgan was looking, instead, to integrate "all aspects of life and all aspects of art." He encouraged troupe members to bring in new objects, tunes, images, to be stirred into the mix: Michael Warren Powell recalls rehearsals with O'Horgan as "a very mutual process. It was completely open, a madhouse of creativity." Nevertheless, everything remained geared to the play-text at hand, and this also meant that another central element of the troupe's aesthetic was an emphasis on storytelling. This was a feature conspicuously absent from many other theatrical experiments of the period, given their emphasis on the immediate "presence of the actor," rather than on characters depicted in another time and place. Yet La Mama Troupe embraced narrative by stressing a sense of childlike play, of "let's pretend": by acting out a story through obviously playful, artificial methods, it was hoped that the spectator would be doubly engaged by the event's immediacy, enjoying the making of the story as well as the story itself.

To this end, the troupe also developed a simple, playful use of props, which could transform their function from one moment to the next. "The big blue" was one such item: this large blue bolt of cloth, ideal for packing and touring, was used in *Tom Paine* to create images as different as billowing ocean waves and the spectacular "Termite Queen" tableau—which functioned as a short-hand representation of Marie Antoinette, during the French Revolution sequence. Marilyn Roberts would push her torso through a slit in "big blue," and then be lifted up to stand on the shoulders of other (unseen) company members, as if suddenly growing into a skirted giant. With the edges of the cloth stretched out by other actors, making strange insect noises, the giant would then move downstage and Roberts—her thighs braced from below—would lean out over the audience like the prow of a ship to utter the words "Eat Cake!" The troupe's reputation for colorful, vivid stage imagery sprang from the use of such simple but telling methods.

As La Mama Troupe developed their idiosyncratic brand of "storytelling for adults," they also necessarily became more selective about the texts they worked with. Instead of simply treating whatever script Stewart gave them as a new challenge with its own, individual solutions, they began to prioritize wilder, looser works that encouraged a kind of chaotic playfulness: "We were looking for plays that would support this style," O'Horgan acknowledges. La Mama's playwrights proved happy to oblige by writing *for* this style. The repertory of four plays with which the troupe embarked on their third European tour, in June 1967, included three new plays written with their working methods in mind. Foster's *Tom Paine*, written in two acts, was the longest and most directly O'Horgan-oriented, but Sam Shepard's *Melodrama Play* and Leonard Melfi's *Times Square* also invited ensemble creativity in the rehearsal process. *Melodrama Play* signaled a striking departure for Shepard: this was the first play in which he used songs, a live band, and satirical cartoon figures. Similarly, Melfi's play was built not around dialogue but around a gaudy theatricality, complete with music and offbeat dance sequences, features a gang of cartoonlike Times Square types, from street hustler to sandwich-board wearer, each embodying aspects of the bittersweet sense of loneliness that was the hallmark of Melfi's writing. "They all begin to pantomime eating, and then drinking," one stage direction reads: "They are getting high on drinking. The sky is getting darker, but the lights are bright and flashing now from all the neon signs. Music is heard everywhere. They are all dancing everywhere" (Melfi 1967, 168). Given that kind of license, the troupe could have a ball.

Yet the play O'Horgan now cites as his personal favorite among the troupe's repertoire was also the only one of the four written without prior knowledge of their work. Rochelle Owens's *Futz*, written in 1958 when its author was just twenty-three, had been slated for production by the Living Theatre in 1963, prior to their departure for Europe. Owens offered it to Judson Poets' Theater following their successful productions of Owens' *Istanbul* and *The String Game*, but then (much to the consternation of Larry Kornfeld, who had already assembled a cast) gave it to O'Horgan, on the strength of his touring production of *Homo*. The play, a grotesque rural fantasy about a farmer who copulates passionately with his pet pig, Amanda, proved perfect for the troupe, and was catalytic in developing their performance experiments that winter. *Futz* premiered at La Mama in March 1967, as the first production by the newly expanded ensemble, and was immediately recognized by Michael Smith as a major leap forward: "From the start, [O'Horgan's] productions had a personality of their own and seemed adequate and appropriate to the various scripts," he wrote, but they had been distinguished by "scattered, striking theatrical ideas" rather than a coherent performance style. *Futz*, conversely, demonstrated "a dense, fierce continuity of energy, fearless physical vitality, primitively expressed vocalization. [The] performance is dance and music as well as drama, [with] a life of its own, independent of the play" (Smith 1967b).

Futzing Around

The itinerary for La Mama's third European tour reflected the troupe's standing. They played eight cities in Germany, Holland, Italy, Denmark, and Sweden, from where—following the Stockholm dates—journalist Ingmar Bjorksten wrote to the *Village Voice*, confirming the troupe's renown by hailing them as "prophets from a new land of theatre" (1967). It was the troupe's reception at the Edinburgh Festival in August, however, that really got people talking back home. *Tom Paine*, appearing as part of the official celebrations, was described by *The Times'* Michael Billington as "far and away the most adventurous and exciting offering in this year's Festival drama programme." Meanwhile, despite being part of the unofficial "fringe," *Futz* attracted still more attention, thanks to the attempts of some of the British tabloids to have Owens's "bestiality play" banned as an obscenity. The campaign succeeded only in boosting box office, however, as indeed did the reviews: "It is unlikely that any other dramatic event at this year's festival will be as stunning," commented the conservative *Daily Telegraph* (qtd. Russell 1996, 170).

The troupe's success in Edinburgh led directly to an engagement at the Mercury Theatre in London's Notting Hill, from which they moved, in October, to the larger Vaudeville Theatre in the West End theater district. The reviews were again highly enthusiastic, emphasizing the cohesion of the ensemble playing, and the acrobatic verve of the performers. A dissenting voice was provided by expatriate American director Charles Marowitz, who dismissed the company's overt theatricality as "puerile," in a *New York Times* article (1967). His comments, however, drew a strongly worded letter to the *Times* from leading British playwright John Arden: "What they have managed to do with both *Futz* and *Tom Paine* is to arouse a quite remarkable degree of excitement among informed and receptive theatre workers in this city. . . . La Mama Troupe's visit here is going to have a very great effect upon the work done in England over the next few years. I know my own writing is already being influenced considerably" (1967).

The company's international acclaim created considerable curiosity in New York, precisely as Ellen Stewart had always hoped. Capitalizing on this, she negotiated off-Broadway openings for both *Futz* and *Tom Paine*. Foster's play opened first, in March 1968, at Stage 73. As a two-act play on an historical topic, it was the more obvious mainstream transfer, and was greeted enthusiastically by critics increasingly acclimatized to the kind of alternative presentational techniques it employed: "*Tom Paine* contains more theatrical imagination than any production seen in New York since the *Marat/Sade*," asserted the *Saturday Review*'s Henry Hewes. The show eventually ran for 295 performances, closing in December, but in June, La Mama Troupe themselves moved to the Theatre de Lys to perform *Futz*, leaving only Kevin O'Connor to continue as Paine, with a replacement company who had to be taught their roles, move for move, by the departing actors. *Futz* ran for a healthy 233 performances, despite the predictably outraged reaction from certain sections of the press, and became something of a cult hit. Rochelle Owens recalls meeting audience members who had seen it eight or nine times. The interest generated by the show was such that the troupe was asked to make a film version: after closing off-Broadway on New Year's Eve, they began work on this early in 1969.

The film of *Futz* is now the best surviving record of the troupe's work, although it never quite succeeds as a film, per se, because the source material is so inescapably theatrical. O'Horgan now expresses regret that he acceded to Owens's request that the troupe cooperate with an American producer's plans to rework it as a location-shot "movie," rather than pursuing Elsa Gress's European-backed scheme to create an accurate film documentation of the stage event itself. Nonetheless, the film provides a vivid sense of the troupe's playfulness (sometimes bordering on joyous silliness), and of the rich interplay of imagery, physicality, and music that was the hallmark of O'Horgan's work as a director. Moreover, many details from the stage production survive intact, thanks to his decision to frame the story as a play within a film. The troupe appear as traveling players who bring their bare, platform stage to a remote farming community, and the film cleverly intercuts their performance with more cinematic renderings of the scenes they enact. This strategy allows for the preservation of *Futz's* essential character as a play. Just as in the Elizabethan theater, scenes and locations move quickly, with chorus-style narration describing the settings not visually apparent on the bare stage: "small fetid room," Owens's opening speech suggests of Cyrus Futz's less-than-idyllic rural home, "with lots of automobile rags and other signs of terrible city existence, brewed still more stinky with the worst the country has to offer" (5).

That first speech, with its allusive introduction both of Cy's predilection for animals, and his dislike of women, epitomizes the pungency and verbal density of Owens's writing: "Let's give it a strange passion to a story," announces the first line, "some handyman handy in the barn with animals—'someone to watch over him'—somethings, the udders of the moo-moo especially. . . . No stupid pretty girl to rely on him, like a home-made stunt between his feet, to knock up his knees—bad onions—spoiling him eternally" (Owens 1968, 5). As the film makes clear, the troupe's delirious delivery of such passages does little to elucidate the text's linguistic subtleties (as a Kornfeld production might have), yet what is lost in the detail is more than made up for in the troupe's generation of atmosphere. By splitting the narrator's speeches up among the whole cast, to present a layered, echoing babble of a chorus, rather than the single, authorial voice envisioned by Owens, O'Horgan created an immediate sense of the gossiping, scandal-mongering village community that Futz falls victim to. The narrative is thus fully integrated into the texture of the play, rather than coming from some omniscient position external to the action, and even Owens's voice as playwright becomes a character of sorts, to be listened to or not, thanks to the various stage directions written into the narrations. "Maybe sad jazz could be played now," suggests one such line (19), prompting a burst of melody that is not jazz at all, but—like all O'Horgan's compositions for this production—haunting, gut-bucket folk music played by the actors on fiddle, recorder, harmonica, guitar, and even a boxy, homemade bass fiddle.

The vibrant physicality of the performance also evolved directly from suggestions in Owens's text. "All the time he's buttering his wrists with his red hands, making bird and other noises," reads an early description of Cy Futz, as he contemplates sex with his pig, Amanda: "he is very excited and seems absolutely certain to explode all his love or whatever over the world which is the room where he is in now" (6). This passage invited an overtly pantomimed enactment of Futz's state of sexual arousal, while the reference to "bird and other noises" provided the rest of the troupe with one of its cues to develop an entire symphony of nonverbal sounds for the play—grunting, groaning, farting, scuffling—to emphasize the animalism at its heart. Significantly, though, the troupe also succeeded in rendering Futz's infatuation with his (necessarily invisible) pig not simply as grotesque depravity, but as an innocent obsession. Responding to lines in which, for example, Cy wonders sadly whether Amanda would prefer a pig partner rather than himself—"Piglets I can't give you" (15)—actor John Bakos rendered Futz as a wide-eyed, moonstruck lover. Even when, in scene 1, Futz persuades the local "slut," Majorie Satz, to join him and Amanda for a threesome, this seduction was depicted (as is vividly apparent from the film) in terms of an unsettlingly childlike eroticism: Cy and Majorie gambol around playfully, teasing and leading each other on, while he explains that he is only attracted to her because she, like Amanda, is a (healthily voluptuous) fat pig. The consummation of this three-way passion is then obscured from spectatorial view as the rest of the cast voyeuristically gather around to watch, comment and judge.

The strange innocence of the scenes depicting Futz's desires is thrown into stark relief by the parallel narrative concerning Oscar Loop, who is discovered in prison, awaiting hanging for the murder of Ann Fox. Interrogated by his captors, it eventually becomes clear, in flashback, that Loop and Fox stumbled upon Futz's deviant threesome, while conducting an illicit liaison of their own. Driven insane at the sight, Loop (in a truly loopy performance by Seth Allen) turns on his date and brutally murders her for tempting him to sin: "Hell isn't as bad as a whoring girl" (14). In the film, this sequence is rendered in nightmarish but wholly cinematic imagery, which offers few clues as to the stage rendition, but Loop's twisted sexual repressions are still more disturbingly illustrated in a later scene (depicted on film almost exactly as it had been onstage) when his mother comes to visit him in jail. Here, the text's suggestion that Loop has an Oedipal infatuation with his strictly religious mother—"Why couldn't I ha' been my own father" (19)—is literalized in strikingly physical terms. First, Mother opens her dress to breast-feed her full-grown son, in a grotesque evocation of traditional Madonna and child iconography: "Mother, you are like the holy virgin." She then cradles his limp body in a pietà image, as if he is already hanged, while passing vengeful judgment on Loop's victim: "No woman is good, all want one thing from a man, his lust stick!" (19). Simultaneously, Loop's insane ramblings about "S[h]iva . . . a holy thing with a lot of arms" (18), prompt an archetypically O'Horganesque counterpoint image: to the side of the stage, an undulating tower of naked actors, arms writhing, outwardly expresses the simmering eroticism underlying the Loops' self-righteously moralistic relationship.

This darkly disturbing scene makes Futz's frank acceptance of his lusts seem positively healthy, by comparison. As Futz himself points out, the villagers turn him into a scapegoat because they see in him an intolerable reflection of their own suppressed desires: "They came to me and looked up my trousers all the way to their dirty hearts" (28). Such implications, of course, prompted the outrage of moral guardians in the press. "The point of all this is that society hounds the non-conforming individual," John Simon frothed in "Hogwash," his *New York* review of the off-Broadway opening, "but the choice of a simple-minded zoophiliac as the standard-bearer of individualism seems to me less than effective" (1968). Yet these accusations ignored the play's loaded ambiguity, as epitomized in the narrator's opening description of Futz's bestiality: "It's pure sickness, but in its pureness it's a truth" (5). Far from offering some simplistic comment about sexual liberation, the play is a multilayered and fundamentally unresolved exploration of the often-frightening complexity of human sexuality, which shows just how closely and discomfortingly entwined eroticism, innocence, and violence can be. Take, for example, Majorie's relationship with her father and brother—"The first is simple. The second is complex" (19)—whose affectionately protective attitude toward her is vividly realized in the film performance (as it presumably was onstage) as they embrace her and carry her around like a little girl. This sequence is playfully amusing, yet the fact that Majorie is a buxom, full-grown woman lends it an unsettlingly sexualized, incestuous undertone. These two men, moreover, can only comprehend Majorie's "sluttish" reputation if they assign blame to Futz as the culprit who has "corrupted" her—a culprit who must therefore be violently punished. Owens's concerns as a "proto-feminist" are perhaps apparent here: women are repeatedly depicted as being denied ownership of their own sexuality, and are treated, instead, as a means of exchange between men. In the play's final scene, brother Ned breaks into Futz's jail cell to exact vengeance, and in O'Horgan's production, his brutal knifing of Futz had clear overtones of forced phallic penetration. Ned's only explanation for his actions is that "you make my brains red" (30), a fittingly blunt summation of the hysteria that Futz's lusts have unleashed. The play then ends with chilling abruptness, as the chorus announces, in a bleakly "ironical" tone, "Amanda—there's someone here he needs you. Yes" (30).

On film as onstage, the closing tableau that accompanies this line presents Futz standing on the bent knees of another actor, arms aloft and falling forward, but held from behind as if suspended in midair. Meanwhile, the rest of the cast gathers around, framing the image like some Renaissance painting of Christ's ascension. Far from being frozen, though, the bodies tremble slightly, breathing hard. This closing image sums up the combination of emotional power and raw, seemingly unpolished physicality that typified La Mama Troupe's work, but that also outraged the company's critical detractors. The *Times*' Walter Kerr, for example, was appalled at the rough imprecision of the performances in *Futz*, and professed himself "scandalized that such slovenliness should be permitted to masquerade as new art" (1968, 1). He explicitly contrasted *Futz* with Joe Chaikin's cool, sharp directorial work with the Open Theatre ensemble on "the first third of *America Hurrah*"—ignoring the elementary fact that van Itallie's *Interview* needs to be so directed because it depicts the militaristic regimentation of urban life. *Futz*, depicting the violent eruption of repressed passions, demands something altogether wilder in the staging, but to Kerr, O'Horgan's troupe was fundamentally lacking in discipline: "When an army of elbows shoots into the air, it is an uncoordinated army, a flailing assortment of random and independent quiverings"; "a man is hanged, and the entire stage erupts into a dance of jerked heads and clacked tongues" (1968, 5). Ironically, these descriptions attest to the unfettered vitality that others so admired in the troupe's work, and that—according to observers of the rehearsal process—was anything but uncoordinated. "The truth is that the dauntless crew would not survive two of their organized madnesses," wrote the troupe's Danish patron, Elsa Gress, "if they were half so spontaneous as both the enemies and supporters of O'Horganism believe" (1969, 117). Aesthetic objections to the troupe's work, she suggested, were mere decoys: "The people who are disgusted at the physicalities are morally disgusted" (117). Looking back in 1991, *Voice* critic Michael Feingold concurred that O'Horgan's rampantly physicalized production of *Futz* had "opened an erotic door, bringing theater a step back toward its beginnings in the worship of Dionysus. To see it happen, in 1967, was like seeing the sexual impulse itself appear onstage for the first time."

Paine's Progress

La Mama Troupe's production of *Tom Paine*, though less controversial than *Futz*, was closely related to it in many respects. Like Owens's play, Foster's text provides a dark, earthy depiction of a convention-breaking antihero, and marries strangely poetic language with an emphasis on physicality that required the company to respond by literalizing its concerns through the actors' bodies. This consistency of vision between the two plays (not shared by the less successful, somewhat more lightweight *Times Square* and *Melodrama Play*) was in part a result of Foster's close relationship with the troupe: witnessing the development of their rehearsal work on *Futz*, he was uniquely placed to respond with new material that could capitalize on the strengths of their evolving aesthetic. As a result, *Tom Paine* engaged La Mama Troupe in a still more layered performance process than *Futz*. Taking the form of a play within a play within a theater, the piece operates simultaneously on three different levels of "reality." Foster's opening stage directions specify that the actors are onstage warming up as the audience enters, and that they should casually improvise lines to each other, as "themselves," as they prepare to perform. The play proper then opens, like *Futz*, in a filthy space for animals—a disused bear-pit in eighteenth-century New York, inhabited by homeless drunks. Believing that the destitute Tom Paine can be found here, a pair of soldiers arrives seeking to arrest him. On the sergeant's demand for "in-for-MATION! About this trai*tor*. This warmon*ger*" (Foster 1967a, 13), the inhabitants of the flophouse launch into an extended enactment of Paine's life. The play flashes back to depict the rise and fall of this agitator for liberty, tracing his catalytic role in the American Revolution (act 1), and his later involvement in the French Revolution (act 2).

This outline bears obvious similarities to Peter Weiss's *Marat/Sade*, in which the inhabitants of a madhouse act out the "persecution and assassination" of the French revolutionary leader Marat, under the direction of the Marquis de Sade. Yet Foster (always a writer who borrowed freely from others) makes mock of his own premise: the notion that this bizarre historical cartoon-strip is being acted out, in tightly choreographed formations, by homeless drunks, is clearly not one intended to "suspend disbelief." Instead, the play constantly draws attention to its own theatricality, often colliding and blurring its three different levels of "reality." The sergeant, for example, orders the recommencing of the performance in part 2 by demanding that the theatre's houselights be taken out and the dimmers lowered, "across the light board!" (46). Similarly, when one of Paine's inquisitors later calls for him to burned at the stake, he is quietly reminded, "We can't start a fire on stage" (61).

The text also includes numerous prompts for casual or "natural" behavior by the actors: "Break. Be yourself. Light a cigarette if you want to" (22). Conversely, though, an actor is at one point enjoined to "just say the words the writer wrote for you" (50), rather than to improvise any of his own. Foster's script, written for and with La Mama Troupe, seems constantly to encourage a playful tug-of-war between text and performance. Far from dictating actions to be carried out, the stage directions make suggestions, ask questions, and goad the company to respond creatively. At one point, Foster addresses the lighting designer with the injunction to "do brilliant things" (63), while leaving the specifics entirely undetermined. In the play's most extraordinary moment, Foster calls for turtles with birthday cake candles on their backs to wander across the stage, so as to conjure a floating sea of stars for the night voyage scene. "We actually tried," O'Horgan notes, laughing: "We got some turtles and tried to put candles on them, but of course they wouldn't move, so we thought that part should just be read because it was so beautifully written." Once again, the simple act of storytelling came to the rescue.

Tom Paine is a tour de force of theatrical set pieces, mapped out by Foster but left to the company to realize in three dimensions. The ensemble skipped through a rite of exorcism (complete with the ritualistic creation of a scapegoat); a disorienting Atlantic boat crossing accompanied by the rabble-rousing "Gin Song" ("GIN! GIN! GIN! Enough to float the navy in!"); a meeting of church, state, and military authorities speaking with cutout cartoon speech bubbles; a life-size chess game outlining international espionage strategies; and a trumped-up English trial scene condemning Paine for sedition, as he thumbs his nose at the court from France. Physicalizing all of this on stage through a kaleidoscopic use of character transformations and tableaux vivant, O'Horgan's troupe were—according to Walter Reid in *The Scotsman*—"all movement, fluidity, ballet. Leaping around the dimly-lit stage like little black devils, they form and reform into one image after another. This is *The Rights of Man* by Batman and Robin, but it's also true to the feel of the eighteenth century in its lusty irreverence. Many scenes could be East End tavern entertainment" (qtd. Russell 1996, 171).

For all its gleeful theatricality, though, the play is also deadly serious in its implications—and was inescapably relevant at a time when talk of political revolt, even revolution, was very much in the air on both sides of the Atlantic. Like Cy Futz, Paine is depicted as a figure caught in a whirlwind, whose actions provoke a chaotic series of consequences over which he has no control. Foster's text constantly emphasizes not only the importance of Paine's writing during this historical crisis period, but the very real bloodshed and misery that his ideas helped to unleash: "The smell of the barracks / A woman is raped / A boy is raped / An army starves in the snow / A WHOLE ARMY! / A young boy is eaten in secret / The cannibals weep as they eat / They pick his brains to mould . . . *The United States of America*" (27–28). The play asks sticky, unanswerable questions about the human costs of this revolutionary upheaval, and also about Paine's own motives. Depicted as a complex, contradictory figure, an alcoholic tormented by personal demons, he seems driven partly by dreams of freedom and democracy, but also partly by more questionable motives. The play suggests that Paine harbored a very personal loathing of the English king, George III, and perhaps even dreamed of replacing him—of being the new Cromwell. Such ideas remain speculative on Foster's part, however, and there is no pretense in the play at offering a rounded, psychological portrait of the "true" Paine. Instead, Foster literalizes the internal conflicts from which he imagines Paine to have suffered, by splitting him into two characters: "Tom Paine" himself is a pitiful, railing drunkard, "Tom Paine's Reputation" an articulate advocate for liberty. Eventually, at the abrupt (anti)climax of the play, the actors leave the stage refusing to offer any conclusive explanation of Paine. "Well, did he want to be king, or didn't he?" demands one, perhaps voicing the audience's curiosity; "That's an easy way to explain him away," comes the reply; "IT'S A COP OUT!!" yells another; "Well, that's it, there's no more script left" (71). The actor playing Tom Paine (Kevin O'Connor) is left alone on stage to speak only the raw facts about what became of "the raw stuff" of Paine's body, which was disinterred, and hung out in public for jeering mobs to ridicule: "Nobody knows where [his bones] are today. So went Tom Paine, who shook continents awake" (71). After all the sound and fury, this is an ending every bit as bleakly "ironical" as that of *Futz*.

Invading the Mainstream

If *Futz* and *Tom Paine* both spoke, albeit ambivalently, to the sexual and political upheavals of the later 1960s, it was perhaps O'Horgan's Broadway production of *Hair* that expressed the cultural zeitgeist most directly. Opening in April 1968 at the Biltmore Theatre, between his two off-Broadway openings with La Mama, it made O'Horgan the most talked-about director in New York. *Hair* was written by, and starred, Gerome Ragni and James Rado. The former was a founder member of the Open Theatre, and had performed in *Viet Rock*. He envisaged *Hair* as a similar attempt to respond theatrically to contemporary cultural developments. With psychedelic rock topping the pop charts in 1967, the play's celebratory depiction of the flower-powered hippie lifestyle had clear commercial potential, and Ragni quickly found an interested producer in Joseph Papp, of the New York Shakespeare Festival, who saw *Hair* as a moneyspinner that might subsidize the development of less populist work at his new, foundation-funded Public Theater (A *Chorus Line* later became another famous example of this strategy). *Hair* opened as the inaugural production at the Public's Lafayette Street venue in October 1967, in the wake of San Francisco's "summer of love." Gerald Freedman's production, however, was widely considered to be "hoked up and conventionally show-bizzed in the writing, acting and staging, to the point of betraying everything it was trying to represent" (Smith 1968c).

Despite such responses, Papp moved *Hair* uptown to a nightclub called the Cheetah (at Fifty-seventh and Broadway) after its initial run at the Public. It survived there as a curiosity for a few months, until O'Horgan, who had always been Ragni and Rado's first choice as director, became available to redirect the piece for Broadway. O'Horgan agreed to take the job on the condition that he could build a new production from scratch. To him, Freedman's production was "this very weird piece which had been totally miscast with people who were like very glossy printed [models]." Keeping only the authors in their roles, O'Horgan sought a more authentically "hippie" cast, eventually adopting the old Cino tactic of "just following people down the street who looked right and trying to get them to come and audition." The show's setting was also reconceived in line with the street-level trash aesthetic of off-off-Broadway staging: "Robin Wagner's beautiful junk-art setting," Clive Barnes noted in the *Times*, was "a blank stage replete with broken-down truck, papier-mache Santa Claus, juke box, neon signs" (1968b).

Most significantly, O'Horgan initiated a radical overhaul of the show's structure, abandoning large parts of the book and narrative in favor of emphasizing the collagelike theatricality that he saw as its underlying strength. Ragni and Rado participated enthusiastically in stripping down their script to its theatrical essence, as Galt McDermot's infectiously catchy pop-rock score was pushed right into the foreground of the event. Matching the bubbly spirit of the melodies with a truckload of theatrical stunts and gimmicks, O'Horgan collapsed songs and scenes into each other to create an ongoing fusion of music, spectacle, and action, structurally reminiscent of some of the Kornfeld-Carmines collaborations at Judson Poets'. "Instead of being a patronizing portrait of hippies, *Hair* is now a direct freak-out," Michael Smith noted of the Broadway opening: "Never has a show been so chock full of shock effects, so manic in its pursuit of novelty." Its importance, he stressed, lay not in "anything it says about hippies, [but in] the plain fact that O'Horgan has blown up Broadway" (1968c). Viewing the London production the following year (which O'Horgan tailored to the specifics of that city and its people, rather than simply duplicating the New York version), Charles Marowitz concurred that "O'Horgan has discarded the representation of states-of-being for the states-of-being themselves," abandoning narrative and illusion in favor of vibrant immediacy: "This is what puts *Hair* into a class of its own" (1969).

O'Horgan himself claims to have been somewhat taken aback by the production's success: "When we first went up to Broadway," he notes, "I thought we'd be there for about twelve seconds. I looked on it as a kind of sit-in. We were just gonna go up and make a protest in the middle of this plaster palace, and then they'd dismiss us and we'd go." Looking back, Michael Smith agrees that O'Horgan's *Hair* had a disarmingly rough-edged, almost casual feel about it, which set it at some remove from other commercial musicals: "It was *not* a slick uptown production," he recalls, "it just had the impact of one." Smith's qualifier is telling. *Hair* pumped a new, youthful energy into the largely moribund genre of the Broadway musical, but its "impact" was that of an entertainment that offered little to challenge audiences, emotionally or intellectually. "One can't *not* consent to this merry mind-blowing exercise in holy gibberish," enthused the *New Yorker*, neatly summing up the emphasis on style over substance (Gill 1968). For many of *Hair*'s admirers, moreover, one of its principal attractions was MacDermot's score—an essentially lightweight, sanitized take on psychedelic rock. "Its noisy and cheerful conservatism," Clive Barnes noted, with its "strong soothing overtones of Broadway melody," made it "just right for an audience that might wince at *Sergeant Pepper's Lonely Heart's Club Band*" (1968b). *Hair* succeeded, in short, because it had successfully fused middle-brow entertainment values with the now-fashionable appeal of "alternative lifestyles." Tellingly, when the smooth running of the commercial machine was threatened, action was swift and merciless: in February 1969, ten months into the run, producer Michael Butler barred

Rado and Ragni from the Biltmore for "increasingly offensive behavior," and recast their roles.

Perhaps the most insidiously "conservative" aspects of *Hair*, however, lay in the social values of Ragni and Rado's book. The show's underlying narrative, such as it is, concerns the impact of the Vietnam draft on a fun-loving hippie tribe. Claude (originally played by Rado), has been called up, but for reasons unclear does not think to burn his draft card, as so many were doing at this time. At heart, it seems, he is a patriotic American: his tribe are, as they sing, "CRAZY FOR THE WHITE RED AND BLUE" (Ragni and Rado 1969, 97). Claude's friend Berger (Ragni) resolves that, before going to war, Claude will get to realize his unfulfilled ambition and sleep with Sheila, a member of the tribe who is in love with Berger. Sheila is thus placed under enormous pressure, as Berger tries to persuade her that it is her duty as a member of this free-love community to consent to this union, whether or not she is attracted to Claude. In scene 3, "Sheila's Rape," Berger demonstrates his emotional control over her by ritualistically raping her, an action that is treated, unquestioningly, as his right (78–79). Sheila finally submits to sex with Claude, and Claude—appetite sated—goes poignantly off to war.

Hair thus staged a bizarre variant on the age-old patriarchal right of men to use and trade women as if they are property, and as such stood in striking contrast to *Futz*'s altogether more subversive treatment of sexuality. It is unsurprising that this conveniently heteronormative take on "free love" proved far more acceptable to mainstream critics. Moreover, one of *Hair*'s biggest commercial draws was the brief sequence in which the cast stripped down to nudity at the end of act 1. This moment was carefully handled by O'Horgan, and no cast member was obliged to strip if they did not feel comfortable about it. Nonetheless, given that this was the first such display of nudity in a Broadway show, there was obvious voyeuristic appeal here—and the exposure of the female cast members, in particular, was widely regarded as a strong "selling point."

Fade Out

For some, O'Horgan's work on *Hair* was little short of a betrayal of La Mama Troupe—a crass commercialization of lovingly developed ensemble techniques. "I was disgusted by *Hair*," Michael Warren Powell notes, "because it was filled with the things that we had developed, but it had been sifted down to its basic components. It was just movement, whereas for us every gesture had meaning, a psychological meaning. There were no empty gestures, but *Hair* was absolutely empty gestures." Whether or not such judgments were fair or accurate, it is clear, with hindsight, that their adventures in the commercial theater arena cost O'Horgan and his troupe dearly in terms of their group identity. The lengthy off-Broadway runs of *Futz* and *Tom Paine*, combined with O'Horgan's repeated absences from New York, mounting versions of *Hair* in London, San Francisco, and Chicago, meant that the troupe lost a critical degree of momentum and focus as a collaborative unit.

There were occasional, somewhat isolated new productions. The troupe premiered *Massachusetts Trust*, by Megan Terry, at Brandeis University in August 1968 (leaving *Futz* to be performed, temporarily, by a stand-in cast), and staged Paul Foster's *Heimskringla; or, The Stoned Angels* for National Educational Television in 1969. Broadcast that November, this was a still wilder, more theatrical play than *Tom Paine*, although—as a retelling of Nordic myths recounted to Foster by Elsa Gress—it lacked the human-scaled, social-political bite of the earlier play. It might well have been developed further, but sadly *Heimskringla* was never restaged theatrically by La Mama Troupe. The company ceased to be that same fall, after O'Horgan parted ways with Ellen Stewart. He assembled a group known simply as the New Troupe, comprising both old and new faces, and embarked on a winter college tour with plays including the premiere version of Sam Shepard's *The Holy Ghostly*. In 1970, the New Troupe played a series of major European festivals, with an unwieldy company of twenty or so, that never quite achieved the old troupe's cohesion. O'Horgan subsequently became caught up in work for the two major Broadway premieres he directed in 1971—Andrew Lloyd Webber's rock opera *Jesus Christ Superstar*, and Julian Barry's portrait of Lenny Bruce, *Lenny*. The New Troupe never reconvened.

The remaining troupe members went their separate ways, many of them subsequently struggling to find fresh direction. The successes of La Mama Troupe proved difficult for its members to recapture individually. "This company had goaded me to the top of the mountain," recalls Paul Foster, "and I just couldn't get down again." His next play, *Elizabeth I*, was produced off-Broadway in 1972, with a cast including Jerry Cunliffe, but the results were disappointing: "My brain was still locked into the capabilities of that core unit," Foster explains, "but this other company was not part of that experience. They couldn't do it." O'Horgan himself feels similarly about some of his own later work: although he continued to find regular work both on Broadway and off, he remained an iconoclastic figure, an outsider in the established theater world. Looking back, he regards the plays he developed collaboratively with La Mama Troupe as his most significant theatrical accomplishments.

11 The Play-House of the Ridiculous: Beyond Absurdity

> My definition of an actor was that, if I was hit by a car and was dying in the street, if an actor came over to me, instead of helping me he would tell me what he was doing. Actors are cowards and egocentrics. My group was not made up of that type of people. They were hippies that I found on the street. Some of them were drug addicts, and I thought that if I gave them something to do, they wouldn't do that.
>
> —John Vaccaro

If O'Horgan's La Mama Troupe represented a rougher-edged take on the ensemble-based physical acting style pioneered by the Open Theatre, the Play-House of the Ridiculous—which also debuted in 1965—was something else again. Pushing performative wildness to demented and sometimes violent extremes a world away from the quiet self-discipline promoted by Joseph Chaikin, the Ridiculous positively reveled in camp excess. Seeing "acting" as a form of cowardice—a hiding behind the facade of character or stagecraft— director John Vaccaro focused instead on the unbridled expression of his performers' outrageous personalities. This was a development of sorts on Judson's use of untrained "stars" and "divas," but the Ridiculous also dispensed with the choreographic precision characteristic of Kornfeld's directing, introducing instead a kind of improvisatory onstage chaos. As with jazz performance, or commedia dell'arte traditions (both of which Vaccaro counted as influences), the execution of a piece could vary substantially from night to night, as performers pursued ad-libs and spontaneous impulses, sometimes taking the performance careering off on tangents from its scripted backbone. "It was chaos," Vaccaro notes, "but it had its parameters; it was directed chaos. . . . And we had such fun!"

Since precision and subtlety in the delivery of texts were usually the first casualty of the Play-House's unhinged approach, Vaccaro (even more than O'Horgan) was often accused of caring little for the scripts he worked with. He would, moreover, often publicly deride the work of collaborating playwrights like Ronald Tavel and Charles Ludlam, both of whom eventually quit the company over disputes with him. And yet, as critic Michael Feingold observed, "There is no point to being John Vaccaro and inviting audiences to experience the Ridiculous if you have no genuinely Ridiculous experience to offer them, and for that a text, a shape for the show, material for the acts, is required. . . . Vaccaro, more honest in this line than some of his colleagues, has never tried to put his own words on the stage" (Bernard 1971, 4). Rather, he formed alliances with a series of writers whose (anti)aesthetic interests were complementary to his own. Their "ridiculously ill-made plays, reflecting an ill-made world" lent themselves to, and indeed catalyzed, his transgressive directorial approach (Brecht 1986, 35).

Indeed, if the company's history was defined in part by ongoing creative tensions between its members, these conflicts seem — in themselves — to have been perversely fundamental in shaping what appeared onstage: "Each production is a three-way fight between the acting dramatist, the acting director, and the cast" (Brecht 1986, 40). In effect, the Ridiculous took to extremes the contemporary emphasis on the here and now of the theatrical moment, by staging the immediate relational dynamics between its participants. This was a neodadaist, "antiart" brand of theater designed to make delirious nonsense of the conventional virtues of consistency and clarity of form, and to emphasize instead the awkward, messy, ludicrous nature of placing people together on a stage, to be looked at.

From Underground Film to Underground Stage

Although firmly rooted in the make-it-up-as-you-go trash aesthetic that had been a feature of the off-off-Broadway movement from its inception, the Ridiculous owed its genesis to New York's underground film community, and particularly to the work of Jack Smith and Andy Warhol. Both these directors sought, in different ways, to make film more "real" precisely by making it more obviously "fake"—believing that the distinct personal qualities of their performers would become more immediately apparent if they were engaged in the construction of blatantly tacky, artificial "illusions." The logic of this position was brilliantly articulated by Smith in his 1962 *Film Culture* article, "The Perfect Film Appositeness of Maria Montez." The 1940s B-movie star, derided by many as "the World's Worst Actress," was for Smith the medium's greatest luminary, precisely because of her failure to convince in dramatic roles, and the transparently cheap production values of her vehicles. Montez in a movie is never merely a character, Smith argued, but always perfectly Montez: she is the "Moldy Movie Queen, Shoulder pad, gold platform wedgie Siren," whose very flaws made her glorious: "M.M. dreamed she was effective, imagined she acted, cared for nothing but her fantasy. . . . Her real concerns (her conviction of beauty/her beauty) were the main concern—her acting had to be secondary" (Smith 1997, 34–35).

There is, certainly, a degree of irony in Smith's observations. Gay men have often selected unfashionable figures from the margins of mainstream pop culture to be the objects of camp adoration. Yet Smith's devotion to Montez was also utterly sincere: "Corniness is the other side of marvelousness," he stressed (31). To him, Montez was the magical source of all inspiration, an alchemist-goddess who had turned dross into gold through the force of her screen personality. He built an entire cosmology around her, even renaming one of his male photographic models "Mario Montez" in her honor, and casting him in his one-hundred-dollar film epic, *Flaming Creatures* (1962). This plotless, ravishingly beautiful piece of monochrome, Spanish-Gothic spectacle is Smith's most famous work, partly because of the censorship controversy that blew up around its orgiastic use of nude bodies, male and female. Yet sexually explicit as it is, *Flaming Creatures* is also strangely innocent, a celebration of real bodies in real contact with each other, totally free of pornographic exploitation value: indeed, the title of Smith's next film, *Normal Love*, might be equally appropriate for it. That piece, however, is a riot of color: shot the following year, and originally titled *The Great Moldy Triumph*, it depicts strange and wonderful creatures, garbed in fantastic costumes of vibrant pink, frolicking in a sunlit meadow. It perfectly embodies Smith's conviction that "to admit of Maria Montez's validities would be to turn on to moldiness, glamorous rapture, schizophrenic delight, hopeless naivete and glittering technicolor trash!" (Smith 1997, 26). John Vaccaro, a close friend of Smith's and one of the key performers in *Normal Love*, openly acknowledges his creative debt to him: "He was nuts, but the only genius I have ever known."

The Ridiculous, however, sprang more directly from writer Ronald Tavel's work as scenarist for Andy Warhol. Tavel was another Montez devotee and had worked as a set assistant on *Flaming Creatures*, but had been drawn into Warhol's orbit partly because he, unlike Smith, had the financial resources to make films regularly. Warhol had appropriated (and made famous) Smith's term *superstar*, to describe the unknown actors whose unvarnished personalities he regarded as the main subject of his films. Compared to Smith's lush, tacky opulence, however, Warhol's work was stark and visually impoverished, often uncomfortable to watch. Adopting a coolly passive gaze not dissimilar to that implied by his paintings, his films were shot from a single, static camera position, and left completely unedited: they would simply "vacuum up" whatever action happened to occur in front of the lens. After shooting a series of silent pieces, documenting such subjects as a man sleeping *(Sleep)* and a man eating *(Eat)*, Warhol acquired a sound camera in 1964. It became Tavel's job to come up with scenarios for possible dialogue and action, which could be improvised around during a shoot. He began simply, with another "still life" piece called *Harlot*—in which a blonde-wigged Mario Montez luxuriates in the consumption of phallic-looking bananas, while offscreen voices discuss the enduring appeal of Jean Harlow. Gradually, though, Tavel moved on to more ambitious projects such as *Vinyl* (1965), loosely adapted from Anthony Burgess's *A Clockwork Orange*, in which Gerard Malanga played a juvenile delinquent arrested and tortured by menacing authority figures. This piece foreshadowed the work of the Ridiculous in several respects, particularly in its disturbing new twist on Smith's conjunction of the blatantly fake with the apparently "real." The actors mumble their lines without charisma or conviction, visibly reading from scripts. Yet much of the improvised violence enacted in both the foreground and, almost casually, in the background of the frame, appears to be anything but artificial. (The one edit in the film comes after Malanga appears to flail helplessly for breath, after being strapped roughly into a black leather face mask.) Shot in starkly contrasting black and white, with loud rock-and-roll music periodically drowning out the dialogue, the film is simultaneously gripping and repellent, leaving the viewer tense and disorientated.

Tavel's collaboration with Warhol, which is only now being properly appraised by film critics, came to an abrupt end with the abandonment of *Shower*, Tavel's most dialogue-heavy scenario thus far. Edie Sedgwick, Warhol's "It Girl" of the moment, who had made her first film appearance as a passive observer in *Vinyl*, reportedly refused to participate in any more of "Tavel's perversities," and Warhol, placing superstar ahead of scenarist, sided with her. Since *Shower* would have required Sedgwick to frolic seminaked in a shower with her costar, her reaction was perhaps understandable. Tavel, however, decided to strike out on his own, and succeeded in persuading the proprietor of the Coda Galleries—a narrow, white-walled space at 89 East Tenth Street, specializing in psychedelic art—to let him stage *Shower* there. He also proposed filling out the evening with *The Life of Juanita Castro*, a short script filmed by Warhol earlier that year.

In search of a director, Tavel turned initially to Jerry Benjamin, who had recently mounted the Present Stages production of Frank O'Hara's *The General Returns from One Place to Another*. This choice was telling, given that Benjamin had cast underground film actor Taylor Mead as his star, thereby achieving results very much in line with the Smith-Warhol approach to film performance. "Taylor Mead is perfectly indescribable as the general," Michael Smith had written: "It is an all-time masterpiece of miscasting" (1964a). Susan Sontag concurred that this "skinny, balding, pot-bellied, round-shouldered, droopy, very pale young man—a sort of consumptive, faggot Harry Langdon" was a ridiculous choice as the MacArthuresque general, "but one simply cannot takes one's eyes off him" (Sontag 1967, 157). Given Mead's bizarrely individualistic performance, the production was a notable precursor to the Ridiculous. Benjamin, however, claimed he was too busy to direct Tavel's double bill, and instead recommended John Vaccaro, who had never directed theater in his life.

An Opening at the Coda

"I read them," Vaccaro recalls of *Shower* and *The Life of Juanita Castro*, "and my friends read them, and they said [*hushed, horrified tone*]: 'DON'T do these! They're HORRIBLE!' And they were. Precisely why I wanted to do them." Having recently worked as an actor with the American Theater for Poets, experiencing firsthand James Waring's ability to make extravagantly theatrical pieces from the most unpromising of texts, Vaccaro had in mind to attempt something similar. Yet his approach was not founded on simple disrespect for Tavel. These plays were knowingly trashy and poorly constructed, having been designed as loose scenarios for Warhol's undisciplined "superstars" to stumble around in, and as such, they appealed to Vaccaro's sensibilities. "They were stupid," he stresses: "What he was writing was very corny, but there was a *thing* that I got from them." If marvelousness is indeed the other side of corniness, Vaccaro seems to have seen that potential in this collaboration with Tavel.

Given a royal budget of twenty dollars, Vaccaro assembled an unlikely cast of friends and associates, such as underground movie actress Beverly Grant, who starred as *Shower*'s heroine, Terrine the Terrible Tart from Terra Cotta (aka Lula La Goulu, the Lady from LaLuna), who is in search of her lost cherry. The wiry, bespectacled Vaccaro implausibly cast himself opposite her as the dashing secret agent, X-35 (aka Mark Stark Naked). As the names indicate, *Shower* is a spy-thriller pastiche that aims at the lowest of low camp humor, and the script is littered with outrageously lewd one-liners: "Say that again and I'll close my fly and starve your mother" (Tavel 1967, 312). The smut is of a kind that would have appealed to Warhol, but the play's tone is so relentlessly cheap and nasty that no poignant emotional charge can emerge in counterpoint to the silliness—as it does, for example, in the "camps" of H. M. Koutoukas. Yet for Tavel, *Shower*'s very vacuity was a statement of sorts, implying an existential void at the heart of American culture more horrifying than anything in Beckett. His program note called for a "Theatre of the Ridiculous," on the grounds that "we have passed beyond the absurd: our position is absolutely preposterous" (Schroeder 1968, 173).

Though Tavel claims that he originated the company name, Vaccaro insists the label *ridiculous* was coined by his friend, actress Yvette Hawkins, in describing a rehearsal of *Shower*. Regardless, the two critics who reviewed the play—Elenore Lester for the *Voice* and Jerry Tallmer for the *Post*—thought it simply trite and juvenile: "Ridiculous?" Lester scoffed, "Man, it's not even absurd." The play's chief attraction, she argued, was the titular shower: two working cubicles had been jerry-rigged on stage to provide very real water in which the blatantly faking actors got drenched—initially while fully dressed, then later in their underwear. These sequences were clearly intended by Tavel as a parody of cheap erotic fiction: "[They] embrace madly," X-35 declares in a self-referential aside to the audience, "unaware that they are both being watched—by eyes filled with DESIRE!!!!!" (313). The irony, however, may have been lost on the watching eyes, since the sight of "Beverly Grant, Queen of Underground Movies, stripped down to her transparent little panties and snaky black hair, past[ing] herself cheek by jowl against her partner" had obvious attractions of its own (Lester 1965b). In 1965, this onstage nudity was sufficiently taboo-breaking to prompt police enquiries, and to pack out the sixty-five-seat house for the six scheduled performances: "They stormed the seating," Vaccaro recalls.

For the critics, *The Life of Juanita Castro* was "by far the better of the two productions" (Lester). Tavel's wit here was much sharper, and aimed at a far less abstract target, in the form of Fidel Castro—who had recently been targeting homosexuals as the scapegoats for Cuba's ills. More a conceptual scenario than a play, *Juanita Castro* had been tailor-made for Warhol, and ingeniously sidestepped the need for his Factory "stars" to learn any lines, by framing them within a static group portrait shot, representing Castro's family. "This play should never be rehearsed," the stage directions stress (Tavel 1966,

120): instead, a director figure—played in the film version by Tavel himself, sitting at the back of the group—simply instructs the performers to kiss, weep, argue, and repeat lines as they are read out to them:

> Juanita, say to Fidel, "You never really cared for the poor peasants." Get very emotional. Say again, "You never really cared for the poor, starving, freezing peasants." Now think about the poor peasants. It makes you sad to think about the peasants. Juanita, start crying. Now, everyone cry with her. (121)

On film, Tavel's strategy creates some genuinely bizarre effects, as the actors react awkwardly to these abrupt instructions, forcibly faking passion, laughter, and even—in the sequence above—thinking. The patent artifice of the characterizations is matched by a very real sense of the uncertainty, even the helplessness, experienced by the actors as they find themselves caught, unprepared, in the camera's gaze. Moreover, Tavel's setup plays cleverly off his ostensible subject. The presentation of the Castros and Guevaras as overacting soap opera characters prompted film critic Andrew Sarris to proclaim *Juanita Castro* "the only valid statement I have seen on [Cuba] in the past several years," since Castro's revolution "has long since been consigned to camp. The whole show was given away when word got out that Castro wanted to be played on screen by Marlon Brando and Raul by Frank Sinatra" (1965). In Tavel's text, the characters bicker over whether or not "the revolution" has "turned out good" for them, and Juanita's love life is treated as the core of an absurd melodrama. She announces (shock!) that she really loves her own brother, Raul, more than Fidel. Both Raul and Che make to kiss her, while Fidel smokes his cigar pensively and stares at the camera.

The movie version was one of Warhol's better-regarded film works, but *Juanita Castro* scaled fresh heights of ridiculousness with its translation to stage. For one thing, Tavel's drag concept was more fully realized here. At the Factory, the speaking parts were all played by women, but all were dressed in their everyday clothes, and performed without much charisma or conviction. Vaccaro ditched Warhol's blank lack of ornamentation in favor of a flamboyant theatricality inspired by Jack Smith, who designed the appropriately Latin-looking costumes. Jeanne Phillips played Fidel in a bushy black beard and a skirt, puffing on a huge, phallic cigar (the film uses only cigarettes), while drag queen Rai Saunders played Juanita: "Full of erotic energy, Latin vivacity," Lester noted, "he-she is ravishing in a brilliant flowered gown and a tossing black lace mantilla." The Guevara brothers, played by Elsene Sorrentino and Barbara Simmons, were "so comically sexually ambiguous they'd fall in the dead center of a Kinseyan masculine-feminine rating scale" (Lester 1965b).

The Life of Juanita Castro thus initiated the use of drag performers, of both sexes, which was to become one of the trademarks of the Ridiculous. "People thought it was something homosexual," Vaccaro notes, "but my main reason for having a man playing a woman is that he was better at it than a woman was. He could play it better." The words "play it" indicate Vaccaro's sense of conventional gender behavior as absurdly artificial role-play, rather than anything innate to the sexes. Decades before Judith Butler theorized the performativity of gender, Vaccaro was using the studied pose of drag queens to expose "femininity" as a set of acquired manners. For him, though, the point was less political than farcical: the more obviously male the performer's body, the more outlandish his determination to appear "feminine" seemed. "The thing I loved about drag queens," remembers Ridiculous actress Mary Woronov, "[is that] no matter how ridiculously things didn't match, they would sacrifice everything for the pose" (2000, 51). Woronov herself was to become one of Vaccaro's favorite performers—as a tall and strikingly beautiful woman playing at full-on masculine brutality.

Gender-bending aside, *Juanita Castro* set another vital precedent for the subsequent work of the Ridiculous, by suggesting that "a certain amount of improvisation . . . is expected" of the onstage director figure (120). Vaccaro cast himself in the director role, and tended to deviate freely from the set script, manipulating the proceedings "live," night by night, according to his own whims. This ensured that the play retained an unrehearsed spontaneity even during repeat performances—an element also complemented by Vaccaro's incorporation of a group of jazz musicians into the proceedings. The musicians (including the Velvet Underground's John Cale) would improvise free-associative noise, while drinking the cocktails provided to them by way of payment for their services.

As a result of these experiments, Vaccaro began to see the potential in treating theater not as a tightly rehearsed edifice, but as an opportunity for "live" improvisation around certain structural parameters (i.e., the script). The Ridiculous subsequently developed as a kind of latter-day commedia dell'arte company, whose rehearsal process was directed not toward arriving at a single, ideal performance to be consistently reproduced, but toward drilling performers in a scenario's improvisational possibilities. The challenge for performers was to find ways to spark off each other's individual styles and personalities, so that the show could evolve spontaneously—moment by moment and night after night. Indeed, Vaccaro would deliberately frustrate any tendency on the part of actors to fall back on comfortably predetermined performance choices. "They would be doing a thing and I'd say, 'No, do it again,'" he recalls, describing a typical rehearsal:

> And they'd do it, I'd say "No, do it again." "No, do it again." "No, do it again." Finally, I'd say, "*Yes!*" And the next day they'd be doing that thing I'd said yes about, and they'd say, "You liked it yesterday," and I'd say, "That was *yesterday!*" We had fun, but then eventually it was set so well that the spontaneity could come out of the fact that we *knew*.

The only drawback was that Vaccaro's ruthlessness in playing this game of perpetual dissatisfaction was sometimes perceived as dictatorial cruelty by those who did not understand that he himself was playing a "role." "I have seldom seen anyone put so much of his person in his work," Tavel wrote of Vaccaro: "He considers a nervous breakdown and the breakdowns of each member of the cast to be a par for the course price to pay for excellence" (1966a, 103n).

The Play-House Evolves

Shower and *Juanita Castro* proved sufficiently popular over the two weekends of performances at the Coda Gallery that a revival was quickly mounted at St. Mark's Playhouse. Emboldened by their success, Tavel and Vaccaro began to plan an ongoing company, teaming up with lighting designer Bill Walters and Tavel's brother, Harvey, to help bring this about. Meanwhile, Jack Smith seems to have been sufficiently inspired by the show to attempt a theatrical experiment of his own, *Rehearsal for the Destruction of Atlantis*, which was presented at the Filmmakers' Cinematheque in December 1965. Though nominally part of a festival of "Expanded Cinema," *Rehearsal* made only limited use of film projection: Smith's script, like *Juanita Castro*, was a loose scenario for onstage improvisation, including only a few lines of dialogue and an extended, voiced-over monologue. The bizarre sequence of action—involving two Siamese twins, the quarreling, pot-smoking queens of North and South Atlantis, who are forcibly separated by chainsaw-wielding "rat narcos"— alluded obliquely to U.S. interference in Vietnam (just as *Juanita Castro* referenced Cuba). It was the immediate sensory impact of the performance, however, that impressed observers most: this was, Jonas Mekas noted in the *Voice*, "an orgy of costumes, suppressed and open violence, and color. The centerpiece creation was a huge red lobster, a masterpiece creation of costume and character" (Smith 1997, 94). As played by Vaccaro, the lobster sought poignantly to cover the queens' corpses with lettuce leaves, while Mario Montez danced around the bodies to "dying swan" music from *Swan Lake*.

Accounts of *Rehearsal for the Destruction of Atlantis* suggest that Smith would have made a superb writer-director for the Ridiculous. Tavel and Vaccaro seem to have envisaged him playing such a role in their nascent company, but Smith proved too erratic and undisciplined to build further on this experiment at the time. His major contribution to the Ridiculous continued to be as designer: he provided another "orgy of costumes" for Tavel's next play, *The Life of Lady Godiva*. Premiering in April 1966, this was the first presentation at the new Play-House of the Ridiculous—a large, rectangular loft at 12 West Seventeenth Street. The group had rented this former parlor room using money donated by Panna Grady, a Hungarian countess (she had divorced an Irishman) who fancied herself an aristocratic patron to the downtown arts scene. The second-floor location meant that, as at Café La Mama, audience capacity was legally limited to seventy-four. Yet there was very little "legal" about this enterprise: indeed, Tavel claims that the designation "Play-House," with its disarming hyphen, was chosen as a means to sidestep the licensing implications of having a "theater" or "playhouse." The name also suggested a sense of "playing" at theater—an idea equally apparent in the makeshift proscenium stage and the obviously recycled fabrics of Smith's designs. To Michael Smith, the "dingy" loft environment and low-budget aesthetic seemed perfectly suited to Tavel's play, despite its insistence on decadently lush, art nouveau–inspired visuals: "It's that roughness that lets it become robust and hearty rather than effete and precious" (1966c).

The Life of Lady Godiva was the first play Tavel had written explicitly for the stage, and it broke from the single-focus approach dictated by Warhol's static camera, suggesting instead a three-ring circus of semi-improvised insanity. Mother Superviva, the head nun of a "sick-riligious" convent, holds court and hears confessions on a "very long chaise longue," lit by a Tiffany lamp, at stage left. Upstage, behind a gauze curtain embroidered with Beardsleyesque tendrils and peacock feathers, Lady Godiva and her chauffeur, Tom, sit on a similarly elongated white wooden horse (which, equipped with steering wheel and rearview mirror, also suggests a stretch limousine). Midway through the play, an enormous ladder is erected center stage to provide a "stairway to heaven" for the nuns. Using these three set elements as focal points for the action, Vaccaro created a rampant, multiple-focus spectacle. He also located himself onstage in the role of Superviva, again giving himself the opportunity to bark commands and improvise on the spot.

Exterior of the Caffe Cino, showing poster for Lanford Wilson's *This is the Rill Speaking*, July or August 1965. (Photo: James Gossage. Reproduced courtesy of the Billy Rose Theatre Collection, New York Public Library for the Performing Arts, and the Astor, Lenox and Tilden Foundations.)

Interior of Caffe Cino, June 1964. Yvonne Rainer performing her piece *Incidents*, with Larry Loonin. (Photo by Peter Moore. © Estate of Peter Moore/VAGA, New York/DACS, London 2003.)

Robert Dahdah, Ron Link, Charles Stanley, and Candace Scott in H. M. Koutoukas's *All Day for a Dollar*, Caffe Cino, December 1965. (Photo: James Gossage. Courtesy of Robert Dahdah.)

Doric Wilson in the Caffe Cino, 1961. Behind him the Cino window and poster-board, and the cast of his play, *And He Made a Her.* Jane Lowry, Allen Zamp, Gary Fillsinger. 1961. (Photo courtesy of Doric Wilson.)

Left, Joe Cino with Edward Albee, at a benefit for the Caffe Cino, March 1965. (Photo: James Gossage. Courtesy of Robert Dahdah.)

Mom is eaten by her children in David Starkweather's *You May Go Home Again*, Caffe Cino, June 1965. Shellie Feldman, Kay Carney and Ron Hansen; Ron Faber with back turned. (Photo: James Gossage. Reproduced courtesy of the Billy Rose Theatre Collection, New York Public Library for the Performing Arts, and the Astor, Lenox and Tilden Foundations.)

Larry Burns (facing away) and Jim Jennings in Robert Heide's *The Bed*. Caffe Cino, July 1965. (Photo courtesy of Robert Heide.)

Charles Stanley in H. M. Koutoukas's *Medea*. Caffe Cino, October 1965. (Photo: Conrad Ward. Reproduced courtesy of the Billy Rose Theatre Collection, New York Public Library for the Performing Arts, and the Astor, Lenox and Tilden Foundations.)

David Christmas and Bernadette Peters in *Dames at Sea*, Caffe Cino, summer 1966. (Photo courtesy of Robert Dahdah.)

Robert Patrick performing solo
at the Caffe Cino, circa 1966.
(Photo: James Gossage. Courtesy of
Robert Patrick.)

Al Carmines, Maria
Irene Fornes, H.
M. Koutoukas,
and Lawrence
Kornfeld at the
Caffe Cino, circa
1965. (Photo: James
Gossage. Reproduced
courtesy of the
Billy Rose Theatre
Collection, New York
Public Library for the
Performing Arts, and
the Astor, Lenox and
Tilden Foundations.)

Jerome Raphael, Peter Boyle, Al Carmines, and Katherine Litz in George Dennison's *The Service for Joseph Axminster*. Judson Poets' Theater, March 1963. (Photo by Peter Moore. © Estate of Peter Moore/VAGA, New York/DACS, London 2003.)

Gertrude Stein's *What Happened*, Judson Poets' Theater, September 1963. Left to right: Masato Kawasaki; Hunt Cole, Lucinda Childs, Arlene Rothlein, Aileen Passloff, John Quinn, Joan Baker (partially hidden), Al Carmines, Yvonne Rainer. (Photo by Peter Moore. © Estate of Peter Moore/VAGA, New York/DACS, London 2003.)

Maria Irene Fornes's *Promenade*, Judson Poets' Theater, April 1965. Left to right: Howard Roy, Florence Tarlow (as Miss Cake, singing), Frank Emerson, David Vaughan, George Bartenieff, John Toland, Gretel Cummings, Crystal Field, Joan Fairlee, Christopher Jones. (Photo by Peter Moore. © Estate of Peter Moore/VAGA, New York/DACS, London 2003.)

Gertrude Stein's *In Circles*, Judson Poets' Theater, October 1967. Left to right: Nancy Zala, David Vaughan, George McGrath, Lee Crespi, Arthur Williams, Elaine Summers (singing), Jacque Lynn Colton, Theo Barnes, Al Carmines at piano (bottom right corner: the knees of Arlene Rothlein). (Photo by Peter Moore. © Estate of Peter Moore/VAGA, New York/DACS, London 2003.)

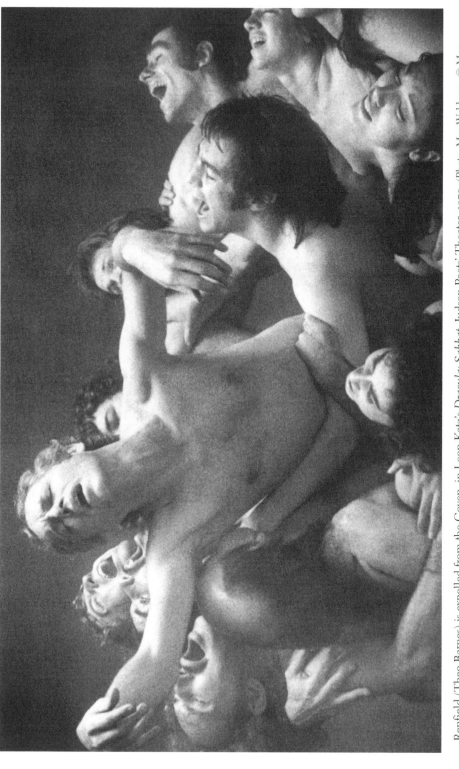

Renfield (Theo Barnes) is expelled from the Coven, in Leon Katz's *Dracula: Sabbat*, Judson Poets' Theater, 1970. (Photo: Max Waldman. © Max Waldman Archive, USA. All rights reserved.)

The audience at Café La Mama, March 1966. Under the lamp-shade: Robert Patrick; two heads from the left of him: Joe Cino. (Photo: James Gossage. Reproduced courtesy of the Billy Rose Theatre Collection, New York Public Library for the Performing Arts, and the Astor, Lenox and Tilden Foundations.)

Café La Mama, during a rehearsal break for Tom
Eyen's *Miss Nefertiti Regrets*, December 1965.
(Photo: James Gossage. Reproduced courtesy of the Billy
Rose Theatre Collection, New York Public Library for
the Performing Arts, and the Astor, Lenox and Tilden
Foundations.)

The cast and crew of Paul Foster's *Balls*, outside Ellen Stewart's apartment, 1964. Back row: Paul Boesing, James Barbosa, Lola Richardson. Middle row: Sydney Schubert Walter (director), Claire Leyba, Gary Friedman, Shirley Stoler. Front row: Amy [?], Paul Foster, Norman Long, Anthony Bastiano, Shellie Feldman. (Photographer unidentified. Courtesy of Special Collections and University Archives, Rutgers University Libraries.)

Robert Wilson's giant doll-people in Jean-Claude van Itallie's *America Hurrah* (later *Motel*), Café La Mama, April 1965. (Photo: Phill Niblock.)

La Mama Troupe in Paul Foster's *Tom Paine*, 1967. Left to right: Claris Nelson, Mari-Claire Charba, Jerry Cunliffe, Michael Warren Powell, Victor LiPari, Rob Thirkield. In back: Peter Craig. Kneeling: Kevin O'Connor and John Bakos as Paine and his Reputation. (Photographer unidentified. Courtesy of Special Collections and University Archives, Rutgers University Libraries.)

Seth Allen (lit) and Peter Craig (right) in Rochelle Owens's *Futz*. Café La Mama, March 1967. (Photo: James Gossage. Reproduced courtesy of the Billy Rose Theatre Collection, New York Public Library for the Performing Arts, and the Astor, Lenox and Tilden Foundations.)

Tom O'Horgan directing Jerry Cunliffe in rehearsals for Paul Foster's *Heimskringla*, 1969. (Photo courtesy of Tom O'Horgan.)

Left, Ellen Stewart and Rochelle Owens at the new La Mama ETC, 1969. (Photo: James Gossage. Reproduced courtesy of the Billy Rose Theatre Collection, New York Public Library for the Performing Arts, and the Astor, Lenox and Tilden Foundations.)

Leonard Melfi on the set of *Birdbath*, Theatre Genesis, June 1965. With stage manager Georgia Lee Phillips and Betsy Broden. (Photo courtesy of Walter Hadler.)

Kevin O'Connor in Sam Shepard's *Chicago.* Premiered at Theatre Genesis in 1965, and seen here in a revival directed by Tom O'Horgan at Café La Mama, March 1966. (Photo: James Gossage. Reproduced courtesy of the Billy Rose Theatre Collection, New York Public Library for the Performing Arts, and the Astor, Lenox and Tilden Foundations.)

Tom Sankey with autoharp in *The Golden Screw,* Theatre Genesis, 1966. (Photo: Bert Andrews.)

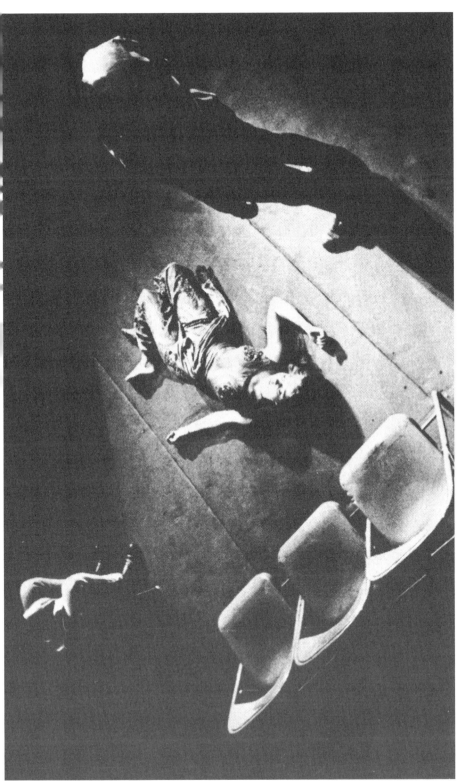

Lee Kissman as the Double, O-Lan Johnson as the Second Victim, and Tony Serchio as the Hawk in *The Hawk*, Theatre Genesis, 1967. (Photo: Ralph Gibson.)

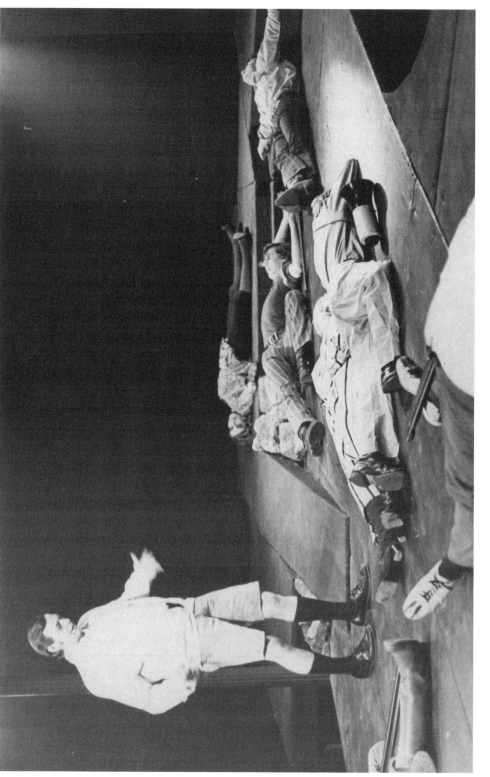

Richard Bright surrounded by corpses in Walter Hadler's *The Waterworks at Lincoln*, Theatre Genesis, November 1969. Upstage: Eileen Ellsworth,

Nevele Adams and Charles Stanley in Michael Smith's *Country Music*, Theatre Genesis, 1971. (Photo: Conrad Ward. Courtesy of Michael Smith.)

Open Theatre ensemble rehearsing Jean-Claude van Itallie's *Pavane* (later *Interview*) at Café La Mama, April 1965. (Photo: Phill Niblock.)

Open Theatre ensemble in *The Serpent*, 1968. Tina Shepard as Eve, with James Barbosa, Ron Faber, Ralph Lee, Peter Maloney, and Ray Barry as the serpent. (Photo: Freddy Tornberg.)

The cast and crew of Ronald Tavel's *The Life of Lady Godiva*, Play-House of the Ridiculous, April 1966. Director John Vaccaro in foreground with Elsene Sorrentino. Dorothy Opalach as Godiva; behind her, Tom Shibona as Leoffric; to her left, Dashwood von Blocksburg as Sheriff Thorold; at her hip, Charles Ludlam as Peeping Tom. Mario Montez in the wig, far left, as part of the nuns' chorus. (Photo courtesy of John Vaccaro.)

Bruce Pecheur as Jack, assaulted by the townsfolk in Kenneth Bernard's *The Moke Eater*, Play-House of the Ridiculous, 1968. (Photo courtesy of John Vaccaro.)

Playwright, actor, and director, Julie Bovasso, in an early portfolio shot, circa 1952. (Reproduced courtesy of the Billy Rose Theatre Collection, New York Public Library for the Performing Arts, and the Astor, Lenox and Tilden Foundations.)

Charles Ludlam in *Bluebeard*, Ridiculous Theatrical Company, 1970. (Photo: Diana Davies. Reproduced courtesy of the Billy Rose Theatre Collection, New York Public Library for the Performing Arts, and the Astor, Lenox and Tilden Foundations.)

Jeff Weiss in Gertrude Stein's *Doctor Faustus Lights the Lights*, Judson Poets' Theater, October 1979. Double-exposed image shows Esteban Chalbaud, Sarah Kornfeld, and Zoelle Montgomery. (Photo by Peter Moore. © Estate of Peter Moore/VAGA, New York/DACS, London 2003.)

Joe Cino in the burned-out rubble of the Caffe Cino, Ash Wednesday, 1965. (Photo: Conrad Ward. Reproduced courtesy of the Billy Rose Theatre Collection, New York Public Library for the Performing Arts, and the Astor, Lenox and Tilden Foundations.)

Tavel's script proved an ideal vehicle for Vaccaro's emerging brand of orchestrated chaos. "You will discover that from this point on, every line is better than the next," announces Superviva in the very first line, as if to signpost the play's delirious decline into incoherence (Schroeder 1968, 175). In the utterly alogical sequence of action, Godiva visits and attempts to join the convent, but is aggressively seduced by Leofric Goodrich, leather-clad lord of Coventry, and raped by the none-too-female Superviva. Eventually, she performs her obligatory striptease, egged on by a chorus of singing Rockette-nuns. Line by line, the text reads like a misassembled jigsaw puzzle of smutty puns, vulgar aphorisms, and random pop culture references, in which characters frequently change accents, change costumes, and even repeat whole sequences of each other's dialogue without explanation. And yet, for all the surface confusion, it was apparent to Michael Smith that "this is a real play, solidly constructed and intelligently written" (1966c). Tavel's underlying concern with satirizing Western culture's "pornographic imagination" (to borrow a term of Susan Sontag's) is apparent from the play's outset, as Tom ogles Godiva's shapely legs in his rearview mirror. It eventually transpires that he is "*The* Peeping Tom of history, if you please" (206). As the play develops, though, it is the audience's voyeurism that is manipulated, as the implied promise of Godiva's nudity is used to taunt the salaciousness of anyone expecting a rerun of *Shower:* "They got hotter shows every night at the Warwickshire Burlesque," Superviva quips at one point, "and there ain't such a long build-up before they take it off, either" (191). When Godiva finally strips, concealing her charms behind a long mane of fake blonde hair, she wittily underlines her own willingness to exploit public fascination with her body: "Will you be getting any money for your ride, Lady Godiva?"; "No: I'm doing it for the exposure" (202).

Vaccaro gleefully added his own twists to Tavel's perverse script, giving bizarre sexual peccadilloes to each of the characters. Sister Kasha Veronicas, for example, played by *Shower* veteran Elsene Sorrentino, became a shoe fetishist with a license to upstage. "She was crawling all over that stage looking for feet [to lick]," Vaccaro recalled: "She was brilliant" (1968). Before every performance, moreover, Vaccaro would whip his cast up into a frenzy. Critic Dan Isaac noted hearing "hysterical shrieks" from the dressing room before the show: "When the curtain went up, the actors were merely doing in public what they had been doing in private just a few minutes before. . . . At times, the play seemed a mere pretext for the acting out of feelings I had never seen exhibited with such unabashed exhilaration." The improvisatory hilarity of their performances, he added, made these actors "the funniest I have ever seen. . . . I felt that I was watching *commedia dell'arte* as a joyous celebration of homosexuality, a revelatory and liberating experience for actors and audience alike" (Isaac 1968, 108).

Perhaps the most revelatory performance was that of Charles Ludlam's Peeping Tom. Just twenty-three, Ludlam was a recent graduate of Hofstra University's drama program—where he had always been told that his acting was too "hammy" for him to succeed professionally. However, after being introduced to Vaccaro by art curator and Warhol confidant Henry Geldzahler, Ludlam swiftly found a theatrical home with the Ridiculous. "In a way, Vaccaro gave my whole theatrical life back to me," he noted later: "I had really given it up, [but] he allowed me to flip out all I wanted on stage. He never felt that I was too pasty, corny, mannered, campy. He let me do anything I wanted" (Ludlam 1992, 13). For his part, Vaccaro recalls Ludlam's Peeping Tom with delight: "The [wooden] horse had this appendage, and Charles was doing things to that horse's appendage that were just *vile!*" Ludlam also had to perform a comic parody of a striptease, in which he valiantly attempted to hide his "particulars" behind the bus conductor's coin-exchanger suspended from his neck. He was, by all accounts, hilarious.

Ludlam impressed even more in Tavel's *Screen Test*, later that year. Another dusted-down Warhol scenario, this was originally conceived as a drag vehicle for Mario Montez. The film is an extended close-up of Montez as Hollywood starlet, being instructed by an offscreen voice (Tavel) in the deportment and vocal skills she needs to develop if she is to get ahead: she is, for example, forced to enunciate the word "di-ah-rrea" repeatedly, as an exercise in elocution. Thus the starlet becomes the helpless puppet of the sadistically manipulative director. In the Ridiculous version, Montez reprised his role, but this time as a less submissive character, more in control of her performance. This polished piece of female impersonation was now juxtaposed with another screen test subject—a young woman whose awkward attempts to live up to the movie-star image paled in comparison to Montez's studied charisma. For Dan Isaac, *Screen Test* thus "became an incisive comment on American stylization of femininity. . . . One suddenly realized that every teenage girl in America goes to the movies in order to be a better female impersonator during her next screen test, or date" (1968, 110). Michael Smith, however, recalls that the impact of the piece lay in its very real sense of danger, as Vaccaro, again improvising freely in the onstage director role, sadistically goaded his "starlets" for more. At times, he seemed to push the performance beyond mere theatricality toward actual emotional assault—his players responding with seemingly genuine hurt, anger, or contempt.

A further twist was added to the scenario when, a few days into the run, Ludlam marched onstage midshow as a third, completely unscripted screen test subject. Wearing an extravagant wig of Salvador Dalí's that Henry Geldzahler had recently given him, Ludlam announced himself as "Norma Desmond," the fading silent-movie queen from Billy Wilder's *Sunset Boulevard*: "I put on the wig and—pow!—there was Norma" (Ludlam 1992, 13). Explaining, in character, that s/he was here to show the starlets how it was done, Ludlam began improvising his own take on feminine movie glamour. "And it was brilliant," Tavel recalls: "He was Norma Desmond to a T" (Kaufman 2002, 57). This choice of character was particularly inspired because Wilder's Desmond is an aging has-been, deludedly obsessed with her own self-image as a much younger, more attractive woman. Accordingly, Ludlam created a drag performance that highlighted its own artifice, exposing its own flaws by retaining a distinctly "masculine" dimension: "It's that teetering on the edge of being a man and woman that throws the audience," Ludlam discovered (1992, 13). His contribution to *Screen Test* proved so inspired that Vaccaro simply let him run with it. "The legendary Mario Montez had to fight tooth and nail to keep Charles Ludlam, the interloper, from stealing the show," Joseph LeSueur reported in the *Voice* (1966a). Other members of the company also began interpolating themselves spontaneously into the proceedings: Harvey Tavel, for instance, once appeared in the Erich von Stroheim role as Desmond's butler. Thus, between the opening of the show in September 1966 and its closing in December, *Screen Test* expanded from a half-hour sketch into an outright war of theatrical egos that could run for up to two hours.

Tavel Defects

Although Ludlam's contribution to *Screen Test* extended the conceptual logic of Tavel's scenario, it also functioned to upstage the latter's new play, *Indira Gandhi's Daring Device*, for which *Screen Test* was supposed to be raising the curtain. This still-unpublished play, a satire on the Indian population crisis, had Indira Gandhi proposing to place the country's lowest caste, the "untouchables," in cryonic suspension. Much of the show's verve, however, stemmed from Vaccaro's own interpolations, including a "daring device" of his own—a huge stage phallus with which Indira became unsuitably enamored. The show's scurrilous depiction of Prime Minister Gandhi so shocked students at Columbia and Rutgers universities, to which the play toured, that the show was reported to the Indian consulate, which sued the Play-House for defamation. Although the company eventually escaped this "international incident" with only a small fine, the legal costs proved crippling. To cut their losses, they closed and vacated the Seventeenth Street loft in March 1967. After only a year, the Play-House of the Ridiculous had lost its playhouse.

Vaccaro kept the name for his newly itinerant company, but Tavel and his brother Harvey had already quit, angered by the extent to which Vaccaro had begun to ride roughshod over Tavel's intentions for his plays. The breaking point had come when Vaccaro proposed to cut two-thirds of Tavel's new script, just to make it stageable. At seventy pages, as opposed to the usual twenty or so, *Gorilla Queen* was, Vaccaro still maintains, "an insult to the people in the group," since its verbal density left little scope for the improvisatory freedom that had become the company's trademark. To Vaccaro, this was Tavel's attempt to impose his own vision for the company over everyone else's. Tavel, however, having come to the conclusion that "Vaccaro could only do something with my worst plays" (Isaac 1968, 112), took *Gorilla Queen* to Judson Poets' Theater, where, he believed, more careful attention would be paid to the internal dynamics of the text itself.

An outrageous pastiche of Hollywood's jungle movies and exotic musicals of the 1930s, *Gorilla Queen* consists largely of the knowingly disgusting puns and self-referential naughtiness that had characterized Tavel's other works: "Was that bikini hard to come by?" "Not at all, I creamed in my grass skirt the second I spotted it in the store window" (Smith 1969, 200). Amusing as such upbeat vulgarity may be, however, it is easy to understand Vaccaro's reservations: the tone of the play is so relentlessly arch that, spun out for so long, it seems increasingly tiresome—on the page, at least. Judson director Larry Kornfeld concluded that he needed to look beyond the play's surface frivolity, and emphasize the mythic subtext he perceived in it. "I didn't want to just sit down and do a camp piece," he recalls: "I wanted the production to be as outrageous, as excruciatingly funny, as the play. And it was. But the play is also filled with images of metamorphosis, change, transcendence. It's a tale of spiritual transformation and a meditation on loneliness, viewed through the icons of trash culture." Implausible as that might sound, it seems to have been precisely what Tavel had in mind: "I just choked up when Larry spoke to the cast [at the first rehearsal]," he told the *New York Times:* "He saw the whole thing" (Lester 1967, 3)

At root, *Gorilla Queen* is indeed a meditation on religion—just as *Lady Godiva* is a meditation on voyeurism. A tribe of all-singing, all-dancing orang-utans called the "Glitz Ionas" worship a transvestite ape god called "Queen Kong," to whom they sacrifice helpless white women, Fay Wray–style. Kong, however, proves to be a vulnerable god who is killed and then resurrected—by unlikely means—four times during the course of the play. Meanwhile, Tavel's use of gender swapping and even color crossing implies a playful blurring of the binary structures of good and evil, black and white, masculine and feminine, which underlie so much religious thought. The play includes such characters as Sister Carries, a male witch doctor in a grass skirt and bikini; Taharahnugi White Woman, "a brownskin male actor, ravishing in a tight white sarong, a wig of long raven hair [and] huge round falsies"; and Karma Miranda, a hugely overweight, powder-white parody of the famously beautiful, dark-skinned Brazilian star, "got up like a lovely rococo shepherdess made of porcelain" (Smith 1969, 185). In this play, nothing is what it seems: identities, sexes, and colors become wildly unstable as they flip back and forth. Building the Judson production around these formal oppositions and reversals, Kornfeld created an extraordinary theatrical spectacle—complete with rope-swinging gorillas and unicycling, roller-skating orangutans—which he purposely crammed into the tiny, upstairs choir-loft space at Judson (rather than using the more expansive downstairs area). The idea was to create an overflowing, "in your face" extravaganza, and to achieve this, Kornfeld choreographed the show with inch-perfect precision: "I had to block every step." If this suggested a marked contrast to Vaccaro's methods, Kornfeld also exploited the particularities of the actors' extravagant personalities just as the Ridiculous would have: *Gorilla Queen*, recalls one spectator, Robert Patrick, "was interpreted by one of those dream casts . . . a mob of utterly free refugees from the suburbs who believed every line they said. When Eddie McCarty [as Sister Carries] screamed, 'Haste in the execution is at the core of camp,' the audience stopped the show with applause."

Gorilla Queen proved such a hit at Judson that it quickly transferred to an off-Broadway run at the Martinique Theatre. As with *Home Movies*, however (Judson's previous such transfer), the downtown community's enthusiasm for the piece was not matched by mainstream critics, who dismissed it as tiresome and offensive. As a result, the Martinique production ran for just forty-two performances. Subsequently, Tavel sought to extend his career by pursuing productions in various off-off-Broadway contexts: *Vinyl* played successfully at Caffe Cino in 1967, under his brother's direction, and he himself directed the universally disliked *Arenas of Lutetia* at Judson in 1968. Tavel struggled, however, to find a new creative home: without regular collaborators to give theatrical substance to his provocative scenarios, his later works often tended to collapse under the weight of their own complex aspirations.

Gay Abandon

Tavel's replacement as writer-in-residence at the Play-House of the Ridiculous was Charles Ludlam. Indeed, looking back, Tavel believes that Ludlam consciously angled for this position—conspiring to drive him away from the company by turning others against him (cf. Kaufman 2002, 60). Be that as it may, Ludlam's early plays were clearly indebted to those of his predecessor, particularly in their rejection of such conventional restraints as coherent narrative and "good taste." Yet where Tavel was essentially a conceptual artist, striving to make bold new statements, Ludlam was a collagist, intent on creating new theater by pasting together (and scribbling over) preexisting fragments culled from a vast range of sources. The practice of quoting from or parodying both high- and pop-cultural sources, a feature of off-off-Broadway plays since the movement's inception, was taken to new extremes in Ludlam's first play. *Big Hotel*, the last play premiered at the Seventeenth Street loft, in February 1967, was initially intended simply as an exercise in cutting and pasting—as "fun for Ludlam to have with a notebook" (Ludlam 1989, xii). At Vaccaro's behest, however, it was fleshed out as a hasty replacement for *Gorilla Queen*.

An affectionate spoof of the Greta Garbo movie *Grand Hotel*, Ludlam's play is set in a hotel lobby, constantly traversed by a collection of bizarre characters (Garbo's Grusinskaya, for instance, is reincarnated here as "Birdshitskaya"). The dialogue is openly plagiarized from a wide array of sources: "I was doing aleatoric writing then," Ludlam noted later, "cutting up other plays, scenes, things I'd heard on radio or TV" (1992, 14). Thus the unmistakable comic patter of the Marx Brothers is present here alongside *Sunset Boulevard*'s Norma Desmond (played again by Ludlam himself) and borrowings from Oscar Wilde's *Salomé:* "I weel kiss thy lips, O Magic Mandarin. I weel kiss thy lips," Mofonga declares in the play's opening line, spoofing Salomé's famous threat to Jokanaan (Ludlam 1989, 3). A Maria Montez type played by Mario Montez, Mofonga later utters the B-movie star's immortal words from *Cobra Woman*, "Geef me that Cobra Jewel! Geef me that Cobra Jewel!" (21). Jack Smith, who once described this as "possibly the greatest line of dialogue in any American flic" (1997, 26), was also present as the mysterious Mr. X, delivering his lines extremely slowly, to bizarre effect.

Ludlam's writing, here and subsequently, anticipated Roland Barthes's 1968 essay "The Death of the Author," which argued that any text should be seen as "a multi-dimensional space in which a variety of writings, none of them original, blend and clash. The text is a tissue of quotations drawn from the innumerable centers of culture" (Barthes 1977, 146). Yet *Big Hotel* was less intellectual exercise than gay fantasia, campily appropriating both famous and obscure sources, while challenging the audience to spot the quotations, and to appreciate the comic value of their recontextualization. The results are often wildly funny, but the play lacks the perversity or transgressive edge of Tavel's plays. Vaccaro found more to get his directorial teeth into with Ludlam's next play, which was an altogether darker, more depraved affair.

Drawing equally on Flash Gordon–style science fiction and the bloody revenge tragedies of the Renaissance, *Conquest of the Universe* follows the attempts of the warlord Tamberlaine to conquer all nine worlds of the solar system, and to humiliate the defeated planetary monarchs by ritualistically sodomizing them. This practice gives rise to some truly appalling jokes—"How do I pay you when I use you as a woman?" "In piles, Master!" (Ludlam 1989, 32)—but also results in Tamberlaine's coming to resemble that other Marlovian king, Edward II, in his preference for sleeping with the defeated Bajazeth, king of Mars, rather than Queen Alice. By scene 9 he is also directly quoting Shakespeare's King Claudius, in his despairing attempts at prayer: "My words fly up. My thoughts remain below. Words without thoughts never to heaven go" (40). Meanwhile, the would-be revenger Cosroe looks on as if he were Hamlet: "If I do it now his soul goes to heaven . . ." (39). Scene 10 then sees Cosroe walking through a parody of *Hamlet*'s gravedigger scene. The references pile up ever further, with the climactic revenge scheme being lifted from *Titus Andronicus*. However, where Shakespeare's Titus bakes Tamara's sons in a pie, Ludlam's Tamberlaine is obliged to eat a dish made from the "nine little ones" borne to him from the buggered asshole of Bajazeth. (He is made, in other words, to eat shit and die.)

Grotesque, scatological, and unwieldy as it is, *Conquest of the Universe* demonstrates the deft grasp of dramatic genre that was to become Ludlam's trademark. As director Neil Bartlett observes, "Ludlam expanded the notion of drag to include not just the wearing of frocks but the philosophical, self-conscious 'wearing' of theatrical culture itself" (1990, 50). His disorienting use of both female impersonation and dramatic convention highlighted "the act of self-creation and self-dramatization," which, for Bartlett, is both "a specifically gay project" and, in a too-closeted world, "a necessary one" (50). It was here, however, that Ludlam and Vaccaro diverged. Ludlam was beginning to conceive of the Ridiculous as an outrageous celebration of queer identities—as in the Tamberlaine-Bajazeth relationship, for example—and believed that, in this respect, Vaccaro was "too conservative. He didn't want homosexuality or nudity onstage because he was afraid of being arrested. I wanted to commit an outrage" (Ludlam 1992, 13). Vaccaro, for his part, had never seen the company as overtly gay in orientation: his attitude was much closer to Tavel's original conception of the Ridiculous as expressing a nihilist philosophical position (the universe as preposterous), and he saw *Conquest of the Universe*—with its pitch-black humor and near-constant stream of images involving violence and twisted sexual assault—as a pretext for the Play-House's most discomforting theatrical experience yet.

With its loose stage directions allowing him a free hand to realize the play according to his own vision, *Conquest* seemed tailor-made for Vaccaro's patented brand of stage chaos. Yet the fundamental differences between Ludlam's and Vaccaro's conceptions of *Conquest* resulted in a permanent parting of the ways, during rehearsals for the play's November premiere at the 199-seat Bouwerie Lane Theatre (a booking arranged by producer Wyn Chamberlain, an admirer of the company). Vaccaro felt that Ludlam was interfering too much with his directing; Ludlam that Vaccaro was ignoring his conception of the play. Whether Ludlam quit or was fired depends on whose account one believes, but when he went, he took with him most of the rest of the cast, including Ridiculous mainstays like Mario Montez. They had all, Ludlam claimed, had enough of Vaccaro's volatile working methods: "He criticizes ideas without giving any suggestions for improvements, and then makes you do it over and over again. It's psychological torture" (1992, 13). To Vaccaro, Ludlam's mutiny was somewhat more self-serving: "Charles wanted to be exactly what he became, which was a megalomaniac." Ludlam and his cohort founded the Ridiculous Theatrical Company (see chapter 16) and instantly arranged to stage their own version of *Conquest* under its subtitle, *When Queens Collide*. The Play-House, however, owned the legal rights to the play's premiere, and it was Vaccaro's production that thus attracted most of the press attention when it opened, on schedule. Having recruited a replacement cast from among contacts in the underground film community—including Beverly Grant, Taylor Mead, Ondine, and Ultra Violet—Vaccaro had put the show together in just twelve days: "the whole Factory came down," he recalls, "and I kept them around the clock rehearsing." With a rock band called the Third Eye backing the action with a near-constant aural assault, the production was "an explosion of talent that leaves the mind in tatters" (Smith 1967f, 33).

Vaccaro's emphasis in *Conquest* was, as ever, on personality rather than text: "Our actors are acting themselves as well as their roles," read the Play-House's press release; "the real person [is] more interesting than the plot." Taylor Mead, for example, appeared simply as himself, an unscripted "Guest Star." Yet it was Mary Woronov's towering self-performance as a drag Tamberlaine in military fatigues that stole the show. Woronov has written that acting for the Ridiculous allowed her a productive outlet for a dark, violent streak within her own personality—a side of herself that she named "Violet," and which she sought to suppress in everyday life. In *Conquest of the Universe*, however, "Violet" was allowed out to play with a vengeance, thanks to "our homicidal genius of a director. . . . Every night he hissed in my ear, 'Do anything you like to them, I want fear in their eyes.' I was all-powerful" (Woronov 2000, 114). Under Vaccaro's direction, argued Stefan Brecht in his *TDR* review, actors like Woronov were capable of achieving an extreme emotional authenticity that had nothing to do with adherence to dramatic convention: the Play-House of the Ridiculous, Brecht wrote, "is the first and only good theatre in New York since the Living Theatre was exiled," and Woronov "is a superb performer. . . . The raving maniac she portrays is of plausible efficacy, a bestrider of the world. . . . With hysteria, paranoia, she plays a bare core of sadistic energy" (1978, 56–57). Michael Smith further observed that "the core" of Vaccaro's production was "a point of view that faces the horror of history, and personal horrors too, and somehow glories in them." The result was "a staggering experience. . . . See it all on stage at the Bouwerie Lane and shudder for the future of the theatre and the species" (1967f, 33).

Beyond Artaud?

Conquest ran for three months and garnered praise from all quarters. Marcel Duchamp reportedly declared it the best piece of theater he had ever seen. Despite the acclaim, however, this show almost marked the end of the Play-House. Vaccaro now admits that, having fallen out so publicly with two writers in quick succession, and without either a permanent playing space or ensemble, he contemplated quitting theater altogether. It was at this point, however, that he received a packet of scripts from playwright Kenneth Bernard, who had been struck more forcibly by *Conquest* than by anything he had seen since van Itallie's *Motel*. His approach initiated a writer-director collaboration that functioned intermittently until 1984. Bernard, a college professor with a wife and family, had little of the queer flamboyance of Tavel or Ludlam—although his plays feature a strong dose of scurrilous humor and sexual absurdity. What he and Vaccaro found that they shared, more importantly, was a similarly dark, apocalyptic worldview.

Bernard's work allowed Vaccaro to develop further his peculiar brand of grotesque, post-Artaudian burlesque. Almost always constructed using a show-within-a-show premise, Bernard's plays demanded an overtly theatrical treatment in production, but were also usually better structured than Tavel's or Ludlam's. Indeed *The Moke Eater*, the play that marked the beginning of this new collaboration, was arguably the most dramatically cohesive and conceptually uncompromising of all the Play-House's works. Premiering in September 1968, it played at weekends after midnight in the back room at Max's Kansas City, the East Village bar-restaurant frequented by the Warhol entourage. A cult hit, it went on to play further engagements at the Café Au Gogo and the Gotham Art Theatre in 1969.

As a text, *The Moke Eater* superficially resembles Tennessee Williams's *Camino Real*: Jack, an all-American everyman figure similar to Williams's Kilroy, stumbles into a town on the border of reality and fantasy, and becomes the "patsy"—ridiculously renamed "Fwed! Fwed!"—in a series of manipulative theatrical games played by the locals. Yet where Williams's play is essentially romantic, Bernard's is the stuff of nightmare, a sadistic ritual in which Jack is systematically tortured and taunted, seduced and abused by a cackling collection of ghouls. Vaccaro borrowed from Kabuki tradition to paint his performers' faces stark white, with black markings like a series of horrific death-masks, and he orchestrated the action as if the play were a contemporary rendition of a Bosch or Breughel painting, filling the stage with grotesque detail in every corner, to create "a kind of pandemonium"—as suggested by one of Bernard's stage directions (Bernard 1971, 68). Far from creating mere undifferentiated chaos, though, Vaccaro exploited the play's rhythmic punctuating devices (a state trooper riding silently across stage; the sound of a guillotine blade creakily being pulled up and then dropped) to pace the play and build its underlying tension into an elongated scream. Inspired by LaMonte Young's musical experiments with chordal drones, Vaccaro also instructed his ensemble to underpin the entire performance with a constant guttural growling that he describes as "the sound of evil. "The noise level," Robert Pasolli noted in the

Voice of the combined sound effects, music and overlapping voices, "is staggering" (1968b).

The performance demonstrated just how much Vaccaro's theatrical vision had darkened and intensified since the camp silliness of *Shower*. Yet *The Moke Eater* resembles Tavel's play insofar that both suggest a strong sense of the farcical-horrific vacuity of American culture. The mythical setting, Monte Waite, seems to represent small-town America at large—"our way of life [is] The American way of life" (66)—and the inhabitants enact a demented pageant of the nation's history. A waitress (played in Vaccaro's production by Elsene Sorrentino, sole survivor from *Shower*) performs a rapid series of costume changes to appear as a southern belle, a pioneer, and a Puritan, while the hapless Jack is forced to perform an appalling parody of an Amos and Andy skit, in clumsily applied blackface, before being told to make like Abraham Lincoln. Meanwhile, the sadistic ringmaster, Alec, seems to represent every small-minded, conformist prejudice of conservative America, condoning a lynch-mob assault on a frail old man on the grounds that he is "the leader of the opposition party. . . . He's always agitating. You saw him. When he gets a taste of his own medicine he whines like a sick dog" (76).

Repellent as Alec undoubtedly is, however, there is also something compellingly seductive about his charisma and savage wit. Rather than allowing the spectator the comfort of a neatly distanced, moralistic position, Bernard presents Alec as a dazzling virtuoso, whose mercurial shifts of tone and attitude keep Jack in a bewildered daze:

> I hope you didn't take me seriously back there. I had to do all that. Part of the show. They're very sensitive. Surely you see that now. Listen, the last man we had drawn and quartered, well . . . *(he giggles)* Shall we say he was a fool? *(He giggles again)* We strung him up till he turned a rainbow purple, then cut him down and threw water on him. The fellow didn't know where he was. . . . You didn't think I meant anything did you, Fred? Oh really, now. *(Earnestly)* It's all part of the show. (74–75)

A further emotional complication for the audience is that they are allowed little empathy for Jack in his plight. He is depicted from the start as a patronizing, arrogant tool of big-city exploiters, a traveling salesman intent on making a fast buck. Once assaulted, he can only spout pitiful clichés in his defense: "Please mister, have a heart. I mean, a joke is a joke. I don't want to get you in any trouble. Live and let live. Listen, I mind my own business. I—I got a territory to cover" (68). On some level, Jack's humiliation might even be enjoyed by the spectator. When he finally escapes Monte Waite at the play's conclusion, only to arrive there once again after "three hours" of driving, his (deserving?) condemnation to this particularly gruesome circle of all-American hell is horrifically confirmed.

Neatly realized as this climax is, however, the messy reality of Vaccaro's production was that, as the knowingly "bad" acting made clear, "a great deal of the violence is actual rather than represented" (Pasolli 1968b). Vaccaro took literally Bernard's stage direction specifying that Jack should be "genuinely crying from fear" (73), and egged his cast on to do their worst to Bruce Pecheur, the male model playing Jack: "I'd be backstage, and I'd say [*whispering*] 'Kill, Kill that motherfucker! Kill him!'" An added twist was that Pecheur's wife, Sierra Bandit, was cast as Alec: taking over the function of tall and lethal drag dominatrix from Mary Woronov, Bandit orchestrated her husband's torments with terrifying verve. A true theater of cruelty, Vaccaro declared in an interview that year, depended on the performers being willing to be cruel not just to the audience, but to each other: "I have gone beyond Artaud," he declared (1968). As Pasolli's review makes clear, though, the impact on the audience was also directly felt:

> The Ridiculous apparently wants to drag the theatre kicking and screaming into a new phase. No more business as usual; no more entertainment, illusion, or representation of our everyday surface realities. For the Ridiculous, the theatre is the place to represent—or to actualize—the psychic monsters which we repress by means of our learned civilized assumptions. . . . As Jack is assaulted, the audience is assaulted. . . . Like Jack, I wanted to run the other way. Like him, I didn't. (1968b)

While hailing Vaccaro "a visionary," Pasolli also asked pointedly whether such a theater could sustain itself for long—not because its vision was invalid, but because audiences might not, ultimately, wish to receive much more of this treatment: "I don't know what the Ridiculous can do about our resistance." Vaccaro seems to have been aware of the problem, and in subsequent work, the assaultive terrors of *The Moke Eater* were often replaced by lighter-hearted, more entertainingly lewd stage antics. Nevertheless, in *Nightclub* (1970), *The Magic Show of Dr. Ma-gico* (1973), and other collaborations with Kenneth Bernard, the starting time (at least metaphorically) was always midnight.

12   Other Kinds of Cruelty: Ritual, Participation, and the Plague

> It is the group that creates instead of me. [Thanks to the group,] I would find myself interesting. It would suffice me to be who I am. Whatever I might do—walk, howl, shout—I would feel absolved by the group. If I wished to show myself human, I would seek contact: touch the hands of my partners, look them straight in the eyes. I'd see nothing at all there, but no matter, the essential thing is to be human and do improvisations.
>
> —Jerzy Grotowski, "External Order, Internal Intimacy"

The year 1968 represented a high-water mark for alternative theater in the United States, just as it marked a peak in countercultural activity more generally—from antiwar demonstrations and student revolts through love-ins, be-ins, and psychedelic rock. The notion of ensemble-based collaboration, pioneered over the previous several years by groups such as the Open Theatre and La Mama Troupe, became widely celebrated at this time as the appropriate theatrical manifestation of the antihierarchical, communitarian spirit of the day. By 1968, though, ensemble explorations of the theatrical "here and now" (as opposed to the "then and there" of representational drama) had acquired a significant new twist. Concern with the immediate "presence of the actor," onstage, began to be complemented by a desire to highlight the presence of the audience—by inviting spectators to participate directly in the theatrical event. Inspired, in particular, by the suggestions for a ritualistic "holy theater" envisaged in Antonin Artaud's widely circulated book, *The Theatre and Its Double*, these experiment with audience participation were seen as a way of transforming spectators into celebrants.

The Living Theatre was at the forefront of this development, as they had been with so many others. Returning to the United States in September 1968 after five years in Europe, they toured nationally for six months with a repertory of four collectively created works, including their most recent and controversial, *Paradise Now*, which had been specifically conceived to facilitate audience involvement. Constructed as a series of eight "rites," rooted in anarchist principles, *Paradise Now* invited spectators to participate in enacting their symbolic liberation from the social, political, and bodily restraints of the status quo. In the notorious "Rite of Universal Intercourse," for example, audience members would "make love, not war" by disrobing and taking to the stage to engage in tangled caresses with both the seminaked performers and each other. At the show's climax, performers and audience exited the theater together to "retake the streets," and thus symbolically invoke "the Permanent Revolution of Change." As is clear, however, from Judith Malina's journal of their U.S. tour (*The Enormous Despair*), performances of *Paradise Now* sometimes did not get this far, having been derailed by audience members intent on making their own points or doing their own thing. As advocates of anarchism, the Living Theatre would allow these alternative "scenes" to play out as the mood dictated.

Another celebrated piece of interactive, ritual-based theater (which also included a participatory "group grope") was *Dionysus in 69*. The Performance Group, which established itself in a downtown garage space on Wooster Street, performed this knowingly titled adaptation of *The Bacchae* from June 1968 through July the following year. Fusing Euripides' primal narrative with images based on the ritual practices of the Asmat people of New Guinea—which the group's director, New York University professor Richard Schechner, had been researching—this piece also tackled the conflict between the desire for personal liberation and the realities of social control. Somewhat more circumspection was brought to this treatment of the subject than to the overtly didactic *Paradise Now*—as was appropriate, given that the Greek narrative emphasizes the perils of Dionysian excess as well as the evils of tyranny. The increasingly Dionysian spirit of the performances themselves, however, meant that measured debate tended to be the first thing to be sacrificed on the altar of audience participation.

Paradise Now and *Dionysus in 69* have both been well documented and analyzed elsewhere, and it is not my purpose here to revisit them in any detail. One underrecognized fact about these pieces, however, is that their fame and notoriety as countercultural landmarks—deserving though it may be—was in large part a product of the distinctly noncountercultural mechanisms of press and publicity. Despite being presented in a downtown garage, *Dionysus in 69* was deftly marketed and run as a commercial operation, charging off-Broadway ticket prices of four to ten dollars per head. It was "packaged as a cultural commodity like any other," John Lahr observed of the production's longevity: "There will be a movie and a book" (1969). Similarly, on their return to American shores, the Living Theatre were promoted by independent producers as high priests of revolutionary agitation. The company's keynote appearances at the Brooklyn Academy of Music in September 1968—the month after the violent clashes in Chicago between police and protesters during the Democratic convention (see chapter 15)—became a media circus, a locus for all the cultural and generational tensions of the day. "The level of fever-pitch excitement preceding *Paradise Now*," Maurice Blanc wrote in the *Village Voice*, "left the actors very little on which to build; an apogee of sound had already been reached. Fist-sized spitballs were flying and Grand Army Plaza matrons were aiming them at any man on stage that they identified as Julian Beck, before he even appeared" (1969, 43).

These points are worth emphasizing for two reasons. First, this selling of countercultural values at mainstream ticket prices raised difficult questions about the intimately physical interaction of cast and audience: "Too often the performers—especially the women—felt used, prostituted," Schechner later acknowledged of *Dionysus*: "The real question was: would we acquiesce in being a function of the audience's fantasies?" (1994, 42–43). Second, these shows were indicative of the way that the counterculture was itself in danger of being reduced to a set of fashion statements—an easily marketed "sound and fury," stripped of any real oppositional significance. The symbiotic relationship at this time between ostensibly alternative theater and commercial mechanisms is nowhere more clearly demonstrated than in the impact of *Hair*, whose successful Broadway premiere in April 1968 not only helped prepare the public arena for further, more radical hippie theatrics, but also had a marked demographic effect. That year saw a further influx of young people into the already crowded Lower East Side, many of whom were apparently seeking to live out the musical's fantasy "tribal" lifestyle. By the fall, a fanzine named *Off-Off* had appeared, which devoted several of its early articles to filling newcomers in on the history of "the early theaters—Genesis, La Mama, Cafe Cino [*sic*]." The front page of *Off-Off*'s second issue featured a piece titled "It was a Hairy Scene before *Hair*," in which the musical's success on Broadway was taken to be the logical consequence of, and best evidence for, the off-off-Broadway movement's vitality (Erlatinger 1968). The article sat next to the edition's other leading piece, on *Dionysus in 69*.

The fact that precious few off-off productions prior to 1968 had borne even a cursory resemblance to these shows was neatly sidestepped by such revisionism. The theatrical values of the scene prior to this date became thoroughly obscured by the new vogue for improvisatory, ensemble-based performances,

which began appearing at obscure venues across the city, and which frequently lacked any kind of aesthetic vision or coherence. Off-off-Broadway
was now seen by many as—in the words of another *Off-Off* headline—"the
World's Largest Romper Room," and Grotowski's scathing caricature of
American ensemble work, cited at the head of this chapter, aptly sums up the
attendant childishness. Against this cultural backdrop, many of the more
significant underground collaborations of the day went largely unacknowledged. Vaccaro and Bernard's *The Moke Eater*, for example, ritualistic though
it arguably was in structure, was violently antithetical to the peace-and-love
pieties of the hippie generation, and—playing after midnight in a bar—
attracted little publicity beyond word of mouth. In this chapter, I want to focus
on two further pieces—*The Hawk*, at Theatre Genesis, and Judson's *Dracula:
Sabbat*—which took the ensemble-ritual format in directions very different
and much darker than those of their more famous counterparts. These are
worth examining in some detail because they provide strong counterresponses
to the question of what an "Artaudian" theater might look like.

How Best to Be Cruel?

Experiments like *Paradise Now* and *Dionysus in 69* were symptomatic of widespread attempts, at this time, to realize Artaud's call for a "theater of cruelty"
that would set aside the familiar comfort of prerehearsed representations and
seek, instead, to overwhelm audiences with the sheer force of its unmediated
reality. In pursuit of this ideal, Artaud had argued both for the removal of the
traditional stage-auditorium divide (so that spectators were caught up in the
midst of a "total" theatrical event, which resisted containment and rationalization) and for the ending of theater's reliance on the playwright to create
dramatic fictions. Hence the Living Theatre's commitment to what they
called "collective creation." "A group comes together," explained Julian Beck:
"There is no author to rest on who wrests the creative impulse from you.
Destruction of the superstructure of the mind. Then reality comes" (1972,
n.p.). However, such antihierarchical rhetoric conveniently ignored the fact
that—as had already been demonstrated by the collaborative creations of the
Judson Poets' Theater, the Open Theatre, La Mama Troupe, the Ridiculous,
and others—it was perfectly possible to bring a sense of the performers' personal, collective "realities" to bear on prewritten texts, without being unfaith-
ful to authorial intentions. The notion that actors and directors are enslaved to
the intentions of the playwright had been effectively disproved by these

groups, each of which worked interactively with writers as an integral part of the creative process.

In practice, the only really concrete results of dispensing with writers were to minimize the use and importance of language in the theatrical event, and to leave the director (or the group itself) in ultimate charge of structural decisions. Perhaps unsurprisingly, the Living Theatre and Performance Group were frequently criticized for the banality and even triteness of their spoken sentiments, and for the seemingly chaotic organization of their performances. By contrast, a group-devised piece like the Open Theatre's *Serpent*—with words and structure by Jean-Claude van Itallie—was far more aesthetically coherent. Of course, such coherence was not a priority in either *Paradise Now* or *Dionysus in 69*, since they were conceived more as open-ended communal happenings than as plays. It was this openness to participation that made these pieces so exciting to their admirers. Yet it also made them highly questionable to skeptics, who often pointed out that ostensibly spontaneous interventions, whether on the part of spectators or performers, were not necessarily any more "real" or "authentic" (whatever that might be) than the rehearsed gestures of a conventional actor. Indeed, many of the observers who participated most enthusiastically in these pieces—including Schechner himself, who stripped naked at *Paradise Now*, in response to the chanted line "I am not allowed to take my clothes off"—freely admitted to being exhibitionists (cf. Malina and Beck 1969, 29).

Direct interaction with audiences had, in fact, been experimented with prior to 1968 by various off-off-Broadway artists, but had not been pursued far precisely because of the fear that such gestures would simply become rote or insincere. *Viet Rock*, for example, had ended with "a celebration of presence" in which the actors left the stage and entered the audience, each choosing an audience member and gently touching his or her hands, head, face, or hair (Terry 1966a, 227). The more the piece was performed, however, the more forced and artificial the gesture seemed to become: in subsequent Open Theatre productions a clear, respectful divide was observed between actors and audience, even as a sense of intimacy was sought through physical proximity and a blurring of stage/auditorium demarcations. Thus, at the end of *The Serpent*, the actors would simply exit down the aisles between spectators, warmly singing "Moonlight Bay." Similarly, O'Horgan's La Mama Troupe frequently crossed the proscenium line to move among audiences, but rarely required any direct participation in response. A notable exception was in *Tom Paine*, at the point in Foster's script where the stage directions call for the actors to

"Break. Be yourself," and to quiz the actor playing Paine about what he really thinks of the historical figure (Foster 1967a, 22). To avoid the loss of spontaneity that would inevitably come from repeating the same debate among themselves night after night, the troupe decided to open this discussion out to involve the audience. This also necessitated an opening of the subject matter, however, since audience members could not be expected to discuss Paine himself with much authority. The Vietnam War usually arose as a topic, since it seemed to lurk obliquely behind the dialogue on the American Revolution that immediately precedes this pause in the action: "The seed crop of a whole generation dying to the last man to protect what?" (21). The effectiveness of the discussion sequence could vary radically from night to night, however, and the actors had to learn when to cut it short and move on. "The talk about imperial power, Vietnam, etc., did not work on opening night," John Lahr reported of *Tom Paine*'s off-Broadway premiere: "I am told it can be dynamic on nights when the audience does not feel bludgeoned. Unfortunately, this relationship is too often precarious, turning performers into ethical bullies which their intelligence and the evidence of the play never quite bear out" (1968, 10).

"Bullying" (as distinct from "cruelty") was one of the offences most frequently charged to *Paradise Now*, whose performers were at times guilty of aggressively hectoring those members of the audience whom they concluded were unenlightened or counterrevolutionary. "Don't scream at me, you fucking idiot!" one spectator reportedly retorted, "I don't hate you because you're black. I hate you because you're spitting in my face!" (qtd. Bigsby 1985, 92). It was incidents of this kind that led Judson director Lawrence Kornfeld to conclude that, much as he still supported his old mentors Julian Beck and Judith Malina, their attempts to remove the actor-spectator divide were disingenuous at best: "Those events that play amidst the people are playing a sleight-of-hand trick: they are trying to convince us that they are not separate from us, [like] a grown-up coming into the midst of children and playing with them as if there were no differences in age between them and the kids" (Kornfeld, unpublished notes, 1968). A basic separation between theater event and audience was, Kornfeld believed, not only inevitable but desirable, if spectators were to engage meaningfully with the proceedings. Sam Shepard made much the same point in caricaturing the Performance Group: "If an audience walks into the building and people are swinging from the rafters and spaghetti's thrown all over them . . . it doesn't necessarily mean . . . that their participation in the play is going to be any closer. In fact it might very well be less so, because of the defenses that are put up as soon as that happens" (Marranca 1981, 202–3).

The setting up of mental defenses was, of course, precisely the opposite of what Artaud had envisaged—but then, there is a strong argument to be made that the calculated randomness of participatory theater would have been anathema to him also: "From a mental viewpoint," he wrote, "cruelty means strictness, diligence, unrelenting decisiveness, irreversible and absolute determination" (1970, 79). Though Artaud's writings are often cryptic and even contradictory, it seems clear that he was far less interested in physical interaction or confrontation with an audience than with creating—through implacably rigorous means—a kind of psychic "plague" that would profoundly disturb the spectators' basic assumptions about *themselves*: "A real stage play upsets our tranquil sensibility, releases our suppressed subconscious . . . urging forward the exteriorization of a latent undercurrent of cruelty through which all the perversity of which the mind is capable, whether in a person or a nation, becomes localized (1970, 19, 21). To achieve this, the theater needed to "rediscover figures and archetypal symbols which act like . . . incendiary images surging into our abruptly awoken minds" (18).

As the writer of *Dracula: Sabbat*, Leon Katz, dryly remarks, "People howling and that sort of thing is not really the essence of Artaud." While stressing, as have many others, that Artaud's ideas for a theater of cruelty are unrealizable in their entirety, Katz insists that his central objective was to assault and undermine the audience's "moral sensibility," rather than their physical comfort (a proposition that Grotowski would no doubt have agreed with). With this in mind, Katz conceived *Dracula: Sabbat* around the enactment of a satanic mass—one of the few images of evil by which a largely secular contemporary audience is still likely to feel unsettled. ("I found it shocking," Clive Barnes confessed in the *Times:* "perhaps it needs an agnostic to be discomforted by blasphemy" [1970b].) Similarly, the creators of *The Hawk* constructed an implacable ritual of repetitive murder. In order that the psychic implications of these pieces could strike home, both were placed within what Katz calls "an extreme aesthetic envelope," sealed off from the audience. Yet if Artaud's notion of surrounding the spectator with theatrical action was ignored, his underlying vision of the theater as the "double" of life—that is, as the mirror image not of our comfortable, conscious mask-lives, but of our suppressed, subconscious "realities"—was honored. Indeed, the makers of *The Hawk* took the metaphor of the mirror-double quite literally: although some of the actors' speeches were addressed directly toward the audience, spectators were also informed that they were separated from the stage by a huge, invisible, two-way mirror. Implicitly, the spectators could see in, but the performers could not see out: when the characters appear to look out at the watchers, they are only seeing their own reflections. Or was the mirror, perhaps, the other way around?

The Hawk

The one major ensemble project to be developed for Theatre Genesis, *The Hawk* was created every bit as "communally" as *Paradise Now*—having its origins in a two-month retreat period during the summer of 1967, when a group of Genesis affiliates lived and worked together on the Keystone Dairy Farm in rural Pennsylvania. The objective was to make a new piece using improvisatory methods, and inspired by the ideas of Artaud and others. Yet this was a project spearheaded by two writers, Murray Mednick and Tony Barsha (the latter acting as director), and was therefore distinctive in paying close attention, from an early stage, to the precise use of language, and to the development of a taut, coherent dramaturgical structure. The result was a performance built around cyclical, ritualistic actions, but which was—as one might expect of Genesis—grounded in the bleak street reality of the Lower East Side.

A heroin dealer, the Hawk, welcomes a series of clients into his apartment, working symbiotically with a mysterious doppelgänger figure known simply as the Double (another conscious echo of Artaud). He converses with each client before administering a lethal overdose: he then cleans up, showers luxuriously, and awaits his next victim. The Hawk seems to crave the kill as compulsively as the victims crave their junk, but the helpless hunger for food, for sex, for love, and for death itself also become part of the equation in this dark portrayal of obsession and addiction. In the final scene, lacking any more victims, the Hawk turns on his Double, and, in a moment reminiscent of the climax of Poe's classic short story "William Wilson," maniacally kills this "demon which he confuses with himself" (Mednick and Barsha 1968, 106). Finally, he finds himself utterly alone.

The play's relentlessness of focus is grimly disturbing, but as actor Walter Hadler stresses, its stylised depiction of murder was intended neither as an abstract aesthetic device nor as a moralistic statement, but as a heightened reflection of reality. *The Hawk* is, in effect, the anti-*Hair*, an uncompromising depiction of the counterculture's criminal underside:

We weren't being sensationalistic. That kind of burning, obsessive energy was all around us at the time. Everybody on earth was coming to the Lower East Side, all the hippies and dippies and zippies, and there was enormous exploitation going on—you know, guys picking up chicks and maybe murdering them, or whatever. A lot of naive middle-class people were coming into that situation looking for some kind of [bohemian freedom], and just getting eaten up by this meat grinder. (Walter Hadler)

Work on what became *The Hawk* began with a series of regular acting workshops initiated at Genesis by Tony Barsha. While Ralph Cook continued to focus on finding and directing new scripts, Barsha was interested in exploring some of the physical acting ideas current at the time, such as the Open Theatre's transformation exercises. The group's experiments were then given focus during the Keystone retreat with the introduction of Mednick's loose "scenario" for a possible performance—actually a few pages of oblique, semipoetic reflections. Sections of this were cut into the final play as a rumbling ur-text spoken by the Double as each victim's body is being cleaned away: "Yes, I have known a lot of psychopaths—bad amphetamine heads, bad junkies, father haters, killers, hard guys. . . . The one thing they all have in common is a certain freedom of action—they just don't give a shit" (53). (There is an echo here, perhaps, of Artaud's awe at the absolute amorality of the incestuous protagonists of John Ford's *'Tis Pity She's a Whore*.) The text's prevailing thematics of addiction and murderous obsession were also used as a starting point in improvising scenes and characters. With four actresses in the group, it was quickly decided that each one should be a victim to Tony Serchio's Hawk and Lee Kissman's Double—a choice that lent an edge of twisted sexual obsession to the proceedings. The women then developed characters representing different types of dope-hunter—the out-of-town innocent trying to be "cool," the hippie pot-head, the wealthy socialite, the narcissistic fantasist—each of which evolved into an unsettling blend of satirical caricature and emotional complexity. There is, moreover, an implicit social critique in this cross-section of types: all are hooked, but not all of them will admit it, and to the socialite, "junkies" are the scum of the earth.

As these characters developed, the focus of the acting experiments also evolved—away from the full-bodied physical expression of the Open Theatre and toward a fusion of downbeat character-acting with a precise, detailed use of mime. Thus, despite its ostensibly domestic setting, *The Hawk* uses no set or props. The all-black space of the Genesis stage was a void filled only by folding metal chairs, standing in as a blue sofa. As the play begins, the Hawk describes the otherwise invisible contents of the room to the audience in intricate detail (almost all the items, we are told, are blue), indicating the presence of these objects through precise physical gestures. Subsequently, the handling of all "props" is meticulously mimed: this close attention to the simplest of actions brings a tight, obsessive focus to sequences such as the Double's preparation of the (invisible) heroin syringe, prior to each victim's overdose. "The inside of the box is lined in blue velvet and contains a syringe and two needles. The syringe has two parts. . . . The plunger and the receptacle. Of the two needles, one is long and the other is short. One is gold and the other silver. I'll put these back in the box here and close it" (12).

This taut, clean presentational style provided a baseline from which the actors' language could take off. While other ensemble groups of the period tended to focus less on the performers' facility with words than on their bodies, Barsha's group worked insistently to develop an ease and fluency in improvising sharp, witty dialogue and imagistic monologues. Genesis writers like Mednick and Shepard had for some time been seeking to achieve a theatrical equivalent to the spontaneous freedom of jazz music, but if the actors themselves could develop the skills to do this in performance, then they could really "jam." Thus, the overall structure eventually developed for *The Hawk* was unmistakably jazzlike, in utilizing certain insistent, recurring passages—particularly those between the Hawk and his Double—and then launching into more spontaneous "breaks" during the Hawk's scenes with his victims. The performance, all participants stress, really did change from night to night: Barbara Young recalls that she eventually acquired the confidence to walk onstage and "just leap into space," knowing that all she had to do was hit certain "signposts" during her scene, to stay on track. That sense of freedom, combined with the trust she had in her fellow performers, made this "the best acting experience I ever had." Perhaps, too, the genuinely risky "liveness" of these performances can be seen as pursuing Artaud's desire for onstage "reality" rather than fixed representations—while maintaining the kind of rigorous self-discipline that he also demanded.

The published text of *The Hawk*, while attributed to Mednick and Barsha, is in truth simply a transcription of tapes from one, improvised performance, rather than any finalized authorial script. Indeed, the printed dialogue is littered with exchanges that smack of the kind of back-and-forth wordplay and bizarre non sequiturs characteristic of improvational comedy. Yet these moments are always underpinned by, and held in tension with, a continuing sense of menace. The two-way mirror conceit was important here, in helping the actors to maintain a certain cool detachment: "We wanted them to be like masterful improvisational comedians in their timing," Mednick notes, "but not to play *to* the audience." In his *Voice* review, Michael Smith suggested that Mednick's writerly influence was also strongly apparent in the actors' control of their performances—"in the nearly faultless tone of the language, despite its range; in the avoidance or reanimation of cliché, [and] in the direct, honest precision of what is told" (1967c).

Equally striking, from the published text, is the extent to which the actors' semi-improvised dialogue exchanges, and particularly their keynote monologues, demonstrate their ability to play off and reintegrate the verbal imagery and thematic motifs already introduced by other voices—just as a jazz musician would play around established themes in a solo break. The most extreme example of such jazz-play is apparent in the character of the Dealer, a kind of über-connection played by Walter Hadler, who appears at the end of the play after the deaths of all four victims. In an extraordinary, unhinged monologue, he would nightly create a rapid-fire restatement of each of the major themes established by those victims, while sardonically mimicking their voices and mannerisms. Seizing on their key turns of phrase, twisting and intercutting them, and building to a kind of frenetic peak, the Dealer's speech implied a violation of the victims' identities that echoed and transcended the physical murders. "Walter was just astonishing," Barbara Young recalls: "You can't get it from the text, it's so dead on the page. But I shut my eyes and I can still hear him doing it."

To an extent, Young's suggestion that the transcribed text is "dead on the page" is accurate: the longer monologues are often difficult to make sense of when reading, and one can now only imagine their impact in performance. Nevertheless, the text retains a structural integrity and an underlying sense of chilling unease that speak volumes about the company's achievements. Particularly striking is the insistent manner in which the wild, almost hallucinogenic freedom of the victims' scenes is again and again dragged back to ground zero as the next corpse hits the floor, and as the same, oblique epitaph is calmly restated: "She was skinny but she had a great walk. A sequin dress in the early darkness and a certain oriental roll to her hips. She was anything but cherry. She had the sweet, pale look of the damned. Just like Jean Harlow" (21). When the Hawk and his Double first recite this passage, they are describing their very first, invisible victim, whom they appear to have fantasized. Yet as they repeat the mantra with reference to each subsequent, visible woman—

even though they look nothing like Harlow—the words begin to suggest some twisted erotic obsession with an inaccessible ideal. When Barbara Young turns up, lastly, as a woman who wants to be Jean Harlow, the description now seems like a prophecy—and yet here the passive victimhood implied by the description seems most inappropriate, since the fourth victim also seems to be the most self-possessed, deftly repelling the Hawk's physical advances. What are we to make of all this? Perhaps only that, as with any addiction, the desire must remain perpetually unsatisfied. So too, though, must the spectator's desire for neatly rational answers: it remains impossible to draw any reliable conclusions about where the line between fantasy and reality exists in this play—a fact already implicit in the disparity between the ostensibly realistic setting and the stark, oblique presentational style. Gnawing away at the darker edges of the imagination, this is—in Michael Smith's words—"too strong a play to explain itself" (1967c).

The Hawk is remembered by many observers, including outsiders to the off-off scene such as critic Ruby Cohn, as one of the single most remarkable downtown performances created during this period. It was, Smith wrote, not only "a pioneering use of the communal/improvisational concept to create a thematically and formally coherent fictional drama" (Mednick and Barsha 1968, viii), but also "the most important single achievement of Theatre Genesis" to date: "It is convincingly detailed yet mysterious, the point of view is sharply contemporary, the form is strange but not obstructive; it is performed with exceptional immediacy and authority" (Smith 1967c). If *The Hawk* is largely forgotten today, it is because—unlike other major ensemble pieces of the period—it played only the usual, limited engagement at Theatre Genesis in October–November 1967 before disappearing. In April 1968, the month of *Hair*'s Broadway opening, it was revived for an off-Broadway run at the Actors' Playhouse, but this uncompromising restaging—"there was no effort to soften the blow" (Mednick)—closed after only fifteen performances, having been met by the mainstream press with a mixture of anger and bewilderment. The anger was mostly in response to the frank use of street language that, as Barsha dryly notes, "was mild by comparison to what you'd hear in a public school today." The bewilderment was at what, exactly, the piece was trying to "say": writing in the *Times*, Clive Barnes responded to the play's mysterious disquiet by concluding that it must signify "an awful lot I could only dimly begin to understand" (1968a). It may be that the bare-stage-with-metal-chairs approach made less theatrical sense on a conventional stage than in the intimacy of Genesis's "black cube." Yet it seems, more fundamentally, that *The Hawk* was simply too cool, too "cruel," to be digestible to mainstream tastes at a time when the boisterous sentimentality of *Hair* was considered radical.

The Keystone Company, as *The Hawk*'s creators called themselves, attempted no further projects as an exclusive ensemble, preferring instead to resume working with the wider Theatre Genesis family on projects with varying rosters of participants. Nevertheless, one result of the piece was that group improvisation became established at St. Mark's as an important means for creating new work. Sam Shepard's play *Forensic and the Navigators*, for example, which followed *The Hawk* at Genesis in December 1967, was partially created through workshop means, and featured three of the *Hawk*'s cast, including Shepard's wife-to-be O-Lan Johnson as "Oolan"—clearly another case of the character being built for and around the actor.

The one subsequent use of the Keystone name came in March 1969, when another piece developed at the Pennsylvania farm opened at Genesis. Again directed by Tony Barsha, *Keystone Communal* was partly inspired by his experience of seeing *Paradise Now* the previous fall—"it was sort of an intimate version of that"—and was thus as loose and haphazard as *The Hawk* had been taut. One of the few Genesis shows to be staged in the round—in a magic circle—this scriptless piece was divided into two parts. In the first, "Vision of the New Body," the half-naked cast, covered in Sioux-style body paint, performed a series of "visions" based on accounts of peyote-induced mystical experiences. In the second part, "Spontaneous Vision," audience members were called upon to tell of their own visions, which the actors would then respond to by "doubling" the speaker's behavior—in an improvisatory practice partly inspired by possession rituals described in the writings of the occultist Aleister Crowley. Barsha recalls, for example, how one participant described his pain and horror at witnessing someone set himself on fire in Central Park, as an antiwar protest, and how his interaction with the actor doubling his words built up into an astonishing moment of catharsis. As "an affirmation and sharing of the communal life of its members," Robert Pasolli reported in the *Voice*, *Keystone Communal* was both "stirring" and "joyous." It was inappropriate to review the event as a play, he added, "but even if I wanted to, I don't suppose I could. [Critics] are speechless in the face of magic" (1969a).

Dracula: Sabbat

The interest in magic and the occult apparent in *Keystone Communal*, and widespread in countercultural circles at the end of the decade, was given more focused and disciplined form in *Dracula: Sabbat,* which — opening in September 1970 — marked Judson Poets' Theater's belated contribution to the genre of ritualistic ensemble performance. "Belated," because the focus of the theater's energies over the previous few years had been on taking the Carmines-Kornfeld musicals to new audiences, through a series of off-Broadway transfers. Judson's previous such ventures, *Home Movies* and *Gorilla Queen*, had been poorly received and did not run for long, but that all changed when Stein's *In Circles* became an unexpected "sleeper hit." The production moved to the Cherry Lane Theatre following its October 1967 run at the church, for what was initially to be a six-week engagement, but its inspired fusion of text, music, and direction proved so popular and accessible that the run was extended all the way to June. At that point it transferred to the Gramercy Arts Theatre in order to meet continuing demand. *In Circles,* Dan Sullivan noted in the *Times* on the occasion of this third opening, was far from being the only crossover success of 1968, but was distinctive in catering to those "with a high capacity for theatrical innovation, but a waning tolerance for shock" (1968b).

The Judson team followed up *In Circles* with two further off-Broadway successes. *Peace,* a rollicking musical adaptation of Aristophanes' antiwar satire, opened at the church in November 1968, before transferring directly to the Astor Place Theatre. It continued to run through much of 1969, winning Carmines a Drama Desk Award for best score, and was still playing when, in June, a newly expanded, two-act version of Maria Irene Fornes's *Promenade* inaugurated and named the new Promenade Theatre (an off-Broadway house on Broadway, in the Upper West Side). Hailed as "a dazzling and bewildering extravaganza . . . there is nothing quite like it to be seen anywhere else in the theatre today" (Mishkin 1969), *Promenade* proved the biggest Judson hit yet. Attracting a largely young, inquisitive audience rather than the mainstream musical crowd, it enjoyed a yearlong run, which was cut short only by a miscalculated hike in ticket prices.

These successes, however, were also leading toward a parting of the ways for Kornfeld and Carmines, in terms of creative priorities. Carmines was now primarily interested in writing full-scale musicals, and even accepted a commission from a Broadway producer to write music and lyrics for a show about W. C. Fields, starring Mickey Rooney. (*W.C.* was roundly panned by critics during its 1971 tryout tour, and never reached Broadway.) Kornfeld, however, had mixed feelings about such commercial ventures, and felt strongly that much was being lost, aesthetically, each time a Judson show moved out of the church. *In Circles*, for example, which had used the full width of the church sanctuary to create "a sense of those Chekhovian distances," had to be totally reblocked for its move to the comparatively cramped stage of the Cherry Lane: "I had to twist the hell out of it to make it work." Similarly, while he recalls the uptown *Promenade* as "quite wonderful"—particularly in its musical qualities, and in Madeline Kahn's virtuoso performance as the Servant—"it did lose some of the focus of the original." In its expanded form, *Promenade* became very much a musical, as opposed to a play with music, and its emphasis on entertainment values meant that the subtleties of Fornes's script were some-what obscured. The set by Rouben Ter-Arutunian, for example, was beauti-fully ornate, but essentially static: the play's sense of picaresque journeying, so clear in the original Judson production, with its giant, page-turning storybook, was thus substantially lost. Understandably, Fornes herself preferred the origi-nal, although her revised, two-act script had some intriguing additions to both dialogue and lyrics (cf. Bottoms 1997).

Whatever compromises there may have been with commercialism, another underlying problem was that Judson's emphasis on ironic-absurd musicals was in danger of becoming predictable even in its home space. Although Kornfeld, Carmines, and their colleagues regarded each project as a fresh challenge, audiences at the church had begun to expect a certain type of archly humorous material, and began to respond knowingly, as an "in-crowd." The result, Ross Wetzsteon argued in his *Village Voice* review of *Peace*, was that Judson shows—while always highly accomplished—were beginning to show "an increasing self-consciousness, an increasing coyness, an increasing emphasis on winking at the audience at the expense of smiling at the play" (Wetzsteon 1968, 39). Whether or not such accusations were justified, a radical shake-up of expectations was clearly necessary, and *Drac-ula: Sabbat* provided just that.

Based on a text by Leon Katz, a close friend of Kornfeld's, *Dracula: Sabbat* ingeniously combined material from three distinct sources: sequences of nar-rative action based on Bram Stoker's *Dracula* are intercut with extracts from *The Tibetan Book of the Dead* (as adapted into English by LSD guru Timothy Leary) and with the enactment of a black mass. Katz's objective in bringing these disparate sources together was to create an Artaudian vision of "magic and horror" by constructing a play in the shape of an unsettling acid trip. At the outset, a "Speaker" informs the audience (using extracts adapted from Leary) that the coming journey of "strange sounds, weird sights, disturbed visions" will seem alarming, but that they should not fear: "They are old friends. / Blood-drinking demons, machines, monsters, devils, / Exist nowhere but in your own skull" (Katz 1992, 142). This speech is juxtaposed with highly visual stage directions in which Stoker's Renfield finds himself surrounded by wolves and demonic figures, on his journey to Dracula's castle. The play then follows an arcing path as the visions gradually grow more intense and disturbing—climaxing in the mass itself, administered by a masked goat priest who is also Dracula, and who uses the naked body of Stoker's Lucy as an altar. In the latter stages of the play, however, Dracula is hunted down and killed by Van Helsing and company, and his body strung up like a ritual scapegoat. These events run parallel with the gradual ebbing away of the "trip," and the reentry to reality.

This take on the material has the intriguing effect of reversing the good-evil polarities of Stoker's narrative: Dracula's followers, one reviewer astutely observed, "are left saved from damnation but silently in mourning for the beauty of what has been removed from their lives" (Hewes 1971). Katz emphasizes this inversion by selectively staging sequences from the novel that focus on those characters—Renfield and Lucy, particularly—who willingly surrender themselves to the vampiric dark side (and to the "trip") rather than seeking to resist or conquer it. Van Helsing and the forces of Victorian Christian rectitude are treated, conversely, as "demons of righteousness" (173), obsessively hunting down and killing that which they fear but do not understand. Katz's purpose in this reversal is not to celebrate Satanism but to present the Dracula/Devil figure as an Artaudian "holy fool" or "lunatic saint," who dares to reject and oppose, absolutely without compromise, the ruling ideology of the majority. In this sense, the play carries an implicitly political subtext. (If the ruling order were sadism rather than Christianity, as in Katz's 1977 play *Justine*, then the hero is she who opposes de Sade.) Beyond that, though, this is also a deeply religious piece, in its presentation of Dracula as an inverted mirror image of Christ himself, unswervingly committed to his own vision of the truth, even at the cost of his life. Al Carmines, Katz recalls, saw this dimension of the script immediately, and programmed the piece for production at Judson without hesitation.

For his part, Kornfeld had little interest in the acid-trip dyamic of the play, but was fascinated by the religious element. A devotee of the great musical masses of Bach and others, he commissioned John Herbert McDowell to write an organ score that—"at times sonorously weighted, at times poisonously uplifted" (Sainer 1970)—provided an aural underpinning for the whole show. Kornfeld also carefully researched the formal progressions of masses, both Christian and anti-Christian, and developed the performance using the stages of the black mass as a subtextual structuring device, running throughout. He brought visual and physical emphasis to these ritualistic dimensions by casting no less than seventeen actors as "the coven"—a choruslike body additional to the seven Stoker characters in the narrative scenes. The result was a performance whose careful, repetitious solemnity was such that it stretched the running time of Katz's relatively short text to well over two hours. Unsurprisingly, this caused some irritation from certain members of the press: "There is one exit, for Dracula and Lucy," Walter Kerr reported of the production's 1971 revival, "that literally moves an eighth of an inch every five seconds over what must be a hundred feet of floor space." (Such an exit would, in fact, have taken upwards of thirteen hours.) This show was, perhaps, the missing link between *Paradise Now* and Robert Wilson's painstakingly slow "theater of images," and for other observers, the careful and deliberate pacing was crucial to its impact. *Dracula: Sabbat*, wrote Jack Kroll in *Newsweek*, was "a work of absolute authenticity—with beauty, dignity, gravity and sensuality, rare to the point of near extinction in any part of our contemporary theatre" (1970).

The ritualistic performance was given added weight by its location within a church. The sanctuary at Judson provided a superb environment for the play, with its tall windows and high, decorated ceiling, with music from the church's organ "pealing through the vault" (Kroll 1970), and with Beverly Emmons's eerie lighting creating shafts of illumination surrounded by impenetrable shadow. Moreover, with the performance taking place on a large platform built out from the church's altar area, the climactic moment of unholy communion was genuinely shocking. After the coven had all taken the host from her and kissed her naked body, Crystal Field, as Lucy, sat up on the stage's altar slab and held a burning crucifix aloft, declaring: "I defy you, Jesus . . . to strike me with lightning and turn my flesh to dust this moment, before the eyes of my faithful coven, if your power is greater than my Lord's and Master's" (160). A frozen pause would follow as the coven waited for a response: Theo Barnes (Renfield), by his own account a "dyed-in-the-wool Episcopalian," recalls that at every performance he was "expecting lightning at any minute."

Tellingly, though, the production was also careful not to take itself overly seriously: the solemnity of the coven's ritual was counterweighted somewhat by the narrative sequences from Stoker's book. With the humans dressed in white and the vampires and witches in black, these scenes were invested with an edge of heightened absurdity reminiscent of Victorian melodrama: "The story of Renfield and Dracula is told in campy, magic-jewels-from-the-late-late-movie style," Clive Barnes noted, "but this is only the background to the ritual" (1970). The resulting, oppositional tension between the strangely silly and the intensely serious was in fact an integral part of Katz's conception of the piece ("You can't afford to lose one or the other"), as is also apparent in his instructions for occasional moments of gross-out theatricality, such as the milking of a dead baby for urine, or the spurting of blood from Lucy's heart when she is staked—moments as potentially disturbing as they are ridiculous. As Artaud too had noted, "humour and its anarchy" could be as important to a theater of cruelty as "poetry and its symbolism and imagery" (1970, 69).

All observers are agreed, however, that what gave the Judson production its particular beauty and power was the extraordinary group choreography of the seventeen-strong coven. Katz notes that, although the play had been produced earlier in 1970 at Purdue University (where he was then teaching), and had caused something of a stir, the Judson production took it to another level entirely through its vividly imagistic response to his open-ended stage directions—which make up about half of the printed text. At one point, for example, following a description of Dracula's coven building up a wild, jerky dance sequence, Katz adds a final, one-word instruction: "Frenzy" (147). "Larry would say to me, 'You sonofabitch, you write one word, it took me a week,'" Katz laughs: "Every moment of Larry's production was his own version of what he was reading of my instructions. It was his version, nevertheless it was my instructions. So that's a true collaboration." The coven was used by Kornfeld in a variety of ways: they created, for example, the visual contexts for the principals to play in, fluidly morphing into different groupings to change scenes. In a sequence described by one critic as "the most imaginative use of actors I've ever seen on stage" (Colman 1970a), the coven created a horse-drawn wagon with their bodies, in which Renfield was transported, and then dissolved that image to become Dracula's castle as the journey ended. But what particularly struck Katz was the coven's own rituals, such as the so-called orgy sequence, in which the coven would come together, remove each other's vestments, and enact simulated copulations across the wide steps leading up to the altar area, in a series of dimly lit, chillingly erotic nude tableaux.

Nudity had become a controversial but fairly familiar feature on American stages in the late 1960s, particularly thanks to shows like *Hair* and *Dionysus in 69*. Most notorious was *Oh! Calcutta!* (1969), a commercially oriented erotic revue devised by British critic Kenneth Tynan and directed by former Open

Theatre associate Jacques Levy. Kornfeld, however, approached *Dracula: Sabbat* with the explicit intention of avoiding the titillation value that these shows had often been accused of: "I wanted to cut right through the sensationalism of it, and the pruriency of that kind of sex scene with nude bodies," he notes. In preparation for rehearsals, Kornfeld watched a string of porn movies precisely in order to figure out how to avoid doing porn, and then worked with the cast through many hours of "body workshops" to make them comfortable with working nude—and so that the onstage body contact would have a genuine intimacy and tenderness about it. The resulting performances were a long way from the awkward, unfamiliar fumbling of the interactive "group gropes" in *Paradise Now* and *Dionysus in 69*, and consciously avoided the kind of sadomasochistic grotesquerie one might expect of a "satanic rite." A chilling counterpoint was brought to the scene, however, by the presence of Theo Barnes's Renfield, who was chained to the floor downstage, horrifically tormented in his isolation from the group ecstasy.

According to *Voice* critic Arthur Sainer, the ensemble work of the *Dracula* company made this "an extraordinary theatrical event . . . one of the most ambitious attempts in recent history": "Figures are draped and then revealed, events are hidden and then revealed. And always circular. Coiling and uncoiling, folding and unfolding, [the performers] create hallucinatory tremors, splendid mass tableaux which at times are almost pagan friezes, and spasmodic outbursts of horror and sensuality" (1970). However, Sainer also had reservations about the piece—chief among them being that the performers, as a temporary group assembled only for the extended workshop and rehearsal period leading up to this production, could not generate the same sense of "communal belief" and emotional investment in their work as could permanent ensembles like the Living and Open Theatres. That may well have been the case, but this was no scratch cast: the core of the company (including Barnes, Field, and Florence Tarlow) had by that time been working together at Judson for several years. In suggesting that the production was dominated by Kornfeld's choreography rather than by a true group dynamic, Sainer (who was heavily invested in the ensemble ideal as both critic and practitioner) seems really to have been objecting to the coolly ornate, distanced feel of the production, by comparison with the more directly personal, interactive dynamic of so much recent experimentation. Yet the production had been constructed within this "extreme aesthetic envelope" precisely in order to appear discomfortingly aloof from its audience—to seem, like *The Hawk*, implacably cruel rather than heatedly confrontational.

Indeed, Kornfeld acknowledges that the production was, for him, a very deliberate response to the "fully participatory" theater of Schechner and the Becks. Spectators were called on to bear witness to the ritual from the outside, and only in the play's final moments was their copresence in the space acknowledged explicitly, "as an act of theatre." Katz's stage directions suggest an alternative to the conventional curtain call: "the COVEN extends its hands to the spectators, and takes one or two steps toward them" (183). The Judson company took this idea, but amended the details. The murdered scapegoat would remove the wolf mask in which he had been disguised, to reveal his Dracula mask, and then remove that to reveal the actual, handsome face of actor Duane Tucker—gazing steadily out at the audience. The rest of the coven, wherever they were onstage, would then turn their heads outward also, to confront the audience with this inscrutable look, "but without polemic, without explanation, without hostility," Kornfeld explains: "It was very, very purified because the ritual was over and the actors were always drained at that moment." Implicated directly in the proceedings for the first time, the audience would gradually realize that the performance had ended. Yet the cast would simply remain there, watching them—sometimes for as long as fifteen or twenty minutes—until every last spectator had left the theater space.

Part 3   Changing Times, 1966–73

13 Going Overground: Changing Profiles in the Later 1960s

> A new unpredictable factor is publicity, which has been increasing in the past few months. Off Off-Broadway has been almost private, exuding a sense of community. . . . But the public eye is cold and sees in categories. A few heads will be turned by publicity, but Off Off-Broadway as a whole will be unaffected.
>
> —Michael Smith (1966), "The Good Scene"

> There was probably a long moment when the off-off-Broadway movement promised hugely as an alternative theatre. That moment is now past. The mood at present is a confirmed make-it-ism. . . . Careerism is ascendant; the desire to be has ceded to the desire to please.
>
> —Robert Pasolli (1967b), "Theatre: A Non-Review"

Having traced, in part 2, some key developments in collaborative playmaking, up to and beyond the tumultuous year of 1968, it is necessary to turn the clock back slightly, in order to look at some of the broader changes affecting the off-off-Broadway scene in the middle to late 1960s. For while the long-running successes of *Hair* and *Dionysus in 69* were indicative of the newly fashionable status of "alternative lifestyles," the developments of 1968 were indicative of a popularization of countercultural ideas that had begun in earnest a couple of years earlier. 1965 had marked a peak, of sorts, for the vibrant, one-act playwriting scene that had been gathering momentum since the start of the decade. Yet from 1966, there was a marked shift in the public profile and underlying dynamics of the theatrical underground, which resulted in a greater emphasis being placed on the work of its leading writers and directors, and on their potential for recognition beyond the downtown scene. That year, as we have seen, saw the first successful transfer of off-off-Broadway material—in the form of *America Hurrah*—into a commercial context. Equally significant, though, was the growing interest of the mainstream press in the movement itself, which provoked ambivalent and uneasy responses from many of the artists involved. Prior to 1966, Jean-Claude van Itallie recalls, "We were ignored, and it was a blessing too: we were allowed gestation in a warm, dark place." Yet his choice of womb metaphor implies that, sooner or later, emergence into the "real world" of marketing and publicity was both inevitable and necessary for the artists' development. The question was, at what cost? The off-off-Broadway scene's sudden exposure, mid-decade, to the often harsh realities of the American culture industry—including the vicissitudes of press, unions, and state and corporate funding bodies—led ultimately to the community's disintegration. The beginnings of that decline are signaled by the juxtaposed quotations above, published little more than a year apart. Yet as Michael Smith would continue, justifiably, to claim, not everybody's head had been "turned."

The Press Moves In

For the first half of the 1960s, New York's daily newspapers had studiously ignored the underground theater scene. The consequent absence of the theatrical press's usual hit-or-miss mentality had been an important factor in the sense of community and common endeavor that had developed off-off-Broadway. As the only newspaper to take any regular interest, the *Village Voice* had adopted a role that was more bulletin board and discussion platform than judge or arbiter of taste. According to Michael Smith, there was a sense, at least during the first half of the decade, that one was writing for an identifiable community of readers, sharing similar interests and perspectives, with whom one could share opinions that might then be debated or refuted. In capturing the growing countercultural mood of the times so effectively, however, the *Voice* steadily acquired more readers and more cachet, with its distribution expanding first citywide, then nationally and even internationally. "More and more people began to read [the *Voice*]," actor-director Crystal Field suggests: "The *Times* was afraid that if they didn't follow suit they would lose their readers" (Marranca 1977, 18).

In April 1965, the *New York Times* ran its first article on the scene, "Making It *Off* Off Broadway" (Keating 1965). The exclamatory italics indicate the generally condescending tone of the writing, which poked fun at this peculiar new downtown fad. In September, a similar, if more informed tack was taken by an article for the *Herald Tribune* (Gruen 1965). By December, however, the *Times* was treating the movement with sufficient import that it devoted an extended Sunday supplement feature to "The Pass-the-Hat Theater Circuit." Wedged in alongside perfume ads and fashion features, this piece—by sometime *Voice* reviewer Elenore Lester—seemed to indicate that theatrical slumming in drafty cafes had suddenly become a chic lifestyle choice.

Lester's article was a fairly pedestrian piece of journalism, but its publication marked a watershed for the movement itself. "Everyone looked miserable, as if the worst had finally happened," Robert Heide wrote of the scene at the Caffe Cino the day the article appeared: "Joe was afraid the uptown media would destroy his tiny crystal dream theatre, and he seemed to be suffering some kind of loss" (Heide 1979, 9). Robert Patrick's account of the same day, however, suggests that this fatalist gloom was accompanied by an unexpectedly bitter intensification of the previously friendly rivalries between the scene's playwrights. Patrick's photograph appeared in the article, along with one of Sam Shepard—whose caption cited him as the "generally acknowledged 'genius' of the Off Off Broadway circuit" (Lester 1965c, 98). Patrick believes that his and Shepard's photographs were probably chosen because they looked the most suitably dissipated, but

> the frost I got when I walked into the Cino was unbelievable. Paul Foster came in and almost physically attacked me, saying, "You told them to put Sam in didn't you! You told them Sam was a genius!" Then David Starkweather came up to me on the street and *threw* the *New York Times* at me. . . . It wasn't as if there was money or a career in it. It was my picture in the paper, and we had all laughed about this sort of thing, but then we had never been in the *Times* before. It's the same as when, even if you've never thought about money or career or any of that, if the person sitting next to you at the table says, "Look, I got a royalty check!" there's a sort of, "Oh, that would be very nice to have a royalty check." It builds up. It's inevitable.

The tensions exposed by the uneasily ambivalent responses to Lester's article were only intensified further during the next year, as a string of similar pieces began to appear in other publications. Significantly, 1966 also saw the publication of *Eight Plays from Off-Off Broadway*, the first such anthology. Bob Amussen, an editor for the publisher Bobbs-Merrill and a member of St. Mark's Church, had asked Theatre Genesis actor-director Nick Orzel to edit the volume: Orzel collaborated with Michael Smith to put together key works by Fornes, Foster, O'Hara, Oppenheimer, Shepard, Terry, van Itallie, and Lanford Wilson. Yet this selection, again, created rivalries and resentments, because judgments had necessarily been made about whom to include and omit. With four of these writers also having featured in *Six from La Mama*, it was clear that a "front rank" of off-off playwrights was beginning to be identified.

Eight Plays was a valuable collection, distinguished by a thoughtful, considered attitude toward both the plays and the venues for which they were written. The same could rarely be said, however, of other media coverage: as novelist Ronald Sukenick has noted, 1965–66 marked a cultural moment in which "the selling of the underground" took hold right across the downtown arts scene, a phenomenon that was marked by "neither an effort of analysis nor an attempt at description," but simply by fashion-conscious hype (Sukenick 1987, 174). As was demonstrated most clearly by the unexpected commercial success of Andy Warhol's 1966 split-screen epic *The Chelsea Girls,* and the sudden media-stardom of his protégée Edie Sedgwick, the counterculture had gone pop.

The Golden Screw

The play that most astutely summed up the implications of this cultural shift was Tom Sankey's *The Golden Screw,* which premiered at Theatre Genesis in September 1966. A folk singer as well as a playwright, Sankey structured the piece so as to alternate its short, sketchlike scenes with performances of his own songs, and took as his subject the recent move of folk music into the pop mainstream. The play alludes, in particular, to Bob Dylan's transformation from acoustic minstrel, hero of the early-1960s folk revival, into the snarling front-man of an electric blues-rock band. During 1965 and 1966, Dylan released three highly influential albums showcasing his changing aesthetic—*Bringing It All Back Home, Highway 61 Revisited,* and *Blonde on Blonde*—and the question of whether or not he had betrayed his grassroots authenticity and "sold out" to the venal mainstream became one of the most heated cultural debates in America. Sankey ingeniously reflected the core of the Dylan controversy by dividing his play into two acts, just as Dylan's shows were then in two sets—acoustic and electric. During the first, Sankey performed solo, singing with guitar or autoharp, but during the second, he was joined by a full band, the Inner Sanctum, with electric bass and drums.

The Golden Screw was, in effect, as much a concert as a play: songs and scenes were given equal weight in performance (indeed the songs often lasted longer), with musicians and actors juxtaposed on separate but adjacent stage areas. Moreover, rather than commenting musically on the material in the dramatic scenes, as in a conventional musical, the songs remained independent, hermetic even, with each one presenting its own lyrical scenario and being allowed to make its own emotional statement. Likewise, each scene presented a different circumstance, with the cast of three (two men, one woman) playing different characters in each. "The play never says what it's doing or what it's about or even that it is a play," Michael Smith noted admiringly of the Genesis premiere: "No meanings or connections are given; they occur, if at all, in the spectator's seeing. . . . The form is very cool" (Smith 1966d, 22–23).

The piece was given dramatic cohesion by a simple staging conceit. All of the scenes were played directly out to the audience, who were consistently addressed by the actors as if they were a single character within the action. Since most of these scenes imply that the addressee is a rising musician, the spectators could thus conclude that they were watching the play from the "point of view" of the singer. At the same time, Sankey himself studiously avoided looking at the audience: closing his eyes, or looking down at his instrument, his delivery seemed almost painfully introspective, rather than an extroverted "star" performance. The songs, one might conclude, represented the singer's inner feelings, and the scenes his encounters in the external world. Although Sankey's music (available to posterity through a soundtrack album), was nowhere close to emulating Dylan's in quality or subtlety, it nonetheless made for highly effective theater, given both his nuanced delivery, and this dramatic contextualization.

During the course of the play, the style and tone of Sankey's songs shift markedly, moving from initially wry, humorous folk ditties to a more jaded, disillusioned attitude and a more noticeably urban landscape in the later material. This trajectory prompted some observers to conclude that *The Golden Screw* was a fairly straightforward attack on the perils of "selling out"—a reading perhaps supported by the title. Several of the scenes feature neatly comic caricatures of the kind of plastic "phoneys" that one might encounter in the rise to fame—the fake-smiling producers who "just *love*" the singer's work; the jive-talking Top 40 DJ who wants his pound of flesh; the vacuous party guests "trying to be hip insiders of the pop-camp scene," who giggle childishly about being cool and smoking pot: "It turns me *on!*" (Schroeder 1968, 71). Significantly, though, the play makes no simplistic distinction between grassroots authenticity and mainstream superficiality. In scene 6, a trio of folk fans at the Newport Folk Festival are presented just as scathingly as the "hip" crowd. They eagerly attach themselves to the now-successful singer, while tut-tutting hypocritically about his hit song: "Aren't you sorry you wrote it? I mean it must be a terrible drag, all the money, and being so popular and all . . . / And everybody jumpin' on the bandwagon" (62).

Newport had been the site of Dylan's first public use of an electric guitar in 1965, which almost provoked a riot among the outraged faithful. Sankey's inclusion of this scene clearly indicates his own impatience with folk purists: indeed, as he made clear in interviews, he was one of those who regarded Dylan's fusion of folk lyricism and electric rock not as a betrayal but as a logical progression. The play, moreover, implies that achieving success in "alternative" circles may involve just as much compromise and artifice as achieving success in the mainstream. In the third scene, a sales assistant in an army-navy store addresses the audience as if serving a customer, who is looking for a work shirt, a railroad engineer's hat, and "blue jeans that fade"—precisely the outfit that Sankey himself is wearing on the adjacent stage (56). The salesman's gently ironic mockery of these various requests highlights the calculated way in which this "working-class hero" image is being constructed for folk-scene consumption. In his next song, "Jesus, Come Down," the implicitly compromised singer then appeals to Christ himself to descend from the cross, on the grounds that his messianic posture has not had the intended impact, that he is now trapped by an image: "He chose to be, he wanted to be / The symbol of life everlasting / But now we see, eternally / The dead Christ nailed upon the cross" (57). The juxtaposition of scene and song speaks volumes: in America, *The Golden Screw* repeatedly implies, everyone buys into an image of some sort; everyone is selling something.

That impression is summarized, in the final scene, by an extraordinary solo tirade from a self-appointed poet-prophet of the underground. Money, he declares, is for sticking up one's ass: the entire economic system is irrelevant because the world is moving inevitably toward a revolutionary evolution of "the great total . . . the universal human soul!" (74). This climactic "rap" suggests a hawking of countercultural "alternatives" as repellent and vacuous as anything in the mainstream. Yet Sankey's singer then moves into his final song, and with a thumping beat behind him, sums up his feelings on the preceding events with a snarl worthy of Dylan:

I have a little message here
That was whispered in my mind
By my fairy godhead holy cow
For to tell to all mankind
But I'm thinking first of you my friends
You're the first I'll tell it to . . .

—at which point Sankey would finally look directly out at his audience, the East Village underground audience, and say, quietly and coolly, "Fuck you" (75). He would then move into a final, acoustic coda, ironically evoking lost innocence—"I'm looking for my little white dog"—during which the force of that momentary confrontation was given time to sink in.

The Golden Screw, as one critic later wrote, "was, and is, an important piece of Americana" (Goldstein 1967, 23). Deceptively simple on the surface, its implied critique of an image-obsessed culture addressed the contradictions and ambivalences of its mid-1960s moment with pinpoint accuracy. The final irony, however, was the unexpected success of the play itself. The Theatre Genesis production proved so popular that its run was extended, eventually playing to around fifteen hundred people instead of the usual six hundred. Many more were turned away at the door. Sankey then proved he was no underground purist by accepting a producer's proposal of an off-Broadway run at the Provincetown Playhouse. This opened in January 1967, but in its new setting the play suffered on several fronts. In the intimacy of Genesis's tiny black cube, Michael Smith noted, it had been presented with "utter simplicity and directness," but the addition of a more decorative set was distracting rather than helpful, and the final "Fuck you" rang fundamentally false when addressed to an audience of paying customers (1967a). Smith also believed that the decision to have the actors refer consistently to their invisible addressee as "Tom"—presumably to make the connection between songs and scenes clearer for a commercial audience—robbed the play of much of its sense of mystery. More seriously still, it led several critics to jump to the conclusion that the play was a self-indulgently autobiographical exercise on Sankey's part. Unlike his character, of course, Sankey had never been a successful pop star, but this did not stop Mel Gussow, in a *Newsweek* review headed "All about Tom," from dismissing the play as a series of "self-serving . . . ego-commercials" (1967). Following a number of such wrongheaded reviews, *The Golden Screw* fared poorly at the box office and closed after just forty performances, despite the topicality of its subject. Sankey thus discovered at first hand that, while the underground scene may not have been any more morally pure than the mainstream, it did at least allow artists to express themselves on their own terms, with less creative compromise.

Equity Turns the Screw

In the fall of 1966, as Sankey's play was making waves at Theatre Genesis, another, very different drama of compromises was being played out at La

Mama—one that suggested that off-off-Broadway's creative independence was itself starting to come under threat. The Actors' Equity Association, which had previously been largely blind to (or had turned a blind eye to) the underground theater, had finally begun to take notice, not least because of the increasing press attention directed at the scene. In late August, two Equity-affiliated actors performing at La Mama were brought up on disciplinary charges by the union for working without pay. A statement was also issued forbidding other actors to work in any theater deemed to be in violation of union regulations. La Mama was thus effectively blacklisted for Equity actors, on whose goodwill Ellen Stewart depended to staff her productions. Although many of her performers were not Equity-affiliated, and were unaffected by the ruling, Stewart was hit badly enough by enforced cast dropouts that she had to cancel La Mama's scheduled shows for the next four weeks.

La Mama, as ever, bore the brunt of the authorities' scrutiny because, with its one-dollar weekly membership dues, it was the only one of the key off-off venues to charge its audiences to watch theater. As far as Equity was concerned, money was being made without actors being remunerated. Ellen Stewart wrote immediately to the union, pointing out that the dues were not even enough to cover operating expenses (which included rents and overheads on both theater and rehearsal space, as well as production budgets), let alone turn any sort of profit. She estimated that, up to that date, she had poured around fifteen thousand dollars of her own earnings as a designer-seamstress into the theater, without taking a penny out. Equity responded by suggesting that a rise in the dues might allow actors to be paid the off-Broadway minimum, but Stewart pointed out that hers was not a commercial venture, and could not survive as one. Meanwhile, she tried to raise awareness of her theater's plight more widely. Recognizing a threat to its future, the off-off community galvanized itself around La Mama's cause, and a barrage of letters was written to Equity and to the *New York Times*. Stewart also secured vital support from the League of Off-Broadway Theatres: the not-for-profit alternative theaters were complementary to, rather than in competition with, their own, profit-making operations, the League assured Equity, and were providing an important laboratory environment for developing new ideas that might subsequently prove commercially viable (as *America Hurrah* had demonstrated).

Faced with such protests, Equity ruled in November that La Mama and other off-off venues could continue to operate as before, provided that they brought their activities in line with the union's new Showcase and Workshop

Code. Instituted in 1965, with the intention of clarifying the legality of workshop productions such as those being staged by the Playwrights' Unit, the code allowed that union members could work without pay for short-run productions. There could, however, be no more than ten performances over a three-week period; shows could not be advertised to the general public, and audience numbers were strictly limited to a maximum one hundred "guests" per night. The final stipulation was that no admission fees could be charged—although La Mama was granted a special dispensation to continue collecting weekly membership dues, provided that the moneys collected could be seen to be going toward operating overheads and nothing else.

On the face of it, Equity's ruling seemed like a victory for Stewart: since La Mama had never made any money from its operations, and had rarely advertised (beyond brief, gnomic listings in the *Voice*), the Showcase Code's stipulations did not force any major changes in her operating practices. The ten-performance limit was tight, however, and the option to run shows for longer—as Joe Cino had done with *The Madness of Lady Bright* and *The Bed*, among others—was no longer open. In effect, the union's conditional acceptance of off-off-Broadway's existence meant that the venues' operations were now being policed: Stewart found herself saddled with applying to Equity for permission every time she wanted to use union-affiliated actors in a new production, and this meant a constant trail of repetitive paperwork. A further, grimly ironic twist was that Equity placed a ban on the practice of passing a hat around at the end of each performance (presumably because this kind of collection could not be properly audited): La Mama's actors were thus deprived of their one source of income.

In the longer term, a still more serious effect of the showcase ruling was the implication that off-off-Broadway productions were now being "organized for, conducted for and participated in by Equity members for the . . . benefits of the participating Actors" (Equity document dated March 1967, held in La Mama archives). The creative interests of writers, directors, and composers were irrelevant to the union, and with any show in which Equity members remained unpaid now designated an "actors' showcase," there was a sudden influx to the off-off-Broadway scene of career-oriented actors who would never previously have dreamed of working in these "illegitimate" spaces. The tiny, ad hoc stages of the East and West Villages were now platforms on which actors could "showcase" their talents to potential agents and producers—assuming, of course, that any could be persuaded to turn up. By March 1968, Equity was reporting that it had signed showcase agreements with no fewer than 140 theater groups that it considered "off-off-Broadway"—a figure that, while no doubt including many short-lived enterprises, was vastly larger than any previous estimate of the number of off-off companies. Precious few of these new ventures had any orientation toward the experimental values of the original scene: "You started to get your conservatory-trained actors coming in," Helen Hanft remembers, "and they were getting classical training at Juillard or Yale, so they were wanting to do more conventional theater." Tony Barsha states bluntly that "when the union came in, it ceased to be a movement. It became a place for the actors."

Initially at least, the rapid expansion in nominally off-off-Broadway activity during 1967 served simply to underline, rather than undermine, the position of the four leading venues. So much of the work in other, newer spaces was so poor or predictable that, as Robert Pasolli noted in the *Voice* that November, "the more able and experienced playwrights and performers are limiting themselves to the Judson, the La Mama, and to a lesser extent Cino and Genesis" (1967b). Nevertheless, it was clear to many that the terms of the Showcase Code represented a threat to the autonomy of these experimental venues, and there were those who sought to contest its terms almost from the outset. One actors' petition addressed to Equity, for example (a draft of which is held in the La Mama archives) argued that the underground venues, far from being exploitative of performers, were directly beneficial to them: "In them we are free from the pressures of commercial theatre—even the pressures of a 'showcase'—to put up or shut up." On this basis, the argument ran, these theaters should be treated *not* as showcase venues but as workshops, whose real value lay in the experimental, process-based work that actors were pursuing behind closed doors, and whose public performances were merely a testing ground for these endeavors. Equity responded to this somewhat disingenuous campaign by declaring that, if this was indeed the case, then off-off-Broadway was in illegal competition with professional acting schools. Actors, it seems, were not to perform for free, but nor were they to be allowed to learn anything for free.

In short, Equity's entire perspective was steeped in precisely the kind of market economics that the off-off-Broadway movement had always resisted. Indeed, there are those who still believe that the union's interventions in the workings of La Mama, Cino, and the other venues were motivated more by political expediency—by an active opposition to the movement's core values—than by concern for the welfare of actors. "Equity helped kill off-off-Broadway; there's no question about that," playwright Doric Wilson argues, laying out his own version of a widely held conspiracy theory:

If they were trying to keep actors from being exploited, all they had to do was limit the size of the audience and the amount of money charged at the door, and they could have controlled it. But if you limit the number of performances, you're killing it, because the longer something runs, the more chance it has to move! If someone sees that a play can run for eighty performances at the Cino, they're going to put it on at the Theatre de Lys, and then everybody can get a union card. But the bottom line was that Equity didn't want us to exist. Because of the old McCarthy era, the Equity board was very conservative. It's never been admitted, but they went out of their way to destroy off-off-Broadway. We were told, "We don't want you atheist Jew faggot commies in the theater anyway." Those were the terms used.

Such accusations, of course, cannot now be verified. What is undeniable, however, is that by complying, however reluctantly, with the Showcase Code, venues like La Mama became considerably less illicit and more "respectable"—and as such could now attract funding from the new wave of grant-making bodies, both governmental and corporate, that were transform-ing the economic viability of the arts in America during this period. Equity's highly conditional approval of off-off-Broadway's existence thus opened the door to the possibility of its artists being paid for work that was not commer-cially oriented. Thus, for all their principled opposition to the union's inter-ference, those artists could be forgiven for having mixed feelings about the new developments.

Granted Wishes

In another ironic twist, it was the most explicitly antiestablishment of the off-off venues, Theatre Genesis, which first received major external sponsorship. In that pivotal autumn of 1966, St. Mark's Church was awarded a federal grant, intended to support its arts programs in their work for and with the "alienated youth" of the Lower East Side. The deal, brokered by a professor at the New School for Social Research, was worth $185,000 for the year 1966–67, with the money coming from the Office of Juvenile Delinquency and the Department of Health, Education and Welfare. The funds were to be divided between the church's theater, poetry, and film projects, and a related socio-logical study administered by the New School. In a paranoid era, there were those who suspected that there was more to this deal than met the eye: Tony Barsha still wonders if the "sociological study" may have been a pretext for covert surveillance operations in a neighborhood reputedly rife with subver-sive elements. What the funds certainly did mean, however, was that each

Theatre Genesis production could now be given a production budget of up to $200, and that writers, directors and performers could all be paid something for their work; a first for off-off-Broadway. Actors were paid about $45 per week ($15 per performance, and $1.50 per hour during rehearsals), a figure that, though still well below the Equity-approved off-Broadway minimum, was sufficient to exempt the theater from the union's crackdown.

The Genesis deal was unique, however, and other small theaters could not come close to gaining federal funds on this scale. The National Endowment for the Arts, founded as part of President Johnson's "Great Society" program in 1966, made its first grants to "experimental theatres and workshops" in September 1967, with La Mama, the Open Theatre, and Judson Poets' Theater among the beneficiaries. The sums involved, though—$5,000, $5,000, and $2,500 respectively—did little more than ease the pressure of running costs. It was the corporate foundations (looking for philanthropic ways to write off their taxes) that began to make a real financial difference, particularly in the case of La Mama. That same fall, Stewart secured grants of $25,000 from the Ford Foundation and $65,000 from the Rockefeller Foundation. The whole of the former grant and $15,000 of the latter were intended for the purchase and renovation of a building on East Fourth Street that Stewart planned to convert into a new, permanent theater space: "I told them [I needed] my own legal premises. I wouldn't always be running" (Stewart 1982, 12).

The Rockefeller Foundation stipulated that their other $50,000 should go toward maintaining Tom O'Horgan's La Mama Troupe for the next two years, with each actor being paid $50 per week for six months out of the year. This offer set an important precedent for the right of actors to be paid not only for rehearsals and performances but for sustained periods of research and experiment. Once again though, Equity intervened, declaring that if the Troupe's actors were to be paid, then any Equity actor working in any show at La Mama would also have to be paid at the same rate. Stewart again refused to comply, but Equity had had enough of her resistance campaigns, and decreed that from now on, all actors in La Mama "showcases" must be paid a minimum of $55 per week for performances. Failure to comply would mean permanent blacklisting. Stewart reluctantly consented to the ultimatum, thereby necessitating her continuing search for further grant funding, and conceding a major step in the direction of La Mama's "professionalization."

Elsewhere, the influx of foundation cash was welcomed less ambivalently. The push was now on, across lower Manhattan, to escape the rough-and-ready, amateur spirit of off-off-Broadway's earlier years. A whole new culture of patronage began to emerge, in which grants began to be seen as a starting point for new theaters, rather than as a reward for work achieved. Indeed, a number of enterprises that had existed as little more than concepts prior to 1967 were granted large amounts of money and ushered into reality. The ranks of purportedly off-off-Broadway theaters were thus swelled by the likes of the Chelsea Theatre Center. This had been established in 1965 at St. Peter's Church on Twentieth Street, with a stated remit to serve the Chelsea neighborhood in ways similar to those in which the Judson arts programs served Greenwich Village. However, given that its founder, Robert Kalfin, was also the associate director of Equity's "Department to Extend the Professional Theater," it is unsurprising that the CTC was always more self-consciously industry-oriented than its Village counterparts. Its program began with a series of staged readings designed to attract the attention of financial backers, to which end Kalfin drafted in many well-known Broadway actors to read for him. Having thus secured an initial grant from the fledgling Peg Sandford Foundation, Kalfin presented CTC's first fully staged play in 1967: *Junebug Graduates Tonight*, a piece of questionable merit by jazz musician Archie Shepp, was mounted on a budget of over twelve thousand dollars (colossal by off-off-Broadway standards), most of which went in Equity wages to the cast and crew (see Russell 1996, 102). Subsequently, that September, the National Endowment for the Arts awarded Chelsea Theatre Center a grant of fifteen thousand dollars—three times what it gave either La Mama or the Open Theatre in the same funding round, despite the fact that it had almost no track record. Clearly, the available grant money was heading in the direction of those whose aspirations were toward assimilation into the professional theater world, rather than those with more "underground" roots.

Over the next few years, an ever-expanding range of theater groups emerged to compete for a limited range of grants. "We're up to our ears in requests for help from Off Off Broadway," Ford Foundation vice president W. McNeil Lowry told the *New York Times* in March 1968. "We're getting an awful lot of mail," a Rockefeller spokesman concurred, "and we have to decline a lot of it" (Schumach 1968). Naturally enough, applicants began to tailor their bids and programming intentions to what they thought the foundations wanted to hear. The literature for the Rockefeller Foundation, for example, stated its policy of supporting "artistic endeavor that furthers humanistic values"—but what exactly did that mean? Certainly nothing anarchic or subversive.

There were those in the off-off community who actively resisted the pressures on artistic decisions implicit in the grant system. In 1966, the same year it accepted federal assistance, Theatre Genesis turned down what Michael Smith described as "a large grant" from the Ford Foundation, "by the terms of which it would have sacrificed its present identity, which it is committed to" (Smith 1966, 175). Ralph Cook explained this decision by commenting that "we live in a system and must affect that system." Rather than unquestioningly accepting corporate support, and thus becoming dependent on the existing system, Cook argued, it was the responsibility of progressive artists to seek "a whole new economic structure that will subsidize the kind of theatre that is already being done" (ibid.). Such revolutionary sentiments were, however, more easily voiced than fulfilled. After renewing the New School funding deal for a second year, St. Mark's curtailed the arrangement in 1968 because of what Pastor Michael Allen calls "excessive entanglement with the government." Unless it were to take a backward step and return to mounting unfunded productions, Theatre Genesis now had no choice but to solicit grants from other external bodies, and it was the Ford Foundation—the same body it had spurned two years earlier—that stepped into the breach. A subsequent cut in funding for the 1969–70 season, however, obliged Genesis to cut its annual program of six productions to just three.

"The foundations have created situations where money is suddenly available to underground activity, but never enough or self-sustaining," John Lahr wrote in the *New York Free Press* in January 1969: "What happens to La Mama or [other theaters] when Rockefeller funds (given for 2 or 3 year periods) run out? Do the institutions merely stop functioning?" Lahr observed grimly that the future lay with those groups who were prepared to abandon their underground roots and play not only the grant system but the whole game of consumerist packaging. Richard Schechner's Performance Group, he suggested, was the exemplar of this new direction. The original off-off ethos of creating free theater for an involved community was rapidly giving way to the desire for a sustainable assimilation into existing economic structures.

La Mama Turns "Professional"

The institutionalization of the alternative theater was symbolized most strikingly by the opening of La Mama's new, foundation-funded premises at 74 East Fourth Street, on April 2, 1969. The red-brick venue, which La Mama still occupies today, featured two main performance spaces—a small, end-on space upstairs, which seated around 60 spectators, and a larger, open-plan studio downstairs, seating up to 140. Julie Bovasso's four-hour extravaganza *Gloria and Esperanza* inaugurated the first, while Tom Eyen's offbeat musical, *Caution: A Love Story*, opened in the second. The grand reopening, covered by the uptown press and even by television, was witnessed on behalf of the *Voice* by Ross Wetzsteon, who confessed to mixed feelings:

> I'd be less than honest not to mention my sense of impending disappointment—for in a way, it seemed that this gala double opening night might mark not the triumph but the death of the Off-Off-Broadway movement, its funeral meats coldly furnishing forth the bridal feast, as an independent way of life finally joined the mainstream. But it'd be less than honest, also, not to realize that this attitude is essentially snobbish. . . . For what's missing, really? Nothing but the sense of struggling against impossible odds, nothing but being ignored by the *New York Times*. (1969c)

Wetzsteon was surely correct to stress that the changes were broadly positive. La Mama finally had the security and legitimacy it needed to survive, and over the next few months, it celebrated by opening new shows at a dizzying rate. Now, more than ever, La Mama seemed to function as "off-off-Broadway Central," with almost everyone who was anyone wanting to work there (several works of this period are discussed in chapter 16). Ellen Stewart, too, remained the same determinedly maverick creative force she had always been, as the board of directors of the newly incorporated "Theater La Mama, Inc." soon learned. In January 1971, when Stewart used $35,000 of La Mama's then-annual $60,000 Ford Foundation grant to make a down payment on a five-story brownstone at 47 Great Jones Street, the board promptly quit in protest. "The building cost $165,000," she explains, "and they could see this big debt to pay. But I felt that we had to have some place to rehearse, rather than rehearsing in subway stations as we used to, or rehearsing in a living room. We needed a rehearsal space, so I paid down on the building." The Great Jones Street rehearsal building is today still a vital part of La Mama's operations.

Even while maintaining her independence, however, Stewart necessarily had to adapt many of La Mama's working practices to its newly institutionalized circumstances. Helen Hanft recalls with regret how the original, all-hands-on-deck cooperative approach vanished with the move to East Fourth Street, to be replaced by a kind of "visiting companies" ethos: "La Mama went from being a place where they'd provide the stage manager, the set, the lights, etcetera, to being a place where you go into the space and have to bring everything else yourself." This situation led to some real tensions. In March 1970, for example, Charles Ludlam's Ridiculous Theatrical Company came in as visitors to premiere his new play *Bluebeard* at La Mama, in a four-week run. Yet when Ludlam was belatedly presented with La Mama's now-standard contract, stipulating that the venue—as originating house—was entitled to a percentage of any subsequent royalties earned by the play, he simply refused to sign. The play and company were his, he insisted, not Stewart's. *Bluebeard*'s run was promptly cut back to a single week, with no press admitted. Ludlam never forgave Stewart, and never again worked at La Mama.

The theater's ticketing policy was also becoming less community-oriented, and more businesslike. The old system of paying weekly membership dues to see the show as often as one liked was reinstituted at East Fourth Street, but these were now pegged at two dollars rather than the one dollar charged at Second Avenue. The new arrangement was still cheap, and was maintained as long as the theater could realistically sustain it. By 1971, however, La Mama had moved over fully to a conventional, show-by-show ticketing system. According to arrangements announced in June, members could still see a show for two dollars and their guests for three dollars, provided a new annual membership fee of five dollars was also paid. Yet by December of the same year, the club membership system was replaced by general public admission at five dollars per ticket. "La Mama has crossed the great divide," *Plays and Players* noted in its January 1972 edition: "It has 'gone public,' selling subscriptions, discount tickets and the like, and playing a season of repertory downstairs while continuing more experimental work upstairs."

Judson Turns "Amateur"

Intriguingly, La Mama's professionalization as a theater was mirrored by Judson Poets' Theater's simultaneous moves in the opposite direction. In 1969, following his series of off-Broadway musical hits, Al Carmines decided to recommit the church's theater work to an avowed amateurism: "Judson was amateur in the highest sense," he insists. "We did it for the love of doing it, period." His new policy was to produce large-scale "oratorios," choral pieces reliant on casts of anywhere between forty and sixty actor-singers, and which therefore required the participation of a sizable chunk of the Judson congregation, inexperienced though many of them were as performers. The emphasis was now very firmly on community endeavor (simply costuming these pieces was itself a monumental task), and Carmines's pastoral role as the church's associate minister became inextricably entwined with his creative leadership, as he took charge of not only composing but also writing and directing these pieces.

By his own account, Carmines was seeking with these oratorios to stake out a trajectory visibly different from that taken by La Mama: "I admire Ellen incredibly," he notes, reflecting on the changes that took place at the end of the decade:

> She's not only a great producer but a great artist. And yet her wealthy friends and wealthy donors in a strange way deluded what was happening at La Mama in 1962 when I saw my first Pinter play there. . . . It's a natural desire to go after funding, but it's sad too. I think that money began to corrupt the original power and beauty of the imagination of off-off-Broadway. Before 1965 and 1966, when we were scrounging for lights, and even scrounging for costumes in trash bins and so forth, some of the work was terrible but some of it was tremendously powerful. Then the grants began to come, and without ever consciously think-ing, one began to fashion one's work toward the grant, so that whereas in 1963 one would not have used a broom to sweep the floor before the audience came in, from 1965 you made sure there was one. Now that's a very tiny, silly exam-ple, but that kind of influence and power and money began a slow process of corruption which finally ended what off-off-Broadway was originally intended to be.

Carmines's analysis here is intriguing, but it is hard to escape a sense that Jud-son's relative "innocence" is being somewhat romanticized, retrospectively. The reality is that La Mama and Judson had found themselves competing with each other for slices of the same corporate cake. In 1969, Judson had nar-rowly missed out on securing a sizable Rockefeller grant of its own: "They were thinking of making us their example of what dance and theater and com-munity could be," Carmines acknowledges, "but I think they were bothered by the church-art relationship; they didn't know how to deal with it." Others speculate that the bid's failure may also have owed something to the fact that Carmines did not have Stewart's persuasive charisma, or indeed her adminis-trative team. Whatever the reason, Carmines's subsequent decision to involve the church membership more directly in the theater's productions repre-sented an implicit recognition of the fact that Ellen Stewart had decisively won the race for institutionalization. Deprived of comparable funds, there was little point in Judson trying to compete on the same terms.

Carmines's first large-scale choral work, produced in October 1969, was *The Urban Crisis*, a broadly satirical reflection on current events that (in what was perhaps an oblique form of personal revenge?) made New York's Gover-nor Rockefeller the chief target of its mockery. The piece was poorly received by critics, but Carmines swiftly followed it up in December with the hugely popular *Christmas Rappings,* which restaged the Nativity story to brightly playful music, and went on to be revived almost annually for the next decade of festive seasons. *About Time,* co-devised with Theo Barnes, appeared in April 1970, and that October *The Playful Tyrant*—which starred Barnes as a Roman dictator composited from texts by Camus and Shakespeare—was described by *Show Business* as "an oratorio of musical greatness" (Colman 1970b).

Barnes points out that these oratorio works were cherished by participants and audiences alike because of the sheer impact of their massed choral singing. Carmines continued to be served, moreover, by a core group of first-rate actor-singers, such as Margaret Wright, Julie Kurnitz, and Lee Guilliatt, who regularly took the principal roles. For Barnes, though, the dynamic sense of push-and-pull tension between creative equals that had so characterized the best of Judson's previous work was now replaced almost entirely by Carmines's individual vision. This shift was, in itself, typical of the period: as is discussed further in chapter 16, the turn of the decade was marked by an increasing desire among individual artists to realize their own theatrical ideas more fully, rather than participating in the open-ended, collaborative processes characteristic of the 1960s off-off scene. These changes related both to the maturing ideas of the artists, and to the changing economic circumstances: with grant funding came the inevitable reintroduction of creative hierarchies, named recipients, and so forth, and a concomitant diminution in freewheeling "community spirit." In Judson's case, however, Carmines's embrace of an explicitly amateur aesthetic led directly to the departure of several members of the Poets' Theater's long-standing core of professionally trained practitioners. Following a number of disputes with Carmines, Theo Barnes quit Judson at the end of 1970 along with Larry Kornfeld, Crystal Field, and George Bartenieff, to cofound a new company, Theater for the New City—which was grant-dependent from its inception.

For Kornfeld, in particular, this move had become inevitable: the emphasis on Carmines's oratorios at Judson meant that, by the time he directed *Dracula: Sabbat* in September 1970, it was his first production there in over a year. "I left because it was over," he states simply: "The movement itself was over, and I wanted my own theater. *Fully* my own theater." Theater for the New City found a performance space at the new Westbeth housing complex, and inaugurated its work in April 1971 with a revival of *Dracula.* Within a year, however, the four Judson exiles had reached an impasse of their own over creative priorities and leadership. As a grant-funded theater, they needed to present a clear profile to sponsors, but Field and Bartenieff did not accept, as Barnes did, that this meant positioning Kornfeld as artistic director. Tensions came to a head over *Swellfoot's Tears*, a dark variation on the Oedipus myth that Leon Katz had written specifically for Kornfeld to direct, but which Field intensely disliked. Rehearsals collapsed amid mutual recriminations, and Kornfeld and Barnes quit the company claiming that Field had become impossible to work with. Whatever the rights and wrongs of the dispute, Judson's old collaborative spirit was clearly dead and buried.

For many observers, though, the Poets' Theater's reincarnation as "fully" Al Carmines's theater gave it a whole new lease of life. "Carmines is a goddam genius," *New York*'s Alan Rich declared in May 1972, reviewing the premiere of *A Look at the Fifties*: "To my way of thinking, the brand of musical theater that Carmines has developed at Judson, abetted by a repertory company of bright, eager, variably talented, unpaid and enormously engaging young people, is the most captivatingly original development in music drama since Brecht-Weill" (Rich 1972). As Rich's phrasing indicates, the charm of Judson's work now lay in a certain sense of youthful, amateur naïveté, and this tone was particularly appropriate to *A Look at the Fifties*, in which a high school basketball game, circa 1956, was played out on a "court" filling most of Judson's gymnasium-sized sanctuary. (As the game progressed, scenes depicting the players' lives, hopes, and dreams were staged as "time-outs.") There were some drawbacks, though, to the frank nonprofessionalism nurtured at Judson in this period. As reviewers often noted, the energy and ingenuity of Carmines's music was rarely matched by his directing, which was efficient but lacked visual flair, or by his writing, which was often accused of a naïveté all its own. Entertaining as they undoubtedly were, his productions tended to lack the more challenging and innovative qualities of Judson's work of the 1960s.

There were, certainly, some standout productions: *The Journey of Snow White* (1971), for example, an "opera" that Carmines now rates as his most satisfyingly complete work, brought real pathos and intriguing philosophical reflections—on death and love, narcissism and self-giving—to the familiar fairy-tale. Yet the ambivalence that many observers learned to feel toward Carmines's productions in the 1970s is summed up by Michael Feingold's *Voice* review of *Why I Love New York* (1975), a piece that affectionately presented the city as a haven of charming eccentrics, while avoiding any real engagement with its pressing social and political problems. This was, Feingold concluded, "one of [Carmines'] bad musicals, which is to say that the childishness outweighs the delight in intensity, and that there are only enough good songs and good performances to make the reputation of six commercial musicals, instead of sixty" (1975).

Looking back on the divisions and oppositions that opened up in the off-off-Broadway movement during the late 1960s—on the arguments over professional standards versus purist amateurism, over who was awarded funding and who was not—Tony Barsha concludes simply that "the money fucked it up. It killed it. . . . We were cooperating, now we're competing. It's that simple. The grant system is the death of art." A striking number of the off-off-Broadway veterans whom I interviewed for this book, almost all of whom have benefited individually from that system at one time or another, expressed similar sentiments. And yet it must also be pointed out that the alternative to grant funding—perpetual pennilessness—was not a condition that could have been sustained indefinitely. In his 1966 introduction to *Eight Plays from Off-Off-Broadway*, prior to the appearance of the first grants, Michael Smith commented that, while the scene was "viable artistically," despite or even because of its physical limitations, "financially it is in urgent need of a new idea, and none is in sight" (6). As actor-playwright Claris Nelson observes pointedly, "the business of working [for money] eight hours a day and then rehearsing your show—it wears thin. And you do eventually start saying, 'Boy I'm tired, hmmm, what is wrong with this picture?'" Nowhere was this sense of dead-end exhaustion more clearly apparent than in the fate of the Caffe Cino.

14 Death and Disaster: Leaving the Caffe Cino

Off-off-Broadway once meant Joe Cino stepping out from behind an ancient coffee machine into the glow of the thousand miniature Christmas lights that shone every night of the year to announce that it was "magic time." Off-off-Broadway now means a brisk and business-like personage signalling the stage manager, stowing away the cash box and counting the house. . . . The professionals will bring craft, reliability, an ordering of responsibilities and a smooth felicity. Along with these, they will bring *a priori* concepts as to what can and cannot be done. When I look back on [the highlights of] four or five years of off-off-Broadway theater attendance . . . I wonder if those juxtapositions of inspiration, emotion, insight and perseverance could have occurred under the more rational circumstances a professional presence would be expected to provide.
—Robert J. Schroeder (1969), "The Rise/Fall of Off Off Broadway"

Of the original off-off-Broadway venues, the Caffe Cino was the only one to find no accommodation with the new realities of grant funding. As the first and, in many ways, the purest incarnation of the underground movement's anarchic, makeshift spirit, it was ill equipped to survive in the increasingly professionalized and competitive atmosphere generated by the influx of foundation funding. The Cino's closure in 1968 was a direct (if delayed) consequence of its owner's suicide the previous year, but it was also a telling reflection of the broader changes in the downtown scene. "I think you have to ask why Joe Cino killed himself at this crucial time," Larry Kornfeld notes: "What happened? Not just to Joe—what was happening, what was falling apart in that world?"

The immediate causes of the tragedy were several, but probably the most important factor was simply that Joe Cino had reached the point of exhaustion in trying to keep the Caffe afloat. A punishing schedule of week-in, week-out performance rotations, with the cafe open six nights out of seven, had been going on almost without let-up since 1960. On top of scheduling shows and being there for almost every performance, Cino had to run the Caffe itself, coordinate catering supplies, and worry about how to scrape together the money for the next month's rent. After seven years of this, it was hardly surprising that he was near breaking point. The city authorities continued breathing down his neck almost daily, and, to make matters worse, Cino was grappling with an addiction to amphetamines. According to Bob Dahdah, he had initially begun taking speed as a means to stay awake longer, when working at both the Caffe by night and day jobs for pay. His usage had developed, however, into a seriously damaging habit: Cino was, Johnny Dodd recalled, an "upper-fanatic madman" (McDonough 2001, 63).

Perhaps not coincidentally, Cino's self-destructive drug use seemed to intensify just as other off-off-Broadway venues were starting to achieve more public respectability. "He probably knew it couldn't go on," remarks Robert Heide: "Everything was becoming more slick and more professional and more geared toward getting to off-Broadway." Cino, however, was derisive of the idea of applying for grants or expanding his operation: "Grants were offered him," his friend Charles Loubier wrote, "but he refused them every time. He said grants would kill it. Even when we were half-starving, he refused" (1979). For many, Cino came to symbolize the inspiring but ultimately unsustainable defiance of the New York underground toward mainstream absorption: to Theatre Genesis's Walter Hadler, "Joe Cino was the Artaud figure burning at the fucking stake."

Dames at Sea

Cino was not, however, quite the inflexible idealist that some imagined. When Michael Smith interviewed him early in 1966, he was seriously considering changing his open-door programming policies: "The thing I've been thinking about is how to be more selective," he confessed, acknowledging that several recent productions had been disappointing. Attendance at certain shows had slacked off somewhat, income was down, and he was under real financial strain. And yet, he stressed, "I like to feel that we're open to everything. . . . Sometimes I've let people do things here for no particular reason and their work has turned out to be very special" (Orzel and Smith 1966, 54). It was a dilemma he never fully resolved, but temporary relief was provided that summer when *Dames at Sea*, an affectionate pastiche of 1930s musical comedy conventions, proved a runaway hit with audiences. After its May opening, Cino let the show run for sixteen weeks, during which time it clocked up well over two hundred performances, to become the longest-running show in the Caffe's history. Previously, Cino had always sought to rotate his programming, but the length of this residency was purely pragmatic: as the show's director, Bob Dahdah, recalls, "Joe was making money for the first time, paying bills for the first time. He even took an apartment on West Broadway, where previously he'd been sleeping on a mattress on the floor of the Cino."

Dames at Sea was at once quite atypical as a Cino show, and the apotheosis of the Caffe's magic-from-trash ethos. Dahdah had literally found the draft script in the garbage, after Cino decided to throw out a teetering stack of manuscripts that had accumulated over several years. Essentially an extended revue skit—a collection of songs held together by comic patter and a loose narrative—the piece had been concocted in the 1950s by George Haimsohn and Robin Miller (book and lyrics) and Jim Wise (music), but had failed to attract any interest from producers. Exactly when and how Cino came to have the manuscript remains a mystery, but Dahdah was sufficiently intrigued by it to contact the authors about mounting a production. Although Miller had long since gone home to England, Dahdah worked with Haimsohn and Wise to flesh out the sketchy script, adding new songs and scenes to create a seventy-minute show.

The simple plot thread of *Dames at Sea* knowingly collides two popular genres of the 1930s, beginning as a backstage drama on the lives of struggling chorus girls (see *Stage Door*) before transmuting implausibly into a *Follow the Fleet*–style tale of sailors and their gals (the theater is closed down, and the chorines find themselves providing shipboard entertainment instead). The songs, cleverly evoking the music of Gershwin and Cole Porter, are also distinguished lyrically by their deadpan, referential wit. In the love song "It's You," for example, the romantic leads identify each other in relation to a series of silver-screen stars: "It's not Leslie Howard or even Noel Coward, it's you, it's you, it's you. . . . Not Claudette or Cary / Jack Benny or Mary / It's you, it's you, it's you" (transcribed from original cast recording). This material was complemented perfectly by Dahdah's casting: Dick Powell lookalike David Christmas played the hero, Dick, and the role of Ruby (named for Ruby Keeler) was filled by the precocious, sixteen-year-old Bernadette Peters, in her first major role. The show's six principals also doubled up as its chorus, so that everything could fit onto the Caffe's tiny stage. This ingenious solution of Dahdah's required a careful reworking of the original text.

Visually, Dahdah conceived the entire production as if it were a black-and-white film—"everything had to be silver, platinum, white boas"—and gathered leftovers and found objects for this purpose. The women's costumes, for example, featuring acres of silver sequins and ostrich feathers, were from a stash of old *Salomé* costumes that Dahdah had acquired some time previously, and which he lovingly adapted to suit his new project. Old film canisters were painted to resemble giant silver dollars, in homage to the "We're in the Money" sequence from *Golddiggers of 1933*, and six white umbrellas had silver sequins stitched onto them, in order to catch the light like raindrops when being twirled during the song "Raining in My Heart"—thus echoing another Busby Berkeley sequence from the same film. As backdrop, Dahdah installed a number of large mirrors, salvaged from the walls of a closing-down restaurant, which referenced the mirrors with which Berkeley had created some of his kaleidoscopic visual effects, and multiplied the cast again into a massed chorus of reflections. "No one can imagine what a polished little gem *Dames at Sea* was at the Cino," Robert Patrick remembers: "I know [the material] sounds trivial, but it was perfect, and perfection is its own genius. And Bob Dahdah made it that way."

Perfectly trivial and trivially perfect; *Dames at Sea* was, perhaps, off-off-Broadway's *Importance of Being Earnest*. And as with Wilde, there was a frisson of camp irony to the piece, which would have been fully appreciated by the Cino regulars. Take, for example, the gender ambiguities of the title song, with its sexually frustrated sailor boys, which mainstream audiences of the period would likely have missed:

Dick & Lucky:	In the Atlantic, we get so frantic,
	For girls we left on the shore.
	In the Adriatic, when things get static,
	We'd love to have a matey with a name like Sal or Sadie.
Lucky:	He's a nice guy Dick, he's really a pal.
Dick:	And Lucky's my best friend but he ain't no gal,
Both:	We need some frilly skirts to boost our morale,
	Some dames at sea!

Whether or not the teasing innuendo was fully picked up on, *Dames at Sea*'s endearing fusion of Hollywood glamor and makeshift materials succeeded in drawing a whole new audience of "straight" musical fans to the Cino. The show was even listed among Burns Mantle's "Best Plays of 1966–67." This new clientele quickly drifted away, however, as the Caffe's post-*Dames* activities became even wilder and more unhinged than they had been before—thanks primarily to a precipitate increase in the quantity and variety of drugs being consumed. "God knows what kind of sickness was going on down there," comments Dahdah, who began avoiding the Caffe after *Dames* closed.

Chas. Dickens' Christmas Carol

For many observers, the chief culprits in this post-*Dames* "decline" were a group of extreme speed-freaks associated with Andy Warhol's Factory, whose ringleader, Ondine (real name Robert Olivo), had performed in several of Warhol's films. Ondine began hanging out regularly at the Caffe during 1966, and became friendly with Joe Cino, whose own drug use escalated as a result. "Into Camelot came the serpents," Paul Foster wrote, summing up the disgust of many of the older Cinoites toward this development: "The Pop Art golems, spawned in a silver factory. When these slimy drug slaves entered the door they infected the place and made it unclean. . . . They are directly responsible for the death of Joe Cino" (Foster 1979). To some extent these accusations seem justified: Ridiculous actress Mary Woronov, a close friend of Ondine's, suggests with hindsight that the popular image of their group—as "the undead, vampires . . . sucking the energy out of scene after scene"—was not inaccurate: "We left each party behind like a wasted corpse, raped and carelessly tossed aside" (Woronov 2000, 121). Yet there is also an element of scapegoating in the various accusations against "the Warhol crowd." Joe Cino's own circle were hardly blushing innocents themselves: indeed Ondine claimed to have been introduced to peyote and hallucinogens *at* the Cino. The newcomers did not so much change the Cino as bring about an intensification of the operatic, potentially self-destructive energies that had always flourished there. Looking back, Johnny Dodd described the months after *Dames at Sea* as "the golden age of the Cino," suggesting that—as the decor of the space and the behavior of its inhabitants became ever more outré—those playwrights given to more conventional material "knew they had to get out of there" (McDonough 2001, 58). The stage was left, instead, to a "hard core" of Cino playwrights whose works were often inspired by, or reflective of, drug experiences. Robert Heide's bleakly existential *Moon*, for example, which opened on Valentine's Day 1967, communicated an immediate sense of "bad trip" nausea to its audiences, through the visual contrast of its set—"the room and the objects in it are of a dark, bilious color"—and lighting: "blazing white light like the high-power-intensity lighting that might be used inside of a microscope" (Smith 1969, 50).

The intoxicated flavor of the Cino's work at this period is perhaps epitomized by Soren Agenoux's *Chas. Dickens' Christmas Carol*, which was commissioned by Cino for a slot opening on December 21, 1966, and written on doses of "high test Lower East Side speed" (Smith 1969, 119). Agenoux, another Warhol associate, wrote the central Scrooge role specifically for Ondine, providing him with a collection of careering, mad-poetic monologues, and even referencing his Warhol-movie persona as the "Pope of Greenwich Village." Scrooge proclaims at one point that he is "Pope for the few who really care . . . my flock consists of human beings of any sort—homosexuals, junkies, thieves, criminals, the rejected by society . . . Come in closer to me, Marley, and confess. You know the cameras are rolling" (Smith 1969, 132–33).

This moment is typical of a play so unhinged that it is often dominated by wild tangents and non sequiturs, yet it is also consistent with Agenoux's underlying design. This Scrooge is a multilayered creation, built of allusions to figures as diverse as Disney's Scrooge McDuck and Warhol himself: "I help support certain establishments, certain recognized charities—*The Girls of Chelsea Amphetamindell*—THE VELVET UNDERGRINDLE" (128). These diverse threads are pulled together by the character's flat rejection of society's conventional pieties and virtues. "I suppose Scrooge is definitive camp," Ross Wetzsteon noted in his *Voice* review, acknowledging the logic of Agenoux's queer spin on Dickens: "the outcast heaping malice on the straight world, one of the greatest put-downs in history" (1966b). In this version, the Ghost of Christmas Past is portrayed as a woman (La Mama Troupe's Jacque Lynn Colton), who seeks to reawaken the heterosexual impulses Scrooge felt in adolescence, by reminding him of his first love, and tempting him with erotic-poetic imagery. Yet Scrooge curtly dismisses her advances: "Girls are nowhere nowadays to Ebenezer Scrooge, can't afford their care, procrastination and upkeep. Boys can comb down any grown man's rumpelstiltskin, sexy and chunky . . . sweet" (135).

In this radical revision of the familiar tale, the Ghost of Christmas Future is also Cardinal Spellman—the reactionary, homophobic churchman widely believed to be a closet homosexual. He announces, in a "tone Sinatra-proud," that Christmas will continue to perpetuate its nuclear-family sentimentalities forever: "Awesome, absolutely awesome how totally I'm recollected and exactly re-enacted" (146). The extent to which Christmas is bound up with conservative American values is further underlined when Spellman reappears as the mysterious Señor Oro, who attempts to brainwash Scrooge into taking an airplane and parachuting into the "Dismal Swamp." The threat of the Vietnam draft haunts the play throughout, and enables Agenoux to provide an ingenious twist on Dickens's narrative climax. Scrooge awakes on Christmas morning and rushes to Bob Cratchit's house to announce a pay raise, not out of newfound philanthropy but in order to save Tiny Tim from dying: Cratchit cannot be drafted, he reasons, "with a son on the Christmas side of the grave—disabled," and so will remain in Scrooge's employ. "God bless us, Every One," Tiny Tim cries on hearing of his salvation, and everyone cheers as the lights fade (149).

There is, of course, a savage sense of black comedy about all this—underlined in the Cino production by having the tall, gangling Charles Stanley play Tiny Tim on his knees, holding a little crutch. But the comedy is mixed also with real pathos, which emerges out of the general chaos at unexpected moments. Marley's ghost, for example, is condemned to walk the night forever dressed in cellophane "saranwrappings" (a neat use of cheap, easily available materials to substitute for ghostly stage effects), which are "inextricable from what I now am" because

> they were sutured to me daily, or
> nearly daily, during the life of our partnership
> in making deals, and great deals of money.
> No office lunches, you ruled, for either [of us,]
> so these plastickings of my wind-weighty movements
> were the containers of the sordid unhappy sandwiches
> you forced me to bring and eat at my desk to *economize*.
>
> (132)

This Scrooge, however, ridicules all moralizing condemnations of his miserliness: "THERE IS NOTHING ON WHICH THE WORLD IS SO HARD AS POVERTY." he points out forcefully, "AND THERE IS NOTHING IT PROFESSES TO CONDEMN WITH SUCH SEVERITY AS THE PURSUIT OF WEALTH" (139).

Agenoux's play is dense, complex, and often beautiful, but it is also an unwieldy piece of theater writing whose longer, speed-driven speeches are sometimes impenetrably convoluted. Michael Smith, who directed the play for the Cino, was attracted by this very quality—by a sense that the play, far from being neatly comprehensible, teetered on the verge of the unutterable. His production sought to bring theatrical form to the piece while allowing it a sense of crazed mystery: he used two staging areas, on opposite sides of the Cino space, to accommodate the play's rapid, almost filmic cuts from scene to scene. Smith's partner Johnny Dodd was credited with both designing and "performing" the complex lighting plan, which required both subtle atmospheric changes and lightning-fast shifts between different scenes and states of mind. It was the performances themselves, however, that divided audiences.

Rather than attempting any kind of conventional acting, the production followed the example of the Play-House of the Ridiculous (with whom Ondine was later to perform), by emphasizing the projection of the performers' own extravagant personalities. This approach was intensely disliked by Ross Wetzsteon: Ondine, he wrote, "refused to allow himself to be responded to as an actor," and his performance was "so self-consciously inept that . . . we're left with nothing but empty mockery. Unrelieved facetiousness is like a parody of the void" (1966b). To H. M. Koutoukas, however, Ondine was "a demented diva" whose performances had an extraordinary authenticity all their own: "Maria Callas was his whole consciousness."

Individual responses to *Christmas Carol* seem to have depended, in large part, on which performance one happened to witness. Smith recalls, with some frustration, that the unchecked drug use of several members of the cast resulted in performances that, like the script itself, were sometimes inspired, and sometimes wildly erratic. Indeed, Smith himself had to stand in as Scrooge on opening night, because "Ondine was too speed-paranoid to go on." Much as he attempted to focus the performers on giving an accurate rendition of Agenoux's text, the director was forced to accept rough edges. In *Temple Slave*, a fictionalized account of his Cino days, Robert Patrick, who belatedly took a part in the show as a favor to Joe Cino, suggests just how out of control the production became. In this version of events, the entire cast cook up a batch of speed backstage: "We took one last sniff and parachuted onto the stage in a brain-damaged parody of professionalism. [Yet] we wired, screaming ganglia-shaped-like-showfolk apparently always gave a great show" (1994, 406).

Last Days

Immediately following the run of *Christmas Carol*, Joe Cino's already fragile state of mind received a shattering blow. On January 5, 1967, his lover, Jon Torrey, was electrocuted while working on power cables in a New Jersey factory. His death was recorded as accidental, but Torrey, as Joe Davies points out, "knew electricity in and out—I mean he wrote the book!" Notoriously erratic and self-destructive (he was widely believed to be responsible for starting the fire that had gutted the Cino in 1965), Torrey could well have taken his own life. His death sent Cino into a deep despair, and instead of coming off amphetamines—as doctors had warned him he must—he plunged still deeper into drugged oblivion. "As Joe began to deteriorate the mood around the place became desperate, baffled, and a lot of people began to move on," Robert Patrick recalls: "He was flaccid and bleary and had incomprehensible mood swings, cosmic mood swings, disappearances and reappearances in very bad states." Michael Smith recalls arriving at "a kind of crazed tripping party" to find Cino in a suicidal condition: "I hid the razor blades and tried to calm him down and reassure him, [but] he was totally isolated and totally freaked out and we just didn't know what to do with him."

On the night of Thursday, March 30, following a performance of yet another revival of *The Madness of Lady Bright* (one of a season of "Torrey's favorite plays," mounted in memoriam), Cino went on a desperate tour of friends' apartments, visiting Bob Dahdah, Kenny Burgess, and Neil Flanagan, apparently searching for some kind of solace. Try though they did, however, they could not help him. Finally, in the small hours, he returned to the Caffe, alone — although the landlady, Josie Lemma, who lived upstairs, claimed she was woken by a voice yelling at Cino, daring him to "do it!" What happened after that has become a matter of speculation, rumor, and myth. One version has Cino placing the final aria of *Madame Butterfly* on the record player and slitting his stomach, in a Japanese-style ritual suicide. H. M. Koutoukas heard that the music chosen was Haydn's "Come, Sweet Death": "And he'd set the lights for the theater too; the lights were adjusted and set." Yet the most reliable account of Joe Cino's final "performance," as of so many others, comes from Michael Smith. At 6:00 A.M., he woke to answer the telephone in Johnny Dodd's Cornelia Street apartment, and heard Cino's voice: "He sounded in desperate straits. I think he was calling Johnny to say goodbye." Unclear as to what exactly was happening, Smith rushed down to the Caffe with the spare keys:

> There I found Joe, on the floor, in a mess of blood. He had been hacking at both his arms with a kitchen knife — still had it in his hands. Weak beyond talking, he saw me but it hardly distracted him. He tried to stab himself in the chest as I stood there horrified, but the knife-blade only bent. He was wild with frustration. He had two or three more big knives around him on the floor. He grabbed another one and tried with that. He could hardly hold the knives, he was so bloody. (2001, 106)

Smith tried disarming him, but Cino resisted fiercely. Unable to get a safe grip on his friend, or to calm him down, Smith ran desperately for help.

Joe Cino was taken to St. Vincent's Hospital where, that Friday, more people came to donate blood than on any day since World War II. Bob Dahdah and Ellen Stewart took responsibility for maintaining a round-the-clock vigil for the next three nights. However, despite doctors' predictions of a recovery, Cino died on Sunday, April 2—Jon Torrey's birthday. As the news spread, a crowd of theater people and Caffe regulars gathered outside the hospital, many openly weeping. The memorial service at Judson Church, several days later, was packed with mourners from all branches of the theater movement that Cino had helped initiate. "Remy Charlip danced," Rosalyn Drexler remembers, "dressed in a plain suit, shoeless, challenging God: why did you take this man out of the world? It was the first time I'd seen anyone do the 'Fuck you' with the arm, in a formal dance. So beautiful."

Caffe Cino reopened in May and continued to operate for almost a year after its founder's death, but amid mounting difficulties. Charles Stanley initially took responsibility for managing the Caffe, and sought, as far as possible, to keep things running as Cino himself would have. In the first instance, that meant overseeing *Donovan's Johnson*, Soren Agenoux's follow-up to *Christmas Carol*, again starring Ondine and directed by Smith. Programmed by Cino before his death, this piece about a pair of queer ex-convicts (who inexplicably metamorphose into cats in scene 2) had moments of surreal beauty, but was largely incoherent. So too were the performers: one of them, Smith recalls despairingly, "would take sleeping pills and just completely space out during the performance." Stanley was so disgusted that he put an abrupt end to the engagement: after the first of two scheduled performance weeks, he took a hammer and smashed a crucial prop—a valuable glass sculpture.

Stanley worked hard to repair the Caffe's tarnished reputation, but audiences declined steadily through 1967. *Voice* critic Robert Pasolli later confessed to having been "finally turned off completely to the scene" during Stanley's regime, which had "confirmed and deepened the Cino's homosexual orientation" (1968a). Stanley's own reputation as a flamboyant drag actor perhaps encouraged such homophobic judgments, but so too did some of his programming choices: "*Vinyl* was what finally did it for me," Pasolli remarked of Ronald Tavel's play, mounted at the Cino by Tavel's brother Harvey in November 1967. Replete "with fetish props, chains, black leather, whips, boots," this staging upped the S-M quotient considerably on Warhol's 1965 movie version, with dominatrix Mary Woronov subjecting an offending delinquent to "unremitting acts of sadistic torture" under harsh red lighting: "I couldn't make much sense of it," Michael Smith acknowledged in his *Voice* review, but "it's highly effective theatre" (1967d).

Serving medicine this strong, it is perhaps unsurprising that the Cino strug-

gled not only to keep its audience, but to attract new playwrights. Regulars like
Robert Patrick and H. M. Koutoukas continued to have new work staged regularly during this period, but Stanley also had to resort, rather too frequently,
to programming semi-improvised comic-book adaptations. The first such
piece had appeared a few months before Cino's death, in December 1966,
when the scheduled show (John Guare's novice playlets *Something I'll Tell
You Tuesday* and *The Loveliest Afternoon of the Year*, first seen at the Cino in
October) was canceled at short notice, without explanation. Asked by Cino to
plug the gap, director Donald Brooks suggested that Patrick run out to the
nearest newsstand for whatever comic he could find most copies of. He
returned with *Wonder Woman: The Secret of Taboo Mountain*. H. M.
Koutoukas took on the title role, with Patrick as her alter ego Diana Prince,
and they camped their way through the story with the comics in their hands.
For the climactic avalanche on Taboo Mountain, they hurled cardboard
boxes at one another, to the delight of the audience.

Following Cino's death, comic-book shows became a staple of the Caffe's
repertoire, with dramatizations of everything from superhero stories to "Classic Comics" retellings of legends such as *Faust* and *Snow White*. Magie
Dominic remembers being dragged in to play Snow White at a moment's
notice: "We leaped through the door, ran through a packed house down to the
back of the Caffe where Harry Koutoukas was in makeup as the wicked step-
mother. Bob Patrick was ready as Doc, and David Starkweather as Sneezy
with a box of Kleenex" (1979). As this description makes clear, the comic-book
shows epitomized the gang spirit and creative spontaneity of the Cino regulars. Yet the madcap jollity could not disguise the fact that the Cino no longer
held the same attraction for young playwrights that it once had. As Robert
Patrick notes, "The sad fact was that there were other places to go where there
was more money, more facilities, maybe things were run better. It was over."

Stanley eventually cracked under the pressure of trying to keep the Caffe
afloat: "He was freaking out," Michael Smith recalls. "It was too much for
him, and he was hiding in his apartment, not seeing anybody. It was just
falling apart." When Smith himself offered to take over the reins, Stanley con-
sented willingly—the succession being marked by a little ceremony in which
Johnny Dodd used a gold sword to bless the transfer of power from one to the
other: "You had to do the right thing by the magic spirit," Smith explains. The
problem for many, however, was that Smith did not "do the right thing." In
partnership with Wolfgang Zuckermann, with whom he had been coordinating a summer arts festival in Pennsylvania, Smith closed the Cino for the first

few weeks of 1968, to refurbish the space. When they reopened, regulars were shocked to discover that the encrusted layers of collaged memorabilia had been taken down from the walls, which had been painted white. "It was just like a museum," Bob Dahdah recalls, "It was no longer the Cino. The Cino had heart, it had love, it had beauty, and he took it all down." Smith himself offers the reasonable defense that "the tattered stuff on the walls was completely full of cockroaches. . . . It wasn't supposed to be dirty!" Yet many of the old Cino regulars refused to set foot inside the newly cleaned, gallery-style space.

The dispute over decor was rendered moot by the intervention of the city authorities, almost immediately after the venue reopened. Suddenly the issue was simply survival: the Cino, Smith was told, needed a cabaret license, and faced a mandatory $250 fine for every day it continued to mount performances without one. There was nothing new here, legally: Joe Cino had periodically faced similar demands, and had always faced them down, by pointing out that the Caffe was not a cabaret, did not sell alcohol, and so did not need a license. There were also persistent rumors that Cino's Buffalo family may have had links with the Mafia—and that their "gay black sheep" was thus afforded a degree of "protection" by these links, which vanished after his death. (As Sicilians, the Cinos were perhaps bound to attract such speculation: Claris Nelson saw the family at St. Vincent's Hospital, "and to look at them, they were mafiosi from central casting—the outfits, the little black shoes".) Rumors aside, though, the most immediate cause of the Caffe's demise was a body called the MacDougal Area Neighbors' Association, founded by local Democratic leader Ed Koch, which was at this time attempting to pressure the city into cleaning up the neighborhood, by enforcing its licensing laws to the letter. The Caffe fell victim to the resulting crackdown because there was, quite simply, no legal way for it to stage live entertainments without also having a liquor license (which it could not afford, even if it wanted one). "We are bizarrely caught in a political double crossfire," Smith wrote in his *Voice* column: "Everyone we talk to professes to value the Cino's existence, no one to desire its destruction . . . but no one can stop the process, even those who started it, and I can't help thinking that the Cino is somehow, indirectly, accidentally, being sacrificed to Ed Koch's political ambitions" (1968b).

After a stream of summonses, Smith bowed to the inevitable and closed the Cino in March, after a two-week run of Diane di Prima's *Monuments*—only the third new show mounted under his stewardship. As a collection of monologues memorializing the exploits of di Prima's friends and colleagues in the underground arts scene, this was, perhaps, a fitting piece to bow out with. For Smith, though, it was the very weight of the past that finally persuaded him to stop fighting for the Caffe's future. "Maybe what I loved was not the Cino but simply Joe," he acknowledged in the *Voice:* "Maybe his was the life of the room, maybe this new life was artificial, backward-facing, forced. . . . Maybe Joe Cino is dead" (1968b).

Brave New World

In April 1968, the month after the Cino's closure, *Hair* hit Broadway: the underground had gone triumphantly commercial. A still more telling opening from the Cino point of view, however, was the same month's off-Broadway premiere of Mart Crowley's play *The Boys in the Band.* Transferred by Richard Barr from its successful tryout at the Playwrights' Unit, this was, in formal terms, an entirely conventional domestic tragicomedy. In a year of theatrical "shocks," however, its treatment of the lives and bitchy wisecracks of a group of semicloseted, self-loathing gay men was seen by critics as groundbreaking. The Cino playwrights tended to disagree: "Any one of us could have written it better," Lanford Wilson later remarked, "but Mart Crowley beat us to it" (Flatley 1973, 21). Particularly depressing for those writers who had pioneered the depiction of "out" gay characters was the way this play had been sold to the mainstream. Although the play was fairly accurate in its depiction of a particular subset of New York's gay community, the production created the impression for curious straights that this was an insight into the lives of "homosexuals" in general. Barr even went so far as to take out press advertisements quoting a line from one of Crowley's characters—"Show me a happy homosexual and I'll show you a gay corpse"—and underlining it with the claim that *The Boys in the Band*, "with surgical precision, reveals the inner corpses."

Capitalizing still more directly on the Cino's achievements, the off-Broadway production of *Dames at Sea* opened that December. Staged in a more "professional," less endearingly makeshift manner, it became a more conventional musical comedy, and proved an instant hit. The *Post* summed up the general press response in declaring it "indisputably the best musical of the year or maybe several years" (Tallmer 1968). Bob Dahdah, however, was incensed to discover that the production, credited to director Neal Kenyon, had intricately reproduced numerous details of his Cino staging, without offering acknowledgment. (To this day, *Dames at Sea* stands out among musicals in requiring only six performers.) Dahdah had, at one stage, been offered the chance to direct, but only on the condition that he waived any claim to coauthorship of the show he had played such a major part in shaping (and thus any claim to royalties). He had rejected this deal—"there was nothing to prevent them from firing me, and then they'd have everything"—and instead attempted to sue the authors Haimsohn and Wise, but his case foundered in legal technicalities. It did not help, of course, that the Cino had never legally been a theater to begin with.

It seemed that Joe Cino's former colleagues now faced a simple choice. They could continue to pursue the Caffe's insistently antiestablishment spirit, risking marginalization, penury, and burnout, or they could look for ways to accommodate themselves to the existing theatrical economy, in the interests of surviving to develop their work further. That choice was neatly demonstrated over the next couple of years by the emergence of the Old Reliable Theatre Tavern and the Circle Repertory Company. The former became home to those seeking to perpetuate something of the spontaneity and willful "nonprofessionalism" of the Cino, while the latter was founded by those attempting to build on its more polished achievements.

The Old Reliable was, quite literally, a long way from the West Village bohemia of Cornelia Street: this "funky, junky, divey bar on Third Street between Avenues B and C" lay further East than any other significant off-off-Broadway venue, in the rough, financially deprived neighborhood of "Alphabet City" (Poland and Mailman 1972, lvii). "It was downtown Lebanon," Robert Patrick recalls: "there was a famous jazz joint right across the street, right next to that was a reeking barbecue joint, sometimes there were cars burning in the street." The local community was an indiscriminate mix of races, classes, and sexual orientations, creating a rowdy clientele for the bar "where all tastes and preferences easily intermingle" (Gruen 1990, 23). That integrative element was also apparent from the start in the Old Reliable's theater program: the first play there, Tony Preston's *Rags an' Old Iron*, staged in the summer of 1967, consisted of a pointed conversation between two old women, one black and one white.

Preston was a regular at the bar who, along with director Hugh Gittens, persuaded the owner, Norman "Speedy" Hartman, to let them put the show on in the back room—a claustrophobic space about two-thirds the size of the bar itself, which could accommodate about forty spectators and a small, platform stage. Preston's experiment went so well that Hartman began programming a new bill of one-act plays every month, playing at weekends, with free admission. Word of this new venue swiftly spread on the grapevine, and in March 1968, the month of the Cino's closure, Robert Patrick's *Un Bel Di* and *Help, I Am* appeared alongside two other new short works. Patrick struck up an immediate understanding with Hartman: "It really is true," he told whomever would listen, "Speedy is the only other person besides Joe [Cino] who thinks you should do what you have to do" (LaGuardia 1969, 8).

Over the next two years, the Old Reliable staged more than thirty new Robert Patrick plays of varying lengths, during what became the most prolific phase of his career. At the Cino, he had always had to compete for attention with the other resident playwrights, but here he became the clown prince. Patrick's work had always had the underlying quality of revue-sketch comedy, full of snappy one-liners and fast, back-and-forth banter. For example, his first play, *The Haunted Host*, has a realistic domestic setting, but is essentially constructed as a double act for wisecracking queen and "straight man" (in both senses of the term). The Old Reliable, with its claustrophobic cabaret atmosphere and an audience who needed little encouragement to talk back to the stage, proved perfect for him. "[Bob] had needed a place where he could improvise on stage, with an audience twice a night, changing his show," Lanford Wilson wrote: "He had needed the freedom to take completely untalented actors and mold them into his idea of glamor" (Patrick 1972, 2).

The most extreme example of Patrick's madcap approach was *Joyce Dynel* (April 1969), a carnivalesque travesty on the life of Christ. With a cast of more than twenty, the piece must have completely overrun the Old Reliable's small back room. Even on the page it comes across as "an enormous love riot" (Patrick 1972, 177), in which freaked-out hippies enact episodes from the Bible under the direction of a gay poet (played by Patrick himself). Filled with irreverent songs, group tableaux, and acrobatics, much of the material would not have been out of place in *Hair* on Broadway, were it not for all the simulated screwing and the outrageous treatment of its subject matter. For the immaculate conception, for example, God rapes Mary, but stops midcoitus to ask his divine member, "What's a nice joint like you doing in a lousy girl like this?" (190). Later on, the child Jesus is rescued from his education at the temple, where the elders have been treating him as a test site for dildos.

William M. Hoffman, who appeared as Cupid in *Joyce Dynel*, brought a subtler treatment to very similar subject matter in XXXXX, which premiered at the Old Reliable in August 1969. The title, which is actually a constellation of crosses, like a dance-step notation, refers to the piece's basic blocking sequence. In an ingenious structural game, Hoffman has his five characters—

God, Jesus, Holy Ghost, Mary, and Joseph—run repeatedly through the same progression of moves around the stage. These represent the immaculate conception and birth of Jesus, but are played with multiple variations: faster, slower, more or less formal, accompanied by showtunes, and so forth. Filled with comic non sequiturs, the piece is almost as irreverent as Patrick's, but Hoffman's objectives seem a little less delirious, a little more serious. The repetitions with variations accumulate to create an alternative liturgical progress, which suggests an aspiration to spiritual experience, even as the Christian narrative is rendered absurd. "A little bit of magic. A little bit of religion," explains Hoffman's narrator-God at the outset: "A little bit. A nickel bag. Just to let you know it's possible" (Smith 1972, 133).

Among the other Cino veterans to feature at the Old Reliable were Neil Flanagan, who in January 1969 directed what Patrick recalls as a "monstrous, unforgettable" Classic Comics version of Mark Twain's *Pudd'nhead Wilson*, and Haal Borske, the Cino's long-serving waiter, whose one play *The Brown Crown*—a bizarre, mythical fantasy—was revived the same month. Yet if the Old Reliable became, for some, a kind of East Side Caffe Cino, its chaotic creativity proved still less viable as a long-term proposition. "Anyone who took any kind of responsibility was asking for it," Albert Poland remembered: "No money, no props, no sets, muggers on the streets. Once when I was playing a scene with Neil Flanagan we heard six shots ring out next door. We just shrugged and went on" (Poland and Mailman 1972, lvii). Given such conditions—and indeed the casually blasphemous or anarchic tone of so many of the shows—it is hardly surprising that Speedy Hartman's various attempts to gain grant funding for the Old Reliable fell on deaf ears. Lacking either the resources to develop the theater program or the limitless energy necessary to sustain it indefinitely in its present state, Hartman called an end to the proceedings in the summer of 1971. He proved understandably unwilling to sacrifice himself, as had Joe Cino, to an unsustainable future.

Circle Rep

The Circle Repertory Company, founded a year after the Cino's closure by a group of the Caffe's more career-minded alumni, was conceived as a more formal, professionally oriented theater. Its raison d'être, from inception, was to provide a stable, longer-lasting home for its resident artists, by establishing itself as a permanent repertory company. Under the directorial leadership of Marshall Mason, Circle Rep set out to create a fixed ensemble of actors and playwrights, all of whom would work collectively to develop and promote the company. "They were making a situation where they could go on doing their work," Michael Smith notes: "The problem [with off-off-Broadway] was that you would blow all your energy and resources on one show and then what? You wanted to do more work, you wanted to pursue what you'd learned about your work, but it would take six months or a year to get it together to do another one."

The need for a stable creative home was felt acutely by Mason, who had experienced a number of damaging blows to his professional ambitions throughout the 1960s. After having directed two plays by fellow Northwestern University graduate Claris Nelson at the Caffe Cino in 1962, Mason had formed an off-Broadway production company with Nelson and some other former classmates. "Northwestern Productions" raised thirty-six thousand dollars in capital, secured a contract to perform at the Actors' Playhouse, and in March 1964 mounted a full Equity production of Ibsen's *Little Eyolf*. Yet despite an excellent review from the *New York Times*, the production closed with substantial losses after five weeks—a tale symptomatic of the difficulties that producers of serious drama were experiencing off-Broadway by that time. A second production by the group fared similarly, and with their financial reserves exhausted, they were back where they had started. Mason swallowed his pride and returned to the Cino, where he subsequently met Lanford Wilson. In 1965, the pair initiated a long-term collaborative partnership with *Balm in Gilead* at La Mama. In 1968, however, when Mason directed Wilson's first commercially oriented play, *The Gingham Dog*, in a showcase production for the New Dramatists Committee, he was again confounded by the system. The play, a broadly conventional slice of socially concerned domestic realism, bravely tackling the heated topic of interracial marriage, was picked up for Broadway. The producers, however, went for an established "name" director, Alan Schneider, whose uninspired production closed quickly following negative reactions from both critics and audiences. Mason and Wilson were obliged to face up, once again, to the brutal realities of the commercial theater system.

Both men had also been hit extremely hard by Joe Cino's death. While neither had been very active at the Caffe in its last couple of years, both had regarded Cino as a mentor, and Wilson has confessed to experiencing bouts of self-destructive depression for years after the suicide. Following the *Gingham Dog* fiasco, and the closure of the Caffe, Mason gave up theater altogether for several months, to give himself time to make sense of the chaos of the last few years. During that time, he began to think about turning back to the off-off-Broadway scene, but with the hope of establishing a permanent company that might be able to negotiate the yawning gulf between underground recognition and the "legitimate" theater. The opportunity for such a venture appeared fortuitously when actor Rob Thirkield—a member of O'Horgan's La Mama Troupe, and a friend of Mason's since Northwestern—struck an unlikely deal with his psychiatrist. Dr. Harry Lerner was founder of a non-profit association of public leaders known as the Council of International Recreation, Culture and Lifelong Education (CIRCLE), and was looking for a theater company to affiliate with the organization as its cultural "arm." He even had a performance space lined up—a loft on Broadway at Eighty-third Street. Thirkield took the proposal to Mason, who jumped at the idea, even though the long, narrow, dingy room was far from ideal as a theater.

Presenting their vision of a sustainable future to old friends and colleagues, Mason, Wilson, Thirkield, and actress Tanya Berezin (Thirkield's partner, who had worked with Mason on several occasions) gathered together a sizable ensemble, including ex-Cino playwrights David Starkweather, Doric Wilson, and Claris Nelson, and actors such as Jane Lowry and Stephanie Gordon (one of the original acting company at Theatre Genesis). "The initial list of members was pretty impressive in terms of off-off-Broadway credentials," notes Doric Wilson, who, in line with the company's collaborative ethos, became its first front-of-house manager: "It was probably the biggest attempt to gather together that many people under one roof." Serious attempts were made to forge a strong sense of group identity: for the first five months of the company's existence—August to December of 1969—the sole order of business was a series of company workshops in which everybody participated. Marshall Mason, in accordance with his own primary interests, foregrounded work with classic dramatic texts, while Rob Thirkield, as an O'Horganite and Grotowski enthusiast, pressed for the exploration of various "new theater" techniques. "We tried literally everybody's ideas," Doric Wilson recalls: "Somebody even brought in one of those Isadora Duncan teachers! And it got very funny because the playwrights were better at the improvs than the actors."

The company's original, idealistic goal of allowing space for every possible theatrical approach was, in effect, an attempt to bring Joe Cino's laissez-faire spirit to bear in a more structured, ensemble-based context. The company's first season of work reflected that diversity, placing a new, experimental play alongside two alternative takes on a classic text. David Starkweather's *A Practical Ritual to Exorcise Frustration after Forty Days of Rain* was mounted in

January 1970, as directed by Thirkield and Starkweather, and was followed by Mason's two, radically contrasting productions of Chekhov's *The Three Sisters*—the first so hypernaturalistic that attempts were made to light scenes only with onstage candles; the second a wildly revisionist version with a rock soundtrack, which drew connections with the current political situation (Chekhov's Russian soldiers, for example, became tie-dyed hippie peace activists). One prospective foundation sponsor thought the latter production "a classic example of over-kill" in its excess of staging gimmicks, "but in its innocent exuberance, it [made for] riveting theatre" (Russell 1996, 200).

The company earned five-thousand-dollar grants from two different funding bodies, on the strength of the two Chekhovs. Starkweather's play, however, proved less successful. A reworking of the Noah's ark story, *A Practical Ritual* followed members of Noah's family back and forth in time over fifteen hundred years. For some, though, the play also felt that long: clocking in at three and a half hours, it began brightly and inventively but, reviewers concurred, had far outlived its welcome by the end, becoming preachy, and laying on its metaphors too thickly. (At the climax, God is placed in a bag and smashed to pieces, apparently to liberate Noah's family from their guilts and inhibitions.) The acting company was praised for its cohesion and energy, but Jane Lowry, who played the trapeze-artist wife of one of Noah's sons (Spalding Gray), confesses that the cast themselves "didn't really believe in this play. We had no idea what it was, although we liked David." *A Practical Ritual* remains unpublished, but Starkweather's play *The Poet's Papers*, anthologized that same year (see Hoffman 1970), gives some idea of how bewilderingly complex his writing was becoming.

The difficulties presented by Starkweather's play underlined the dilemma Circle Rep faced that first season. While the company attempted to envision itself as a broad church, the programming of Starkweather and Chekhov had effectively separated out and "labeled" the threads of experimentalism and traditionalism that had always been intertwined at the Cino. As a result, the company appeared to face a clear-cut choice about its future trajectory, and it is unsurprising that over the next couple of years, Mason began to guide Circle Rep toward specializing in the production of poetic-realist texts. (Doric Wilson, recognizing that his own, primarily satirical writing style did not really fit within this emerging profile, left the company in 1972: "I loved Circle Rep, but my instincts told me that was not where I needed to be.") Mason's drive and discipline became central to the company's survival, and his vision was for Circle Rep to emulate the Group Theatre of the 1930s—by developing a tight-knit ensemble that specialized in forging a theatrical lyricism from ordinary American lives and speech patterns. Mason's Clifford Odets was, of course, Lanford Wilson, and the company's breakthrough production, clearly establishing its goals and strengths, was Wilson's *Hot l Baltimore*, which premiered in 1973.

Wilson had taken a backseat during the company's first few years, suffering depression and writer's block, but working on various backstage tasks (he designed the set, for instance, for Starkweather's *Practical Ritual*). During that time, he had developed an intimate knowledge of the acting company, and *The Hot l Baltimore* was tailor-made for their voices and abilities. Set in the lobby of the eponymous establishment (a shabby residential hotel with a letter missing from its neon sign), the play uses a cast of fifteen characters, who constantly come and go through this hub. There is no overarching narrative, however, just a series of incidental micronarratives: as with Chekhov, it is the precisely observed minutiae of character interaction and stage business to which the spectator's attention is directed, and which become the source of both humor and pathos. The links to Wilson's earlier, more unorthodox off-off-Broadway plays are also clearly apparent. *Hot l Baltimore* is, like *Lady Bright* or *Balm in Gilead*, a portrait of stasis; a dramatic circumstance whose tensions arise from the characters' apparent inability to move or change. Yet in Circle Rep's narrow, proscenium-style space, Wilson was able to specify a detailed, naturalistic setting in which the physical details (such as the hand-operated hotel switchboard) acquire theatrical force and dramatic meaning.

The play's resemblance to the single-set dramas common in the 1930s was not lost on critics. "Mr. Wilson's play is delightfully old-fashioned, and purposely so," Clive Barnes suggested in the *Times*: "It is like a William Saroyan play without a story. . . . There are no villains, only circumstances, [and] every whore has a heart of gold" (1973). "Does all this sound corny?" Michael Smith asked in the *Voice*: "It is. [And] I don't actually know any people like these" (1973a). Both critics agreed, however, that the play was enjoyable precisely because of its loving evocation of fading theatrical traditions, which seemed mirrored by the fading grandeur of the hotel itself: "Nostalgia," Smith wrote, "permeates Wilson's form, content, sensibility. It is there to be enjoyed." *Hot l Baltimore* opened at Circle Rep in February, but before the end of March had transferred to the Circle in the Square, for an off-Broadway run that lasted over a year. It also won the New York Drama Critics Circle Award for best new play of 1972–73. That success was followed in the 1973–74 season by off-Broadway transfers for two other new naturalistic dramas from Circle Rep—Mark

Medoff's *When You Comin' Back, Red Ryder?* and Edward J. Moore's *The Sea Horse*. The company swiftly took advantage of the respect it now commanded, cutting its ties with the CIRCLE organization and moving back downtown, to take up long-term residence in the 150-seat Sheridan Square Playhouse.

It would be easy, perhaps, to dismiss Circle Rep as a company that survived and prospered by reverting to a traditional, even conservative form of dramaturgy, rather than by seeking to perpetuate the diversity and risk-taking that had characterized the 1960s underground. Indeed, the group might be seen as embodying the efficiency of the new professionalism referred to so regretfully by Robert Schroeder at the start of this chapter. Yet the fact remains that Circle Rep was built squarely on Joe Cino's ethos, "Do what you have to do." Lanford Wilson could never have dreamed of writing *Hot l Baltimore* for fifteen actors had he been looking directly toward a commercial production: by the 1970s, that kind of cast size was almost exclusively the purview of Broadway musicals. Circle Rep needed to prove the play's worth in production before it could go anywhere else. The very size of the company, moreover, was further evidence of its independent spirit: all involved believed in the value of maintaining a repertory ensemble, even though that meant that, as late as 1974 (after which serious grant funding began to kick in), the actors were still only being paid $12.33 per performance—less than Theatre Genesis had been paying in 1966, thanks to its federal grant. The company's pay policy was challenged early on by Equity, who insisted that they must either pay actors the union off-Broadway minimum (which the company could not then afford), or else function under Showcase Code regulations, offering no payment to actors. "We said, we want to pay our actors something, we don't want to get them for nothing," Mason recalls, "but there was no mechanism for doing it, so we just did it." To avoid appearing foolish, Equity finally conceded that Circle Rep could function as an exception to their rules.

Yet the most important, long-term evidence of Circle Rep's off-off-Broadway roots was the ongoing writer-director collaboration between Mason and Wilson, which—nurtured during their years at the Cino and La Mama—continued to flourish for decades afterward. This partnership could never have been maintained in the commercial theater, as the *Gingham Dog* episode demonstrated, yet each firmly believed that he needed the other to bring out the best in his work, and Circle Rep provided them with the platform they needed. "Ever since 1973, Circle Rep's *raison d'etre* is really to support that collaboration," Tanya Berezin noted in a 1980s interview: "Circle Rep *is* Lanford and Marshall" (Williams 1993, 41). Wilson and Mason each became much sought-after by larger theaters, but for many years their first commitment remained to Circle Rep, whose small scale of operations allowed a degree of flexibility and creative freedom that would have been impossible elsewhere. "All that money kills a sense of experimentation," Mason once noted of both the commercial sector and the regional, not-for-profit theater: "For $200,000, you can't take risks" (Gussow 1974, 6). That figure refers to the reported budget for the Mark Taper Forum's Los Angeles production of *Hot l Baltimore*—a play Circle Rep had originally staged for just one thousand dollars.

15 The Absence of Peace: Changing Politics, Changing Communities

> I wanted to be political. I wanted desperately to be political, and to do a piece that was a political piece. But the story was that it was political if you *talked* about politics, or if you took a stand on an issue. And I guess what most of us realized, either at that time or later, was that what we were doing was in itself political. The action of being involved in a theater that is, in its very bones, critical—or ecstatic—about aspects of our life today; that's a political action, because it *changes perception.*
>
> —Lawrence Kornfeld

Given that the "radicalism" of the off-off-Broadway movement had always been of the loosest, least specific kind, it was perhaps no surprise that some veterans of the scene reverted to more conservative dramatic forms in the 1970s—as Lanford Wilson did with *Hot l Baltimore*. Robert Patrick probably speaks for many when he notes, "My politics were always limited to 'I don't want anyone telling me what to do.'" Overtly politicized statements and debates very rarely appeared in off-off-Broadway plays and performances, not least because—in the context of downtown bohemia—anyone arguing for alternatives to the American status quo would have been preaching to the choir. The antiauthoritarian spirit of the times also meant that anyone trying to teach or preach to their audience would have been looked on with suspicion or even derision. Yet the aesthetic open-endedness of much off-off-Broadway theater was also its most "political" feature, in the sense that audiences were empowered to watch, listen, and think for themselves, rather than being told something they were assumed not to know already. The importance of a play like Wilson's *The Madness of Lady Bright* lay partly in its very avoidance of treating Leslie's homosexuality or transvestism as an "issue" (despite the initial shock factor in that subject matter, even for Cino audiences). It is, at root, a play about loneliness, in which the individual's particular circumstances provide a context but not a thesis. The audience is invited to view Leslie less as "a drag queen"—that is, as a generalized social type—

than as a person. For some, this would certainly, in Kornfeld's words, have "changed perceptions." In 1966, Joe Chaikin went as far as to suggest that "the whole off-off-Broadway movement is very political even when it's not dealing with political subjects. It has to do with the overthrow of public opinion—it's a very radical point of view" (Smith 1966, 169).

That said, the urge to find some way of engaging more directly with the political issues of the period was strongly felt in certain quarters, and such concerns intensified markedly during the latter half of the 1960s, particularly as the war in Vietnam came into focus as the central protest issue of the era. The problem was how to address the issues without trivializing them. In hindsight, one of the problems with the Open Theatre's *Viet Rock* was simply its political naïveté. This group of earnest young people wanted to say something, but much of what they said was clumsy, at best. Their trite representation of Muhammad Ali, for example, as an antiwar witness in a congressional hearing, failed either to capture the infectious rhythms of Ali's rapping or to comprehend the importance of his draft resistance for many African Americans: "Yeah, yeah, oh yeah. I'm the prettiest. I'm the greatest, and I ratest with the girls. And to stay this way, I want to say: we got no quarrel with the Northern race. And that's the place where I stand. And I'm grand" (Terry 1966, 209). Similarly, the play's representation of South Vietnamese soldiers—using female actors to mindlessly repeat the instructions given them by the male GIs—succeeded only in reinforcing the media stereotypes of Asians as the feminized and infantilized "other," apparently in need of strong Western leadership: "Ooooooooooo we get. No shoot the boot boot. Shoot the heart heart" (214).

Such "satire" contrasts starkly with *A Vietnamese Wedding*, the Judson Poets' Theater's response to a call for material for an "Angry Artists Against Vietnam" event, staged at Washington Square Methodist Church in February 1967. Maria Irene Fornes's script for this piece—less a "play" than a participatory happening—is strikingly un-angry in its approach: it simply lays out a sequence of events in which Aileen Passloff, Florence Tarlow, Remy Charlip, and Fornes herself described and enacted the customs observed in a traditional Vietnamese wedding, using volunteers from the audience to stand in as the bride, groom, and family. No mention is made of the war: instead Fornes's text provides for a simple and moving explication of these "alien" customs, which turn out to be very similar in essence to those of a Western wedding. For observers, "the Vietnamese" thus became a little less abstract as a concept, and a little more comprehensible as a culture and a people. This was a "change of perception" that most antiwar campaigning failed to attempt, much less achieve.

As political tensions steadily increased toward fever pitch in the nation at large, however, such benign evasion of explicit protest began to seem less and less adequate as a response. Other theater artists, such as Peter Schumann's Bread and Puppet Theatre, were finding ways to participate in the increasingly theatricalized antiwar movement without compromising their artistic integrity: Schumann's huge, mute puppets, many of them seeming to embody a profound sense of pain or rage, appeared in marches across the country and became widely recognized as the iconic embodiment of pacifist protest. By contrast, the off-off-Broadway movement, confined as it was to the tiny, self-reflexive world of downtown Manhattan, and now seemingly "compromised" by involvement with commercial producers and corporate foundations, was widely felt to have lost its cutting-edge relevance. "Six years ago," commented Bread and Puppet's Maurice Blanc in January 1969, "I could appreciate the urbane, brutal, tender, witty complexity of such plays [as Judson's *Home Movies*]. Now they nauseate me. . . . One can no longer focus on Hamlet without focusing on Denmark at the same time" (1969, 44).

Director Jacques Levy is just one of the artists who sought more direct engagement with the wider world during this period, by becoming one of the first members of the Yippie organization. From its inception in 1967, this East Village–based alliance of radicalized hippies and leftists sought, under the inspirational leadership of Abbie Hoffman, to use a playful, highly theatrical brand of public protest as a means of capturing media attention and sparking debate: "as Abbie Free says, all Demonstrations / Lives / Actions / are now Theatre" (Malina 1972, 160). The Yippies' situationist high jinks were designed to subvert the mystique of the nation's authorities—from their poignantly farcical attempts to "levitate" the Pentagon, to their hilarious "playing along" with the procedures of the House Un-American Activities Committee, when called to appear before it in 1968. Most famous of all was the Yippie presence during the large-scale street demonstrations accompanying the Democratic Convention of 1968 in Chicago (at which President Johnson's intended successor was to be nominated). "We burlesqued the whole process of electoral politics," Hoffman notes of the Yippie antics, which included proposing "Pigasus the Pig" as a presidential candidate (Schultz 2001, 321). (The pig was arrested by police.) For Levy, involvement with the Yippies felt like a logical extension of the cultural critique implicit in his work with the Open Theatre on shows like *America Hurrah:* "We needed to move it out into the world. That's what the Yippies were doing, and there's nothing that we'd ever done in the Open Theatre that had anything like the breadth or excitement or effectiveness of going to Chicago for the National Convention."

What none of the Yippies had expected, however, was the brute force with which the thousands of young protesters were met by Mayor Daley's riot police. "There is nothing like getting clubbed by a policeman, or being in the middle of tear gas, to commit you to being in a movement," Levy remarks dryly. The events surrounding the Chicago convention, and other developments such as the assassination of Martin Luther King the same year, prompted a further radicalization of the protest movement. Many began to argue that fire must be fought with fire—that armed revolutionary violence was a legitimate response to the sophisticated repressive apparatus of local and national governments. "Sixty-nine is the year the United States goes down," ran one gung-ho witticism; yet the revolutionary movement was divided into so many different parties and splinter groups—from Black Panthers to White Panthers, Weatherpeople to SDS—that their political impetus was always confused and fragmented. In *The Enormous Despair*, Judith Malina's diary of the Living Theatre's 1968–69 U.S. tour, she records both her admiration for the burning energy of groups like the Yippies and the Up Against the Wall Motherfuckers, and her distress, as a pacifist, at the increasingly violent rhetoric on all sides. How could a better society be created with guns?

Genesis at War

Of the original off-off-Broadway theaters, the one most consistently in tune with the heightened political tensions of the later 1960s was Theatre Genesis. Slightly younger than the other leading venues, Ralph Cook's theater was just coming into full creative flower as the Cino wound down toward closure, and as the socially engaged aesthetic that Cook had always sought to foster became increasingly pertinent. Genesis was the only off-off theater to engage consistently with the tensions and passions aroused by the war in Vietnam, and while Cook was no more interested in plays that made propagandist antiwar statements than were his counterparts at other venues, his advocacy of "subjective realism"—of the expression through theatrical image and metaphor of the playwright's individual anxieties in relation to the world at large—made the war inescapable as a subject.

Of course, such expressionism could sometimes be every bit as crude as agit-prop. Murray Mednick now confesses to acute embarrassment over his early play *Sand* (April 1967), in which two utterly repellent parents have their son's bloody corpse delivered home to them, on a meathook, by vulgar and abusive soldiers. Other Genesis plays, however, succeeded in avoiding such overboiled angst, by blending hard-edged commentary with a bleak, sardonic wit, to provide provocative perspectives on the war. A prime example is Grant Duay's *Fruit Salad* (January 1967). Duay was primarily a screenwriter for independent films, and his basic premise in *Fruit Salad* was to juxtapose brightly colored film sequences of a woman making a fruit salad, as if on a television cookery program, with scenes depicting three soldiers lost and under fire in the jungle. The soldiers, however, are dressed not in khakis but in sci-fi-serial silver helmets and in bright yellow, green, and red coveralls to signify their identities as, respectively, (Sergeant) Banana, (Corporal) Melon, and (Private) Cherry. On screen, the woman smilingly selects these very fruits, chops them up and mixes them in a bowl, accompanied both by perky television music and sounds of gunfire. The play thus creates a chillingly blithe metaphor for the seemingly casual sacrifice of American lives in Vietnam, while also commenting—far more succinctly than had *Viet Rock*—on the way that stateside war coverage had become enmeshed with the saccharine trivialities of the mass media.

Fruit Salad also suggests further, underlying levels of meaning, by exploring ways in which the pressures of warfare can act to undermine ostensibly rational structures—from military command chains to mental self-image. Melon, for example, is constantly second-guessing Banana's authority and strategies, and uses Banana's rampant homophobia as a lever by which to manipulate his decisions: "Are we going to risk our skins for that—that FAG Sergeant, and his boys up the hill? For a fag?" (Schroeder 1968, 122). As the play progresses, it becomes clear that the competition between Melon and Banana is also, obliquely, a competition for the affections of young Cherry— whose name, of course, indicates his ripe virginity. Banana's homophobia stems from his own repressed sexual urges, to which he finally succumbs amid the pressurized chaos of battle. He and Cherry are mown down by gunfire during their climactic sex act: "They are cut up like fruits, and they are fruits," Michael Smith wrote pointedly, "but mainly they are victims assailed and overpowered from inside and out, by themselves, each other, and the world" (1967, 27).

Fruit Salad, rooted in Duay's own "subjective realist" perspective as a gay man threatened by the draft, was untypical Genesis fare insofar that it deals so openly and sympathetically with homosexual characters. In all other respects, however, the play and its production were entirely consistent with the Theatre Genesis aesthetic. Tony Barsha's distinctly noncamp directorial approach was praised by Smith for the "vivid, simple and arresting" manner in which it articulated the play's "intricate series of subtle and intriguing formal relationships," both between juxtaposed media and contrasting characters. The result was a production whose "bitter, painful, almost despairing vision" was nevertheless presented with "lightness, fluidity, conciseness and cunning" (27), a description that might equally apply to many other Genesis pieces of the period.

However, the regular Genesis playwrights—Barsha, Mednick, Shepard, and Hadler—tended to be concerned less with reflecting directly on the violence in Vietnam, than with the increasing violence of the revolutionary movement at home. This is hardly surprising, given that St. Mark's in the Bowery had become a virtual headquarters for East Village radicals. The theater's writers and actors found themselves rubbing shoulders on a daily basis with members of groups like the Black Panthers, the Socialist Workers Party, and the Puerto Rican Independence Party, who used the church's meeting rooms. (The Panthers also ran a breakfast program from the church, providing free food to the area's poor.) Sometimes, moreover, the political and theatrical activities overlapped: in an old courthouse building at Second Avenue and Third Street, rented by St. Mark's using part of its federal grant, Tony Barsha began running workshops for anarchist groups like Black Mask, the New York Federation of Anarchists, and, he recalls, "some other crazies who'd been turning in scripts to Theatre Genesis that were unproduceable messes." The participants were let loose to devise theatrical "consciousness-raising" events, such as one in which hapless audience members were locked in the courthouse's cells and aggressively interrogated.

For the most part, however, the Genesis crew maintained a careful distance from these groups. They were well informed on the issues (Walter Hadler, for example, was versed in the writings of figures like Marx, Lenin, and Kim Il Sung), but viewed the radical rhetoric with skepticism. "It was bullshit," Mednick remarks bluntly: "There were some genuine elements in all that, but I think we knew that the chances of [a revolution] happening were slim to none." Even Barsha's sympathies for the anarchists were severely tested when members of Black Mask, now restyled as the Up Against the Wall Motherfuckers, began advocating the murder of police officers as a progressive strategy. Rather than speaking for or with these groups, the Genesis playwrights found themselves reflecting on this new urge to rebellion in relation to the social and existential questions already apparent in their work. They viewed the posturing of groups like the Motherfuckers, for example, as being directly related to America's age-old mythology of the outlaw. This historical perspective tended to make them fatalistic about the chances of liberating change, but the bleak honesty of their theatrical visions provided a cathartic charge of their own.

The first Theatre Genesis play to tie Wild West iconography to the contemporary suppression of political dissent was Sam Shepard's *Forensic and the Navigators* (December 1967). Forensic and Emmet are a pair of cowboy-and-Indian outlaw revolutionaries planning a daring jailbreak for fellow dissidents, but they are in hiding, on the run, and hopelessly divided over the best course of action to achieve their goals. They are also being hunted down by invisible authorities, who have sent bug-control-style "exterminators" after them. The tone of the play is broadly parodic, and includes comic diversions such as Oolan's disquisition on how best to eat Rice Krispies: Shepard portrays his inept heroes and villains alike with a wild, cartoon-strip humor. The play's underlying sense of paranoia is brought to the fore in its conclusion, however, as the exterminators pump poison gas into Forensic's room. In the Genesis production, colored smoke filled up the entire theater to the extent that spectators could not see their own hands in front of their faces, while Shepard and his rock band, the Holy Modal Rounders, struck up a deafening assault of drumming and electric noise. "[Shepard's] themes of disaster are so vast," Clive Barnes later wrote of *Forensic*, and "his offhand methods are so casual," that they leave the observer with a "disenchanting and disturbing" aftertaste (1970a).

More serious treatments of similar themes are apparent, post-Chicago, in Walter Hadler's 1969 plays *Flite Cage* (May) and *The Waterworks at Lincoln* (November). The first, set in the stillness and vast open spaces of the southwestern desert—itself a weirdly disorientating concept when staged within a tiny black studio—seems to allude simultaneously to America's frontier past and the imperialistic foreign policies of the present, by suggesting that this seemingly unconquerable territory is in the process of being tamed and "civilized" by government forces. These are symbolized by the jet fighter aircraft heard rocketing overhead on training flights, breaking the sound barrier with great sonic booms and shattering the desert's eerie peace. For Moss and Wilma, the play's central characters, this location thus moves from being a natural haven for the wanderer to being "a testing lab" within which they are strangely confined. "They're making a figure eight," Moss notes of the jets:

"Must be over fifty thousand feet. Wow. It's like someone ice-skating. It's like we're under water. All you can see is blades on the ice" (Smith 1972, 247).

That sense of entrapment is still more pronounced in *The Waterworks at Lincoln*. Here, the setting is lush parkland rather than desert, a territory that has already been fully colonized. In this nightmare fantasy, the land is a private estate whose gates shut promptly at 5:15: any visitors still inside at that time are mercilessly gunned down by patrolling helicopter gunships. Written at a time when the United States was secretly bombing Cambodia and Laos, even while claiming to be scaling down its military presence in Vietnam, the play was appropriately paranoid: "It was kind of an apocalyptic vision of the war coming home," Hadler explains. Beyond that, though, America's callous separation of the haves and the have-nots is also very much part of the equation: "The gates feel it is not their concern: such questions as which is inside and which is outside" (Hadler 1969, 25). On the "inside" are characters such as Mrs. Meyer, ostensible owner of the estate (named for the owner of the *Washington Post*). On the "outside" are Gene and Cody, two working-class hippie types who come to the estate to gawk at the ducks in the lake—by staring out into the space occupied by the audience. The pair, however, cannot agree on whether to leave when instructed. Cody, in a small act of rebellion, proposes staying in the park after dark. Gene, concerned for his family and his job as well as himself, refuses: "Shit man. Why do you have to be so difficult? I don't like breaking laws. . . . They were nice enough to let us use this place. Let's not abuse it" (5). Cody stays behind, meets Mrs. Meyer and her daughter Hattie, 5:15 arrives, and all three are duly gunned down by the helicopters. (Perhaps Mrs. Meyer was not in charge after all.)

Hadler's dramatic style is eerily oblique, full of strange, tangential conversations and abrupt entrances and exits. "So much of it is unexplained," Martin Washburn noted in his *Voice* review of *Waterworks*, yet "the timing and transitions and juxtapositions created the flavor of a significant engagement with reality. . . . I felt myself in the presence of a genuine question" (1969). The question, insofar as it can be apprehended, seems to hinge around Cody and Gene's uncertainty about how to act in this paradisically hostile environment; whether to stay or go. The play simultaneously evokes the existential dilemma of Beckett's Vladimir and Estragon—"'Shall we go?' 'Yes, let's go.' *They do not move*" (Beckett 1956, 94)—and the more immediate choice faced by those excluded and disempowered by American society. Does one meekly accept the status quo, or attempt to challenge it in some, probably futile way? For Hadler, this was a very real issue. Having grown up a "hick" in a poor,

western Pennsylvania mining town (where the mine company's callous disregard for employees' safety resulted in his father losing an eye and fracturing his
skull in industrial accidents), he understood the revolutionary impulse.

In scene 2 of *Waterworks*, his bloody death mysteriously erased, Cody reappears with Gene, and this time they have chosen the radical option. Both are
armed to the teeth with guns and ammo belts. Yet since the power controlling
the estate seems so invisible and arbitrary, their next move is unclear. Instead,
Cody's pent-up aggression gets misdirected toward personal hang-ups, and
particularly toward resentful memories of his mother, who appears to him as a
Betty Grable–like apparition, belittling him with a stream of patronizing
abuse: "You're just like [your father] the stupid bastard. Only he worked in the
coal mine for a living while all you do is leech around like some pimp off poor
little rich girls. Gotta hide from me like a convict" (16). Cody, expressionless,
shoots her dead, and then proceeds—in a moment of gruesome psychological
revelation—to "cannibalize" her, by pouring Karo syrup onto the corpse's
stomach and gradually licking it off. As he does, he reels off childhood memories of abuse and violence: "When you killed a deer with a 30.06 from two
hundred yards, I said no. When you mashed his face through a broken wind-
shield into a cinder block, I said no. When I broke your lover with a two by
four while you staggered by puking and drowning on my bed, I said no" (16).
Cody, it seems, has nowhere to direct his bitter "no" against his poverty-
stricken upbringing except into these twisted, Oedipal resentments.

While Cody and Gene roam the park like armed bandits, a group of shot-
gun-toting redneck hunters appear and take potshots at the "ducks"—by
pointing their weapons and firing (blanks) directly at the audience. With
many Theatre Genesis spectators literally diving for cover in terror, this deafening assault provoked real anger from some, and prompted Martin Washburn to note that the moment was "not only bad for already over-strained city
ears, but tore at the texture of the play itself." Hadler, however, must surely
have intended this disruption of the play's otherwise distanced, reflective
mood: as a means of "crossing the audience divide," this sudden, almost
casual gesture proved as shocking and unsettling as any of the audience participation experiments of the period, and confronted the spectators' "city ears"
with the latent violence of the country. The hunters function, in effect, as the
mirror image of Cody and Gene—as the conservative, reactionary face of
working-class America—and their presence alludes, again, to the connection
between limited choices and misdirected violence. Rocky, Stu, Seth, and Bob
casually destroy nature and persecute those different from themselves: they

subject Gene to a kangaroo court trial and then lynch him, simply because they dislike the look of him and the length of his hair.

In the play's final scene, surrounded by the bodies of those shot down by the omniscient helicopters, Cody confronts the one surviving hunter, Rocky. The tragic irony of their meeting is that, in the course of their almost desultory exchange, they gradually warm to each other, realizing their essential similarities: "You play ball?" / "Yeah." / "Any good?" / "Nah." / "I was good." / "You look it." / "You dig it." / "Yeah" (27). Yet they seem somehow compelled to shoot each other down as enemies, even though, as Cody notes in the play's anticlimactically final line, "I've never seen you before" (28). They both fire, they both fall wounded, and the helicopters arrive to finish them off in a cacophony of gunfire. "Silver and red confetti through the strobe lights," Hadler suggests: "They die" (28). *The Waterworks at Lincoln* depicts, through allusive and highly theatrical means, an America forever divided against itself, blindly unable to see the real enemy—or even to articulate the question. Hadler's work, wrote Robert Pasolli, "reflect[s] our deep suspicion that what is wrong in our lives is so fundamental, yet so elusive, that we can do nothing to set it right" (1968c).

Such "dark diagnoses," Pasolli pointed out, were also common to the work of Shepard and Murray Mednick. With *The Deer Kill* (1970), however, Mednick broke ranks by attempting to shed a little light on the situation. Rather than condensing his concerns into an intense, unsettling one-act experience, revolving around a single central image or theatrical metaphor, Mednick opted here for the more immediately accessible form of a linear, character-based narrative, worked out over three acts. The characteristic Genesis features are all still there—abrupt dream and memory sequences; incantatory monologues; the occasionally jarring juxtaposition of images. Mednick seems concerned, though, to articulate with greater clarity the stark choices faced by countercultural radicals at the turn of the 1970s. *The Deer Kill* is a sustained examination of loss and confusion that in many ways transcends the period it depicts: ambitious in every respect (its tripartite stage arrangement also required that it be mounted in the sanctuary of St. Mark's Church itself, rather than in the tiny Genesis space), it deservedly won the 1970 Obie for best play—the year after Theatre Genesis itself had been awarded an Obie for "sustained excellence." Like *Waterworks*, it was sharply directed by Ralph Cook.

The choices faced in the play are neatly articulated in the prologue, in which three self-styled "psychedelic bandit freaks" celebrate their "comradery as Motherfuckers"—implicitly of the "Up Against the Wall" variety (Mednick

1972, 1). Yet Luke, John, and Peter, whose apostolic names are no coincidence, are divided over the correct course of radical action for the future. Peter seems simply lost in his own drugged-up haze. John wants to "join up with the Panthers and get it on once and for all . . . there's going to be a revolution in this country" (2, 4). Yet Luke strongly doubts this: "I'm sick and tired of violence," he insists: "the best thing we can do is fan out around the country and be our own selves" (2–3). Like many other radicals at this time, Luke has concluded that, rather than attempt to combat the system directly, the answer is resistance through separatism, and the formation of alternative, self-contained communities. A former drug dealer, Luke had once thought his trade was helping to free the minds of his comrades, but has come to realize that he and they were simply becoming the dependent slaves of gangsters. Luke urgently needs to get the social and economic pressures of the city out of his system.

He finds refuge, as the play proper begins, at the home of Thomas and his wife Martha, whose house in the country appears to operate as a kind of communal drop-in center for the disaffected. Thomas (played by the Open Theatre's Ralph Lee) is the son of an Appalachian miner, and a singer of old-time mountain music: the presence of this grounded figure implicitly ties the Motherfuckers' contemporary voices of resistance to the anarchic, independent spirit of pioneers and farmers. A believer in natural justice, Thomas stands up for old-fashioned common sense when the police visit his home to demand that they be permitted to execute his dog (a large, invisible hound created via sound effects and actors' gestures). The dog has reportedly attacked and killed a deer while roaming loose. Thomas points out that the dog has simply helped control the size of the deer population: the state authorities have themselves killed 145,000 deer in the previous year. Yet the dog, it seems, is not free to contribute to the cull, and must be kept on a leash. Since Thomas refuses to confine it in this way, and even denies the property-based assumption that it is "his" to confine, he must be punished. His pointed and often hilarious dispute with the cops over the dog's "deer kill" deftly raises a series of questions over the coercive power of the state and the apparent absence of traditional, down-home freedoms in contemporary America. Crucially though, Thomas eventually caves in and pays the twenty-five-dollar fine, since the alternative is imprisonment. The long arm of the law stretches even into this supposed haven of liberty: there is no "getting away from it all," as Luke had hoped.

Moreover, the refugees in Thomas's casual commune prove as incapable as the Motherfuckers of agreeing how to organize themselves. Elliott, for example, is a member of a black revolutionary group (implicitly the Black Panthers: a large poster of the party's founder, Huey Newton, hangs on Thomas's wall) and believes he is being hunted: "That vicious motherfucking Nixon is trying to destroy us." His solution is apparently to kill the president, or, failing that, some of the rednecks "going around with Old Glory on their automobiles saying fuck the niggers and the hippies, they ought to love it or leave it" (21). Thomas points out that this is the wrong target: "I know the kind of people you're talking about. I grew up with them. And they're ignorant, just plain ignorant . . . They act like they been told to" (22). Elliott, though, has little time for such pleading, pointing out, with a kind of paranoid logic, that "nobody's going to change, [if] you don't give them a goddamn good reason to change . . . Take Kenya—the British wouldn't do shit in Kenya until the Mau Mau put the fear of death in 'em. . . . It is necessary to pick up the gun in order to get rid of the gun" (76–77).

The contextual irony here is that Elliott's rhetoric seems completely detached from the reality of his personal situation. His white wife, Dolores, is not interested in his agenda, and is instead obsessed with ecological issues, seeing pesticides as the enemy: "It's absolutely incredible how the system is poisoning our bodies" (24). Her solution is to completely detoxify the body through fasting, and then eat only direct-from-the-land organic produce. Former junkie Luke, attracted by this program, embarks on a starvation fast that leaves him emaciated and spaced out. He also conducts a brief affair with Thomas's wife, Martha, which seems based on a genuine mutual attraction, and which Thomas appears to give his blessing to. For Martha, however, the free-love ideal proves cruelly incompatible with her responsibilities as a housekeeper and mother. Indeed, the glaring mismatch between the utopian outlooks of Thomas's houseguests and the day-to-day reality of running the place, with little or no money, begins to drive Martha to distraction. The seeds are visible here of the 1970s feminist movement's abandonment of the various, male-run revolutionary efforts of the previous decade, in favor of all-too-necessary self-help.

The Deer Kill's careful and complex articulation of its various characters' dilemmas makes them comprehensible and, for the most part, sympathetic figures (even given the subtle layering of black-comic irony). Yet Mednick also leaves no doubt as to the dysfunctionality of the whole situation: this "convincing, harrowing" play, Martin Washburn wrote, "depicts the black disaster which befalls members of a group who ultimately share little with each other aside from dissociation" (1970b). "It gets to where many of us are today as we turn to the possibility of the commune and 'the country thing' to save us," Arthur Sainer concurred: "Mednick must have written this one in blood" (1970a). In retrospect, the play seems prescient of horror stories surrounding communes that emerged during the 1970s. What is the dissenting individual to do, *The Deer Kill* asks, when an acceptance of the established order would constitute capitulation, and yet one can find no coherent way to put progressive dreams into action?

For Luke's friend John, the answer is to put his personal revolution into action by killing a cop. He describes the event to Luke in an extraordinarily vivid, extended monologue: "I've done it," he keeps repeating, "I've crossed over" (68). John was played to great acclaim in the Genesis production by Walter Hadler, whose *Flite Cage* had depicted a similar cop-killing, as Moss's answer to his sense of entrapment: "It's a study of murder," Hadler comments of that play, "when it was sort of becoming fashionable to accept it." Far from liberating them, both Moss and John find that the act of killing traps them further into a state of numbed shock. On the run from the law and his own demons, John finally decides to blow his own brains out, and Luke, finding himself with no more options, quietly asks to join him. "I am ashamed before the earth," Luke chants, in a depressive corruption of his favorite Native American chant: "I am ashamed before the heavens. . . . I am ashamed before that standing within me that speaks with me. . . . Therefore I must tell the truth" (69). So must John, for whom the most painful truth of all lies in the last words spoken by his victim (words that also echo the climax of Hadler's *Waterworks*):

> "I'M KILLIN' YOU, COP, THE OLD JOHN IS DEAD, I'M MAKING THE BIG MOVE, COP." "Don't do it," he says. "Me and you are the same, we're brothers; I got a mother in Wheeling, West Virginia and a cousin in the army." "OH NO, COP, THIS IS IT, COP, THIS IS IT. NO WAY BACK FOR YOU AND ME, BANG! BANG! BANG!" (34–35)

Genesis Exodus

On May 4, 1970, just four days after the opening performance of *The Deer Kill*, Ohio National Guardsmen opened fire, without provocation, on students demonstrating against the war at Kent State University, killing four of them and generating mass panic. News of the event struck a heavy blow to countercultural radicals of all hues, and, for many, seemed to douse what little optimism remained that real social and political change might be achieved in the near future. "That kids were shot, kids were killed, by their contemporaries," Jean-Claude van Itallie explains; "the people who killed them were not more than a year or two older than the people who were killed. That it should some-how come to that? [There was a sense] that the world would not change this fast; that maybe it would take a long, long time." Some responded to the killings with calls for further escalation of the revolutionary effort, but many more opted for retrenchment and withdrawal—sometimes into communes. The defiant but rather vague idealism of the 1960s, during which there were almost as many different revolutions being proposed as there were revolution-aries, now gave way to hard decisions. Many radical organizations disinte-grated rapidly in the new decade.

This sense of fragmentation was as apparent in the alternative theater com-munity as it was among political alliances. 1970 saw the Living Theatre's itin-erant collective split up into different factions, ostensibly for strategic political reasons. It was also the year of the Judson Poets' Theater's breakup, and the year in which Ralph Cook quit his beloved Theatre Genesis. Recollections as to exactly what prompted his departure differ: Barsha recalls a dispute about the ethics of grant funding; Mednick believes he had simply reached the point of burnout; Hadler remembers Cook becoming increasingly dogmatic and overtly Marxist in his political opinions, and starting to demand that his play-wrights adopt a more didactic, propagandistic approach (this was against the backdrop of upheaval in St. Mark's Church itself, as the traditionally liberal pastor Michael Allen was deposed by his Marxist associate, David Garcia). Whatever the reason, Cook stepped down and moved to California, well away from the pressure cooker atmosphere of the East Village. The directorship of Theatre Genesis was taken over collectively by Shepard, Hadler, and Med-nick, but with the project's father figure having gone, the sons fell increasingly to squabbling among themselves: "The fighting was fierce; the stakes were so little," Barsha quips dryly, recalling disputes over whose plays should be scheduled, and how much foundation money should be parceled out to which. Barsha quit Genesis in 1971 over his colleagues' refusal to program his play *The Tragedy of Homer Stills*, which he took instead to La Mama. Shepard also jumped ship later that year, fleeing New York to get off drugs and forge a new life in London.

These departures were symptomatic of a more general exodus of artists and activists from downtown Manhattan at the turn of the decade. The primary cause was economic, as rent hikes made the pursuit of alternative lifestyles increasingly difficult. "I see the shooting at Kent State as very significant," Robert Heide remarks, voicing an appropriately paranoid conspiracy theory,

> because after that it was as if a group of people met in a boardroom somewhere and said, "Well, let's get them where it hurts." Because we were against the whole societal concept of landlordism. Most of the people that I knew as a playwright, our rents had been under one hundred dollars, so that afforded us the chance to do something different with our lives. But there's a big difference between your rent being one hundred dollars and it being twelve hundred dollars. That's a new kind of landlord fascism.

The question now, Ronald Sukenick observes, was "what would make money, or where could you get along with less of it?" With the streets of the Lower East Side descending into an ever more frightening spiral of drug-fueled crime and violence, the remaining residents

> had to start thinking about a way to live that made it possible to get home at night without getting mugged or raped on the way, to open the door without finding the place burglarized again, to send the kids to decent schools, to earn money without putting in long hours at mind-granulating low pay jobs. . . . Subterraneans started moving at a rapid rate to Vermont and Maine, the west coast, or hospitable college campuses all over the country. (Sukenick 1987, 42)

In 1973, Murray Mednick too quit Theatre Genesis, heading to California in Ralph Cook's footsteps. His final Genesis play, produced earlier that year, was *Are You Lookin'?*, a brutally honest and grimly depressing document of his own experiences as a Lower East Side heroin addict, scrounging on the streets for money and dope, instead of living the idealized life of art and intellect he had once hoped for. "We've lost it, Kay," the lead character Mickey remarks to his girlfriend, voicing the feelings of many of New York's departing "subterraneans": "We ain't tied into things no more. It's a sickness. . . . There has to be a balance, Kay, between the pollution of things, and the glory. The beautiful, and the diseased. . . . We've upset the balance. We've gone too far. Too gross, too ugly, too much, too selfish, too many" (Mednick 1973, 3.3–4).

Open Theatre: *Terminal*

In counterpoint to the attempts of the Genesis writers to reflect on the cultural specifics of turn-of-the-decade political violence, the Open Theatre were simultaneously attempting to investigate the more universal question of death itself, in their show *Terminal*. Developed during 1969 and premiered in New

York in April 1970, this piece emerged from the company's desire to find subject matter open-ended enough to allow for a genuinely collaborative exchange of ideas and experiences—and indeed to be comprehensible to the culturally diverse audiences they encountered while touring. The piece eventually created by the company was, like *The Serpent* before it, structured as a kind of stage ritual. *Terminal* opens with an extended sequence of incantatory chanting, with the actors beating short wooden sticks on the floor to create a polyrhythmic, shamanistic cacophony: by this means, the spirits of the dead are conjured up from beneath the earth, and given voice by the "possessed" performers in the piece's subsequent scenes. Seeking to inhabit a gray area between the neatly opposed concepts of life and death, *Terminal* characterizes its audiences as "the dying": "We come among the dying to call upon the dead," runs the opening chant (Sainer 1975, 113). This confrontation of spectators with the fact of their own mortality is then underlined by an unnerving sequence in which a series of performers are told that this is "your last chance to use your eyes" (or voice, or legs), before being deprived of those capacities. The eyes and mouth are sealed off with black tape, the legs give way, and in these moments the vulnerability of the individual performers is made vividly apparent. *Terminal*, one critic noted, is "an unforgettable sequence of simply executed images, an experience that will jar you out of your half-life if anything can" (Hewes 1970).

Crucially, however, the Open Theatre's investigations of such universal thematics were inseparable from the group's heartfelt commitment to finding an appropriate creative response to America's immediate political tensions. As Joe Chaikin put it in one interview, "My struggle is involved now with the political because there can no longer be a divided sensibility [between art and politics]. One eats food that is poisoned because it helps someone to profit, one listens to commercials that destroy someone" (Croyden 1970). Chaikin was personally committed to grueling work as a counselor for draft resisters, but his company's social consciousness was most immediately apparent in its collectively taken decisions regarding where and why to perform. Its first two New York performances of *Terminal*, for example, were given as benefits for the Black Panther Party's Legal Defense Fund, while a subsequent benefit raised funds for the Native American activists then occupying Alcatraz Island. The company also committed itself at this time to tour not only to colleges and arts venues but to prisons, performing for those incarcerated by a system whose concept of justice they fundamentally distrusted.

These choices provided evidence of the group's radical sentiments, even as their theater work maintained a (politically principled) avoidance of proselytizing for progressive causes: "If a group of people say, 'We're going to do political theatre—direct political theatre, agit-prop theatre,'" Chaikin commented, "it's simply another kind of salesmanship at this time. They're saying, 'I would like to sell you my view of this tumult we're in,' and that very often is not effective in terms of the audience going through a change of perceiving things" (1974, 41). The potentially liberating results of resisting didacticism were summed up for Susan Yankowitz—the writer with whom the group collaborated on *Terminal*—by the comments of one young prison inmate who spoke up during a discussion after one show: "I see why this is different from the soap operas we watch," she recalls him saying, "because there they tell you everything that you can think and feel, and here, you have an opening for your own feelings."

Terminal's openness to individual response was, as with *The Serpent*, very much a product of the way it fused rich visual imagery with loaded silences and an evocatively minimal use of pared-down language, so as to allow for a reflective, meditative experience. Abstracted and aestheticized as its concerns were, however, *Terminal* was as much a "view of this tumult we're in" as any agit-prop piece of the period. Its most insistent metaphor is that of death within life; the idea that while the dead may be imprisoned in their graves, many of the living-dying are also jailed by the behaviors imposed on them. The performance thus returns repeatedly to images of enslavement. In one sequence, for example, the "dying" enter the "terminal ward" to be stripped naked of clothing and individual initiative: "We know what you need" (120). The sequence seems to allude both to the patronizing humiliations to which old people can be subjected in care homes, and to the ritualized hazing of convicts entering prisons or conscripts entering military training. Elsewhere, a soldier marches obsessively on the spot, mouthing "Yes sir, yes sir" over and over: "Said yes when I wanted to say yes, Said yes when I wanted to say no . . . And dead because I said yes / And dead because YOU said yes . . . Dead before and dead again / Because I never knew / What the FUCK I was saying yes to / yes / yes / yes" (127).

The antiwar stance of the soldier sequence is unambiguous, as indeed are the antiestablishment sentiments apparent in the "visions" of a chanting prophet figure: "I see the thief go into business / Now he can steal and not get caught / I see the killer become a policeman / Now he can murder, that's his job" (128). In other sequences again, the use of repressive violence as a weapon to enforce consent is vividly evoked: in a shorthand scene reminiscent of Orwell's 1984, one man is systematically hit over the head until he learns to give all the "correct" answers about his personal feelings (135). Even so, *Terminal* avoids becoming simplistic in its political imagery by repeatedly implying that the oppressors, too, are imprisoned in their lives and roles: "Your hatred was your prison / but your hatred set me free," declares "The One who was Hit" (132), perhaps evoking memories of how the nationwide campaign for civil rights had been ignited by resistance to the racism of southern conservatives. One of *Terminal*'s most moving visual sequences depicts the power of such nonviolent resistance, as the obedient "patients" on the dying ward gradually begin to lose patience with the mind-numbing uniformity of walking in circles (the group task they have been given by their jailers). "You are each responsible for keeping the circle moving," they are told, encouragingly: "Everyone is useful / You are each keeping the circle alive" (124). One by one, the patients drop out of the circle, their chant of "out" quietly counterpointing the leaders' rhythmic chant of condescending approval: "Very / good / Nice."

Terminal, then, even while taking an ostensibly universal subject, was inseparable from the concerns of its time. Its importance was felt, particularly, by those who saw in the painstaking care and integrity with which it had been constructed an inspirational alternative to the self-defeating violence into which much countercultural resistance had descended. In his review for the *Village Voice*, John Lahr juxtaposed his experience of seeing *Terminal* with that of watching Harvard students rioting on campus, the same week. The significance of the Open Theatre's "haunting litany became clear in the face of this fatuous violence," Lahr wrote: "The riot was a living tableau of how deeply this society has been touched by death and how numb it is to life. [The] radicals who pelted police cars with bricks and punched out parking meters [did so] in the name of the dead and the dying: those who die in Vietnam and in the ghettos," and yet they had, he felt, "lost a reverence for life in the process of petty rebellion." By stark contrast, *"Terminal* makes you conscious of death and the limits of time. . . . The call to action is mixed with a compassion and commitment approaching love" (Lahr 1970, 43).

Idealized as the Open Theatre was by many observers, the company itself was often divided over the efficacy of its approach. Several members argued forcefully for a more explicitly engaged stance, particularly after the shootings at Kent State, which had taken place just as the company was preparing to take *Terminal* to that campus. The feelings of actor Peter Maloney, for example, are expressed in a television documentary shot at this time:

We can stand up in front of the audience before we perform our "artistic," "universal" work, and bring it down to newspaper facts, and say how many people were killed, and say that we deplore it, and ask that they deplore it too—which they probably do—but it's increasingly frustrating, because that's as far as we can go. And I really don't know how practical a theatre can be. That's something we're going to find out next year, I guess. (Venza 1970)

Maloney's comments imply that a serious debate was brewing within the company; that there were "issues" to be thrashed out. In the event, however, that debate was forestalled by Chaikin's decision, in the fall of 1970, to exclude Maloney and all but six of the Open Theatre's other performers from future participation in his workshops. This drastic move was understandable, given that the sheer logistics of leading an eighteen-strong company had become a severe drain on Chaikin's energies (as paternal arbiter, he was often called on to resolve the interpersonal disputes that could crop up with monotonous regularity). In reducing his company to a third of its former size, Chaikin also proposed that some of the excluded actors might continue to work together separately, taking a proportion of the company's grant funds with them. (Indeed, former Open Theatre members went on to cofound groups such as the Medicine Show and the Bridge Collective.) Yet the sense of betrayal over this splintering of the company was profoundly felt, particularly since Chaikin—loved and revered by his actors—proved unable to summon the courage to notify them of their exclusion in person: "Joe sent out the equivalent of pink slips," Yankowitz recalls. Among those left out of the new group were actors such as James Barbosa, Barbara Vann, and Lee Worley, who had been key members of the Open Theatre since its inception. Chaikin's reconstruction of the company thus not only closed the debate about whether a more activist political stance should be taken, but was seen by some as an abandonment of the company's collaborative ideals. Certainly, it was symptomatic of a shift toward the more distinctively director-led approach that was to emerge as a hallmark of alternative theater in the 1970s.

Like many leading members of off-off-Broadway's "first generation," Chaikin had by this time matured to the point where he needed final say over the shape of his work. This was also apparent in his changing relationship with the Open Theatre's writers. Chaikin's decision to work with Susan Yankowitz on Terminal, rather than with an older, more "equal" colleague such as Jean-Claude van Itallie or Megan Terry, meant that he was assured total control over the creative process. Fresh out of drama school, Yankowitz was grateful for his support and encouragement, and was usually happy to defer to his judgments: "If Joe liked it and I didn't like it that much, it would stay in, and I would work with it. But I couldn't get something I liked, and Joe didn't, to stay in the piece." Moreover, Yankowitz was asked only to furnish words for individual sequences, rather than to create an overall structure for the piece, as van Itallie had for *The Serpent*. Structurally, *Terminal* was simply a series of loosely related images, separated by brief blackouts. Subsequent Open Theatre works displayed still less concern for overall dramatic shape. *Mutation Show* (1972) was created without a dedicated playwright, and explored its theme of life changes by presenting a series of freak-show acts, which used only a few short fragments of spoken text. *Nightwalk* (1973) incorporated commissioned contributions from van Itallie, Terry, and Sam Shepard, on the theme of dreaming, but again lacked cohesive structure. Indeed, *Nightwalk* was never considered fully finished: the group disbanded in the fall of 1973, while it was still work in progress. These later pieces, though marked by mature, highly focused performances from their six actors, were never as highly regarded as *The Serpent* or *Terminal*: "In the recent Open Theatre works," Michael Smith wrote in his obituary for the group, "the fragments are finely polished and rich in implications, but always fragments" (1973c).

It seems that the sketchbook quality of these later works directly reflected Chaikin's temperament: "Joe distrusts structure," van Itallie contended in a 1995 interview: "While improvising he's very happy, but the moment you get to the point of a performance, where you need a structure, he's uncomfortable." Finally, this distrust of fixed structures was also what prompted Chaikin to disband the company. At the time he stated simply that he wanted to avoid the Open Theatre becoming ossified as a grant-dependent institution that would perpetuate itself for the sake of perpetuating itself. The essential character of the company, he pointed out, had always been "this thing of changing, of getting rid of, like *snakeskins*," and ultimately this meant shedding the company umbrella itself—though the members might (and did) continue to work together in other contexts (Feingold 1973). Chaikin seems also to have sensed, though, that the company had reached a point where his unchallenged control of the group was in danger of becoming a handicap: "I find that it is absolutely essential to work with a writer," he told another interviewer after the group disbanded: "It isn't incidental at all, that the effectiveness of a piece depends on how effective the writer is. . . . We can do these various things, but we need a form and words as well" (1974, 38).

With hindsight, it seems clear that the Open Theatre was a company whose major achievements were based more on the push-pull of group endeavor than on individual creative vision. Chaikin was always at his best as a catalyst and a facilitator, rather than as an "auteur," and it was the large-group incarnation of the Open Theatre—for all the strains and stresses it entailed—that ultimately rendered the richer results. (Indeed, though the smaller company adapted *Terminal* to be performed by six, video evidence suggests that this was at some cost to the layered, multifocus quality of the original—particularly in full-ensemble sequences such as the cacophonous opening incantations, and the circle walk of "the Dying Resist.") However, the need to preserve the vitally "open," collaborative nature of the Open Theatre's work, while simultaneously developing a clear creative direction of his own, in the end proved too difficult a balancing act even for Chaikin. Years later, in an unduly harsh piece of self-criticism, he confessed to feeling he had been "a real imposter in the way I chose to appear self-sacrificing toward the wishes of the group. . . . I manipulated a lot in terms of my own wishes and interests, while appearing to think that the only thing I was concerned about was a strictly Maoist idea of The People" (Blumenthal 1984, 26).

There is a paradox here, of course, since even the most democratic of theater ensembles needs strong creative leadership. Nevertheless, it might be argued that the "political" significance of the off-off-Broadway movement lay primarily in its various experiments with the micropolitics of theater-making: its major achievements had been created by communities of artists, often working with and for specific, community-based audiences. With the arrival of the 1970s came the gradual disintegration of those communities, as physical exhaustion and financial pressures began to take their toll, and as artists as diverse as Chaikin and Al Carmines began seeking greater individual control over their work.

Going Solo:
Auteurs, Poseurs, and La Mama

> Ellen was after me for years. After 1967 she didn't let me alone. . . . Then one day
> I'm walking down from my loft with this kid who had brought me a play—seven
> little scenes called *Cock-Strong*—and we're walking down Fourth Street and
> Ellen's outside sweeping. And she says, "John, *please* do a play!" And I turned to
> the playwright [Tom Murrin], and I said, "Would you like your play done?" He
> said yes. I said, "Can I turn it into a musical?" He said, "You can do anything
> you want." So I asked her, "When do you want it?" and she said in two weeks. I
> said, *"Two weeks?!"* So I went home, called a friend of mine, a composer [Ralph
> Czitron]. He came over, we smoked a whole lot of grass, we wrote thirty-three
> songs in two and a half hours, and I used like twenty-two of them in the play. I
> did it in her theater, with a rock and roll band, and she gave me one hundred
> dollars to do the show.
>
> —John Vaccaro

Off-off-Broadway, as it had initially evolved, had been a scene dedicated to the
new playwright. Viewed in relation to the commercial theater of the 1950s and
early 1960s—in which even the most accomplished writers were frequently
required to alter scripts according to the commercial or theatrical demands of
powerful producers and directors—this championing of the playwright's
vision had, for many, represented an important restatement of theater's potential as an art form, rather than as "show business." Initially, the function of
directors off-off-Broadway was widely assumed to be that of realizing the
writer's intentions onstage, as clearly as possible—an approach that some,
such as Ralph Cook, continued to pursue throughout the decade. As the
scene developed, however, directors began to be appreciated as creative artists
in their own right, and—as we have seen—formed a variety of rich, collaborative alliances with playwrights that became central to off-off-Broadway's experimental profile.

By the end of the decade, however, the delicate balance of power between
writers and directors had shifted to the point where the latter tended to enjoy
more creative autonomy. John Vaccaro's anecdote regarding the beginnings
of *Cock-Strong*, embroidered as it may be, demonstrates clearly that by 1969—
with La Mama having opened in its new premises on East Fourth—Ellen

Stewart's priorities lay with securing the services of leading directors, almost regardless of what they might choose to direct. Stewart had developed a strong preference for work that was highly visual and musical, and thus had greater potential to cross national and cultural borders: "I wanted to appeal to the world," she explains, "and you can't appeal to the world with these words." With its boisterously nonsensical rock songs and its central prop—a gigantic, ejaculating phallus—*Cock-Strong* proved "an *immense* success" (as Vaccaro laughingly notes) both at La Mama and on a subsequent European tour. Although Vaccaro now sees the piece as little more than a stop-gap joke (a kind of "Ridiculous Lite," perhaps, after the apocalyptic intensity of *The Moke-Eater*), it proved a big enough hit to prompt a 1970 sequel, *Son of Cock-Strong*, also at La Mama. "Oh, that was *terrible*," Vaccaro recalls, beaming: "But it was fun!"

The situation was somewhat less fun for many of off-off-Broadway's playwrights, who now found it increasingly difficult to get their work mounted. With the Cino closed forever, with Judson dedicating itself almost exclusively to the production of Al Carmines's musicals as of 1969, and with Genesis mounting only a handful of pieces per year, mostly by its resident writers, La Mama was the only one of off-off-Broadway's four leading venues still maintaining an open-door policy for new work, and a regular programming schedule. However, with Stewart prioritizing the work of favored directors, the days of playwrights simply being allocated a production slot on request were over. "Before," Irene Fornes recalls, "if any of us had a new play, we could go to wherever, La Mama or Judson, and the person running the theater would be so happy and say, 'When can you do it?' . . . And then, it seemed to me suddenly, you would say to somebody, 'I have a play,' and they would say, 'Well, I don't think I have a slot for next season. I'll try to see if I can fit it in.' It seemed almost like a cold shoulder."

The writers best placed at La Mama now fell into two broad categories. First, there were those who had established collaborative partnerships with directors, or who were willing to develop them. For example, Kenneth Bernard's *Nightclub*, which premiered to critical acclaim in September 1970, was an automatic programming choice now that Vaccaro's Play-House of the Ridiculous was in residence at La Mama. Composed of a series of demented, perverse cabaret acts compered by Bubi, a freakish master of ceremonies, as civilization shudders to a cataclysmic halt outside, *Nightclub*'s loose, compartmentalized structure gave Vaccaro and his performers free rein to expand theatrically on Bernard's text. Vaccaro cast both Ondine and Mary Woronov as dual incarnations of Bubi, "like mirror images of doom," as Woronov puts it: "I repeated the same line seconds behind Ondine; he sincere, I mocking; he feminine; I masculine" (2000, 131). Similarly, Leon Katz's chilling new version of the Jewish ghost story, *The Dybbuk* (1971), positively invited directorial intervention. Commissioned to be directed by Rina Yerushalmi, a young Israeli director then being championed by Stewart, and a former student of Katz's, this piece (like *Dracula: Sabbat*) is full of "supernatural" stage directions wide open to personal interpretation. "Rina's sense of theater is extraordinary," Katz notes, "so I really wrote it for her to do."

The second category of writers favored at La Mama around the turn of the decade consisted of those who, rather than looking to directors to bring their own theatrical ideas to bear on a raw text, had chosen either to direct or to star in their own work (or both). In so doing, they could stamp their material with a particular personal vision. Such solo strategies, virtually unheard of in the professional theater, were relatively unusual even off-off-Broadway throughout most of the 1960s, but, perhaps not coincidentally, became an increasingly familiar feature of the scene just as directors were gaining more clout.

Camp Travesties

The trailblazer of this new direction was Tom Eyen. Having established himself, mid-decade, as one of off-off-Broadway's leading playwrights, with one-acts such as *The White Whore and The Bit Player* and *Why Hanna's Skirts Won't Stay Down*, Eyen built on these successes by repackaging himself, from 1967, as a "repertory company," the Theatre of the Eye. He drew on a small group of regular collaborators, but this was not really a company in anything but name. Eyen simply used the title as a means of maintaining control over his work: venue programmers were promised a complete package rather than a play that would need resourcing. A prolific writer (one 1970 estimate cited twenty-two plays and ten musicals to date), Eyen almost always directed his own texts, although he occasionally entrusted cohorts like Neil Flanagan and Ron Link with the task, or credited his (fictitious) identical twin brother, "Jerome." Eyen's work appeared all over the off-off scene, and with particular regularity at La Mama.

Eyen's control over the production process meant that his work, which had always drawn on his previous experience as a revue-club sketch-writer, began increasingly to resemble a kind of Lower East Side version of the Ziegfeld Follies. Where his early plays had each needed just two or three actors, Theatre of the Eye productions habitually boasted all-singing, all-dancing casts of over a dozen. The texts for these pieces feature few stage directions and tend to read simply as strings of rhythmic comic patter and one-liners. Eyen would leave staging and choreography to the rehearsal process, where, like a show-man arranging his chorus line, he would build the presentation using—as Michael Smith noted of *Sarah B. Divine* (La Mama, 1967)—"varieties of cho-rus speaking and crisply patterned movement. . . . The flow is maintained almost perfectly from beginning to end—a tour de force of both writing and staging" (1967c).

The high-theatrical antics could also give rise to moments of unexpected poignancy or tenderness. *Sarah B. Divine* sends a cast of thirteen on a whistle-stop musical tour of the life of Sarah Bernhardt, with cameo appearances by the likes of Oscar Wilde and Eleanora Duse. Yet the relentlessly snappy pace of the play becomes indicative of Bernhardt's own tragic-heroic inability to slow down or age gracefully. In the final scene, set in 1922, Eyen's four differ-ent incarnations of Sarah (is any one of her performed personae the "real" Bernhardt?) discuss with each other the next job, and the next one: "What are we doing tonight?" / "*Joan of Lorraine*—the four thousandth performance!" / . . . "Do not forget to pack for our Fifth Farewell American tour!" . . . "I am nineteen—going on seventy-four" (Eyen 1971, 163–64).

Pointed as it often was, however, Eyen's work was increasingly dominated by his kaleidoscopic staging arrangements. In 1969's *The No Plays*, for exam-ple (also La Mama), there was "no play" as such, just a series of sketches mer-cilessly parodying the theatrical excesses of *Paradise Now, Dionysus in 69* and *Oh! Calcutta!* (or *Oh! Cowfucker!* as Eyen preferred), played by a highly phys-ical ensemble much given to partial nudity and sudden group gropes. Eyen pushed the joke further in *The Dirtiest Show in Town* (1970), which satirized New York's new trend for commercial sexploitation shows, and was itself quickly picked up for off-Broadway production. ("Makes *Oh! Calcutta!* look like *Little Women!*" the advertising declared gleefully.) Ostensibly "a docu-mentary on the destructive effects of air, water and mind pollution in New York City," *The Dirtiest Show* was performed on a dazzling white set by actors constantly jumping in and out of clean white costumes. Its skitlike scenes invariably ended with the delighted discovery that someone or something was "dirty"—whether physically, morally, or spiritually. The comedy was broad, and the sex simulations graphic, but Eyen's underlying attack on contempo-rary hypocrisies was nonetheless clear. "[It's] much less prurient, though not less explicit, than *Oh! Calcutta!*" wrote *Variety*'s Sege, "and nowhere near as self-conscious as *Hair*." Eyen's directorial orchestration of his material attracted particular attention: "It resembles the structure of a Godard movie, complete with cuts and cross-cuts" (Sege 1970); "some critics have compared the abstract, surrealistic style of *The Dirtiest Show* to Jerzy Grotowski's Polish Laboratory Theatre productions" (Klemesrud 1970, 5). Thanks partly to such implausible comparisons, the Theatre of the Eye was that year awarded an eight-thousand-dollar Guggenheim grant. Eyen professed himself both amused and astonished: "I ask myself, 'Why did they give it to a person like me?'" (Klemesrud 1970, 5).

The year 1970 saw a breakthrough of a different sort for Charles Ludlam's Ridiculous Theatrical Company, another group where creative control rested with the resident playwright-director. Following Ludlam's acrimonious split with Vaccaro over *Conquest of the Universe* in 1967, his newly formed splinter company had taken up residence at Tambellini's Gate Theatre, a run-down cinema where they could perform at midnight, after the movie program was over. With a proscenium stage and curtains, this satisfied Ludlam's desire to perform his pasted-together plays in a "real theater." Performing in a haze of incense and pot smoke, the company built up a nocturnal cult following with new plays like *Turds in Hell* and *The Grand Tarot*—large-cast pieces that, in the established Ridiculous manner, were consciously unwieldy, grotesque, and "ill-made." By 1969, however, it was clear to Ludlam "that we couldn't continue in that direction indefinitely. I took the winter off . . . and wrote a play that was very formal and traditional, much more focused and carefully worked out than our previous ones" (1992, 24). He cannily arranged to premiere *Bluebeard* at La Mama, in March 1970, so as to capture a broader audience than previously, and though his contractual dispute with Stewart (see chapter 13) cut the run short, the company's ejection from La Mama had publicity value of its own. Critics from major papers like the *Times* and *Wall Street Journal* now sought the company out at their unlikely substitute venue, Christopher's End—a dingy gay bar at the foot of Christopher Street, where a platform had to be erected on the bar to extend the playing area. The reviews were mostly raves, and helped earn Ludlam's company their first grants.

Bluebeard can be considered "formal and traditional" only in relative terms. Though it has a tighter narrative through-line, this is every bit as much a collage play as Ludlam's earlier pieces, drawing prominently on H. G. Wells's *The Island of Doctor Moreau* and Marlowe's *Doctor Faustus*. This Bluebeard, rather than simply killing his wives, conducts horrific experiments on them in the name of science—experiments that, like Faustus's black arts, threaten his eternal soul and prompt furious conflict between his "good" and "bad" angels. In tone, the play is balanced somewhere between Victorian melodrama and B-movie schlock horror (genres that are not, perhaps, that far apart): Bluebeard's servants are terrorized into submission with dark threats of torture, to which they respond, recurringly and hilariously, "No, no, not the House of Pain!" (Ludlam 1989, 117). Bluebeard also does a nice line in villainous mustache-twirling. When asked, "Have you no desire for Miss Cubbidge?" he replies, thoughtfully: "She is not without a certain cadaverous charm" (122). He subsequently seduces her in a ludicrous, seminude romp of a sex scene that became one of the *Bluebeard*'s most famous sequences.

The play's use of camp pastiche would be easy to overplay, but Ludlam had tailor-made it for his established ensemble. Where the appeal of Eyen's work was largely in his staging, Ludlam's was all about the actors. The Ridiculous Theatrical Company had evolved into a theatrical family, which Ludlam led in the fashion of a Victorian actor-manager. Their plays developed organically, with scripts being constantly revised and developed through rehearsals and performances, so that roles gelled perfectly with performers. *Bluebeard*'s principals were all praised individually by critics, for their comic mastery of the stock "types" they reinvigorated—Bill Vehr as matinee idol Rodney, Black-Eyed Susan as the ingenue Sybil, Lola Pashalinski as the matronly Miss Cubbidge, John Brockmeyer as the grotesque servant Sheemish. In each case, there was a vivid sense that the actors were playing themselves playing at character-acting: Ludlam had taken the actor-as-personality principle pioneered by Kornfeld and Vaccaro, and returned it to a kind of playful innocence, in the childlike "make-believe" of traditional theatrical artifice. Ludlam himself wore a bristling, bright blue paste-on beard, and added delightfully twisted touches, such as a pinky ring worn over rubber laboratory gloves. "Bluebeard is not a role for Ludlam, the actor," Martin Washburn argued in the *Voice*: "He *becomes* Bluebeard, because he knows all the passwords, the right way to do this and that movement. . . . He is like a child who is making a magic ogre puppet work" (1970a).

Crucially, though, this playfulness also contained very adult undertones: for Stefan Brecht, Ludlam's Bluebeard seemed reminiscent of "mad doctors" as diverse as Albert Einstein, Henry Kissinger, and Wernher von Braun (1986, 83). This points to the darker edge of satire beneath the overt hilarity: in this version of the myth, the baron's experiments are aimed at creating an "unnatural" blurring of sex and gender binaries: his wives are experimented on in his attempts to create a "third sex"—a Victorian term for homosexuals. Drag artist

Mario Montez appeared as one of *Bluebeard*'s failed experiments, Lamia the Leopard Woman: "Eecht! Is that a mound of Venus or a penis?" declares Rodney when shown Lamia's privates, to which s/he replies, "*(perplexed)* I wish I knew" (130). In the final scene, as the latest victim of Bluebeard's experiments, Sybil appears, naked but for high-heeled "fuck-me pumps" and a grotesque "third genital" protruding from her crotch. Such experimental gender-bending renders *Bluebeard* as a wicked satire on quasi-scientific, pathologizing attitudes to sexuality.

In this respect, *Bluebeard* was very much in tune with its times, appearing the year after Greenwich Village's Stonewall Riots—three nights of protest and unrest sparked by police harassment of the Stonewall Inn's gay and lesbian clientele, which marked the beginning of the gay liberation movement. Camp performance of all varieties was now firmly in vogue, at least among the young and hip for whom downtown gay had become radical(ly tacky) chic, and this trend produced some unlikely stage stars. Jackie Curtis, for example, one of a bevy of drag queens who were then part of the Warhol entourage, also became a protégé of Ellen Stewart's—initially via John Vaccaro, who directed Curtis's 1970 play *Heaven Grand in Amber Orbit*, and then as writer-director-performer in his own right. Curtis's most ambitious project was *Vain Victory*, which opened at La Mama in May 1971 before transferring to a four-month run at another off-off space, the Workshop for the Player's Art (WPA), on the Bowery. This glitter-speckled low-camp travesty of Hollywood musical clichés featured a sixteen-strong cast, including Curtis himself (out of drag this time as glam rock singer Blue Denim) and fellow Warhol "superstars" Candy Darling, Eric Emerson, and (the ubiquitous) Mario Montez. This show was, Mel Gussow suggested in the *Times*, best treated as "unabashed trash [that] does not even try to raise the level of the material, to turn it, as Ludlam does, into myth—and art." Poorly structured and badly written as it may have been, however, "the delivery is so ingenuous as to make almost the worst line excusable" (Gussow 1971). Curtis, in particular, was celebrated as a performer whose attraction lay in his ability to seem "somehow truthful and touching even when the material is trashy and patently false; he is graceful in his clumsiness, beautiful in his plainness" (Smith 1974b).

The Presentation of Self

Given that the impact of a camp line lies as much in the tone and attitude of its delivery as in its phrasing, it is no surprise that the camp-travesty genre was largely defined by multitasking theater artists like Ludlam, Eyen, and Curtis. Satire and pastiche were not, however, the only forms of individualistic theater-making to develop during this period. At the Old Reliable, for example, Robert Patrick's love of overtly campy material—best showcased in *Joyce Dynel*—did not prevent him coming up with a much more "sincere" piece like *One Person* (1969), a self-performed monologue delivered to a former lover who is ostensibly seated among the audience. This piece uses direct verbal address and mimed visual indicators to tell the story of a short but apparently passionate relationship. Constantly shifting pace and location—from, for example, a quiet bedroom scene to a manic barroom—the play is, for its period, unusually frank and vivid in its portrait of gay sexuality and community. Funny, moving, and often neatly understated, *One Person* is similar in approach to the brand of monologue-based solo performance developed by Tim Miller, also on the Lower East Side, more than a decade later. Miller's approach is overtly autobiographical, but observers of *One Person* also sensed a disarming honesty, an "absolute unity between actor and material. Patrick is so utterly believable that you cannot help feeling these experiences are his. Yet the artist's hand is clearly there. He presents his material, he doesn't impose it" (Brukenfeld 1969).

This period saw the beginnings of the loosely defined solo performance genre that would become known as performance art. Developments in visual art practice, in which artists were beginning to place themselves within their works, using their own bodies as their primary media, were paralleled in the alternative theater world by actors presenting themselves, as performative variations on themselves. Charles Stanley, for example, became known not only for his show-stealing performances in other people's plays, but for untitled, semi-improvised spectacles—not quite dance; not quite theater. One of his earliest such pieces, at the Caffe Cino on July 4, 1967, was performed in homage to Joe Cino, as Stanley worked through his own agony at his friend's death using monologue, movement, and bizarre shifts of costume. In the same year, Jack Smith also began to present a series of solo performances, advertised as the work of the "Reptilian Theatrical Company," at his own loft apartment at 36 Greene Street. These pieces frequently ran on into the small hours, as Smith pottered around the space, exhibiting slides, toying with objects, and improvising strange, elongated monologues full of lengthy silences. The fascination for Smith's small but devoted band of spectators was the sheer strangeness of his presence, his ability to create moments of magic out of the most seemingly banal details. Several of these pieces are docu mented in loving detail by Stefan Brecht in the opening chapter of *Queer Theatre.*

The most celebrated self-performer of the period, however, was Jeff Weiss—yet another artist sponsored by La Mama. Weiss wrote and appeared in his own material under the direction of his lover, Ricardo Martinez, with whom he shared a close personal understanding. The results were extraordinary, as the superlatives showered on Weiss by interviewees for this book demonstrate: "He's just the greatest" (O'Horgan); "a dazzling virtuoso, a consummate theater craftsman in every area" (Patrick); "in Ludlam's league as an actor" (Hoffman); "The best things ever done at La Mama were by Jeff Weiss" (Kornfeld). Very much his own creation, Weiss was untrained as an actor, having quit Stella Adler's class—which he saw as an "offensive lesson in group therapy" (Gruen 1967)—after just one session. In 1964, he was spotted waiting tables at La Mama by playwright Robert Sealy, who asked him to star, as a waiter, in his café-set play *Waiting Boy*. Weiss was an instant hit, and became fascinated by his ability to manipulate audience reactions.

Weiss's first, one-man play, *And That's How the Rent Gets Paid*, premiered at La Mama in August 1966. Welcoming the audience into his "home," he regaled them with tales of his attempts to raise the cash to pay his back rent, while indulging tangentially in "a cascade of fantasies, reminiscences, meditations, poetry-readings and miscellaneous schticks" (Novick 1966). Full of ad-libs and improvised asides, Weiss's performance was as compelling as a good stand-up routine, but it also grew increasingly disturbing, as the exhibition of wit gradually gave way to the exhibition of seemingly very real neuroses. The underlying dramatic premise of this "frightening study in paralyzing anxiety" (Gruen 1967) was that—as William Hoffman explains—"the actor you're seeing appears to be having a nervous breakdown. [And] I don't know anyone who saw through it, who felt that he was merely acting. It was totally convincing."

In person as well as onstage, Weiss was wildly eccentric, given to adopting a bewildering array of voices and personae. Indeed, among the downtown theater community, he was widely believed to be not quite sane: Robert Patrick recalls him carrying a draft exemption certificate in his wallet, stating he was schizophrenic—though this may also have been part of his "act." All of Weiss's self-performed stage characters were mentally unstable in one respect or another, yet as those who worked with him stress, he was never less than totally focused and disciplined in rehearsal and onstage. The lava-flow intensity of his performances apparently stemmed from his ability to focus and channel his eccentricities into utterly believable characterizations. Larry Kornfeld's wife Margaret, then in training as a psychotherapist, recalls Weiss's second play, *A Funny Walk Home*, as revelatory, because it helped her to balance the clinical, objective view of insanity she had encountered in textbooks with a more personal, compassionate understanding of the interior life of a troubled mind. "Jeff made being unhinged seem human, not frightening," she notes, "and that's a gift."

A Funny Walk Home was one of the late, great Caffe Cino performances: premiering in February 1967, just a month before Joe Cino's death, it had audiences lining up around the block, in the snow, trying to get in. Weiss starred as Stephen Kleppinger (in a hand-corrected manuscript, "Steve" is repeatedly substituted for the crossed-out "Jeff"), a young man returning home to his family after thirteen years in a mental asylum. "Home," however, is again the theater space itself: prior to the performance proper, the two actors playing Stephen's parents (Claris Nelson featured as Mom) moved about the Cino audience along with the waiters, handing out streamers, balloons, and invitations to the homecoming party. In the first scene, they then explain to these "guests"—in a kind of stiff double-act—that Stephen was sent away for smiling and giggling too much as a child: unable to take life "seriously," he was institutionalized, has been subjected to fifteen sets of shock treatment and a lobotomy, and is now "as serious as they come," and ready to return home (Weiss 1967, 6). These assertions, however, are undermined by the next stage of the play, in which Steve's three letters home are played as voice-overs, interspersed with too-jolly party music, while his parents make ready for his arrival. These darkly ironic letters indicate that Steve is fully aware of what role he must play to be freed from the asylum: "I am so moved by my joylessness! I know you'll be more than pleased when you see me! I wept all day yesterday" (10). More disturbingly, they are also punctuated by unsettling outbursts of paranoia, religious fervor, anti-Semitism, and self-contradictory political remarks (apparently designed for both his reactionary-Republican father and his bourgeois-liberal mother). There is even a sideways, manifestly self-indulgent swipe at the *Village Voice* critic who had accused *And That's How the Rent Gets Paid* of "soul baring . . . self-indulgence": "is Julius Novick one of ours, [Mom]? Another little Jewish boy from the Bronx, moneyed and over-educated, slumming it for a price" (9).

The letters build both anticipation and apprehension prior to Weiss's arrival, through the street door of the Cino itself. The ensuing family reunion, the stage directions specify, is "most awkward and distressing," as the parents fumble to hug and kiss the prodigal son, and then struggle to find things to say to him, talking in polite banalities. The scene is both excruciating and hilarious as an evocation of middle-class repression, but abruptly changes gear as Steve is introduced to his younger brother, Richard Nixon Kleppinger, whom he has never met. Suddenly overcome by an outpouring of pent-up need for emotional contact, Steve clamps his sibling in a vicelike embrace,

> turning slowly in a kind of emotionally charged dance: he's touching Richard's hair now . . . feeling him . . . pressing Richard ever more closely, as if to absorb his younger brother's body. The parents are moved. Richard gasps and begins desperately trying to push his brother away. His body is off the floor now, dangling in Steve's grip. . . . Steve is staring up into the lights, sobbing, blinded, turning in a trance. (17)

Worriedly wondering whether she should do something to help, his mother climbs up on a chair to judge the expression on Steve's upturned face: "Bill. Oh, Bill," she cries with relief, "Get on up here. I want you to share this moment with me . . . I think they're real tears, Bill. Emotion, feeling, pouring out of him" (17–18).

The scene is authentically grotesque—simultaneously horrific and absurdly funny—as the family attempts to respond to an intensity of feeling for which they have no reference points. Yet this is only the beginning: as the play goes on, Steve's behavior becomes ever more erratic, veering through virtuoso fascist monologues on the need to burn art, destroy great architecture, and establish "a world of plastic and Saran Wrap" (21). The content is clearly satiric, but the force of Steve's convictions—even on the page—is unnerving. So too are his vivid memories of having been "cuddled" rather too closely by his father as a child. This revelation prompts a stomach-turning sequence in which first father and son, and then father and mother, roll around on the floor in each other's embrace like children playing a wrestling game. Then, just as mother is requesting rather too forcefully to roll around the floor with her son, a further twist is provided by the arrival of the priest, Father Duncombe, whose "phony liberal" sympathies have prompted him to dress up in blackface, with a falsely bulbous "Jewish" nose.

By this stage, the play has become hallucinatory—psychotic even; a savagely funny externalization of all-American trauma. The audience, however, is never allowed simply to sit back and laugh: they are the guests at Steve's homecoming, and they have become, he suggests eventually, the fascinated voyeurs at "a street accident." Why don't they intervene to stop this, he asks:

"You're the only ones capable of pulling us up short, if you care enough to make the effort" (30). Cino audience members recall the plea as direct and genuine, rather than merely rhetorical. When no one from the audience attempted to stop the action, however, Weiss would initiate the final stage of the depravity: "I'm gonna write a poem. But the only one worth writing anymore. A poem of anarchy and passion and sickness and death" (30). Throwing his mother to the floor, Steve rapes her, while father covers them with a sheet, for decency's sake. Under the sheet, Mom swells up pregnant; father is then born, "as Steve," through her legs—completing their role reversal. Meanwhile, Steve physically assaults the priest, smearing his blackface, pulling off his nose, and driving him out of the Cino. His parents turn on him, beating and kicking him for his lack of hospitality, demanding he apologize to the guests/audience. In response, he strangles his father.

Read off the page, the climax to the piece seems altogether too excessive—unstageable, even. This is, perhaps, why Weiss never allowed his plays to be published: the written texts are inseparable from his own conception and execution of the performance. Certainly, those who saw it agree that Weiss made the demented conclusion to A *Funny Walk Home* terrifyingly persuasive: "The audience were furious," Claris Nelson recalls, "because they'd been made somehow responsible for this [mayhem]. Except that during the last performance, he stopped it, because many of the audience were people who had seen it before, and they'd sneaked back in, and they still wouldn't stop it. So he said well, I started this, so I think I'll stop it." At several performances, audience members did in fact intervene to stop the show when invited to (at which point the cast would simply bow and exit): "Those of us who know too much about the lobotomized intertness of theatre audiences," Ross Wetzsteon wrote, "should marvel at the fact" (1967).

By the end of the play, Wetzsteon reported, Weiss was "totally exhausted—emotionally, physically, spiritually [and] drenched in sweat and tears." This absolute commitment to the role was for Wetzsteon the antithesis of the campy evasiveness he had so disliked in Ondine's performance as Scrooge in the Cino's *Christmas Carol*, two months earlier. Indeed, Weiss brought such "unrelieved intensity" and "passionate honesty" to the role of the madman (shades of Artaud?) that the play seemed to Wetzsteon to blur the line between drama and life itself: this was "easily the most powerful and stirring performance I've seen in years," but also "one of the most moving and harrowing experiences I've ever had—and I don't just mean 'in the theater.'"

A *Funny Walk Home* won Weiss an Obie award, an achievement he repeated in 1969 with his next play, *The International Wrestling Match*, at La Mama. Staged within a wrestling ring, this was presented as a confrontation between two figures representing different sides of the same psyche. As "Quentin" (an irreverent allusion to Arthur Miller's autobiographical hero in *After the Fall*), Weiss swapped fascist demagoguery for radical agitation, planning a vague, maniacal coup against oppressive state forces, while being interrogated, shrinklike, by Richard Portnow, as "Jean Paul van Fostex" (a punning conflation of La Mama's most celebrated playwrights). This premise, Wetzsteon suggested in the *Voice*, could be read as "an objectification of schizophrenia" (1969a): Weiss the playwright listening to Weiss the madman. The second act developed this scheme by presenting a play-within-a-play purporting to be van Fostex's stylized dramatization (pastiching Foster and van Itallie) of the material previously introduced in Quentin's unhinged ranting. Here, however, Weiss the playwright may have overreached himself somewhat: while the first act was as good a demonstration as ever of his "wildly undisciplined, even volcanic genius," Wetzsteon wrote, the second "attempts to objectify his emotions, and that's simply not his style." With a painfully unwieldy running time of almost four hours, *The International Wrestling Match* demonstrated the perils, as well as the advantages, of Weiss's "self-indulgently" individualistic approach.

Apocalypse Hurrah

Weiss's piece had originally been scheduled, along with Eyen's *No Plays*, to inaugurate La Mama's new, foundation-funded premises on East Fourth Street, in January 1969. Owing to delays in the building-conversion schedule, however, these productions—the first La Mama shows since vacating the Second Avenue premises in April 1968—had to be staged in temporary accommodations on St. Mark's Place. When the new venue finally opened in April, it was with another Eyen production, *Caution: A Love Story,* and another Jeff Weiss vehicle, Julie Bovasso's *Gloria and Esperanza,* in which Bovasso costarred, and which she also directed. She too had joined the ranks of off-off-Broadway "auteurs," more than a decade after her last production with Tempo Theatre.

Bovasso's one previous La Mama outing as writer-director-performer had been *The Moondreamers,* in February 1968. Consisting of well over three hours of revue acts, dance routines, minstrel songs, and self-referential showbiz shtick, it too was widely dismissed as unforgivably self-indulgent. Michael

Smith, however, while sympathizing with the many who walked out early, argued that the excessive length of the show was central to its impact: the "elaborately tacky, overcrowded manner" in which it "interminably balloons into elephantine low farce" seemed to him "a deviously subtle formal irony," given that Bovasso's subject matter was "contemporary America, its pernicious excess and grotesque, ill-proportioned overabundance" (1968a, 33). The *Times* concurred that "unlike the 'camp' crowd, [Bovasso] finds nothing charming in the empty rattle of a 1934 tap routine. . . . She finds the hollowness and brutality of yesterday's and today's pop culture the stuff of nightmares, and she [has] transferred the nightmare to the stage of the La Mama with grisly finesse" (Sullivan 1968a).

Running a full four hours, and with a cast of forty-three crammed onto the postage-stamp proscenium stage in La Mama's new, sixty-seat studio, *Gloria and Esperanza* pushed this "bloated revue" strategy still further, and to greater acclaim. Opening with an extended soft-shoe patter from Bovasso and Weiss as the title characters, it quickly moved on to present an eight-foot-tall dancing chicken and an aggressive, large-scale confrontation between soldiers and Maoist agitators, staged as a tango routine—and all this within the first scene. "Considered solely as showmanship, as a collection of skits," Ross Wetzsteon wrote, "the evening is nothing less than brilliant, [displaying] a masterful sense of stage gamesmanship and theatrical imagery" (1969c). The extended psychiatrist's office sequence, in which Weiss was grilled by a midget shrink (Leonard Hicks) clearly crazier than he, was for Wetzsteon "one of the most hilarious scenes I've ever seen, through Miss Bovasso's skilful directing of facial nuance and artfully bizarre use of the most ordinary dialogue." Similarly, Tom O'Horgan recalls a moment in which the entire cast vacated the stage and crammed themselves in among the audience, watching the empty stage to the sound of a chorus of dogs barking "Jingle Bells," as "the most remarkable thing I've ever seen in the theater."

Bovasso clearly set out to entertain, but there is far more to the play than that: indeed, her bleakly sardonic use of farce and black comedy was in many ways congruent with Weiss's own work. As the Candide-like poet, Julius Esperanza, Weiss played bewildered innocence rather than mounting insanity, but with the same underlying conviction. Julius is haunted by dark, prophetic visions, and foresees an apocalypse he is powerless to stop: "You don't seem to realize what's going on out there. Don't you know what's going on out there?" he demands in his opening speech, of fellow players and audience alike (Poland and Mailman 1972, 319). Not wishing to hear about it, his girlfriend Gloria hands him a straw hat and cane and begins high-kicking. He joins in, reluctantly, but they are clearly incompatible: as the play develops its soap-opera-style parallel narratives, Esperanza finds himself rejected, psychoanalyzed, and arrested, always by ridiculous cartoon figures, while Gloria—in his absence—uncovers the book in which he records his most secret, most terrible visions, and tries to find a buyer for it. (He is, after all, a famous poet, so he has to be worth something.) She has to cut her landlord in on the deal (in lieu of rent), as well as her mailman (who blackmails her), and her tax inspector, Von Schtutt (whom she has been evading). On reading the secret book, however, Von Schtutt declares that "there's no dramatic action, the central character hasn't got any balls, and the visions and revelations stink" (347). He proposes a radical overhaul of the material—"muck it up a little"—in order to sell it to a theatrical producer.

It gradually becomes clear that the audience is watching the very show that has been made from Von Schtutt's bastardized version of Esperanza's visions, "the Revelations Revue" (350). As the play develops, it moves from a vaudeville version of late 1960s America, with its hippies and agitators, soldiers and politicians, into a high-Victorian version of the declining Roman Empire—with centurions and gladiators who brutally massacre the helpless Christians in artfully choreographed slow motion, accompanied by the music of *L'Orphee* and "anguished cries, recorded in the ancient Greek" (346). From here, the play moves inexorably toward its final, nightclub-cabaret scene, starring an array of Catholic saints (a drag version of St. Theresa performs a languorous striptease), warring angels and devils, and the four horsewomen of the Apocalypse. Finally, in a spectacular dance sequence, a dragon steals an infant from the arms of "the Woman Clothed in the Sun," just as in St. John's Revelations. (The old ones, it seems, are still the best.)

Bovasso thus staged a kind of demented, showbiz version of the apocalyptic fears apparent in the writings of many American playwrights and novelists of this period (something similar, though less effective, is apparent in Sam Shepard's *Operation Sidewinder*, staged the following year at Lincoln Center). The excess would have seemed merely gratuitous, however, were it not underpinned by a sense of Esperanza fighting for his very soul. His key dramatic confrontation is with Black Jack Sinistre, a cool figure clad in black leather, with one hand forever hidden deep in his pocket: this hand, we are told, held the hand-grenade that Jack blew up in the face of God. Even given his B-movie-villain appearance, the mythic resonances of this figure hover eerily around him: Sinistre is the Devil, the orchestrator of the apocalypse, but he is also Esperanza's own left hand, his own dark fears. This literalization of internal conflict is reminiscent of Weiss's *Wrestling Match*, and indeed, in the play's final moments, Julius and Jack become locked in a wrestling grip (which, given the biblical context, also evokes Jacob's Old Testament confrontation with the angel). The showstopping finale to the Revelations Revue grinds to a halt as Julius invades the stage to tackle his nemesis, and then, as "the struggle reaches a climax . . . the death grip gradually becomes an embrace" (351). After all the sound and fury, the audience is left with this simple, silent image, and an oblique, unspoken question. *Gloria and Esperanza* was regarded by Jerry Tallmer as "a miracle, a mythopoeic 'fireworks display' with strands going back to Joyce, Cocteau, Fellini, Jean Vigo, Ionesco himself" (1991, 31), and netted Bovasso three Obie awards for acting, writing, and directing. "[It] justifies everything La Mama and Ellen Stewart—and Julie Bovasso—have been struggling for all these years," Tallmer wrote, "but Julie, dear—edit, edit" (1969).

Troupe Escalations

With Weiss, Bovasso, and Eyen dominating both of La Mama's "grand reopening" programs in 1969, it seemed that Ellen Stewart was now championing the the playwright-auteur model as the next "big idea." All three had further shows at the venue over the next couple of years, but Stewart shifted gear again, prioritizing the promotion of director-driven ensembles. In the spring of 1970, following the departure of Tom O'Horgan the previous fall, she announced the creation of a whole raft of new La Mama troupes. In addition to hosting the Theatre of the Eye and the Play-House of the Ridiculous, La Mama would now also sponsor the activities of three new, ethnically specific companies—the Asian American Repertory Company (directed by Ching Yeh, formerly of *The Hawk*'s Keystone Company), the Jarboro Troupe (African American), and the Bilingual Company (Hispanic). Meanwhile, Joel Zwick would take the reins of "La Mama Plexus," a group primarily dedicated to ongoing workshop experiments rather than public performance. There were also two, more public standard-bearers for the La Mama name. La Mama Repertory Company, effectively the flagship replacement for O'Horgan's troupe, was to be directed by Andrei Serban, a young Romanian director whom Stewart had discovered on her travels to European theater festivals. (In 1969, she invited him to work at La Mama, persuading the Ford Foundation to sponsor his move.) Meanwhile, La Mama ETC Company would be co-directed by Wilford Leach and John Braswell, both professors at Sarah Lawrence College. With Leach also a writer and Braswell a composer and actor, they generated their own new, musically oriented work, often adapting existing literary texts—such as the Victorian vampire tale *Carmilla* (1970).

Stewart's creation of this new collection of companies demonstrated once again her canny ability to make the most of the evolving grant-funding situation. The diversity of these new groups meant that La Mama could now target all kinds of niche grants aimed at promoting intercultural understanding and international exchange. Yet these ensembles were no mere fund-raising gimmick: the seeds of La Mama's culturally inclusive profile had been sown during its earliest days, and from Stewart's point of view, her best-laid plans were now coming to fruition. Serban's work, in particular, came to epitomize her dream of a truly international theater dependent on sound, spectacle, and music rather than the English language (of which he initially had only a limited command). The first production by the new La Mama Repertory Company, in the spring of 1970, was a complementary double bill of *Arden of Faversham* and *Ubu*. With the first, a domestic tragedy by an anonymous Elizabethan playwright, Serban pared the text down to its bare bones, to create a production using

> every possible sensory device to embody in theatrical terms the violence, lust and duplicity that constitute the play's basic elements. Actors' faces, contorted with fury, sensuality, mendacity, panic, were caught in the flare of candlelight or glare of flashlight on the black stage. Sibilant whisperings, hisses, gasps, scrapings, rhythmic tappings and poundings on the floor suggested unnameable evils. (Lester 1970)

Similarly, with *Ubu*, fragmented segments of Alfred Jarry's plays were rearranged into a collage of theatrical excess, full of slapstick and offal. Serban's strengths, as these pieces indicated, lay in using classic texts as malleable raw material for creating his own theatrical visions, rather than in working with living playwrights.

Serban's concern with developing a sensory and essentially antiliterary theater was further underlined as he began work on what became his most famous production, the five-hour long *Greek Trilogy*. Consisting of heavily adapted versions of Euripides' *Medea*, Sophocles' *Electra*, and Euripedes' *The Trojan Women* (first produced, respectively, in 1972, 1973, and 1974), the finished trilogy first appeared in October 1974, to near-universal acclaim. Eschewing English translations, Serban selected and adapted freely from various renditions of the ancient Greek and Latin texts, read aloud to him by scholars. Working closely with the young composer Elizabeth Swados, he then constructed a sound score from the chosen fragments, which the actors memorized phonetically—to create what Julius Novick described in the *Times* as a startling symphony of "singing, chanting, keening, whispering, moaning, guttural shouting" (1974). The absence of anything resembling communicative speech, Novick observed, meant that "a great deal is lost . . . but a great deal is gained as well. The high strangeness of the unfamiliar sounds make us listen differently, and feel differently."

The trilogy also made impressive use of contrasting spatial dynamics. *Medea*, for example, was originally staged in a long, narrow basement rehearsal room at La Mama: the audience were led downstairs via an eerie, candlelit journey, and seated down either side of the claustrophobic space. For *The Trojan Women*, by contrast, Serban adopted a promenade approach, with performers leading the audience from site to site across a large expanse of floor. This latter configuration was possible because the completed *Greek Trilogy* was presented as the premiere performance in La Mama's newest theater space, the hangarlike "Annexe"—located in a large building a few doors west from the East Fourth Street headquarters. (Further foundation grants financed the conversion of this former television studio, when it became clear that Serban needed more spatial options than were available in La Mama's existing, still relatively small theaters.) Despite its name, the Annexe quickly became La Mama's showcase space, its size and flexibility enabling further development of the visually oriented, director-led theater that Stewart was now prioritizing. It also eventually enabled her to host work by visiting directors of international stature, such as Tadeusz Kantor, in 1979, and Peter Brook, in 1980. Brook had been a mentor figure for Serban, whose *Greek Trilogy* itself became recognized as a seminal work of the "international avant-garde"—eventually touring to forty festivals in fifteen different countries over a five-year period.

Serban's work for La Mama deserves extended critical examination, but it also falls beyond the proper scope of this book. Far from being products of the New York "underground," as the plays of Eyen, Bovasso, and Weiss still clearly were, Serban's productions were instead indicative of two new, director-led trajectories that came to characterize the alternative theater of the 1970s. On the one hand, there was an increasing preference for staging reexamined classics, rather than new plays—a tendency also apparent in the foundation of "next generation" off-off-Broadway companies such as the

Classic Stage Company, the Roundabout Theatre, and the Jean Cocteau Repertory Company (all of which quickly sought professional, "off-Broadway" status). On the other hand, the *Greek Trilogy* was also a leading example of the new trend for a spectacle-based theater that used language (if at all) in a largely abstract, nonreferential manner. Other prime exponents of this "theater of images" were Robert Wilson and Richard Foreman, both of whom also came to prominence in New York around the turn of the decade.

Unsurprisingly, these new developments were met with skepticism by many first-generation off-off-Broadway playwrights. "In the theater, the director becomes important when you don't have a live product," William Hoffman contends, "so you have to produce classics. You have to come up with radical new theories for doing dead plays." For Robert Patrick, the new decade's emphasis on imagistic spectacle was indicative of the experimental theater's changing cultural standing: publicity and exposure, he argues, brought a new, fashion-conscious, "avant-garde" audience whose interests lay less in being challenged than in experiencing off-the-wall sensation. That development was illustrated quite literally, Patrick suggests, by Serban's *Trojan Women*:

> When Andromache, or whoever, jumps off the wall of Troy, there was this huge slanted wall built, with two-by-fours laying across it as if it were a ladder. And the girl fell down it for five minutes, catching onto these various things, just as if she were falling on a wall. For five minutes, with great long blonde hair, she rolled down it striking pose after pose. This is high Victorian theater! Come and see Andromache fall down the wall! See bare-breasted priestesses goad the captured Trojan women! It was lovely, but it was big, tableaux-vivant Victorian theater.

A few dissenting critics also felt that the high-artistic seriousness of the new avant-garde spectacles might simply be masking the emperor's new clothes. "Most of [Swados's] ritualistic music is merely bad Carl Orff, meaning rather bad," *New York*'s Alan Rich wrote of *The Trojan Women*, adding that "even with two years of Xenophon under my belt, I could pick out only one phrase [from the chanted text]: 'Hey, moussaka, nonny no'" (1974).

An Accidental Auteur

Whether or not such criticisms are fair, the views of Hoffman, Patrick, and other unimpressed playwrights were clearly bound up in part with a sense of betrayal. La Mama, it seemed, was no longer "dedicated to the playwright." "It is becoming clear," Michael Smith wrote in the fall of 1971, "that playwrights . . . must not only write plays but create the theatre to present them. Nobody's going to do it for us." Significantly, Smith himself had just become co–artistic director of Theatre Genesis, the only established off-off venue still explicitly committed to serving the playwright's intentions (and indeed, by the early 1970s, the only one still offering free admission). Following Sam Shepard's departure for London, Smith was asked by St. Mark's to replace him, joining Mednick and Hadler on the guiding triumvirate. That December, Smith took on the role of all-round auteur to stage his first Genesis play, *Country Music*. He not only wrote and directed, but also designed the lights and contributed substantially to the set design.

Smith would, he admits, have liked very much to find a directorial partner who would bring an insightful objectivity to bear on his playwriting—just as, say, Marshall Mason did for Lanford Wilson. His experience working with Jacques Levy on *The Next Thing* in 1966 had been productive, but that collaboration was a one-off. When Smith's next play, *Captain Jack's Revenge* (see Hoffman 1971), was scheduled for production at La Mama in 1970, Smith was alarmed to discover that the director appointed by Ellen Stewart was interested only in the play's first and last acts, and proposed cutting almost the whole of the second. This act, a "play within the play" in which the naturalistic setting of a downtown artist's apartment suddenly transmutes into a Wild West campfire scene, was for Smith the conceptual hinge of the whole piece, setting up a provocative parallel between the disintegrating emotional and spiritual state of bohemian New York at the turn of the decade, and the historical decimation of Native American culture at the hands of treaty-breaking whites. Since Stewart's director seemed intent on staging another play entirely, Smith opted to step in and direct for himself—casting Ondine, once again, in the dual central role of Jack the multimedia artist and Captain Jack of the Modoc tribe.

Although the resulting production was highly praised by some, Smith himself was never quite sure about it: didn't a play this complex need a committed, outside eye to make it cohere for spectators? Lacking a directorial partner, he resolved his dilemma by writing *Country Music* as a piece that might actively benefit from direction by its author. Set in a country farmhouse kitchen, the play is built from moods and textures rather than conventional dramatic action: "There is no light in the kitchen except what spills in the windows from outside and, later, candles," the opening stage directions specify, indicating the fade into evening over the course of the first act (Poland and Mailman 1972, 496). Within moments of the play's opening, an old man, Boppo, notes that "this is my favorite time, to feel the slowness of the light leaving, leaving" (496). By giving himself control over the play's lighting and pacing, Smith could create precisely the atmosphere he imagined.

The country house setting and the evocation of mood inevitably conjured the ghost of Chekhov—a factor that Smith playfully acknowledged by pasting in a whole passage of dialogue from *The Cherry Orchard*, toward the end of the play. This provoked criticism from Michael Feingold, in the *Voice*, who lamented that Smith's grasp of characterization paled in comparison with Chekhov's. Yet, as even the play's title and dialogue makes clear, Smith's intention was less to create human drama than to evoke a sense of the eternal, natural rhythms of the country itself: "We could make it into a theatre," one character says of a tree-filled meadow, "but it already is a theatre. Free show, continuous. I don't need a lot of psychology. No explanations—over and over is good enough for me" (498). That sense of the continuous "over and over" of time and seasons is also apparent in the play's overall structure: the evening of the autumnal first act is also "the evening of the year, and my life," old Boppo notes, while the bright sunshine of morning, in the second act, brings spring-time. All the same characters are present, but some of them have mysteriously aged, as if the rhythms of life have affected them differently. A baby bear seen in the first act has also become a full-grown bear in the second, even though, in some sense, just one night has passed.

Country Music creates an exquisite blend of surreal, dreamlike images and hypernaturalistic details. The pace moves from the inexorably slow, with extended pauses focusing on the slightest of movements, to the quick, bustling activity and back-and-forth conversation of an evening meal. Music from the piano works of Beethoven is used both as an external, atmospheric accompaniment, played over the theater's sound system, and as an element internal to the action, performed on an actual piano from an offstage room. Lighting fades in and out with the subtlety of dusk and dawn. The characters punctuate the passing of time by sharing reminiscences, stories, and observations, and engage in simple, everyday activities—from chopping up vegetables to extended, passionate kissing.

Beneath the seemingly casual activity, though, there are also intimations of deeper emotional undercurrents. Something is clearly going strangely awry, for example, in the relationship between Petey and Marcus (Nevele Adams and Charles Stanley): toward the play's conclusion, Petey dresses and makes himself up as a specimen of perfect, feminine beauty, as if somehow to draw his lover's eye back to him. Yet even these relational tensions are merged with the seasonal life rhythms of the play—a factor that this couple's recitation of the Chekhov extract further underlines: "You look boldly ahead, but isn't it because you neither see nor expect anything dreadful, since life is still hidden from your young eyes? . . . You see, I was born here, my mother and father lived here, and my grandfather. I love this house, without the cherry orchard my life has no meaning for me" (507).

Knowing exactly what he was seeking, on all levels, Smith created what Michael Feingold (despite his reservations about the text) described as "a superb evening. . . . Everything in this staging tells, and tells double. The disparate cast works together as if blended by [James] Waring" (1971). Smith won an Obie award for direction, but in this context, that was really an award for the production as a whole: writing, lighting, pacing, and spacing were all of a piece. "I wanted a marriage of . . . pictorial literalism and musical patterning, that would draw the audience in and offer pure aesthetic delight," Smith later wrote: "I wanted to make something as beautiful as Robert Wilson's spectacles, but not so lacking in content" (2001, 180).

Thus, even in defending the creative autonomy of the playwright, Smith was also responding to the changing rhythms of the theatrical world around him, a world inseparable from his own emotional life. Indeed, the widening gulf between Petey and Marcus in *Country Music* probably reflected Smith's own recent breakup with Johnny Dodd, his long-term partner. Dodd had that year poured everything he knew into designing lighting for Robert Wilson's breakthrough production at the Brooklyn Academy of Music, *Deafman Glance*—a show that, according to the *New Yorker*'s Edith Oliver, featured "the subtlest and most dramatic lighting I have ever seen" (1971, 95). Dodd, however, is not even mentioned in Oliver's review—an omission typical of the critical amnesia that was already settling over the off-off-Broadway movement and its leading artists.

17 Signals through the Flames: The Afterlife of a Movement

The disbanding of the Open Theatre this winter seems to mark the closing of that era [of ensemble experiment], as the departure of the Living Theatre in 1963 ended the possibility of a committed poetic theatre Off-Broadway, and the end of the Caffe Cino after Joe Cino's death in 1968 broke the new wave of playwrights. A busy, compulsively productive scene sprang up in the wake of all that, but it's continuing now mostly on administrative momentum and vague careerism.

— Michael Smith, *Village Voice*, January 1974

And so ended the off-off-Broadway movement. As this summary judgment by its chief critic and advocate neatly points out, it had moved through two major phases—the initial, playwright-driven scene documented in part 1 of this book, and the freewheeling collaborative exchanges that grew out of it, discussed in part 2. The work of the various leading off-off theaters had latterly branched off in a variety of different directions, as part 3 has attempted to demonstrate, but by the time the Open Theatre disbanded at the end of 1973, the momentum and energy of the original movement had largely dissipated. As the older companies and venues adapted for survival or simply closed down, new theaters were springing up at an exponential rate. In most cases, however, these were speculative ventures that folded swiftly, unable to make ends meet in an environment where too many groups were scrambling for too few resources.

Some idea of off-off-Broadway's suicidally rapid expansion during the early 1970s can be gained simply by glancing at survey figures. In 1968, *Cue* magazine noted the existence of around 40 off-off-Broadway companies and venues—already well up on the situation a couple of years previously, when the underground theaters could still be counted in single figures. In 1972, the first volume of *The Scene* (a series of new play anthologies edited by Stanley Nelson) listed 117 off-off-Broadway enterprises. In 1975, the third volume listed 316. Many of the new theaters were paid-up members of the Off-Off-Broadway

344

Alliance (OOBA), which was formed in 1971 with the intention of defending the interests of, and advocating the development of, alternative theater in New York. Such a body would have been invaluable in the 1960s, when the Cino and La Mama were facing constant pressure from the city authorities, but in the 1970s, the big idea was to raise money. One early indication of OOBA's objectives was its unsuccessful attempt in February 1972 to persuade the city of New York to donate $1.2 million, annually, for OOBA to spread among its members according to need.

OOBA offered no indication as to what artistic standards, if any, would be applied as criteria in sharing out their anticipated municipal funds. Generally, though, concerns for creative originality were fast giving way to a more conventional brand of "professionalism." The hyperinflation of the scene was largely a result of the proliferation of career-oriented Equity showcases: off-off-Broadway became widely regarded by actors as a (rather scummy) stepping stone to greater things. A documentary video from this period, held in the La Mama archive, features a typical group of hopefuls calling themselves "the Times Square Players," after Leonard Melfi's *Times Square*—a play they had chosen to stage not on any aesthetic grounds, but because "it had a part for everybody and a monologue for each of us." As one of them happily admits, "A lot of actors work off-off-Broadway to get *off* of off-off-Broadway. There's no money involved, [but] a showcase gives you the opportunity to be seen, to bring in the casting directors and agents." Looking to get a foot on the ladder to professional success, young actors would show up in droves to audition at any hole-in-the-wall venue: in July 1972, one young playwright with a group called the New York Theater Ensemble informed the *New York Times*' Mel Gussow that 250 people had shown up to audition for the ten parts in her new play. This was a far cry from the days when Caffe Cino playwrights had press-ganged passers-by into trying out for roles.

Most of the new programmers were also a far cry from Joe Cino. Often, budding artists felt that, rather than being encouraged and assisted in their endeavors, they were simply being exploited. In a 1972 *Dramatists Guild Quarterly* article, aspiring playwright Tom Topor noted that the average off-off-Broadway theater would allocate a tiny budget to a programmed show ("usually, it allows $25"), and then flout the provisions of the Equity Showcase Code by charging for tickets or "suggesting" a specific entry donation. "Though most OOB operators are all charm and love, they will not begin working on a production until the writer has signed his contract," Topor wrote: "Most of these contracts take everything and give next to nothing, [and]

demand 10 percent of the writer's proceeds from any [future productions]—
films, television, published versions, tours, everything" (1972, 11). Topor's article is bitterly resentful of these conditions, but the fact is that, even for the
most exploitative producer, off-off-Broadway was a losing proposition. With
the scene having become so diffuse, precious few shows could hope to attract
much of an audience. "El Dada is the most famous of the four hundred and
twelve underground theatres listed in the *Village Voice* this week," quips a
character in Robert Patrick's 1973 play *Kennedy's Children* (alluding, of
course, to La Mama): "Which means that if you're lucky enough to work there
for a week, you might pull out with a fast five dollars and play to a house of
twelve" (Patrick 1976, 8).

It became impossible even for the press to keep track of what was happening off-off-Broadway. As early as 1970, Robert Schroeder estimated that an
accurate mapping of "the Other Theatre" would now "require some 25
reporters and perhaps 25 pages of review space per week." To do this, moreover, would be pointless, given that so many shows had nothing to recom-
mend them: "Some expertise is required if the prospective auditor is to avoid
evenings not only lost but also esthetically distressing" (1970, 38). Similarly,
Michael Smith—who finally quit his post at the *Village Voice* in 1974—recalls
the expansionary early 1970s with weary resignation:

> It got to be impossible to be a critic: there was too much going on, there were
> too many people, too many artists. And there were some new kinds of things
> being done, but I just couldn't work up much enthusiasm. As a reviewer I always
> felt like I had to like it, but I had periods where I just dreaded going. I'd just sit
> at home and say, "I can't write reviews." I had to force myself to go. It was just
> over, you know? It wasn't interesting anymore.

Cry for the Sixties?

The off-off-Broadway movement's disintegration was, of course, symptomatic
of much broader changes in American culture. The Caffe Cino had staged its
first theater productions in 1960, the year of Kennedy's election, and *America
Hurrah* had "gone mainstream" in 1966, just as the counterculture went
"pop." It was perhaps poetically appropriate, then, that the Open Theatre
should close in 1973—the year in which a cease-fire was finally agreed in the
Vietnam War. With the end of "the sixties" came the end of the "free theater"
ethos that had animated the underground—free of charge; free of creative

interference from backers; freewheeling, reciprocal collaboration between artists. Many of off-off-Broadway's leading lights proved ill equipped to handle the new realities of having to compete for grant funding and public recognition, and struggled to find contexts in which to pursue their work. Thus, by the mid-1970s, underground voices of all varieties had either found accommodations with the establishment or fallen largely silent.

Robert Patrick's play *Kennedy's Children* provided a bleak epitaph for the decade passed, and first appeared in that pivotal year of 1973, in an unheralded production at Playwrights' Horizons (founded in 1971 by Robert Moss, after the closure of the Barr-Albee Playwrights' Unit, which he had managed in its final year of operations). It then became an unexpected hit on the London fringe, and eventually transferred to the West End. Via this circuitous route, Patrick's play reached Broadway in the fall of 1975, but its run there was brief, and in hindsight it is easy to see why: this is no "feel-good" play for commercial audiences. Though showcasing Patrick's trademark comic patter, *Kennedy's Children* is a harrowing attempt to map out the "enormous despair" felt by many in the 1970s — the numb disillusionment that inevitably followed on from a period of such heightened idealism and creativity. "The seventies are just the garbage of the sixties," one character remarks (1976, 13), and indeed all five speakers seem to regard themselves as little more than detritus. Standing or sitting in lonely, isolated spots in a Lower East Side bar, lost in their own overpowering memories, each one speaks only to the audience (or to the air, or the floor). Never interacting with each other, they make only slight, habitual gestures to the silent bartender for drinks.

The play is, in effect, composed of five long, intercut monologues. Wanda recalls the Kennedy assassination as a turning point in her life, as a loss of innocence from which she has never recovered. Carla, contrarily, recalls the death of Marilyn Monroe as marking the start of a "pop" decade in which ordinary people imagined they could aspire to be "superstars" (at least for Warhol's famous fifteen minutes), and often wound up selling themselves in the search. Meanwhile, Mark pores over the letters and diaries from his traumatic tour of duty in Vietnam, trying helplessly to make some sense of the experience, as Rona traces her involvement in radical political campaigns — from her days as a student on civil rights marches, through to the chaos of 1968 and the disillusionment that followed, as Berkeley, Haight-Ashbury, and the Lower East Side turned into junk-infested slums. Obliquely connecting the tales of Rona and Carla, there is also Sparger (loosely based on Charles Stanley), who reminisces about his days in the underground haven of the Caffe Cino—thinly disguised here as "Opera Buffo"—and how it too descended into a nightmare of drugs and death.

On its Broadway opening, *Kennedy's Children* drew predictable criticism for its use of broad, representative character-types (stereotypes?), and for its refusal to engage them in conversation. The play's success in London, some New York reviewers felt, must have been a result of English eagerness to look down pityingly on these poor, benighted Americans. Yet with hindsight, these objections seem indicative of just how discomforting the play was in its attempt to tackle recent history. "Patrick oversimplifies a complex decade," Jack Kroll wrote in *Newsweek*, and

> there is an element of exploitation in the playwright's seizure of his subject. [Yet] for me all these flaws vanish in the face of the play's emotional impact and authenticity of feeling. With real pain, a rich black wit and a scathing gift of language, Patrick launches his theatrical howl for the wasted energy that turned the '60s into a scorched junk sculpture of aspiration. [The play] goes all the way, touching the nerve of terror. But it is the terror of truth that any new marshaling of hope will have to confront. (1975)

Today, decades later, it is all too easy to idealize the 1960s as a golden era of libertarian creativity, but as Kroll implies, any discussion of the period must also address the sense of loss and betrayal felt by so many who watched alternative communities disintegrate in exhaustion and bitterness. Many of those interviewed for this book were keen to share their recollections and perspectives, but also found that the process stirred up painful memories they had not confronted in years.

Ultimately, though, *Kennedy's Children* seems flawed in allowing so little possibility for new hope, or new directions. The 1960s were over, but not everyone was lost in backward-looking despair. For example, even as New York's underground theater movement was disintegrating (or hyperinflating, depending on one's perspective), the thriving new fringe scene that was emerging in London could be seen to owe a demonstrable debt to the New York example. It was not simply that plays like *Kennedy's Children* proved popular and influential: the London scene was in large part developed and driven by expatriate Americans. In 1968, for example, the year after *Futz* and *Tom Paine* had played acclaimed runs in London, La Mama Troupe's Beth Porter founded La Mama Wherehouse, which quickly became one of the leading venues of the new theatrical fringe. So too did Charles Marowitz's

Open Space, where early productions included plays by the likes of Drexler, Melfi, and Shepard. "The fringe in London is, if you can picture it, like a corner of the East Village tucked among the stodgy symmetry of Westchester county," Marowitz reported to *Village Voice* readers in March 1970, adding that many productions were "American-dominated, American-oriented, and riddled with obsessions that seem remote to the majority of its English public." Sam Shepard immediately felt at home when he arrived in London in 1971, and one of the first productions he saw was an accomplished version of his 1965 play *Icarus's Mother*, directed by yet another American, Nancy Meckler (who had moved on from the Wherehouse to form her own Freehold Company). Shepard found a temporary creative home at the Royal Court Theatre, which had established its tiny "Theatre Upstairs" in response to fringe developments.

A number of small-scale American theaters were also founded around the same time, partly in response to the off-off-Broadway model. The Open Theatre's Jo Ann Schmidman, for example, set up Nebraska's Omaha Magic Theatre in 1968, which became long-term home to Megan Terry. Another Magic Theatre, in San Francisco, was established in 1969, and became Shepard's home base on his return from London. In New York, of course, La Mama was the only one of the original off-off-Broadway theaters that continued to flourish—in its newly institutionalized form—throughout the 1970s and beyond. But while the theater programs at both St. Mark's Church and Judson Memorial Church gradually petered out over the course of the decade, some important new work was nonetheless produced in the process.

Michael Smith, for example, helped bring a new lease of life to Theatre Genesis, during his membership of the directorial triumvirate between 1971 and 1974. The venue's "straight boys only" profile was finally shed as, alongside the usual diet of new plays by Hadler and Mednick, Genesis presented revivals of plays by female writers like Adrienne Kennedy and Irene Fornes, and new work by gay male writers including Ronald Tavel (whose *Bigfoot* and *The Queen of Greece* were premiered in 1972 and 1973, respectively) and Jeff Weiss (whose *Horsemeat: A Play to See While Sipping Tea* appeared in 1974). This eclectic profile was maintained even after the departures of Smith and Mednick, which left Hadler in sole charge at Genesis. A young Harvey Fierstein, for example, who had been forbidden by Ellen Stewart to appear in drag at La Mama, was given the opportunity to play a street queen in Hadler's drama of Bowery life, *The Silver Bee*, in the fall of 1974. The following year, Tony Barsha returned to direct the irrepressible Taylor Mead in Michael

McClure's *Spider Rabbit*—a demented, satirical monologue about a peace-loving warmonger. (Genesis also produced several other short plays by McClure during the 1970s: the California-based poet, whose controversial play about Jean Harlow and Billy the Kid, *The Beard*, had been produced off-Broadway in 1967, was a natural Genesis associate, given his preoccupations with sharply rhythmic dialogue, incantational monologues, and American pop-myths.) Throughout this period, Genesis managed to maintain its commitment to idiosyncratic social commentary, and also to free audience admission. However, it gained little public attention (never having been much given to trumpeting its activities beyond its immediate neighborhood), and when St. Mark's was badly damaged by fire in 1978, the theater program was quietly shelved.

At Judson Poets' Theater, the program during the 1970s consisted almost exclusively of Al Carmines's large-cast "oratorio" works. Carmines's once prolific creativity gradually tailed off, however, and by the end of the decade, Judson was mounting just one or two shows a year. The oratorios remained popular with audiences (although critics often accused Carmines of repeating himself), but where the Poets' Theater continued to shine during its later years was in the infrequent but always eagerly attended collaborations between Kornfeld and Carmines on plays by Gertrude Stein. Although Kornfeld's presence as a regular contributor at Judson had ended in 1970, both men were devoted to continuing their work with Stein. They joined forces with playwright and Stein scholar Leon Katz in 1972 to stage an adaptation of Stein's major historical novel, *The Making of Americans*, and followed this with productions of Stein's plays *Listen to Me* (1974), *A Manoir* (1977), and finally *Doctor Faustus Lights the Lights* (1979). Other Poets' Theater veterans also returned to collaborate on these shows: Theo Barnes, for example, acted in both *Listen to Me* and *A Manoir*, and designed costumes for *Doctor Faustus*, for which Florence Tarlow also returned as a performer.

By contrast with the essentially lighthearted feel of Judson's earlier Stein collaborations (*What Happened* and *In Circles*), these productions were based on darker, bleaker texts, written during the depression and prewar era of the 1930s. In the disillusioned, after-the-orgy atmosphere of the 1970s, Kornfeld and Carmines seem to have opted consciously for this shift of emphasis. Their staging of *Listen to Me*, for example, was built around the line "Sweet William had his genius and he looked for his Lillian"—the problem being, as the *Voice*'s Michael Feingold pointed out (citing another line), that "when 'the world is all covered with people, and no one knows who anyone looks like,' it is impossible to find another person" (1974). Kornfeld, who won a third Obie for his direction (adding to those for *What Happened* and *Dracula: Sabbat*), conceived of the piece as a variant on the Orpheus myth, with Theo Barnes's Sweet William searching the contemporary (under)world for his lost love. *Listen to Me* was thus revealed as "a genuine twentieth-century tragedy," Feingold noted, which might well be "the best thing I have ever seen anywhere . . . Lawrence Kornfeld's production, a painstaking lesson in weaving complexities out of simple statements, is so attuned to the text that at times he appears to be breathing with Stein." Meanwhile Carmines's score, even at its most boisterous, seemed to contain "a tinge of pure evil; the chill of despair is plainly felt under the bubbly music." Five years later, Feingold also hailed *Doctor Faustus Lights the Lights* as "a major event of our lifetime" (1979b), staged with "an unerring sense of beauty and clarity" (1979a). Here, though, the highest praise was reserved for Jeff Weiss, making his one Judson appearance in the title role. "To say that he possesses a vocal and physical skill rarely matched in any theater doesn't describe the galvanic energy that he brings to the stage," James Leverett commented in the *Soho Weekly News*: "This force is, in fact, Faustian" (1979). Weiss was provided with an ideal foil by Al Carmines, who, for once forsaking his piano, played a disturbingly genial, urbane Mephistopheles.

The Judson Poets' Theater remains unrivaled in American theater history for the consistency and complexity of its attention to Gertrude Stein's often-neglected plays. *Doctor Faustus*, however, proved the theater's last hurrah. The following year, after one last oratorio *(The Agony of Paul)*, Carmines suffered a cerebral aneurysm, which forced him to retire his ministry and take a period of convalescence. In 1981, the church formally wound up its theater program. Judson's influence continued to be felt, however, in the activities of several of its former collaborators. Theater for the New City, for example, still operates today under Crystal Field's leadership, and in some respects still perpetuates the antiestablishment spirit of the original off-off-Broadway movement.

Theater for the New City, as we have seen, had a troubled beginning, with Kornfeld and Barnes walking out over clashes with Field in 1971. Then, in 1972, the lease on its original Westbeth performance space was abruptly canceled. Yet Field and her husband George Bartenieff showed a tenacity to rival Ellen Stewart's, in finding a new space—a "grand ballroom" on Jane Street—and transplanting their equipment there using handcarts, an old station wagon, and volunteer helpers. (In 1977, they moved again, this time to the

East Village.) From its inception, this theater sought a more explicitly political engagement with the "new city" than had its 1960s predecessors, and its social concerns were epitomized by the introduction of free, agit-prop-style plays, toured annually around the parks and streets of New York's five boroughs. These shows, similar to those pioneered on the West Coast by the San Francisco Mime Troupe, used a broad, cartoon-strip approach in tackling social concerns of immediate relevance to city audiences. The first such was *Minding the Store* (1971), by another former Judsonite, Robert Nichols, in which four homeless children, hiding out in a garbage-filled playground, were harassed by a succession of pompous authority figures.

Other projects initiated during the 1970s, and also oriented toward serving the needs of particular communities within the city, included a Hispanic theater program, a women playwrights' program, and an annual Native American Dance Concert. Throughout this period, though, Theater for the New City also sought to perpetuate the experimental playwriting profile of the 1960s movement, providing a much-needed home for work by writers as diverse as Rosalyn Drexler, Jean-Claude van Itallie, Ronald Tavel, Robert Heide, Sam Shepard, and H. M. Koutoukas. The somewhat fragmented nature of Field's programming occasionally attracted criticism from those—particularly funding bodies—who wanted to see a more coherent profile, but she saw this diversity as a strength, and as a continuation of the freewheeling spirit of the previous decade. "We have been accused of never having found a style," Field acknowledged in 1979: "Well, I hope and pray we never do. . . . We feel that we are the survivors in the quest for the avant-garde. One theater does not a movement make, but we can't let up" (Gould 1979, 2).

Irene's Theater Strategy

That refusal to "let up" has been apparent in the post-1960s work of many off-off-Broadway veterans. By way of demonstrating some of the strategies employed, I want to focus on the activities of one, exemplary figure—Maria Irene Fornes. Yet another Judson alumnus, and a close colleague and collaborator with Field, Fornes launched her own, somewhat more cohesive attempt to serve the interests of experimental playwrights in 1971. The New York Theatre Strategy was an advocacy agency that fought to provide Fornes's fellow dramatists with the opportunity to have work produced in their own ideal production circumstances. The idea was that writers should be able to choose the context and collaborators for any given project, rather than having to make do with the circumstances and personnel offered by existing venues.

The prototype production, in this regard, had been Fornes's own *Molly's Dream* (1968)—a haunting musical fantasia, full of hallucinatory twists and turns, on the subject of romantic love and *its* many twists and turns. Though its whimsy and theatricality might have made it an obvious choice for production at Judson, Fornes found that she had very particular ideas about how she wanted it staged, and was hesitant about simply handing it over to Carmines and Kornfeld (or indeed to another director-led venue like La Mama). Instead, she first approached Julie Bovasso, whom she believed would be ideal for the central role of the lovelorn waitress, Molly. Bovasso advised Fornes to do as she would, and to direct the play herself. Fornes did so in a workshop production at the New Dramatists' Studio on East Fourth Street, with an "ideal" cast also including Crystal Field as Alberta (a full-grown Shirley Temple lookalike), and the Open Theatre's Ray Barry as Jim, the handsome object of Molly's fantasies.

New Dramatists, an arm of the Dramatists' Guild, was not an obvious home for such a piece, having always been oriented toward showcasing relatively conventional work by would-be commercial playwrights. However, the agency had a stated commitment to serving the interests of the playwright, and Fornes exploited this in arguing for the right to direct the play herself: "I said that if this organization exists to help dramatists, then it should support what the dramatist thinks is best for her work." The resulting production went unreviewed in the press (as was customary with New Dramatists presentations), and Fornes herself now recalls little about its details. Yet it is remembered by Robert Patrick, for one, as "the greatest play I ever saw. Produced as Irene wanted it, with the people she wrote it for, it was beyond doubt the single most perfect and memorable and dazzling production of any play I've ever seen anywhere in the world."

Molly's Dream convinced Fornes of the creative advantages of such independent strategizing. Three years later, in founding New York Theatre Strategy, she once again sought the collaboration of Julie Bovasso, who came on board as the organization's president. The pair gathered an initial membership roster of twenty-three, including "virtually the whole first generation of playwrights from Off-Off-Broadway" (Smith 1973b), and by May 1973 had coordinated a public launch for the organization, in the form of an unfunded, five-week festival of twenty different plays, mounted at the Manhattan Theatre Club on East Seventy-third Street. This do-it-yourself off-off jamboree—which included revivals of 1960s favorites such as Shepard's *Chicago* and

Eyen's *The White Whore and the Bit Player*—achieved its goal of attracting the attention of foundation sponsors. The following year, the Strategy was able to coordinate a season of four, fully professional productions.

New York Theatre Strategy never had its own permanent venue, and was not concerned to emulate the rapid turnover of new work that had characterized off-off-Broadway in the previous decade. Instead, the objective was to ensure that a small, manageable number of projects was properly resourced and administered annually. In each case, the playwright's preferences for venue, casting, and production team were prioritized in the creation of a project proposal. Playwrights were not the only beneficiaries of the scheme, however: directors like Lawrence Kornfeld and John Vaccaro were asked to direct productions for Strategy playwrights like Rochelle Owens, Rosalyn Drexler, and Kenneth Bernard, and were given professional-standard production budgets to do so. The collaborative spirit of the 1960s thus found a new outlet in such projects, although Fornes was keen to ensure that playwrights were given the opportunity to direct their own work if they so desired. Indeed, one of the Strategy's most significant productions was her own new play *Fefu and Her Friends*, which she directed in 1977 at the Relativity Media Lab—an unorthodox venue that she chose to serve her conception of the piece as an environmental promenade performance. The play cycles different groups of spectators around four small rooms during act 2, while uniting them in a seated auditorium for acts 1 and 3. This approach tellingly contrasts the more "public" and "private" lives of the play's eight female characters, while uncomfortably implicating the audience themselves as "fly on the wall" voyeurs in the second act. By turns witty, delicate, and devastating in its depiction of the women's varying attempts to define themselves within a male-dominated world, *Fefu and Her Friends* became a significant landmark in the emerging feminist theater movement of the 1970s, and was revived at the American Place Theatre the following year, in association with its Women's Project.

However, the success of *Fefu* also prompted Fornes to review her own priorities: the commitment of time and energy required in running the Theatre Strategy had too long proved a distraction from her own writing, and so, when no one else proved willing to take on the burden of administration, 1977–78 proved to be the organization's final season. Yet no sooner had the Strategy been wound up than Fornes committed herself to another new self-support scheme for playwrights. Southern California's Padua Hills Playwrights' Festival was founded in 1978 by another exemplary figure, Murray Mednick, with the intention of providing a mentoring context for writers, similar to that which Ralph Cook had created at Theatre Genesis. Running annually right through to 1995, Padua Hills was a kind of residential summer retreat for playwrights and other theater artists, which each year created a temporary but highly productive creative community. If economic conditions did not allow such a community to exist year-round, Mednick had reasoned, an intensive festival was the next best thing.

Many of Padua's key personnel were directly transplanted from the Theatre Genesis "tribe": over the years, participants included Walter Hadler, Sam Shepard, Lee Kissman, Robert Glaudini, and—forming a creative partnership of their own—Shepard's and Mednick's ex-wives, O-Lan Jones and Kathleen Cramer. "In many ways," Mednick feels, "Padua was a furthering and even a fulfilment of what began at Genesis." A wide variety of new plays was written and staged at the festival each year, often using Padua Hills' expansive outdoor spaces to create intriguing, "site-specific" stagings. Mednick's own *Coyote Cycle*, for example—an ambitious sequence of seven short plays developed over a six-year period between 1978 and 1984—was an anarchic take on Native American myths concerning nature gods like Coyote and Spider Woman, and made superb use of the site's contrasting landscape of open, prairielike spaces and wooded enclosures. Actors would "magically" appear from hiding places in trees, or from dirt-covered holes dug into the ground. Just as they had in New York in the 1960s, Mednick and his colleagues took the resources available to them, and made theatrical virtues out of necessity.

Irene Fornes was among those who particularly benefited from the festival's supportive environment: several of her major plays of the 1980s—including *Mud*, *The Danube*, and *The Conduct of Life*—had their first, work-in-progress airings at Padua, before being staged in finished form at Theater for the New City (always under her own direction). Fornes more than repaid that debt, though, by becoming one of the festival's most regular and inspirational playwriting teachers, and thus helping to mentor a whole new generation of writers. She shared with students (including now-familiar names like Jon Robin Baitz and Eduardo Machado) the various exercises and writing strategies that she had been developing ever since writing *Promenade*, when she first used shuffled cards to generate chance juxtapositions and so "take the subconscious by surprise." According to playwright David Henry Hwang, a student at the first Padua Hills festival in 1978, Fornes is "one of the best playwriting teachers on earth. Basically I learned to access my subconscious from that. . . . That summer I started a play that eventually became *F.O.B.*" (Savran 1988, 119–20).

Hwang's Obie Award–winning *F.O.B.* — "fresh off the boat" — became the first in a trilogy of plays exploring his Chinese-American heritage, and there is, as his comments here imply, an important connection between Fornes's playwriting methods and Hwang's starting to tap into the particular cultural history of which he was a part. In encouraging her students to explore, intuitively, their own "inner libraries" of personal material (rather than to obey the usual guidelines for "proper" dramatic structures insisted on by more conventional playwriting teachers), Fornes has played a significant part in helping to liberate the distinct creative voices of a generation of younger dramatists from different "minority" backgrounds. Indeed, in the early 1980s, she founded the Hispanic Playwrights' Lab at the New York–based INTAR company — becoming a mentor to writers such as Milcha Sanchez-Scott, Migdalia Cruz, and Caridad Svich.

Such links should come as no surprise when one considers that the multiculturalism of today is built foursquare on the ground cleared by the countercultural upheavals of the 1960s. Significantly, though, Fornes herself tends to resist the pigeonholing beloved of contemporary identity politics, preferring to think of herself simply as a continuing exponent of New York's alternative theater, rather than allowing herself to be labeled as a "feminist playwright," a "Latina playwright," a "lesbian playwright," or anything else. Despite (or perhaps because of?) the acclaim deservedly accorded to plays like *Fefu and Her Friends*, Fornes has been particularly wary of the political expectations that have sometimes been attached to her as a woman: "If my expression is honest, it is inevitable that it will often speak in a feminine way," she notes, "[but] I don't sit down to write to make a point *about women*" (1985, 13). In this respect, as in many others, Fornes is typical of her generation: many former members of the off-off-Broadway movement have contributed directly to the identitarian liberation politics of the 1970s and beyond, while always maintaining their own, independent status as creative iconoclasts. In what remains of this final chapter, I want to sketch in a few of the ways in which this tendency has been particularly apparent in the emergence of a distinctively queer theater culture in America.

Queerly Incorrect

"Off-Off-Broadway is rugged individualism," Charles Ludlam quipped, butchly, in 1973, "the last stronghold in a corporate society" (Leogrande 1973).

At first glance, that comment seems indicative of the newly auteur-oriented trajectory of alternative theater in the 1970s, and might appear to sit oddly with this book's emphasis on collaborative creative endeavor. Yet "rugged individualism" can also be seen as the flip side of the communitarian coin: as Fornes and Mednick demonstrated, any theater artist needs a supportive context in order to "do what you have to do," and Ludlam's nurturing of his own creative family, the Ridiculous Theatrical Company, provided him not only with performers but with a self-contained community dedicated to the furtherance of his idiosyncratic aesthetic. Ludlam's insistence on maintaining creative control over his work meant that he always resisted the approaches of commercial producers, and his company thus remained determinedly "off-off-Broadway." Despite constant financial hardship, however, Ludlam's core ensemble continued to work together throughout the 1970s. Changing personal circumstances led to the dissolution of the original group in 1980, but Ludlam kept the company itself going right up until his death in 1987, from AIDS-related illnesses (at which point his partner, actor Everett Quinton, took over the reins—calling on Larry Kornfeld to direct the next production). The Ridiculous Theatrical Company's resilience and longevity made it one of the single greatest sources of inspiration for a newly emerging, post-Stonewall generation of gay theater artists.

The fascination of Ludlam's work lay not only in the fact that it was outrageously entertaining, but also in its ability to subvert all kinds of received assumptions in the process. A prime example is *Camille*, which premiered at the Thirteenth Street Theatre in May 1973. Almost as if Ludlam were marking his own break with "the sixties," the play departed strikingly from the company's previous, relentlessly irreverent approach. An adaptation of the classic melodrama (drawing not only on the original Dumas novel, but also the Garbo film version and recordings of stage performances), *Camille* was conceived as a faithful rendering of this sentimental story, as well as a travesty on it. The first act lulled Ludlam's audience into a false sense of familiarity by presenting a formal dinner party as wildly burlesqued as anything in his previous work. Yet the second and third acts present a remarkably sincere narrative of found and lost love—punctured only occasionally by what Clive Barnes called "subtitles of humor" (1974a). As a result, the comic excesses of the first act come to embody, retrospectively, the shallow vulgarity of Marguerite's previous life as a high-society courtesan. Indeed, in act 2, one of the other courtesans is pointedly chastised by her lover for a catty comment on Marguerite's fate: "Don't be a camp, Olympe" (Ludlam 1989, 241). In context, of course, that line is itself truly camp—an indication of the game of double bluff that Ludlam's script seems constantly to play with its audience.

The heart of the production, however, was not the text but Ludlam's performance as Marguerite. By 1973, male-to-female drag had become almost too familiar in downtown theater, and objections were starting to be raised—particularly by feminists—over the derogatory view of women that often seemed to be implied. Ludlam, however, responded not by dropping drag, but by taking it to another level. Appearing in a low-cut gown that showed off his plentiful chest hair, and making no attempt at speaking falsetto, he emphasized his own status as a man playing a female role—even as he moved seamlessly "back and forth between Dumas' sentiments and contemporary comments on them," so that "every conceivable contradictory mood, emotion, impulse exists side by side" (Malpede 1973). This Marguerite, far from being a misogynistic caricature, was a virtuoso piece of character acting: "The remarkable thing is," Clive Barnes noted, "that while Mr. Ludlam takes very little pains to convince us that he is a woman . . . he is a completely convincing Camille" (1974). By highlighting the irrelevance of biological sex in the performance of gender, the show was, for critic Karen Malpede, implicitly progressive: "the Ridiculous company . . . appeals to feminists as well as homosexuals and also to straight men who feel locked into and limited by traditional sex roles" (1973). Ludlam himself regarded *Camille* as "a profoundly feminist work. . . . It allows audiences to experience the universality of emotion, rather than to believe that women are one species and men another, and that what one feels the other never does" (1992, 44).

That thought was also implicit in an element of the performance that went unmentioned by reviewers—namely that, thanks to Ludlam's double-edged performance, the heartfelt love affair between Marguerite and Armand (played by Bill Vehr) was at least as homosexual as it was heterosexual, particularly in its onstage physicality. The apparent impossibility of the couple's love surviving in a society scandalized by it thus gained added poignancy. Characteristically, though, the most overtly "queer" moment in the play was also the most outrageously hilarious. At the beginning of act 3, after the heartbreaking dramatic twists of act 2, and with Marguerite lying in visible pain on what will become her deathbed, she tells her maid (played in drag by Jack Mallory), "I'm cold. Nanine, throw another faggot on the fire!" Nanine informs her, "There are no more faggots in the house." *Plaintively looking out at the audience,* Marguerite responds: "No faggots in the house? Open the window, Nanine. See if there are any in the street" (1989, 246). With his deftly understated performance of that one line (described with still-lingering awe by several interviewees for this book), Ludlam always brought the house down, shattering the tragic air of the scene, before instantly retrieving it again a moment later. The line also performed the unprecedented move of acknowledging and celebrating the homosexual gaze of much of Ludlam's audience.

Camille, then, engaged implicitly with changing attitudes to gender and sexuality, as both the gay and women's liberation movements gathered pace in the early 1970s. Another important piece from 1973 proved more controversial, however, by tackling homosexuality directly, as subject matter. Al Carmines's *The Faggot* was a gay-themed musical revue (despite its title, it had no central character, and was composed of a series of loosely connected skits) which, like *Camille*, proved popular with audiences and earned a second run. Moving to the Truck and Warehouse Theatre in July after its initial Judson dates in May, this was to prove Judson's last-ever off-premises transfer. Carmines's ragtime-based piano score was regarded by reviewers as one of his best, and the production was praised as "a warm and courageous tribute to personal sexual liberation" (Baker 1973). Yet *The Faggot*—which was clearly rooted in its author's own "coming out" as a gay man—also drew vehement criticism from some of the more vocal advocates of gay liberation.

From the outset, Carmines's play makes clear its opposition to society's traditional proscription of homosexuality. The pressures placed on individuals to deny their orientation are satirized mercilessly: "Seventy years or so," goes one tune, "Seventy years to find reasons not to do something / What a wonderful way to live" (Carmines 1973, 2). Laughing in the face of such repression, Carmines brought his subject right out of the closet, going as far as presenting a gay male sex scene in the form of a sung duet (whose lines give clear indications as to the onstage action): "Please do it again and again / Yes—yes / No, don't shift / Just lift / Oh yes / And please keep on" (5). The ire of activists was aroused, however, by *The Faggot*'s tendency to juxtapose such celebratory material with other scenes depicting some gay lives as less than ideal. A politician figure, for example, confesses that "gay liberation came just about five years too late for me," that he is addicted "to secrecy and furtiveness and pain" (8–9). Several subsequent scenes focus on this underworld of "lonely walks on dark streets . . . bright and empty barrooms / filled with flashing teeth and empty eyes" (17).

Carmines's attempt to underline the wrongs of societal oppression by stressing the consequently seedy, secretive nature of some gay lives was, perhaps, easy to misinterpret. To *Voice* critic Arthur Sainer, *The Faggot* seemed to approach homosexuality "not as a liberating erotic force but as a social and psychological problem" (1973). That concern also prompted a letter to the *New York Times* from activist Martin Duberman, describing *The Faggot* as "more than a failure. It is an affront" (July 22, 1973). Carmines's response, published on the letters page a week later, protested that "politics is not art," and that his only responsibility was to depict his subject honestly, as he saw it (July 29). This prompted another letter from Jonathan Katz, arguing that the play "adds to the oppression of gays," and attacking Carmines's claims to apoliticism. This, he contended, was a willfully naive stance, given that all representations of homosexuality are ideologically loaded: the cause of liberation therefore demanded positive character portrayals. Not coincidentally, Katz was himself the author of the first gay agit-prop play, *Coming Out.* Mounted the previous year by the Gay Activists' Alliance (GAA), this documentary drama presented a collage of scenes outlining the historical oppression of homosexuals.

By contrast with *Coming Out*, which stated its liberatory message very clearly, Carmines's revue-style writing seemed somewhat unfocused. Moreover, his decision to open out the second act to deal with historical examples of sexual deviation was an open invitation to his critics. Here, Oscar Wilde and Lord Alfred Douglas are depicted as a sadomasochistically self-tormenting couple, while Catherine the Great's famous fondness for horses is interpreted as full-on bestiality. Alongside these scenes, the touchingly depicted love of Gertrude Stein and Alice B. Toklas seems refreshingly uncomplicated. Whatever its flaws and contradictions, though, *The Faggot* also demonstrated a shrewd awareness that the gay liberation movement was already generating a certain political orthodoxy of its own, and hence a censorship of "incorrect" voices. "I go around with faggots all the time," declares a character generically named Fag Hag: "Only now, I don't say faggot—you're not supposed to; you use other terms. Like, the term for me used to be fag hag—but now I'm called a gay mascot. I guess that's better—I don't know" (36). Later, a street queen named Philip, aware that his own effeminate style is now considered politically retrograde, observes sardonically that "revolutions are never good news for queens" (47). "And that's dead right," asserts Doric Wilson, "but it upset the Katz-Duberman types, because it didn't hold party line."

Significantly, Wilson had himself been heavily involved in the early gay liberation movement: he was present at all three nights of the Stonewall riots in 1969, and subsequently fought for the reclamation and championing of the confrontational term *faggot*, in preference to what he considered the weaker, less pertinent *gay*. (This move, though unsuccessful, anticipated the later retrieval of *queer* as a defiantly affirmative descriptor.) For Wilson, *The Faggot*'s rejection of any dictates but that of its own personal vision—combined, of course, with its musical uplift—made it seem oddly more "liberating" than Katz's more coherent, controlled drama. "*Coming Out* was more professional, more intelligent, better done," he recalls, "whereas *The Faggot* meandered here and there and was amateur and was meant to be. But what was strange was that you came away from the one feeling 'that was very nice,' and you came away from the other, *The Faggot*, feeling deeply moved. And very proud that you were gay. And a little taller."

Katz had claimed in his *New York Times* letter that "the Duberman-Carmines debate raises publicly for the first time some basic questions about a new, developing gay culture; the answers will affect its future character." Wilson agreed, but drew different conclusions. For him, the saving grace of "out" gay theater, as it subsequently developed, was that it tended to follow not the politically didactic model pioneered by Katz, but Carmines's archetypically "off-off-Broadway" approach. Personal, homemade, emotionally charged, and resistant to totalizing conceptualizations, *The Faggot* set an important precedent for gay playmaking—one that Wilson himself followed in founding New York's first explicitly gay-oriented theater company, TOSOS (The Other Side of Silence), in 1974.

Building on his experience as one of the very first Caffe Cino playwrights, Doric Wilson conceived of TOSOS as an "off-off" venture in the Cino tradition, allowing its members to pursue whatever work interested them, without imposing a particular aesthetic or party line. Having converted a large basement space in Tribeca, the company inaugurated its work with another musical revue, Peter del Valle's *Lovers*, and over the next three years went on to stage revivals of key gay-themed Cino plays like *The Madness of Lady Bright* and *The Haunted Host*, as well as new pieces by up-and-coming writers like Martin Sherman *(Passing By)* and Terrence McNally *(Noon)*. A number of older works by "closeted" dramatists were also mounted: the latent gay subtexts of pieces like Noel Coward's ménage à trois play *Design for Living* and Gilbert and Sullivan's "fairy" operetta, *Iolanthe*, now became clearly apparent to audiences.

In 1975, Wilson revisited his own early Cino play, *Now She Dances!* (1961). This satirical reworking of Oscar Wilde's *Salomé*, in the idiom of *The Impor-*

tance of Being Earnest, had originally been little more than a one-act caprice, but he now reworked it into a more sophisticated, two-act comedy. Here, the John the Baptist figure is a radical gay activist, persecuted by Miss Salome for resisting her charms. By contrast, *Earnest*'s oh-so-proper butler, Lane, remains firmly in the closet even when put mockingly "on trial" over his sexuality. (Wilson thus raised an implicit question mark over the conduct of Wilde himself, in his trials for "gross indecency.") Operating on multiple levels—the characters are simultaneously Victorian, biblical, and actors in a play—*Now She Dances!* keeps its audience guessing throughout. Wilson's political concerns are as heartfelt as Jonathan Katz's, but his dramatic methods considerably more playful and circumspect.

By 1977 TOSOS, like so many other off-off-Broadway ventures, was proving economically unsustainable and was closed down. By then, however, Wilson had (like Irene Fornes) decided he needed more time to devote to his writing. Over the next five years he wrote a series of plays—*The West Street Gang*, *A Perfect Relationship*, *Forever After*, and *Street Theater* (a satirical account of Stonewall)—that still stand up as pioneering gay plays, and as important documents of the mores and concerns of the gay community in the period prior to the onset of AIDS. In the absence of a dedicated theater space, all but one of these plays was produced in an improvised staging in a gay bar, prior to the late-night "rush." Indeed, *The West Street Gang* followed Wilson's Cino play *Babel Babel Little Tower* in being written directly for a particular environment—the Spike leather bar, on West Street, where the author worked as a bartender.

Wilson was not the only Cino veteran promoting the cause of gay theater during this period. William M. Hoffman published the first anthology of *Gay Plays* in 1979, and by 1985 had become one of the first playwrights to have a sympathetic portrait of gay men's lives produced on Broadway—in the shape of his AIDS play, *As Is*, which had been developed by Circle Rep. Three years earlier, Harvey Fierstein's *Torch Song Trilogy*, developed at La Mama, had achieved the same feat. Significantly, though, this admission into the mainstream was almost coterminous with a renewed vitality in the gay theatrical underground. The 1980s saw the emergence, in the far eastern reaches of the East Village, of a thriving new nighttime landscape of semilegal storefront clubs and cabarets, specializing particularly in solo performance pieces, predominantly by queer artists. The "performance art" label commonly applied to such work misled many observers into assuming that the roots of this new movement lay in the visual art world: *The Drama Review*, for example, in its spring 1985 edition devoted to "East Village Performance," again demonstrated its historical myopia by equating the scene with "the Happenings movement of the early 1960s" (Kirby 1985, 4). However, as Uzi Parnes's article "Pop Performance" in that same issue makes abundantly clear, the campy, trashy, "disposable aesthetic" that dominated the new scene represented a revival and continuation of certain underground theater trends initiated in the 1960s. Indeed, among the notable players on the East Village circuit were Jack Smith, Jackie Curtis, Tom Murrin (author of *Cock-Strong*), and Jeff Weiss, who had helped inspire the do-it-yourself solo performance trend by turning his own East Tenth Street apartment into a seventeen-seat theater in 1976. (Weiss presented solo pieces there for several years, performing to spectators sitting mere inches away on shabby, red-felt seats salvaged from an old movie theater.) Among the younger gay artists to cut their teeth in this new scene were the autobiographical monologuist Tim Miller, and drag-artist playwrights Charles Busch and Ethyl Eichelberger—both of whom had appeared with the Ridiculous during the 1970s.

This period also saw the emergence of an entire community of lesbian performers—including Holly Hughes, Lois Weaver, Peggy Shaw, Carmelita Tropicana, and many others—who found their spiritual home at the WOW Café on East Eleventh Street. There was an important historical progression here: although many of the female artists of the 1960s off-off-Broadway movement were lesbians, theirs was a love that—given the societal prejudices of the day—dared speak its name even less openly than male homosexuality. Two decades later, though, the WOW Café came to serve a very similar function to that which the Caffe Cino had served for young gay male theatermakers of the 1960s. In its ethos and organization, WOW can be viewed as very much the twisted younger sister of the Cino—always insisting on low-budget self-sufficiency and refusing to apply for grant funding, while maintaining a laissez-faire creative policy of "anything goes." Critic Jill Dolan recalls her discovery of the venue, in the early 1980s, as a breath of fresh air. Previously, she had seen a lot of "terrible" lesbian-feminist theater work that seemed "political and ideological more than aesthetic or even theatrically interesting": by contrast, WOW "encouraged work that was much more daring formally and much less reverent politically. . . . Rather than eschewing popular culture, performers and writers at WOW delighted in queering it, so that everything from detective fiction to forties radio shows were ripe for satire and sexualizing" (Dolan 2001, 106). The WOW Café now holds a hallowed place in the pantheon of queer American theater history, right alongside the Ridiculous Theatrical Company and the Caffe Cino itself.

Afterword

The off-off-Broadway movement may have run its course by the early 1970s, but as examples such as those outlined above indicate, its independent, underground spirit did not die out. Having mutated over the years, like an adaptable, resilient virus, it continues to survive in a variety of contexts. Perhaps, when the conditions exist once again for its contagion to spread, it will resurface to "plague" us once again. Beyond that fond hope, this book has no conclusion: I will leave it up to readers to take what lessons they will, just as so many of the playwrights I have discussed left conclusions up to their audiences. I would, however, crave your indulgence by finishing where I began—on a personal note. In my preface, I noted my own preference for work in unorthodox spaces, by artists who challenge the usual assumptions of "professional theater." Yet while working on this book, I have been struck by how many of the professional theatermakers whose work I most admire today can trace their own heritage more or less directly back to the underground experiments of the 1960s. During the academic year 1993–94, for example—my first in university employment, during which I first decided to begin researching the off-off-Broadway movement—I saw three standout theater productions that still linger powerfully in my memory. All three were radically contrasting, but all three, I later realized, owed conscious creative debts to the New York scene of the 1960s.

First, at the Edinburgh Festival, I saw Penny Arcade for the first time in her controversial show *Bitch! Dyke! Faghag! Whore!* Accompanied by go-go dancers of both sexes, bumping and grinding their way around the audience, Arcade delivered her knowingly "incorrect" monologue performance, which succeeded in throwing all kinds of received assumptions about gender and sexuality into question. One of the more distinctive solo voices to emerge from the East Village club scene of the 1980s, Arcade identifies her mentors as Jack Smith and John Vaccaro. In 1970, she began her stage career by originating the role of Shigushitsume, the psychotic diva from the "Grand Kabuki Theatre of America," in Vaccaro's production of Kenneth Bernard's *Nightclub.*

Second, at home in Glasgow, I saw Chicago's Goat Island performance group for the first time, in *We Got a Date*—a grimly disturbing show mapping the connections between societal conditioning and twisted, repressed sexualities. This brilliant, unorthodox dance-theater troupe began working together in 1987, after its core members first met at the Padua Hills Playwrights' Festival (writer-performer Matthew Goulish was a long-term member of Mednick's *Coyote Cycle* team). In their group creation process, they still draw on ideas culled from Irene Fornes's playwriting classes, as well as on the inspirational work of the Judson Dance Theater (cf. Bottoms 1998b). Funding regimes have dictated that, while highly respected across Europe, Goat Island remain very much in the margins back home: working out of a church gymnasium, company members still keep up "day jobs" to pay the bills.

My third, somewhat less marginal example, is playwright Tony Kushner's seven-hour, two-part "gay fantasia," *Angels in America*, which I saw in its mind-blowing entirety on a single day at London's National Theatre. Kushner himself, in labeling his much-debated play an example of "the Theatre of the Fabulous," positions his work in a line of direct descent from the Theatre of the Ridiculous—acknowledging both the Vaccaro and Ludlam branches (Savran 1994, 24–25). Leon Katz, however, who worked as a dramaturg on *Angels* at the Mark Taper Forum, points out that its roots lie equally in the distinctive blend of character-based realism and camp theatricality pioneered by Caffe Cino plays like *The Madness of Lady Bright*. William M. Hoffman concurs: "The flamboyance, the out-front-ness, the challenge, the 'dare me' [of *Angels*]—that sensibility is very Cino." Joseph Cino himself may have died in tormented despair in 1967, but more than three decades later, the movement he kick-started stands as one of the most significant influences on the subsequent evolution of contemporary American theater. It is long past time to acknowledge this.

Appendix A: Chronology of Notable Events and Productions

1949–50   Season sees only 59 new plays on Broadway. Actors' Equity rules that members may work off-Broadway, at lower pay rate.

1951   First performances of Living Theatre, first in Julian Beck's living room, then at Cherry Lane Theatre.

1952   Circle in the Square presents Tennessee Williams's *Summer and Smoke*. First notable success for off-Broadway theater.

     John Cage's *4′33″* premieres. Cage, Merce Cunningham, and Robert Rauschenberg collaborate on "Theater Piece" at Black Mountain College.

1954   Joseph Papp founds New York Shakespeare Festival.

1955   *Village Voice* established.

     Julie Bovasso's Tempo Theatre opens with U.S. premiere of Jean Genet's *The Maids* (theater closes 1957).

1956   Samuel Beckett's *Waiting for Godot* flops on Broadway.

     Allen Ginsberg's poem *Howl* published.

1957   Jack Kerouac's novel *On the Road* published.

1958   Caffe Cino opens at 31 Cornelia Street.

1959   Living Theatre opens its Fourteenth Street venue with Jack Gelber's *The Connection*.

     Allan Kaprow's *18 Happenings in 6 Parts* at Reuben Gallery.

1960   Election of President Kennedy.

     Edward Albee's *The Zoo Story* premieres at Provincetown Playhouse.

     First fully staged productions at Caffe Cino.

     Village Voice initiates "Off Off-Broadway" listings column.

1961   Judson Poets' Theater established at Judson Memorial Church. Opens with Joel Oppenheimer's *The Great American Desert*.

     New York Poets' Theatre launches at Off-Bowery Theatre.

     Cino: Doric Wilson's *And He Made a Her*; *Babel Babel Little Tower*.

1962   Café La Mama established on East Ninth St. Opens with Tennessee Williams's *One Arm*. Also presents U.S. premiere of Pinter's *The Room*.

Peter Schumann founds Bread and Puppet Theatre.

Cino: Claris Nelson's *The Rue Garden*.

Judson Poets': George Dennison's *Vaudeville Skit*.

Judson Dance Theater established.

Jack Smith films *Flaming Creatures*.

1963   Assassination of President Kennedy.

Open Theatre workshop established.

Barr-Albee Playwrights' Unit established at Village South Theatre.

Café La Mama moves to 82 Second Avenue.

Living Theatre's Fourteenth Street venue closed by IRS, during run of Kenneth Brown's *The Brig*. Company leaves for exile in Europe.

Cino: David Starkweather's *You May Go Home Again*; Lanford Wilson's first play *So Long at the Fair*.

Judson Poets': George Dennison's *The Service for Joseph Axminster*; Gertrude Stein's *What Happened*.

La Mama: Paul Foster's *Hurrah for the Bridge*.

1964   Theatre Genesis established at St. Mark's in the Bowery.

Café La Mama moves to 122 Second Avenue.

Cino: Lanford Wilson's *Home Free!* and *The Madness of Lady Bright*; Robert Patrick's *The Haunted Host*.

Judson: Rosalyn Drexler's *Home Movies*.

La Mama: Paul Foster's *Balls*; Tom Eyen's *The White Whore and the Bit Player*.

Genesis: Sam Shepard's first plays *Cowboys*, *The Rock Garden*.

Open Theatre: showcase evenings at Sheridan Square Playhouse.

Present Stages: O'Hara's *The General Returns from One Place to Another*, LeRoi Jones's *The Baptism*.

Playwrights' Unit: LeRoi Jones's *Dutchman*: moves off-Broadway.

1965   Lyndon Johnson begins first full term as president, unveiling his "Great Society" program, and committing more troops to Vietnam.

Theatre of the Ridiculous launches at Coda Gallery with Ronald Tavel's *Shower* and *The Life of Juanita Castro*.

Caffe Cino damaged by fire. Benefit nights at La Mama and elsewhere.

New Playwrights bill at Cherry Lane Theatre: plays by Foster, Shepard, Wilson.

La Mama launches first European tour.

Open Theatre begins La Mama residency.

Cino: Robert Heide's *The Bed*; H. M. Koutoukas's *Medea, With Creatures Make My Way, All Day for a Dollar.*

Judson: Maria Irene Fornes's *Promenade*; Rochelle Owens's *The String Game, Istanbul*; Ruth Krauss's *A Beautiful Day.*

La Mama: Wilson's *Balm in Gilead*; Jean-Claude van Itallie's *America Hurrah* (aka *Motel*); Eyen's *Why Hanna's Skirt Won't Stay Down.*

Genesis: Shepard's *Chicago*; Leonard Melfi's *Birdbath.*

Open Theatre: Van Itallie's *Almost Like Being*; Megan Terry's *Calm Down Mother, Keep Tightly Closed in a Cool Dry Place*; Fornes's *The Successful Life of 3.*

Jack Smith's *Rehearsal for the Destruction of Atlantis*: "expanded cinema" event at Filmmaker's Cinematheque.

1966   *Six from La Mama* appears off-Broadway at Martinique Theatre.

La Mama Troupe forms under Tom O'Horgan's direction.

Play-House of the Ridiculous established on West Seventeenth Street.

Ntoni Bastiano establishes Playwrights' Workshop Club in Chelsea.

Jean-Claude van Itallie's triple bill *America Hurrah* and Megan Terry's *Viet Rock* open in off-Broadway productions.

La Mama temporarily blacklisted by Actors' Equity.

Theatre Genesis receives federal grant funding.

Eight Plays from Off-Off-Broadway published.

Cino: Musical *Dames at Sea*; Soren Agenoux's *Chas. Dickens' Christmas Carol.*

Judson: Shepard's *Red Cross.*

La Mama: Michael Smith's *The Next Thing*; Jeff Weiss's *And That's How the Rent Gets Paid.*

Genesis: Tony Barsha's *The Trunk*; Tom Sankey's *The Golden Screw.*

Ridiculous: Tavel's *The Life of Lady Godiva, Screen Test*, etc.

1967   Formation of Black Panther Party and Yippie organization.

Joseph Cino dies of self-inflicted wounds; Charles Stanley takes over as manager of Caffe Cino.

La Mama Troupe's third European tour includes acclaimed runs at Edinburgh Festival and in London. Plays: Owens's *Futz*; Foster's *Tom Paine*; Melfi's *Times Square*, Shepard's *Melodrama Play*.

Tavel quits the Play-House of the Ridiculous, which also loses its playhouse, and becomes itinerant. Charles Ludlam also subsequently quits to form Ridiculous Theatrical Company.

First NEA grants to experimental theaters and workshops. La Mama wins grants from Rockefeller and Ford Foundations.

Old Reliable Tavern initiates theater program.

Cino: Jeff Weiss's *A Funny Walk Home*, Robert Heide's *Moon*, Tavel's *Vinyl*.

Judson: Tavel's *Gorilla Queen*, Stein's *In Circles* (both move off-Broadway).

La Mama: Eyen's *Sarah B. Divine*.

Genesis: Grant Duay's *Fruit Salad*; Keystone Company's *The Hawk*; Shepard's *Forensic and the Navigators*.

Ridiculous: Charles Ludlam's *Big Hotel, Conquest of the Universe*.

1968   Assassinations of Martin Luther King and Robert Kennedy.

Abortive revolution in Paris (Living Theatre occupies Odeon).

Police brutality sparks rioting by protesters at Chicago Democratic Convention; sections of anti-war movement adopt revolutionary rhetoric.

Caffe Cino closed by Michael Smith, due to licensing pressures.

Ragni and Rado's *Hair* opens on Broadway.

Mart Crowley's *The Boys in the Band* opens off-Broadway, after Playwrights' Unit try-out.

Futz, Tom Paine, and *Dames at Sea* opens off-Broadway.

Living Theatre returns to U.S. with *Paradise Now* etc.

Richard Schechner's Performance Group premieres *Dionysus in 69*.

Judson: Aristophanes' *Peace* (moves off-Broadway, 1969).

La Mama: Julie Bovasso's *The Moondreamers*.

Genesis: Murray Mednick's *The Hunter*.

Open Theatre: *The Serpent* premieres on tour in Europe.

Play-House of the Ridiculous: Kenneth Bernard's *The Moke-Eater*.

New Dramatists: Lanford Wilson's *The Gingham Dog*; Maria Irene Fornes's *Molly's Dream*.

1969   President Nixon takes office: announces troop withdrawals from Vietnam, while ordering U.S. incursion into Cambodia.

Stonewall Riots spark beginnings of gay liberation movement.

La Mama ETC reopens in foundation-funded premises, East Fourth Street.

Tom O'Horgan leaves La Mama, forming the New Troupe.

Play-House of the Ridiculous takes up residence at La Mama, opening with Tom Murrin's *Cock-Strong*.

Revised version of Fornes's *Promenade* opens off-Broadway.

Circle Repertory Company founded.

Grotowski's Polish Laboratory Theatre performs in New York.

Kenneth Tynan's *Oh! Calcutta!* opens in New York.

Judson: *The Urban Crisis*: first of Al Carmines's large-cast oratorios.

La Mama: Julie Bovasso's *Gloria and Esperanza*; Jeff Weiss's *The International Wrestling Match*; Tom Eyen's *The No Plays*.

Genesis: Walter Hadler's *Flite Cage, The Waterworks at Lincoln*.

Old Reliable: Robert Patrick's *Joyce Dynel* and *One Person*; William M. Hoffman's *XXXXX*.

1970   Four student protesters shot dead by troops at Kent State University.

La Mama announces formation of new ensembles under direction of Andrei Serban, Ching Yeh, Wilford Leach, etc.

Ralph Cook leaves Theatre Genesis. Replaced by triumvirate of Mednick, Shepard, Hadler.

Judson: Leon Katz's *Dracula Sabbat*; Carmines's *The Playful Tyrant*.

La Mama: Eyen's *The Dirtiest Show in Town*; Serban's *Arden of Faversham* and *Ubu*.

Genesis: Mednick's *The Deer Kill*.

Open Theatre: *Terminal*.

Play-House of the Ridiculous: Bernard's *Nightclub*, Jackie Curtis's *Heaven Grand in Amber Orbit*.

Ridiculous Theatrical Company: Ludlam's *Bluebeard*.

Circle Rep: David Starkweather's *A Practical Ritual to Exorcise Frustration after Forty Days of Rain*.

1971   Tom O'Horgan directs *Lenny* and *Jesus Christ Superstar* for Broadway.

Robert Wilson's *Deafman Glance* at BAM.

Theater for the New City launches with revival of *Dracula: Sabbat*, but Kornfeld and Barnes subsequently quit; Field and Bartenieff in control.

Shepard emigrates to London; Michael Smith takes his directorial position at Genesis.

Old Reliable ends theater program.

Playwrights' Unit closes.

La Mama begins charging for admission by ticket.

Formation of OOBA (Off-Off-Broadway Alliance).

Fornes and Bovasso form New York Theatre Strategy.

Judson: Carmines's *The Journey of Snow White*.

La Mama: Curtis's *Vain Victory*, musical *Godspell*.

Genesis: Michael Smith's *Country Music*.

Theater for the New City: Robert Nichols's *Minding the Store*.

1972 Watergate scandal breaks, as Nixon reelected president.

Judson: Stein's *The Making of Americans*, adapted by Leon Katz.

Open Theatre: *The Mutation Show*.

Gay Activists' Alliance: Jonathan Katz's *Coming Out*.

1973 U.S. signs cease-fire in Vietnam.

Joseph Chaikin disbands Open Theatre, with *Nightwalk* unfinished.

New York Theatre Strategy launches with festival of one-act plays at Manhattan Theatre Club.

Judson: Carmines's *The Faggot*.

Genesis: Mednick's *Are You Lookin'?*

Play-House of the Ridiculous: Bernard's *Magic Show of Dr. Ma-Gico*.

Ridiculous Theatrical Company: Ludlam's *Camille*.

Circle Rep: Lanford Wilson's *Hot l Baltimore* (moves off-Broadway).

Playwrights' Horizons: Robert Patrick's *Kennedy's Children*.

1974 President Nixon resigns.

Mednick and Smith quit Genesis, leaving Hadler in sole charge.

Doric Wilson founds TOSOS in Tribeca basement.

Judson: Stein's *Listen to Me*.

La Mama: Serban's *Greek Trilogy* completed.

1975 Patrick's *Kennedy's Children* plays briefly on Broadway.

1978   Theatre Genesis closes after fire at St. Mark's.
        New York Theatre Strategy wound up.
        Mednick launches Padua Hills Playwrights' Festival.
1981   Judson Poets' Theater wound up by church.

Appendix B: Interviewees, Correspondents, and Discussants

Unless otherwise indicated, contacts were interviews by the author conducted in New York. Interviews were tape-recorded and transcribed.

Allen, Michael	Letter to the author, August 25, 1995
Arcade, Penny	February 28, 2002
Barnes, Theo	April 22, 1999
Barsha, Tony	Los Angeles, January 17, 1997
Carmines, Al	September 13, 1995
Chaikin, Joseph	San Francisco, September 7, 1994
Charba, Mari-Claire	Roundtable discussion, New York, April 13, 2003
Craig, Peter	Roundtable discussion, New York, April 13, 2003
Cunliffe, Jerry	Roundtable discussion, New York, April 13, 2003
Davies, Joseph C.	August 11, 1996
Dahdah, Robert	February 12, 1997
Drexler, Rosalyn	August 14, 1996
Field, Crystal	September 16, 1995
Fornes, Maria Irene	August 17, 1994, September 16, 1995
Foster, Paul	Roundtable discussion, New York, April 13, 2003
Hadler, Walter	February 24, 1997, September 23, 1999
Hanft, Helen	February 27, 1997
Heide, Robert	February 13, 1997
Hoffman, William M.	September 14, 1995
Katz, Leon	Los Angeles, January 14, 1997
Kornfeld, Lawrence	September 12, 1995, September 27, 1999
Koutoukas, H. M.	September 18, 1995, September 14, 1998
Levy, Jacques	February 18, 2002
Lowry, Jane	February 25, 2002
Malina, Judith	February 17, 1997
Mason, Marshall W.	February 26, 1997

Mednick, Murray   Los Angeles, January 14, 1997
Nelson, Claris   Los Angeles, January 13, 1997
O'Horgan, Tom   September 17, 1995; roundtable discussion, New
                                York, April 13, 2003
Owens, Rochelle   Letter to the author, September 14, 1995
Patrick, Robert   Los Angeles, January 13, 1997
[Robert Patrick may be contacted at rbrtptrck@aol.com]
Powell, Michael Warren   February 27, 2002
Sainer, Arthur   September 15, 1995
Smith, Michael   Santa Barbara, January 18, 1997,
                                November 20, 2001
Stewart, Ellen   August 23, 1995
Vaccaro, John   September 15, 1995
Van Itallie, Jean-Claude   September 14, 1995
Wilson, Doric   August 23, 1995
Young, Barbara Eda   February 18, 1997
Yankowitz, Susan   February 20, 2002

Bibliography

Plays and Play Collections

Albee, Edward. 1961. *The American Dream* and *The Zoo Story*. New York: Signet.
———. 1971. *Tiny Alice, Box*, and *Quotations from Chairman Mao*. Harmondsworth: Penguin.
Barsha, Anthony. 1966. *The Trunk*. Manuscript, 30 pp., courtesy of the author.
Beckett, Samuel. 1956. *Waiting for Godot*. London: Faber and Faber.
Benedikt, Michael, ed. 1968. *Theatre Experiment: An Anthology of American Plays*. New York: Anchor.
Bernard, Kenneth. 1971. *Nightclub and Other Plays*. New York: Winter House.
Brown, Kenneth H. 1965. *The Brig*. New York: Hill and Wang.
Carmines, Al. 1973. *The Faggot*. Manuscript, 52 pp., Judson Church archives.
Crowley, Mart. 1969. *The Boys in the Band*. New York: Secker and Warburg.
Dennison, George. 1962. *Vaudeville Skit*. Manuscript, 18 pp., collection of Lawrence Kornfeld.
———. 1963. *The Service for Joseph Axminster*. Manuscript, 27 pp., collection of Lawrence Kornfeld.
———. 1964. *Patter for a Soft-Shoe Dance*. Manuscript, 5 pp., collection of Lawrence Kornfeld.
———. 1979. *Oilers and Sweepers and Other Stories*. New York: Random House.
di Prima, Diane. 1963. *Murder Cake*. Manuscript, 7 pp., Judson Church archives.
Drexler, Rosalyn. 1967. *The Line of Least Existence and Other Plays*. New York: Random House.
Eyen, Tom. 1971. *Sarah B. Divine and Other Plays*. New York: Winter House.
Ferlinghetti, Lawrence. 1963. *Unfair Arguments with Existence*. New York: New Directions.
Fornes, Maria Irene. 1978. *Fefu and Her Friends*. New York: PAJ Publications.
———. 1987. *Promenade and Other Plays*. New York: PAJ Publications.
Foster, Paul. 1967a. *Tom Paine*. London: Calder and Boyars.
———. 1967b. *Balls and Other Plays*. London: Calder and Boyars.
———. 1970. *Heimskringla, or The Stoned Angels*. London: Calder and Boyars.
Gelber, Jack. 1960. *The Connection*. New York: Grove.
Genet, Jean. 1954. *The Maids and Deathwatch*. New York: Grove.
Hadler, Walter. 1969. *The Waterworks at Lincoln*. Manuscript, 28 pp., courtesy of the author.
Heide, Robert. 1965. *The Bed*. Manuscript, 2 pp., courtesy of the author.
Hoffman, William M., ed. 1968. *New American Plays*. Vol. 2. New York: Hill and Wang.

————. ed. 1970. *New American Plays: Volume 3*. New York: Hill and Wang.

————. ed. 1971. *New American Plays: Volume 4*. New York: Hill and Wang.

————, ed. 1979. *Gay Plays: The First Collection*. New York: Avon.

Jones, LeRoi. 1965. *Dutchman* and *The Slave*. London: Faber and Faber.

————. 1966. *The System of Dante's Hell*. London: MacGibbon and Kee.

Katz, Leon. 1992. *Midnight Plays*. Los Angeles: Wavecrest.

Koutoukas, H. M. 1965a. *Medea; or, The Stars May Understand*. Manuscript, 17 pp., collection of Michael Smith.

————. 1965b. *With Creatures Make My Way*. Manuscript, 12 pp., collection of Michael Smith.

Lahr, John, and Jonathan Price, eds. 1974. *The Great American Life Show: Nine Plays from the Avant-Garde Theater*. New York: Bantam.

Ludlam, Charles. 1989. *The Complete Plays of Charles Ludlam*. New York: Harper and Row.

Machiz, Herbert, ed. 1960. *Artists' Theatre: Four Plays*. New York: Grove.

Malpede, Karen. 1974. *Three Works by the Open Theater*. New York: Drama Book Specialists.

Marranca, Bonnie, and Gautam Dasgupta, eds. 1998. *Theatre of the Ridiculous*. Rev. ed. Baltimore: Johns Hopkins University Press.

McClure, Michael. 1971. *Gargoyle Cartoons*. New York: Delta.

Mednick, Murray. 1972. *The Deer Kill*. Indianapolis: Bobbs-Merrill.

————. 1973. *Are You Lookin'?* Manuscript, 85 pp., courtesy of the author.

————. 1993. *The Coyote Cycle*. Los Angeles: Padua Hills Press.

Mednick, Murray, and Tony Barsha. 1969. *The Hawk*. Indianapolis: Bobbs-Merrill.

Melfi, Leonard. 1967. *Encounters*. New York: Samuel French.

Miller, Arthur. 1958. *Collected Plays*. London: Cresset.

Nelson, Claris. 1962. *The Rue Garden*. Manuscript, 41 pp., courtesy of the author.

Nelson, Stanley, and Harry Smith, eds. 1972. *The Scene 1: Plays from Off-Off-Broadway*. New York: New Egypt.

O'Hara, Frank. 1978. *Selected Plays*. New York: Full Court.

Orzel, Nick, and Michael Smith, eds. 1966. *Eight Plays from Off-Off-Broadway*. Indianapolis: Bobbs-Merrill.

Owens, Rochelle. 1968. *Futz* and *What Came After*. New York: Random House.

Parone, Edward, ed. 1965. *New Theatre in America*. New York: Delta.

Patrick, Robert. 1972. *Robert Patrick's Cheep Theatricks*. New York: Winter House.

————. 1976. *Kennedy's Children*. New York: Samuel French.

Performance Group. 1970. *Dionysus in 69*. Ed. Richard Schechner. New York: Farrar, Straus and Giroux.

Pinter, Harold. 1976. *Plays: One*. Vol. 1. London: Methuen.

Poland, Albert, and Bruce Mailman, eds. 1972. *The Off-Off-Broadway Book*. Indianapolis: Bobbs-Merrill.

Ragni, Gerome, and James Rado. 1969. *Hair: The American Tribal Love-Rock Musical*. New York: Pocket Books.

Schroeder, Robert J., ed. 1968. *The New Underground Theatre*. New York: Bantam.

Shepard, Sam. 1967. *Five Plays*. Indianapolis: Bobbs-Merrill.

————. 1986. *The Unseen Hand and Other Plays*. New York: Bantam.

Smith, Michael, ed. 1969. *The Best of Off-Off-Broadway*. New York: Dutton.

————, ed. 1972. *More Plays from Off-Off-Broadway*. Indianapolis: Bobbs-Merrill.

Stein, Gertrude. 1975. *Last Operas and Plays*. Ed. Carl van Vechten. New York: Vintage.

Tavel, Ronald. 1966. *The Life of Juanita Castro*. Tri-Quarterly 6:119–26.

———. 1967. *Shower*. In *The Young American Writers*, ed. Richard Kostelanetz, 310–34. New York: Funk and Wagnalls.

Terry, Megan. 1966. *Viet Rock*. Tulane Drama Review 11, no. 1: 196–227.

———. 1967. *Viet Rock and Other Plays*. New York: Simon and Schuster.

Tynan, Kenneth, and Jacques Levy. 1969. *Oh! Calcutta!* New York: Grove.

van Itallie, Jean-Claude. 1978. *America Hurrah and Other Plays*. New York: Grove.

Walcott, Derek. 1970. *Dream on Monkey Mountain and Other Plays*. New York: Noonday.

Weiss, Jeff. 1967. *A Funny Walk Home*. Manuscript, 34 pp., collection of Michael Smith.

Wilson, Doric. 1961a. *And He Made a Her*. Manuscript, 30 pp., courtesy of the author.

———. 1961b. *Babel Babel Little Tower*. Manuscript, 28 pp., courtesy of the author.

———. 2000. *Now She Dances!, A Perfect Relationship, The West Street Gang, Street Theater, Forever After*. Revised versions of these previously published plays may be downloaded from the author's website: www.doricwilson.com.

Wilson, Lanford. 1969. *The Gingham Dog*. New York: Dramatists Play Service.

———. 1973. *Hot l Baltimore*. New York: Mermaid.

———. 1988. *Balm in Gilead and Other Plays*. New York: Noonday.

———. 1993. *Twenty-One Short Plays*. New York: Smith and Kraus.

Books, Articles, and Other Sources

Some of the following references lack page numbers or other bibliographical information. In these cases, the sources are archived clippings with incomplete information. Every effort has been made to provide all relevant details.

Absher, Kathryn Ann. 1990. "Caffe Cino: The Cradle of Lanford Wilson's Career." M.A. thesis, University of Nebraska. Includes interview with Wilson.

Albee, Edward. 1964. "Where the Action Is, or, Notes on the Future." *New York Herald Tribune*, December 27, pp. 12–14.

Alter, Nora M. 1996. *Vietnam Protest Theatre: The Television War on Stage*. Bloomington: Indiana University Press.

Arden, John. 1967. Letter to the *New York Times*, November 26, pp. 8, 14.

Aronson, Arnold. 2000. *American Avant-Garde Theatre: A History*. London: Routledge.

Artaud, Antonin. 1970. *The Theatre and Its Double*. Trans. Victor Corti. London: Calder and Boyars.

Banes, Sally. 1993a. *Democracy's Body: The Judson Dance Theater, 1962–64*. Durham: Duke University Press.

———. 1993b. *Greenwich Village, 1963: Avant-Garde Performance and the Effervescent Body*. Durham: Duke University Press.

Barba, Eugenio. 1965. "Theatre Laboratory 13 Rzedow." *Tulane Drama Review* 9, no. 3: 153–65.

Barthes, Roland. 1977. *Image Music Text*. Trans. Stephen Heath. London: Fontana.

Bartlett, Neil. 1990. "Just Ridiculous." *American Theatre*, April, pp. 50–51.

Battcock, Gregory, ed. 1995. *Minimal Art: A Critical Anthology.* Berkeley and Los Angeles: University of California Press.

Beck, Julian. 1972. *The Life of the Theatre: The Relation of the Artist to the Struggle of the People.* San Francisco: City Lights.

Benevy, Robert. 1955. "For $250—a Theatre in the New 'Village.'" *Mirror Magazine,* n.d., n.p.

Bigsby, C. W. E. 1985. *A Critical Introduction to Twentieth Century American Drama.* Vol. 3, *Beyond Broadway.* Cambridge: Cambridge University Press.

Bjorksten, Ingmar. 1967. "Report from Stockholm." *Village Voice,* August 24, p. 18.

Blanc, Maurice. 1969. "Participations and Responses." *Village Voice,* January 30, pp. 43–44.

Blumenthal, Eileen. 1984. *Joseph Chaikin: Exploring at the Boundaries of Theater.* Cambridge: Cambridge University Press.

Bottoms, Stephen J. 1997. "Language Is the Motor: Text and Performance in Maria Irene Fornes' *Promenade.*" *New England Theatre Journal* 8:45–71.

———. 1998a. *The Theatre of Sam Shepard: States of Crisis.* Cambridge: Cambridge University Press.

———. 1998b. "The Tangled Flora of Goat Island: Rhizome, Repetition, Reality." *Theatre Journal* 50, no. 4: 421–46.

———. 2002. "Shepard and Off-Off-Broadway: The Unseen Hand of Theatre Genesis." In *The Cambridge Companion to Sam Shepard,* ed. Matthew Roudane. Cambridge: Cambridge University Press.

———. 2003. "The Efficacy/Effeminacy Braid: Unpicking the Performance Studies/Theatre Studies Dichotomy." *Theatre Topics* 13, no. 2: 173–87.

Brecht, Bertolt. 1964. *Brecht on Theatre.* Trans. John Willett. New York: Hill and Wang.

Brecht, Stefan. 1986. *Queer Theatre.* London: Methuen.

Brustein, Robert. 1970. *The Third Theatre.* London: Jonathan Cape.

Bryer, Jackson. 1995. *The Playwright's Art: Conversations with Contemporary American Dramatists.* New Brunswick, N.J.: Rutgers University Press.

Burke, Tom. 1969. "And I Call That God." *New York Times,* February 23, p. 7.

Chaikin, Joseph. 1972. *The Presence of the Actor.* New York: Atheneum.

———. 1974. "Closing the Open Theatre: An Interview with Joseph Chaikin." Interview by Richard Toscan. *Theatre Quarterly* 4, no. 16: 36–47.

Cleto, Fabio, ed. 1999. *Camp: Queer Aesthetics and the Performing Subject: A Reader.* Ann Arbor: University of Michigan Press.

Cohn, Ruby. 1991. *New American Dramatists 1960–1990.* New York: Grove.

———. 1998. *From Desire to Godot: The Pocket Theatre of Post-war Paris.* London: Calder.

Corrigan, Robert W. 1964. "Corrigan on TDR." *Tulane Drama Review* 8, no. 4: 13–16.

Croyden, Margaret. 1974. *Lunatics, Lovers, and Poets: The Contemporary Experimental Theatre.* New York: McGraw-Hill.

———. 1970. "For Joe Chaikin, Burning Bridges is Natural." *New York Times,* March 29, pp. 1, 3.

Dace, Tish. 1981. "Wilson's Tale Told." *Other Stages,* June 4, p. 10.

di Prima, Diane. 2001. *Recollections of My Life as a Woman: The New York Years.* New York: Viking.

Dolan, Jill. 2001. *Geographies of Learning: Theory and Practice, Activism and Performance*. Middleton: Wesleyan University Press.

Dominic, Magie. 1979. "Caffe Cino: Part VI." *Other Stages*, July 12, p. 5.

Drexler, Rosalyn. 1986. *Intimate Emotions*. N.p. Catalog accompanying touring exhibition of Drexler's paintings.

Erlatinger, J. Lance. 1968. "It Was a Hairy Scene before *Hair*." *Off-Off*, October, pp. 1–2.

Esslin, Martin. 1962. *The Theatre of the Absurd*. London: Eyre and Spottiswoode.

Feingold, Michael. 1973. "A New Way of Making Theater—and It's Over." *New York Times*, October 7, p. 3.

Feldman, Peter. 1966. "Notes for the Open Theatre Production [of *Keep Tightly Closed in a Cool Dark Place*]." *Tulane Drama Review* 10, no. 4: 200–208.

Flatley, Guy. 1973. "One 'L' of a Playwright." *New York Times*, April 22, pp. 1, 21.

Foreman, Richard. 1992. *Unbalancing Acts: Foundations for a Theater*. New York: Theatre Communications Group.

Fornes, Maria Irene. 1985. "Creative Danger." *American Theatre*, September, pp. 13–15.

Foster, Paul. 1979. "A Nurse in a Madhouse." *Other Stages*, March 22, p. 7.

Gnys, Charles. 1968. [On the Playwrights' Unit.] *New York Times*, February 25.

Goffman, Erving. 1969. *The Presentation of Self in Everyday Life*. Harmondsworth: Penguin.

Gordy, Douglas W. 1998. "Joseph Cino and the First Off-Off-Broadway Theater." In *Passing Performances: Queer Readings of Leading Players in American Theater History*, ed. Robert A. Schanke and Kim Marra. Ann Arbor: University of Michigan Press.

Gould, Christopher. 1979. "George and Crystal." *Other Stages*, February 22, p. 2.

Gress, Elsa. 1969. "Ohorganism: the Lost Years." *The Drama Review* 13, no. 3: 115–19.

Grotowski, Jerzy. 1969a. "External Order, Internal Intimacy: An Interview with Jerzy Grotowski." Interview by Marc Fumarole. *The Drama Review* 14, no. 1: 172–77.

———. 1969b. *Towards a Poor Theatre*. Ed. Eugenio Barba. London: Methuen.

Gruen, John. 1965. "The Off-Beat Beat: Off Off Broadway." *New York Herald Tribune*, September 12, Magazine section, pp. 20–24.

———. 1967. "The Pop Scene: Talented Young Actor Chooses Poverty to Easy Compromise." *New York World Journal Tribune*, February 16.

———. 1990. *The New Bohemia*. Chicago: A Cappella.

Gussow, Mel. 1970. "Playwrights Lift the Curtain on Success." *New York Times*, February 4.

———. 1972. "Off-Off-Broadway Aims to Be Right On." *New York Times*, July 12, p. 28.

———. 1974. "Suddenly, Real Plays about Real People." *New York Times*, May 12, pp. 1, 6.

Harding, James M., ed. 2000. *Contours of the Theatrical Avant-Garde: Performance and Textuality*. Ann Arbor: University of Michigan Press.

Heide, Robert. 1979. "Cockroaches in the Baubles." *Other Stages*, February 22, pp. 8–9.

———. 1985. "Magic Time." *New York Native*, May 19, p. 30.

Isaac, Dan. 1968. "Ronald Tavel: Ridiculous Playwright." *The Drama Review* 13, no. 1: 106–15.

Kaufman, David. 2002. *Ridiculous! The Theatrical Life and Times of Charles Ludlam.* New York: Applause.

Kaplan, Donald. 1965. "Homosexuality and American Theatre: A Psychoanalytic Comment." *Tulane Drama Review* 9, no. 3: 25–55.

Keating, John. 1965. "Making It *Off* Off Broadway." *New York Times*, April 25, pp. 1, 3.

Kempton, Sally. 1966. "Beatitudes at Judson Church." *Esquire*, March, pp. 106–7.

Kirby, Michael. 1965. *Happenings: An Illustrated Anthology.* New York: Dutton.

———, ed. 1985. Special issue on East Village Performance. *The Drama Review* 29, no. 1.

Klemesrud, Judy. 1970. "Dirty Is a State of Mind." *New York Times*, August 16, pp. 1, 5.

Kolin, Philip C., ed. 1988. *Conversations with Edward Albee.* Jackson: University Press of Mississippi.

Kornfeld, Lawrence. 1990. "How the Curtain Did Come: The Theatre of Gertrude Stein." In *Gertrude Stein Advanced*, ed. Richard Kostelanetz, 135–42. Jefferson, N.C.: McFarland.

LaGuardia, Robert. 1969. "A Role for Every Soul at Old Reliable." *Off-Off*, March, pp. 3, 8.

Lahr, John. 1969. "Getting By with No Help from Her Friends." *New York Free Press*, January 30.

Leffingwell, Edward, et al., eds. 1997. *Jack Smith: Flaming Creature.* London: Serpent's Tail.

Leogrande, Ernest. 1973. "Night Owl Reporter." *New York Daily News*, June 12, p. 1.

Lerman, Leo. 1966. [On La Mama.] *Mademoiselle*, March, pp. 146–47.

Lester, Elenore. 1965d. "The Pass-the-Hat Theater Circuit." *New York Times*, December 5, Magazine section, pp. 90–108.

———. 1967. "In the Parish Hall, the Hippies Go Ape." *New York Times*, March 26, pp. 1, 3.

———. 1968. "O'Horgan: 'Of Course, There Were Some Limits.'" *New York Times*, May 19, p. 14.

———. 1970. "Mama Makes 'Wonton Soup.'" *New York Times*, April 5, p. 5.

Levin, Peter. 1965. "Hardware House." *New York Herald Tribune*, February 24.

Loubier, Charles. 1979. "Caffe Cino, Part VII." *Other Stages*, June 14, p. 8.

Loughery, John. 1999. *The Other Side of Silence: Men's Lives and Gay Identities, a Twentieth Century History.* New York: Henry Holt.

Ludlam, Charles. 1992. *Ridiculous Theatre: the Scourge of Human Folly.* New York: Theatre Communications Group.

Malina, Judith. 1972. *The Enormous Despair.* New York: Random House.

Malina, Judith, and Julian Beck. 1969. "Containment Is the Enemy: An Interview with Judith Malina and Julian Beck." Interview by Richard Schechner. *The Drama Review* 13, no. 3: 24–44.

Marcus, Greil. 1997. *Invisible Republic: Bob Dylan's Basement Tapes.* New York: Henry Holt.

Marowitz, Charles. 1967. "La Mama 'Alienates' London." *New York Times*, November 12, p. 17.

———. 1969. "Dateline London: Existential Thunder." *Village Voice*, February 20.

———. 1970. "Dateline London." *Village Voice*, March 5.

Marranca, Bonnie, ed. 1977. "American Experimental Theatre: Then and Now." *Performing Arts Journal* 2, no. 2: 13–24.

———, ed. 1981. *American Dreams: The Imagination of Sam Shepard.* New York: PAJ Publications.

Marranca, Bonnie, and Gautam Dasgupta. 1981. *American Playwrights: A Critical Survey.* Vol. 1. New York: Drama Book Specialists.

McDonough, Jimmy. 2001. *The Ghastly One: The Sex-Gore Netherworld of Filmmaker Andy Milligan.* Chicago: A Cappella.

Menta, Ed. 1995. *The Magic World behind the Curtain: Andrei Serban in the American Theatre.* New York: Peter Lang.

Owens, Rochelle. 1989. "The Androgynous Muse: An Interview with Rochelle Owens." Interview by C. B. Coleman. *Yale/Theater,* spring, 19–23.

Pasolli, Robert. 1970. *A Book on the Open Theatre.* New York: Avon.

Patrick, Robert. 1979. "The Other Brick Road." *Other Stages,* February 8, pp. 3, 10.

———. 1994. *Temple Slave.* New York: Masquerade.

Russell, Donn. 1996. *Avant-Guardian: A Theater Foundation Director's Twenty-five Years Off-Broadway, 1965–1990.* Pittsburgh: Dorrance.

Sainer, Arthur. 1975. *The Radical Theatre Notebook.* New York: Avon.

———. 1984. "Is the Best Now behind Us?" *Village Voice,* April 3, p. 87.

Sandford, Mariellen. 1995. *Happenings and Other Acts.* London: Routledge.

Savran, David. 1988. *In Their Own Words: Contemporary American Playwrights.* New York: Theatre Communications Group.

———. 1994. "Tony Kushner Considers the Longstanding Problems of Virtue and Happiness." *American Theatre,* October 20–27, pp. 100–104.

Schechner, Richard. 1963a. "Who's Afraid of Edward Albee?" *Tulane Drama Review* 7, no. 3: 7–10.

———. 1963b. "TDR: 1963–?" *Tulane Drama Review* 8, no. 2: 9–14.

———. 1981. "The Decline and Fall of the (American) Avant-Garde." *Performing Arts Journal* 5, no. 2: 48–63.

———. 1994. *Environmental Theater.* New York: Applause.

Schroeder, Robert J. 1969. "The Rise/Fall of Off Off Broadway." *Dramatists Guild Quarterly* 5, no. 4: 32–34.

———. 1970. "The 'Other Theater': A Survey." *Dramatists Guild Quarterly* 7, no. 1: 38–43.

Schultz, Bud, and Ruth Schultz. 2001. *The Price of Dissent: Testimonies to Political Repression in America.* Berkeley and Los Angeles: University of California Press.

Schumach, Murray. 1968. "Off Off Broadway Theater in Squeeze." *New York Times,* March 20.

Shepard, Sam. 1971. "Autobiography: Sam Shepard." *News of the American Place Theatre* 3: 1–2.

Smith, Jack. 1997. *Wait for Me at the Bottom of the Pool: The Writings of Jack Smith.* Ed. J. Hoberman and Edward Leffingwell. New York: High Risk Books.

Smith, Michael. 1966. "The Good Scene: Off Off-Broadway." *Tulane Drama Review* 10, no. 4: 159–76.

———. 1969. *Theatre Trip.* Indianapolis: Bobbs-Merrill.

———. 1985. "The Caffe Cino: Homage to a Patron of the Arts." *The Day* (New London, Conn.), March 24, p. B13.

———. 1991. "Obituary: John P. Dodd, 1941–91." *Village Voice,* August 6.

———. 2001. "One Single Time." Autobiographical manuscript, 669 pp., courtesy of the author.

Sontag, Susan. 1967. *Against Interpretation and Other Essays.* New York: Farrar, Straus and Giroux.

Stein, Gertrude. 1985. *Lectures in America.* Boston: Beacon Press.

Stewart, Ellen. 1982. "La Mama Celebrates Twenty Years." *Performing Arts Journal* 6, no. 2: 6–17.

Sukenick, Ronald. 1987. *Down and In: Life in the Underground.* New York: Beech Tree.

Tallmer, Jerry. 1991a. "Death of a Hell-Raiser." *New York Post,* September 17, p. 29.

———. 1991b. "A Life on the Edge: Julie Bovasso Remembered." *Theater Week,* October 14, pp. 30–31.

Tavel, Ronald. 1966a. "The Theatre of the Ridiculous." *Tri-Quarterly* 6:93–109.

Terry, Megan. 1966a. "*Viet Rock* Escalates." *New York World Tribune,* November 6.

Tomkins, Calvin. 1968. *The Bride and the Bachelors: Five Masters of the Avant-Garde.* New York: Viking.

Topor, Tom. 1972. "Off Off Broadway: Bewitched, Bothered, and Bewildered, but Produced." *Dramatists Guild Quarterly* 9, no. 3: 6, 11–14.

Tytell, John. 1995. *The Living Theatre: Art, Exile, and Outrage.* New York: Grove.

Vaccaro, John. 1968. "I Come from Ohio: An Interview with John Vaccaro." Interview by Dan Isaac. *Drama Review* 13, no. 1: 142.

van Itallie, Jean-Claude. 1979. "*War* and We." *Other Stages,* May 17, p. 6.

———. 1981. "Memories." *Other Stages,* November 19, p. 8.

Venza, Jac, prod. and dir. 1970. *The Open Theatre: The Serpent.* Documentary film for NET Playhouse, Educational Broadcasting Corporation.

Wallach, Allan. 1968. "He's Gertrude Stein's Soul Mate." *Newsday,* July 11, p. 56.

Wetzsteon, Ross. 1975. "Chaikin and O'Horgan Survive the '60s." *Village Voice,* November 3, pp. 81–86.

———. 1982. "The Most Populist Playwright." *New York,* November 8, pp. 40–45.

Williams, Philip Middleton. 1993. *A Comfortable House: Lanford Wilson, Marshall W. Mason, and the Circle Repertory Theatre.* Jefferson, N.C.: McFarland.

Wilson, Doric. 1979. "Everything but the Dates." *Other Stages,* March 8, p. 7.

Wilson, Lanford. 1978. Interview by Robb Baker. *After Dark,* June, p. 40.

Wolf, Reva. 1997. *Andy Warhol: Poetry and Gossip in the 1960s.* Chicago: University of Chicago Press.

Woronov, Mary. 2000. *Swimming Underground: My Years in the Warhol Factory.* London: Serpent's Tail.

Reviews

Albee, Edward. 1965. "Theatre: *Icarus's Mother.*" *Village Voice,* November 25, p. 19.

Baker, Robb. 1973. "Al Carmines' *The Faggot.*" *After Dark,* July, pp. 36–37.

Barnes, Clive. 1967. "Theater: Gertrude Stein Words at the Judson Church." *New York Times,* October 14.

———. 1968a. "Theater: *The Hawk,* a Play of Improvisation, Opens." *New York Times,* April 18, p. 54.

———. 1968b. "Theater: *Hair*—It's Fresh and Frank." *New York Times,* April 30, p. 40.

———. 1968c. "Theater: Camping It Up." *New York Times,* November 10.

———. 1968d. "Theater: Musical Pastiche of the 30's with Panache." *New York Times,* December 21, p. 46.

————. 1970a. Review of *Forensic and the Navigators* and *The Unseen Hand*. *New York Times*, April 2.

————. 1970b. "Drama: The Ritual of *Dracula: Sabbat*." *New York Times*, October 2, p. 28.

————. 1973. "Lanford Wilson's *Hot l Baltimore*." *New York Times*, March 23, p. 21.

————. 1974. "Stage: An Oddly Touching *Camille*." *New York Times*, May 13, p. 31.

Brukenfeld, Dick. 1969. "Theatre: Two Solos." *Village Voice*, September 4, p. 36.

Buck, Richard M. 1970. Undated press bureau typescript regarding Open Theatre's *Endgame*.

Calta, Louis. 1964. "Theater: *Home Movies*." *New York Times*, May 12.

Colman, Sam. 1970a. "*Dracula: Sabbat*: Demonic Erotica." *Show Business*, October 10, p. 13.

————. 1970b. "Off-Broadway: *The Playful Tyrant*." *Show Business*, November 7.

Feingold, Michael. 1971. "Theatre: *Country Music*." *Village Voice*, December 23, p. 59.

————. 1974. "Triumph, the Stein Way." *Village Voice*, October 24, p. 85.

————. 1975. "Theater: *Why I Love New York*." *Village Voice*, October 20, p. 111.

————. 1979a. "Stein et Lumiere." *Village Voice*, November 12, p. 107.

————. 1979b. "Voice Choices." *Village Voice*, November 19, p. 67.

————. 1991. "Sex and the Single Pig." *Village Voice*, October 29, p. 98.

Gill, Brendan. 1968. Review of *Hair*. *New Yorker*, May 11, p. 84.

Gilman, Richard. 1967. Review of *Snow White*, by Donald Barthelme. *New Republic*, June 3, p. 27.

Goldstein, Richard. 1967. "Turn of *The Golden Screw*." *New York World Journal Tribune*, February 12, pp. 22–23.

Gussow, Mel. 1967. "All About Tom." *Newsweek*, February 13.

————. 1971. "Stage: *Vain Victory*, Campy Transvestite Musical Spectacle." *New York Times*, August 25, p. 46.

Herschberger, Ruth. 1961. "Theatre." *Village Voice*, December 14.

Hewes, Henry. 1968. Review of *Tom Paine*. *Saturday Review*, May 4.

————. 1970. Review of *Terminal*. *Saturday Review*, May 2, p. 12.

————. 1971. Review of *Dracula: Sabbat*. *Saturday Review*, May 15, p. 17.

Johnston, Jill. 1961. "Dance: James Waring and Co." *Village Voice*, January 5, p. 9.

Kauffmann, Stanley. 1966a. "Theater: La Mama Bill." *New York Times*, April 12.

————. 1966b. "Last 3 Plays of '6 from La Mama' Offered at the Martinique." *New York Times*, April 13.

————. 1966c. "Music by Al Carmines." *New York Times*, July 3.

Kerr, Walter. 1966a. "The Theater: A Whisper in the Wind." *New York Times*, November 7, p. 66.

————. 1966b. "One Succeeds, the Other Fails." *New York Times*, November 12, pp. 1, 3.

————. 1968. "*Futz*: Is It a Fiasco?" *New York Times*, June 30, pp. 1, 5.

————. 1971. "What Did Dracula Ever See in Lucy?" *New York Times*, April 18, pp. 1, 18.

Krim, Seymour. 1960. "Café Theatre: *No Exit*." *Village Voice*, December 15.

Kroll, Jack. 1970. "The Count." *Newsweek*, October 5, p. 87.

————. 1975. "Howl for the '60s." *Newsweek*, November 17, 93.

Lahr, John. 1968. "What to Do with Tom Paine Who Liked Words." *New York Free Press*, April 4, pp. 7, 10.

———. 1970. "On-Stage" [*Terminal*]. *Village Voice*, April 23, p. 43.

Lester, Elenore. 1965a. "Theatre: Genesis." *Village Voice*, June 24.

———. 1965b. "Theatre: *The Bed.*" *Village Voice*, July 8.

———. 1965c. "Theatre: Two by Tavel." *Village Voice*, August [?].

LeSueur, Joseph. 1966a. "Theatre: Two Plays by Ronald Tavel." *Village Voice*, October 13, p. 25.

———. 1966b. "Theatre: *Viet Rock.*" *Village Voice*, November 17.

———. 1966c. "Theatre: *The White Whore and the Bit Player.*" *Village Voice*, December 22.

Leverett, James. 1979. "Gertrude Stein Lights the Lights." *Soho Weekly News*, November 8, p. 63.

Malpede Taylor, Karen. 1973. "Toodooloo Marguerite." *The Press*, May 19, p. 12.

Marlowe, Alan. 1963. "Wieners and Stein at Judson." *The Floating Bear*, No. 27, n.p.

Mishkin, Leo. 1969. "*Promenade* Witty Melodious Musical." *Morning Telegraph*, June 6.

Novick, Julius. 1966. "Theatre: *And That's How the Rent Gets Paid.*" *Village Voice*, September 1.

———. 1974. "La Mama Rekindles the Fire of Ancient Greek Drama." *New York Times*, November 17, p. 5.

Oliver, Edith. 1971. Review of *Deafman Glance*. *New Yorker*, March 20, pp. 95–96.

Pasolli, Robert. 1965. "Theatre: Hardware Poets." *Village Voice*, May 13, p. 16.

———. 1967a. "Post-Mortem of an Off-Off-Broadway Casualty." *Village Voice*, February 23.

———. 1967b. "Theatre: A Non-Review." *Village Voice*, November 30.

———. 1968a. "Theatre Journal." *Village Voice*, February 1, p. 39.

———. 1968b. "Theatre: *The Moke-Eater.*" *Village Voice*, September 26.

———. 1968c. "The Theatre of the Hung-Up." *Village Voice*, December 19, p. 49.

———. 1969a. "A Communal Theatre Experiment in Progress." *Village Voice*, March 20.

———. 1969b. "Irene Fornes: You Take a Yes and a No." *Village Voice*, April 17, pp. 45, 57–60.

Rich, Alan. 1972. "Life Is Like a Basketball Game, Isn't It?" *New York*, May 8, p. 74.

———. 1974. Review of Serban's *Greek Trilogy*. *New York*, November 11, p. 117.

Sainer, Arthur. 1970a. "Theatre: *The Deer Kill.*" *Village Voice*, May 14, p. 44.

———. 1970b. "Theatre: *Dracula Sabbat.*" *Village Voice*, September 17.

———. 1973. "Theatre: *The Faggot.*" *Village Voice*, June 28, p. 66.

Sarris, Andrew. 1965. "Films." *Village Voice*, December 9.

Schmidt, Sandra. 1961. "Theatre." *Village Voice*, November 2.

Sege. 1970. Review of *The Dirtiest Show in Town*. *Variety*, July 1.

Simon, John. 1968. "Hogwash." *New York*, July 1, p. 52.

Smith, Michael. 1961. "Theatre" [Judson Gallery Players]. *Village Voice*, March 30.

———. 1962a. "Theatre: Two at Judson" [*Vaudeville Skit*]. *Village Voice*, August 30.

———. 1962b. "Theatre: Two at Judson" [*Malcochon*]. *Village Voice*, November 8.

———. 1963a. "Theatre: Two at Judson" [*Murder Cake* and *The Service for Joseph Axminster*]. *Village Voice*, March 14.

———. 1963b. "Theatre: Judson Poets" [*Asphodel* and *What Happened*]. *Village Voice*, October 3.

———. 1964a. "Theatre: Present Stages." *Village Voice*, March 26, pp. 9, 15.

———. 1964b. "Theatre: *Home Movies*." *Village Voice*, May 14.

———. 1964c. "Theatre: *The Madness of Lady Bright*." *Village Voice*, May 21.

———. 1964d. "Theatre: *Cowboys* and *The Rock Garden*." *Village Voice*, November 19.

———. 1964e. "Theatre: *Sing Ho for a Bear!*" *Village Voice*, December 24.

———. 1965a. "Theatre: Two by Wilson." *Village Voice*, February 11.

———. 1965b. "New Playwrights: 1." *Village Voice*, February 18.

———. 1965c. "Theatre: *Devices* and *The Promenade*." *Village Voice*, April 15, p. 20.

———. 1965d. "Theatre Journal" [*America Hurrah* and *Chicago*]. *Village* Voice, 15 May.

———. 1965e. "Theatre Journal" [*Medea*]. *Village Voice*, October [?] .

———. 1965f. "Theatre Journal" [*A Beautiful Day*]. *Village Voice*, December 16.

———. 1965g. "Theatre Journal" [*All Day for a Dollar*]. *Village Voice*, December 22.

———. 1966a. "Theatre Journal" [Hardware Poets]. *Village Voice*, February 3.

———. 1966b. "Theatre Journal" [La Mama Troupe]. *Village Voice*, March 17, p. 19.

———. 1966c. "Theatre Journal" [*The Life of Lady Godiva*]. *Village Voice*, April 28, p. 27.

———. 1966d. "Theatre Journal" [*The Golden Screw*, Genesis]. *Village Voice*, September 29, pp. 21–23.

———. 1967a. "Theatre Journal" [*The Golden Screw*, Off-Broadway]. *Village Voice*, February 2.

———. 1967b. "Theatre Journal" [*Futz*]. *Village Voice*, March 9.

———. 1967c. "Theatre Journal" [*Sarah B. Divine*]. *Village Voice*, June 8.

———. 1967d. "Theatre Journal" [*The Hawk*]. *Village Voice*, October 26.

———. 1967e. "Theatre Journal" [*Vinyl*]. *Village Voice*, November 9.

———. 1967f. "Theatre Journal" [*Conquest of the Universe*]. *Village Voice*, November 30, pp. 33, 37.

———. 1968a. "Theatre Journal" [*The Moondreamers*]. *Village Voice*, February 8, pp. 33–34.

———. 1968b. "Theatre Journal" [Caffe Cino closure]. *Village Voice*, March 14.

———. 1968c. "Theatre Journal" [*Hair*]. *Village Voice*, May 2.

———. 1971. "Theatre Journal" [Ronald Tavel]. *Village Voice*. December 2, p. 61.

———. 1973a. "Theatre Journal" [*Hot l Baltimore*]. *Village Voice*, Feburary 8, p. 61.

———. 1973b. "Theatre Journal" [New York Theatre Strategy]. *Village Voice*, May 17, p. 81.

———. 1973c. "Theatre Journal" [Open Theatre closure]. *Village Voice*, October 18, p. 71.

———. 1974a. "Theatre Journal" [Survey of scene]. *Village Voice*, January 31, p. 65.

———. 1974b. "Theatre Journal" [Jackie Curtis]. *Village Voice*, April 4, p. 74.

Sullivan, Dan. 1967. Review of *The White Whore and the Bit Player*. *New York Times*, February 2.

———. 1968a. "At Café La Mama, a Floor Show in Hell." *New York Times*, February 5.

———. 1968b. "Another Delightful Look at *In Circles*, a Drama of Obfuscation." *New York Times*, June 28.

Swan, Jon. 1959. Review of *Faust*. *The Villager*, May 20.

Tallmer, Jerry. 1961. "Theatre: Apollinaire and Oppenheimer." *Village Voice*, November 23.

———. 1963. "Theatre in the Church Stages Two Short Plays." *New York Post*, October 6, p. 14.

———. 1964a. "The Corpse Sits Up." *New York Post*, March 23, p. 34.

———. 1964b. "The Face in the Mirror." New York Post, June 25.

———. 1965. "A Wild One at Judson." *New York Post*, September 24.

———. 1968. "To the 30s, With Love." *New York Post*, December 21, p. 54.

———. 1969. "Julie of the Spirits." *New York Post*, April 5, p. 28.

Washburn, Martin. 1969. "Theatre: *The Waterworks at Lincoln*." *Village Voice*, November 27, p. 49.

———. 1970a. "Theatre: *Bluebeard*." *Village Voice*, April 16, p. 53.

———. 1970b. "Theatre: *The Deer Kill*." *Village Voice*, May 7, p. 49.

Wetzsteon, Ross. 1966a. "Theatre: *America Hurrah, Three Views of the U.S.A.*" *Village Voice*, November 10.

———. 1966b. "Theatre: *Chas. Dickens' Christmas Carol*." *Village Voice*, December 29.

———. 1967. "Theatre: *A Funny Walk Home*." *Village Voice*, February 16.

———. 1968. "Theatre Journal" [*Peace*]. *Village Voice*, November 7, pp. 39, 41.

———. 1969a. "Theatre Journal" [*The International Wrestling Match*]. *Village Voice*, January 16, p. 35.

———. 1969b. "Theatre Journal" [*The Serpent* and *Hair*]. *Village Voice*, March 6, pp. 39, 44.

———. 1969c. "Theatre Journal" [*Gloria and Esperanza*]. *Village Voice*, April 10, p. 45.

———. 1969d. "Theatre: Two by Grotowski." *Village Voice*, November 27, p. 46.

Wilson, Lanford. 1984. "Unexpected Shocks: An Interview with Lanford Wilson." Interview by Terry Miller. *New York Native*, December 3–16, pp. 31–32.

Soundtrack Albums:

Carmines, Al. 1973. *The Faggot*. Blue Pear Records, BP 1008.

Carmines, Al, and Maria Irene Fornes. 1969. *Promenade*. Producer: Andy Wiswell. RCA Records, LSO-1161.

Carmines, Al, and Tim Reynolds. 1969. *Peace*. Producer: Chuck Cassey. Metromedia Records, MP 33001.

Carmines, Al, and Gertrude Stein. 1968. *In Circles*. Avant-Garde Records, AV-108.

Haimsohn, George, Robin Miller, and Jim Wise. 1969. *Dames at Sea: The New 30s Musical*. Producer: Thomas Z. Shepard. Columbia Records, OS 3330.

Ragni, Gerome, James Rado, and Galt MacDermot. 1968. *Hair: The American Tribal Love-Rock Musical*. Producer: Andy Wiswell. RCA Records, LSO-1150.

Sankey, Tom. 1967. *The Golden Screw*. Producer: David Lucas. Atco Records, SD33–208.

Index

Aaron, Joyce, 118, 177
About Time, 276
absurd, theater of the, 15, 21, 70, 86,
    128–29, 171, 220
acting approaches, 6, 29–30, 111, 141,
    157–58, 165, 170–74, 179–81, 186,
    192–93, 197–200, 215, 216–17, 222–23,
    233, 327
Actors' Equity Association, 19–20, 43, 51,
    266–69, 270, 271, 299
Actors' Playhouse, 43, 47, 248, 295
Actors' Studio, 44
Adams, Charles, 164
Adams, Nevele, 342
African American theater, 4, 86, 337
Agenoux, Soren, 14, 283–86, 288
Albee, Edward, 12, 21–22, 83–86, 115, 137,
    347
Alexander, Ross, 88, 92, 195
All Day for a Dollar, 59–60
Allen, Michael, 106–7, 109, 272, 314
Allen, Seth, 197, 204
Almost Like Being, 175, 182
America Hurrah (triple bill: for one-act
    play, see *Motel*), 181–85, 192, 197,
    206, 259, 266, 304, 346
American Place Theatre, 3, 354
American Theater for Poets. *See* New
    York Poets' Theatre
Anderson, Jim, 161
And He Made a Her, 49–50, 51, 55, 68, 85
And That's How the Rent Gets Paid, 330,
    331
Angels in America, 365
Antigone, 163, 179
antitextualism, 4, 9–11, 12
Apollinaire, Guillaume, 69–70
Arcade, Penny, 6–7, 364

Arden, John, 202
Arden of Faversham, 338
Are You Lookin'? 315
Aristophanes, 168, 250
Aronson, Arnold, 7, 11
Arrabal, Fernando, 48, 86
Artaud, Antonin, 4, 9, 15, 30, 98, 183, 187,
    234, 236, 237, 240, 243–46, 251–52,
    254, 280, 333
Artists' Theatre, 25
Ashbery, John, 25
Asian American Repertory Company,
    337
Asphodel, in Hell's Despite, 79–80, 81
audience participation, 237–43, 249, 256
audience response. *See* spectatorship
avant-garde, conceptions of the, 4, 7,
    9–12

Babel Babel Little Tower, 50–51, 59, 104,
    362
Babuscio, Jack, 158
Baker, Joan, 150, 152
Bakos, John, 204
Balls, 33, 92–94, 98, 103, 127
Balm in Gilead, 96–97, 104, 295, 298
Bandit, Sierra, 236
Banes, Sally, 150, 161
Baptism, The, 81
Baraka, Amiri (LeRoi Jones), 4, 18,
    62–63, 81, 86
Barbosa, James, 176, 319
Barnes, Clive, 167, 168, 210, 211, 243, 248,
    254, 298, 307, 357
Barnes, Theo, 163, 165, 167, 253, 255,
    276–77, 350, 351
Barr, Richard, 21, 51, 83–86, 103, 291, 347
Barry, Ray, 353

Barsha, Tony, 110–11, 116–17, 119, 121–23, 244–49, 268, 269, 278, 306, 314, 349–50
Bartenieff, George, 163, 276, 277, 351–52
Barthelme, Donald, 14
Barthes, Roland, 231
Bartlett, Neil, 231–32
Bastiano, Ntoni, 124
BbAaNnGg! 100
Bean, Orson, 162
Beard, The, 350
Beat movement, 16–17, 22, 28, 40, 115–17, 119, 120
Beautiful Day, A, 164
Beck, Julian, 24–26, 28, 61–62, 65, 71, 78, 154, 170, 239, 242, 256
Beckett, Samuel, 21, 28, 34, 70, 73, 86, 92, 93, 108, 115, 121–22, 125, 128, 155, 220, 308
Bed, The, 128–30, 134–35, 267
Benedikt, Michael, 153
Benjamin, Jerry, 79, 81, 219
Berezin, Tanya, 296, 299
Bernard, Kenneth, 233–36, 240, 323, 354, 364
Bernstein, Leonard, 95
Big Hotel, 230–31
Bigsby, Christopher, 1
Billington, Michael, 201
Birdbath, 102, 114–15
Black-Eyed Susan, 327
Black Mountain College, 32
Black Panther Party, 304, 306, 312, 316
Blanc, Maurice, 239, 303
Blau, Herbert, 140
Blau, Isabelle, 176
Bluebeard, 274, 326–28
Bolotowsky, Ilya, 65
Bond, Sudie, 157
Borske, Haal, 294
Bouwerie Lane Theatre, 232–33
Bovasso, Julie, 25–28, 62, 194, 273, 334–37, 339, 353
Boys in the Band, The, 291
Braswell, John, 337–38
Bread and Puppet Theatre, 1, 10, 303
Breasts of Tiresias, The, 69–70

Brecht, Bertolt, 76, 141, 170–72, 177, 178, 187, 277
Brecht, Stefan, 13, 216, 233, 327, 329–30
Bridge Collective, the, 319
Brig, The, 30, 61, 80, 154, 163
Broadway theater, 2, 19, 52, 170, 185, 192, 209–13, 250, 347, 362
Brockmeyer, John, 327
Brook, Peter, 95, 169, 183, 186, 339
Brooklyn Academy of Music, 239, 343
Brooks, Donald, 289
Brown, Kenneth H., 30, 80
Brown Crown, The, 294
Brukenfeld, Dick, 329
Brustein, Robert, 9, 28, 180, 184
Bullins, Ed, 4
Burgess, Anthony, 93, 218, 287
Burgess, Kenny, 42, 287
Burns, Larry, 128
Busch, Charles, 363
Butler, Judith, 222
Butler, Michael, 211–12

Café Au Gogo, 234
Café Bizarre, 40, 89
Café La Mama. *See* La Mama ETC
Café Manzini, 40
café theaters, 18, 40–41, 61, 68, 83, 84, 91, 95, 103–4
Caffe Cino, 1, 5, 7, 10, 12, 14, 22, 39–60, 61, 64, 66, 72, 73, 83, 84–85, 87, 88–90, 94, 96, 97, 99, 100, 102, 106, 110, 121, 124, 127, 128, 131, 134, 142–43, 159, 173, 174, 194, 210, 229, 239, 261, 268, 269, 278, 279–92, 293, 294, 295, 299, 323, 329, 331–33, 344, 345, 346, 348, 363, 364, 365
    closure of, 290–91, 344
    layout and decor, 42, 45–46, 57–58
    programming, 42–45, 49, 51–52, 55–57, 280
    staging and lighting, 45–48, 49, 113
Cage, John, 31–32, 33–34, 75
Calm Down Mother, 175–76
Camille, 357–59
camp, 59–60, 64, 113, 131–34, 158–62, 169, 215, 217, 219–22, 224–26, 228–30, 235,

254, 263, 282, 284, 286, 323, 324–29, 333, 336, 357–59, 363, 365

Capote, Truman, 45

Captain Jack's Revenge, 341

Carmilla, 338

Carmines, Al, 65, 67, 69, 70, 72, 74–75, 78, 87, 105, 110, 120, 148, 150–52, 154–55, 157, 159–60, 163–68, 177, 211, 250–51, 252, 274–77, 321, 323, 350–51, 353, 359–61

Carroll, Vinnette, 4

Caruana, Jerry, 52

Cernovich, Nikola, 46, 62

Chaikin, Joseph, 4, 6, 31, 169–77, 179, 181–82, 185–88, 193, 197, 206, 215, 302, 316–17, 319–21

Charba, Marie-Claire, 101, 195–96

Charlip, Remy, 75, 163–64, 183, 288, 302

Chas. Dickens' Christmas Carol, 14, 283–86, 288, 333

Chekhov, Anton, 167, 251, 297, 298, 342, 343

Chelsea Girls, The, 129, 262, 284

Chelsea Theatre Center, 271

Cherry Lane Theatre, 19, 21, 23, 24, 85, 86, 103, 104, 162, 250, 251

Chicago, 102, 112, 117–18, 353

Childs, Lucinda, 150, 152

Chilton, Nola, 170–72

Christianity. *See* theology

Christmas, David, 281

Christmas Rappings, 276

Cino, Joseph, v, 12, 41–42, 44, 46–48, 50, 51, 52, 54, 55–60, 69, 87, 89, 100, 104, 105, 110, 128, 141, 261, 267, 279–81, 283, 286–91, 292, 293, 294, 295, 296, 299, 304, 329, 331, 344, 365

Circle in the Square Theatre, 20, 27, 102

Circle Repertory Company, 292, 294–300, 362

Cixous, Hélène, 144

Classic Stage Company, 340

Clockwork Orange, A, 93, 218

Cock-Strong, 322–23, 363

Cocteau, Jean, 24, 45, 337

Coda Galleries, 218–20, 223

coffeehouse scene, 18, 40–41, 61. *See also* café theaters

Cohn, Ruby, 248

Coleman, Ornette, 17, 116

collective creation. *See* ensemble-based creation

Colman, Sam, 254, 276

Colton, Jacque Lynn, 101, 195, 197, 284

comic-book plays, 289, 294

Coming Out, 360, 361

commercialization, 2, 83, 184–85, 192, 212–13, 238–39, 259, 262–63, 291

Connection, The, 28–30, 60, 61, 71, 75, 130, 170

Conquest of the Universe, 231–33, 326

Cook, Ralph, 12, 105–11, 113–20, 245, 272, 304, 310, 314, 315, 322, 355

Corrigan, Robert, 8

Corso, Gregory, 116

Country Music, 341–43

Coward, Noel, 44, 45, 159, 281, 361

Cowboys, 107–8, 112

Coyote Cycle, 355, 365

Craig, Peter, 197, 199

criticism, role of, x, 7–8, 260, 346

cross-disciplinarity. *See* interdisciplinarity

Crowley, Mart, 291

cruelty, theater of. *See* Artaud, Antonin

Cummings, Gretel, 157, 163

Cunliffe, Jerry, 197, 198, 213

Cunningham, Merce, 31, 32, 150, 164

Curtis, Jackie, 328, 329, 363

Customs Collector in Baggy Pants, The, 117–18

Dahdah, Robert, 44–45, 48, 59, 128, 280–82, 287–88, 290, 291–92

Dames at Sea, 280–83, 291–92

Darling, Candy, 328

Davies, Joseph C., 42–44, 45, 47, 57, 89, 286

Davies, Mimi, 109, 119

Deafman Glance, 343

Deathwatch, 26, 48

Deegan, Denis, 54

Deer Kill, The, 310–14

de Ghelderode, Michel, 26, 70

de Kooning, Willem, 17

Delucia, Jack, 48

Dennison, George, 73–74, 75–77, 121
de Pury, Marianne, 180
Devices, 80
Dine, Jim, 31, 66
Dionysus in 69, 186, 238–41, 254, 255, 259, 325
di Prima, Diane, 62–64, 65, 86, 290–91
director, role of, 4, 6, 72, 73, 104, 110–11, 152, 154, 177, 194, 196, 321, 322–23, 337, 339–40
Dirtiest Show in Town, The, 325–26
Doctor Faustus Lights the Lights, 24, 350, 351
Dodd, Johnny, x, 46, 48, 59, 112–13, 158, 164, 280, 283, 285, 287, 289, 343
Dolan, Jill, 363–64
Dominic, Magie, 289
Donovan's Johnson, 288
Dracula: Sabbat, 240, 243, 250–56, 276, 324, 351
drag, 53, 64, 113, 131, 194, 221–22, 226–27, 229, 231, 233, 288, 301–2, 327–28, 349, 358–59, 363
Drama Review, The, 8–9, 12–13, 169, 233, 363
Drexler, Rosalyn, 78, 144, 149, 154–58, 162, 288, 349, 352, 354
drugs, 108, 112, 119, 120–21, 129, 215, 244–46, 251–52, 280, 282–84, 286–87, 288, 314, 315
Duay, Grant, 305–6
Duberman, Martin, 360–61
Duchamp, Marcel, 233
Duncan, Robert, 63
Dunn, Judith, 150
Dutchman, 86
Dybbuk, The, 324
Dylan, Bob, 18, 262–64

East Village, 2, 3, 17–18, 105–6, 108, 121, 239, 244–45, 269, 303, 306, 314, 315, 347, 362–63
Eichelberger, Ethyl, 363
18 Happenings in 6 Parts, 31, 32, 34, 66
Eighth Ditch, The, 63
Eight Plays from Off-Off-Broadway, 7, 92, 105, 119, 261–62, 278
Einstein on the Beach, 10

Eliason, James, 92
Elizabeth I, 213
Emerson, Eric, 328
Emmons, Beverly, 253
Endgame, 21
ensemble-based creation, 1, 150–55, 163–66, 179–81, 186–89, 192–93, 195–201, 237–41, 244–49, 253–55, 295–99, 316–21, 327, 337, 357
environmental theater. *See* site-specificity
Equity. *See* Actors' Equity Association
Esslin, Martin, 86, 129
Euripides, 130, 238, 338
Eyen, Tom, 56, 98–100, 101, 273, 324–26, 329, 334, 337, 339, 354

Faber, Ron, 176
Faggot, The, 359–61
Faust, 68, 69, 197, 289
Faustina, 25–26
Fefu and Her Friends, 354, 356
Feingold, Michael, 10–11, 179, 206–7, 216, 277–78, 342, 343, 350–51
Feldman, Peter, 172, 176, 179
feminism, 120, 134, 312, 354, 356, 358, 359, 363. *See also* protofeminism
Ferlinghetti, Lawrence, 117–18
Field, Crystal, 163, 253, 255, 260, 276–77, 351–52, 353
Fierstein, Harvey, 349, 362
film, uses of, in theater, 194, 305
Filmmakers' Cinematheque, 223
Finnerty, Warren, 31, 60, 118, 126, 170
Firehouse Theatre, 92, 196
Five Spot jazz club, 17–18, 21
Flaming Creatures, 217
Flanagan, Neil, 54, 55, 89, 287, 294, 324
Flite Cage, 307–8, 313
Floating Bear, The, 62, 63, 78, 152
Flyspray, 44
folk music, 18, 180, 204, 262–64, 311
Ford, John, 74, 88, 245
Ford Foundation, 23, 270, 271, 272, 273, 337
Foreman, Richard, 10, 13, 111, 149, 340
Forensic and the Navigators, 249, 307
Fornes, Maria Irene, 5, 27, 33, 58, 78,

120, 139–42, 144, 149, 152, 155–56,
    158–60, 162, 164, 174, 175, 250–51,
    261, 302–3, 323, 349, 352–56, 357,
    362, 365
Foster, Paul, 33, 41, 47, 58, 84, 88–89, 90,
    92–94, 98, 100, 101, 102, 103, 126–27,
    134, 162, 192, 193, 195, 197, 199–200,
    202, 207–9, 213, 241–42, 261, 283
foundation funding. See grant funding
Fourteen Hundred Thousand, 197
Francine, Frankie, 64
Frankenstein, 179
Freeman, Gerald, 210
Fried, Michael, 127
Fruit Salad, 305–6
Funny Walk Home, A, 331–33
Futz, 9, 192, 201–7, 209, 213, 348

Gans, Sharon, 176, 177
Garbo, Greta, 230, 357
Gaslight Café, 40–41
gay liberation movement, 328, 359–62
gay theater, 39, 45, 53–54, 231–32, 284,
    291, 328, 329, 357–64. See also
    camp; homosexuality
Gelber, Jack, 28–29, 130
Geldzahler, Henry, 226, 227
General Returns from One Place to
    Another, The, 80–81, 219
Genet, Jean, 21, 26–27, 29, 48, 140, 194
Gide, André, 45
Gilman, Richard, 14, 154, 155
Gingham Dog, The, 295, 299
Ginsberg, Allen, 2, 16–17, 75, 116–17
Giraudoux, Jean, 43
Glaspell, Susan, 19
Gloria and Esperanza, 273, 334–37
Gnys, Charles, 85, 103
Goat Island Performance Group, 364–65
Goffman, Erving, 172–73
Golden Screw, The, 262–65
Goodman, Paul, 25–26, 150
Goodnight I Love You, 39
Gordon[e], Charles, 67–68
Gordon, Stephanie, 109, 119, 296
Gorilla Queen, 228–29, 230, 250
Grand Tarot, The, 326
Grant, Beverly, 219–20, 232

grant funding, 23, 210, 269–73, 275, 276,
    278, 279–80, 294, 297, 299, 314, 320,
    326, 337–38, 339, 345, 353–54, 363
Gray, Spalding, 297
Great American Desert, The, 69–72, 77,
    80, 116
Greek Trilogy, The, 338–40
Greenberg, Clement, 11, 13
Greenwich Village, 2, 3, 17, 19, 66, 106,
    328
Gress, Elsa, 195, 203, 206, 213
Grotowski, Jerzy, 8, 10, 13, 169, 186,
    192–93, 197, 199, 237, 240, 243, 296,
    326
Gruen, John, 260, 292, 330
Guare, John, 84, 289
Guilliatt, Lee, 163, 276
Gussow, Mel, 265, 328, 345
Guy, Shirley, 120

Hadler, Walter, 112–13, 119, 123, 244–45,
    247, 280, 306, 307–10, 313, 314, 341,
    349, 355
Haimsohn, George, 281, 292
Hair, 9, 192, 210–13, 239, 244, 248, 249,
    254, 259, 291, 293
Hanft, Helen, 99, 268, 273
happenings, 4, 14, 31–34, 62, 64, 65–67,
    69, 116, 126, 156, 194, 241, 302, 363
Hardware Poets' Playhouse, 61, 64–65
Harlot, 218
Harlow, Jean, 74, 99, 218, 247–48, 350
Harris, Cynthia, 176
Hartman, Norman "Speedy," 292–94
Haunted Host, The, 56, 293, 361
Hawk, The, 240, 243–49, 255, 337
HB Studio, 43
Heaven Grand in Amber Orbit, 328
Heide, Robert, 22, 47, 84, 128–30, 135,
    261, 280, 283, 315, 352
Heimskringla, or, The Stoned Angels, 213
Hendricks, Jon, 73
Herko, Fred, 62, 64, 157–58
heterosexuality, 12, 109, 119–20, 204–6,
    212, 312
Hewes, Henry, 203, 316
Hoffman, William M., 12, 39, 49–50, 56,
    101–2, 293–94, 330, 340, 362, 365

Hoffmann, Hans, 156
Hollywood movies. *See* popular culture
Home Free! 53, 96, 101, 102, 103
Home Movies, 78, 80, 149, 154–63, 185,
    229, 250, 303
homosexuality, 7, 12–13, 16, 22, 27, 39, 45,
    54, 120, 137, 157–58, 160, 161–62, 217,
    220, 222, 226, 231–32, 284, 288, 291,
    301, 305–6, 327–28, 358–61. *See also*
    camp; gay theater
Hot l Baltimore, 298–300, 301
Howard, James, 44
Hurrah for the Bridge, 92–94, 101, 195–96
Hwang, David Henry, 355–56

Ibsen, Henrik, 295
Icarus's Mother, 174, 349
Iceman Cometh, The, 20, 27, 97
Importance of Being Earnest, The, 133,
    282, 361–62
I'm Really Here, 175, 182
In Circles, 149, 165–67, 250, 251, 350
Indira Gandhi's Daring Device, 227–28
Inge, William, 44, 45, 74
interdisciplinarity, 3, 18, 25, 31–32, 33,
    64–67, 73, 78, 116, 147, 150–53,
    164–65
International Wrestling Match, The, 334,
    337
Interview (formerly *Pavane*), 182, 197, 206
In the First Place, 68, 69
Ionesco, Eugene, 21, 26, 27, 52, 140, 155,
    171, 337
Isaac, Dan, 225–26
Isherwood, Christopher, 160
Istanbul, 163, 201

Jarry, Alfred, 23, 155, 338
jazz music, 17–18, 28–30, 116, 117, 215,
    222, 246–47, 271
Jean Cocteau Repertory Company, 340
Jennings, Jim, 128
Jesus Christ Superstar, 213
Johnson, Larry, 44
Johnson, Lyndon B., 178–79, 184, 270,
    303
Johnson, O-Lan (aka O-Lan Jones), 119,
    249, 355

Johnston, Jill, 64
Jones, LeRoi. *See* Baraka, Amiri
Journey of Snow White, The, 277
Joyce Dynel, 293, 329
Judson Dance Theater, 2, 11, 150, 154,
    157, 365
Judson Gallery, 66, 73
Judson Memorial Church, viii, 65–69,
    107, 116, 153–54, 162, 171, 197, 253,
    274–75, 288, 349, 351
Judson Poets' Theater, ix, 1, 5, 11, 14, 61,
    65–80, 82, 83, 84, 85, 104, 106, 110,
    120, 121, 124, 138, 139–40, 144,
    147–68, 173, 174, 177, 185, 201, 215,
    228–30, 240, 250–56, 268, 270,
    274–78, 302–3, 314, 323, 350–51, 353,
    359
    collaborative methods of, 73–75,
        77–78, 150–58, 163–68, 254–55
    finances of, 73, 270, 275
    layout and staging, 68, 71–72, 78–79,
        152, 253
    programming, 69, 72–73, 80, 274–75

Kahn, Madeleine, 251
Kahn, Michael, 98, 183
Kalfin, Robert, 271
Kantor, Tadeusz, 339
Kaplan, Donald, 12–13
Kaprow, Allan, 4, 31, 32, 34, 66, 73, 126
Katz, Jonathan, 360–62
Katz, Leon, 20, 243, 251–54, 277, 324, 350,
    365
Kauffmann, Stanley, 102, 104
*Keep Tightly Closed in a Cool Dark
    Place*, 175–76
Kennedy, Adrienne, 349
Kennedy, John F., 187–89, 193, 346, 347
Kennedy, Robert, 187, 189
Kennedy's Children, vii, 346, 347–48
Kent State University, 313–14, 315, 318
Kerouac, Jack, 17, 75, 116
Kerr, Walter, 181, 184, 206, 253
Kessler, Bruce, 92, 101
Keystone Company, 244–49, 337
King, Martin Luther, Jr., 187, 189, 304
Kissman, Lee, 109, 118, 177, 245, 355
Kline, Franz, 17

Koch, Ed, 290
Kopit, Arthur, 22
Kornfeld, Lawrence, 6, 25, 31, 35, 65, 67,
    71–75, 77–78, 79, 80, 97, 141, 147,
    149–54, 157, 159–60, 163, 165–68,
    171, 177, 193, 201, 203, 211, 215,
    228–29, 242, 250–56, 276–77, 279,
    301, 327, 330, 331, 350–51, 353, 354,
    357
Kornfeld, Margaret, 331
Koutoukas, H. M., v, viii, 7, 27, 59–60,
    98, 113, 124, 126, 130–34, 137, 220,
    286, 287, 289, 352
Krapp's Last Tape, 21
Krauss, Ruth, 144, 164
Krim, Seymour, 45
Kroll, Jack, 253, 348
Kurnitz, Julie, 163, 276
Kushner, Tony, 365

La Bar, Tom, 197
Lahr, John, 238, 242, 272, 318
La Mama ETC, viii, 1, 14, 33, 41, 47, 72,
    83, 87–104, 106, 124, 173, 176–80,
    183, 186, 192, 194–97, 201, 224, 239,
    266–70, 272–75, 295, 299, 314,
    322–26, 328, 330, 334–41, 345, 346,
    349, 353, 362
  club status of, 91, 95
  European tours by, 53, 101–2, 114, 176,
    195–96, 197, 200–202
  finances of, 95, 266, 270, 273–74, 337
  layout, staging, and decor, 88–89 (East
    Ninth St.), 94–95 (122 Second Ave.),
    272–73 (East Fourth St.), 339
    (Annexe)
  programming, 89, 92, 337
La Mama Repertory Company, 337–40
La Mama Troupe, 101, 192–93, 194–209,
    212–14, 215, 237, 240–42, 270, 284,
    296, 348
language, uses of, 4, 33, 69, 78, 108,
    115–18, 121, 131–34, 144, 151, 155–56,
    182, 189, 196, 241, 246–47, 338–39
Lazy Baby Susan, 90, 114
Leach, Wilford, 337–38
Leary, Timothy, 251
Lee, Ralph, 311

Lenny, 213
LeSeuer, Joseph, 63, 181, 227
Lester, Elenore, 3, 130, 220, 221–22, 261
Leverett, James, 351
Levin, Peter, 65
Levy, Jacques, 6, 177–78, 180, 182–85,
    186, 188, 254–55, 303–4
licensing issues, 24, 40–41, 43, 52, 62,
    90–91, 94, 224, 290
Life of Juanita Castro, The, 218–22, 223
Life of Lady Godiva, The, 224–26, 229
Lights, Fred, 88
Lincoln Center, 163, 336
Line of Least Existence, The, 155
Link, Ron, 324
LiPari, Victor, 195, 197
Listen to Me, 350–51
Living Theatre, 1, 9–10, 23–26, 28–31, 46,
    61–62, 63, 66, 69, 71, 75, 80, 120,
    153–54, 163, 164, 169–71, 172, 179,
    186, 201, 233, 237–42, 255, 314, 344
Look at the Fifties, A, 277
Loscasio, Michael, 90
Loubier, Charles, 42, 280
Love's Labor, 63–64
Lower East Side. *See* East Village
Lowry, Jane, 50, 52, 296, 297
Ludlam, Charles, 7, 216, 226–27, 230–32,
    234, 274, 326–28, 329, 356–59, 365

Machiz, Herbert, 25
Madness of Lady Bright, The, 53–55, 58,
    59, 64, 97, 100, 101, 102, 267, 287,
    298, 301–2, 361, 365
Magic Show of Dr. Ma-gico, The, 236
Maids, The, 26–27, 48, 194
Mailman, Bruce. *See* Poland, Albert
Malanga, Gerard, 218
Malcochon, 74
Malina, Judith, 23–26, 59, 71, 170, 238,
    242, 256, 303, 304
Maloney, Peter, 318–19
Manhattan Theatre Club, 353–54
Man Is Man, 170
Mann, Theodore, 102
Mantle, Burns, 282
Marat/Sade, 183–84, 202, 207
Mark Taper Forum, 300, 365

Marlowe, Alan, 62, 64, 72, 78, 152
Marlowe, Christopher, 231, 326
Marowitz, Charles, 202, 211, 348–49
Martinez, Ricardo, 330
Martinique Theatre, 102–4, 115, 173,
    180–81, 229
Mason, Marshall W., 52, 56, 96,
    294–300, 341
Massachusetts Trust, 213
Max's Kansas City, 234
McCarthyism, 16, 269
McCarty, Eddie, 229
McClure, Michael, 63, 349–50
McDermot, Galt, 210–11
McDowell, John Herbert, 62, 79, 252
McNally, Terrence, 361
Mead, Taylor, 219, 232, 233, 349–50
Medea, or, The Stays May Understand,
    113, 130–34
Medicine Show, the, 319
Mednick, Murray, 112, 116, 118, 119, 121,
    244–48, 304–5, 306, 310–13, 314, 315,
    341, 349, 354–55, 357, 364
Medoff, Mark, 298–99
Mee, Charles L., 113
Mekas, Jonas, 223
Melfi, Leonard, 90, 102, 114–15, 118, 200,
    345, 349
Melodrama Play, 200, 207
Midler, Bette, 99
Miller, Arthur, 12, 54, 137, 163, 334
Miller, Tim, 329, 363
Milligan, Andy, 48–49, 88–89, 90, 194
Milne, A. A., 154
Milton, David Scott, 119
Minding the Store, 352
Mingus, Charles, 17, 108, 116
minimalism, 14, 33, 112, 127
Miss Nefertiti Regrets, 99
Mitchell, Mary, 101
modernism, 13, 14
Moke Eater, The, 234–36, 240
Molly's Dream, 353
Monday Night Series, 31, 62, 64, 71
Monk, Meredith, 65
Monroe, Marilyn, 99, 100, 347
Montez, Maria, 216–17, 230
Montez, Mario, 217, 218, 224, 226–27,

230, 232, 328
Monuments, 290–91
Moody, Howard, 66–67, 68–69, 106–7
Moon, 283
Moondreamers, The, 334–35
Mooney, Phoebe, 43
Moore, Edward J., 299
Moore, Jim, 88
Moss, Robert, 347
Motel (formerly *America Hurrah*), 98,
    101, 126, 182–84, 234
Murder Cake, 63–64, 65
Murrin, Tom, 322–23, 363
music, uses of, 29–30, 74–75, 78, 80, 130,
    134, 151, 156–57, 159–60, 165–66,
    180, 198–99, 200, 204, 210–11, 222,
    232, 250–51, 252–53, 262–64, 274–77,
    281, 307, 323, 338, 339, 342
Mutation Show, 320

National Educational Television, 197,
    213
National Endowment for the Arts, 270,
    271
Negro Ensemble Company, 4
Nelson, Claris, 52, 57, 142–43, 197, 278,
    290, 295, 296, 331, 333
Nelson, Stanley, 344
New Dramatists, 295, 353
New Lafayette Theatre, 4
New School for Social Research, 24, 32,
    59, 269, 272
Newsweek, 253, 265, 348
New Troupe, the, 213
New York, 205, 277, 340
New Yorker, 211, 343
New York Poets' Theatre, 61, 62–64, 219
New York Post. See Tallmer, Jerry
New York Shakespeare Festival, 210
New York Theatre Strategy, 352–54
New York Times, 3, 8, 28, 162, 202, 228,
    243, 260–61, 271, 295, 326, 360, 361.
    See also entries for Times *critics:*
    Barnes, Clive; Gussow, Mel; Kauff-
    mann, Stanley; Kerr, Walter;
    Novick, Julius; Sullivan, Dan
Next Thing, The, 6, 141–42, 177–78, 341
Nichols, Robert, 68–70, 74, 352

Nightclub, 236, 323–24, 364
Nightwalk, 320
Nixon, Richard, 313, 332
No Exit, 44, 45
No Plays, The, 325, 334
Normal Love, 217
Northwestern University, 52, 295, 296
Novick, Julius, 330, 331, 339
Now She Dances! 51, 361–62
nudity, 205, 212, 220, 225, 226, 232, 238, 241, 254–55, 325

Obie Awards, 27, 100, 153–54, 310, 333–34, 337, 343, 351
O'Connor, Kevin, 102, 109, 114, 118, 126, 195, 202, 209
Odets, Clifford, 122, 298
off-Broadway theater, 2, 19–23, 66, 83, 84, 85–86, 102, 137, 140, 162, 180–81, 185, 192, 202, 248, 250, 265, 266, 279, 291–92, 295, 298–99, 325, 344
Off-Off, 239, 240
Off-Off-Broadway Alliance, 344–45
Off-Off-Broadway Book, The, viii, 4
off-off-Broadway movement
    "death" of, 268–69, 278, 344–47
    definitions of, 1–5, 9, 11–12, 14–15
    evolving profile of, 40, 61, 83, 124–28, 137–38, 140–41, 147, 259–60, 267–68, 279, 303, 322
    initial influences on, 18, 22, 23, 31
O'Hara, Frank, 25, 63, 80–81, 219, 261
Oh! Calcutta!, 254–55, 325
O'Horgan, Tom, 6, 9, 33, 104, 192–201, 203–14, 215, 241, 270, 296, 330, 335, 337
Oldenburg, Claes, 31, 33, 34, 66, 69, 156
Old Reliable Theatre Tavern, 292–94, 329
Oliver, Regina, 44, 49
Ondine (Robert Olivo), 7, 14, 232, 283–84, 286, 288, 323–24, 333, 341
one-act plays, 5, 56–57, 124–27, 310
One Arm, 48, 89
O'Neill, Eugene, 19, 20, 89, 97
One Person, 329
Open Theatre, 1, 3, 4–5, 10, 92, 135, 169–91, 192, 193, 196, 197, 206, 210,

215, 237, 240–41, 245, 254–55, 270, 302, 303–4, 311, 315–21, 344, 346, 349, 353
Operation Sidewinder, 336
Oppenheimer, Joel, 69–72, 116, 261
Ordway, Sally, 120
Ortman, George, 26
Orzel, Nick, 261
Osgood, Lawrence, 86
Owens, Rochelle, 9, 31, 138–39, 143–44, 163, 192, 197, 201–7, 354

Packard, William, 68
Padua Hills Playwrights' Festival, 354–55, 365
Page, Geraldine, 20
Pagoon Kang Wook, 90
Papp, Joseph, 210
Paradise Now, 186, 237–42, 244, 249, 253, 255, 325
Parker, Charlie, 116
Parone, Edward, 86
Pashalinski, Lola, 327
Paskin, Murray, 119
Pasolli, Robert, 65, 155, 170, 182, 234–35, 236, 249, 259, 268, 288, 310
Passloff, Aileen, 150, 152, 163, 302
Patrick, Robert, vii, 15, 16, 17, 41, 51, 56, 89, 100, 120, 229, 261, 282, 286, 287, 289, 292–94, 301, 329, 330, 340, 346, 347–48, 353
Patter for a Soft Shoe Dance, 75
Peace, 168, 250, 251
Pecheur, Bruce, 236
Perez, Rudy, 150
performance art, 6–7, 116, 126–27, 329–30, 362–63, 364
Performance Group, the, 1, 186, 238, 241, 242, 272
performance poetry, 5, 18, 61, 116
Peters, Bernadette, 281
Phillips, Georgia Lee, 119
Phillips, Jeanne, 221
Philoctetes, 45
Pinter, Harold, 90–91, 115, 275
Pirandello, Luigi, 24, 29
Piscator, Erwin, 24, 59
Playful Tyrant, The, 276

Playhouse Café, 42
Play-House of the Ridiculous, 2, 6, 13,
    64, 149, 158, 215–16, 219–28, 230–36,
    240, 286, 322–23, 337
playwright, role of, 4–6, 137–38, 179, 187,
    193, 208, 240–41, 319–20, 322–24,
    337, 352–54
Playwrights' Horizons, 347
Playwrights' Unit, 83–87, 101, 103, 106,
    267, 291, 347
Playwrights' Workshop Club, 124
poetic drama, 24–25, 61–66, 70, 71, 78,
    80–82. *See also* performance poetry
Poland, Albert, viii, 4, 59, 292, 294
Polish Laboratory Theatre. *See* Gro-
    towski, Jerzy
political theater, 1, 121–23, 138–39,
    143–44, 169–70, 175–76, 179–81,
    301–4, 316–19, 352, 360
Pollock, Jackson, 17, 116
pop art, 14, 27, 79, 98, 113, 131, 156, 189,
    283
popular culture, 14–15, 34, 70, 72, 73,
    99–100, 108, 122, 130, 135, 156–57,
    174–75, 180, 220, 225, 228, 230,
    281–82, 289, 305, 327, 328, 334–35,
    363
Porter, Beth, 348
Portnow, Richard, 334
postmodernism, 13–15, 75
Powell, Michael Warren, 52–53, 195, 197,
    198, 199, 212–13
*Practical Ritual to Exorcise Frustration
    after Forty Days of Rain, A*, 296–97,
    298
presence of actor/performer, 147–49, 157,
    167–68, 171, 174, 193, 194, 199, 207,
    237, 240–42
*Presentation of Self in Everyday Life,
    The*, 172–73
Present Stages, 81–82, 219
Preston, Tony, 292
pricing policies, 3, 51, 89, 95, 186, 266,
    274
professionalism, 2, 8, 20, 84–85, 105,
    270–75, 278, 292, 345, 354
Promenade, 78, 80, 139–42, 149, 154–56,
    158–60, 162, 163, 250–51, 355

protofeminism, 49, 142–44, 163, 176,
    205–6
Provincetown Playhouse, 19, 42, 162,
    265
Public Theater, 210

Quintero, Jose, 20, 27
Quinton, Everett, 357

Rado, James, 210–12
Ragni, Gerome, 210–12
Rags an' Old Iron, 292
Rainer, Yvonne, 150, 153
Rauschenberg, Robert, 5–6, 27, 32, 47,
    168
Ray Gun Theatre, 33, 66
Recluse, The, 47, 92, 101, 102, 197
Red Cross, 177
regional theaters, 8, 23, 300
Rehearsal for the Destruction of Atlantis,
    223–24
revolutionary movement, 239, 303–4,
    306–13
Rexroth, Kenneth, 24
Rich, Alan, 277, 340
Richardson, Jack, 22
Ridiculous Theatrical Company, 13, 232,
    274, 326–28, 357–59, 363, 364
Rimers of Eldritch, The, 96
ritual theater, 186–87, 237–40, 316
Rivers, Larry, 25
Robards, Jason, 27
Roberts, Marilyn, 197, 200
Rockefeller Foundation, 23, 270, 271,
    272, 275
Rock Garden, The, 107–9, 112
rock music, 210–11, 233, 262–64, 307
Rogoff, Gordon, 169
Rook, The, 86
Rooney, Mickey, 250
Rothlein, Arlene, 150, 163
Roundabout Theatre, 340
Rue Garden, The, 52, 142–43
Russell, Donn, 297

Sainer, Arthur, 1, 30, 90, 92, 255, 313, 360
Salomé, 178, 230, 282, 361–62
Sand, 304–5

Sandcastle, The, 96
San Francisco Mime Troupe, 1, 352
Sankey, Tom, 262–65
Sarah B. Divine, 325
Sarris, Andrew, 221
Sartre, Jean-Paul, 44
Saunders, Rai, 221
Savage, Robert Cosmos, 178
Schechner, Richard, 4, 8, 11, 12, 238, 239, 241, 256, 272
Schisgal, Murray, 22
Schmidman, Jo Ann, 349
Schneider, Alan, 21, 295
Schroeder, Robert J., 279, 299, 346
Schumann, Peter, 303
Screen Test, 226–27
Sealy, Robert, 92, 101, 330
Sedgwick, Edie, 218, 262
Serban, Andrei, 337–40
Serchio, Tony, 245
Serpent, The, 186–91, 241, 316, 317, 320
Service for Joseph Axminster, The, 75–78, 80, 104
Shakespeare, William, 231
Shepard, Sam, vii, 1, 5, 87, 102, 103, 104, 106, 107–9, 112, 113, 115–18, 119, 138, 162, 174, 177, 197, 200, 242–43, 246, 249, 261, 306, 307, 314, 320, 336, 341, 349, 352, 353, 355
Shepp, Archie, 271
Sheridan Square Playhouse, 43, 173–76, 182, 299
Sherman, Martin, 361
showcase productions, 2, 266–69, 270, 295, 299, 345
Shower, 218–20, 223, 225, 235
Simmons, Barbara, 221
Simon, John, 205
Sing Ho for a Bear! 154
site-specificity, 5, 50–51, 59–60, 75, 96–97, 103–4, 250–51, 354, 355, 362
Six from La Mama, 102–4, 115, 180, 185, 261
Smith, Jack, 7, 216–17, 218, 219, 221, 223–24, 230–31, 329–30, 363, 364
Smith, Michael
  as critic, ix–x, 8, 23, 26, 27, 31, 40, 41, 46, 54, 57, 59–60, 65, 67, 68, 72–73, 74, 77, 80, 81, 91, 92–93, 95, 96–97, 98, 103, 108, 118, 121, 132, 134, 149, 153, 154, 157–58, 159, 162, 164, 171, 174, 201, 210, 211, 219, 224, 225, 226, 233, 247, 248, 259, 260, 261, 263, 265, 272, 278, 280, 287, 288, 289, 295, 298, 305, 320, 325, 328, 335, 344, 346, 353
  as playwright and director, x, 6, 141–42, 143, 171, 174, 177–78, 196, 285–86, 288, 289–91, 341–43, 349
Solarium, 112–13
So Long at the Fair, 52, 58
Sontag, Susan, 86, 131, 137–38, 156, 158, 159, 161, 162, 219
Sorrentino, Elsene, 221, 225, 235
So Who's Afraid of Edward Albee? 52, 101
spectatorship, 34, 79–80, 121, 124–30, 132–34, 136–38, 148–49, 162–63, 186–88, 241–44, 248, 256, 332–33
Spooner, Malcolm, 140
Stanley, Charles, 113, 131, 285, 288–89, 329, 342, 348–49
Starkweather, David, 52, 56, 101, 134–37, 141, 261, 289, 296–97, 298
Stein, Gertrude, ix, 6, 24, 25, 70, 78, 80, 147–53, 155, 165–67, 250, 350–51, 360
Stewart, Ellen, 24, 41, 83, 87–92, 94–95, 97, 98, 100–102, 104, 105, 110, 125, 138, 176, 192, 194, 196, 200, 202, 213, 266–67, 270, 273–75, 288, 322–24, 326, 328, 337–39, 341, 349, 351
St. Mark's Church in the Bowery, 105–7, 109, 116, 120–21, 123, 261, 269, 306, 310, 314, 341, 349, 350
St. Mark's Poetry Project, 116, 118, 269
Stoker, Bram, 251–53
Stonewall Riots, 328, 357, 360–61, 362
Strasberg, Lee, 44
Strindberg, August, 57
String Game, The, 138–39, 201
subjective realism, 115–19, 121, 304–5
Successful Life of 3, The, 174, 175
Sukenick, Ronald, 11–12, 13–14, 262, 315
Sullivan, Dan, 57, 167, 250, 335
Summers, Elaine, 166
Swados, Elizabeth, 339, 340
Swellfoot's Tears, 277

Take 3 Coffeehouse, 23, 40
Tallmer, Jerry, 26–27, 28, 40, 54, 66, 70, 71, 80, 108, 151, 162, 163, 220, 291, 337
Tango Palace, 140
Tarlow, Florence, 158, 163, 164, 177, 255, 302, 350
Tavel, Harvey, 223, 227, 228, 288
Tavel, Ronald, 64, 216, 217–21, 223–30, 234, 235, 288, 349, 352
Teer, Barbara Ann, 157, 161
Tempo Theatre, 26–27, 62, 334
Ter-Arutunian, Rouben, 251
Terminal, 315–18, 319, 320, 321
Terry, Megan, x, 4, 135, 175–76, 178–81, 186, 187, 213, 261, 302, 319, 349
Thank You, Miss Victoria, 101–2
Theater for the New City, 276–77, 351–52, 355
theater of cruelty. See Artaud, Antonin
theater of the ridiculous. See Play-House of the Ridiculous; Ridiculous Theatrical Company
Theatre Genesis, 1, 12, 14, 102, 105–23, 124, 173, 239, 240, 244–49, 262–65, 268, 269–70, 272, 296, 299, 304–15, 323, 341–43, 349–50, 355
    evolving aesthetic of, 115–21, 123, 304, 306–7
    finances of, 269–70, 272
    programming, 107, 109–10, 113–14
    space and staging, 107, 111–13
Theatre of the Eye, 324–25, 337
theology, 67, 107, 109, 148–49, 187, 190–91, 252, 294
Thirkield, Rob, 296–97
This Is the Rill Speaking, 53, 96, 102
Three from La Mama, 197
Tidy Passions, or Kill, Kaleidoscope, Kill, 98
Times Square, 200–201, 207, 345
'Tis Pity She's a Whore, 88, 245
Tom Paine, 192, 199–202, 207–9, 213, 241–42, 348
Topor, Tom, 345–46
Torrey, Jonathan, 46–47, 286, 287, 289
TOSOS (The Other Side of Silence), 361–62

Trojan Women, The. See Greek Trilogy
Trunk, The, 119, 121–23
Tucker, Duane, 256
Tulane Drama Review. See Drama Review, The
Turds in Hell, 326
Two Executioners, The, 48, 86
Tynan, Kenneth, 28, 254

Ubu plays, 23, 24, 155, 338
underground, conceptions of the, 11–14, 264–65, 280
Up Against the Wall Motherfuckers, 304, 306, 310–12
Up to Thursday, 103
Urban Arts Corps, 4
Urban Crisis, The, 275–76
US, 186

Vaccaro, John, 6, 7, 64, 215–17, 219–36, 240, 322–24, 326, 327, 328, 354, 364, 365
Vain Victory, 328
van Itallie, Jean-Claude, 4, 5, 33, 85, 89–90, 98, 102, 125, 174–75, 181–89, 192, 197, 234, 241, 259–60, 261, 314, 319, 320, 352
Vann, Barbara, 319
Vaudeville Skit, 73–74, 75
Vaughan, David, 163, 165, 166
Vehr, Bill, 327, 358
Velvet Underground, the, 2, 222, 284
Vietnamese Wedding, A, 302–3
Vietnam War, 14, 81, 178–81, 186, 223, 242, 284, 302–6, 308, 316, 317, 318, 346, 347
Viet Rock, 178–81, 182, 187, 197, 241, 302, 305
Village South Theatre, 84, 101
Village Voice, viii, ix, 2, 8, 10, 27, 40, 43, 44, 45, 54, 61, 63, 71, 90, 95, 201, 239, 260, 267, 346, 349. See also entries for Voice critics: Brukenfeld, Dick; Feingold, Michael; Lahr, John; LeSeuer, Joseph; Lester, Elenore; Novick, Julius; Pasolli, Robert; Sainer, Arthur; Sarris, Andrew;

Smith, Michael; Washburn, Martin; Wetzsteon, Ross
Vinyl, 218, 229, 288

Waiting for Godot, 21, 28, 108, 122, 308
Walcott, Derek, 74
Waldman, Ann, 116
Walter, Sydney Schubert, 92, 196
Walters, Bill, 223
War, 85, 90, 102
Ward, Douglas Turner, 4
Warhol, Andy, 2, 14, 79–80, 128–29, 158, 216–19, 220–21, 224, 226, 234, 262, 283, 284, 288, 328, 347
Waring, James, 62, 64, 65, 78, 168, 219, 343
Washburn, Martin, 308, 309, 312–13, 327
Waterworks at Lincoln, The, 307–10, 313
Wax Engine, The, 74–75, 80
W.C., 250
Weill, Kurt, 75, 277
Weiss, Jeff, 7, 330–34, 335, 337, 339, 349, 351, 363
Weiss, Peter, 183, 207
Wetzsteon, Ross, 10, 184, 189–90, 192, 251, 273, 284, 286, 333, 334, 335
What Happened, ix, 78, 79, 80, 97, 149–54, 157, 350, 351
Whitehead, Paxton, 85
White Whore and the Bit Player, The, 99–100, 101, 324, 354
Whitman, Robert, 31, 66, 156
Who's Afraid of Virginia Woolf? 12, 22, 84
Why Hanna's Skirt Won't Stay Down, 99, 324
Why I Love New York, 277–78
Wieners, John, 63, 79
Wilde, Oscar, 45, 133, 159, 178, 230, 282, 325, 360, 361–62

Wilder, Clinton, 83, 86
Williams, Tennessee, 12, 19, 20, 43–44, 45, 48, 53–54, 89, 234
Williams, William Carlos, 25
Wilson, Doric, 39–40, 43, 45, 49–51, 55, 57, 68, 84, 85, 268–69, 296, 297, 360–62
Wilson, Lanford, 46, 52–55, 56, 58, 96–97, 102, 103, 137, 162, 261, 291, 293, 295, 296, 298–300, 301, 341
Wilson, Robert, 10–11, 13, 46, 98, 183, 253, 340, 343
Wise, Jim, 281, 292
With Creatures Make My Way, 60
Wolf, Reva, 79
Workshop for the Player's Art, 328
Worley, Lee, 319
Woronov, Mary, 222, 233, 236, 283, 288, 323–24
WOW Café, 363–64
Wright, Margaret, 163, 276
Wurlitzer, Rudolph, 113

XXXXX, 293–94

Yankowitz, Susan, 4, 317–20
Yeh, Ching, 337
Yerushalmi, Rina, 324
Yippie organization, 303–4
You May Go Home Again, 52, 134–37, 141
Young, Barbara Eda, 109, 110, 111, 114, 119–20, 246–48
Young, LaMonte, 65, 234

Zimet, Paul, 190
Zoo Story, The, 21–22, 28, 86
Zuckermann, Wolfgang, 289
Zwick, Joel, 337